DIAGRAM
OF STATE AND FEDERAL POWER

AB Federal and State Powers (4)

A Federal Powers (17)

AZ Federal Powers forbidden to States (43)

B Powers expressly reserved to the States (simply) (3)

BX Powers expressly reserved to the States and forbidden to U.S. (2)

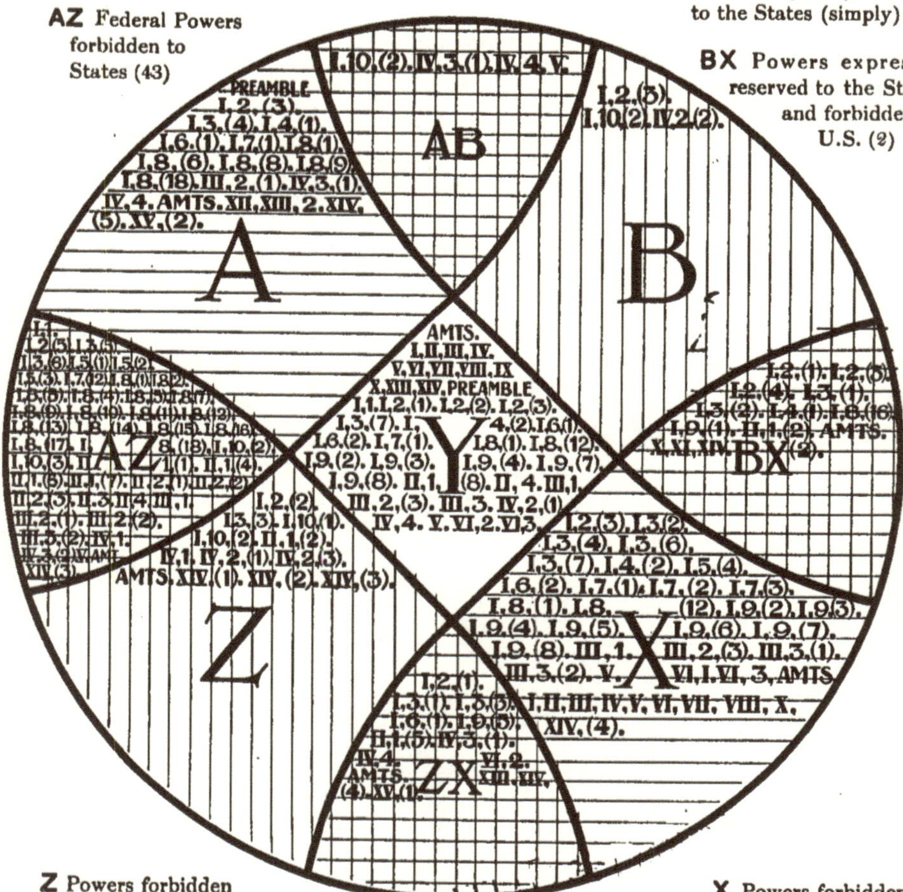

Z Powers forbidden to the States (simply) (11)

X Powers forbidden to U.S. (simply) (37)

Y Rights or Powers reserved in the People (39)

ZX Powers forbidden to both States and U.S. (12)

See Appendix

THE LAW

OF THE

FEDERAL AND STATE CONSTITUTIONS

OF THE

UNITED STATES

WITH AN HISTORICAL STUDY OF THEIR PRINCIPLES
A CHRONOLOGICAL TABLE OF ENGLISH
SOCIAL LEGISLATION
AND
A COMPARATIVE DIGEST OF THE CONSTITUTIONS
OF THE FORTY-SIX STATES

BY

FREDERIC JESUP STIMSON

Professor of Comparative Legislation in Harvard University; Late Advisory Counsel to the United States Industrial Commission; Massachusetts Commissioner on Uniformity of Laws; Member of Massachusetts Committee on Corporation Law
Author of "American Statute Law," "The American Constitution" "Handbook of Labor Law of the United States" etc., etc.

THE LAWBOOK EXCHANGE, LTD.
Clark, New Jersey

ISBN 978-1-58477-369-6

Lawbook Exchange edition 2004, 2026

The quality of this reprint is equivalent to the quality of the original work.

THE LAWBOOK EXCHANGE, LTD.
33 Terminal Avenue
Clark, New Jersey 07066-1321

Please see our website for a selection of our other publications and fine facsimile reprints of classic works of legal history:
www.lawbookexchange.com

Library of Congress Cataloging-in-Publication Data

Stimson, Frederic Jesup, 1855-1943.
The law of the federal and state constitutions of the United States : with an historical study of their principles, a chronological table of English social legislation, and a comparative digest of the constitutions of the forty-six states / by Frederic Jesup Stimson.
p. cm.
Originally published: Boston : Boston Book Co., 1908.
Includes bibliographical references and index.
ISBN 1-58477-369-3 (cloth : alk. paper)
1. Constitutional law—United States—States. 2. Constitutional law—United States. I. Title.

KF4550.Z95S7 2003
342.73'02—dc21 2003053950

Printed in the United States of America on acid-free paper

THE LAW

OF THE

FEDERAL AND STATE CONSTITUTIONS

OF THE

UNITED STATES

WITH AN HISTORICAL STUDY OF THEIR PRINCIPLES
A CHRONOLOGICAL TABLE OF ENGLISH
SOCIAL LEGISLATION
AND
A COMPARATIVE DIGEST OF THE CONSTITUTIONS
OF THE FORTY-SIX STATES

BY

FREDERIC JESUP STIMSON

Professor of Comparative Legislation in Harvard University; Late Advisory Counsel to the United States Industrial Commission; Massachusetts Commissioner on Uniformity of Laws; Member of Massachusetts Committee on Corporation Law
Author of "American Statute Law," "The American Constitution" "Handbook of Labor Law of the United States" etc., etc.

BOSTON
THE BOSTON BOOK COMPANY
1908

THE UNIVERSITY PRESS, CAMBRIDGE, U. S. A.

PREFACE

AMERICAN constitutional law has had its broadest development in the last twenty years. Since the cardinal meaning of the Federal Constitution was settled by the early great decisions, and the relation of the States to the Federal Government once decided by the Civil War, there has, in a century, been comparatively little growth until the last decade or two. The enormous mass of litigation on the meaning of the "obligation of contract" and of the words "commerce among the States" related, after all, to but two short phrases in that great document; and in the latter of these two instances the decisions of the last twenty years far exceed, both in number and importance, all that went before. Constitutional law, therefore, like the law of labor and free contract, is in the United States "a live science." Both in the States and in the nation it has had its most active discussion recently; and the matter bids fair to increase still more at the hands of the next generation. The great social principles, of the right of the individual, both to property and even to personal liberty, as against the will of a majority or an organized minority having the ears of the executive and the legislative branches of government, have got to be resettled — the great political questions of the social and jurisdictional (not political) relation of the States to the Federal Government, the right of the States to their own customary law and their own police power, have, it seems, once more to be fought over. No apology, therefore, is offered for presenting this work at this time. It is prepared primarily for the author's use in his classes at Harvard University; not, therefore, in the first instance, for a practising lawyer; rather for the citizen and the student of politics. Moreover, considerations of space and otherwise have made it advisable to duplicate no work that has been done before. No effort, therefore, has been made to supersede such classics as, in America, Cooley's "Constitutional Law"; and for

English history I have largely relied upon Dicey's "Law of the Constitution"; Taswell-Langmead, "On English Constitutional History," Hannis Taylor, and Stubbs' Charters; while for most of the sources of information I have gone directly to the "Statutes of the Realm," the usual edition of which is Ruffhead's "Statutes at Large," London, 1769, but the original folio "Statutes of the Realm," when procurable, is to be preferred, as the "Statutes at Large," like most digests or selections, has a curious faculty for omitting what is historically most interesting. Mention in the United States should also be made of "Miller's Lectures," Patterson's "The United States and the States under the Constitution," and McClain's "Constitutional Law." The book is not, however, intended for a case lawyer. I have cited cases only when the proposition is in some doubt or my authority not easily discoverable. In like manner, at least in the prefatory essays (Book I), I have sought to lay down the general principles and the broad antitheses, not too much delaying the line of discussion to consider exceptions or qualifications. These are usually to be found in the footnotes to Book III.

What has been principally sought is to give the history, origin, and present tendency of American Constitutions, both Federal and State; and for this purpose the bulk of the work is made up of a careful comparative presentation of the forty-six State Constitutions annotated with the corresponding provisions of the Federal Constitution, and voluminous footnotes. In Book II is presented a chronological digest of the more important statutes referring to English constitutional principles, or even common law principles which became in the lapse of centuries so universal as to be almost part of the "unwritten Constitution"; and also a table of excerpts from all the great constitutional documents, arranged chronologically, thus showing their growth from the simple phrasing of Magna Carta to the verbose essays of the Massachusetts Bill of Rights. Books II and III, therefore, represent an attempt at comparative study never, I believe, hitherto made; [1] while the first Book is intended for a broad historical essay, not too technical, on those parts of constitutional law which now most concern us, and have, indeed, been most neglected by other writers; for it is very recently

[1] That is, before 1886, when the first edition of the present Book I appeared, without footnotes, in the author's "American Statute Law," Vol. I. Dr. J. Q. Dealey, of Brown University, has recently published a valuable essay on salient features of the State Constitutions, but without citations. (Am. Acad. Pol. & Soc. Science, Supp., November, 1907.)

that students of constitutional law have begun to turn their attention from the political provisions, which were most important in English history, to the broader principles of individual rights which most concern us to-day.

The reason of this is obvious. Personal freedom was established in England, substantially as we know it now, in the 12th century. It was taken almost as a matter of course by our ancestors, both in England and here, until within a very few years. It was the assertion of political power, and notably of the right to tax and impose military rule or law, that remained in question. But when our Constitution was adopted, these principles also were so engrained in the popular mind as to need hardly more than expression. Since then more than a century has gone by. Our population has grown from four millions to eighty millions, a majority with no inherited training in English institutions, and even the American minority, in their very security, forgetful of them. Two potent forces are now at work; first that of philanthropy, general benevolence, ethical amelioration, seeking results rather than liberty, traceable in theory directly back to Austin, Bentham, and Hobbes; the other the class-conscious multitude of organized labor, seeking (and for the same reason) to reimpose regulations and control upon the actions of others either through or beside the State, which was tried but only partially tried in the thirteenth or fourteenth centuries in England. For the English agitations, when not mere risings of the peasants, resulted rapidly in an exclusive, almost aristocratic, trade-guild. To show how striking is the present activity of these two forces I need but to refer to the decisions of the Supreme Court of the United States. In all the ninety years from 1796 to 1886 they found only one thousand constitutional cases to consider, and in these declared some two hundred statutes of States or Acts of Congress to be unconstitutional. In the twenty years from 1886 to 1906 they considered more than thirteen hundred cases of this sort, more than half of which, and these much the most important, were set in motion by the two forces I have named, and probably a larger proportion than before were held unconstitutional.[1] For State Constitutional law it is only necessary to refer to the valuable annual bulletins of the New York State Library. One hundred and four laws of the States or of the United

[1] The admirable digest of Mr. Bancroft Davis, at the end of 131 U. S., has, I believe, been ordered by the President to be brought up to date by the present Reporter; it will then show precisely the figures which the author can only estimate.

States were declared unconstitutional in the one year 1906. It is a fact not possibly unconnected with this that during the same year forty-six new constitutional amendments were adopted and thirty rejected, making the attempted output seventy-six, just about two thirds of the one hundred and six nullifications; but only about one third of these amendments found the favor of the people. If these amendments embodied in all cases the same provisions which had been declared void by the courts, one might draw the inference that in about two thirds of the cases the people sustained the courts. The true number, however, is far greater than this. Nothing is more interesting than the unanimity with which the people, as a rule, welcome the decision of their highest court declaring a law unconstitutional; that is, in conflict with their own will as permanently expressed. Of late years only do we see an ominous tendency in the other direction, due to the unfortunate fact already adverted to, that so many unconstitutional statutes embody the rash attempts of philanthropic and labor interests to impose their will upon others by law, rather than by persuasion or the legitimate powers of the trades union.

In closing, a word should perhaps be said as to the form of this work. A table of the Constitutions referred to will be found before the preface; the citations are always made by numbers of chapters, sections, etc., without any other abbreviations; thus, 1, 2, 3, will mean Chapter 1, Section 2, Clause 3, or whatever other may be the division in the Constitution referred to. To have done otherwise would have been to add inconceivably to the bulk of the work. The index cites Book III by sections and not by pages in order to avoid the necessity of star pages in any future edition. Article 99, Constitutional Amendments, has been reserved for later constitutional amendments which shall be adopted after April 1, 1908 (that being the final date of publication of this work). Fortunately most of the States do not adopt Constitutions very frequently, and the amendments they adopt, though numerous, frequently relate to such matters of petty detail, the appointment of local officers, etc., as fall outside the scope of this work. Thus, Connecticut, Iowa, Oregon, Maine, Massachusetts, and several other States, have never had but one Constitution; while the amendments proposed in all are more often than not rejected. In 1903, for instance, the forty-five States then existing adopted twelve amendments and rejected twenty-six, and this is about the usual proportion. This would cease to be the case, however, if the Western States continue their present unscientific tendency of embodying all that the present majority wish to be law into the framework of the Constitution. This, however, I have discussed more fully in Book I, Chapter XI.

F. J. S.

CAMBRIDGE, MARCH 31, 1908.

TABLE OF CONTENTS

BOOK I

ORIGIN AND GROWTH OF THE AMERICAN CONSTITUTIONS

BOOK II

CONSTITUTIONAL PRINCIPLES AS EXPRESSED IN THE ENGLISH STATUTES OF THE REALM AND AMERICAN CONSTITUTIONS

CHAPTER I

CONSTITUTIONAL PRINCIPLES PROTECTING PERSONAL LIBERTIES AND PRIVATE RIGHTS AS EXPRESSED IN CONSTITUTIONAL DOCUMENTS FROM MAGNA CARTA TO THE UNITED STATES CONSTITUTIONS

I. LIBERTY

BOOK III

THE STATE CONSTITUTIONS DIGESTED, ANNOTATED, AND COMPARED WITH THE FEDERAL CONSTITUTION

PART I

BILL OF RIGHTS

CHAPTER I

BILL OF RIGHTS: CIVIL

CHAPTER II

Bill of Rights: Criminal

PART II

Political Provisions

PART III

LEGISLATION

PART IV

JUDICIAL SYSTEM

PART V

CONSTITUTIONAL AMENDMENTS

TABLE OF CITATIONS

THE Constitutions, State and Federal, are cited by section number only if, as in many States, it is continuous; otherwise by number of Chapter, Article, or other subdivision, separated by commas. The Statutes, State or National, are cited in like manner from the latest revision or the volumes of Annual Laws, but are always distinguished by an asterisk.

For the amendments I am indebted to the industry and courtesy of the New York State Library in its "Yearbooks of Legislation," founded by Robert H. Whitten and continued by Edwin H. Anderson, Director. My thanks are also due to the Secretaries of State of the several States who have nearly all obliged me with editions of the several State Constitutions in pamphlet form; in Georgia, however, it is "not procurable." The inaccessibility of State Constitutions is greatly to be deplored. Some States, like New Hampshire and Ohio do not print them at all with their general laws. Oregon and other States entirely omit constitutional amendments, while hardly any State follows the example of Massachusetts in printing the Constitution in its correct form every year. Texas, West Virginia, and many another State do not date their Constitution or the amendments; while the usual compilations of the laws of New York and the official compilation of Georgia and several other States commit the last inanity of printing the State Constitution alphabetically under *C*, as if it were an ordinary law. The following table, however, is believed to be accurate so far as is possible under the circumstances.

Alabama (Ala.), (Constitutions of 1819, 1868, 1867, 1875)	Constitution of 1901
Arkansas (Ark.), (1836, 1864, 1868)	Constitution of 1874
California (Cal.), (1849)	Constitution of 1879
Colorado (Col.)	Constitution of 1876
Connecticut (Conn.), (1776)	Constitution of 1818
Delaware (Del.), (1776, 1792, 1831)	Constitution of 1897
Florida (Fla.), (1838, 1865, 1868)	Constitution of 1885
Georgia (Ga.), (1777, 1789, 1798, 1865, 1868)	Constitution of 1877
Idaho (Ida.)	Constitution of 1889
Illinois (Ill.), (1818, 1848)	Constitution of 1870
Indiana (Ind.), (1816, 1851)	Constitution of 1851
Iowa (Io.), (1846)	Constitution of 1857
Kansas (Kan.), (1855, 1857, 1858)	Constitution of 1859
Kentucky (Ky.), (1792, 1799, 1850)	Constitution of 1891

Louisiana (La.), (1812, 1845, 1852, 1864, 1868, 1879)	Constitution of 1898
Maine (Me.)	Constitution of 1820
Maryland (Md.), (1776, 1851, 1864)	Constitution of 1867
Massachusetts (Mass.)	Constitution of 1780
Michigan (Mich.)	Constitution of 1850
Minnesota (Minn.)	Constitution of 1857
Mississippi (Miss.), (1817, 1832, 1868)	Constitution of 1890
Missouri (Mo.), (1820, 1863, 1865)	Constitution of 1875
Montana (Mon.)	Constitution of 1889
Nebraska (Neb.), (1867)	Constitution of 1875
Nevada (Nev.)	Constitution of 1864
New Hampshire (N. H.), (1784, 1792)	Constitution of 1903
New Jersey (N. J.), (1776)	Constitution of 1844
New York (N. Y.), (1777, 1821, 1846)	Constitution of 1894
North Carolina (N. C.)	Constitution of 1868 as amended 1876
North Dakota (N. D.)	Constitution of 1889
Ohio (O.), (1802)	Constitution of 1851
Oklahoma (Okla.)	Constitution of 1907
Oregon (Ore.)	Constitution of 1857
Pennsylvania (Pa.), 1776, 1790, 1838)	Constitution of 1873
Rhode Island (R. I.)	Constitution of 1842
South Carolina (S. C.), (1776, 1778, 1790, 1865, 1868)	Constitution of 1895
South Dakota (S. D.)	Constitution of 1889
Tennessee (Tenn.), (1796, 1834)	Constitution of 1870
Texas (Tex.), (1845, 1866, 1868)	Constitution of 1876
Utah (Uta.)	Constitution of 1895
Virginia (Va.), (1776, 1830, 1850, 1864, 1870)	Constitution of 1902
Vermont (Vt.), (1777, 1786)	Constitution of 1793
Washington (Wash.)	Constitution of 1889
West Virginia (W. Va.), (1863)	Constitution of 1872
Wisconsin (Wis.)	Constitution of 1848
Wyoming (Wy.)	Constitution of 1889

BOOK I

ORIGIN AND GROWTH OF THE AMERICAN CONSTITUTIONS

CHAPTER I

INTRODUCTORY

THE English Constitution is expressed in writing in the Magna Carta of King John (1215); with certain omissions and a few additions in the Magna Carta of Henry III (1216), and the Confirmation of the Charter granted by Edward I in 1297; in the Petition of Rights extorted from Charles I in 1628, and finally enacted in the Bill or Declaration of Rights subscribed to by William of Orange in 1689; in the Habeas Corpus Act of Charles II (1679); and in the Act of Settlement of Queen Anne (1700). Besides this there are certain fundamental statutes which by long observance or by frequent re-enactment have grown to be such essential parts of the English notion of liberty or government as to be in effect constitutional documents; such, notably, is the Statute of Monopolies of 1623 and the principle against restraint of trade and monopoly of commerce or of industry embodied in the long series of statutes against forestalling, engrossing, regrating, and against by-laws in restraint of trade or depriving one of his legal rights, which all begin as early as 1285,[1] and only end under George III, when such principles were immutably established in the popular mind as well as in the law-making of Parliament and the law-giving of judges.

But the English Constitution should hardly be regarded as embodied only in these documents; nor the American Constitution, outside the frame of government, be considered as first expressed in 1787. Magna Carta and the other constitutional documents are but

[1] See Book II, Historical Digest. James C. Carter (Law, its Origin, History, and Function, N. Y. 1907) seems to confuse these statutes with those fixing prices, and states that they began in 1552. On the contrary, they were *made perpetual* soon after (13 Eliz.) and began under Edward I (1285). Statutes at Large (Vol. I, p. 188) calls the date uncertain, but before Ed. III; and the statute punishes forestalling of "grain or any other Thing to be sold coming by Land or Water, oppressing the Poor and deceiving the Rich." For a discussion of their relation to the modern laws against Trusts, see Chapters V, VI.

the record of the victories of the people in the long fight which they waged for their liberties against the Crown; they mark the definite establishment of Anglo Saxon notions of liberty and law over the feudal or Norman, European, Roman or Civil Law view, which the Norman kings after the Conquest, and, later, even the Tudors and the Stuarts, endeavored to impose on the English people. Indeed the notion of the sovereignty of the Crown, of personal government, only ended with George III of the House of Hanover. Magna Carta is in form a treaty between the Norman king and his English subjects, assembled for the first time in a representative assembly in which the Commons also took part, whereby he recognizes the general body of liberties of the English freemen as known to them at that time. The form of these early constitutional documents, confirmations of charters, coronation oaths, etc., is always a recognition of prior laws, customs, or liberties, as already existing: "All the laws and customs of the men of Kent as they existed in the time of King Withraed." For statute-making in the modern sense was yet unknown. Indeed, the very notion of a statute, that is, a law made by a sovereign and addressed to his people, with a *sanction* or threat of punishment if disobeyed, is a notion of Roman or Continental law; foreign to the genius of the English folk, who made their laws themselves or, more correctly, recognized all law as but the growth of the free customs of the people.[1] English legislation before the Conquest does not consist in what we should now call making laws, but rather in decreeing the scale of punishment for their breach; when they do make a law, it is never regarded as a new law, but is merely recognized by the Great Council as part of the existing law of England. Their law-making was not statute-making, in the modern sense; but at most a recognition, or an expression, in writing for the first time, of the law already existing; the primal distinction being that, in England, the people made the law, and the king but recognized it. During four centuries after the Conquest the kings vainly endeavored to impose upon the English people the Continental view that law is the command of a sovereign to a subject, not the customs and usages of the people; an effort which proved futile, and by the eighteenth century did not survive even in the royal veto, but only

[1] The admirable lectures of James C. Carter above referred to argue strongly for this principle. There are doubtless some Continental examples of such custom-law; but this book is intended to state broad principles, without regard to exceptions and qualifications, for which the reader is referred to the footnotes in Book III.

in the formula *le roy le veut*, by which the king expresses his assent to the legislation of Parliament, a perfunctory act. For since the days of Queen Anne, no monarch has ventured to use even the gentle formula which indicated the royal veto — *le roy s'avisera.*

The history of the regaining by the people of their power to legislate, almost forgotten in the middle centuries, is now, by the effort of German and English scholars, well known. We owe it, like our own Revolution, to unconstitutional taxation. No Englishman was bound to pay taxes but under a general law passed by his representatives in the Great Council and for the general good of the whole people; no arbitrary exaction, aid, impost, or levy by the Crown or its officers was tolerated. This fundamental principle, expressed with the greatest distinctness in John's Charter, was intentionally omitted by Henry III in his, sixteen months later (the usual one printed in the statutes), and only restored in 1297 by Edward I when the needs of the war in Flanders compelled this concession. But the principle was never lost sight of, and there never has been a period in the history of England when the people permitted any taxation for a considerable length of time in contravention thereof; and from the very beginning they used this principle to extort legislation restoring their own law; that is to say, decrees or statutes of the king recognizing the common law of England "as it was in the time of Edward the Confessor." For three or four centuries after the Conquest there was no new legislation, in the modern sense; only the old laws restored. The Commons, with that practical good sense which characterizes the English people, caring not for the form provided they got the substance, when asked for grants of money would put the matters they desired to be recognized as part of the law of England into a petition, which would be the foundation of a statute; then, in theory, made by the king, but practically dictated by the Parliament. Thus, gradually, all the customs of England, with the common law of the Saxon kingdoms, was recognized as the law. Finally the form of petition and decree (which still exists in the machinery of legislation in many of our State Legislatures) was dropped, the House of Commons finding that the law did not always emerge from the king's law officers as they had drawn it in their petition; and the statutes were drawn in Parliament as well as enacted there, and only sent to the king when in the form of complete Acts for his signature. Thus the power of the purse, the taxation power, residing only in the House of Commons, drew back to it the power to legislate and the English view of the law, — as customs, grown, not made, based on natural justice, common usage, and the liberties of the people; laws not newly ordered, but the result of evolution and experience. Hence their wisdom and their strength. It is hard to fix precisely the first date at which anything like *constructive* legislation, as to ordinary matters concerning the people, first appears in England. For two centuries the statutes of the realm are concerned with matters of taxation, with recognizing or re-establishing the common law, and with political matters, defining the powers of the Crown and excluding the control of the Roman Church and of the Roman law over secular matters. The Statute of Merton, it is true, in 1235 has a word about usury and about the legitimacy of children; but in both cases it is merely to enforce the Common Law of England instead of the Civil Law of the Church. For a century more they concern merely what we should now call procedure, or the penalties for the infraction of laws already existing, feudal tenures, and the effort to fix the prices of bread and other necessities which was extended in 1349 to the wages of labor. The first constructive legislation that we do find is concerned with those same questions that most concern us to-day, — the regulation of charges, and the prevention of the cornering of markets or the making of artificial prices by individuals or by combinations. The price of bread, and ale and tolls of mills were regulated by the Assize in 1266; and in 1275 the Statute of Westminster I forbids "excessive toll contrary to the common custom of the Realm in market towns." Notice that it is still "the common custom of the realm" that toll should be reasonable, it is not a new law; and in 1285, ten years later, appears the statute against forestalling or engrossing; that is to say, monopolizing the market, — a common complaint against the modern trust. In 1691 the rates of carriers are fixed.

When we come to the American Constitution, though now all expressed for the first time in one document, its principles must, so far as they express the English Constitution, be regarded as a continuation, not as a new enactment, and must be taken with all the historical meaning and import with which they were viewed in the minds of our ancestors, far more familiar with historical law, with constitutional history, than we Americans have had to be since. It was at first believed by our greatest judges and jurists that the whole English Constitution was implied in the Federal Constitution; that there is, as it were, an unwritten Constitution which we inherited in America and which consisted, not only of the English Constitution where not expressly altered by our own, but of all matters of natural right and justice. Doubtless this is the intended meaning of the Ninth Amendment: "The enumeration in the Constitution of certain rights shall not be construed to deny or disparage others retained by the people." Such is not, perhaps, the modern view; but the question has become, in fact, academic, for the reason that in 120 years of interpretation our Supreme Court has ever found some clause in the Federal Constitution into which to read any English constitutional principle not therein expressly altered.

But while we must insist that the American Constitution is not an instrument or a code of rules created for the first time by a body of gentlemen however wise, and therefore subject to the errors of an ordinary new-made document, we must hasten to accentuate the point that it is a different Constitution, the Constitution of another country; while it embodies all the liberty principles of the English Constitution, what we may call all its human or social side, yet also it creates an entirely new frame of government, and it invents two or three great new principles, — principles as profoundly important as those of Magna Carta, principles now recognized throughout the world as America's great contributions to the science of government. First of all these we should put that invention, be it Franklin's or Pelatiah Webster's, by which a centralized national government is given all the political power necessary for the protection of the whole country and the conduct of foreign relations, while the States are carefully preserved to secure to the people their own laws and governments and courts at home, — the marvellous dual system whereby power, in so vast a country, is made compatible with liberty. Second, the great principle of the separation of the powers, suggested, indeed, to Montesquieu and others by the practical working of things in England, but never formally embodied in the Constitution of any country, not even to-day, except our own; that principle that they who make the laws may not administer them, and he who administers them may not judge them, "to the end it be a government of Laws and not of Men." [1] Third, most novel, perhaps, and still but half understood, the first great attempt of democracy to found a nation without entrusting the sovereign power away from itself, or in the hands of any one branch of government. This, to me, is the most wonderful political occurrence in modern history; that

[1] See Chapters VIII, X, below.

the people, having (for eleven years from 1776 to 1787) for the first time in the history of the world gained all the reins of power, should, voluntarily and of their own high intelligence and patriotism, have put certain things beyond the power of their own Congress, of their own Legislatures, of the very government they were about to create.[1] Theirs was the high experiment, to found a nation that should forever be without Imperial power; wherein the Bill of Rights, the cardinal principles, should be kept from the hands of sovereignty itself, and all the powers of autocratic nations, of continental empires and kingdoms, should be given neither to Congress nor to President, but sleep in the lap of the people until they woke to further need.

Lastly, with us the people are sovereign; not, as in England, the Parliament; nor, as in continental countries, the king; and this led, logically and necessarily, to the invention and the function of our Supreme Court. In all other countries, either there is one sovereign, or there are branches of the government co-ordinate and of equal dignity; and it would be presumptuous for the judicial branch to question the acts of either other. But in England we had the history of the judgments by the courts, of the king's own acts, or those of his officers under his orders. "What power the king hath, he hath but by law." This English heritage, joined with the logic of our Constitution, led to the creation of our great tribunal. When a people has granted to its government only certain powers, it may not trust to the wisdom of that government to judge of its own oversteps. When it has parcelled out those powers between Congress and Executive, between Federal government and State, neither branch, neither forum, may safely be entrusted to determine its own power or to limit its own realm. Therefore the people said, This Constitution we establish for the government of our country; it shall stand until we, the people, by amendment alter it; and beside the Executive and the Congress we place our Supreme Court, which shall judge matters arising between States or citizens of different States, or which involve any principles of this our Constitution; and the judges of that Court shall be bound by this Constitution and its provisions as against any

[1] "Though this Government possesses sovereign power, it does not possess all sovereign power; and so the State governments, though sovereign in some respects, are not so in all. Nor could it be shown that the power of both, as delegated, embraces the whole range of what might be called sovereign power." James B. Thayer, "Legal Essays," p. 203, quoting Daniel Webster, in *Luther* v. *Borden*, 7 How. 1.

State or power, civil, executive, or military, and as against the acts of their own representative assembly.

This is the great difference, the great distinction of our Constitution. It is a commonplace to say that there is nothing like it in England, nor indeed elsewhere in the world. No other country has dared as yet to grasp the idea that the people may have a guardian above the laws made by their representatives. Many countries have written Constitutions, but in none can a statute be declared void by the courts.

And there is another important practical difference between the English Constitution and our own. Theirs in the main is composed of limitations upon the Executive. Ours limits (what is to-day far more important) the legislative assemblies as well. In theory still, the English Constitution is a pact between the King and Parliament, which is sovereign and brooks no constitutional control. Ours is the written will of the people, who are with us sovereign, addressed to their servants, the three branches of government, and defining and delimitating their powers among themselves. Both constitutions embody the frame of government; but in this the English is much simpler, for it provides but for the supremacy of Parliament, the power of the Commons in money matters, and the limitations imposed upon the king. Even the Cabinet, that committee of the House of Commons which now rules the nation, is not mentioned in the English Constitution. But it was necessary for our Constitution, besides setting up the frame of government, and that more complicated and explicit, as befits a Republic, also to set forth, in words so exact as to be undoubted, both the powers and the prohibitions given to Congress and the division of power between the Federal government and the States.

Most important in our Constitution to-day is that portion which is not the frame of government, but the liberties of the people; the part most neglected by historians and in treatises upon constitutional law. In this great domain the English and American Constitutions are practically identical; only that the American Constitutions, Federal and State, express in many words what the English Constitution puts in a very few, while of course the English restraint upon Parliament, though equally (some think more) effective, is a moral one. The growth of words in which these cardinal principles are swathed is curiously shown in Book II of this work. Besides we have, in our Federal Constitution, not only to secure these liberties to the individual as against the Federal government, but in some cases against the State governments as well; and our State Constitutions, which, after all, with us are the charters of the people's liberties in the ordinary relations of mankind, seek to protect the individual also against the State Legislatures. In this, indeed, they go much too far, as we shall later (Chapter XI) discuss.

This branch of constitutional law forms the main subject of this work. There are many political treatises in which matters relating to government, hitherto deemed most interesting and perhaps most important, have been exhaustively treated; but in no work has attention been concentrated on those constitutional documents which embody the people's liberties; and in none is the Federal with all the State Constitutions compared and brought together. My last predecessor in this attempt (William Smith) wrote in Philadelphia what he calls "A View of the State and Federal Constitutions Compared" in 1797. It fills about twenty-eight pages, and his attention is entirely concentrated on the frame of government, the terms of governors and judges, and the methods of electing them and the members of the State Legislatures. Nothing whatever is said about the Bills of Rights, or other matters even such as the Interstate Commerce Clause, the clauses limiting State and Federal legislation, or the Fifth Amendment, which have proved to be of infinitely greater importance; nor of course of those modern restrictions, relating to labor, corporations, liquor laws, and the like, so voluminous in the newer State constitutions.

These cardinal rights may, for convenience at least, be divided into the four great realms of Rights to Liberty, to Property, to Law, and Rights of the people as against the Government. Logically and historically the first is the right to law, for there can be no property, no government and no real liberty without law.

CHAPTER II

THE RIGHT TO LAW

The Right to Law, peculiar to the English people, is the right of any one, irrespective of rank or station, to appeal to the ordinary law courts for trial of any dispute between him and any other person, or body of persons, or even any officer of the government. This applies as well to criminal as to civil cases, and to any infringement, by any person or officer, acting under whatever authority, upon the individual rights to liberty and property, or other civic rights. In England, and with us, there is no Administrative Law; no peculiar *corpus juris* extending to the doings or relations of government or any officer thereof, such as exists in all continental countries. The notion that the doings of the government itself, or even of the king, in the person of any of his officers, can be questioned by any subject in the ordinary law courts — conjoined with the right of instant inquiry into the reason or pretext of the detention of any man's person by the officers of government, civil and military as well as judicial — is the principal reason that England has been called free. The law required by this general right, furthermore, must be the Common Law of the English people. That is to say, in origin, the body of their free customs and usages, made by themselves, not by a king, and also, in earliest days, enforced by themselves; and furthermore it must be the Common Law, not the Roman or Civil Law, nor the Canon or Church Law, nor any supposed Administrative Law, or orders or decrees of the king, or king in Council. Even chancery jurisdiction, which rests originally on the royal power as wielded by the king's chancellor (whence the writs of injunction, mandamus, prohibition, etc., are called Prerogative writs), is hardly an exception. For many centuries we find statutes restraining or limiting chancery jurisdiction. It arose comparatively recently (we can almost fix the time of the first use of equity process, in matters of trade and domestic affairs as now used, at the time of Jack Cade's Rebellion in 1452) and as we all know, the prejudice against the injunction, and the interference of Chancery courts with ordinary criminal jurisdiction and the principles of the Common Law, has not yet disappeared (see Chapter IV). Equity therefore, may truly be said to be a modern growth upon the body of the Common Law. All its other competitors or intruders were early got rid of. Statutes against the Roman law will be found in the fourteenth century, while the ouster of Canon Law, of the Church courts, from their jurisdiction in England, begins with the Constitutions of Clarendon. The three great heads of the growth of the English Constitution, from the Conquest until modern times, are indeed but the resumption by the whole Parliament of its power to make laws, by the Commons of their power to regulate taxation, and by the people generally of their right to be tried in their local courts by their neighbors under the Common Law, and to have no royal officer or Civil Law or church tribunal hold himself above it. The procedure must always be the people's; and, since the time of Henry II, by grand and petit jury; for the Saxon method of trial by ordeal was abolished by the Lateran Council in 1213, and about the same time the English got rid of the Norman method of trial by battle. The broad principle remained that an Englishman could only be put in peril by a grand jury of his neighbors, and definitely condemned or his property forfeited by twelve men of his peers. It is true that the machinery of the Norman Inquest was applied to the jury system; but the principle of the latter pre-existed, even as we go back to the earlier times when a man's neighbors helped him to enforce his law, or the earliest times when he enforced the law himself. For it results logically, and did result historically, from the Anglo-Saxon conception of law that it might be enforced by anybody; these were the times of the "unwritten law," and the law, like the moral code, was supposed to be known of every one and justified a man's right hand. Earliest statutes, therefore, never declared the law, but merely defined the penalties for its enforcement; just as the modern statutes against trusts add nothing to the old common law except to define the penalties for its infringement. In early English trials, therefore, what was tried was rarely whether the man did the deed (it was usually admitted or known), but whether he was right in doing it: that is to say, was he *in his law?* Was he acting upon a state of facts whereon the unwritten law gave the right of reparation or vengeance into his own hands? If not, he was out of law, *outlaw;* that is, he had lost his right to law as against any one molesting him in person or property.

As Stubbs remarks, the early English statutes, before the Conquest, are hardly statutes in the modern sense. When they have not to do with matters of procedure, or penalty, they are but vague statements of the moral law. The underlying law, like the Ten Commandments, is supposed to be known of every one. Written statutes busied themselves only with the amount of the *were*, or fine, or (for the first century after the Conquest) with the method of procedure.

Furthermore, the right to law involved the right to trial by a man at home by his local courts according to his local customs, originally by his neighbors. The jealousy of the King's judicial power, of the Court following the person of the king or even centralized in London to the exclusion of the jurisdiction of the county courts, is shown in every constitutional document, beginning with Magna Carta, in a long line of statutes, in the Declaration of Independence, and in the American Constitution.

"The great original principle of the English judicial system was that of trial in local courts properly constituted — trial *per pais*, in the presence of the county, as opposed to a distant and unknown tribunal." [1] And the law enforced was the law as it was in the time of Edward the Confessor, — the customary law of the people, not the statutes of the Norman sovereign. Thus, in 890, "I, then, Alfred, king, gathered these (laws) together, and commanded many of those to be written which our forefathers held, those which to me seemed good; and many of those which seemed to me not good I rejected them, by the counsel of my 'witan.' . . . I, then, Alfred, king of the West Saxons shewed these to all my 'witan', and they then said that it seemed good to them all to be holden." [2] After the Conquest every Norman king was made on his coronation oath to promise this, the law of Edward the Confessor, until Magna Carta; after that they promised to respect Magna Carta instead, which was thus reissued or confirmed thirty-two times in the eighty-two years which intervened between Runnymede and the final Confirmation of charters under Edward I. Thus, William the Conqueror himself, in his charter to the City of London says, in Anglo Saxon: "And I do you to wit that I will that ye two be worthy of all the laws that ye were worthy of in King Edward's day." [3] So the Domesday Book records "the customs," that is to say, the laws, of various towns and counties; these bodies of customs invariably containing a mere list

[1] Taswell-Langmead, 6th ed., p. 28.
[2] Stubbs' Charters, p. 62.
[3] Ibid., p. 83.

of penalties for the breach of the established law, while later charters usually give the inhabitants of a town all the customs and free privileges enjoyed by the citizens of London. In 1100 Henry I in his Charter of Liberties promises in the first section relief to the kingdom of England from all the evil customs whereby it had lately been oppressed, and finally returns to the people the law of Edward the Confessor "with such emendations as my father made with the consent of his barons."[1] In his charter to the citizens of London[2] he promises general freedom from feudal taxes and impositions, from dane-geld, and from the fine for the murder of a Norman; and the Charter of Liberties issued by Henry II in 1154 confirms their "liberties and free customs to all men in the kingdom."[3] In Magna Carta the right to law is of course primarily guaranteed in Cap. 39, that no freeman is to be molested except "by the law of the land"; also by Cap. 24, prohibiting minor royal officers from trying criminal cases; and Cap. 13, which extends the ancient liberties and the free customs of the citizens of London as well by land as by sea to all other cities, burghs, towns, and ports in the realm as to their own law. In 1309 (see Historical Digest) we already find a statute restraining chancery jurisdiction and forbidding arrest, conviction, or forfeiture without a jury, a principle only recently revived in the Constitution of Oklahoma;[4] in 1331 a statute against invasion of common law jurisdiction by the chancellor; in 1383 a protest against Roman law and a definite prohibition of it to the courts of England; in 1391, no man is to be compelled to answer before a Lord (of matters determinable at common law), and there is another statute limiting admiralty jurisdiction and again prohibiting the Roman law. In 1406 the House of Commons present their Petition of thirty-one articles, of which the tenth provides that the Council should determine nothing cognizable at common law unless by the advice of the judges; and other clauses are that all officers shall personally perform their duties[5] and be sworn to observe "the common law of the land"; but in 1452, after Jack Cade's Rebellion, the Act 31 Henry VI, C. 2, provides that in case of riots or disorder an offender may be commanded to appear in Chancery and, if he disobey, the chancellor may issue writs of proclamation to appear within one month or suffer forfeiture or outlawry; and although this statute continued

[1] Stubbs' Charters, p. 101 (clause 13).

[2] Ibid., p. 108.

[3] Ibid., p. 135.

[4] See Book III., §§ 650, 662.

[5] For this principle in modern American State Constitutions, see Book III, § 215.

only seven years, its principle remained and is the historical origin of the use of the injunction process to prevent disorder or crime (see Chapter IV). So, in 1487, a statute of Henry VII gives special authority to the Court of Star Chamber over riots and disorders. But the abuse of the royal prerogative continued under the Tudors and Stuarts, until the Petition of Right in 1627 complains (Article 3) that although it is declared (quoting Magna Carta) that no man be imprisoned nor put out of his freehold, nor franchises, nor free customs unless it be by the law of the land, and established that from thenceforth none shall be taken by petition or suggestion made to the king or his Council unless it be by indictment or presentment of good and lawful people of the same neighborhood or by process by writ originally at the common law, and no one shall be forejudged but by the courts of the law, nevertheless of late times divers commissions have issued giving authority to proceed under martial law whereby (§ 8) some have been put to death when and where if by the laws and statutes of the land they had deserved death, by the same laws and by no other they ought to have been judged. And finally, the long history of invasion of the common law is closed by the entire abolition at the hands of the Long Parliament of the Star Chamber and of all but common-law courts. After the Revolution, the Bill of Rights complains that James II endeavored to subvert the laws and liberties of the kingdom, among other things by issuing a commission for a court to be called "The Court of Commissioners" (clause 3), and (Part II, clause 3) that both this commission and all other commissions and courts of like nature are illegal and pernicious. The right to the common law exclusively was too well established to need much expression in the Federal Constitution, but the Declaration of Independence complains (clause 17) that George III " has combined with others to subject us to a jurisdiction foreign to our Constitution and unacknowledged by our laws," and (clause 24) arraigns him for "abolishing the free system of English laws in a neighbouring province, establishing therein an arbitrary government." The Federal Constitution recognizes the principle in the seventh Amendment of the ten which are our national Bill of Rights, providing for suits at common law and trial by a jury, and that no fact so tried shall be otherwise re-examined in any court of the United States than according to the rules of the common law; while many State Constitutions declare the people entitled to the common law of England.[1]

[1] See Book III, § 76, and note 6.

The *equal* right to law was established as early as the Charter of Liberties of Henry II, and extended not only to the barons but to all persons except actual slaves; for even the villeins had full law rights. Magna Carta recognizes the principle of equality in Caps. 39, and in 40, — "To none will we sell, to none will we deny right or justice," and in the preamble conceding these liberties also "To all free men of our kingdom," and expressly in Cap. 60, extending all the foregoing customs and liberties not only to the king's tenants, but they are to be observed by all others, both clergy and laity, and in Cap. 65 (omitted by Henry III) granting the aforesaid liberties to all men. "By 1485," says Hallam, "the principle that all officers, administrators, or soldiers are liable at the common law for their acts, that is, the prohibition of the continental Administrative Law, had been fully established"; while in 1566 Speaker Onslow tells Elizabeth herself that she is subject to the common law. So in the Massachusetts Body of Liberties, clause 2, the same justice and law is extended to every one, whether an inhabitant or a foreigner;[1] and in the Declaration of Independence appears the famous statement that "All men are created equal," thus extending the principle established under Henry II, six hundred years before, that they are only equal before the law.

What is due process of law will be discussed later more particularly. It is particularly notable that the words of Magna Carta, "legal judgment of his peers or the law of the land," are, in the Statute of 28 Edward III replaced by the words "due process of the law," and the Petition of Right (Article 4) quotes the provision in the same words. It is probable that historically the words are synonymous; that is, "the law of the land" means by indictment and procedure at the common law, and "judgment of his peers" trial by jury, while "due process" includes both. There is still a feeling that the words "due process of law" will not justify prosecution by information or in any other manner than a common law indictment or trial except by jury.[2] The Supreme Court of the United States has, however, held that "due process of law" does not necessarily include trial by jury or, in certain cases, any court trial. The principle is embodied in the Fifth Amendment nearly in the words of the Statute of Westminster, "No person shall be

[1] See Book II, Constitutional Principles.

[2] See the recent amendment to the Wisconsin Constitution, Book III, § 127, and § 130, note 10.

deprived of life, liberty, or property without due process of law," and in the Fourteenth Amendment is required, in the same words, by the Federal Government of the States. It exists in this language in New York and in the newer States copying the Federal Constitution, but still stands in the words of Magna Carta in New England and the older States.[1] Finally, the principle that this common law under due process must be afforded to every person in his home or in local courts is expressed in Magna Carta, Cap. 17 in the exact terms demanded by the barons (clause 8 of the barons' demands),[2] that common pleas shall not follow the King's Court, but be assigned or held in some certain place; in Cap. 18, that recognitions shall only be held in the court of the county where the lands lie and that the king shall send two justices into each county four times a year to hold assizes where, if all matters cannot be tried on the day appointed, a sufficient number of knights and freeholders present at the assizes shall stay to decide them. It is further especially provided that the writ *præcipe* (Cap. 34) shall not in effect be issued so as to cause a freeman to lose his court; and this is also the exact words of the barons (clause 24), the object being to protect the local jurisdiction against the royal courts; and in Cap. 45, "justices . . . shall only be appointed of such as know the law and mean duly to observe it," — also taken literally from the barons' request; the meaning being to require local common law courts held by common law judges and allow no other jurisdiction. So in 1391 the law above quoted preserving the common law as against a Lord's courts; while by 1485 Hallam mentions as one of the six liberties now established the right to be tried by a jury of the county. In the Declaration of Independence the twenty-third clause complains of the king's "transporting us beyond seas to be tried for pretended offences" and the Virginia Bill of Rights (clause 8) provides for trial in the vicinage. The principle is preserved in the Federal Consitution, Art. 3, § 2, requiring all trials to be held in the State where the crime is committed; and so in most of the States.[3] The same principles are true of civil cases. Cap. 40 of Magna Carta applies to civil as well as criminal matters, slightly expanding the demand of the Barons (clause 30) "that justice shall not be sold nor deferred nor forbidden"; and the clause is adopted in almost the same words in all the State Constitutions.[4]

[1] See Chapter III, *infra;* Book III, § 130.

[2] Printed in Stubbs' Charters.

[3] See Book III, § 133.

[4] Ibid., §§ 70, 73, 79.

CHAPTER III

THE RIGHT OF LIBERTY

CIVIC liberty, as understood and enjoyed by the English people, has, like the right to law, important differences from the conception held in other countries. For the right to have one's person free of arrest, detention, or control applies as well to the government, the actions of officers of the courts of law, as to the trespass of any fellow-citizen; and the right of liberty in trade or industry involves the notion of protection from any monopoly or any privilege even if granted by the State, as well as from any combination of guilds or other workmen. Moreover, the right is guarded by the great institutions of trial by jury and *habeas corpus;* the former of which indeed has lately been copied in continental countries, but the latter, so far as I am informed, not even yet. There is on the Continent nothing corresponding to the constitutional right of any individual when arrested by an officer of government to demand instant information of the cause of his arrest and to be set at large unless indicted by a grand jury for a crime not bailable or for which the person accused is unable to give satisfactory bail.

The right of personal liberty includes, therefore, the right to life, that is, the right not to be deprived of life except under a general law of the land previously made, the facts to be found by a jury (Magna Carta, Cap. 39); and the right to liberty of the person, that is, freedom of bodily restraint either by imprisonment, detention, or the being refused locomotion to any place desired, even to the extent of leaving the kingdom. In this country this right has been found by the Supreme Court to involve the constitutional right to move from one State to another free of tax or hindrance,[1] and this is expressly decided not to rest upon the Interstate Commerce clause, but upon the right to personal liberty of the American citizen. On the other hand it involves the right not to be banished even

[1] Crandall *v.* Nevada, 6 Wall. 39.

for crime, presumably, therefore, not to be banished even from a State of the Union.[1]

The right to personal liberty is guarded by the writ of *habeas corpus*, preceded by the writ *de odio et atia* referred to in Cap. 36 of Magna Carta: "Nothing shall be given or demanded of another for the writ of inquisition of life or limb, but it shall be given gratis and never denied." The right to be informed at once upon arrest of the nature and cause of the accusation is a different and independent constitutional right from that to a grand jury or the process of indictment; although many State Constitutions confound the two. The right to be informed of the nature and cause of the accusation [2] is instantaneous upon arrest, or at least arises as soon as the accused is brought before a magistrate. The requirement that the person accused or arrested can only be tried on a finding of a body of twenty-three men, the grand jury, antedates the petit jury, going back to the time when the trial of facts was by ordeal. The English people persistently struggled for many years after the Conquest to have this the only method of accusation; the practice of beginning a criminal suit by information to the king or to a Crown officer, obviously Norman in origin, was obnoxious to the people; it cannot, however, be said that it was not finally established, though many of the American State Constitutions evidently contemplate that procedure by information is not "due process of law." Some of the western States, however, have shown a tendency to do away with the grand jury and use the process of information exclusively.[3]

There were twenty-five thousand slaves in England at the Domesday Book,[4] probably the result of earlier conquest or punishment, possibly of voluntary sale; but they soon disappeared, either by exercising a trade (see Chapter V) or by acquiring land, just as under the Dawes Act the allotment of land in severalty makes an Indian a United States citizen. Villeins were not regarded as slaves under the law; and they also disappeared, largely as a consequence of the rebellions of Jack Cade and Wat Tyler, which successfully established their right to land in severalty and to be paid money wages. Subject to this exception the right to liberty was

[1] The word "Banishment" is used in the sense of compulsory transportation beyond the limits of the British Empire. In early days it was defined to mean not beyond the four seas, Tangier and the Islands. A pardon, however, granted by a State governor on condition that the offender leave the State might possibly be upheld.

[2] See Book III, § 120, notes.

[3] See Book III, § 127.

[4] Taswell-Langmead, p. 18.

general in England from the earliest times. Henry VIII even, in 1514, manumits two villeins, using the words of the Declaration of Independence, "Whereas God created all men free."

The Statute of Westminster I, 1275, again refers to the writ *de odio et atia*, and the Statute of Edward III, 1354, in quoting Cap. 39 of Magna Carta, also says that "no man of what estate or condition that he be shall be . . . imprisoned nor disinherited, nor put to death without being brought in answer by due process of law," expressing for the first time that there must not only be lawful trial, but that the person accused must be present; and chapter 9 of the same Statute forbids the sheriffs by virtue of commissions and general writs to take inquest to cause to indict the people at their will, — expressly, therefore, providing for indictments.

"By 1485," says Hallam, "the right not to be imprisoned without warrant" was established; and in 1617 we find the last legislation concerning villeinage. During these centuries, however, there had been a persistent effort by all the kings to avoid the writ of *habeas corpus*, to arrest people without warrant or indictment, detain them without cause or trial, try them without a jury, or punish them by martial law. Finally, in the petition of Right (clause 5) the Parliament complains of this and that when they were brought up on *habeas corpus* they were still detained, without cause certified, by the king's special command; and in clause 10 they pray that no free man in such any manner be imprisoned or detained. Fourteen years later the Massachusetts Body of Liberties (Preamble) defines the denial of liberty to be the ruin of the Commonwealth, and first definitely adds to the principles above stated, that no person can be deprived of liberty or *property* or *reputation* unless by some express law of the country, *i. e.*, a general law warranting the same, established by a legislature, and sufficiently published; and (clause 18) "No man's person shall be restrained or imprisoned by any authority whatsoever, before the law hath sentenced him thereto, if he can put in sufficient security, bail, or mainprise for his appearance, and good behavior in the mean time, unless it be in crimes capital, and contempts in open court, and in such cases where some express act of court doth allow it." This was enacted nearly forty years before the Habeas Corpus Act, in 1679, first cured the defect in the writ by providing against delay and for bail, and extending the number of judges who are required to grant the writ; and still later the English Bill of Rights, prohibiting excessive bail, and a statute providing that it should apply as well to commitment upon civil as criminal cases; which is followed generally in American constitutions.[1]

The Massachusetts Body of Liberties (clause 17) provides for liberty to remove from the Commonwealth, and (clause 91) that there shall never be any bond slavery, villeinage, or captivity, unless lawful captives or such strangers as willingly sell themselves. Massachusetts, however, departed from this principle later, and a few slaves existed as late as the Revolution, when the Massachusetts Constitution in its Bill of Rights, Article 1, put an end to it by declaring that all men are born free and have inalienable right to liberty; so, the Declaration of Independence, clause 2, and the Virginia Bill of Rights (§ 1), but this was believed not to apply to negroes.

The objection to information or proceedings other than indictment is also foreshadowed in Magna Carta, Cap. 38, that no one shall be put to his law, that is, trial, by ordeal or otherwise, upon the bare saying of a bailiff (prosecuting officer), without credible witnesses to prove it, and by 1354 indictments are expressly required. The modern law of the English Constitution on this point is first fully expressed in the Virginia Bill of Rights, clause 8, that "in all . . . criminal prosecutions a man hath a right to demand the cause and nature of his accusation, to be confronted with the accusers and witnesses, to call for evidence in his favor[2] and to a speedy trial by an impartial jury of his vicinage without whose unanimous consent he cannot be found guilty," anticipating exactly the words of Hallam above quoted as early established in England.

Whatever may be the meaning of due process of law, there is no doubt that the words "judgment by his peers," in the great clause in Magna Carta, means trial by jury, or what then corresponded to it; and the reading of the clause developed with the growth of the institution to make our modern understanding that it must be a unanimous verdict of twelve who are not witnesses of the crime accused.[3] The Statute of Wales (1284) already provides a complete code of procedure with jury trial; but the system of punishing juries for a wrong verdict by attaint existed until 1670, and only at that time

[1] Va. B. Rts. 9; U. S. C. Amt. VIII. See Book III, § 122.

[2] This right is not expressed in the English Constitution. See Book III, § 135, note 6.

[3] See § 131, note 4.

was finally established their right to be judge of all the facts, a right extended in many of our State Constitutions to the law as well as to the facts, conjoined with a prohibition to judges to charge the jury on the facts or even to state them.[1]

The Virginia Bill of Rights requires a jury in criminal cases, and holds it preferable to any other mode of trial in civil suits; the Declaration of Independence complains of the deprivation of trial by jury. There has been no further development of the principle except in the direction of allowing verdicts by a smaller number than twelve, or, in civil cases, not unanimous.[2]

The provision against excessive bail, as has been said, dates only from the Bill of Rights. That against cruel or unusual punishments as well as excessive fines goes even back to Magna Carta, Cap. 20, providing that a free man shall only be fined for a small offence after the manner of the offence, for a great crime, according to the heinousness of it, saving to him his contenement; that is to say, his necessary tools of trade. The former provision is found in all our State Constitutions as well as the Federal;[3] and the latter in many,[4] and probably always by statute if not at the common law. Banishment was early held an unusual punishment, and there was probably never any legal torture in England, though once or twice the rack was introduced. The Massachusetts Body of Liberties, however (clause 43), says that no man shall be beaten with above forty stripes nor shall any true gentleman nor any man equal to a gentleman be punished with whipping, etc.; and clause 45, "no man shall be forced by torture to confess any crime . . . unless in some capital cases where he is first fully convicted, after which if the cause be of that nature that it is very apparent there be other conspirators or confederates with him, then he may be tortured, yet not with such tortures as be barbarous or inhuman"; and in clause 46, the usual constitutional provision is anticipated for bodily punishments, — "we allow amongst us none that are inhuman, barbarous or cruel," thus anticipating the provision of the Bill of Rights, clause 10, that excessive bail ought not to be required nor excessive fines imposed, nor cruel and unusual punishments inflicted, copied in the Virginia Bill of Rights, § 9; in the Federal Constitution, both as to the States and the nation; and in all the State Constitutions.[5]

[1] See § 675.
[2] See Book III, §§ 72, 132.
[3] Ibid., § 140.
[4] Ibid., §§ 81, 331.
[5] Ibid., §§ 122, 140.

The only exception to this common-law right to personal liberty and court trial (except that exercised under chancery jurisdiction discussed in Chapter IV) is the practice of finding a man guilty of a criminal offence, usually, but not necessarily, treason, by a bill of attainder; that is, a legislative act of the Houses of Parliament declaring the person guilty without trial and even in his absence. This practice was freely employed by the Tudors and Stuarts especially under Henry VIII.[1] It has never been declared unconstitutional in England, though the abuse was so well known to our ancestors that they expressly put it in the Federal Constitution as applied to the nation and to the States as well.[2] This has been followed in nearly all the State Constitutions.[3]

Some of the State Constitutions forbid imprisonment for debt in civil cases, a principle first embodied in the Massachusetts Body of Liberties, clause 33, providing that no man should be imprisoned for debt if the law could find competent means of satisfaction otherwise from his estate. The Body of Liberties also anticipates the modern right to counsel (clause 26), which, as a constitutional right, does not yet exist in England,[4] and (clause 47) requires two witnesses in capital cases.

Finally, the right not to be placed twice in jeopardy goes back also for its first clear expression to the Massachusetts Body of Liberties, which gave many principles both to later English constitutional documents and to the Federal and State Bills of Rights. Clause 42 reads: "No man shall be twice sentenced by civil justice for one and the same crime, offence, or trespass." The Habeas Corpus Act forty years later provided that no person once delivered by *habeas corpus* should be recommitted for the same offence. And while the Fifth Amendment to the Federal Constitution only provides that no person shall be subject for the same offence to be twice in jeopardy of life or limb, thereby limiting the principle to capital cases, many of the State Constitutions extend it to any criminal prosecution for which the punishment may be imprisonment.[5]

[1] See § 138, note 10.
[2] Art. I, § 9, (3); Art. I, § 10 (1).
[3] See Book III, § 138.
[4] See § 134, note 17.
[5] See Book III, § 137, notes.

CHAPTER IV

CHANCERY AND THE INJUNCTION ORDER

THE common law sounds in damages. In early times it was enforced, civil and criminal, only by a money penalty; or by personal redress or vengeance. Thus, the earliest codes or statutes merely fix a scale of penalties. The notion of compelling a freeman to do something or to abstain from doing something was foreign to Anglo-Saxon ideas of liberty. Like the doctrine of free will carried to its extreme, a freeman was lord of his own acts; only liable for the consequences of the same, to the person injured; later only to the Crown if a criminal act, and to the individual injured if a private wrong. Even when the judgment of the court went against him, the defendant was never compelled to *do* a thing, or even, in ordinary cases, to make restitution, as in the Oriental system of rendering justice. This principle must never be lost sight of, for it explains many things both in local history and in popular prejudice. Probably the power of the chancellor to issue injunction writs went as far towards prejudicing our ancestors against the courts of chancery and Star Chamber (which was merely its criminal side) as the absence of the jury and the local county court. Repeated attempts to limit or do away with this jurisdiction are found in the Statutes of the Realm, and the general prejudice against Chancery courts came to our ancestors by direct inheritance. As is known, some States, notably Massachusetts, for some time withheld chancery jurisdiction entirely, and when adopted it was in a limited and tentative way. On the other hand Congress, for the Federal courts, adopted the full English practice in the first judiciary act;[1] Art. III, § 2 of the Constitution expressly provides that the Federal judicial power shall extend to all cases, in law and equity.

[1] Act of Sept. 20, 1789 c. 20 § 11. By Rule XXXIII of the first (1822) Rules of Practice, equity practice is regulated by that of the High Court of Chancery in England; and so to-day, where applicable, by its "present" practice.

The use of the injunction to quell disorder or control the action of large bodies of men, with the vigorous use of contempt process, to an even greater extent, stirs public opinion to-day, though it also has very early precedents going back, like chancery jurisdiction itself, to the first century after the Conquest. It was used in early times to quell disorder; but its use to control the action of bodies of men in labor disputes may be said to date from the case of Spring Head Spinning Co. *v.* Riley, decided in 1868 (L. R. 6 Eq. 551). The principle of this case has had vast extension in the United States, due not only to the prevalence of labor disputes and the activity of organized labor, but still more to the inefficiency in many parts of the country of the local courts and of the State police; and most of all to our State and Federal system and the fact that the Constitution gives the Federal courts jurisdiction for suits between citizens of different States, as railroad, mining and manufacturing industry is with us almost entirely carried on by corporations. Frequently chartered in other States than where the trouble occurred, it was a convenient thing for the corporation which feared prejudice in the local courts, or distrusted their strength or the strength of the local police to enforce their orders, to go into the Federal courts and obtain injunctions for the enforcement of which they could, in last resort, depend upon the entire military force of the United States.

English notions of liberty, it is true, resisted the chancellor's power in its most dangerous path; that is to say, in applying the doctrine of specific performance to the contract of labor; though we see an effort to arrive at the same result in the so-called "peonage laws" in the south, as well as in recent injunctive orders or mandatory injunctions of Federal and other courts ordering a man or bodies of men not to quit work. Specific performance of a contract to render services, like a contract for indefinite or long term service, too much resembled slavery to be tolerated at the common law. And indeed contracts to do work "in gross," piece-work, not paid by the day, had to be expressly authorized by a statute of Edward III (1360). Nevertheless, statutes requiring a man to labor at *some* work continued for several centuries.

Bearing in mind firmly the principle that the English law sounds only in damages, and that the notion of ordering or even forbidding any act (except under a criminal statute) is utterly foreign to its system; and the cardinal principle that no fact can be found without the intervention of the petit jury; we shall be able to understand both the historical reason and the present meaning of the objection of the American people to the injunctive powers of chancery and the *ex parte* sentences for contempt made by the judge who issued the injunction and upon the facts as found by him showing the infringement of the same. It must also continuously be borne in mind that this chancery power to sentence for contempt of an injunction writ is wholly different, both in historical origin and in logic, from the necessary inherent power of any common law court to punish for contempts committed in the presence of the court itself; for this is a power inherent in the Court, and the Massachusetts Body of Liberties in 1641 only anticipates the Oklahoma Constitution of 1907 in recognizing it only as to "contempts in open court." [1]

We have already cited many statutes indicating the dislike of our ancestors to courts of Chancery and the Star Chamber; Coke himself speaks of the latter complainingly as "a court of criminal equity." In 1327 King Edward III found it necessary to adopt some more effectual measures of police than those which already existed. For this purpose justices of the peace were first instituted throughout the country, with power to take security for the peace and bind over parties who threatened offence; [2] and only four years after this we find the first statute against invasion of common law jurisdiction by the chancellor, forbidding the arrest or conviction of a man or the forfeiture of his property without a jury trial in a common law court. In 1382 the Commons themselves complained to the king of grievous oppression by the great barons which rendered the remedies of common law courts of no avail. Accordingly the judges of these courts themselves were placed under the special supervision of the chancellor, who began to exercise his authority in repressing disorderly obstructions to the courts of law and in affording civil remedy in cases of outrage which could not be effectually redressed through the ordinary tribunals (precisely the reason advanced for the great use made of the injunction writ to-day); but thereupon the Commons took great umbrage at the exercise of such authority by the chancellor, claiming that this jurisdiction was an interference with the common law, but the king persevered, stating that he would preserve his prerogative.[3] Later the Court of Star Chamber had the

[1] Mass. Body Liberties § 18; Book III, § 662.

[2] Spence, Equity Jurisdiction, pp. 342–344.

[3] F. J. Stimson, "Modern Use of Injunctions," printed as Senate Document, Report 827, 54th Congress, 1st Session; Political Science Quarterly, Vol. 10, No. 2.

same jurisdiction and Coke particularly mentions as part of it "the suppression . . . of great and horrible riots, routs, and unlawful assemblies, leaving ordinary offences to the courts of law."[1] In 1348, according to Herbert Spencer, the court of Chancery became the Court of Equity with power to relieve in certain cases and a fixed abode; and it is a curious coincidence that the very next year was passed the first Statute of Laborers, the first law requiring compulsory labor save of slaves or villeins in England; confirmed in 1360 by a statute which also contains the first prohibition against combinations by trade alliances in restraint of trade or to fix wages, and in 1388 villeinage was abolished or commuted to a fixed money payment. That is to say, the freedom of labor and the principle forbidding combinations to control labor grew up together. Then, in 1452, after Jack Cade's Rebellion, we have the definite invention of chancery process to control riotous laborers already (Chapter II) referred to; and in 1487 the Court of Star Chamber is given special authority over riots and disorders. Finally, in the 5th of Elizabeth, the great Statute of Laborers was enacted, consolidating all previous laws and still maintaining the principle of compulsory labor and fixed wages, but it was only enacted to be forgotten, save for the principle that it bequeathed to English law that strikes and trade unions were unlawful combinations.

Many further authorities can be cited to sustain this position; but these are sufficient to establish the general principle that the injunction process and contempt in chancery procedure, as well as chancery jurisdiction itself, is looked on with a logical jealousy in Anglo-Saxon countries as being in derogation of the common law; and that, while an injunction to prevent irreparable injury to property or private rights will not be refused because the injury be also a crime or misdemeanor, yet the naked principle is undoubtedly true, as indeed is the history and the logic of the thing, that under the English legal system the power of the king's chancellor may not be invoked to forbid or punish a crime as such, thus taking away the jurisdiction of the common law courts and depriving the person accused of his trial by jury.[2] The objection, therefore, to the abuse of the injunction is

[1] F. J. Stimson, "Handbook to the Labor Law of the United States," 1st Edition, pp. 315–316.

[2] "A court of equity has no criminal jurisdiction, but it lends its assistance to a man who has, in view of the law, a right of property, and who makes out that an action at law will not be a sufficient remedy and protection against intruding upon his possession." (Macauley *v.* Shackell, 1 Bligh, N. S., 96, 127.)

". . . 'If an act be illegal,' said Vice-

sound, and this in our country not only for the historical reason we have explained, but because it tends to make the courts no longer judicial but in effect part of the Executive branch of government. This is the sense of the popular phrase — and most popular phrases have some sense — "government by injunction." [1]

There has, of course, been no constitutional limitation of the powers of equity in England, nor is there in the Federal Constitution, which clearly contemplated giving all judicial power which then existed in England to the Federal judiciary in cases where they had jurisdiction; but the State Constitutions are beginning to deal with the subject and several States have attempted statutes. The matter is likely to be of large importance in the future, for bills to limit or prohibit punishment by contempt for disobedience to injunctions granted by courts of equity, at least in labor or trade disputes, are pending before Congress and in nearly every State of the Union. The constitutional provisions will be found in Book III, § 662. They have so far been adopted in the Constitutions of seven States. Whether, in the absence of a constitutional provision, a statute to that effect would be valid, is a matter so untouched as yet by any decision of a high court that the author can only hazard his own opinion. While a legislature cannot take away the power of a common law court, at least, to sentence for actual contempt committed in its presence, necessary to preserve the dignity of the court, there would seem no reason why, in the absence of a constitutional provision recognizing chancery jurisdiction, a State legislature should not do away with contempt process in equity or even with chancery jurisdiction entirely, though perhaps it may not legislate especially and only for labor disputes, under the Fourteenth Amendment. In some States, as has been pointed out, chancery jurisdiction did not originally exist; there are, however, several States which recognize it in their Constitutions,[2] while other States declare that common law and chancery shall be "fused" or that all the courts shall exercise chancery jurisdiction. In these States, as the doctrine of specific performance and the contempt power is the very right arm of chan-

Chancellor Kindersley, in Solteau v. De Held, 2 Sim. & Stu. 153, 'I am not to grant an injunction to restrain an illegal act merely because it is illegal. I cannot grant an injunction to restrain a man from smuggling, which is an illegal act,' nor could he for any merely criminal or penal offence." F. J. Stimson, "Handbook to the Labor Law of the United States," p. 318.

[1] U. S. Senate Report 827, 54th Congress, 1st Session, p. 116. Charles Claflin Allen, "Injunction and Organized Labor," 17 American Bar Association Reports, p. 299.

[2] See Book III, § 651.

cery, it may be questioned whether a State statute may forbid the writ of injunction, require a jury trial, or deny the power to enforce it by fine or imprisonment; and so Congress, under the Federal Constitution, may have no such power. But it may surely limit the extent of punishment to be inflicted, as is done by statute in Kentucky, to imprisonment for ten or thirty days, or at most six months, — the extreme sentence now usually imposed. A shorter limit would be adequate to any emergency and equally well protect the dignity of the Court.

CHAPTER V

THE RIGHT TO LABOR AND TRADE

Coming last to the liberty of labor or trade, it is the more important to trace the appearance of the great principles falling under this head for the reason that they have largely been lost sight of in American jurisprudence. The frequent enactment of acts against trusts, monopolies, or contracts in restraint of trade, both State and Federal, show that our Legislatures, if not our Bench and Bar, must have substantially forgotten the body of the common law, to say nothing of the course of English constitutional history upon these matters.

For the broader understanding of the liberty right involves as well as the liberty of life and person, the liberty to support life and family. That is, to exercise one's labor freely and without control, to acquire possessions, to earn wages and to exercise one's faculties in any lawful way, without competition by the State or any organism of the State and without restraint or hindrance by the government or by individuals. The extent of this right is the matter most discussed to-day and therefore it is far the most important one to be considered. Closely connected with it is the right to private property, at least in so far as such property is the result of a man's labor,[1] and the right to freedom of contract for such labor or in the exercise of such trade both as to reward or profits and conditions. There is probably no constitutional principle more often invaded by modern statutes than is this.

Both liberty of the person and liberty of trade are guaranteed by the great clause of Magna Carta, especially by the explanatory words added in the Charter of Henry III: "No free man shall be taken or imprisoned or disseised of his freehold *or his liberties or his free customs*, unless by the lawful judgment of his peers or by the law of the land," which latter expression was, as we have found, changed in the recital of later statutes to "due process of law."[2] Sir

[1] This kind of property is expressly declared to be the only one guaranteed by the Constitution of Oklahoma; see Book III, §§ 13, 14; also see Chapter VIII, *infra*.

[2] See §§ 127, 130, notes.

Edward Coke's famous exposition of this clause points out that it protects, and was understood at the time to protect, a man's liberties or free customs, meaning both the laws of the realm, any franchises and privileges that may have been bestowed upon him, and the national freedom possessed by the subjects of England; and, as being opposed to these last, forbids monopolies;[1] and we may add to these many other matters as we follow the development of this clause in the statutes. Moreover, the Preamble begins by saying "We have granted to all the freemen of our kingdom all the under written liberties"; and a very important result of the constitutional right to trade or labor lay in the fact that a villein, although escaping from the Lord of his manor, who worked at a trade in a town a year and a day, thereby became free. Another great development of this principle was the successful insistence of laborers that their wages should be paid in money and not in produce; for money is the badge of free labor; as we instinctively feel about peonage. Still another clause of Magna Carta (Cap. 13) provides that the City of London shall have all its ancient liberties and free customs, and so of all other cities, etc., which means not only the right to law, as described in the last chapter, but the freedom of trade and labor as well. Cap. 33 in Magna Carta providing for the destruction of all weirs or impediments to navigation, early suggests the general freedom of trade under the English Constitution; so Cap. 41, providing for the liberty of merchants, and prohibiting any evil tolls other than the ancient and allowed customs; and the Charter of Henry III (Cap. 30) amplifies this. Earlier local charters recognizing freedom of trade were granted to London by Henry I;[2] to all men by Henry II in his Charter of Liberties,[3] and so in his Charter to the Town of Winchester,[4] and later by Richard I to the same town.[5] In 1200 the Charter of Nottingham [6] recognizes the trade gild with similar liberties. The usual phrase in all these charters is "the ancient and free customs which are enjoyed by the citizens of London of which were enjoyed by the town itself when they had them 'best or most free.'"[7] So the Charter of York [8] recognizes especially its merchant gild. While, finally, the Charter of John to London [9] grants them to have "well and in peace freely,

[1] Taswell-Langmead, p. 104.
[2] Stubbs' Charters, p. 108.
[3] Ibid., p. 135.
[4] Ibid., p. 165.
[5] Ibid., p. 266.
[6] Ibid., p. 309.
[7] Charter of Winchester, A. D. 1190, Stubbs, p. 266.
[8] A. D. 1200, Stubbs, p. 312.
[9] A. D. 1215, Stubbs, p. 314.

quietly and in full all its liberties which they were used to have up to that time as well in the town of London as outside, by sea or by land and in all other places." All these, it will be noted, preceded Magna Carta, and that instrument goes beyond trade, to recognize what we should call commerce; as in Cap. 33, providing for freedom of navigation of all rivers, and Cap. 42, granting liberty to all to leave the kingdom and return to it at will. So, a statute of 1335 allows free trading in England to foreign merchants, and in 1340 all merchants are allowed to come freely into the kingdom, and in 1344 all persons may buy or export wool and the seas shall be open to merchants. The Statutes of Staple are full of provisions requiring freedom of trade. In 1362, 36 Edward III, there is a statute requiring merchants to deal in only one kind of goods, and handicraftsmen to use but one mystery or trade, but it is notable that the former part of the statute was repealed the following year; the part concerning handicraftsmen, only under Elizabeth. In 1383 Wat Tyler for the villeins demanded among other things freedom of commerce in market towns. In 1436 is the first statute against by-laws in restraint of trade "by persons in confederacy for their singular profit and the common damage of the people," using modern language, but recognizing such combinations as unlawful by existing law. It would be easy to multiply examples of statutes recognizing the general right of the English freeman to labor or to trade without being coerced in any manner and without combination or privilege against him.[1] In the Declaration of Independence the king is complained of "for cutting off our trade with all parts of the world," but the principle was so thoroughly established as to require no express mention in our Federal Constitution other than that contained in the ordinary due-process-of-law clause of the Fifth Amendment, and of the Fourteenth Amendment requiring for all persons the equal protection of the laws; the word "liberty" being well understood to include this most important liberty-right as well as the mere right to life and personal freedom. The broad principle is probably nowhere better defined than by the Supreme Court of the United States, speaking through Mr. Justice Field in the Slaughterhouse Cases[2] "Among these inalienable rights as proclaimed in that great document [the Declaration of Independence] is the right of men to pursue their happiness, by which is meant the right to pursue any lawful business or vocation in any manner not inconsistent with the equal rights of others, which may

[1] See more particularly Chapter VII. [2] 111 U. S. 757.

increase their property, or develop their faculties, so as to give them their highest enjoyment. . . . The common business and callings of life, the ordinary trades and pursuits, which are innocuous in themselves, and have been followed in all communities from time immemorial, must, therefore, be free in this country to all alike upon the same conditions. The right to pursue them, without let or hindrance, except that which is applied to all persons of the same age, sex, and condition, is a distinguishing privilege of citizens of the United States, and an essential element of that freedom which they claim as their birthright." And by the same Court through Mr. Justice Peckham in Allgeyer *v.* Louisiana:[1] "The liberty mentioned in that amendment [the fourteenth] means not only the right of the citizen to be free from the mere physical restraints of his person, — as by incarceration, — but the term is deemed to embrace the right of the citizen to be free in the enjoyment of all his faculties; to be free to use them in all lawful ways; to live and work where he will, to earn his livelihood by any lawful calling; to pursue any livelihood or avocation; and for that purpose to enter into all contracts which may be proper, necessary, and essential to his carrying out to a successful conclusion the purposes above mentioned." Nevertheless, a few of the newer State Constitutions express the right and express it very well.[2]

As we have said, both the right to labor and the right to property necessitate the right of free contract; and while it may be admitted that a legislature in the exercise of the police power may enact a statute forbidding for the future a specific class of contracts when the court can see that the object of such statute bears an intelligible relation to the health or safety of the community or to protect it against imposition or fraud, an arbitrary statute, especially when directed against certain races or certain classes of the community, should not be held constitutional.

The constitutional freedom of labor and trade involves, as has been said, matters commonly invaded by modern statutes; such as our laws fixing the hours of labor of adult men in special occupations, and of women of full age in all, in States which adopt the theory or express in their Constitution the civic equality of women in all particulars with men;[3] Massachusetts, however, allows the labor of adult women to be limited by law, at least in ordinary mills and

[1] 165 U. S. 589.

[2] See Book III, §§ 6, 13, 14, 16, 20.

[3] See Book III, §§ 23, 24, and 25 with notes.

factories; and a law of Oregon prescribing her hours of work in all mechanical employment has recently been declared by the Supreme Court not to violate the Fourteenth Amendment. In all States such regulation is permissible as to persons under age. And in all States, it would seem, the labor of women may be restricted or forbidden in occupations tending to immorality or to provoke immorality in others, such as serving in drinking saloons; and the labor of adult men may be regulated in such employments as are dangerous to the health or safety of the public. But the better law is that the hours of labor of adult men may not be limited for the benefit merely of the health of those employed. So, of the rate of the wages and the payment of wages. It will be seen in the Historical Digest that a long series of acts endeavoring to fix the rate of wages and, indeed, general prices, began in England as early as 1266, was abandoned, and tried again until finally definitely given up for the last time about the time of Elizabeth.[1] The result may be said to be that the fixing of wages is part of the freedom of contract with which the State cannot interfere, at least in ordinary cases (for the exception of seamen is perhaps as old as the principle itself). One State Constitution states this expressly;[2] but the expression is probably unnecessary. New York alone, in a recent Constitutional Amendment, makes a step in the direction of allowing the State to fix wages in public employments. The question whether the time or kind of payment of wages may be regulated by statute is much more difficult. This interference with the freedom of contract has led to wide differences of opinion in the courts. In Massachusetts a weekly payment law has been held not an infringement upon personal liberty; in most of the western and southern States, otherwise.[3] Laws requiring wages to be paid in money or in cash orders, not in commodities or store credits, have been more usually held constitutional, as tending to protect the public, or a large class of the public, against fraud; and as has been said, the contracts of seamen have been regulated from time immemorial. The whole question comes down to this, whether there is such a constitutional principle as the right to freedom of contract; that is to say, a constitutional right to make

[1] See "Historical Digest," *Annis* 1266, 1349, 1350, 1353, 1362, 1388, 1389, 1427, 1444, 1514, 1562. The effort to regulate the labor contract ended with Elizabeth; laws fixing prices for commodities were given up much sooner.

[2] See Book III, § 14.

[3] For a full statement of all these matters, see the author's "Handbook to the Labor Law of the U. S."

what contract the two parties choose, so long as it be not criminal or immoral. It is still impossible to make a final and definite decision on this point. The courts, from the Supreme Court of the United States down, while they have shown a tendency to sustain a law prohibiting future contracts of a certain kind when they can see an element of fraud or protection to the people, have, at the same time, when their attention is not called primarily to the question of legislative power, found, or still more, taken as a matter of course, in hundreds of decisions, that there is such a thing as a constitutional right to freedom of contract derived from either of two sources, — the right of freedom to labor or the right to acquire property; neither right being of value unless one can make contracts concerning it.

The scene of battle to-day, for this principle, is the question of contracts agreeing or not agreeing to employ, or not to discharge, or not to employ, either Union or Non-Union labor (for the legal principle must be the same whether the contract concern Union labor or Non-Union labor, whether the promise be by the employer or by the employees, whether the illegal combination or compulsion complained of be exercised by one or the other side to the dispute). Many States have passed statutes forbidding discrimination against Union labor, that is, forbidding an employer to discharge, or not to employ, or to threaten to discharge a person for being a member of a Union. In most of the States where such statutes have been construed by the courts they have been held unconstitutional; and so recently by the U. S. Supreme Court.[1]

[1] Adair *v.* U. S., 28 Sup. Ct. Rep. 277.

CHAPTER VI.

THE RIGHT TO PROPERTY

All personal property is the result, in last analysis, of free labor, while ownership of land was a cause of freedom in itself. This species of property, indeed, preceded the right to labor discussed in the last chapter, and while it is probable that there was always property in a man's personal belongings, yet the written law was not much concerned with personal property until some time after the Norman Conquest when (1100) we find a statute giving a man the right to bequeath it at his death. The abstract word "property" is not mentioned in any constitutional document before the Virginia Bill of Rights; but the Massachusetts Body of Liberties protects a man's "goods or estate," while the words "freehold" and "cattle" in Magna Carta itself substantially comprise all varieties of property then commonly enjoyed. It is noteworthy that the property right is guaranteed by the same words and in the same clause in all constitutional documents from Magna Carta to Oklahoma, although Oklahoma afterwards qualifies it by saying that a man has an inherent right only to such property as results from his own natural industry.[1] On the other hand, Washington and Utah expressly say that the object of government is to protect and maintain individual rights. The Petition of Rights recites both Magna Carta and the Statute 28 Edward III requiring "due process of law"; while the Massachusetts Body of Liberties (Section 1) seems to think that a statute might deprive a man of his property, wife, children, or estate if it were only general and published beforehand; while if there be no common law or statute for the case, it may be "by the Word of God." So, "Christianity is part of the common law." The right of the State to take property upon due compensation will be found expressed repeatedly in Magna Carta[2] and indeed in many other constitutional documents; while the American Constitutions[3] only add that the compensation must be made before the taking, and the amount found by a jury.[4]

[1] See Book III, §§ 14, 130, 183.

[2] Caps. 28, 30, 31.

[3] See Book III, §§ 90, 91.

[4] See Book III, §§ 93, 94.

The usual infringements of the property right are by way of taxation, regulation of rates or charges, and the police power.[1] The earliest tax, in the modern sense, other than the feudal Aids, was the Saladin tithe on personal property (1188).[2] The right to regulate the charges of those exercising franchises or enjoying monopolies granted by the State does not properly fall under the head of either eminent domain or the police power, though often confounded with one or the other, and is equally ancient.

We have already pointed out how Clauses 12 and 14 of Magna Carta, requiring that no aid or tax should be taken except by the Common Council of the Realm and prescribing how the Common Council of the Realm should be held, — that is, by a summons to the bishops and greater barons by special writ and to other chief tenants by general writ, — were omitted one year later in the Reissue of Henry III and not restored until the Confirmation of Charters of Edward III in 1297; when the important phrase is furthermore added that they must not only be by the common assent, but also for the common profit of the Realm; and by 1353 this was established to apply also to indirect taxation, and by 1407, that all money bills must originate in the lower house. These principles have neither been added to nor improved upon in the very latest State Constitutions, which, indeed, have rather shown a tendency to infringe upon them, as in the betterment tax, and in the extension of the right of eminent domain to private uses, recently, however, held unconstitutional in the State of Wyoming.[3] The Massachusetts Body of Liberties (Clause 8) extends the principle of eminent domain only to cattle and goods. The Petition of Rights repeats Magna Carta as to taxation by assent of Parliament; and the several State Constitutions merely repeat the general principle, though they sometimes forbid the right to tax to be given or granted away.[4] So, also, the Federal Constitution,[5] that taxes must be for the general welfare of the United States and be uniform, and [6] that bills for raising revenue shall originate in the lower house. The principle that money raised by taxation must be used for purposes to which it is expressly appropriated, established in England in 1666, is repeated.[7] The Bill of Rights complains of the king's levying money without the grant of Parlia-

[1] See Mr. Justice Brewer's "Address to the Yale Law School," June 23, 1891.

[2] For other early tax laws, see Historical Digest, *Annis* 1193, 1203, 1275, 1309, 1322.

[3] Sterritt *v.* Young, 82 Pac. 946.

[4] See Book III, § 330.

[5] Art. I, § 8, Clause 1.

[6] Art. I, § 7, Clause 1.

[7] Art. I, § 9, Clause 7.

ment, and the Declaration of Independence that he imposed taxes on the Colonies without *their* consent.

Neither police power nor the regulation of charges is mentioned in any constitutional document; but the early statutes are full of instances independent of the attempted fixing of the price of bread and beer according to the price of wheat and barley respectively by the Assize of bread and beer;[1] nine years later the great Statute of Westminster I prohibits excessive toll contrary to the common custom of the Realm in all market towns; and many such statutes might be found applying to ferries, wharves, toll roads, or any other franchise or monopoly made by law. And finally, in the year 1691, there is a general statute fixing the rates of common carriers. Moreover the early reports are full of indictments against persons keeping a ferry, etc., for extortion.[2] Logically, it would seem that the right of the State to regulate charges by those enjoying franchises it has granted would be absolute; it has no connection with the eminent domain principle requiring property not to be taken without compensation; but American courts have held the right subordinate to the constitutional provisions securing property right.[3]

The principle against monopoly or restraint of trade, though not expressed in any constitutional document, is quite as old as many that are, and may fairly be considered as part of the law of the land. Indeed there is no principle in any of the modern statutes against trusts which cannot be traced to an historical prototype. It is only necessary to look at our Historical Digest to see how frequently these principles find expression in statutes from the very earliest times, when statutes were understood but to express the common law.[4] The common law against contracts in restraint of trade and engrossing of the market having been thus established, we begin to find the same evil reappearing under State grants of monopoly; much as to-day when the trusts were forbidden by the Sherman Act of 1890 against trusts, they proceeded to form corporations, thereby securing a franchise under the shield of some State. Indeed it is hardly too much to say that the so-called anti-trust legislation, by preventing any reasonable agreement even when meant only to

[1] "Historical Digest," *Anno* 1266.

[2] *I. e.*, discrimination. See Rex *v.* Burdett, 1 Ld. Raymond, 143; Roberts' case, 4 Mod. 101; Rex *v.* Wadsworth, 5 Mod. 13.

[3] See Book III, § 13 and note; U. S. C. Amts. 5 & 14.

[4] See Book II, "Historical Digest," *Annis* 1285, 1335, 1350, 1362, 1425, 1436, 1503, 1533, 1552. In this year the statute against forestalling was made perpetual, and not repealed until the latter part of the 18th century.

make rates equal and prevent discrimination, compelled in itself the formation of the thing it was designed to prevent.

Noticing as we pass an early appearance of the prejudice against middle-men, especially coal dealers (1553) and the statute of 1555, which seems to anticipate the notions of modern socialists that there is a monopoly in the instrumentalities for the production of wealth, we find in 1571 a definite complaint of monopoly. In 1601 the abuse increases so much that indignant speeches are made about it in the House of Commons.[1] Nevertheless, James I found it too easy a method of raising money to abandon, and he awarded patents for dealing in articles which were not even inventions or matters of special trade. About this time too arose the trading corporation, then really first invented, historically derived from the religious corporation or the gild, but now directed to private gain and having one of the essential modern attributes, perpetual succession, though the other, that of non-liability of members, was not, as far as I can learn, imagined until a statute of the State of Connecticut enacted in May, 1818. These early corporations, however, such as "The Turkey Company," "The India Company," "The Hudson Bay Company" often gave a monopoly of trade with the respective countries indicated; but the objection would not be felt to be the same as that against a monopoly at home. Finally, in 1623, the great Statute of Monopolies was passed, just after the famous case of monopolies was decided, holding that such were against the common law of the Realm and prohibiting the king from dispensing with the common law by granting licenses. This statute, 21 James I, is extremely like a modern anti-trust statute in that it gives remedy in double or treble damages to anybody injured, and makes exception of copyrights and certain corporation charters.

It may fairly be stated, therefore, that the principles against what we now call "trusts," against monopoly and against combinations to fix prices, limit output, or secure a monopoly in restraint of trade, are derived from fundamental principles of the common law. The modern statutes against trusts, while possibly necessary as to a Federal statute, there being no Federal common law in civil matters, and therefore comprising but the enunciation of common-law principles as to interstate commerce, with the imposition of a penalty and the provision of remedies, were not really necessary as to State Legislation. Nearly one-half, indeed, of the State anti-trust laws have

[1] See F. J. Stimson, "American Constitution," page 114.

been declared unconstitutional, either by the U. S. Supreme Court or by the courts of the State enacting them; while the half that is valid hardly do more than enunciate the principles of the common law.[1] In England no more legislation was necessary. The Massachusetts Body of Liberties copies the Statute of Monopolies passed eighteen years before: "No monopolies shall be granted or allowed amongst us but of such new inventions that are profitable to the country and that for a short time." And finally the American principle against class legislation, of which in our next chapter.

[1] See Book III, Art. 58. The East India Co., chartered under Elizabeth, is said to have been the first trading corporation in the modern sense; that is, an association for making money and dividing the profit, although it allowed the members to trade separately. In 1643 came the charter to the merchant adventurers of England "for the better maintenance of trade" closing with the words "said Fellowship shall be a corporation and shall have power to levy moneys on the members of the corporation and other goods for their necessary charge and maintenance of their government," thus anticipating the principle of stock assessments; and the charter gave a monopoly of trade "into those parts limited by their incorporation." In the same year is a charter to merchants trading in the Russian seas, and in 1650 a charter to the weavers of Norwich giving power to adopt by-laws, to impose fines for imperfect weaving — lately forbidden by statute in Massachusetts, which statute was declared unconstitutional (Croth *v.* Perry, 155 Mass. 117). A few years later come the Hudson's Bay and Greenland Companies.

CHAPTER VII

OTHER CONSTITUTIONAL RIGHTS

THERE are several other cardinal rights of less importance than those to liberty, which may be considered as consequences either of it or of the right to law. All of these have been preserved, and many of them amplified, in our Constitutions; while hardly a new one is added, unless it be the right to reputation, which, indeed, Blackstone mentions as a cardinal right, and the recently felt notion of right to privacy (this is recognized in a very striking manner in the Constitution of Washington [1]), and the provision against imprisonment for debt which appears in the Massachusetts Body of Liberties and in a few State Constitutions. But most important of all, the principle against class legislation found in the Virginia Bill of Rights (Clause 4), "That no man or set of men are entitled to exclusive or separate emoluments or privileges from the community," the Fourteenth Amendment, § 1, that "no State . . . shall deny to any person within its jurisdiction the equal protection of the laws," and much more definitely expressed in the State Constitutions;[2] an American principle, for the great clause of Magna Carta, extending the law of the land to all, is no guaranty against class legislation contained in an Act of Parliament. Closely allied to this is the provision against hereditary privileges, titles of nobility, etc., contained in both State and Federal Constitutions, and deemed of such importance that it is forbidden in the Federal Constitution to the States.[3] It is difficult to see how the provision in the North Carolina and other Southern Constitutions against hereditary privileges is consistent in principle with that extending an hereditary right to vote.[4] Equal law is furthermore extended to all races[5] and sexes.[6] American Constitutions, of course, prohibit slavery, but so, in modern times, does the English. A striking statement of the principle of equality

[1] See Book III, § 71.
[2] See Book III, §§ 16, 395.
[3] See Book III, § 17.
[4] See Book III, § 246.
[5] Fourteenth Amendment; Book III, §§ 20–21.
[6] Book III, §§ 23–27.

before the law will be found in the Massachusetts Body of Liberties, Clause 2.[1]

The principle of equality by birth declared in the Virginia Bill of Rights and the Declaration of Independence is not carried into the Federal Constitution, though it is found in nearly all State Constitutions.[2]

The right to bear arms was inherent in the English people; in fact, under early laws, was compelled. The barons were required to support their king in war but they early complained against being led out of the kingdom, and King John's insistence upon this was the principal cause leading to Runnymede. This right is expressed in every American constitutional document as well as all the State Constitutions. On the other hand, the objection to mercenaries or standing armies seems to have always existed. There were practically none in England until the time of the Stuarts, (though Italian and German — "Brabazon" — mercenaries were first employed in 1449, to suppress Jack Cade) a cause to which most students of constitutional history attribute the preservation of English freedom and parliamentary government.

The objection to the use of the army to establish military tribunals or to overawe the people is apparent in a long range of constitutional documents and statutes. Correlative to this, but having its source also in the right to the common law, are many statutes in early times protesting against the laws of the Forest; also the general prohibition of martial law, — the English and American principle being that the military must never be independent of or superior to the civil power.[3]

The militia, the ancient defence of the realm, we find revived only seventeen years after the conquest; and the support of the militia, or even of the army and navy, is therefore entrusted to the legislative branch both in our Federal and in the State governments, their command only entrusted to the Executive, but his use of the army is carefully limited to definite emergencies (invasion, insurrection, etc.); and, as between the State and the Federal power, the President cannot employ the State militia but in a national emergency, nor Federal troops in a State except when requested thereto by the legislative authority thereof — save, indeed, where necessary to maintain the functions or officers of the Federal Government, or when

[1] See Book II., Constitutional Principles.

[2] See Book III, § 11.

[3] See Declaration of Independence, Clause 16.

the State Government ceases to be republican in form but of that it does not appear from the Constitution whether Congress or the President is to be the judge.

These three principles will be found recognized in every one of our constitutional documents, both English and American, and in all the State Constitutions.[1] Even military law, the necessary regulations for the government of the army and navy in actual service, is only made possible in England by an annual re-enactment of the Mutiny Act, and the same effect is secured in the Federal Constitution by the provision that Congress may make no appropriation for the army for more than two years. The right to bear arms, however, does not prevent laws for the punishment of carrying concealed weapons, nor does it authorize bands of men not belonging to the militia to drill or parade armed, while the recent provisions in some new State Constitutions against "Pinkerton" men, or the employment of private armed guards, is curiously reminiscent of the earlier English statutes against "retainers."[2]

Of the other rights which are common to the English and American Constitutions, freedom of speech may be first mentioned, which arose very early as to members of Parliament or debates in Parliament; but is perhaps not otherwise a right recognized in the English Constitution except so far as involved in the political right of assembly and petition, for which see later. It is recognized as a general right, however, in the First Amendment to the Federal Constitution and in all the State Constitutions. Freedom of speech, in political matters at least, is, however, established in England, and freedom of the press even more definitely, so that a man is able to write what he will on all subjects, being only responsible for libellous matter. There is generally no distinction between the two rights made in American Constitutions.[3]

The important political right of assembly and petition is rather the original than a derivation from freedom of speech, and is also related to the general political rights of the English subject. It is recognized first clearly in the Bill of Rights, and generally in American Constitutions,[4] and forms an indispensable part of the political liberty enjoyed by the Anglo Saxons. Indeed this, with the right to bear arms, has always been the essential difference which has

[1] See Book III, §§ 62, 63, 290–295; Book II, Constitutional Principles.

[2] See Book III, § 63, note 5.

[3] See Book III, §§ 60, 61.

[4] See Book III, § 64; U. S. C. Amt. 1.

attended revolutions or popular reforms in England from other European countries. The other political rights are mainly the great right of equal representation in the legislative assemblies, with correlated provisions for free elections and for the judgment of disputed elections by the legislative body itself, not by the Executive, nor even, unless the Legislature so will, by the courts.[1] The requirement that elections shall be free appears in the Statutes of the Realm as early as 1571, but is finally embodied in the Bill of Rights as well as in the Virginia and Massachusetts Constitutions. There appears to be no English constitutional principle respecting the right of suffrage, which, from having been early shared in by all freemen, was in 1429 limited to the forty shillings freeholders; but it is carefully provided for, to a limited extent saving property rights, in the Virginia and Massachusetts Bills of Rights; and in the Federal Constitution, providing that all electors who vote for the lower house of the State Legislature shall vote for the President; and as to race distinctions, or even educational or property qualifications, in the Fifteenth and Fourteenth Amendments respectively. Hardly any property and few educational qualifications remained in the State Constitutions a few years ago; but there is a tendency to re-impose them.[2]

Having thus established the right of the people to be represented in a legislative body and having established in effect the right of that body to participate in all law-making and to originate all laws imposing taxes, it only remained for our ancestors to prevent the suppression of the legislative body by the Executive, or "personal government" attempted without the Parliament or without calling the Legislature together. This principle first appears in the statutes in 1330 and is embodied in the English Constitution in the Bill of Rights, and in the Federal Constitution, Art. I, § 4, requiring annual sessions of Congress.

The important new American principles of government, the separation of the powers, and the effect of the written constitution on statutes, have been discussed in an earlier chapter. The former principle appears in the Federal and in all the State Constitutions with the striking exception, to which attention was called in a recent decision of the Court of Appeals of that State, of New York. The expression of it in the Virginia Bill of Rights is interesting; and they attempt to engraft upon it the possibly more debatable prin-

[1] See Book III, § 270.

[2] See Book III, §§ 240, 245, 246.

ciple of rotation in office. The exclusion of the judicial branch from this last principle is equally striking and counter to prevailing tendencies to-day.[1] The more abstract provisions of American constitutional documents supposed at the time to embody new political principles[2] have so far hardly resulted in more than the sounding phrases in which they are couched, while generally principles embodying the idea that governments are formed for the people and by the people, that all officers are but the servants of the people, and that, when the government fails of its effect in protecting natural rights, the people may and should alter or abolish it, — have hardly more practical result in constitutional law than the possibly moral justification of a future revolution.[3]

The last important addition made by American Constitutions is perhaps that of religious rights[4] and in State Constitutions, education.[5] The former is not completely yet a constitutional principle in England, — for there is still an established Church, — and its expression originated with the Virginia Bill of Rights, though there are foreshadowings of religious freedom even in the Massachusetts Body of Liberties. The inclusion of education as a natural right by our State Constitutions may have interesting consequences,[6] but the Federal Constitution does not recognize it. The former principle prevents any discrimination against any person on account of his religion as well as any sectarian appropriation or established church, but it does not justify, under the guise of religious belief, crime or practices inconsistent with the safety or well being of the State.

The last significant innovation, and not the least important, made by American Constitutions, is the prohibition of general warrants, the exercise by the government of the power to search places or seize persons with no specific charge and without a sworn warrant specifying an offence, the persons to be seized, and the objects of seizure. This principle, originating in Massachusetts ten years before the Revolution,[7] became later (1765) indeed a constitutional principle in England, but is not of course expressed in any of the

[1] See Book II, Virginia Bill of Rights § 5.

[2] See Book III, §§ 5, 185.

[3] See Book II, Constitutional Documents, Chapter III, Clause c., Theory of Government; and Chapter VIII below.

[4] See Book III, Art. 4.

[5] See Book III, Art. 5.

[6] See Book III, §§ 50, 190, note 9.

[7] See Book III, § 71, note 10. But see Petition of Right, Clause 2, complaining of commissions directed to commissioners to raise moneys for the king, who administered an oath not warrantable by the laws or statutes of the realm.

so-called constitutional documents, which are usually considered as terminating with the Act of Settlement. It is most strongly expressed, however, both in the Virginia and Massachusetts Bills of Rights and in the United States Constitution, Fourth Amendment. It is, of course, closely connected with the right of a person not to be compelled to give self-criminating evidence, but it has a far broader historical connection with the general objection of the Englishman to inquisitions, visitatorial expeditions by king or Crown officer, going straight back, indeed, to the great clause of Magna Carta. A man's private affairs cannot be looked into nor his papers searched except in judicial proceedings or upon the charge of some definite offence; while even then he may refuse either to testify or furnish documentary evidence if it may reveal him guilty of a criminal offence, unless under a law guarantying him immunity not only for the offence charged, but for all offences that may be revealed by the process directly or indirectly, either in that court or in any other court of the same sovereign. The immunity does not, however, have to be extended to courts of another State or country, or even, in the Federal courts, to those of any State, and *vice versa;* nor, it appears, is the privilege one which may be claimed by corporations. On the other hand, the privilege undoubtedly relates only to the danger of a criminal prosecution, and can hardly be extended to cover a general right to privacy, either of person or possessions, however much that is to be desired.

CHAPTER VIII

RIGHTS OF GOVERNMENT

In England, if there be a sovereign, it was the king in Parliament and is now practically the House of Commons. In either case, not the people, though they elect their representatives; for Parliament can change either law or form of government. In America, by definition of our Constitution, it is the people; though refiners in substance may trace it back to a majority of an assemblage of three-fourths of the States, by which alone the Constitution can be amended.[1] This, however, seems rather like casuistry; while the people provided that their written Constitution could only be amended regularly in that way, it equally remains true that the people themselves might at any time amend it by a successful constituent assembly; it hardly needs the assurances of the Declaration of Independence and other constitutional documents [2] to assure that principle. We may therefore lay down the proposition that all political power is inherent in the people, that governments derive their just powers from the consent of the governed, except, indeed, when we exercise territorial jurisdiction, and that the people may alter the government when it fails of its design or ceases to be Republican in form.[3] The Declaration of Independence is not part of the American Constitution, although printed at the beginning of the Revised Statutes of the United States, before the Constitution itself, and although certain of the Acts of Congress admitting territories provide that they shall adopt Constitutions in accordance with its principles. However, therefore, it may be questionable in abstract theory, at least for States of the Union, it is true that the people are sovereign.

Representative government was a mediæval — in the forms it has most successfully developed, an English — invention. It did away

[1] See James B. Thayer, "Legal Essays," pp. 200–204.

[2] See Book III, § 181.

[3] See Book III, §§ 181, 182, 183.

with the pure democracy to which "legislation by the people" — initiative and referendum [1] — would seem to return. Therefore they found it necessary to provide particularly for the great Council of the Realm, later Parliament, later the representative House of Commons; and for its frequent meeting. As early as 1330 we find a statute requiring annual sessions of Parliament; in 1362 the principle is repeated. Triennial Acts follow, in 1641 and 1694; and in 1716 the duration of Parliament is extended to seven years. With us the Virginia Bill of Rights expresses the doctrine that all magistrates or officers of government are but the trustees or servants of the people, and the Federal Constitution as well as the Bill of Rights of Massachusetts requires that legislative bodies should meet annually.

It follows that elections must be free and that Parliament must sit without dictation of the executive branch,[2] the efforts of the kings to resist this having proved futile.[3] The long attempt of the Executive to make laws by orders in Council or by proclamation, or indirectly by suspending laws already existing, may be traced through the history of the middle centuries until they ended in the Bill of Rights.[4] It is now an established constitutional principle that the Executive can neither suspend a law nor suspend a penalty nor even pardon an offence in anticipation of trial.

The history of suffrage may be summed up in the statement that originally all free men had the vote; that is to say, when there was a vote. In early times of course only the peers of the realm, the barons or tenants in chief, came to Parliament. Beginning with the time of Magna Carta we may trace the practice of summoning representative commoners by general writ; then for two centuries we find indirect general suffrage through the County Courts; but in 1429 we find a disfranchizing act, restricting the voting qualifications to forty shillings a year freeholders, which, in England, has never been entirely abolished since. In the United States we have, since the Fourteenth Amendment, and under State laws, manhood suffrage without distinction of race; although property, educational, or other distinctions are allowed, subject only to the consequent

[1] See *infra*, Chapter IX; Book III, § 309. The early system was of course the primary assembly or folk-mote, etc. Early European prototypes disappeared; only the English Parliament endured.

[2] See "Historical Digest," *Annis* 1275, 1407, 1485, 1707.

[3] Ibid., *Annis* 1539, 1609.

[4] Ibid., *Annis* 1407, 1414, 1485, 1539, 1609. Stimson "The American Constitution," p. 102.

diminution of representation in the Federal Congress.[1] The effort to control elections and candidates was, indeed, made in England, especially by James I, but was early abandoned, and the principle exists there as here that only the legislative body itself can judge of the qualifications returns of its members unless, indeed, it choose to delegate that power to the courts.[2] Legislative sessions must (except executive sessions of Senate), with us, be open; not necessarily so in England; but in both countries the legislative body has power to protect itself against contempt; and of this it may not be deprived. It may expel a member and it may punish a person not a member, but probably in America only by fine or imprisonment, the latter not to last beyond the duration of the session. Speech in the Legislature is free in both countries, and the members themselves are privileged from arrest except for felony or, in England, on civil process, which privilege early extended to their servants and members of the household; not, however, to attachment for contempt of *habeas corpus*.[3] The principle of freedom of elections was reiterated in the English Bill of Rights and is preserved in American constitutional documents,[4] and our State Constitutions usually require vote by ballot and secrecy of the ballot, though by recent amendments voting machines may be used.

Officers of the government are, as has been said, the trustees or servants of the people. They may not hold place in more than one of the three departments or, with us, usually, in both State and Federal preferment. They are sworn to support the Constitution of the United States and must give attention to the duties of their office and not farm it out to others. This principle, dating from the petition of thirty-one articles to Henry IV in 1406, is copied in some modern State Constitutions.[5] They may be impeached by the lower house for crime or mere maladministration, which impeachment is tried by the upper house; and no pardon is available but they are still liable to trial at the common law.[6]

The right of assembly has been already discussed.[7] By an Act of 1549 unlawful assemblies of twelve to alter laws or abate prices were made unlawful, which apparently gave rise both to the modern riot acts and to the notion that strikes were criminal. This, how-

[1] See Book III, §§ 23, 240, 245, 246.
[2] See Book III, § 270.
[3] See Book III, § 273.
[4] See Book III, § 237.
[5] See Book III, § 215.
[6] See "Historical Digest," *Annis* 1485, 1512, 1581; Act of Settlement, Clause 8.
[7] See Chapter VII.

ever, has nothing to do with the *political* right of assembly. In the Massachusetts Body of Liberties, Clause 12, every man shall have liberty to come to any public court, council, or town meeting, and there by speech or writing move any lawful, seasonable, and material question, so it be done in convenient time, due order, and respectful manner. Bowen says that this right was not established in England until the Bill of Rights in 1689, nearly fifty years later.[1]

The early English statutes protecting the subject against attainder or trial for treason [2] and requiring two witnesses to the same overt act are copied in American constitutional documents, Federal and State, and extended in the Massachusetts Body of Liberties (Clause 47) to capital offences.

Finally, the most important of all our governmental principles, that of the separation of the powers into three departments, is expressly recognized in both Federal and all State Constitutions, except, possibly, New York, though by a recent decision of the Supreme Court of the United States, it is not guaranteed by the Federal government to a citizen of a State in the State. We have already discussed this principle as one of the two most important American constitutional innovations. Nevertheless, there are foreshadowings of it in English constitutional documents or statutes outside of the writings of theorists. Thus, in 1615, the attempt of the Executive to control the judicial branch led to the famous rebuke of Chief Justice Coke. He was indeed removed, and from that time until the Civil War judges held office at the king's pleasure, but in the Act of Settlement it was for the first time embodied in writing that their tenure must be for life, and their remuneration not dependent on the caprice of the king. This, also, has been copied in the Federal Constitution and originally in all the State Constitutions.[3] The States have indeed largely departed from this principle since, in so far as their appointment is concerned, judges being now elective in almost all, but their compensation continues to be fixed, not to be changed by the legislature and they may not be removed by the Executive.[4] The Declaration of Independence stated the principle clearly when it complained of King George that he made judges dependent on his will alone for the tenure of their offices and the amount and pay-

[1] See Book II, Constitutional Documents; Bill of Rights, Clause 5.

[2] See "Historical Digest," *Anno* 1552.

[3] See Smith, "The American Constitutions," Philadelphia, 1797.

[4] See Book III, §§ 206, 660.

ment of their salaries. Furthermore, that he was guilty of usurpation in that he refused his assent to laws and forbade the passing of laws until his assent should be obtained, and refused to pass other laws unless the people would relinquish the right of representation, "a right inestimable to them and formidable to tyrants only," and in the Virginia Bill of Rights (Clause 5) we find the principle first expressed that the legislative and executive powers of the State should be separate and distinct from the judiciary, and the two first should at fixed periods be reduced to a private station; which principle of rotation in office, however, is expressly declared not to be applicable to the judicial branch.

Nothing remains but to remark of the American Constitution that it creates a government of limited powers and that those not therein expressed, however usual to sovereignty in other countries, are not given to the present government, but remain with the people; that is to say, the people's will as expressed by the legislatures of three fourths of the States or by conventions of the people in three fourths thereof. The will of the people in these conventions is final, — higher than any other governmental authority, requiring not the consent of the Executive; although Abraham Lincoln, with pardonable satisfaction, appended his name to the Thirteenth Amendment abolishing slavery. And our government must be republican in form, and constitutional; that is to say, it must protect even minorities or individuals in certain cardinal rights. "Absolute, arbitrary power over the lives, liberty, and property of free men exists nowhere in a republic, not even in the largest majority." [1]

[1] See Book III, § 182.

CHAPTER IX

GOVERNMENT ORGANIZATION

This, the matter usually treated of in constitutional history, we may dispose of briefly. The main distinction of the American Constitution, that of the separation of the powers, we have been compelled to anticipate. It is not complete; for instance, the Executive has, under the Federal Constitution, some legislative powers, such as the veto; and during his term of office a certain control over the judiciary, by his power to appoint and promote; the Senate, in its power to confirm appointments and advise and consent to treaties, some executive powers; the judicial branch alone has no part in the other two.[1] But in England there is no clear division, nor even effort to secure it; though the tendency of history has been in that direction and many of the evils complained of by the people have resulted from the confusion of the powers or their usurpation by the king or his officers. Broadly speaking, English history has gone through the following stages: In the beginning the people, all freemen who chose to attend the Great Council, made the laws; later, after the attempt to usurp the law-making power failed under the Norman and Angevin kings, they were made by the king in Parliament; later the king tried to secure legislative power to the king in Council. In the last stage, the power went back absolutely to Parliament and practically to the House of Commons: more practically still, to an inner committee of the Cabinet of the party in power, just as with us, short of a great popular movement, the real power of shaping ordinary legislation rests with the Speaker of the House. English constitutional history clearly establishes two or three other principles: That the king can neither make laws, nor suspend laws, nor grant pardons in advance for a crime or breach of the law, nor ever in cases of impeachment. The first and the last are expressed clearly in the Federal Constitution, and it might be wished that the other two were also. The

[1] It has been claimed by Mr. Hearst and others that the power to declare a law unconstitutional is legislative, but this is not the correct view. See p. 8, *supra;* Stimson's "The American Constitution," pp. 7–10.

power of suspending laws or their application, or agreeing not to prosecute in certain cases or to pardon certain offenders, is a dangerous one in the hands of the Executive. Moreover, there is an increasing tendency to-day in Congress to grant legislative power to the Executive or to boards or commissions of his appointment. Notably has this been done in recent years in the case of making treaties, fixing customs duties, the rates of railways, and in the control of corporations, — all properly legislative matters. The excuse made is that Congress but declares the general principle, and that the act of the president, for instance, in finding a state of affairs to exist upon which he may ratify a treaty or proclaim a commercial arrangement, is merely ministerial. An example of the length to which this theory may be carried is found in the recent railway regulation act or Hepburn Bill, where Congress merely proclaims that the rates shall be reasonable and without discrimination, — both mere expressions of the common law, — and leaves the determination of what is reasonable between the Interstate Commerce Commission and the Supreme Court, neither of them legislative bodies. The common law may, indeed, be decided by a judicial body; but it is difficult to see why the alteration of the common law is not legislation. When, therefore, the Commission fix a "just and reasonable" rate,[1] if they are applying the common law, their act is judicial; if they are fixing other standards, it is legislative. Federal judges have consistently, from the beginning, refused to exercise other than judicial functions, though they have accepted functions which are in a sense judicial but were not conferred by the Constitution; as, notably, in the Venezuela arbitration and in the Electoral Commission of 1884. Recent State Constitutions express this point particularly, independent of the usual section concerning separation of the powers.[2] It may be urged in objection to the too frequent invocation of the courts in trade disputes that they tend to make the courts take part in the administration of affairs.[3]

In England for a time it was urged that the king might make laws punishing offences which were *mala in se*, or might increase penalties in such cases, or suspend laws generally directed at things not *mala in se;* but it may be doubted if much be left of that distinction to-day. Somewhat analogous to it, however, is the growing practice of leaving to the president or the attorney-general or other

[1] U. S. Act of February 4, 1887, as amended June 29, 1906, § 15.

[2] See Book III, §§ 200 n., 650.

[3] See above, Chapter IV.

officers to determine what corporations or combinations are unlawful under Federal legislation, or otherwise, when in principle or in outward form they may all be the same.

Other examples of the confusion of the departments in England may be instanced in the usurpation by the Star Chamber, later the Privy Council, of executive and judicial functions; it is significant that the "Orders in Council" [1] survived to be a principal cause of the War of 1812. It may be questioned whether Parliament to-day would not interfere, were such orders attempted.[2] The interference of the king with legislation by dictating to Parliament or even by his personal presence, notable under Henry VIII through Cardinal Wolsey, and by Charles I himself, is familiar to all readers of history; and his attempt to secure the opinion of judges in advance of their decision, or even to dictate and compel them to decide in a certain way, as well as the practice of attainting juries, has been discussed elsewhere.[3] James I also sat personally in court, but was told by the judges he could not deliver an opinion.[4]

The judicial power has been broadly discussed above.[5] Usurpation by the judicial branch has never existed in this country nor has it been complained of since the time of Thomas Jefferson; nor ever, as to common-law judges, in England; except, indeed, by James I, who complained that "The courts of common law had grown so vast and transcendent as to meddle with the king's prerogative." [6]

The executive power, while probably it was intended by Hamilton and others to be given to the president in much the shape that it was enjoyed by a constitutional English king, nevertheless reveals striking differences in the two Constitutions. Indeed, our Supreme Court has remarked more than once that the American president is not a king even for four years; that though in theory he exercise the rights of an English sovereign it is with the loss of many a flower of the English king's prerogative. On the other hand, he has more powers as to treaty making, more powers in fact (though not in theory) as to making war, and is expressly made commander-in-chief of the Army and Navy. He has the veto power which has

[1] See Declaration of Independence, Clause 7, and 18: "He has combined with others to subject us to a jurisdiction foreign to our Constitution." These words refer to the Orders in Council.

[2] Stimson, "The American Constitution," pp. 102, 130.

[3] Ibid., p. 100; Book III, § 131.

[4] Ibid., pp. 100, 101.

[5] See Chapters I, II, III, IV, and more particularly throughout the footnotes following the text of Book III.

[6] Stimson, "The American Constitution," p. 118.

practically passed from the English king's prerogative, and most important of all, he appoints all Federal officers, even the judges. Practically all these powers are exercised in England by the lower legislative house through its committee, the Cabinet. Moreover, they, or the prevailing majority, in effect designate the prime minister and through him the rest of the Cabinet. With us the president appoints them, and in this instance at least, his appointments are nearly always confirmed. Both king and president make oath that they will support the National Constitution. Neither may dismiss the Legislature (under recent practice, at least in England) and both may call it together.

The American president is, indeed, liable to impeachment, but in England the Parliament or even the House of Commons have many times claimed the power of deposition which is very nearly expressly recognized in the Act of Settlement; indeed, the king has been called but the personification of a majority in the House of Commons. Finally, the American president has far more power, even under the text of the Constitution, in the *execution* of the laws than has the English king.[1]

Coming to the State Constitutions, we have discussed the political powers generally in Book III, Part 2, and the legislative power in full in Part 3. The principle of representative government is recognized in all Constitutions, except that of Oklahoma, and, by recent amendments, in States adopting the general initiative. Representation must generally be apportioned according to population; the separation of the powers is most carefully provided for,[2] and the constitution and functions of the Legislature are the same as in the Federal Constitution. The powers of the governor resemble those of the president, except where (as in war, treaties, etc.) restricted by the Federal power. The terms of office are usually shorter, and sessions of the Legislature not so frequent as in the case of Congress.[3] All Legislatures are paid, though very much less than members of Congress; and the provision in the Federal Constitution against plurality of office is much extended, even so far as to forbid in most States a member of Congress or person holding any lucrative office under the United States from sitting in the State Legislature or being elected as governor.[4] Conversely in New York and Michigan, no

[1] Stimson, "The American Constitution," pp. 164–166.

[2] See Book III, §§ 200, 201.

[3] See Book III, §§ 203, 204.

[4] See Book III, § 220; Stimson's "American Statute Law, Vol. I, § 220 (B).

member of the State Legislature can, during his term, be elected to the United States Senate; and in New York and several other States a member of the State Legislature taking any United States office or being elected to Congress vacates his seat. Thus, the English principle that the holder of a Crown office may not sit in the House of Commons, is extended, with us, to the holding of a legislative function in both sovereignties. Practically all State officers may be impeached and the usual English constitutional powers are given to the State Legislatures.[1] The machinery of legislation is much the same and the constitutional principle that all revenue measures must originate in the lower house and be for the general good of the people is fully recognized.[2] The veto power is extended in all the States except North Carolina and Rhode Island; usually in the same terms as in the Federal Constitution.[3]

But by far the most important innovation in the government organization of the States is, of course, the initiative and referendum, now adopted generally under the Constitutions of seven States,[4] and, as to local referendum, on certain matters of debt and taxation, in many others.[5] The wise modern tendency is to require a referendum as to all acts of State, county, city, or town government creating a municipal debt or granting a public franchise. This, however, though similar in principle, is so different in consequence from a broad general referendum covering all legislation of any sort, especially when coupled with the initiative which enables the people to dispense with the Legislature entirely or even to amend the Constitution by direct intervention of the people, that the narrower referendum first mentioned, limited to certain matters affecting local interest, may be dismissed from our further discussion. The State initiative is, of course, direct legislation by the people; and this, it must be noted, is no new thing, but merely a recurrence to primeval principles, — doing away with that invention of representative government which has served the English people well for a thousand years and has been commended as their peculiar contribution to political science. Direct legislation early existed in England, at least as to the free men or greater barons; indeed, mention is made by historians of a Witenagemot of sixty thousand men meeting on Salisbury Plain not very long after the Conquest.[6] The inconven-

[1] See Book III, §§ 260, 270.
[2] See Book III, §§ 300, 310.
[3] See Book III, § 304.
[4] See Book III, § 309.
[5] See Book III, §§ 316, 363 and 372.
[6] Hannis Taylor, I, 240.

ience and expense of such large assemblies, coupled perhaps with the notion of greater wisdom in their chosen representatives, gave rise to the device of representation. It is difficult to see why the objections of a thousand years ago do not apply to-day, at least as to the initiative, and even as to the referendum. The inconvenience of referring all laws to the people is already shown in the usual provision that they must be allowed to vote on each amendment to the Constitution separately, and that not more than two or three amendments may be submitted in any one year;[1] for submission of a law by referendum is practically the same in working as that of a constitutional amendment. Indeed, we already have the principle of the initiative in full operation in the adoption of new State Constitutions;[2] still more so when the State Constitutions require the submission of a new Constitution or the voice of the people as to whether one is necessary, every seven,[3] ten,[4] or twenty[5] years.

One of our political parties peculiarly favors the referendum and may, perhaps, even adopt it as applicable to Federal legislation. There is no logical difficulty as to this, for, after all, the people made the Constitution and not the States; to the people, therefore, may be referred both any amendment to the Constitution, and any law, by permission of the Constitution when amended so as to allow the referendum. Whether such a system would be workable may be told better when we have the experience in the smaller field of the States.

The objections to the referendum fall into three arguments: First, that of inconvenience above referred to; second, that it takes away responsibility from the legislatures to the extent of belittling both their personnel and their ambition; third, that the people themselves are not wise enough or competent to vote directly upon laws. If all laws are to be subject to a referendum, the legislature becomes nothing but a draughting committee for which it were better to substitute a mere parliamentary counsel.[6] If, on the other hand, the people have the initiative and employ it generally, it is hard to see that any function remains to the legislature whatever.

[1] See Book III, § 993.

[2] See Book III, Art. 99.

[3] N. H., see Book III, § 994.

[4] Io.

[5] Md., N. Y., O.

[6] It is the practice in the English House of Commons to have bills draughted by such a permanent body of experts, and the adoption of the practice in this country has lately been recommended by Bryce. Indeed, the result of the present system may be seen in Oregon, where the Secretary of State complains bitterly of the form in which laws are drawn up by initiative.

Unfortunately, our experience at the time of going to press (March, 1908), is too limited to enable us to form a judgment on this great question. Seven States, as we say, have adopted the referendum, but three of them did so only in the year 1906. The Oregon amendment was itself originated by initiative petition and not by the legislature; and extends the general referendum to items or parts of acts and also to all local or municipal legislation, not more than ten per cent of the voters to be required for the referendum or fifteen per cent for the initiative.[1] The early use of the initiative in Oregon is instructive. Under it the Legislature were allowed to regulate the binding and printing of State documents — a matter of comparative unimportance — and free passes were prohibited to railroads, etc.; but the enacting clause being omitted, this latter law was considered of no effect. The veto of the governor does not usually extend to measures referred to the people by initiative or referendum, any more than it would to constitutional amendments.

In municipal matters the referendum is making much more rapid progress; as has been said, that sphere is peculiarly appropriate to it. Indeed, the famed system of municipal government in New England, the town meeting, like the early Witenagemot, is nothing but the initiative and referendum combined in one assembly. As a matter of fact, however, the articles in the warrant are shaped by a small committee of the town, thus resembling bills prepared by a legislature or draughting committee (the Selectmen) and referred to the people in town meeting. Other measures than those recommended may, however, be adopted directly at such town meeting, which was thus, until the initiative, the only example of direct legislation in modern times.[2]

So far it does not appear that the referendum makes much alteration in legislation; though of course the fear of it may prevent many laws which the Legislature might otherwise pass; nor does it appear that measures begun by the initiative are much more likely to pass the popular suffrage than those drawn up by the Legislature. The practical working of the initiative leaves, as has been said, much to be desired. A constitutional amendment adopted by initiative was not even printed in the Oregon Annual Laws.

[1] Charles Edward Merriam, in N. Y. State Library Bulletin No. 113, Review of Legislation for 1906.

[2] For a full discussion of the municipal referendum, see Delos F. Wilcox on local government, printed in N. Y. State Library Review of Legislation for 1905, p. 191.

A more radical measure still, is that of the recall; that is, any senator or representative, or possibly even a judge or other officer, may be instantly retired by a direct vote of the people. As to this, and indeed the referendum, it may safely be said that the laws should be very careful to require a sufficiently large proportion of the total vote. The writer believes the most serious danger of the initiative and referendum to be its perversion to the very corrupt purposes the institution is designed to prevent. It would be easy enough for a public service corporation, directly or indirectly controlling possibly a tenth of the voters of an entire city, to propose complicated laws, by initiative, which the people might find hard to understand or in which they would take little interest; and so rush them through a popular election by a vote of their tenth of the votes, the rest of the people not taking the trouble to understand the question. The experience of constitutional amendments has shown that the votes upon them are ridiculously small. In New York, for instance, in 1905, a constitutional amendment altering the entire economic law as to the rate of wages to be paid in public work [1] passed the popular electorate by a vote hardly one-tenth of the total vote thrown for governor, — a far less important matter.

[1] See Book III, § 453.

CHAPTER X

FEDERAL AND STATE POWERS

THE division of all governmental powers, judicial as well as legislative and executive, into two sovereignties, whereby a strong national government is made compatible with local courts, laws suited to the conditions and institutions of each several State, and home administration of domestic affairs, — is the most striking of American inventions and has been discussed elsewhere.[1] This it is which chiefly distinguishes the American public from France or most other modern governments; though indeed some resemblance to it may be found in the system of the German Empire. Our frontispiece shows graphically this division of powers: the whole circle representing the sphere of all possible legislation, and every possible division and qualification of power being represented in the several zones; the blue zones "A" and "B" representing powers granted, express or implied, to the Federal Government and to the States respectively; the red zones "X" and "Z" representing powers denied or withheld, expressly or by necessary implication, from the Federal Government and from the States respectively; the perpendicular lines always referring to the States and the horizontal lines always to the Federal Government; while that domain of sovereign power left uncovered in the centre by either the two blue zones of permission or the two red zones of denial represents those cardinal rights and that part of ultimate sovereignty which the people who adopted the Constitution chose to keep in their own hands not only by necessary implication, but by the express iteration of the Tenth Amendment. These divisions of power and negations of power we have endeavored to analyze in detail in Chapter III of Book II; but it remains for us here to study the broad lines and the leading principles of this great division of all constitutional powers between the States and the Federal Government.

The Federal powers are political; that is the great criterion. The State powers, on the other hand, are domestic, social. They relate

[1] See Chapter I; Stimson, "The American Constitution," Chapters V and VI; Book III, Art. 19.

to the relation between a man and his fellow-men, to his control over his own property, taxation for all purposes but national defence, and to the trial of his disputes with his neighbors, of his controversies with all except the Federal Government, and of all his crimes or offences except only those which, like treason, relate directly to his duty to the Federal Government, or are committed in the places subject to its exclusive jurisdiction, such as forts, military reservations, national territory not incorporated into a State, and the high seas. The Federal Government is a political sovereign; but has almost none of the attributes of sovereignty for any other purpose. This broad fact is revealed to us with startling clearness when we note that it has generally neither the power of capital punishment nor, in effect, of direct taxation. It would be hard to find two more necessary attributes of sovereignty, as commonly understood in the science of government, than the power over life and the power over property. Moreover, except for specified purposes of national defence, etc., it cannot hold any land; even the district of the capitol is limited to ten miles square. Even its political power is far less than is commonly enjoyed by sovereign nations; it cannot, for instance, cede territory from any State. Moreover, our national sovereign is controlled by the most fundamental of all limitations. It may not, under the Constitution — that is to say, without going back to the people, which it recognizes as the only source of power — change its form from a republican form of government,[1] not even to a pure form of democracy.[2] It is even possible, under the Fifth and Fourteenth Amendments, that it may not adopt a system of socialism or communism, or permit a State so to do.

To see how completely this division between what is political and what is social, domestic, or relating to private right is carried out in the Federal Constitution, it will repay us to run over its provisions in some detail. The Preamble relates both to social and political objects, such as the common defence, but lays down at the beginning the great principle that it is the people and not the States who made the nation and the Constitution. The first two sections of Article I relating to Congress are political. Section 3 forbids all direct taxes, that is, all taxes directly imposed upon property or individuals, except they be apportioned to the States according to their popula-

[1] Cooley, Const. Law, Chap. XI; 3d ed., p. 213.

[2] Art. IV, 4.

tion, and not according to their wealth. This not only is, but was intended to be, in effect a prohibition to the Federal Government of the power of direct taxation. All the rest of the first seven sections are also political; relating generally to the organization, election, and liberties of the Congress, and the method of legislation. Section 8 of Article I contains almost the only powers given to the Federal Government which may, under our division, be called social; and while no one would desire to change the Constitution in this particular, it is highly significant that this exception has given rise to most of the litigation, most of the discussion, and to the leading division between the two great political parties to-day. That is to say, while the object of the Federal Government is to protect the nation from attack and manage its foreign affairs and impose taxes therefor "for the common defence and general welfare of the United States," the lesson of the existence of the thirteen States under the Confederation showed that they could not be trusted with the regulation of commerce passing from or to other States and crossing their borders. This, therefore, was denied to the States, and necessarily left to the Federal power; doubtless, however, rather with the intention of preventing the States from interfering with such commerce than of allowing the Federal Government to do so. Then, Congress is authorized to make a uniform bankruptcy law throughout the United States; the only matter in which the necessary advisability of uniform laws was recognized in the Constitution and expressly given to the Federal Government; and the power to establish post offices and post roads and issue national patents and copyrights, being a usual national power, is hardly an exception to our rule. Yet these matters, until we come to the Fourteenth Amendment, are the only subjects in which the Constitution clothes the Federal Government with any power relating to the citizen's individual affairs and his private business.

But even the political powers are not broadly given. The eight clauses of Section 9 in the first article consist entirely of negations; and there are many others.[1] On the other hand, the entire sovereignty of the State over individual relations, social and domestic affairs, and property rights is shown by the very few restrictions and exceptions we can find in the Federal Constitution. And these exceptions are purely political,[2] except in so far as they guarantee the

[1] See Chapter III, Book II (X), (ZX).

[2] Ibid., (Z).

rights of citizens of States to equal law in other States. The experience of the Revolution gave rise to Article I, Section 10, Clause 1, prohibiting them from passing a law impairing the obligation of contracts; that is to say, a stay law, or a law preventing any creditor — and it was aimed to protect creditors outside the State — from enforcing lawful contracts or debts. National political powers, as well as powers of national taxation, or taxes upon interstate or foreign trade, are, of course, forbidden to the States. Article II relates entirely to the Federal executive power and is entirely political; Article III to the Federal judicial power, and here we find that the only case where the national courts may be invoked except to interpret and define the Federal Constitution is to guarantee a fair trial in an impartial tribunal between citizens of different States. Article IV, Section 2, does, indeed, provide that a citizen of one State shall have all the social and contractual rights that are given in any other State to the citizens thereof; but this can hardly be said to give the Federal Government any power over social matters; rather it merely guarantees the right to law in each State to all citizens of other States, much as the Fourteenth Amendment later does to all citizens of the United States, and even as Henry II guaranteed it to all freemen of England. Over the territories, indeed,[1] Congress[2] is expressly given full power, social and domestic as well as political; but it is only of late years that it has generally exercised it in any other way than to erect territorial legislatures; and in the older territories, at least, there is no meddling with individual rights.

The first eleven amendments are *all* restrictions; that is to say, they are at great pains expressly to withhold all social and domestic affairs, or cardinal liberty rights, from the Federal Government, and even some that are political; the first ten, therefore, showing a strong reaction in favor of the rights of the States and the liberties of the people, in 1791, while the Eleventh Amendment, in 1798, was a still more decisive step in that direction, withholding all Federal judicial power where a State was directly concerned; much as James I endeavored, though vainly, to get Chief-Justice Coke to rule that he would not consider a case where the interests of the king were involved. The Thirteenth Amendment is striking in that it is the only instance where the Constitution is expressly extended to any place subject to the jurisdiction of the United States, and

[1] Art. IV, Sec. 3.

[2] Not, as in England it would be, the whole government, both President and Congress, but Congress alone.

where, as it has recently been put, "The Constitution follows the flag." Slavery, therefore, can exist nowhere, not even in the Sulu Islands; although even the other cardinal requirement, a republican form of government, may constitutionally be withheld from them as from the other territorial possessions.

The modern reaction in favor of the Federal power is shown first in the Fourteenth Amendment, proclaimed July 28, 1868, though the interpretation which might have revolutionized the whole State and Federal system has substantially been denied by the Supreme Court. The amendment does, however, and for the first time, interfere between the State and the individual, if not between the individual and his neighbors. The State is forbidden to deprive any person of life, liberty, or property without due process of law, or to deny any person within its jurisdiction the equal protection of the laws, and this directly by the Federal Government. The radical upholders of centralization, in reconstruction times, undoubtedly believed that this brought the hand of the Federal Government between a man and his neighbors and indeed into all his private affairs; otherwise it would be surprising that it took nearly twenty years of great decisions by the Supreme Court to read the amendment in strict accordance with its simple words and establish that it applied only to a State, and to due process of law of a State; that it did not give, as had been given to the King's courts after the Conquest, on the mere plea of Englishry or that a Norman was concerned, jurisdiction to the Federal courts of all matters and causes where a Negro was concerned. As it has therefore worked out, it is merely a new national guaranty, like that securing a republican form of government, of the cardinal liberty and property rights against law-making by the States; and it does not, under the plea that a person is being unfairly treated by a neighbor or an official, drag all matters of ordinary trade and private right into the Federal courts.

Whether the extreme interpretation of the interstate commerce clause now proposed will carry us to this length, it is too early now to say; nor, indeed, is this a controversial essay. That there has been for some years a decided trend in that direction, one must admit. The effect of the interpretation by the courts and by Congress of the words "regulate commerce among the several States" has been gradually to extend the meaning of "commerce," from the things transported, the physical instrumentalities of interstate commerce, the necessary documents concerning it, to the corporations and persons conducting it, the conditions of their labor and the rates they may charge, — this by the year 1908,—and the meaning of the words "among the several States" from the natural physical transportation across State lines, to a combination or contract made in one or more States intended to act in others or in effect carried out in others. It is perhaps obvious that we intend to withhold the right of conducting interstate commerce from any *corporation* not conforming to a Federal standard. Whether we shall go further and deny it to individuals; whether, indeed, Congress has the constitutional right to deny it to individuals; and whether, on the other branch of the definition, we shall extend it from commerce, in the sense of interstate traffic, to manufacturing, mining, or producing goods intended to be sold outside of the State where they are manufactured, mined, or produced; and to the returns, or the profits, or the fortunes, or the disposition of the fortunes derived therefrom; and still more, to the contractual relations, the conditions of labor, etc., of the persons so engaged, — are all matters for the future to settle.

Finally, we must never forget that there is a division of power more important still, and also made for the first time in the American Constitution; that is to say, the powers, rights, or liberties reserved in the people of the United States, not delegated by them to the Federal power or always, even, to the State Governments formed or to be formed. This principle we have discussed in Chapter I. It is expressed in the frontispiece in the central domain "Y," left white, "virgin still with the people."[1] It must be particularly noted that this is the only *infinite* domain of power recognized in the Federal Constitution. All the others are definite, delimitated; given, or denied. There has, indeed, of late been a notion that there is something like an inherent national power, indefinite in extent; but this idea can find no place in any logical study of the Constitution; if there be such powers, they simply fall under the head of *implied* powers of the Federal Government. And from the point of view of our study, there is no difference between an expressed power and one implied. After the Supreme Court of the United States has found an implied power to exist, by necessary implication or otherwise, it becomes for our purposes just as much a part of the Federal Constitution as if it were definitely expressed. The wording of the articles of Confederation (Article II) that "each State retains every

[1] See "The American Constitution," p. 197.

power . . . which is not by this confederation *expressly* delegated to the United States . . ." fell to the ground with the adoption of the Federal Constitution eight years later, and received its *coup de grâce* in the Civil War; but because this is so, we must not fly to the other extreme and hold powers to reside in the Federal Government, whether they were ever given to it or intended to be given by the people, expressly or impliedly, or not. The "inherent national power," therefore, finds its natural and legitimate place in our zone of "A"; but is not to be robbed from the central liberties of "Y."

The great right reserved to the people, of course, is that of a republican form of government. The next is that of personal liberty. A republican form of government is forever guaranteed to the States, — not, apparently, to the territories; still less to the insular possessions; for the somewhat contradictory opinions of our judges on the insular cases seem at least to involve this result: that there is a *tertium quid,* something other than a State or a territory as hitherto understood. Just what a republican form of government means, it may be for the future to settle. On the one hand, it may not be a military dictatorship or military power generally, save, perhaps, in the insular possessions; or in time of actual war, or as a consequence thereof; on the other hand, according to the text-writers, it must involve representative government, and by the letter of our Constitution, the institution of private property. The right of personal liberty was originally and expressly guaranteed to citizens of the States alone, but practically, by the Fourteenth Amendment and many decisions, to United States citizens in the territories; while the general institution of slavery, indeed, is the one thing forbidden by the Constitution even in our insular possessions. The rest of the Federal Constitution, however, does not, by the prevailing opinion, extend to the insular possessions, except, at least, in such doses as Congress may choose to administer it. As to the frame of government, the Constitution makes the most sacred thing in it the last sentence in the fifth article, providing that the Constitution itself may never be so amended as to deprive any State of its equal suffrage in the Senate; this, indeed, being the strongest recognition of States' rights in that document, outside of the Tenth Amendment, and, indeed, put more strongly than in the Tenth Amendment, as it is the one instance in which the Constitution itself recognizes the right of secession.

The other cardinal rights reserved to the people are in general all those liberty rights discussed in our seven first chapters; in other words, substantially the English Constitution. These are, for the most part, set forth in the first eight amendments. The people are declared in the Preamble to be the sovereign, though the expression of that sovereignty is, in the Fifth Article, shifted to legislatures or popular conventions in three fourths of the States. The political rights are, broadly speaking, popular representation, equal suffrage for the lower house, control of their own elections and courts, impeachment of Federal officers, the power of the purse in the lower house of Congress, uniform taxation for the general welfare, limitation of military appropriation to two years, practical freedom from direct taxation by the Federal Government, and prohibition of special privilege; most important of all, that the judges shall hold their office for life, not subject to removal by the Executive, and for a fixed compensation; and the careful separation of the powers already referred to.

Many of these rights are doubly safeguarded by being forbidden both to the nation and to the States.[1] Freedom of trade among the States, supremacy of the Federal Constitution, a republican form of government, liberty and racial equality are so guaranteed. It will be noted[2] that Massachusetts (1780) preceded and New Hampshire (1792) followed the Federal Constitution in reserving to the people every power, jurisdiction, and right which was not by them expressly[3] delegated to the United States of America in Congress assembled. A more striking statement still is found in West Virginia (Article I, 2): "The government of the United States is a government of enumerated powers, and all powers not delegated to it, nor inhibited to the States, are reserved to the States or to the people thereof. Among the powers so reserved by the States, is the exclusive regulation of their own internal government and police; and it is the high and solemn duty of the several departments of government, created by this Constitution, to guard and protect the people of this State from all encroachments upon the rights so reserved."

[1] Book II, Chap. III, "ZX."

[2] See Book III, § 193, notes.

[3] *Sic*, in Massachusetts and New Hampshire, but omitted, in accordance with modern doctrine, from the later Constitution of West Virginia.

CHAPTER XI

THE STATE CONSTITUTIONS

MANY of the State Constitutions, notably of Virginia and Massachusetts, were adopted before the Federal Constitution itself,[1] and served to a certain extent as a model for it, and it is always important to remember that the two parties bringing their influence to bear upon the adoption of the State Constitutions changed positions entirely from those occupied by them in considering these, when they came to consider the Federal Constitution. The latter, in its most centralized form, giving largest power to the Federal Government, was backed by the Federalists; generally the educated and propertied classes, who were desirous of a strong central government, not only from motives of personal ambition, but because they desired protection from the absolute democracy of the State Legislatures. They wanted the nation to be strong abroad, their own property and contracts to be protected and respected at home, and their trade and business not to be taxed or interfered with by State regulations. Too great extension of the Federal power was, however, opposed by those whom we should now call Democrats, Thomas Jefferson, Patrick Henry, and others, jealous of too much government of any sort, who desired above all things

[1] Virginia, June 29; New Jersey, July 13; Delaware, Sept. 21; Pennsylvania, Sept. 28; Maryland, Nov. 11; North Carolina, Dec. 18, 1776; Georgia, Feb. 5; New York, April 20, 1777; Massachusetts, March 2, 1780. In Connecticut the charter of Charles II (1662) was ratified, and a simple Bill of Rights added, in 1776. New Hampshire, after one or two abortive attempts, adopted its Constitution June 2, 1784. Charles II, in 1663, granted to Benedict Arnold and other "trustie and well-beloved subjects" a charter for Rhode Island and Providence plantations which lasted until 1842, but this granted autonomy, with the liberties of the common law. Virginia's, followed closely by those of Pennsylvania and Maryland, was the first American Constitution actually adopted, that of South Carolina (March 26, 1776) being a political frame of temporary government for the "Colony." and soon followed by the Constitution of 1778. It uses the word "Commonwealth;" the Declaration of Independence, and the Constitution of Delaware are first to say "State." Pennsylvania, Massachusetts, and Kentucky are also still Commonwealths; Connecticut (1776) calls itself a Republic, Massachusetts a "free, Sovereign, and Independent State;" while Maine is officially the State of Maine, and Rhode Island also "of Providence Plantations." Thus doth one star differ from another in glory!

to maintain the political liberty of the individual, and his freedom in his home affairs; while as to the State Governments, having enjoyed for the first time in modern English history complete legislative power unhindered even by a Constitution or a Protector, popular leaders were desirous of preserving their sovereignty, and therefore wished to give indefinite powers to the State Governments and particularly to the State Legislatures, and withhold as much as they could from the Federal Government. For, the powers of a State government being original, not delegated, its legislature represents a power that at its origin was sovereign. Here, therefore, the Federalists became the upholders of individual rights and property, and imposed the checks in the State Bills of Rights that we find so notable in Virginia and in Massachusetts. It is as true as are most antitheses that the people imposed the Bill of Rights upon the Federal Government, in the form of the first ten amendments; and that the so-called privileged classes imposed similar checks upon the State legislatures. Upon one thing only were they agreed, — personal freedom.

These Bills of Rights have been necessarily discussed already; for they concern, generally, the cardinal principles of that part of the Anglo-American Constitution which is not merely political. Every State without exception has one, though Michigan in her last Constitution chops up its Bill of Rights and distributes its provisions around "under their proper headings."[1] The political framework, also, has been sufficiently discussed in Chapters VIII and IX above. It remains for us to discuss here that extraordinary development of the modern State Constitution which tends to reduce all law-making to constitutional provisions; to require a periodical referendum; and to a great extent do away with representative government.[2] New Constitutions, such as those of Alabama, Louisiana, and the seven Western States, evidently seek to embody all the broad notions of what a present majority thinks the law ought to be into the organic law of the State. Necessarily this leads to the embodying of the prejudice or caprice of the moment into the Constitution itself; for it is human nature

[1] I cannot agree with Professor Dealey that this is "a good precedent." (Am. Acad. P. & S. S. Supp. March 1907, p. 21). Is the great clause 39 of Magna Carta judicial alone? Such an arrangement destroys historical continuity; moreover the Bill of Rights should have a greater sanctity than the organization parts of a modern State Constitution.

[2] See Book III, §§ 182, 200, 209, &c.

to care more for one's peculiar fancies than for commonplace facts. Thus, the Constitutions of several States make liquor selling, or the bribery of officials, necessarily crimes by the organic law; which murder is not. It is part of the Constitution of Oklahoma that corporations shall be denied the rights of ordinary citizens in the courts; of California that stockholders shall not be protected from unlimited liability; and of several States that fiduciaries may not invest in corporate securities.[1] All these fall into that part of our Book III that we call "Legislation," and, it will be observed, they cover one hundred and thirty-six out of two hundred and forty-nine pages of that portion of our work.

It is significant to compare these modern Constitutions with the older Constitutions, such as that of Massachusetts. This is, indeed, owing to its elaborate political framework, much longer than most Constitutions of the original thirteen States; but it contains only a Bill of Rights, and a Part II, setting forth the frame of government, — and nothing whatever else; no directions or instructions or limitations, upon the Legislature, save that they should enact[2] "all manner of wholesome and reasonable laws as they may judge for the benefit and welfare of this State." The only other restriction which can possibly be considered a regulation or direction in the modern sense is a special separate chapter providing for welfare of the university at Cambridge, — Harvard College. The Constitution of Alabama, on the other hand, contains nearly one hundred sections relating to the legislation permitted or denied to the Legislature;[3] and thirty-six long sections concern corporations, the whole Constitution covering sixty-nine pages of fine print. The Oklahoma Constitution runs to one hundred and seventy-five pages, — and that without an index. Such Constitutions, of course, show distrust by the people of their own Legislatures; but such distrust will breed unworthiness.[4] Of such nature also are the curious restrictions upon the passage of bills, and the elaborate constitutional provisions against corruption or abuse of official power.[5] The more reasonable partial referendums, to the people or even to the taxpayers, of all bills involving the raising or expenditure of public money or the increase of State or municipal debt,[6] have al-

[1] See Book III, §§ 424, 508, 509.

[2] See Book III, § 391.

[3] §§ 65 to 111; 204 to 219; concerning taxation and exemptions; and 220 to 255.

[4] See above, Chapter VIII.

[5] See Book III, Articles XXII and XXVII.

[6] See Book III, Articles XXXI to XXXVII, &c.

ready been discussed. The extraordinary number of things which the Legislatures are now forbidden to do by local or special law (following the precedent set by the Constitution of New York of 1848) is another indication of the same distrust.[1]

The main lines on which this third or unscientific part of the modern State Constitution has sought to hamper posterity may be briefly summarized. Land laws, the prohibition of feudal tenures, long leases, and absentee land-holding[2] go back to the first Constitution of the State of New York; but the complete alteration of the common law as to the use of water, both for irrigation purposes and for municipal supply, is the creature of recent Western State Consitutions and Spanish or customary local law.[3] The same may be said of the "apexing" law of mines, though this has not yet crept into any Constitution. The prejudice against dealing in futures, stock jobbing, etc.,[4] is closely connected with the provisions against trusts, of which later. Many States forbid the Legislature to grant any divorces.[5] Otherwise the law of marriage is not interfered with. Laws prohibiting the manufacture or sale of intoxicating liquor or extending the right so to prohibit it to the counties or towns themselves is, of course, the most striking novelty usually indulged in by Constitution-makers;[6] but is now likely to be surpassed in frequency of adoption by the provisions protecting union labor, guarding the labor of women and children, and providing the length of the day's work, even of men, for any work done for the State or a public contractor; and, in such work, the payment of fixed wages.[7] But the greatest innovation by the Constitution on the legislative domain will be found in the law of corporations and of combinations. The laws against "trusts" — which, however, in almost no instance where the law has been held constitutional, do more than restate the principles of the older common law,[8] are put into constitutions. Not only are general incorporations constitutionally regulated, but a special chapter must be given to railroads and banks.[9] The charges of all public service corporations may be regulated, and all discrimination or preference forbidden,[10] and they may not engage in other lines of business,[11] nor can foreign corporations engage

[1] See Book III, § 395.

[2] See Book III, Article XL.

[3] See Book III, Article XLI.

[4] See Book III, Article XLII.

[5] See Book III, §§ 395, 430.

[6] See Book III, Article XLIV.

[7] Chapter V; See Book III, Article XLV.

[8] See Book III, Articles L and LVIII.

[9] See Book III, Articles LIII and LV

[10] Book III, §§ 506, 521–524.

[11] Ibid., § 531.

in business not permitted to State corporations [1] nor one corporation own stock in another.[2] Most interesting will be found the article against trusts, monopolies, combinations to fix prices, limit output, control the market or the actions and business of others.[3] All these, being common-law principles, have stood the tests of the courts; when legislators have gone beyond them, and particularly when even State Constitutions have attempted to exempt certain classes, such as organized or agricultural labor, or certain businesses, such as dealing in farm produce, from the limitations of the general law, they have been held unconstitutional; that is to say, State Constitutions have been held void under the Federal Constitution, and State laws under both; under State Constitutions frequently even by the courts of the same States which adopted them.

A few States have embodied in their Constitution their system of municipal government,[4] but this need not detain us except for the striking novelty in newer Western Constitutions that any city or even town may form its own charter, thereby making its own law and founding its own frame of government, — a recurrence, as in many another case, to the earliest of English precedents; thereby interesting and probably possible, for what has worked well is likely to work again. It is new legislation, made without regard to custom or habit, that is apt to be futile.[5]

With the judicial system alone have State Constitutions rarely presumed to tamper. They have contented themselves with adopting the common law, or such part of it as is suited to their needs and to their previous customs; none of them has so far rejected it; although a good many "fuse" common law with equity; while there is a recent tendency to deprive courts of chancery of the power of specific performance or of enforcing their decrees by contempt process, at least in labor disputes.[6] And they have usually prescribed a scheme of courts, their organization and jurisdiction; though even this is not done in New Hampshire.[7]

[1] Book III, § 505.

[2] Ibid., § 518.

[3] See Book III, §§ 518, 527, 580.

[4] See Book III, Article LX.

[5] See James C. Carter, "Law: its Origin, Growth and Function," *passim*.

[6] See above, Chapter IV, Book III, Arts. LXV, LXVII.

[7] See Book III, Art. LXV, American Statute Law, Vol. I, § 550, "Table of Courts."

BOOK II

CONSTITUTIONAL PRINCIPLES AS EXPRESSED IN THE ENGLISH STATUTES OF THE REALM AND AMERICAN CONSTITUTIONS

CHAPTER I

CONSTITUTIONAL PRINCIPLES PROTECTING PERSONAL LIBERTIES AND PRIVATE RIGHTS AS EXPRESSED IN CONSTITUTIONAL DOCUMENTS FROM MAGNA CARTA TO THE UNITED STATES CONSTITUTIONS

I. LIBERTY

(a) General Right to; Jury Trial

Magna Carta (1215), Cap. 39 "No free man shall be taken or imprisoned or disseised, or outlawed, or exiled, or anyways destroyed; nor will we go upon him, nor will we send upon him, unless by the lawful judgment of his peers, or by the law of the land."

Cap. 42 "In future any one may leave the Kingdom and return at will. . . ."

Magna Carta of Henry III (1217), Cap. 35 Wording identical with M. C. cap. 39, save that the very important words "Of his freehold or his liberties or his free customs" are added after the word "disseised."

28 Edw. III (1354), Cap. 3 The words "Unless by due process of law" are used instead of "the legal judgment of his peers or the law of the land."

Massachusetts Body of Liberties, 1641 (1) "No mans life shall be taken away, no mans honour or good name shall be stayned, no mans person shall be arrested, restrayned, banished, dismembered, nor any wayes punished, no man shall be deprived of his wife or children, no mans goods or estaite shall be taken away from him, nor any way indammaged under colour of law or Countenance of Authoritie, unlesse it be by vertue or equitie of some expresse law of the Country warranting the same, established by a generall Court and sufficiently published, or in the case of the defect of a law in any parteculer case by the word of god. And in Capitall cases, or in cases concerning dismembring or banishment, according to that word to be judged by the Generall Court."

(17) "Every man of or within this Jurisdiction shall have free libertie, notwithstanding any civill power to remove both himselfe, and his familie at their pleasure out of the same, provided there be no legall impediment to the contrarie."

(91) "There shall never be any bond slaverie, villinage or Captivitie amongst us unles it be lawfull Captives taken in just warres and such strangers as willingly selle themselves or are sold to us. . . ."

Virginia Bill of Rights (June, 1776), (Sec. 1) "That all men are by nature equally free and independent, and have certain inherent rights, of which when they enter into a state of society, they cannot, by any compact, deprive or divest their posterity; namely, the enjoyment of life and liberty, with the means of acquiring and possessing property, and pursuing and obtaining happiness and safety."

(8) ". . . That no man be deprived of his liberty, except by the law of the land or the judgment of his peers."

Declaration of Independence (July, 1776) "We hold these truths to be self-evident, that all men are created equal, that they are endowed by their Creator with certain unalienable Rights, that among these are Life, Liberty and the pursuit of Happiness. . . ."

"For depriving us in many cases of the benefits of trial by jury."

Mass. Decl. of Rights (1780), I "All men are born free and equal, and have certain natural, essential, and unalienable rights; among which may be reckoned the right of enjoying and defending their lives and liberties; that of acquiring, possessing, and protecting property; in fine, that of seeking and obtaining their safety and happiness."

Ibid., XII ". . . And no subject shall be arrested, imprisoned, despoiled, or deprived of his property, immunities, or privileges, put out of the protection of the law, exiled, or deprived of his life, liberty, or estate, but by the judgment of his peers, or the law of the land."

"And the legislature shall not make any law that shall subject any person to a capital or infamous punishment, excepting for the government of the army and navy, without trial by jury."

U. S. Constitution (1787), III, 2 (3) "The Trial of all Crimes, except in cases of Impeachment, shall be by Jury. . . ."

Ibid., Amt. V (1791) "No person shall be held to answer for a capital, or otherwise infamous crime, unless on a presentment or indictment of a Grand Jury, except in cases arising in the land or naval forces, or in the Militia, when in actual service in time of War or public danger; nor shall any person be subject for the same offence to be twice put in jeopardy of life or limb; nor shall be compelled in any Criminal Case to be a witness against himself, nor be deprived of life, liberty, or property, without due process of law; nor shall private property be taken for public use, without just compensation."

Ibid., Amt. VI "In all criminal prosecutions, the accused shall enjoy the right to a speedy and public trial, by an impartial jury of the State and district wherein the crime shall have been committed, which district shall have been previously ascertained by law, and to be informed of the nature and cause of the accusation; to be confronted with the witnesses against him; to have compulsory process for obtaining witnesses in his favor, and to have the Assistance of Counsel for his defence."

Ibid., Amt. XIII (1865) "Neither slavery nor involuntary servitude, except as a punishment for crime whereof the party shall have been duly convicted, shall exist within the United States, or any place subject to their jurisdiction."

Ibid., Amt. XIV, 1 (1868) "All persons born or naturalized in the United States and subject to the jurisdiction thereof, are citizens of the United States and of the State wherein they reside. No State shall make or enforce any law which shall abridge the privileges or immunities of citizens of the United States; nor shall any State deprive any person of life, liberty, or property without due process of law, nor deny to any person within its jurisdiction the equal protection of the laws."

(For State Constitutions, see Book III, §§ 10, 12, 13, 14, 130, 184.)

(b) Habeas Corpus and Indictment

Magna Carta, Cap. 36

"The right of inquest of life or limb shall be given *gratis*, and not denied." Substantially the same in the Magna Charta of Henry III, cap. 32.

Petition of Rights, V (1627)

". . . divers of your subjects have of late been imprisoned without any cause showed; and when, for their deliverance, they were brought before your justices, by your Majesty's writs of *habeas corpus*, there to undergo and receive as the court should order, and their keepers commanded to certify the causes of their detainer, no cause was certified, but that they were detained by your Majesty's special command . . ."

Mass. Decl. of Rights, XII

"No subject shall be held to answer for any crimes or offence, until the same is fully and plainly, substantially and formally, described to him. . . ."

U. S. Constitution, 1, 9 (2)

"The Privilege of the Writ of Habeas Corpus shall not be suspended, unless when in Cases of Rebellion or Invasion the public Safety may require it."

(For State Constitutions, see Book III, §§ 125, 126.)

Mass. Body of Liberties (1641) Clause 18

"No mans person shall be restrained or imprisoned by any Authority whatsoever, before the law hath sentenced him thereto, If he can put in sufficient securitie, bayle or mainprise, for his appearance, and good behaviour in the meane time, unlesse it be in Crimes Capital, and Contempts in open Court, and in such cases where some expresse act of Court doth allow it."

Habeas Corpus Act, 1679

Provides, in substance, "that on complaint and request in writing by or on behalf of any person committed and charged with any *crime* . . . any of the twelve judges, in vacation, upon viewing a copy of the warrant, or affidavit that a copy is denied, . . . shall award a *habeas corpus* . . . returnable immediately. . . . That the writ shall be returned and the prisoner brought up, within a limited time according to the distance, not exceeding in any case twenty days. . . . That no person once delivered by *habeas corpus*, shall be recommitted for the same offence, on penalty of £500."

Virginia Bill of Rights, Sec. 8

"That in all capital or criminal prosecutions, a man hath a right to demand the cause and nature of his accusation. . . ."

U. S. Constitution, Amt. V

"No person shall be held to answer for a capital or otherwise infamous crime, unless on a presentment or indictment of a grand jury, except in cases arising in the land or naval forces, or in the militia, when in actual service in time of war or public danger; nor shall any person be subject for the same offense to be twice put in jeopardy of life or limb; nor shall be compelled in any criminal case to be a witness against himself. . . ."

(For State Constitutions, see Book III, §§ 120, 127, 128.)

(c) Extent of Bail and Punishment

Magna Carta, Cap 20

"A Freeman shall only be amerced . . . after the manner of the offence . . . saving to him his contenement . . . a merchant saving his merchandise, and a villein saving his wainage; the amercement in all cases to be assessed by the oath of honest men of the neighbourhood."

Mass. Body of Liberties Clause 46

"For bodilie punishments, we allow amongst us none that are inhuman, barbarouse, or cruel."

Habeas Corpus Act, Clause XI

That no "inhabitant . . . of England . . . shall or may be sent prisoner into Scotland, Ireland, Jersey, Guernsey, Tangier . . . or places beyond the seas . . . within or without the dominions of his Majesty. . . ."

Bill of Rights, Clause 10

"That excessive bail ought not to be required, nor excessive fines imposed, nor cruel and unusual punishments inflicted."

Virginia Bill of Rights, Sec. 9

Copies the English Bill (10).

Mass. Decl. of Rights, Clause XXVI

"No magistrate or court of law shall demand excessive bail or sureties, impose excessive fines or inflict cruel or unusual punishments."

U. S. Constitution, Amt. VIII

"Excessive bail shall not be required, nor excessive fines imposed, nor cruel and unusual punishments inflicted."

(For State Constitutions, see Book III, §§ 121, 122, 123, 140, 141.)

(d) Trial and Evidence

Mass. Body of Liberties, Clause 42

"No man shall be twise sentenced by Civill Justice for one and the same Crime, Offence or Trespasse."

Clause 45

"No man shall be forced by Torture to confesse any Crime against himselfe nor any other unlesse it be in some Capitall case where he is first fullie convicted by cleare and suffitient evidence to be guilty" (after which he may be tortured to obtain evidence against his confederates yet not with such "as be barbarous and inhuman").

Clause 47

"No man shall be put to death without the testimony of two or three witnesses or that which is equivalent thereunto."

Habeas Corpus Act, VI

Forbids a second committal for the same offence.

Virginia Bill of Rights, Sec. 8

". . . to be confronted with the accusers and witnesses, to call for evidence in his favour, and to a speedy trial by an impartial jury of twelve men of his vicinage, without whose unanimous consent he cannot be found guilty; nor can he be compelled to give evidence against himself. . . ."

Mass. Decl. of Rights, XII

"No subject shall . . . be compelled to accuse, or furnish evidence against himself. And every subject shall have a right to produce all proofs that may be favorable to him; to meet the witnesses against him face to face, and to be fully heard in his defence by himself, or his counsel, at his election. . . ."

U. S. Constitution, Amt. V

"Nor shall any person be subject for the same offence to be twice put in jeopardy of life or limb."

(For State Constitutions, see Book III, § 132, 137, 140.)

(e) Bills of Attainder

Mass. Decl. of Rights, XXIV "Laws made to punish for actions done before the existence of such laws, and which have not been declared crimes by preceding laws, are unjust, oppressive, and inconsistent with the fundamental principles of a free government."

U. S. Constitution, 1, 9 (3) "No Bill of Attainder or ex post facto Law shall be passed."

1, 10, (1) "No State shall . . . pass any bill of attainder, ex post facto law, or law impairing the obligation of contracts. . . ."

(For State Constitutions, see Book III, §§ 138, 141.)

(f) Suspending Laws

Bill of Rights (1) "That the pretended power of suspending of laws, or the execution of laws, by regal authority, without consent of Parliament, is illegal."

(2) is to the same effect but forbids the "dispensing with laws" and leaves out the clause about Parliament.

Virginia Bill of Rights, Sec. 7 "That all power of suspending laws, or the execution of laws, by any authority, without consent of the representatives of the people, is injurious to their rights, and ought not to be exercised."

Mass. Decl. of Rights, XX "The power of suspending the laws, or the execution of the laws ought never to be exercised but by the legislature, or by authority derived from it, to be exercised in such particular cases only as the legislature shall expressly provide for."

(For State Constitutions, see Book III, §§ 126, 392.)

(g) Treason

XXV "No subject ought, in any case, or in any time, to be declared guilty of treason or felony by the legislature."

U. S. Constitution, III, 3, (1) "Treason against the United States shall consist only in levying War against them, or in adhering to their Enemies, giving them Aid and Comfort. No Person shall be convicted of Treason unless on the Testimony of two Witnesses to the same overt Act, or on Confession in open Court.

III, 3, (2) "The Congress shall have Power to declare the Punishment of Treason, but no Attainder of Treason shall work Corruption of Blood or Forfeiture except during the Life of the Person attainted."

(For State Constitutions, see Book III, § 150.)

II. LAW

(a) Common Law, Judges

Magna Carta, Cap. 39 (The right to law, in criminal matters, has necessarily been shown above in connection with *Liberty*. This heading relates to general matters.)

"... unless by . . . the law of the land." (See I, above.),

Cap. 40 "To none will we sell, to none will we deny or delay right, or justice."

Cap. 45 "Justices, constables, sheriffs, and bailiffs shall only be appointed of 'such as know the law and mean duly to observe it.'"

28 Edw. III, Chap. III "No man . . . shall be . . . put out of land or tenement . . . nor disinherited . . . without being put in Answer by due Process of the Law."

Mass. Body of Liberties, Clause 2 "Every person within this Jurisdiction, whether Inhabitant or forreiner shall enjoy the same justice and law, that is generall for the plantation, which we constitute and execute one towards another without partialitie or delay."

Petition of Right Cites Magna Carta and 28 Edw. III as above and denounces the acts complained of as "against the laws and free customs of the realm" (clauses II, VI, VII, VIII, IX), "the laws and franchise of the land" (X).

Bill of Rights (3) That the commission for erecting the late Court of Commissioners for Ecclesiastical Causes, and all other commissions and courts of like nature, are illegal and pernicious.

Act of Settlement (1700) "That . . . judges' commissions be made *quamdiu se bene gesserint*, and their salaries ascertained and established; but upon the Address of both Houses of Parliament, it may be lawfull to remove them."

Virginia Bill of Rights, Sec. 6 No men can be "bound by any law to which they have not [by their representatives] assented. . . ." See *Government*, below.

Sec. 11 "That in controversies respecting property, and in suits between man and man, the ancient trial by jury of twelve men is preferable to any other and ought to be held sacred."

Declaration of Independence, Clause 13 "He has made Judges dependent on his Will alone, for the tenure of their offices, and the amount and payment of their salaries."

Clause 24 "For abolishing the free System of English Laws in a neighbouring Province, establishing therein an Arbitrary government, and enlarging its Boundaries so as to render it at once an example and fit instrument for introducing the same absolute rule into these Colonies."

New York Constitution, Clause 41 (1777) ". . . the legislature of this State shall at no time hereafter institute any new court or courts, but such as shall proceed according to the course of the common law."

Mass. Decl. of Rights, XI "Every subject of the Commonwealth ought to find a certain remedy, by having recourse to the laws, for all injuries or wrongs which he may receive in his person, property, or character. He ought to obtain right and justice freely, and without being obliged to purchase it; — completely, and without any denial; — promptly, and without delay; — conformably to the laws."

XV "In all controversies concerning property, and in all suits between two or more persons, except in cases in which it has heretofore been otherways used and practised, the parties have a right to a trial by jury; and this method of procedure shall be held sacred, — unless, in causes arising on the high seas, and such as relate to mariners' wages, the legislature shall hereafter find it necessary to alter it."

Mass. Decl. of Rights, XXIX

"It is essential to the preservation of the rights of every individual, his life, liberty, property, and character, that there be an impartial interpretation of the laws, and administration of justice. It is the right of every citizen to be tried by judges as free, impartial, and independent as the lot of humanity will admit. It is, therefore, not only the best policy, but for the security of the rights of the people, and of every citizen, that the judges of the supreme judicial court should hold their offices as long as they behave themselves well; and that they should have honorable salaries ascertained and established by standing laws."

(The Virginia Bill of Rights implies this principle; see III (d), below.

U. S. Constitution, Amt. VII

In suits at common law, where the value in controversy shall exceed twenty dollars, the right of trial by jury shall be preserved, and no fact tried by a jury shall be otherwise re-examined in any Court of the United States, than according to the rules of the common law.

Amt. V

"No person shall be . . . without due process of law . . ."

Amt. XIV, 1

". . . Nor shall any State deprive . . . , without due process of law, nor deny to any person . . . the equal protection of the laws."

(For State Constitutions, see Book III, §§ 70, 72, 73, 74, 76, 130.)

(b) Local Courts

Magna Carta, Cap. 17

"Common pleas shall not follow the King's Court, but be held in some certain place."

Cap. 20

Fines to be assessed by honest men of the neighbourhood (see I, (c), above).

Cap. 34

The writ called *Præcipe* shall not in future be issued, so as to cause a freeman to lose his court.

Virginia Bill of Rights (8)

". . . jury of his vicinage . . ."

Declaration of Independence, Clause 17

"He has combined with others to subject us to a jurisdiction foreign to our Constitution, and unacknowledged by our laws; giving his Assent to their Acts of pretended Legislation."

Clause 23

"For transporting us beyond Seas to be tried for pretended offences."

Maryland Constitution, Clause 18 (1776)

"That the trial of facts where they arise is one of the greatest securities of the lives, liberties, and estates of the people."

Mass. Decl. of Rights, XIII

"In criminal prosecutions, the verification of facts, in the vicinity where they happen, is one of the greatest securities of the life, liberty, and property of the citizen."

U. S. Constitution, III, 2, (3)

"The trial of all Crimes, except in Cases of Impeachment, shall be by Jury; and such Trial shall be held in the State where the said Crimes shall have been committed; but when not committed within any State, the Trial shall be at such Place or Places as the Congress may by Law have directed."

(See for State Constitutions, Book III, § 133.)

(c) Martial Law, Right to Arms, etc.

Petition of Rights, Clause VI

". . . of late great companies of soldiers and mariners have been dispersed into divers counties of the realm, and the inhabitants against their wills have been compelled to receive them into their houses and there to suffer them to sojourn, against the laws and customs of this realm, . . ."

Clauses VII, VIII

". . . certain persons have been appointed commissioners, with power and authority to proceed . . . according to . . . martial law . . . and by such summary course and order as is agreeable to martial law, and as is used in armies in time of war, to proceed to the trial and condemnation of such offenders, and them to cause to be executed and put to death according to the law martial. By pretext whereof some of your Majesty's subjects have been by some of the said commissioners put to death, when and where, if by the laws and statutes of the land they had deserved death, by the same laws and statutes also they might and by no other ought, to have been judged and executed."

Clause X

". . . and that the foresaid commissions, for proceeding by martial law, may be revoked and annulled . . . that your Majesty would be pleased to remove the said soldiers and mariners, and that your people may not be so burdened in time to come."

Bill of Rights, Clause 7

"That the subjects which are Protestants may have arms for their defence suitable to their conditions, and as allowed by law."

Clause 6

"That the raising or keeping a standing army, within the kingdom in time of peace, unless it be with consent of Parliament, is against law."

Virginia Bill of Rights, Sec. 13

"That a well regulated militia, composed of the body of the people, trained to arms, is the proper, natural, and safe defence of a free State; that standing armies in time of peace should be avoided as dangerous to liberty; and that in all cases the military should be under strict subordination to, and governed by, the civil power."

Declaration of Independence, Clause 15

"He has kept among us, in times of peace, Standing Armies without the Consent of our legislatures."

Clauses 18, 19

"For quartering large bodies of armed troops among us: For protecting them, by a mock Trial, from punishment for any murders which they should commit on the inhabitants of these States."

Mass. Decl. of Rights, XXVII

"In time of peace, no soldier ought to be quartered in any house without the consent of the owner; and in time of war such quarters ought not be made but by the civil magistrate, in a manner ordained by the legislature."

XXVIII

"No person can in any case be subject to law-martial, or to any penalties or pains, by virtue of that law, except those employed in the army or navy, and except the militia in actual service, but by authority of the legislature."

XII "And the legislature shall not make any law that shall subject any person to a capital or infamous punishment (excepting for the government of the army and navy) without trial by jury."

XVII "The people have a right to keep and to bear arms for the common defence. And as, in time of peace, armies are dangerous to liberty, they ought not to be maintained without the consent of the legislature; and the military power shall always be held in an exact subordination to the civil authority, and be governed by it."

U. S. Constitution, I, 8, (12) "To raise and support Armies, but no Appropriation of Money to that Use shall be for a longer Term than two Years."

I, 8, (14) "To make Rules for the Government and Regulation of the land and naval Forces."

I, 8, (15) "To provide for calling forth the Militia to execute the Laws of the Union, suppress Insurrections and repel Invasions."

I, 8, (16) "To provide for organizing, arming, and disciplining, the Militia, and for governing such Part of them as may be employed in the Service of the United States, reserving to the States respectively, the Appointment of the Officers and the Authority of training the Militia according to the discipline prescribed by Congress."

Amt. II (1791) "A well regulated Militia, being necessary to the security of a free State, the right of the people to keep and bear Arms, shall not be infringed."

Amt. III "No Soldier shall, in time of peace be quartered in any house, without the consent of the Owner, nor in time of war, but in a manner to be prescribed by law."

(For State Constitutions, see Book III, §§ 62, 63, 290, 291, 293, 294, 295, 298).

III. PROPERTY AND TRADE

(a) Property

Magna Carta, Cap. 39 The word "disseised" (see I, (a), above) relates to property.

Magna Carta, Caps. 28, 30, 31 No constable or other royal bailiff shall take any man's corn or other chattels without immediate payment . . . nor shall the King, his sheriffs or bailiffs take any horses or carriages of freemen for carriage, or any man's timber . . . unless by consent of the owner.

Magna Carta of Henry III, Cap. 23 No constable nor his bailiff shall take corn or other chattels of any man . . . but he shall forthwith pay for the same.

28 Edw. III, Chap. III (See II, (a), above.) A man may not be "put out of Land or Tenement" but by due process of Law.

Mass. Body of Liberties, Clause 8 "No mans Cattel or goods of what kinde soever shall be pressed or taken for any publique use or service, unlesse it be by warrant grounded upon some act of the generall Court, nor without such reasonable prices and hire as the ordinarie rates of the Countrie do afford. And if his Cattel or goods shall perish or suffer damage in such service, the owner shall be suffitiently recompenced."

Virginia Bill of Rights, Sec. 1 ". . . all men . . . have certain rights . . . namely, the enjoyment of life and liberty, with the means of acquiring and possessing *property*, and pursuing and obtaining happiness and safety."

Mass. Decl. of Rights, I ". . . that of acquiring, possessing, and protecting property; in fine, that of seeking and obtaining their safety and happiness."

U. S. Constitution, Amt. V (No person shall) . . . "be deprived of life, liberty, or property without due process of law; nor shall private property be taken for public use without just compensation."

Amt. XIV, 1 "Nor shall any State deprive any person of . . . property without due process of law."

(For State Constitutions, see Book III, §§ 13, 90–95, 130, 183.)

(b) Trade and Monopoly

Magna Carta, Cap. 13 "The City of London shall have all its ancient liberties and free customs as well by the lands as by the seas and so of all other cities, boroughs, towns and ports." In Henry III this is extended to the barons of the five ports.

Cap. 41 "All merchants shall have liberty safely to enter, to dwell and travel in and to depart from England for the purpose of commerce without being subjected to any evil tolls but only to the ancient and allowed customs except in time of war. . . ." Identical in Cap. 37 of the Charter of Henry III.

Cap. 33 All weirs in the Thames and Medway and throughout England shall be put down, except on the sea-coast.

Magna Carta of Henry III, Cap. 35 "No freeman shall be . . . disseised of his freehold or liberties or free customs." The last words relate to trade, and are expounded by Coke as including a prohibition of monopoly.

Statute of Monopolies, 1623 All monopolies, all licenses to do, use or exercise anything against the tenor or purport of any law or statute, declared void. 21 James I, Cap. 3.

Mass. Body of Liberties (9) "No monopolies shall be granted or allowed amongst us, but of such new Inventions that are profitable to the Countrie and that for a short time."

Declaration of Independence, Clause 20 "For cutting off our Trade with all parts of the world."

Virginia Bill of Rights, Sec. 4 "That no man, or set of men, are entitled to exclusive or separate emoluments or privileges from the community but in consideration of publick services; which not being descendible, neither ought the offices of magistrate, legislator, or judge to be hereditary."

Maryland Constitution, XXXIX (1776) That monopolies are odious, contrary to the spirit of a free government and the principles of commerce; and ought not to be suffered.

Mass. Decl. of Rights, Clause VI "No man, nor corporation, or association of men, have any other title to obtain advantages, or particular and exclusive privileges, distinct from those of the community, than what arises from the consideration of services rendered to the public; and this title being in nature neither hereditary, nor transmissible to children, or descendants, or relations by blood, the idea of a man born a magistrate, lawgiver or judge, is absurd and unnatural."

U. S. Constitution, Amt. XIV, Sec. 1

". . . nor shall any State . . . deny to any person within its jurisdiction the equal protection of the laws."

(For State Constitutions, see Book III, §§ 14, 16, 70, 394, 404, 580, etc.)

(c) TAXATION

Magna Carta, Cap. 12

"No scutage nor aid shall be imposed in our kingdom unless by the common Council of the realm" (*i. e.* the Parliament).

Cap. 14

Describes how the National Council is to be summoned by a writ to all the nobility and tenants in chief.

These two clauses were omitted in Magna Carta of Henry III but restored in the Confirmation of Charters of Edward I in the words "From henceforth we shall not take such manner of aids, tasks nor prises but by the common assent of all the realm and for the common profit thereof."

Petition of Rights, I

". . . your subjects have inherited this freedom, that they should not be compelled to contribute to any tax, tallage, aid or other like charge not set by common consent, in parliament."

X

". . . that no man hereafter be compelled to make or yield any gift, loan, benevolence, tax, or such like charge, without common consent by the act of parliament."

Bill of Rights (4)

"That levying money for or to the use of the Crown by pretence of prerogative, without grant of Parliament, for longer time, or in other manner, than the same is or shall be granted, is illegal."

Virginia Bill of Rights, Sec. 6

". . . all men . . . cannot be taxed or deprived of their property for publick uses without their own consent or that of their representatives. . . ."

Declaration of Independence, Clause 21

"For imposing Taxes on us without our Consent."

Mass. Decl. of Rights, X

"Each individual of the society has a right to be protected by it in the enjoyment of his life, liberty, and property, according to standing laws. He is obliged, consequently, to contribute his share to the expense of this protection; to give his personal service, or an equivalent when necessary; but no part of the property of any individual can, with justice, be taken from him, or applied to public use, without his own consent, or that of the representative body of the people. In fine, the people of this Commonwealth are not controllable by any other laws than those to which their constitutional representative body have given their consent. And whenever the public exigencies require that the property of any individual should be appropriated to public uses, he shall receive a reasonable compensation therefor."

Mass. Decl. of Rights, XXIII

No subsidy, charge, tax, impost, or duties ought to be established, fixed, laid, or levied, under any pretext whatsoever, without the consent of the people or their representatives in the legislature.

(For State Constitutions, see Book III, §§ 90, 330, 335, 340, 310, 311, 312, 314, 320, 322.)

(d) Miscellaneous Rights

Freedom of Speech

Bill of Rights, Clause 9 "That the freedom of speech, and debates or proceedings in Parliament, ought not to be impeached or questioned in any court or place out of Parliament."

Virginia Bill of Rights, Sec. 12 "That the freedom of the press is one of the great bulwarks of liberty, and can never be restrained but by despotick governments."

Mass. Decl. of Rights, Clause XVI "The liberty of the press is essential to the security of freedom in a State: it ought not, therefore, to be restrained in this Commonwealth."

XXI "The freedom of deliberation, speech and debate, in either house of the legislature is so essential to the rights of the people, that it cannot be the foundation of any accusation or prosecution, action or complaint in any other court or place whatsoever."

Right to Petition

Bill of Rights, Clause 5 "That it is the right of the subject to petition the King, and all commitments and prosecutions for such petitioning are illegal."

Mass. Decl. of Rights, Clause XIX "The people have a right, in an orderly and peaceable manner, to assemble to consult upon the common good; give instructions to their representatives, and to request of the legislative body, by the way of addresses, petitions, or remonstrances, redress of the wrongs done them, and of the grievances they suffer."

XXI "The freedom of deliberation, speech, and debate, in either house of the legislature, is so essential to the rights of the people, that it cannot be the foundation of any accusation or prosecution, action or complaint, in any other court or place whatsoever."

Religion

Virginia Bill of Rights, Sec. 16 "That religion, or the duty which we owe to our Creator, and the manner of discharging it, can be directed only by reason and conviction, not by force or violence, and therefore all men are equally entitled to the free exercise of religion, according to the dictates of conscience; and that it is the mutual duty of all to practise Christian forbearance, love, and charity, towards each other."

Mass. Decl. of Rights, III "And every denomination of Christians, demeaning themselves peaceably, and as good subjects of the commonwealth, shall be equally under the protection of the law: and no subordination of any one sect or denomination to another shall ever be established by law."

Search Warrants

Virginia Bill of Rights, Sec. 10 "That general warrants, whereby an officer or messenger may be commanded to search suspected places without evidence of a fact committed, or to seize any person or persons not named, or whose offence is not particularly described, and supported by evidence, are grievous and oppressive, and ought not to be granted."

Mass. Decl. of Rights, XIV

"Every subject has a right to be secure from all unreasonable searches, and seizures, of his person, his houses, his papers, and all his possessions. All warrants, therefore, are contrary to this right, if the cause or foundation of them be not previously supported by oath or affirmation, and if the order in the warrant to a civil officer, to make search in suspected places, or to arrest one or more suspected persons, or to seize their property, be not accompanied with a special designation of the persons or objects of search, arrest, or seizure: and no warrant ought to be issued but in cases, and with the formalities prescribed by the laws."

U. S. Constitution, Art. IV

"The right of the people to be secure in their persons, houses, papers, and effects, against unreasonable searches and seizures, shall not be violated, and no Warrants shall issue, but upon probable cause supported by Oath or affirmation, and particularly describing the place to be searched, and the persons or things to be seized."

(For State Constitutions, see Book III, §§ 71, 136.)

IV. POLITICAL RIGHTS

(a) ELECTIONS

Bill of Rights, Clause 8

"That election of members of Parliament ought to be free."

Virginia Bill of Rights, Sec. 6

"That elections [of representatives] ought to be free, and that all men having sufficient evidence of permanent common interest with, and attachment to the community have the right of suffrage."

Mass. Decl. of Rights, IX

"All elections ought to be free; and all the inhabitants of this Commonwealth having such qualifications as they shall establish by their frame of government, have an equal right to elect officers, and to be elected, for public employments."

U. S. Constitution, Fifteenth Amt.

"The right of citizens of the United States to vote shall not be denied or abridged by the United States or by any State, on account of race, color, or previous condition of servitude.

"The congress shall have power to enforce this article by appropriate legislation."

(For State Constitutions, see Book III, §§ 230, 235, 240, etc.)

(b) LEGISLATURES

Bill of Rights, Clause 13

"And that for redresse of all grievances, and for the amending, strengthening, and preserveing of the lawes, Parlyaments ought to be held frequently."

Mass. Decl. of Rights, XXII

The legislature ought frequently to assemble for the redress of grievances, for correcting, strengthening, and confirming the laws, and for making new laws, as the common good may require.

(For State Constitutions, see Book III, § 277.)

(c) THEORY OF GOVERNMENT

Virginia Bill of Rights, Sec. 2

"That all power is vested in, and consequently derived from, the people; that magistrates are their trustees and servants, and at all times amenable to them."

Virginia Bill of Rights, Sec. 3

"That government is, or ought to be, instituted for the common benefit, protection and security of the people, nation, or community; of all the various modes and forms of government, that is best, which is capable of producing the greatest degree of happiness and safety, and is most effectually secured against the danger of maladministration; and that, whenever any government shall be found inadequate or contrary to these purposes, a majority of the community hath an indubitable, unalienable and indefeasible right, to reform, alter or abolish it, in such manner as shall be judged most conducive to the public weal."

Declaration of Independence, 3, 4

"That to secure these rights, Governments are instituted among Men, deriving their just powers from the consent of the governed. That whenever any Form of Government becomes destructive to these ends, it is the Right of the People to alter or to abolish it, and to institute new Government, laying its foundation on such principles and organizing its powers in such form, as to them shall seem most likely to effect their Safety and Happiness."

Mass. Constitution, Preamble

"The end of the institution, maintenance, and administration of government, is to secure the existence of the body politic, to protect it, and to furnish the individuals who compose it with the power of enjoying in safety and tranquillity their natural rights, and the blessings of life: and whenever these great objects are not obtained, the people have a right to alter the government, and to take measures necessary for their safety, prosperity, and happiness.

"The body politic is formed by a voluntary association of individuals: it is a social compact, by which the whole people covenants with each citizen, and each citizen with the whole people, that all shall be governed by certain laws for the common good. It is the duty of the people, therefore, in framing a constitution of government, to provide for an equitable mode of making laws, as well as for an impartial interpretation and a faithful execution of them; that every man may, at all times, find his security in them."

Mass. Decl. of Rights, IV

"The people of this commonwealth have the sole and exclusive right of governing themselves, as a free, sovereign, and independent state; and do, and forever hereafter shall, exercise and enjoy every power, jurisdiction, and right, which is not, or may not hereafter be, by them expressly delegated to the United States of America, in Congress assembled."

V

"All power residing originally in the people, and being derived from them, the several magistrates and officers of government, vested with authority, whether legislative, executive, or judicial, are their substitutes and agents, and are at all times accountable to them."

VII

"Government is instituted for the common good; for the protection, safety, prosperity, and happiness of the people; and not for the profit, honor, or private interest of any one man, family, or class of men: Therefore the people alone have an incontestable, unalienable, and indefeasible right to institute government; and to reform, alter, or totally change the same, when their protection, safety, prosperity, and happiness require it."

VIII

"In order to prevent those who are vested with authority from becoming oppressors, the people have a right, at such periods and in such manner as they shall establish by their frame of government, to cause their public officers to return to private life; and to fill up vacant places by certain and regular elections and appointments."

(For State Constitutions, see Book III, §§ 4, 6, 11, 181, 182, 183, 184, 185.)

(d) *The Separation of the Powers*

Act of Settlement (1700)

"That no person who has an office or place of profit under the king, or receives a pension from the Crown, shall be capable of serving as a member of the House of Commons."

Virginia Bill of Rights, Sec. 5

"That the legislative and executive powers of the State should be separate and distinct from the judiciary; and that the members of the two first may be restrained from oppression, by feeling and participating the burthens of the people, they should, at fixed periods, be reducted to a private station, return into that body from which they were originally taken, and the vacancies be supplied by frequent, certain, and regular elections, in which all, or any part of the former members, to be again eligible, or ineligible, as the laws shall direct."

Mass. Decl. of Rights, XXX

"In the government of this commonwealth, the legislative department shall never exercise the executive and judicial powers, or either of them: the executive shall never exercise the legislative and judicial powers, or either of them: the judicial shall never exercise the legislative and executive powers, or either of them: to the end it may be a government of laws and not of men."

U. S. Constitution, I, 1

"*All* legislative powers herein granted shall be vested in a Congress of the United States. . . . " (See II, 1; III, 1, similarly expressed as to the other two powers.)

CHAPTER II

HISTORICAL DIGEST OF ENGLISH SOCIAL LEGISLATION

1066 *The Conquest.*

1087 William Rufus

1100 1 Hen. I Charter of Henry I ("of Liberties") restores the laws of Edward the Confessor "with the amendments made by my father with the counsel of his barons." First recognition of *personal property* at a man's death. It is to be divided between his widow and heirs.

1136 1 Stephen Charter of Stephen mainly concerning church matters, simony, and forests; but promises to observe "good and ancient laws and just customs"; and again "all good laws and just customs which they had in the time of King Edward."

1154 1 Hen. II Confirms "liberties and free customs" to "all counts and barons and to all men."

1159 Scutage substituted for military service. Institution of the "Grand Assize" or trial by jury (Taswell-Langmead, p. 71) supersedes old modes of trial by battle (Norman) and compurgation (Saxon).

1164 10 Hen. II Constitutions of Clarendon subjected the church and priests to the secular (common) law (I Taylor, 287), the church courts still retaining jurisdiction over offences between the clergy, marriage, sexual relations, slander, usury, and wills.

1181 28 Hen. II Assize of Arms revives the ancient fyrd (militia). — Glanvil Justiciar.

1188 36 Hen. II Saladin tithe; first taxation of personal property.

1193 Richard I Tax of one-fourth of every person's revenue or goods to ransom the King.

1203 John Tax of one-seventh on the barons, (1207) tax of one-thirteenth on every man.

1213 John surrenders England to the Pope and takes it back in feud for tribute of 1000 marks. Trial by ordeal abolished by the Lateran Council.

1215 John *Magna Carta.* C. 7. Establishment of the *widow's dower.* C. 12. No scutage or aid (tax) shall be imposed in our kingdom unless by the common council of our realm. C. 14. In order to take the common council of the realm in the imposition of aids the King shall summon the archbishops, earls, and barons by separate writ, and all other tenants in chief by general writ, with the 40 days' notice; and the consent of those present shall bind those absent. [These two clauses were omitted in the re-issue of Henry III, and only returned in Edward I, Confirmation of Charters (1297).] C. 13. Confirms ancient liberties and customs of London and of all other cities and free ports. C. 17. Common Pleas: Court shall not follow the King, but be held in some place certain. C. 20. Fines to be reasonable; with exemption of tools, implements of husbandry, stock in trade. C. 39. The great Liberty statute: "No freeman shall be taken or imprisoned or be disseized [of his freehold or liberties or his free customs, in the Charter of Henry III], or be outlawed or exiled or any otherwise destroyed; nor will we go upon him nor send upon him but by lawful judgment of his peers or by the law of the land. C. 40. We will sell to no man, we will deny or delay to no man either right or justice." C. 34. The writ "præcipe" not to issue to oust local courts of jurisdiction. C. 36. The writ of inquest of life or limb [predecessor of *habeas corpus*] to be given gratis and not denied. C. 45. Justices to be appointed of such as know the law. (Omitted in Charter of Hen. III.) C. 41. Merchants to have safe conduct in England in time of peace, subject only to the ancient and allowed customs not to evil tolls; in time of war they shall be attached, without injury, until it be known "how our merchants are treated in such hostile state; and if ours be safe, the others shall be safe also." C. 42. Any one may leave the kingdom, and return at will, except in time of war (omitted in Charter of Henry III). C. 60. Extends these customs and liberties to the whole nation.

1217 Henry III reissues charter, omitting clauses 12, 14, 45; improving clause 39; and adding clause 43 concerning Mortmain.

1225 Charter of the Forest and reissue of Magna Carta.

1235 20 Hen. III C. 2. *Statute of Merton:* no usury permitted against minors. Children born before marriage to be illegitimate.

1253 37 Hen. III In the King's presence, the Archbishop of Canterbury and all the bishops, "apparelled in pontificals, with tapers burning" curse and excommunicate all who break the charters or "the liberties or other customs of the realm of England."

1264 Citizens of towns first represented in Simon de Montfort's parliament.

1266 51 Hen. III *The assize of bread and beer.* Fixes the price of bread according to the cost of wheat, and two gallons of ale for a penny, with barley at 20*s*. The first French statute; previously all were in Latin.

1267 52 Hen. III *Statute of Marlborough.* Concerns actions concerning real estate and trials of clerks for murder. Farmer shall commit no waste.

1275 3 Ed. I *Westminster the First.* First use of the word Parliament. Common right to be done to rich and poor. Statute concerns principally criminal law. Nothing to be a wreck from which a dog or cat escapes quick out of the ship. No disturbance of free elections for parliament. Customs tax on wool. Fines to be reasonable. Slander made criminal. Ravishment of women of full age without their consent, or of maidens under age with or without, is now made a crime by secular law, punished by fine and two years' imprisonment. "Excessive toll, contrary to the common custom of the realm," forbidden in Market towns. Parties indicted, etc., to have the writ *de odio et atia* "lest they be kept long in prison, like as it is declared in Magna Carta." — This great statute the first complete code of English law.

1275 Statute of Bigamy aimed against priests with more than one wife refers to the Pope as "the Bishop of Rome."

1279 Statute of Mortmain.

1283 11 Ed. I (Re-enacted 1285 and called the Statute Merchant.) *Statute of Acton Burnel* provides for speedy recovery of debts due merchants. Foundation of the modern law of pledge, sales of collateral, etc. If he have no goods to be seized the debtor to be imprisoned, but "the creditor shall find him bread and water," and, if a stranger, may recover expenses of his trip to England (1285). Does away with the Droit D'Aubaine. Provides generally for the recovery of ordinary debts; but Jews are excluded from its provisions.

1284 Statute of Wales. A complete code of procedure for Wales, with jury trial.

1285 13 Ed. I *Westminster the Second.* De Donis. A still more complete code than Marlborough. These two codes caused Edward I to be named the English Justinian, but mainly concern criminal law and land ownership. First game law, protecting salmons, c. 47.

1285 13 Ed. I *Statute of Winchester.* Provides for the gates of great towns to be shut at sunset, and no citizen to bear arms, nor taverns to sell drink, after 9 P. M. The duties of the watch described in Dogberry's language.

1285 Statutes for London.

Statute of Bakers. The first pure food law. Punishment of forestallers.

1289 18 Ed. I *Westminster Third,* or Quia Emptores. Affects land tenures.

Statute of *Quo Warranto.* (All offices and privileges may be tried and challenged in the courts.)

1276 or 1290 (Time uncertain.) *Statute concerning Jews:* Usury forbidden. Christian debtors to retain half of their substance. Jews must wear mark of two tables joined, on coat. *Quia Emptores.*

1295 The Model Parliament.

1297 25 Ed. I *The Confirmation of the Charters.* No aid or tax without common consent of the realm and for the common profit.

1300 Articles upon the Charters.

1305 33 Ed. I First statute of conspiracy (in maintaining law suits only). Rise of chancery jurisdiction. Year books begin.

1309 Summary of Grievances: seizure of supplies by King; new customs on wine and cloth and other imports whereby their price to the people is enhanced; current coin debased; petitions of Commons to Parliament not received; delay of actions at law; pardons to felons; trial of civil cases by constables; escheats.

1309
3 Ed. II
5 Ed. Statute of Stamford. All duties suspended "in order to know what advantage will accrue to the people thereby."

Abolition of "new" customs duties. The King shall not go out of the realm. First statute restraining chancery jurisdiction, forbidding arrest, conviction, or forfeiture without jury.

1322
15 Ed. II Assertion of right of commonalty to share in legislation. End of scutage. Customs become part of permanent revenue.

1330 Yearly sessions parliament, law for.

1331 Statute against invasion of common-law jurisdiction by the Chancellor.

9 Ed. III
1335 *Statute of York.* Allows free trading in England to foreign merchants. *Statute de Moneta;* forbids carrying money abroad. About this time (records contradictory, see 1285) the first law making *forestalling* penal.

1336
10 Ed. III Unanimous verdict of jury of twelve now necessary.

De Cibariis. Forbids more than two courses of three dishes each for dinner or supper.

1337
11 Ed. III *Felony to carry wool* out of England or to wear cloth made out of England. No clothes made beyond seas to be brought into England. The right to wear furs to be accorded the nobility only.

1340 or 1328
14 Ed. III All merchants allowed to come freely into the Kingdom. Abolition of the laws of staple. Export of wool restricted.

1340
14 Ed. III "The realm and people of England shall not be subject to the King or people of France."

In the royal edict issued the year he assumed the title King of France, King Edward also deprecates any inference being drawn from his assuming the Flower de Luces in the first quarter of his arms.

1344
18 Ed. III This statute complains that the French king is trying to destroy the English language. The statute itself is

written in French. All persons may buy or export wool; the seas to be open to merchants.

1348 Herbert Spencer notes that at this time the Court of Chancery became the Court of Equity with power to relieve in certain cases and a fixed abode. The Black Death.

1349
23 Ed. III *The first statute of laborers.* Requires all persons able in body under sixty to do labor to such persons as require labor or else be committed to gaol.

No workman or servant can depart from service before the time agreed upon; the old wages and no more shall be given. Victuals shall be sold only at reasonable prices. (Apparently these prices were to be fixed by the mayor.) C. 7 provides that no person shall give anything to a beggar who is able to labor. Barrington notes that this statute is probably illegal because the Commons are not mentioned as having joined in its enactment. It recites the great increase of wages by reason of the plague.

1350 Herbert Spencer has a note that this year *privileges of the trade guilds* were confirmed by statute after two centuries of struggle. This statute, however, cannot be found in the Statutes at Large.

1350 *The amended statute of laborers.* This law was joined in by the Commons and provides elaborately for the amount of wages to be paid all sorts of service, including agricultural service. Thus, common laborers one penny, mowers three pence a day. At this time the Black Prince, the head of the army, was paid 20 shillings a day, carpenters two or three pence, masons three or four pence, servants one-half a penny, tilers three, thatchers of fern and straw 3 pence a day. (Confirmed in 1378.)

1350
25 Ed. III *The statute of cloths.* C. 3 of this statute contains a more severe provision against forestalling wines and victuals, the buyer to forfeit the value of the amount of goods he forestalled, with two years' imprisonment. This law confirmed in 2 R. II, 1378.

1352 Indictments made necessary by statute.

1353 *Statute of the staple* re-established and enlarged; creates staple towns, giving a law for the staple of wood, wool, lead, and leather, and fixing the rent of houses in staple town at a reasonable rate; merchandise to be freely sold at the staple, if not forestalled. Consent of Parliament fully recognized as necessary even to indirect taxation (I Taylor, 490).

1354
28 Ed. III
Another *confirmation of the charters,* notable because this time the great clause in the Magna Carta uses the words "due process of law" instead of the previous phrases "law of the land," "judgment of his peers," etc. The export of iron is forbidden.

1360
34 Ed. III
Confirms the *statute of laborers,* and allows work in gross, *i. e.,* by contract, if well and lawfully done, and declares void all alliances and covins between masons, carpenters and guilds, chapters and ordinances. Laborers refusing work may be imprisoned. C. 10 punishes laborers departing to another county. This, though claimed to have been repealed by general words in the 5 Elizabeth, was not expressly repealed until 1869.

1362
36 Ed. III
Parliament required to be held once a year, and pleas to be in the English language.

Fixes the price of hens and chickens, capons and geese, at from one to four pennies, the reason of such a statute being alleged to be the great dearness of such articles in the kingdom. By c. 5 merchants are forbidden to ingross or enhance the prices of them, and are required to deal in only one kind of goods, and in the same way handicraftsmen were allowed to "use but one mystery." This statute also prescribes in great detail for the apparel of all sorts and conditions of persons, their wives and servants. The part of the law forbidding merchants from using more than one kind of merchandise was, however, repealed the following year, and it was declared that "all people shall be free as they were at all times before."

1376
51 Ed. III
Ordinance that *women might not sue* in court by way of maintenance or reward, especially Alice Perrers.

First impeachment by Commons, Nevil and Latimer.

1377
2 Rich. II
Last severe *statute concerning villeinage,* requiring villeins refusing to labor to be committed to prison without bail at the complaint of the landlord. Villeins fleeing to cities were made free after a year and a day.

1379 2 Rich. II First *statute concerning frauds* by debtors against creditors.

1381 5 Rich. II All persons not great lords or merchants *forbidden to leave the kingdom.* No goods to be exported or imported save in English ships, except (see amending statute of 1381) where no English ships are to be had. Exportation of gold and silver definitely forbidden. Attendance at Parliament made compulsory.

1383 7 Rich. II Wat Tyler leads rising against villeinage. Growth of small freeholders. Villeins demand commutation of service to 4*d* an acre rent, and freedom of commerce in market towns.

First laws against *vagabonds.*

Barons protest against Roman law, and judges forbid it to be cited in the courts (T.-L. 145).

1388 12 Rich. II *Laborers restricted* to their hundred, and following the same trade as father compulsory after twelve. *Wages of agricultural laborers* fixed as well as of handicraftsmen at low rates, — shepherds ten shillings a year, plowmen seven, women laborers six shillings. Servants may carry bows and arrows, not swords; may not play tennis or football. Servants leaving employment required to carry testimonial, and none to receive servants without such letter, — the original of the black list. The first Poor Law; those unable to work are to be supported in the town where born. Villeinage, which began at the Norman Conquest, according to Fitz-Herbert, "because the Conqueror gave lordships with all the inhabitants to do with them at their pleasure to his principal followers, and they, needing servants, pardoned the inhabitants of their lives, and caused them to do all manner of service," — was now abolished by compensation in a money wage payment.

The institution of villeinage is last mentioned in a commission of Queen Elizabeth, 1574, directing Lord Burleigh and others in certain counties to compound with all such bondmen or bondwomen for their manumission and freedom.

First act against nuisances, forbidding corruption of rivers, etc.

1389 *Wages of artisans* and laborers to be fixed at Easter and Michaelmas by a Justice of the Peace, not as before, fixed at a permanent sum.

1391 15 Rich. II No man to be *compelled to answer* before a Lord of matters determinable at common law. Statute limiting admiralty jurisdiction. Roman law prohibited.

17 Rich. II Court of Chancery now established. (Spence, V, 344.)

1400 2 Hen. IV *Foreign merchants* permitted to carry away half the value of their imports in money, spending the other half in English commodities.

1401 2 Hen. IV First secular *law against heresy,* making it a capital offence. Upon conviction by the ordinary the heretic is to be delivered to the secular arm, *i. e.,* burnt. Note that the trial, however, still remains with the ordinary, *i. e.,* the clerical court.

1402 *English burgesses* who marry Welsh women disfranchised.

Laborers not to work feast days, nor for more than half a day before a holiday.

Attorneys to be learned in the law and examined by judges.

Parliament asserts right to ratify treaties and be consulted on wars.

1403 *Transmutation of metals* into gold made a felony, also breach of trust and embezzlement.

1406 Petition of 31 articles.

1407 King ceases to sit in Parliament. Establishment of principle that money bills must originate in the House of Commons.

1412 1 Hen. VI On account of the *felonies committed by Irishmen* resorting to the University of Oxford, all natives of that country obliged to leave England, except University graduates, clergymen, and lawyers.

1414 Legislation still by petition of House of Commons, but now in English.

1422-1461 *Personal property* now legally protected. (Spencer.)

No one with land of less than twenty shillings per annum to apprentice a son or daughter within a city.

1423 *Pound of silver,* though worth 32 shillings, fixed at 30*s*.

1425 *Masons* forbidden to confederate themselves in chapters, etc.

1427 Attempt to *fix wages* by law (1388) again abandoned. To be fixed by justices as in 1389 "because Masters could not get Servants without giving higher Wages than allowed by the Statute."

1429 First disfranchising act, restricts voting qualification to 40*s* a year freeholders. Residence qualifications for both electors and elected — only abolished in 14 Geo. III.

1436 15 Hen. VI *Corn* allowed to be exported when below a certain price. Importation of manufactured articles and of wheat, when under 6*s* 8*d* per quarter, forbidden.

1436 First statute against by-laws in *restraint of trade,* providing for guilds and the corporate companies making unlawful ordinances as to the price of their wares for their own profit and to the common hurt of the people and such made penal and invalid except when approved by the chancellor. This statute re-enacted in 1503, 19 Hen. VII, c. 7.

1439 18 Hen. VI Exportation of *wool* still forbidden.

1444 23 Hen. VI *Servant in husbandry* proposing to depart from his master must give him half a year's warning. Wages again fixed, overseers 20*s*, common husbandry 15*s*, women 10*s*, etc., etc., with meat and drink. Carpenters, in summer 4*d* a day, in winter 3*d*, etc., and meat and drink, or 1½*d* a day in lieu thereof. Women 2½*d* a day and keep at 2*d*. Repealed by 5 Eliz., c. 4.

1452 31 Hen. VI Prototype of *government by injunction.* C. 2 recites Jack Cade's Rebellion, declares that in cases of riots, etc., in the future, if any offender be commanded to appear in chancery or before a council but disobey, the chancellor, on certificate thereof, may issue writs of proclamation to appear within one month or suffer forfeiture or outlawry. Statute to continue only seven years.

1463 3 Ed. IV *First corn law* prohibiting importation of corn, but only effective when the quarter of wheat or barley, etc., does not exceed a certain price. General prohibition of importation of manufactured articles. First example of reciprocity; 4 Ed., c. 5, prohibits importation of merchandise from Burgundy while English cloth is prohibited there. Strict law regulating apparel, but repealed twenty years later.

1483 1 Rich. III Statutes now begin to be in English. C. 12, first precedent of prohibitive tariff imposed on manufactured articles only, and not on raw materials.

1485 1 Hen. VII "No *tanner* shall be a currier, nor any currier a tanner."

[Hallam, Const. Hist. I, 2.] Six liberty rights now established: taxation by parliament; no person to be imprisoned without warrant; legislation by consent of commons; criminal causes triable by a jury of the county, in open court, from whose unanimous verdict no appeal could be made; officers, administrators, or soldiers liable for acts at the common law; impeachment of the King's ministers.

1487 3 Hen. VII Gives special authority to *court of Star Chamber* over riots and disorders.

Dispensing power of Crown now denied as to *mala in se* (things against the common law).

1495 11 Hen. VII First suits in *forma pauperis.*

1503 19 Hen. VII By-laws of guilds, etc., restraining *suits at law* unlawful. So ordinances "against the common weal of the people."

1509 1 Hen. VIII Paucity of legislation due to attempt at personal government.

1511 3 Hen. VIII License required from physicians and surgeons to practise.

1512 *The Strode Case.* Right of Parliamentary privilege established. Benefit of clergy abolished in murder. Statute of laborers repealed in so far as it imposes a penalty on the master for giving higher wages than the law allows.

1514 Henry VIII manumits two villeins in the following form: "Whereas God created all men free . . ."

1514 6 Hen. VIII The most elaborate of all the acts fixing the *wages* and hours of labor, what time he shall begin and end his work, and what time he shall have for his meals and sleep. First general commission of sewerage.

1523 Wolsey's attempt to intimidate the House of Commons. Parliament not summoned for seven years.

1530 Bakers, brewers, surgeons, and scriveners declared not handicraftsmen.

1533 New act against the forestalling, and regrating of *victuals,* corn and especially fish.

1534 Henry VIII declared supreme head of the Church of England. First game law against wild fowl.

1535 *Statute of uses and wills.* Third conviction for joining trade union punished with loss of ear. (H. Spencer, but not in statutes at large.) The law, 27 Hen, VIII, c. 25, is aimed only at sturdy vagabonds and beggars.

1536 First State poor law.

1539 *Dissolution of monasteries.* The "Bloody Statute" against heresy. The sacraments, celibacy, masses, confessions insisted upon. Punishment, burning. The act is entitled "An Act abolishing diversity of opinion on certain articles concerning the Christian religion."

1540 First act against *witchcraft.* First act establishing prescriptions in land titles. First act for the breeding of horses, to be over fifteen hands.

1539 Act giving royal proclamations of the King in Council the force of law.

Abuse of bills of attainder.

1542 34 Hen. VIII C. 4. First *bankruptcy act,* empowering distribution of effects, with penalties against absconders and fraudulent debtors. Prohibits Tindale's translation of the Bible and directs that the New Testament in English shall not be read by women, prentices, and laborers under the degree of yeomen.

1545 *Usury* law — 10%.

1548 Marriage of priests made lawful.

1549 3 & 4 Ed. VI C. 5. *Unlawful assemblies* of twelve to alter laws or abate prices, etc. First (High Church) Prayer Book.

1552 The last act against *regraters, forestallers,* and *ingrossers.* 5 Ed. VI, c. 14, made perpetual by 13 Eliz., and repealed by 12 Geo. III. Origin of anti-trust laws.

Two witnesses required to treason.

1553 7 Ed. VI First precedent of a *coal and fuel* law, prohibiting middlemen. The Thirty-nine Articles.

1555 1 P. & M. *Act for relief of weavers,* prohibiting "the ingrossing of looms," anticipating Marx.

1562 5 Eliz. C. 4. *The great statute of laborers.* Consolidation of all previous laws. Recites that wages were fixed too small, and not reasonable to this time. Provides for many trades, and no person to be hired for less than a year. Compels all persons not having an estate of 40*s* per annum to serve in any of the mentioned handicrafts. Unmarried persons under 30 not having been brought up to any special craft, if not in a nobleman's household, may be compelled to labor at the request of any person using an art or mystery. Other persons between 12 and 60 compelled to serve in husbandry. None may leave or discharge before a year's time, except on order of a justice of the peace, and none may leave his city or town without a testimonial. Hours of labor between March and September from 5 A. M. to 7 P. M. with 2½ hours for meal times, and drink times and sleep 2½ hours. From September to May, dawn to sunset. Wages to be fixed by justice of the peace. Unmarried women between 12 and 40 to serve in like manner; and elaborate rules for the apprentices. None may use any manual art who has not been apprenticed to the same. Masters prohibited from discharging servants before their term without reasonable cause or a quarter's warning. No servant to be hired without testimonial.

1566 Speaker Onslow tells Elizabeth she is subject to the common law.

The Pope forbids attendance at the English Church.

1570 13 Eliz. C. 5. *Fraudulent conveyances* against creditors declared void.

1571 Commons complain of monopolies. First punishment for bribery at elections.

1581 First recorded expulsion of a member of the House of Commons.

1585 Strict censorship of the press.

1572
1601
14 Eliz. C. 5. The first law against *vagabonds* and poor law, completely re-enacted in 43 Eliz., c. 2, establishing the principle of support of the poor by the public, *i. e.*, parish, only that the able who refuse work may be sent to the house of correction by the magistrates.

Many acts regulating trades, and encouraging agriculture, rebuilding villages, etc., passed during this period.

Height of the monopoly abuse. Elizabeth promises to do away with them.

1603 James attempts to control elections. Asserts Divine Right.

1604 The "Form of Apology."

1606 Patents granted for the exclusive sale of article not inventions. Beginning of laws licensing liquor sellers, aimed against drunkenness. James omits to summon Parliament and imposes a duty on imports without its consent.

1609 The Commons object to laws by proclamation, and the King's Bench sustains them.

1615 James attempts to get the opinion of the judges in advance and separately.

1616 Case of Commendams. Disgrace of Coke. Judges now hold office at the King's pleasure.

1617 Last laws of villeinage.

1623
21 James I C. 3. The statute of *monopolies,* prohibiting of such monopolies both granted and to be granted, giving remedy in double or treble damages, making exceptions of the charters to municipal corporations, of the trade guilds and fellowships, and of copyrights and tavern licenses.

Legal rate of interest now 8%.

1628
3 Charles I The *Petition of Right.*

1641 Massachusetts *Body of Liberties. The Grand Remonstrance.*

1642 Arrest of the Five members. Parliament abolishes the Star Chamber and all but common law courts.

1643 First Business Corporation: the Fellowship of Merchant Adventurers.

1653 (Commonwealth) The Instrument of Government.

1666 Appropriation Act.

1667 The Statute of Frauds.

1670 Immunity of jurymen for their verdicts finally established. General verdicts vindicated.

1679 31 Charles II The Habeas Corpus Act.
Standing armies begin, in England. The Mutiny, or Army Act.

1685 Act to encourage the building of ships in England. Tax on foreign ships employed in coasting trade.

1689 William III Bill or *Declaration of Rights.*

1691 Rates of carriers fixed by law.

1700 Act of Settlement. Judges' tenure made for life. No pardon pleadable to impeachment.

1707 Last royal veto of an Act of Parliament.

1716 The Septennial Act.

1765 General warrants declared illegal by Lords Camden and Mansfield.

1776 Virginia *Bill of Rights.*
Declaration of Independence.

1780 Massachusetts *Bill of Rights.*
The Massachusetts *Constitution.*

1787 *Constitution of the United States.*

1789 *First Ten Amendments* U. S. Constitution.

1794 *Eleventh Amendment* U. S. Constitution.

1804 *Twelfth Amendment* U. S. Constitution.

1840 About this time the invention of the business corporation with limited liability to stockholders.

1865 *Thirteenth Amendment* U. S. Constitution.

1866 *Fourteenth Amendment* U. S. Constitution.

1870 *Fifteenth Amendment* U. S. Constitution.

1887 Interstate Commerce Act.

1890 Anti-Trust (Sherman) Act.

1903 Bureau of Corporations established. Discrimination (Elkins) Act.

1906 Pure Food Law.

1906 Railway Rate Regulation (Hepburn) Act.

CHAPTER III

DIVISION OF NATIONAL AND STATE POWER

THE frontispiece graphically represents the exact division of political and legislative power between the States and the Federal Government as well as the large field reserved by the Constitution to the people; and it does this even to the finer shades of distinction, as when powers delegated to the Nation are, at the same time, forbidden to the States or when they are shared by the Nation and the States, or when nothing is said about it, so that the matter must depend upon the interpretation of the Supreme Court. Thus, the entire sovereign and legislative power we will assume represented by the entire circle. Then, drawing a zone "A" on the northwest of the circle nearly to the centre, we will assume that "A," colored blue with horizontal lines, comprises all the powers which are delegated or permitted to the Federal Government. A corresponding zone "B," colored blue with vertical lines, will represent in like manner the powers expressly reserved by the Federal Constitution to the States; though it is obvious that all powers not comprised in the zone "A" must necessarily remain either with the States or with the people. It will be observed that these two zones intersect. The area covered by both "A" and "B" will naturally and mathematically represent the powers given, by the express words of the Constitution, to both the Nation and the States. These, naturally, are few in number.

Now in a manner precisely corresponding, we can represent those powers which are denied or forever withheld, both to the United States and to the States, by the wording or necessary implication of the Constitution. These denied or withheld powers we have colored red. Thus, the zone "X," with horizontal lines, comprises all those matters which are expressly or by necessary implication forbidden to the Federal Government; in like manner zone "Z," drawn red with perpendicular lines, comprises all those matters which are expressly or by necessary implication forbidden to the States. Again, where these two zones intersect, is the area "XZ," comprising many most important matters which, by the Federal Constitution, are forbidden to both the Nation and the States; that is to say, matters which the people expressly withheld from either government they were creating. In a sense, therefore, this area "XZ" is analogous to "Y," the central area, outside of any zone permitted to either Nation or State; the difference being that our area "XZ" will represent those matters which are merely denied to both State and Federal power, while the area "Y" will represent those which are, by the wording of the Constitution itself, expressly reserved or declared to remain with the people.

But we have not yet exhausted all our shades of meaning. The intersection of the zone "B," matters permitted to the States, with the zone "X," matters forbidden to the Federal Government, results in the area "BX," the peculiar domain of States' rights; that is to say, those powers which are both permitted to the States or reserved to the States, and, by the wording of the Constitution, expressly denied or forbidden to the Federal Government. On the other hand, the corresponding area "AZ" in like manner represents those powers delegated to the United States and forbidden expressly to the States; that is to say, "AZ" is the peculiar domain of the imperialist or the supporter of centralization; those great matters, notably interstate commerce, which, by interpretation or otherwise, he would have given over solely to the National Government, and withheld from any control by the States.

It is not too much to say that if we knew exactly what matters fall within the area "AZ" and the corresponding area "BX" and the central domain of "Y," we should have the solution of all the questions that are now vexing both the constitutional lawyer and the general public; for these neutral grounds, these contested areas, graphically represent both what is given or denied to the Federal Government, what is reserved to the States, and finally, what has never been parted with by the people. Under the extreme interpretation at some times proposed by President Roosevelt, the area "Y" almost disappears; while the area "BX," or indeed the whole zone of "X," is much shrunken. On the other hand, according to Thomas Jefferson and the old strict-construction Democrats, it is the area "Y" that largely expands, and the area "AZ," or indeed the whole zone "Z," what is forbidden to the States, largely diminishes. If the reader of this book will take the diagram and carefully, for himself, decide (for on some clauses there may be a difference of opinion) just what sentences or sections of the Constitution, or matters or powers mentioned therein, fall within each of these nine divisions of our sphere of the total powers of government, he will almost, by the very study required, the close examination of the Constitution necessary, become a good American constitutional lawyer. But it is needless to say that hundreds of decisions of the Supreme Court have been required to settle these most debatable areas, "AZ," "BX," and "Y"; and many more are still required before we can be certain on all points. That great power to control commerce among the States, under which it seems it is now proposed to bring the Federal Government into all the domains of law and life in such a manner as to revolutionize our whole system, does it, for instance, all fall within the area "AZ"? or may it go into the rest of the zone of "A," that is, a matter over which some control or power, co-ordinate, not subordinate to the Federal Government, rests or remains with the States? In like manner, does the power of imposing an income tax belong only in the narrow area of "BX"? or may it go into the other divisions of the zone of "B," powers given or reserved to the States, which yet may be exercised concurrently by the Nation?

With this explanation I pass (with some diffidence, for my readers may not agree with me on all points) to the division I have made into our nine possible categories of the matters and powers enumerated in the Federal Constitution:

AZ

FEDERAL POWERS WHICH ARE FORBIDDEN TO THE STATES

ALL legislative powers herein granted shall be vested in a Congress of the United States, which shall consist of a Senate and House of Representatives. I, 1. The House of Representatives shall choose their Speaker and other officers and shall have the sole power of impeachment. I, 2, (5).

The Senate shall choose their other officers, and also a President *pro tempore* in the absence of the Vice-President. . . . I, 3, (5).

The Senate shall have the sole power to try all impeachments. I, 3, (6).

Each house shall be the judge of the elections, returns, and qualifications of its own members, and a majority of each shall constitute a quorum to do business; but a smaller number may adjourn from day to day, and may be authorized to compel the attendance of absent members, in such manner, and under such penalties, as each house may provide. I, 5, (1).

Each house may determine the rules of its proceedings, punish its members for disorderly behavior, and with the concurrence of two thirds, expel a member. I, 5, (2).

Each house shall keep a journal of its proceedings, and from time to time publish the same, excepting such parts as may in their judgment require secrecy, and the yeas and nays of the members of either house on any question shall, at the desire of one-fifth of those present, be entered on the journal. I, 5, (3).

Every bill which shall have passed the House of Representatives and the Senate shall, before it become a law, be presented to the President of the United States; if he approve he shall sign it, but if not he shall return it, with his objections, to that house in which it shall have originated, etc. If approved by two-thirds of [each] house it shall become a law. I, 7, (2).

The Congress shall have power to lay and collect . . . duties, imposts, ... to pay the debts and provide for the common defense and general welfare of the United States. . . . I, 8, (1).

To borrow money on the credit of the United States; I, 8, (2).

To regulate commerce with foreign nations and among the several States, and with the Indian tribes; I, 8, (3).

To establish an uniform rule of naturalization, and uniform laws on the subject of bankruptcies throughout the United States; I, 8, (4).

To coin money, regulate the value thereof, and of foreign coin, and fix the standard of weights and measures; I, 8, (5).

To establish post-offices and post-roads; I, 8, (7).

To constitute tribunals inferior to the Supreme Court; I, 8, (9).

To define and punish piracies and felonies committed on the high seas and offences against the law of nations; I, 8, (10).

To declare war, grant letters of marque and reprisal, and make rules concerning captures on land and water; I, 8, (11).

To raise and support armies, but no appropriation of money to that use shall be for a longer term than two years; I, 8, (12).

To provide and maintain a navy; I, 8, (13).

To make rules for the government and regulation of the land and naval forces; I, 8, (14).

To provide for calling forth the militia to execute the laws of the Union, suppress insurrections, and repel invasions; I, 8, (15).

To provide for organizing, arming and disciplining the militia, and for governing such part of them as may be employed in the service of the United States. . . . I, 8, (16).

To exercise exclusive legislation [over the District of Columbia and] all places purchased by the consent of the legislature of the State in which the same shall be, for the erection of forts, magazines, arsenals, dockyards, and other needful buildings; I, 8, (17).

To make all laws which shall be necessary and proper for carrying into execution the foregoing powers, and all other powers vested by this Constitution in the Government of the United States, or in any department or officer thereof I, 8, (18).

. . . the net produce of all duties and imposts, laid by any State on imports or exports, shall be for the use of the Treasury of the United States; and all such laws shall be subject to the revision and control of the Congress. I, 10, (2).

The executive power shall be vested in a President. . . . He shall hold his office during the term of four years, and together with the Vice-President, chosen for the same term, be elected as follows. II, 1, (1).

The Congress may determine the time of choosing the electors and the day on which they shall give their votes, which day shall be the same throughout the United States. II, 1, (4).

In case of the removal of the President from office, or of his death, resignation, or inability to discharge the powers and duties of the said office, the same shall devolve on the Vice-President, and the Congress may by law provide for the case of removal, death, resignation, or inability, both of the President and Vice-President, declaring what officer shall then act as President, and such officer shall act accordingly until the disability be removed or a President shall be elected. II, 1, (6).

The President shall, at stated times, receive for his services a compensation, which shall neither be increased nor diminished during the period for which he may have been elected, and he shall not receive within that period any other emolument from the United States, or any of them. II, 1, (7).

The President shall be Commander-in-chief of the Army and Navy of the United States, and of the militia of the several States when called into the actual service of the United States; he may require the opinion, in writing, of the principal officer in each of the executive departments, upon any subject relating to the duties of their respective offices, and he shall have power to grant reprieves and pardons for offences against the United States, except in cases of impeachment. II, 2, (1).

He shall have power, by and with the advice and consent of the Senate, to make treaties, provided two-thirds of the Senators present concur; and he shall nominate, and, by and with the advice and consent of the Senate, shall appoint ambassadors, other public ministers and consuls, judges of the Supreme Court, and all other officers of the United States, whose appointments are not herein otherwise provided for, and which shall be established by law; but the Congress may by law vest the appointment of such inferior officers, as they think proper, in the President alone, in the courts of law, or in the heads of departments. II, 2, (2).

The President shall have power to fill up all vacancies that may happen during the recess of the Senate, by granting commissions which shall expire at the end of their next session. II, 2, (3).

He shall from time to time give to the Congress information of the state of the Union, and recommend to their consideration such measures as he shall judge necessary and expedient; he may, on extraordinary occasions, convene both houses, or either of them, and in case of disagreement between them with respect to the time of adjournment, he may adjourn them to such time as he shall think proper; he shall receive ambassadors and other public ministers; he shall take care that the laws be faithfully executed, and shall commission all the officers of the United States. II, 3.

The President, Vice-President, and all civil officers of the United States shall be removed from office on impeachment for and conviction of treason, bribery, or other high crimes and misdemeanors. II, 4.

The judicial power of the United States shall be vested in one Supreme Court, and in such inferior courts as the Congress may from time to time ordain and establish. III, 1.

The judicial power shall extend . . . to all cases affecting ambassadors, other public ministers, and consuls; to all cases of admiralty and maritime jurisdiction; to controversies to which the United States shall be a party; to controversies between two or more States; between a State and citizens of another State; between citizens of different States; between citizens of the same State claiming lands under grants of different States, and between a State, or the citizens thereof, and foreign States, citizens, or subjects. III, 2, (1).

In all cases affecting ambassadors, other public ministers and consuls, and those in which a State shall be a party, the Supreme Court shall have original jurisdiction. In all the other cases before mentioned the Supreme Court shall have appellate jurisdiction, both as to law and fact, with such exceptions and under such regulations as the Congress shall make. III, 2, (2).

The Congress shall have power to declare the punishment of treason. . . . III, 3, (2).

. . . the Congress may by general laws prescribe the manner in which such acts, records, and proceedings shall be proved, and the effect thereof. IV, 1.

The Congress shall have power to dispose of and make all needful rules and regulations respecting the territory or other property belonging to the United States; and nothing in this Constitution shall be so construed as to prejudice any claims of the United States or of any particular State. IV, 3, (2).

New States may be admitted by the Congress into this Union. . . . IV, 3, (1).

The Congress, whenever two thirds of both houses shall deem it necessary, shall propose amendments to this Constitution, or, on the application of the legislatures of two thirds of the several States, shall call a convention for proposing amendments. . . . V.

. . . But Congress may, by a vote of two thirds of each house, remove such disability. Amendment XIV, 3.

A

POWERS GRANTED TO THE UNITED STATES SIMPLY

. . . in order to form a more perfect union, establish justice, insure domestic tranquillity, provide for the common defense, promote the general welfare, . . . do ordain and establish this Constitution for the United States of America. (Preamble.)

. . . direct taxes shall be apportioned among the several States which may be included within this Union, according to their respective numbers. . . . I, 2, (3).

The Vice-President of the United States shall be President of the Senate. . . . I, 3, (4).

. . . the Congress may at any time by law make or alter such regulations [elections for Senators and Representatives]. I, 4, (1).

The Senators and Representatives shall receive a compensation for their services, to be ascertained by law and paid out of the Treasury of the United States. I, 6, (1).

. . . the Senate may propose or concur with amendments as on other bills [bills for raising revenue]. I, 7, (1).

The Congress shall have power to lay and collect taxes, . . . and excises, . . . I, 8, (1).

To provide for the punishment of counterfeiting the securities and current coin of the United States. I, 8, (6).

To promote the progress of science and useful arts by securing for limited times to authors and inventors the exclusive right to their respective writings and discoveries. I, 8, (8).

To make all laws which shall be necessary and proper for carrying into execution the foregoing powers, etc. . . . I, 8, (18). See in AZ.

The judicial power shall extend to all cases, in law and equity, arising under this Constitution, the laws of the United States, and treaties made, or which shall be made, under their authority. . . . III, 2, (1).

The electors shall meet in their respective States and vote by ballot for President and Vice-President [the general method of election]. Amendment XII.

Congress shall have power to enforce this article by appropriate legislation [the article against slavery]. Amendment XIII, 2.

The Congress shall have power to enforce, by appropriate legislation, the provisions of this article [the Fourteenth Amendment]. Amendment XIV, 5.

The Congress shall have power to enforce, by appropriate legislation, the provisions of the article [the Fifteenth Amendment]. Amendment XV, 2.

AB

POWERS COMMON TO THE NATION AND THE STATES

No State shall, without the consent of Congress, lay any imposts or duties on imports or exports. . . . I, 10, (2).

[or] lay any duty of tonnage. . . . I, 10, (3).

. . . nor any State be formed by the junction of two or more States or parts of States, without the consent of the Legislatures of the States concerned as well as of the Congress. IV, 3, (1).

The United States . . . shall protect each of them against invasion [the States] and on application of the legislature, or of the executive [when the legislature cannot be convened], against domestic violence. IV, 4.

The Congress . . . on the application of the legislatures of two thirds of the several States, shall call a convention for proposing amendments. V.

B

POWERS RESERVED IN THE STATES (SIMPLY).

. . . each State shall have at least one Representative. I, 2, (3).

[A State may lay imposts or duties] absolutely necessary for executing its inspection laws. I, 10, (2).

A person charged in any State with treason, felony, or other crime, who shall flee from justice, and be found in another State, shall, on demand of the executive authority of the State from which he fled, be delivered up, to be removed to the State having jurisdiction of the crime. IV, 2, (2).

[House shall vote, by States, for President, in case of no electoral majority, from the three highest on the list, each State having one vote]. Amendment XII.

BX

STATE POWERS FORBIDDEN TO THE UNITED STATES

The House of Representatives shall be composed of members chosen . . . by the people of the several States. I, 2, (1).

When vacancies happen in the representation from any State, the executive authority thereof shall issue writs of election to fill such vacancies. I, 2, (4).

The Senate of the United States shall be composed of two Senators from each State, chosen by the Legislature thereof, for six years, and each Senator shall have one vote. I, 3, (1).

. . . if vacancies happen by resignation or otherwise during the recess of the Legislature of any State, the executive thereof may make temporary appointments until the next meeting of the legislature, which shall then fill such vacancies [in the Senate]. I, 3, (2).

The times, places, and manner of holding elections for Senators and Representatives shall be prescribed in each State by the Legislature thereof; but the Congress may at any time by law make or alter such regulations, except as to the places of choosing Senators. I, 4, (1).

. . . reserving to the States respectively the appointment of the officers, and the authority of training the militia according to the discipline prescribed by Congress. I, 8, (16).

The migration or importation of such persons (slaves) . . . shall not be prohibited by the Congress prior to the year one thousand eight hundred and eight. . . . I, 9, (1).

Each State shall appoint, in such manner as the Legislature thereof may direct, a number of electors, equal to the whole number of Senators and Representatives to which the State may be entitled in the Congress. . . . II, 1, (2).

The powers not delegated to the United States by the Constitution, nor prohibited by it to the States, are reserved to the States respectively. . . . Amendment X.

The judicial power of the United States shall not be construed to extend to any suit in law or equity, commenced or prosecuted against one of the United States by citizens of another State, or by citizens or subjects of any foreign State. Amendment XI.

Representatives shall be apportioned among the several States according to their respective numbers, counting the whole number of persons in each State, excluding Indians not taxed. . . . Amendment XIV, 2.

X

POWERS FORBIDDEN TO THE UNITED STATES SIMPLY

Representatives and direct taxes shall be apportioned among the several States according to their respective numbers . . . excluding Indians not taxed. . . . I, 2, (3).

[The Senators] . . . shall be divided as equally as may be into three classes . . . I, 3, (2).

The . . . President of the Senate . . . shall have no vote, unless they be equally divided. I, 3, (4).

[The Senate when sitting to try impeachments shall] be on oath or affirmation. When the President of the United States is tried, the Chief Justice shall preside: and no person shall be convicted without the concurrence of two-thirds of the members present. I, 3, (6).

Judgment in cases of impeachment shall not extend further than to removal from office, and disqualification to hold and enjoy any office of honor, trust, or profit under the United States. . . . I, 3, (7).

[The meeting of Congress] shall be on the first Monday in December, unless they shall by law appoint a different day. I, 4, (2).

Neither house, during the session of Congress, shall, without the consent of the other, adjourn for more than three days, nor to any other place than that in which the two houses shall be sitting. I, 5, (4).

No Senator or Representative shall, during the time for which he was elected, be appointed to any civil office under the authority of the United States, which shall have been created, or the emoluments whereof shall have been increased during such time. . . . I, 6, (2).

All bills for raising revenue shall originate in the House of Representatives. . . . I, 7, (1).

(Vetoed bills) . . . the votes of both houses shall be determined by yeas and nays, and the names of persons voting for and against the bill shall be entered on the journal of each house respectively. If any bill shall not be returned by the President within ten days (Sundays excepted) after it shall have been presented to him, the same shall be a law, in like manner as if he had signed it, unless the Congress by their adjournment prevent its return, in which case it shall not be a law. I, 7, (2).

Every order, resolution, or vote to which the concurrence of the Senate and House of Representatives may be necessary (except on a question of adjournment) shall be presented to the President of the United States; and before the same shall take effect, shall be approved by him or being disapproved by him, shall be repassed by two thirds of the Senate and House of Representatives, according to the rules and limitations prescribed in the case of a bill. I, 7, (3).

. . . all duties, imposts and excises shall be uniform throughout the United States. 1, 8, (1).

. . . no appropriation of money [to raise and support armies] . . . shall be for a longer term than two years. I, 8, (12).

The privilege of the writ of habeas corpus shall not be suspended, unless when in cases of rebellion or invasion the public safety may require it. I, 9, (2).

No bill of attainder or ex post facto law shall be passed. I, 9, (3).

No capitation or other direct tax shall be laid, unless in proportion to the census or enumeration hereinbefore directed to be taken. I, 9, (4).

No tax or duty shall be laid on articles exported from any State. I, 9, (5).

No preference shall be given by any regulation of commerce or revenue to the ports of one State over those of another; nor shall vessels bound to or from one State be obliged to enter, clear, or pay duties in another. I, 9, (6).

No money shall be drawn from the Treasury but in consequence of appropriations made by law. . . . I, 9, (7).

No title of nobility shall be granted by the United States; and no person holding any office of profit or trust under them shall, without the consent of Congress, accept of any present, emolument, office, or title, of any kind whatever, from any king, prince, or foreign State. I, 9, (8).

. . . The judges, both of the supreme and inferior courts, shall hold their offices during good behavior. . . . (See also in Y.) III, 1.

[The trial of crimes] . . . not committed within any State . . . shall be at such place or places as the Congress may by law have directed. III, 2, (3).

Treason against the United States shall consist only in levying war against them, or in adhering to their enemies, giving them aid and comfort. . . . III, 3, (1).

. . . no attainder of treason shall work corruption of blood, etc. III, 3, (2).

. . . no State, without its consent, shall be deprived of its equal suffrage in the Senate. V.

All debts contracted and engagements entered into, before the adoption of this Constitution, shall be as valid against the United States under this Constitution as under the confederation. VI, 1.

. . . no religious test shall ever be required as a qualification to any office or public trust under the United States. (See also in Y.) VI, 3.

Congress shall make no law respecting an establishment of religion, or prohibiting the free exercise thereof; or abridging the freedom of speech or of the press. . . . Amendment I. (See also under Y.)

. . . the right of the people to keep and bear arms shall not be infringed. (See under Y.) Amendment II.

No soldier shall, in time of peace, be quartered in any house without the consent of the owner, nor in time of war, but in a manner to be prescribed by law. (See under Y.) Amendment III.

The right of the people to be secure in their persons, houses, papers and effects, against unreasonable searches and seizures, shall not be violated, and no warrants shall issue but upon probable cause, supported by oath or affirmation, and particularly describing the place to be searched, and the person or things to be seized. Amendment IV.

No person shall be held to answer for a capital or otherwise infamous crime, unless on a presentment or indictment of a grand jury, except in cases arising in the land or naval forces, or in the militia, when in actual service in time of war or public danger; nor shall any person be subject for the same offence to be twice put in jeopardy of life or limb; nor shall be compelled in any criminal case to be a witness against himself, nor be deprived of life, liberty, or property, without due process of law; nor shall private property be taken for public use without just compensation. Amendment V.

[Trial by jury of the vicinage. Witnesses, evidence, etc.] (See under Y.) Amendment VI.

[Trial by jury in civil cases.] (See under Y.) Amendment VII.

[Bail, fines, punishments.] (See under Y.) Amendment VIII.

[Powers not delegated to the United States forbidden.] (See under BX.) Amendment X.

The validity of the public debt of the United States, authorized by law, including debts incurred for payment of pensions and bounties for services in suppressing insurrection or rebellion, shall not be questioned. . . . Amendment XIV, 4.

Z

POWERS FORBIDDEN TO THE STATES SIMPLY

No State shall enter into any treaty, alliance, or confederation; grant letters of marque and reprisal; coin money; emit bills of credit; make anything but gold and silver coin a tender in payment of debts; pass any bill of attainder, ex post facto law, or law impairing the obligation of contracts, or grant any title of nobility. I, 10, (1).

No State shall . . . lay any imposts or duties on imports or exports, except what may be absolutely necessary for executing its inspection laws. . . . (See also under AB.) I, 10, (2).

No State shall, without the consent of Congress, lay any duty of tonnage, keep troops or ships of war in time of peace, enter into any agreement or compact with another State or with a foreign power, or engage in war, unless actually invaded or in such imminent danger as will not admit of delay. I, 10, (3).

. . . no Senator or Representative, or person holding an office of trust or profit under the United States, shall be appointed an elector. II, 1, (2).

Full faith and credit shall be given in each State to the public acts, records, and judicial proceedings of every other State. . . . IV, 1.

The citizens of each State shall be entitled to all privileges and immunities of citizens in the several States. IV, 2, (1).

Fugitive slave provision, [obsolete.] IV, 2, (3).

No State shall make or enforce any law which shall abridge the privileges or immunities of citizens of the United States; nor shall any State deprive any person of life, liberty or property, without due process of law; nor deny to any person within its jurisdiction the equal protection of the laws. Amendment XIV, 1.

. . . when the right to vote at any election for the choice of electors for President and Vice-President . . . , Representatives in Congress, the executive and judicial officers of a State, or the members of the legislature thereof, is denied to any of the male inhabitants of such State, being twenty-one years of age, and citizens of the United States, or in any way abridged, except for participation in rebellion, or other crime, the basis of representation therein shall be reduced [in proportion]. Amendment XIV, 2.

No person shall be a Senator or Representative . . . or elector . . . or hold any office, civil or military, under the United States, or under any State, who, having previously taken an oath . . . to support the Constitution of the United States, shall have engaged in insurrection or rebellion against the same, or given aid or comfort to the enemies thereof. . . . Amendment XIV, 3.

ZX

POWERS EXPRESSLY FORBIDDEN TO BOTH THE NATION AND THE STATES

. . . the electors in each State shall have the qualifications requisite for electors of the most numerous branch of the State legislature. I, 2 (1).

. . . The number of Representatives shall not exceed one for every thirty thousand. . . . I, 2, (3).

No person shall be a Representative who shall not have attained the age of twenty-five years, and been seven years a citizen of the United States. . . . I, 2, (2).

The Senate of the United States shall be composed of two Senators from each State, chosen by the legislature thereof, for six years. . . . I, 3 (1).

No person shall be a Senator who shall not have attained the age of thirty years, and been nine years a citizen of the United States. . . . I, 3, (3).

No person shall be a Senator who shall not have attained to the age of thirty years . . . and who shall not, when elected, be an inhabitant of that State for which he shall be chosen. I, 3 (3).

[Senators and Representatives] shall, in all cases except treason, felony, and breach of the peace, be privileged from arrest during their attendance at the session of their respective houses, and in going to and returning from the same; and for any speech or debate in either house they shall not be questioned in any other place. I, 6, (1).

No tax or duty shall be laid on articles exported from any State. (See also I, 10, (2).) I, 9, (5).

No person except a natural-born citizen, or a citizen of the United States at the time of the adoption of this Constitution, shall be eligible to the office of President; neither shall any person be eligible to that office who shall not have attained to the age of thirty-five years, and been fourteen years a resident within the United States. II, 1, (5).

. . . no new State shall be formed or erected within the jurisdiction of any other State. . . . IV, 3, (1).

The United States shall guarantee to every State in this Union a republican form of government. . . . IV, 4.

This Constitution, and the laws of the United States which shall be made in pursuance thereof, and all treaties made, or which shall be made, under the authority of the United States, shall be the supreme law of the land; and the judges in every State shall be bound thereby, anything in the Constitution or laws of any State to the contrary notwithstanding. VI, 2.

Neither slavery nor involuntary servitude, except as a punishment for crime whereof the party shall have been duly convicted, shall exist within the United States or any place subject to their jurisdiction. Amendment XIII, 1.

. . . neither the United States nor any State shall assume or pay any debt or obligation incurred in aid of insurrection or rebellion against the United States, or any claim for the loss or emancipation of any slave; but all such debts, obligations, and claims shall be held illegal and void. Amendment XIV, 4.

The right of citizens of the United States to vote shall not be denied or abridged by the United States or by any State on account of race, color, or previous condition of servitude. Amendment XV, 1.

Y

RIGHTS RESERVED OR EXPRESSLY RETAINED IN THE PEOPLE

We, the people of the United States, in order to . . . secure the blessings of liberty to ourselves and our posterity . . . do ordain and establish this Constitution for the United States of America. Preamble.

All legislative powers herein granted shall be vested in a Congress [separation of powers]. . . . (See also II, 1; III, 1.) I, 1.

The House of Representatives shall be . . . chosen . . . by the people of the several States. . . . I, 2, (1).

[Every Senator or Representative must be] an inhabitant of that State in which he shall be chosen. I, 2, (2); I, 3, (3).

. . . each State shall have at least one Representative. . . . I, 2, (3).

[Persons impeached] shall nevertheless be liable and subject to indictment, trial, judgment, and punishment, according to law. I, 3, (7).

The Congress shall assemble at least once in every year. . . . I, 4, (2).

[Privilege of Senators from arrest, etc.] (See under XZ.) I, 6, (1).

. . . no person holding any office under the United States shall be a member of either house during his continuance in office. I, 6, (2).

All bills for raising revenue shall originate in the House of Representatives. . . . I, 7, (1).

. . . all duties, imposts, and excises shall be uniform throughout the United States. I, 8, (1).

. . . no appropriation of money . . . [to raise and support armies] shall be for a longer term than two years. I, 8, (12).

The privilege of the writ of habeas corpus shall not be suspended, unless when in cases of rebellion or invasion the public safety may require it. I, 9, (2).

No bill of attainder or ex post facto law shall be passed. I, 9, (3).

[No direct Federal taxation]. I, 9, (4).

No money shall be drawn from the Treasury but in consequence of appropriations made by law; and a regular statement and account of the receipts and expenditures of all public moneys shall be published from time to time. I, 9, (7).

No title of nobility shall be granted by the United States. . . . I, 9, (8).

(The President) before he enter on the execution of his office . . . shall take . . . oath to . . . preserve, protect, and defend the Constitution of the United States. II, 1, (8).

The President, Vice-President, and all civil officers . . . shall be removed from office on impeachment for and conviction of treason, bribery, or other high crimes and misdemeanors. II, 4.

The judges, both of the supreme and inferior courts, shall hold their offices during good behavior, and shall, at stated times, receive for their services a compensation which shall not be diminished during their continuance in office. III, 1.

The trial of all crimes, except in cases of impeachment, shall be by jury; and such trial shall be held in the State where the said crimes shall have been committed. . . . III, 2, (3).

. . . No person shall be convicted of treason unless on the testimony of two witnesses to the same overt act, or on confession in open court . . . but no attainder of treason shall work corruption of blood or forfeiture except during the life of the person attainted. III, 3.

The citizens of each State shall be entitled to all privileges and immunities of citizens in the several States. IV, 2, (1).

The United States shall guarantee to every State in this Union a republican form of government. . . . IV, 4.

[Amendments to this Constitution shall be valid] when ratified by the legislatures of three fourths of the several States, or by conventions in three fourths thereof, as the one or the other mode of ratification may be proposed by the Congress. . . . V.

. . . the judges in every State shall be bound thereby [this Constitution] anything in the Constitution or laws of any State to the contrary notwithstanding. VI, 2.

The Senators and Representatives . . . and all executive and judicial officers, both of the United States and of the several States, shall be bound by oath . . . to support this Constitution; but no religious test shall ever be required as a qualification to any office or public trust under the United States. VI, 3.

Congress shall make no law [respecting religion — see in X] or abridging freedom of speech or of the press; or the right of the people peaceably to assemble and to petition the government for a redress of grievances. Amendment I.

A well-regulated militia being necessary to the security of a free State, the right of the people to keep and bear arms shall not be infringed. Amendment II.

No soldier shall, in time of peace, be quartered in any house without the consent of the owner, nor in time of war, but in a manner to be prescribed by law. Amendment III.

The right of the people to be secure in their persons, houses, papers, and effects, against unreasonable searches and seizures, shall not be violated, and no warrants shall issue but upon probable cause, supported by oath or affirmation, and particularly describing the place to be searched, and the person or things to be seized. Amendment IV.

No person shall be held to answer for a capital or otherwise infamous crime, unless on a presentment or indictment of a grand jury, except in cases arising in the land or naval forces, or in the militia, when in actual service in time of war or public danger; nor shall any person be subject for the same offence to be twice put in jeopardy of life or limb; nor shall be compelled in any criminal case to be a witness against himself, nor be deprived of life, liberty, or property, without due process of law; nor shall private property be taken for public use without just compensation. Amendment V.

In all criminal prosecutions the accused shall enjoy the right to a speedy and public trial, by an impartial jury of the State and district wherein the crime shall have been committed, which district shall have been previously ascertained by law, and to be informed of the nature and cause of the accusation; to be confronted with the witnesses against him; to have compulsory process for obtaining witnesses in his favor, and to have the assistance of counsel for his defense. Amendment VI.

In suits at common law, where the value in controversy shall exceed twenty dollars, the right of trial by jury shall be preserved, and no fact tried by a jury shall be otherwise re-examined in any court of the United States, than according to the rules of the common law. Amendment VII.

Excessive bail shall not be required, nor excessive fines imposed, nor cruel and unusual punishments inflicted. Amendment VIII.

The enumeration in the Constitution of certain rights shall not be construed to deny or disparage others retained by the people. Amendment IX.

The powers not delegated to the United States by the Constitution, nor prohibited by it to the States, are reserved to the States respectively or to the people. Amendment X.

[President elected by electors chosen as the State legislatures may direct, but in fact by the people]. Amendment XII.

Neither slavery nor involuntary servitude, except as a punishment for crime whereof the party shall have been duly convicted, shall exist within the United States or any place subject to their jurisdiction. Amendment XIII, 1.

All persons born or naturalized in the United States, and subject to the jurisdiction thereof, are citizens of the United States and of the State wherein they reside. No State shall make or enforce any law which shall abridge the privileges or immunities of citizens of the United States; nor shall any State deprive any person of life, liberty, or property, without due process of law; nor deny to any person within its jurisdiction the equal protection of the laws. Amendment XIV, 1.

BOOK III

THE STATE CONSTITUTIONS

DIGESTED, ANNOTATED, AND COMPARED

WITH THE

FEDERAL CONSTITUTION

THE STATE CONSTITUTIONS

SECTION 1. *Explanatory preface.* Of the contents of the various State Constitutions, a threefold division may roughly be made; they usually contain, first, the Declaration of Rights; second, the political constitution and organization of the State; and third, very varied and miscellaneous restrictions and injunctions concerning legislation. I have attempted to incorporate herein the entire Constitution of every State, excepting only minute and detailed provisions, not of general interest, concerning minor administrative offices, courts, and municipal government. Where the wording in the several States is not identical, I have been careful to give the various forms when there is any possibility of a difference of meaning or legal effect.

This third part has grown out of all proportion to the others; in fact, in the newer Constitutions, particularly in the West, it far exceeds the other two in bulk and contains such a code of directions or inhibitions as to leave very little real legislative power to the Legislature. The Louisiana Constitution, for instance, contains one hundred and forty-four pages! But still more notable is that of Alabama, covering sixty-nine pages of fine print, and those of the eight new far Western States. Even in States which do not adopt the initiative and referendum, as some of these Western States do, the adoption of such an elaborate Constitution is practically direct legislation, "Legislation by the people." Naturally, there is a tendency in such cases to more frequent amendment; necessarily so when the Constitution, instead of embodying a few great principles and the broad framework of the State government, attempts to prescribe infinite details of legislation and of administrative machinery. Historically, and from the point of view of a Constitutional lawyer, such Constitutions are entirely unscientific. The late Governor Russell of Massachusetts, in his address before the Yale Law School, well pointed out the objections of putting such a mass of things into the Constitution, both as depriving the Legislature of all sense of responsibility, and as discrediting the Constitution itself. Such a vast mass of directions embodying merely the temporary desires of a present majority, when either necessity or popular opinion requires a change, involves a necessity of such continual amendment and frequent alteration as to bring a written Constitution into contempt.

It must be borne in mind that this is a comparative digest of *constitutional* provisions only; it does not follow, of course, that there may not be in the several States *statutes* on the same subject.

All the forty-six States have Constitutions; not so the Territories, or the District of Columbia. Arizona, however, has a "Bill of Rights," though it has naturally no greater sanction than an ordinary territorial statute. In a few cases I have noted similar provisions in the United States laws which restrict the legislation of New Mexico and Arizona. References are also made in the Bill of Rights to the provisions of the United States Constitution or of the English and American constitutional documents on which such articles are founded; and the principles are fully discussed in the notes, and elsewhere.

It may generally be said that the Constitutions of the Western States are more elaborate, more cumbrous, and more frequently amended than those of the Eastern. One reason for this is, that in the West the State Constitution is frequently made the instrument for enacting laws which are in most States unconstitutional; another, that in the West many things are put in the Constitution which are elsewhere left to the Legislature. The constitutional provisions are, of course, much more stable than ordinary laws. Nevertheless, the practice is, as has been said, an objectionable one.

For the date of the latest State Constitutions and where they may be found, see the Table of Citations. States are cited in alphabetical order, and the words "Article" or "Section" are left out. That is to say, 1, 14, would be Article 1, Section 14, or whatever other division is used in the Constitution in question. If there is no citation, refer to the one of the same State last preceding. Many of the States, however, have the articles of the Constitution numbered continuously. The asterisk sign is used in the rare instances where, to complete the subject, a statute is cited.

Since the first edition of this part, published as the first part of Volume I. of "American Statute Law," in 1886, no less than eighteen new State Constitutions have been adopted, counting Oklahoma. Of these, eight are of new Western States, but the other ten are new Constitutions adopted in the Eastern or Southern States. It is notable that none of the States of the middle West or New England, with the exception of New Hampshire, have adopted new Constitutions during this period of twenty years. The industry of constitution making is confined to the more radical States, or to those which have the greatest distrust of their legislators. My thanks are due to Mr. Robert H. Whitten of the New York State Library for a complete table of constitutional amendments adopted in the last twenty years. Owing to the negligence or stupidity of the State authorities in not printing these with the annual laws, this is a difficult matter to ascertain. In Oregon, indeed, where laws and constitutional amendments are adopted by initiative, the Secretary of State complains that they are "full of bad spelling, punctuation, omissions, and repeated words!" It appears, however, that only two states — Tennessee and Wyoming — failed to amend their Constitutions in the last twenty years, while California did so forty-two times!

§ 2. *Interpretation of the State Constitutions.* — In some of the newer Constitutions we find the provision that the Constitution itself is mandatory and prohibitory, except where otherwise declared by express words.[1]

[1] Cal. 1, 22; Mon. 3, 29; N. D. 21; S. C. 1, 29; Utah 1, 26; Wash. 1, 29. In other States, whether the Constitution is self-executing is sometimes an important question. It has been particularly debated in Kansas and Ohio, where new constitutional amendments relieving corporations and stockholders from liability have not been followed by legislation to carry them into effect; and in States whose constitutions have articles against Trusts, etc. The rule would seem to be, if the Constitution *defines* Trusts or declares the law in any way, it is self-executing; otherwise if it merely says that the legislature shall enact laws to a certain effect. If it do both — as has happened in several States — we are in a quandary. The better rule here would be *valeat quantum valere potest.* White (§ 14), cites some Pa. cases where it was held directory merely.

PART I

BILL OF RIGHTS

§ 3. *Note to Part I.* — The Bill of Rights of the English Statute [1] has been largely adopted in the States of the Union, somewhat modified and largely amplified by the addition of new provisions of a similar nature, founded on Magna Carta, the Declaration of Independence and the Constitution of the United States, old Province charters, and the Virginia and Massachusetts bills of rights.

§ 4. *Bill of Rights Irrepealable.*[2] — Ten States declare that "to guard against transgression of the high powers delegated to the Legislature by the Constitution, everything in the Bill of Rights is declared to be excepted out of the general powers of Government, and shall forever remain inviolate; and all laws contrary to the Bill of Rights are void." [3] Meaning of course constitutions as well as statutes, — a striking attempt to bind posterity.

"When men enter into a state of society they surrender up some of their natural rights to that society in order to insure the protec-

[1] 1 W. & M. Sess. 2. This declaration of rights, however, represents but principles old as Anglo-Saxon freedom, rewon from Norman or Stuart kings and thus finally codified in the Revolution of 1689. Magna Carta, won in like manner from John, was not superseded by it; in theory it had always been in force. The Declaration represents only additions, or, more correctly, precisions, of the old principles. In outward form the Constitution under Edward I. became essentially the same as in the present day. (Taylor, I. 424. See notes to §§ 10, 70, 130.)

[2] Compare U. S. C. Amts. 9, 10. Decl. Ind. § 2.

[3] Ala. 1, 36; Ark. 2, 29; Del. Art. 1, *ad fin.*; Ky. 26; N. D. 24; N. M.* 1851, July 12, § 20; Pa. 1, 26; R. I. Preamble; Tenn. 11, 16; Tex. 1, 29; Va. 1, 17. This attempt to bind posterity would not, however, survive omission in a new State Constitution. A precedent of such attempt may, however, be found in England, where in 1495 an act for the security of a subject serving a *de facto* king declared "Every Act made contrary to this statute shall be void and of no effect." (Taswell-Langmead, p. 295.)

So in Arizona "the Bill of Rights is the supreme law of the land, subject only to the United States Constitution and laws. And it cannot be amended or altered but by the concurrence of a majority of all the members elected to the Legislature, the vote to be taken by yeas and nays entered on the journal." B. Rts. 32. Neither can any other law!

A Bill of Rights is still necessary (R. White, p. 31).

tion of others; and without such an agreement the surrender is void." [1]

In other States also the social compact is recognized. Thus, the Constitutions of five States declare that some rights cannot be surrendered by men when they enter into a state of society, but are inalienable, because no equivalent can be given for them.[2] As, for example, rights of conscience,[3] and other natural rights.[4]

This social compact notion hardly appears in the Federal Constitution except, possibly, by inference, in the Tenth Amendment. This says that "The powers not delegated to the United States . . . by the Constitution, nor prohibited by it to the States, are reserved to the States respectively or to the people." But the second paragraph of the Declaration of Independence states that "All men are . . . endowed by their creator with certain inalienable rights. . . . That to secure these rights governments are instituted.'' . . . This, and not Rousseau directly, is doubtless the prototype of the State provisions.

§ 5. *Construction of Bill of Rights.* — By the Constitutions of most States it is declared that this enumeration of rights shall not be construed to impair or deny others retained by the people.[5]

This section is, of course, founded on the Ninth Amendment to the Federal Constitution, the wording being almost identical, though the phrase "deny or disparage" is used instead of "impair or deny."

And in many States the Constitution declares that a frequent recurrence to fundamental principles is necessary to preserve the blessings of liberty.[6]

[1] N. H. 1, 3. See also § 182.

[2] N. H. 1, 4; Va. 1, 1; W. Va. 3, 1. Ala. 1, 1.

[3] N. H. 1, 4.

[4] (See also §§ 12, 13, 14, 15), Va., W. Va.

[5] Ala. 1, 36; Ark. 2, 29; Cal. 1, 23; Col. 2, 28; Fla. Decln. Rts. 24; Ga. 1, 5, 2; Ida. 1, 21; 1, 25; Io. 1, 25; Kan. B. Rts. 20; La. 15; Me. 1, 24; Md. Decln. Rts. 45; Minn. 1, 16; Miss. 1, 32; Mo. 2, 32; Mon. 3, 30; Neb. 1, 20; Nev. 1, 20; N. C. 1, 37; N. D. 24; N. J. 1, 21; O. 1, 20; Okla. 2, 33; Ore. 1, 33; R. I. 1, 23; S. C. 1, 41; Utah 1, 25; Va. 1, 17; Wash. 1, 30; Wy. 1, 36.

[6] Ill. 2, 20; Mass. 1, 18; N. C. 1, 29; N. H. 1, 38; S. D. 6, 27; Utah 1, 27; Va. 1, 15; Vt. 1, 18; Wash. 1, 32; W. Va. 3, 20; Wis. 1, 22. This reference to fundamental principles is made in several, both of older and of the newer, State Constitutions, and always in a more or less general phrase. Thus in Idaho (3, 24) "Sobriety, morality and the purity of the home" are the words used. In Wyoming (7, 20) "Health and morality." It has not seemed necessary to print these phrases in full.

§ 6. *Individual Rights.* — It is declared that the object of government is to protect and maintain individual rights, in the Constitution of Washington, and in both Washington and Utah it is declared that a frequent recurrence to fundamental principles, etc., is "essential to the security of individual right."[1] This definite recognition of the claims of the individual against socialistic government is a decided novelty, though a Federal judge in Texas has refused to naturalize a socialist on the ground that his doctrine was not compatible with the Federal Constitution.[2] In Oklahoma, on the other hand, "the right of the State to engage in any occupation or business for public purposes shall not be denied or prohibited, except that the State shall not engage in agriculture for any other than educational and scientific purposes and for the support of its penal, charitable, and educational institutions."[3] The question whether a State could under the Federal Constitution was debated, but not decided, in the South Carolina liquor case;[4] and municipal coalyards, etc., have usually but not always been held unconstitutional under State constitutions.[5]

[1] See last note for citations.
[2] *Ex parte Sauer*, 81 Fed. Rep. 355.
[3] Okla. 2, 31.
[4] 199 U. S. 437.
[5] Opinion of Justices, 182 Mass. 605.

CHAPTER I

BILL OF RIGHTS: CIVIL

NOTE. This division of the Bill of Rights into *civil* and *criminal* is purely one of convenience, and has no precedent, either in the statute of William and Mary or in the various State Constitutions, where those rights which we have termed civil and those which relate to criminal proceedings are often treated in the same paragraph, as, notably, the great clause 39 Magna Carta. See § 130.

ARTICLE 1. NATURAL RIGHTS

§ 10. *Freedom.*[1] — The Constitutions of many States have a provision that men are free.

Thus, that all men are born free and independent;[2] that they are by nature free and independent;[3] that they are equally free and independent;[4] that they are born equally free and independent;[5] that they are by nature equally free and independent.[6]

"The inhabitants of this State are not controllable by any other laws than those to which they or their representative body have given their consent."[7]

[1] Compare also §§ 12, 30. The great principles of freedom, both of body and of labor or trade, antedate Magna Carta itself; a month before Runnymede, John granted to the baronies of London the right to elect their Mayor; and the right to liberty is implied in several provisions of the Magna Carta of John ("The City of London shall have all its ancient liberties and free customs as well by land as by water: furthermore we will and grant that all other cities and boroughs, and towns and forts shall have all their liberties and free customs." — Cap. 13), but more expressly stated in that of Henry III., cap. 29: "No man . . . shall be disseized of his liberties or free customs," etc. There were 25,000 slaves numbered in the Domesday book out of about 300,000 registered population. Villeins were free men as the word is used in Magna Carta. Wat Tyler led 100,000 villeins in 1381, but by 1530 villeinage had disappeared (Taylor, I. 510. "By nature equally free and independent" is the phrase in the Virginia Bill of Rights. It is not in the Federal Constitution. Compare §§ 130, 183.

[2] Mass. 1, 1; S. C. 1, 1.

[3] Cal. 1, 1; Fla. Decln. Rts. 1; Ida. 1, 1; Ill. 2, 1; Io. 1, 1; Ky. 1; Nev. 1, 1; N. J. 1, 1; O. 1, 1.

[4] Ala. 1, 1.

[5] Ark. 2, 2; Me. 1, 1; Mon. 3, 3; Neb. 1, 1; N. H. 1, 1; Pa. 1, 1; S. D. 6, 1; Vt. 1, 1; Wis. 1, 1.

[6] N. D. 1; Va. 1, 1; W. Va. 3, 1.

[7] N. H. 1, 12.

So, many States have preambles resembling the United States Constitution (mentioning liberty, justice, etc.).[1]

§ 11. *Equality.*[2] — The Constitutions of most States declare this principle. Thus, that men are born equal,[3] (and this seems to be implied in other States);[4] that they are by nature equal;[5] that they are equal before the law;[6] (and this seems implied in the Constitutions of seven other States);[7] that all men have equal rights when they form a social compact;[8] that "no person shall be denied the equal protection of the laws";[9] that all laws should be made for the good of the whole; and the burdens of the State ought to be fairly distributed among its citizens.[10]

§ 12. *Life and Liberty.*[11] — The Constitutions of most of the States declare that all men have a natural, inherent, and inalienable right to enjoy and defend life and liberty, and (in all of these except Missouri) to the pursuit of happiness.[12] (The same may be implied in other States from the provisions of §§ 10, 71, 184.) And in most of these States, also, that they have such natural right to obtain safety.[13]

§ 13. *Property.*[14] — In more than half the States the Constitu-

[1] Ala., Ida., Ky., La., Mon., N. D., N. Y., S. D., Utah, Wy.

[2] Equality is first mentioned in the Virginia Bill of Rights, § 1: "By nature equally free and independent," and in the Declaration of Independence, "All men are created equal." It is no part of the English Constitution, except as freemen have equal rights at law. This legal (but neither political nor social) equality was re-established in England as early as Henry II. (II. Taylor, 3), and was clearly implied in John's Magna Carta, caps. 39, 40; and the great statute of Westminster I (1275). "Common right shall be done to rich and poor alike without respect to persons."

[3] Ind. 1, 1; Mass. 1, 1; Me. 1, 1; Neb. 1, 1; N. C. 1, 1; N. H. 1, 1; S. C. 1, 1; Vt. 1, 1.

[4] Ark. 2, 2; Mon. 3, 3; Pa. 1, 1; S. D. 6, 1; Wis. 1, 1; Wy. 1, 2. See also §§ 10, 20, and 184.

[5] Ida. 1, 1; Io. 1, 1; Ky. 1; Nev. 1, 1.

[6] Ark. 2, 3; Fla. Decln. Rts. 1.

[7] Ala. 1, 1; Ga. 1, 1, 2; Kan. B. of Rts. 1; O. 1, 2; Va. 1, 1; W. Va. 3, 1; Wy. 1, 3. See §§ 10, 12, 20, 184.

[8] Ct. 1, 1; Ky. 3; N. M.* 1851, July 12, § 2; Ore. 1, 1; Tex. 1, 3.

[9] S. C. 1, 5.

[10] R. I. 1, 2.

[11] Inalienable rights are based on the social compact theory; but have no higher standing than the Constitution at law. The word is not in the Declaration of Independence.

[12] Ala. 1, 1; Ariz.* Preamble B. Rts.; Ark. 2, 2; Cal. 1,1; Col. 2, 3; Del. Preamble; Fla. Decln. Rts. 1; Ida. 1, 1; Ill. 2, 1; Ind. 1, 1 Io. 1, 1; Kan. Bill of Rts. 1; Ky. 1; La. 1; Mass. 1, 1; Me. 1, 1; Mo. 2, 4; Mon. 3, 3; Neb. 1, 1; Nev. 1, 1; N. O. 1, 1; N D. 1; N. H. 1, 2; N. J. 1, 1; O. 1, 1; Okla. 2, 2; Pa. 1, 1; S. C. 1, 1; S. D. 6, 1; Utah 1, 1; Va. 1, 1; Vt. 1, 1; W. Va. 3, 1; Wis. 1, 1; Wy. 1, 2.

[13] Cal., Col., Fla., Ida., Io., Ky., Mass., Me., Mon., Nev., N. D., N. J., O., S. C., S. D., Va., Vt., W. Va.; as cited in § 12.

[14] The property right is recognized in Magna Carta (cap. 28. No constable, etc., shall take corn or other chattels of any man unless he presently give him money for it, etc.; and see also

tion declares expressly that all men have a natural right to acquire, possess, and protect property [1] (it seems the right of property is also recognized in other States by the provisions of § 183,[2] and compare also § 90); but in three, only that all men have such right to the enjoyment of the fruits of their own labor.[3] So, the Constitutions of other States declare that the right of property is "before and higher than any constitutional sanction." [4]

§ 14. *Rights to Labor or Trade.* — "Every citizen of this State shall be free to obtain employment wherever possible, and any person or corporation maliciously interfering or hindering in any way any citizen from obtaining or enjoying employment already obtained from any other corporation or persons is guilty of a misdemeanor." [5]

The rights of labor shall have just protection through laws calculated to secure to the laborer proper rewards for his services and to promote the industrial welfare of the State.[6]

No law shall be passed fixing the price of manual labor.[7]

These provisions are novel and interesting, but may carry the courts further than the Legislature intended; for instance, the first might make unlawful the sympathetic strike, or any strike against union or non-union labor. The right to one's free liberties or customs is, however, guaranteed in Magna Carta itself.

§ 15. *Reputation.* — In four States the Constitution declares that men have a natural right to acquire, possess, and protect reputation.[8]

§ 16. *Special or Exclusive Privileges.*[9] — The Constitutions of many States prohibit to the Legislature any grant of special privi-

caps. 30, 31, 39. No man shall be disseised of his freehold); but the word "property" is first used in the Va. B. Rts. The Declaration of Independence does not mention it at all. The Fed. Const. only in the 14th Amt. (See also § 130 and Art. 9, Eminent Domain.)

[1] Ark. 2, 2; Ariz. Preamble B. Rts.; Cal. 1, 1; Col. 2, 3; Del. Preamble; Fla. Decln. of Rts.; Ida. 1, 1; Io. 1, 1; Ky. 1; Mass. 1, 1; Me. 1, 1; Mon. 3, 3; Nev. 1, 1; N. D. 1; N. H. 1, 2; N. J. 1, 1; O. 1, 1; Pa. 1, 1; S. C. 1, 1; S. D. 6, 1; Utah 1, 1; Va. 1, 1; Vt. 1, 1; W. Va. 3, 1.

[2] Ala. 1, 35; Ga. 1, 1, 2; Ill. 2, 1; Ky. 4; Mo. 2, 4.

[3] N. C. 1, 1; Mo. 2, 4; Okla. 2. 2.

[4] Ark. 2, 22; Ky. 13, 3; and see §§ 90, 130. "Higher" is impossible.

[5] N. D. 23; Utah 12, 19.

[6] Mon. 1, 22; Wy. 1, 22.

[7] La. 51. See Art. 45 for the new New York provision as to public work.

[8] Ark. 2, 2; Del. Preamble; N. D. 1; Pa. 1, 1.

Blackstone mentions this as a natural right; but it appears in no other American or English constitutional document.

[9] The usual provision is that such privileges may not be granted by special act; and compare §§ 20, 21, 392, 394, 395 (15), and Arts. 50 and 60, and see U. S. Constitution 1, 9; Va. B. Rts. 4. There is nothing of this kind in the English Constitution.

leges or immunities to any citizen or class of citizens,[1] or corporation.[2] No man or set of men is entitled to exclusive public emoluments or privileges from the community.[3]

Except in consideration of public services.[4]

No special privileges or immunities shall be granted that may not be altered or revoked by the Legislature.[5]

In Kansas, the wording is that no such special privilege or immunity can be granted *except* by the Legislature.

And in three States the operation of a general law cannot be suspended by the Legislature for the benefit of any individual, corporation or association.[6]

§ 17. *Hereditary Privileges.*[7] — In many States the Constitution declares that no hereditary emoluments, privileges, or honors can be granted;[8] or no hereditary distinctions;[9] no hereditary offices;[10] no title of nobility;[11] no hereditary emoluments.[12]

§ 18. *Pensions* cannot, by the Constitution of one State, be granted but in consideration of public services; and not for more than one year at a time.[13] In two, the Legislature are forbidden to establish any general pension system.[14]

Pensions may be granted only for military or naval service; but officers may not be retired on pay or half pay.[15]

Pensions to confederate soldiers, sailors and their widows are provided for in several Constitutions.[16]

[1] Ark. 2, 18; Cal. 1, 21; Ind. 1, 23; Io. 1, 6; Ky. 3; Mass. 1, 6; N. D. 20; Okla. 5, 51; Ore. 1, 20; S. D. 6, 18; Tenn. 11, 8; Wash. 1, 12.

[2] Io., Okla., Wash., Territories.

[3] Ct. 1, 1; Ky. 3; N. C. 1, 7; N. M. 1851, July 12, § 2; Tex. 1, 3; Va. 1, 4; Vt. 1, 7.

[4] This exception is not made in some (Ct., N. D., S. D., Wash.).

[5] Ala. 1, 22; Cal. 1, 21; Col. 2, 11; Ga. 1, 3, 2; Ida. 1, 2; Ill. 2, 14; Kan. B. of Rts. 2; Mo. 2, 15; Mon. 3, 11; Neb. 1, 16; N. D. 20; O. 1, 2; Pa. 1, 17; S. D. 6, 12; Tex. 1, 17; Utah 1, 23; Wash. 1, 8. See also §§ 212, 503.

[6] Ark. 5, 25; Tenn. 11, 8. See §§ 394, 395 (15).

[7] Compare U. S. C. 1, 9. See also § 212.

[8] Ala. 1, 29; Ark. 2, 19; Ct. 1, 20; Kan. B. of Rts. 19; Mass. 1, 6; Me. 1, 23; N. C. 1, 30; O. 1, 17; Tenn. 1, 30; Wash. 1, 28; W. Va. 3, 19.

[9] Ala.; Del. 1, 19; Ind. 1, 35; Ky. 23; Me.; Md. Decln. Rts. 42; Ore. 1, 29; Pa. 1, 24.

[10] Mass.; N. H. 1, 9; Va. 1, 4.

[11] Ala., Ky., Ind., Md., Ore., Pa., S. C.

[12] Ala.; S. C.

[13] N. H. 1, 36. The same would result from the Constitutional principles of taxation.

[14] Md. 3, 59; S. C. 3, 32.

[15] S. C.

[16] Ga. 1893 p. 19, La. 303; 1902, 129; Miss. 272; S. C. 13, 5; Tex. 1897, p. 275. See U. S. 14th Amt. § 4.

ARTICLE 2. CIVIL RIGHTS

§ 20. *General Provisions.*[1] — The Constitution of Georgia provides that the social status of the citizen shall never be the subject of legislation.[2] So in South Carolina,[3] that no person shall be disqualified as a witness, nor be prevented from acquiring, holding, and transmitting property, nor be hindered in acquiring education, nor be liable to any other punishment for any offence, nor be subject in law to any other restraints or disqualifications in regard to any personal rights, than such as are laid upon others under like circumstances. "All citizens of the State possess equal civil and political rights and public privileges." [4] "Every citizen is entitled to equal representation in the government." [5] "The civil rights of the people shall not be abridged." [6]

"Since equality in the enjoyment of natural and civil rights is made sure only through political equality, the laws of this State affecting the political rights and privileges of its citizens shall be without distinction of race, color, sex, or any circumstance or condition whatsoever other than individual incompetency, or unworthiness duly ascertained by a court of competent jurisdiction." [7]

§ 21. *Color Distinction.*[8] — By the Constitution of Arkansas also no citizen shall be ever deprived of any right, privilege, or immunity, nor exempted from any burden or duty, on account of race, color, or previous condition.[9]

So in Maryland, as to the right of being a witness in a court of law.[10] So, in other States, as to the right of suffrage and holding office.[11] Distinction on account of race or color in any case whatever is prohibited, and all classes of citizens shall enjoy equally all common, public, legal, and political privileges.[12] So, in several, it is specially provided that all the public schools should be free and open, without regard to race or color,[13] or caste.[14]

In Mississippi the Constitution provides that the right of all

[1] Compare §§ 11, 16, 184.
[2] Ga. 1, 1, 18.
[3] S. C. 1, 12.
[4] Ala. 1, 2; S. C. 1, 31.
[5] W. Va. 2, 4.
[6] Ariz. Bill Rts. 6.
[7] Wy. 1, 3.
[8] Compare U. S. C. Amts. 14, 15, which of course apply in all the States; and see §§ 240, 241.
[9] Ark. 2, 3.
[10] Md. 3, 53.
[11] Nev. 18, 1; Okla. 1, 6; S. C. 1, 10; Terr.* U. S. 1860.
[12] Wy. 1, 3.
[13] Col. 9, 8; Ida. 9, 6; Wash. 9, 1; Wy. 7, 10.
[14] Wash.

citizens to travel upon all public conveyances shall not be infringed.[1]

§ 22. *Exceptions.* — By the Constitutions of a few States the right of voting is confined to whites,[2] but this provision is rendered null by the Fifteenth Amendment.

By the Constitutions of many States white and colored children shall not be taught in the same [public] schools.[3]

By that of Oregon no Chinaman can hold real estate, or hold or work a mining claim.[4] And by that of three States no native of China can vote or hold office.[5] The old Constitution of Mississippi legitimated all children, born before or after its adoption [1868], of persons not married, but cohabiting as husband and wife on December 1, 1869; and such persons are to be taken as married.[6] So by the old Virginia Constitution the children of parents, one or both of whom were slaves at or during the period of cohabitation, and who were recognized by the father as his children, and whose mother was recognized by such father as his wife, and was cohabited with as such, shall be capable of inheriting from such father as if born in lawful wedlock.[7] And by the old South Carolina Constitution "no person shall be disfranchised for felony or other crimes committed while a slave." [8]

The Constitution of Oregon provides that the Legislature shall pass laws prohibiting free negroes from coming to or living in the State, and making such action felony.[9] And in several, the intermarriage of white persons with negroes or mulattoes,[10] or their cohabitation as husband and wife, is forbidden.[11]

By that of California the Legislature is to prescribe all necessary regulations for the protection of the State and the counties, cities, and towns thereof from the burdens and evils arising from the pres-

[1] Miss. 1, 24.

[2] Kan. 5, 1; Md. 1, 1; O. 5, 1; Ore. 2, 2.

[3] Ala. 256; Del. 10, 2; Ga. 8, 1, 1; Ky. 187; La. 248; Miss. 207; Mo. 11, 3; N. C. 9, 2; Okla. 1, 5; 13, 1; S. C. 11, 7; Tenn. 11, 12; Tex. 7, 7; Va. 140; W. Va. 12, 8. See § 50.

[4] Ore. 15, 8.

[5] Cal. 2, 1; Ida. 6, 3; Ore. 2, 6. See also Art. 24 for the provisions in full concerning the right of voting. This provision is of course abrogated by U. S. Constitution, Amt. 15, as to voting by U. S. citizens.

[6] Miss. 12, 22, Constitution of 1868.

[7] Va. 11, 9, Constitution of 1870.

[8] S. C. 8, 12, Constitution of 1868.

[9] Ore. 1, 35. Now unconstitutional under the 14th Amt.

[10] A mulatto is a person who has ⅛ or more of negro blood. (S. C., Fla., Miss.) "Colored" or "Negro" means the African race; all others are included in white. Okla. 23, 11. Such laws are valid under the Fourteenth Amendments; for they apply to whites and blacks equally.

[11] Ala. 102; Fla. 16, 24; Miss. 263; N. C. 14, 8; S. C. 2, 33; Tenn. 11, 14.

ence of aliens who are or may become vagrants, paupers, mendicants, criminals, or invalids afflicted with contagious or infectious diseases, and from aliens otherwise dangerous or detrimental to the well-being or peace of the State, and to impose conditions upon which such persons may reside in the State, and to provide the means and mode of their removal from the State upon failure or refusal to comply with such conditions; and no corporation shall employ directly or indirectly in any capacity any Chinese or Mongolian, and the Legislature shall pass laws to enforce this provision; and no Chinese shall be employed in any State, municipal, or other public work except as a punishment for crime.[1] And further the presence of foreigners ineligible to become citizens of the United States is declared to be dangerous to the well-being of the State; and the Legislature is to discourage their immigration by all means within its power; and Asiatic coolieism is declared a form of human slavery, and prohibited, and all contracts for coolie labor are void; and the Legislature may prescribe penalties for companies or corporations formed in any country for the importation of such coolie labor; and the Legislature is to delegate all necessary powers to cities and towns for the removal of Chinese, or their location in prescribed portions of such towns; and also to provide legislation to prohibit the introduction of Chinese into the State.[2]

§ 23. *Sex Distinctions: Voting.* — The Constitutions of all the older States specify that the elective franchise is confined to males.[3]

But in three States the Legislature may at any time enact a law to extend the right of suffrage to women of lawful age, otherwise qualified; and such enactment shall take effect if approved by a majority of the electors at a general election.[4] In Colorado it was so submitted and adopted. In two States it was rejected,[5] while in three States the Constitution provides for female suffrage,[6] making four full suffrage States in all.

[1] Cal. 19, 1–3.

[2] Cal. 19, 4.

[3] Ala. 177; Ark. 3, 1; Cal. 2, 1; Col. 7, 1; Ct. 6, 2; Del. 5, 2; Fla. 14, 1; Ga. 2, 1, 2; Ill. 7, 1; Ind. 2, 2; Io. 2, 1; Kan. 5, 1; Ky. 145; La. 185; Mass. 2, 1, 3, 4; Amt. 3; Md. 1, 1; Me. 2, 1; Mich. 7, 1; Minn. 7, 1; Miss. 247; Mo. 8, 2; N. C. 6, 1; Neb. 7, 1; Nev. 2, 1; N. H. 2, 27; N. J. 2, 1; N. Y. 2, 1; O. 5, 1; Okla. 3, 1; Ore. 2, 2; Pa. 8, 1; R. I. 2, 1; S. C. 2, 3; Tenn. 4, 1; Tex. 6, 2; Va. 18; Vt. 2, 8; Wash. 6, 1; W. Va. 4, 1; Wis. 3, 1. This would be the common law in the absence of statute, though women voted in New Jersey and possibly other States in early times, though never in England. See § 240.

[4] Col. 7, 2; N. D. 122; Wis. See § 240 G.

[5] S. D. 7, 2; Wash. 27, 17. The vote in South Dakota was 45,682 to 22,072.

[6] Ida. Amt. 6; Utah 4, 1; Wy. 6, 1.

But in several States the Constitution provides that women of the age of twenty-one may vote at any election of school officers, or upon any measure relating to schools,[1] or libraries.[2]

And in Louisiana they may vote upon all questions submitted to the taxpayers as such of any municipal or other political subdivisions of the State, subject to ordinary age and residence qualifications, either in person or by their agents authorized in writing.[3]

Upon all questions submitted to the vote of the taxpayers of the State, or any political division thereof, women who are taxpayers and possessed of the qualifications for the right of suffrage required of men by this Constitution, shall, equally with men, have the right to vote.[4]

§ 24. *Sex Distinctions: Schools.* — The Constitutions of some States declare that the Legislature, in providing for the formation and regulation of schools, shall make no distinction between the rights of males and females.[5] So as to admission to the University.[6]

And in several States, women may hold any office pertaining solely to the management of schools.[7]

§ 25. *Sex Distinctions: Occupation.* — The Constitution of California provides that no person shall, on account of sex, be disqualified from entering upon or pursuing any lawful business, vocation, or profession.[8]

In Missouri and Oklahoma, the Constitution specifies that the Governor and members of the Legislature must be male.[9]

Women may be notaries public.[10] They may hold any office except as otherwise provided by the Constitution.[11]

[1] Col. 7, 1; Ida. 6, 2; Minn. 7, 8; Mon. 9, 10; N. D. 128; Nev. 15, 3; Okla., 3, 3; S. D. 7, 9; Wash. 6, 2. "Until otherwise provided" (Ida.). "The legislature may so provide" (Wash.).

[2] Minn. 1897, 175.

[3] La. 199.

[4] Io.* 1121; Mon. 9, 12.

[5] Kan. 2, 23; Wash. 9, 1; Wy. 7, 10.

[6] Mon. 11, 9.

[7] Col. 7, 1; Ida. 6, 2; Minn. 7, 8; Mon. 9, 10; N. D. 128; Pa. 10, 3. "Unless the Legislature otherwise provide" (Ida.). "Or libraries," in Minn.

[8] Cal. 20, 18. At the common law every employment was open to them except political offices, the army or navy, and learned professions. They are now, however, forbidden to engage in many trades or employments by statutes of the more advanced States; see also Art. 45. These statutes have frequently been held unconstitutional as depriving women of their liberties. They are only valid where clearly in the interest of morality or the general health, and probably never in States with constitutional provisions like the above. Of such nature are the laws limiting their hours of labor or age of employment differently from men. These have, in most of the States except Massachusetts, been held unconstitutional.

[9] Mo. 4, 4 & 6; 5, 5; Okla. 6, 3. And so in Oklahoma of the other executive officers. This is common law, in the absence of any statute.

[10] Va. 32.

[11] S. D. 7, 9. In other States, by the common law, not. See Arts. 20, 21.

The rights of citizens in two States, "to vote and hold office shall not be denied or abridged on account of sex. Both male and female citizens of this State shall equally enjoy all civil, political and religious rights and privileges."[1]

§ 26. *Sex Distinctions: Property.* — In many States there are constitutional provisions concerning the property of married women.[2]

In detail: the real and personal property of a female acquired before marriage remains her estate and property, and is not (without her consent in Florida, executed as a conveyance) liable for the debts of the husband, and may be devised and bequeathed by her as if unmarried; and so also all property to which she may become entitled after marriage.[3] The Legislature shall provide for the protection of the rights of women in acquiring and possessing property, real, personal, and mixed, separate and apart from the husband.[4] The Legislature are to provide for the registration of such separate property.[5]

A married woman's separate real or personal property may be charged in equity and sold, or the uses, rents and profits thereof sequestrated for the purchase money thereof; or for money or thing due upon any agreement made by her in writing for the benefit of her separate property; or for the price of any property purchased by her, or for labor and material used with her knowledge or assent in the construction of buildings, or repairs, or improvements upon her property, or for agricultural or other labor bestowed thereon, with her knowledge and consent.[6]

The Legislature shall never create by law any distinction between the rights of men and women to acquire, own, enjoy, and dispose of property of all kinds, or their power to contract in reference thereto. Married women are hereby fully emancipated from all disability on account of coverture. But this shall not prevent the Legislature from regulating contracts between husband and wife, nor shall the Legislature be prevented from regulating the sale of homesteads.[7]

§ 27. *Sex Distinctions: Custody of Children.* — In Kansas the

[1] Utah 4, 1; Wy. 6, 1.

[2] Ala. 209; Ark. 9, 7; Cal. 20, 8; Fla. 11, 1; Ga. 3, 11, 1; Kan. 15, 6; Md. 3, 43; Mich. 16, 5; Miss. 94; N. C. 10, 6; N. D. 213; Nev. 4, 31; Ore. 15, 5; S. C. 17, 9; S. D. 21, 5; Tex. 16, 15; Utah 22, 2; W. Va. 6, 49. By the laws of all States, she has all the rights of a man, save that she is to a certain extent protected.

[3] Ala., Ark., Cal., Fla., Ga., Mich., N. C., N. D., Nev., Ore., S. C., S. D., Tex., Utah.

[4] Fla., Kan., Md., Nev., W. Va.

[5] Ark. 9, 8; Nev.; Ore.; Tex.

[6] Fla. 11, 2.

[7] Miss. 94.

Constitution provides that the Legislature shall provide for women equal rights with the husband in the possession of their children.[1]

Article 3. Slavery and Apprenticeship

§ 30. *Slavery Prohibited.* — In most States slavery and involuntary servitude remain forbidden by the Constitution; and they are prohibited in all the States by the Thirteenth Amendment.[2]

Except [3] as a punishment for crime whereof the party has been duly convicted; and in Vermont, when bound by law for the payment of debts, damages, fines, costs, and the like.

In Maryland there is a constitutional provision that slavery shall not be re-established.[4] In Tennessee, the Legislature can make no law recognizing the right of property in man.[5]

§ 31. *Compensation for Slaves.* — In two States the Constitution provides that the Legislature shall have no power to make compensation for emancipated slaves.[6] The provision in Mississippi to this effect was left out of the new Constitution. It is forbidden, however, by United States Amendment 14 (4).

And in Maryland the Constitution declares that, slavery having been abolished by the authority of the United States, compensation is due the State from the National Government.[7]

§ 32. *Apprenticeships.* — In Vermont service by indentures and apprenticeships is allowed, but must expire at the age of twenty-one in males and eighteen in females.[8]

In Indiana, no indenture of any negro or mulatto made out of the State is valid.[9]

§ 33. *Terms of Service* over the age prescribed in § 32 are forbidden by the Constitution of Vermont unless entered into with the full consent of the party serving.[10]

[1] Kan. 15, 6.

[2] Ala. 1, 32; Ark. 2, 27; Ariz. *B. Rts. 20; Cal. 1, 18; Col. 2, 26; Fla. Decln. of Rts. 19; Ga. 1, 1, 17; Ind. 1, 37; Io. 1, 23; Kan. Bill of Rts. 6; Ky. 25; Mich. 18, 11; Minn. 1, 2; Miss. 15; Mo. 2, 31; Mon. 3, 28; N. C. 1, 33; N. D. 17; Neb. 1, 2; Nev. Ordinance 3 & 1, 17; N. M.* 76, 1; O. 1, 6; Ore. 1, 34; R. I. 1, 4; Tenn. 1, 33; Utah 1, 21; Vt. 1, 1; Wis. 1, 2. See § 10, note.

[3] This exception is omitted in a few (Vt., R. I., N. M.).

[4] Md. Decln. Rts. 24.

[5] Tenn. 1, 34.

[6] Md. 3, 37; N. C. 1, 6.

[7] Md. Decln. Rts. 24.

[8] Vt. 1, 1.

[9] Ind. 1, 37.

[10] Vt. 1, 1.

Article 4. Religious Rights

§ 40. *General Rights of Conscience.*[1] — In all the States except Alabama (for which compare §§ 42, 43), these are recognized by the Constitution, in slightly varying phrases. Thus, "every man may worship God according to his own conscience."[2] "The free enjoyment of all religious sentiments and the different modes of worship shall ever be held sacred."[3] "It is the duty of the Legislature to pass suitable laws to protect every religious community in the peaceable enjoyment of its own mode of worship."[4] "No human authority or law ought, in any case whatever, to control or interfere with the rights of conscience in matters of religion."[5] "No person ought to be molested in person or estate on account of his religious persuasion."[6]

§ 41. *Limitations.* — But the provisions of §§ 40, 45 are not to excuse acts of licentiousness, or justify practices inconsistent with the peace and safety of the State;[7] or polygamy;[8] or bigamy, or advice and propaganda thereto.[9] Nor to excuse disturbance of the public peace.[10] Nor "to justify practices inconsistent with the rights

[1] In newer Western States, these clauses are made irrevocable without the consent of the U. S. (Ida., N. D., S. D., Utah, Wash., Wy.). See U. S. Amt. 1. "Congress shall make no law respecting an establishment of religion, or prohibiting the free exercise thereof." This constitutional right to free worship does not appear to be recognized in any British constitutional document. It first appeared in a statute of Charles I. and in the Va B. Rts. 16.

[2] Ark. 2, 24; Ct. 7, 1; Del. Preamble; Ga. 1, 1, 12; Ida. Sched. 19; Ind. 1, 2; Kan. B. Rts. 7; Ky. 1; La. 4; Mass. 1, 2; Md. Decln. Rts. 36; Me. 1, 3; Minn. 1, 16; Mo. 2, 5; N. C. 1, 26; Neb. 1, 4; N. H. 1, 5; N. J. 1, 3; N. M.* 95, 1; 1851, July 12, § 4; O. 1, 7; Ore. 1, 2; Pa. 1, 3; R. I. 1, 3; S. D. 6, 3; Tenn. 1, 3; Tex. 1, 6; Utah 1, 1; Va. 16; Vt. 1, 3; Wash. 1, 11; W. Va. 3, 15.

[3] Cal. 1, 4; Col. 2, 4; Ct. 1, 3; Fla. Decln. Rts. 5; Ida. 1, 4; Ill. 2, 3; Io. 1, 3; La. 4; Mich. 4, 39; Miss. 18; Mon. 3, 4; N. D. 4; Nev. Ordinance 3 & Const. 1, 4; N. Y. 1, 3; Okla., 1, 2; S. C. 1, 4; S. D. 22, 1; Utah 1, 4; Va. 58; Wash. 26, 1; Wis. 1, 18; Wy. Ordinance, 1, 18.

[4] Ark. 2, 25; Neb.; N. M.* 1851, July 12, § 4; O.; Tex.

[5] Ark.; Del. 1, 1; Ga.; Ind. 1, 3; Io. 1, 3; Kan.; Ky. 6; Mich.; Minn.; Mo.; N. C.; Neb.; O.; Ore. 1, 3; Pa.; Tenn.; Tex.; Utah 1, 4; Vt.; Wis.

[6] Ga. 1, 1, 13; Ida. 21, 19; Mass.; Md.; Me.; Nev.; N. H.; N. M.*; N. D. 203; Okla.; R. I.; S. D. 26, 18; 22, 1; Utah 3, 1; Va. 58; W. Va.; Wy. 21, 2; Wash. 26, 1.

[7] Ariz.* B. Rts. 13; Cal. 1, 4; Col. 2, 4; Ct. 1, 3; Fla. Decln. Rts. 5; Ga. 1, 1, 13; Ida. 1, 4; Ill. 2, 3; Md. Decln. Rts. 36; Minn. 1, 16; Miss. 18; Mo. 2, 5; Mon. 3, 4; N. D. 4; Nev. 1, 4; N. Y. 1, 3; S. D. 6, 3; Wash. 1, 11; Wy. 1, 18.

[8] Ida., Utah.

[9] Ida., Mon.

[10] N. H. 1, 5; Mass. 1, 2; Me. 1, 3; Md.

of others."[1] No person is to disturb others in their religious worship.[2]

§ 42. *Compulsory Support of Churches.* — No man can be compelled, against his consent, to support or attend any church.[3] Nor to send his children to any school to which he may be conscientiously opposed.[4] No person of one particular sect shall be compelled to contribute to the support of ministers of another sect.[5]

§ 43. *Established Church.* — The Constitutions of some States provide that there shall be no established church.[6] Others say that there shall be no preference shown any one sect.[7] No subordination of one sect to another.[8] No union of Church and State.[9] But the Constitutions of two States declare that every sect ought to observe the Lord's day and to keep up some sort of religious worship.[10]

No charter may be granted to any church or religious corporation, but their title to property may be secured to an extent to be limited by law.[11]

§ 44. *State Support.* — By the Constitutions of many States no money can be taken from the public treasury in aid of any church, sect, or sectarian institution.[12] Or in aid of any priest, etc.[13] Nor from any municipal corporation.[14] Nor can property of the State ever be appropriated for such purpose.[15] Nor property of any municipality.[16] Nor shall money be appropriated for religious services

[1] Md., Mo., Va.

[2] Mass., Me., N. H., N. M.*

[3] Ala. 1, 3; Ark. 2, 24; Col. 2, 4; Ct. 7, 1; Del. 1, 1; Ida. 1, 4; Ill. 2, 3; Ind. 1, 4; Io. 1, 3; Kan. B. of Rts. 7; Ky. 5; Md. Decln. Rts. 36; Mich. 4, 39; Minn. 1, 16; Mo. 2, 6; Mon. 11, 9; Neb. 1, 4; N. J. 1, 3; O. 1, 7; Pa. 1, 3; R. I. 1, 3; S. D. 6, 3; Tenn. 1, 3; Tex. 1, 6; Va. 58; Vt. 1, 3; W. Va. 3, 15; Wis. 1, 18.

[4] Ky.

[5] N. H. 1, 6.

[6] Ala. 1, 3; Io. 1, 3; La. 4; N. J. 1, 4; S. C. 1, 4; Utah 1, 4; Va. 58.

[7] Ala.; Ark. 2, 24; Cal. 1, 4; Col. 2, 4; Ct. 1, 4; Del. 1, 1; Fla. Decln. Rts. 6; Ida.; Ill. 2, 3; Ind. 1, 4; Kan. B. Rts. 7; Ky. 5; La. 53; Mass. Amt. 11; Me. 1, 3; Minn. 1, 16; Miss. 18; Mo. 2, 7; Mon.; N. D. 4; Neb. 1, 4; Nev. 1, 4; N. H. 1, 6; N. M.* 1851, July 12, § 4; N. J.; N. Y. 1, 3; O. 1, 7; Pa. 1, 3; S. D. 6, 3; Tenn. 1, 3; Tex. 1, 6; Va. 58; W. Va. 3, 15; Wis. 1, 18; Wy. 1, 18.

[8] N. H., Mass., Me.

[9] Utah.

[10] Del. 1, 1; Vt. 1, 3.

[11] Va. 59.

[12] Ala. 1, 3; Cal. 4, 30; Col. 9, 7; Fla. Decln. Rts. 6; Ga. 1, 1, 14; Ill. 8, 3; Ind. 1, 6; La. 53; Mich. 4, 40; Minn. 1, 16; Miss. 66; Mo. 2, 7; Mon. 5, 35; Okla. 2, 5; Ore. 1, 5; Pa. 3, 18; S. C. 11, 9; S. D. 6, 3; Tex. 1, 7; Utah 1, 4; Va. 67 & 141; Wash. 1, 11; Wis. 1, 18; Wy. 1, 19.

[13] La.

[14] Cal.; Col.; Ida. 9, 5; Ill.; Mo. 11, 11; W. Va. 3, 15.

[15] Cal.; Col.; Ida. 9, 5; Ill.; Mich.; Mo.; Okla.; S. C.; S. D.; Tex.; Va. 10, 13.

[16] Cal.; Col.; Ill.; Mo.; S. C.; S. D. 8, 16.

in the Legislature.[1] Nor shall the State or any county or municipality accept any grant or gift of land, money or other property to be used for sectarian purposes.[2]

But by the Constitution of New Hampshire the Legislature may authorize towns or parishes to provide at their own expense for the support of Protestant ministers.[3] And in Massachusetts [4] and Missouri parishes may do so. So in Maine, religious societies.[5] But in Virginia and West Virginia it is expressly provided to the contrary.[6]

For religious corporations and their support, see also § 323; for schools, § 54.

§ 45. *Religious Test.* — In many States no religious test may be required as a qualification for office,[7] for any public trust under the State,[8] for voting,[9] for serving on juries,[10] or for being a witness in a court of law.[11]

Nor can a man be questioned in a court as to his religious belief, in order to shake his credit,[12] or be deprived of any civil right as a citizen on account of his religious sentiments.[13]

§ 46. *Limitations.* — But by the Constitution in a few States, a man cannot hold office who denies the being of Almighty God or the existence of a Supreme Being.[14] Nor is he competent as a

[1] Mich. 4, 24; Ore.

[2] Ida. 9, 5; Neb. 8, 11; S. D.

[3] N. H. 1, 6.

[4] Mass. Amt. 11.

[5] Me. 1, 3.

[6] The introduction of these provisions into the Virginia Bill of Rights is commemorated on Jefferson's tomb. The Church of England was "established" in Virginia before the Revolution, as, more recently, was the "Congregational" or English Calvinist church in Massachusetts and Connecticut, to the extent that taxes were levied in support of the same.

[7] Ala. 1, 3; Ark. 2, 26; Cal. 20, 3; Del. 1, 2; Ga. 1, 1, 13; Ill. 5, 25; Ind. 1, 5; Io. 1, 4; Kan. B. Rts. 7; Mass. Amt. 7; Md. Decln. Rts. 37; Me. 1, 3; Mich. 18, 1; Minn. 1, 17; Miss. 18; Mo. 2, 5; Neb. 1, 4; N. J. 1, 4; N. M.* 95, 1; 1851, July 12, § 3; N. Y. 12, 1; O. 1, 7; Okla., 1, 2; Ore. 1, 4; R. I. 1, 3; Tenn. 1, 4; Tex. 1, 4; Utah 1, 4; Va. 58; Wash. 1, 11; W. Va. 3, 11; Wis. 1, 19; Wy. 1, 18. See U. S. 6, 3.

[8] Ala., Cal., Del., Ga., Ind., Io., Kan., Md., Me., Mich., Minn., Mo., N. J., Ore., Tenn., Tex., Utah, Wis., Wy.

[9] Ark., Kan., Minn., Utah, W. Va.

[10] Cal.; Md. Decln. Rts. 36; Mo.; N. D. 4; Ore. 1, 6; Tenn. 1, 6; Utah; Wash.; W. Va.; Wy.

[11] Ark.; Cal.; Fla. Decln. Rts. 5; Ind. 1, 7; Io.; Kan.; Md.; Mich. 6, 34; Minn.; Mo.; N. D.; Neb.; Nev. 14; N. Y. 1, 3; O.; Ore.; Tex. 1, 5; Utah; Wash.; Wis.; Wy.

[12] Ore. 1, 6; Wash.

[13] Ala.; Ariz.* B. Rts. 13; Col. 2, 4; Ida.; Ill. 2, 3; Io. 1, 3; Ky. 5; Mich. 4, 41; Mon. 3, 4; N. J.; Okla.; R. I. 1, 3; S. D. 6, 3; Va. 5, 14; Vt. 1, 3; W. Va. 3, 15. This provision would seem to apply generally to the rights of voting, holding office, serving on juries, or being witnesses. Compare § 40, *ad fin.* Religious disqualification only disappeared from England in the nineteenth century.

[14] Ark. 19, 1; Miss. 265; N. C. 6, 5; S. C. 4, 3; 17, 4; Tex. 1, 4.

witness.[1] Nor, it seems, can a man hold office unless he believes in God[2] and in a future state of rewards and punishments.[3] And a man who does not believe in God and a future state of retribution will be deemed incompetent as a witness or juror.[4]

§ 47. *Oaths and Affirmations.* — The provisions of § 40 shall not be construed to dispense with oaths or affirmations.[5] And the mode of administering an oath shall be such as is most binding upon the person sworn.[6] The general form is to be such as shall be deemed by the Legislature the most solemn appeal to God,[7] but an affirmation may be made, instead of an oath, by Quakers.[8] Any oath or affirmation, taken as above, renders the person liable for perjury, if falsely taken, as if the oath were in the ordinary form.[9]

§ 48. *Sundays and Sabbaths.* — By the Constitution of Tennessee no person shall, in time of peace, be required to perform any service to the public on any day set apart by his religion as a day of rest.[10]

§ 49. *Superstitious uses* are not recognized in the American law. White, § 19.

Article 5. Education

§ 50. *General Right.*[11] — In some States the Constitution declares that the people have a right to education, which it is the duty of the State to guard and maintain,[12] "without distinction of race, color, caste or sex." [13]

In others, that a general diffusion of knowledge and intelligence being essential to the preservation of the rights and liberties of the people, it shall be the duty of the Legislature to encourage the promotion of intellectual, scientific, moral, social, and agricultural improvement,[14] "to cherish the interests of literature and the sciences," [15] or "to encourage schools and the means of instruction." [16]

[1] Ark. and so, possibly, by the c. l. in other States. White, p. 65.

[2] Md. Decln. Rts. 37; Pa. 1, 4; Tenn. 9, 2.

[3] Pa., Tenn.

[4] Ark.; Md. Decln. Rts. 36.

[5] Ark. 2, 26; Col. 2, 4; Ida. 1, 4; Ill. 2, 3; Mon.; Neb. 1, 4; O. 1, 7.

[6] Ind. 1, 8; Ky. 232; Md. Decln. Rts. 39; Ore. 1, 7; Tex. 1, 5; Wash. 1, 6.

[7] Ky.

[8] Mass. Amt. 6; N. H.

[9] Mass., N. H., Tex.

[10] Tenn. 11, 15.

[11] See § 21. There is, of course, no constitutional right to free education except where so specified.

[12] N. C. 1, 27; Wash. 9, 1; Wy. 1, 23.

[13] Ida. 9, 6; Wash.; Wy. 7, 10. See § 21.

[14] Cal. 9, 1; Ind. 8, 1; Io. 9, 2, 3; Kan. 6, 2; Mass. 5, 2; Md. Decln. Rts. 43; Mich. 13, 11; Miss. 201; N. D. 151; Nev. 11, 1; W. Va. 12, 12. See also § 391.

[15] Mass.; N. H. 2, 82; Tenn. 11, 12.

[16] Ida. 9, 1; Mass.; Me. 8, 1; N. C. 9, 1; N. D. 147; Neb. 1, 4; N. H.; O. 1, 7; R. I. 12, 1; S. D. 8, 1; Tex. 7, 1.

"All religious societies or bodies of men, united or incorporated for the advancement of religion or learning, or other pious or charitable purposes, ought to be encouraged and protected in the enjoyment of the rights, immunities, and estates which they in justice ought to enjoy, under such regulations as the Legislature direct."[1]

This right or duty of education is not mentioned or referred to in the Federal Constitution, though most of the other fundamental principles are. It would therefore seem without the power of the national government to prescribe, limit or regulate the State common schools (10 Bush, 681), (63 Ky. 49). A treaty to that effect, though valid in favor of a foreign power, would not be binding upon the States except as a consequence of the war power.

§ 51. *Free Schools.* — The Constitutions of nearly all the States provide for a system of free schools.[2] And in most of the newer States there is provided by the Constitution a school fund to be used for that purpose.[3]

§ 52. *Time of Holding.* — The schools must be held, in several States, for at least three months a year in every district;[4] in others, at least four months,[5] and in some six.[6]

[1] Vt. 2, 41.

[2] Ala. 256; Ark. 14, 1; Cal. 9, 5; Col. 9, 2; Del. 10, 1; Fla. 12, 1; Ga. 8, 1, 1; Ida. 9, 1; Ill. 8, 1; Ind. 8, 1; Io. 9, 1, 12; Kan. 6, 2; Ky. 183; La. 248; Md. 8, 1; Me. 8, 1; Mich. 13, 4; Minn. 8, 3; Miss. 201; Mo. 11, 1; Mon. 11, 1; Ord., N. C. 9, 2; N. D. 147; Neb. 8, 6; Nev. 11, 2; N. J. 4, 7, 6; N. Y. 9, 1; O. 6, 2; Okla. 13, 1; Ore. 8, 3; Pa. 10, 1; S. C. 11, 5; S. D. 8, 1; 22, 1; Tex. 7, 1; Utah 3, 4; 10, 1; Va. 129; Vt. 2, 41; Wash. 9, 1; 26, 1; 27, 1; W. Va. 12, 1; Wis. 10, 3; Wy. 7, 1; Ord. (Irrevocable without the consent of the U. S.; Wy., Wash., Utah, N. D., S. D., Mon.) See U. S. Stats. 1889, 180. In Georgia, free schools are to be established only on two-thirds vote of the town or county or district, and the legislature may prescribe who shall vote at such election (1903, p. 23). The Dakotas, Montana, and Washington were authorized admission by Act of Congress prescribing that they should adopt State constitutions containing this, with other similar provisions, upon proclamation by the President. For Utah, see U. S. Stats. 1894, 138. Idaho and Wyoming were admitted by Acts of Congress after they had adopted constitutions which were declared "republican in form" (U. S. Stats. 1890, 656 and 664). One of these enabling acts also required it to be according to the principles of the Declaration of Independence; which would seem to make it, after all, a constitutional document.

[3] Ala. 256, 279; Ark. 14, 2; Cal. 9, 4; Col. 9, 3; Ct. 8, 2; Del. 10, 2; Fla. 12, 4; 1893, p. 491; Ga. 8, 1, 1; Ida. 9, 2; Ill. 8, 2; Ind. 8, 2; Io. 9, 2, 1; Kan. 6, 3; Ky. 184; La. 248; Md. 8, 3; Mich. 13, 2; Minn. 8, 2; Amt. 1903, 25; Miss. 206; Mo. 11, 6–8; Mon. 11, 2; N. C. 9, 4, 5; N. D. 1, 53; Neb. 8, 3; Nev. 11, 2; N. J. 4, 7, 6; N. Y. 9, 3; O. 6, 1; Ore. 8, 2; Pa.; R. I. 12, 2; S. C. 11, 6; S. D. 8, 2; Tenn. 11, 12; Tex. 7, 2; Utah 10, 3; 9, 6; Va. 134; Wash. 9, 2; 16, 1; W. Va. 12, 4; Wis. 10, 2; Wy. 7, 2. (This also is irrevocable without the consent of the U. S. as above in six of the new Western States.)

[4] Col.; Io. 9, 1; Kan. 6, 4; Mich. 13, 5; Mo. 11, 2; Mon. 11, 6; Neb. 8, 7; Wis. 10, 5; Wy. 7, 8.

[5] Miss. 205; Mo. 11, 7; N. C. 9, 3; Va. 136.

[6] Cal., Nev.

In Vermont, there must be one or more schools in each town, and one or more grammar schools in each county;[1] and one in each township, in Minnesota.[2]

§ 53. *Age of Scholars.* — The free schools must provide instruction for all persons between the ages of 5 and 21,[3] 6 and 21,[4] 4 and 20,[5] 5 and 18,[6] 6 and 18,[7] 6 and 20,[8] 7 and 20,[9] 7 and 21.[10] See also § 55.

§ 54. *Unsectarian Schools.*[11] — No public money shall ever be appropriated for the support of any sectarian or denominational school;[12] and the same would follow from § 44 in other States. So, no public money can be appropriated for any school not under the exclusive control of the State or its school department.[13]

No sect shall ever have any exclusive right to, or control of, the State school fund.[14] So, the school fund is for "the equal benefit of the people."[15]

No sectarian instruction or control is permitted, directly or indirectly in any of the State schools.[16] No religious test required, for teacher or student.[17] No teacher or student shall ever be required to attend or participate in any religious service whatever.[18]

§ 55. *Compulsory Attendance.* — The Constitutions of a few States specify that the Legislature may enact laws requiring the attendance at a free school of all persons between six and eighteen years of age for a term of at least sixteen months in all;[19] and

[1] Vt. 2, 41.

[2] Minn. 8, 3.

[3] Io. 9, 2, 7; Kan.; Minn. 8, 2; Neb. 8, 6.

[4] Ark.; Col.; Ida. 9, 9; Mon. 11, 7; N. C.; Pa.; S. C. 11, 5; Wy. 7, 9.

[5] Ore. 8, 4; Wis. 10, 3.

[6] N. J.

[7] Ida. 9, 9; La. Okla.

[8] Mo. 11, 1.

[9] Va.

[10] Ala.

[11] See also §§ 44, 323. For sex distinctions, color distinctions, etc., in schools, see §§ 22, 24.

[12] Ala. 263; Cal. 9, 8; Col. 9, 7; Del. 10, 3; Ida. 9, 5; Ill. 8, 3; Ky. 189; La. 253; Mass. Amt. 18; Mich. 4, 40; Minn. 8, 3; Miss. 208; Mo. 11, 11; Mon. 11, 8; 5, 35; N. D. 152; N. H. 2, 82; N. Y. 9, 4; Pa. 10, 2; S. C. 11, 9; S. D. 8, 16; 26, 18; Tex. 7, 5; Utah 10, 13; Wash. 9, 4; Wis. 1, 18; Wy. 7, 8; Ord. 5. Irrevocable — see § 51 note 2 — in the six new States and in Idaho, by Act of Congress (U. S. Stat. 1890, 656, 658), as to lands granted by the United States.

[13] Cal.; Mass.; Me. 8, 1; Mon. 5, 35; 11, 8; N. D.; Pa. 3, 17; S. C. 11, 9; Va. 141; Wy. 3, 36.

[14] Kan. 6, 8; Miss. 208; O. 6, 2; Tex. 1891, 195.

[15] Ct. 8, 2; N. J.; Tenn. 11, 12; Wash. 26, 1; 9, 4; Wy. 7, 12, Ord.

[16] Cal.; Col. 9, 8; Ida, 9, 6; Mon. 11, 9; N. D. 147; Neb. 8, 11; Nev. 11, 9; S. C.; S. D. 22, 4; 26, 1; 8, 16; Utah 10, 1; 3, 4; Wis. 10, 3 (irrevocable in the new States, see § 51, note 2).

[17] Ida. 9, 6; Mon.; Utah 10, 12 & 1.

[18] Col., Ida., Wy.

[19] N. C. 9, 15; Okla., Wy. (unless educated by other means).

so, of children between eight and twelve,[1] not mentally or physically disabled."[2] So, of all persons between six and eighteen for a term of at least three years,[3] or three months each year.[4]

So, in Nevada, the Legislature may enact laws to insure general attendance.[5] See also § 53.

§ 56. *Universities.* — The Constitutions of many of the States provide for a State university or college.[6]

So, in Massachusetts, Harvard College is specially recognized by the Constitution and provided for;[7] and in Connecticut, Yale;[8] In Virginia, William and Mary;[9] in Louisiana, Southern University for Negroes;[10] in California, Leland Stanford.[11]

And in some States the Constitution provides specially for free normal schools or academies.[12]

And in others for an agricultural school or schools;[13] for a school of mines;[14] for a mechanical school;[15] manual training or technical schools;[16] a school of forestry;[17] a scientific school;[18] kindergartens.[19]

§ 57. *The Language* taught in the schools is, by the Constitution of two States, to be English;[20] but in Louisiana the instruction may be given in French.

§ 58. *Libraries.* — The Constitutions of two States provide that there shall be at least one public library in each township.[21]

So, in Iowa, the State school fund may be applied to the establishment of libraries.[22]

§ 59. *Legislative Restrictions.* — No educational or charitable

[1] Del. 10, 1; Va. 138.

[2] Va.

[3] Col. 9, 11; Wy. 7, 9.

[4] Okla. 13, 4.

[5] Nev. 11, 2.

[6] Ala. 264; Cal. 9, 9; Col. 9, 12; Fla. 8, 2; Ga. 8, 6, 1; Ida. 9, 10; Io. 9, 1, 11; Kan. 6, 7; La. 255; Mich. 13, 6–8; Minn. 8, 4; Miss. 213; Mo. 11, 5; Mon. 11, 11; N. C. 9, 6, 7; N. D. 215; Neb. 8, 10; Nev. 11, 4; N. Y. 9, 2; Ore. 8, 1; S. C. 11, 8; S. D. 14, 4; Tex. 7, 10; Utah 10, 4; Wis. 10, 6; Wy. 7, 1–15.

[7] Mass. 5, 1.

[8] Ct. 8, 1.

[9] Va. 141.

[10] La. 256.

[11] Cal. 1899, p. 493.

[12] Cal. 9, 6; 1901, p. 948; Fla. 12, 14; Kan. 6, 2; La. 256; Me. 8, 1; Miss. 201; Mon. 11, 12; N. C. 9, 14; N. D. 148–215; Nev. 11, 5; N. Y. 9, 1; Pa. 3, 17; S. C. 10, 6; Utah 10, 2; Va. 137; Wash. 9, 2; W. Va. 12, 11; Wis. 10, 2.

[13] Ala. 266; Cal.; La. 255; Mich. 13, 11; Miss. 8, 8; N. C. 9, 14; N. D.; Nev.; Okla. 13, 7; S. C.; Tex. 7, 13; Utah; Va.

[14] Col. 8, 5; N. C.; S. D. 14, 5; Wy. 9, 5.

[15] Ala., La., N. C., S. C., Tex., Va.

[16] La. 256; Va.; Wash. 9, 2.

[17] N. D.

[18] N. D.

[19] La., Utah.

[20] Ga. 8, 1, 1; La. 251; Mich. 13, 4. French was used in the English House of Commons until 1414.

[21] Ind. 13, 12; Mich. 13, 12.

[22] Io. 9, 2, 4.

institution, other than the State institutions now existing, or expressly provided for in this Constitution, shall be established by the State, except upon a vote of two-thirds of the members elected to each House of the General Assembly.[1]

Neither the Legislature nor the State Board of Education shall have power to prescribe text-books to be used in the common schools.[2] In California they must be printed by the State.[3]

The metric system shall be taught in the public schools of the State.[4] So, agriculture, stock-feeding, and domestic science.[5]

No teacher or officer connected with the public school system shall be interested in the sale of text-books.[6] Text-books must be uniform.[7] Separate schools for white and colored must in some States be provided. See § 22.

Article 6. Miscellaneous Rights

§ 60. *Freedom of Speech.* — Nearly all the States [8] provide in some phrase for general freedom of speech; [9] thus, "every man is given the right freely to write, speak, and publish his opinions on all subjects, being responsible for the abuse of that privilege." [10]

No law shall ever be passed to abridge or restrain freedom of speech and of the press.[11] This is the form in the Federal Constitution. And so, in two, of freedom of speech only; [12] and in several, of freedom of the press only.[13]

In others, there is a declaration that the liberty of the press ought

[1] La. 60.

[2] Utah 10, 9; Wy. 7, 11.

[3] Cal. Amt. 1894, Nov. 6.

[4] Utah 10, 11.

[5] Okl. 13, 7.

[6] S. D. 8, 17.

[7] Okla. 13, 6.

[8] (Except Del., N. H., Mass., R. I.)

[9] For speech in the Legislature, see § 272. Freedom of speech and of the press are both guaranteed by U. S. C. Amt. 1. By Eng. Stat. W. & M. S. 2, C. 2, the principle is limited to speech in the Legislature; nor does Blackstone give it as one of the fundamental rights, though he calls liberty of the press "essential to a free State." See following note.

[10] Ala. 1, 4; Ark. 2, 6; Ariz.* B. Rts. 16; Cal. 1, 9; Col. 2, 10; Ct. 1, 5; Fla. Decln. Rts. 13; Ga. 1, 1, 15; Ida. 1, 9; Ill. 2, 4; Ind. 1, 9; Io. 1, 7; Kan. B. Rts. 11; Ky. 8; La. 3; Md. Decln. Rts. 40; Me. 1, 4; Mich. 4, 42; Minn. 1, 3; Mo. 2, 14; Mon. 3, 10; N. D. 9; Neb. 1, 5; Nev 1, 9; N. J. 1, 5; N. M.* 95, 1; July 12, 1851, § 5; N. Y. 1, 10; O. 1, 11; Okla. 2, 22; Ore. 1, 8; Pa. 1, 7; S. D. 6, 5; Tenn. 1, 19; Tex. 1, 8; Utah 1, 1; Va. 1, 12; Wash. 1, 5; Wis. 1, 3; Wy. 1, 20. Substantially the English law, though not in the English Constitution. See White, p. 87.

[11] Ala. 1, 4; Cal.; Ct. 1, 6; Fla.; Ga.; Ind.; Io.; Ky. 1; La. 3; Mich.; Miss. 13; Mon.; Nev.; N. J.; N. M.*; N. Y.; O.; Okla.; Ore.; S. C. 1, 4; Tex.; Utah 1, 15; Va. 12 & 58; W. Va. 3, 7; Wis.

[12] Col., Mo.

[13] Ark., Del., Ky., Mass., Me., N. Y., Pa., Tenn.

to be maintained;[1] or that "the printing-presses shall be free to every person who undertakes to examine the proceedings of the Legislature or any branch of government; and no law shall ever be made to restrain the right thereof."[2]

In one, the general right extends only to freedom of speech, and freedom to publish matters relating to the government or officers thereof;[3] while in three "any man may publish his sentiments on any subject, being responsible for the abuse of that liberty."[4]

Limitations. — But the Constitution of West Virginia specifies that the Legislature may restrain the sale of obscene books, etc.; and that they may provide for the punishment of libel and defamation; and the Federal Government, under U. S. Const. I. 8, (8) denies to such the use of the mails.

§ 61. *Libel.*[5] — The Constitutions of many States provide that in all civil and criminal trials for libel the truth may be given in evidence.[6] [This would seem implied in certain cases by the Constitutions of other States; see below.] So, in seven others, when the matter published is proper for public information, or in prosecutions for libels on officers or men in a public capacity.[7] But in some the principal provision applies to criminal trials only.[8] [This, also, would seem implied by the Constitutions of other States mentioned below.]

And the truth, in all *civil* and criminal trials for libel, is a sufficient defence.[9] But only in the absence of malice,[10] or when published with good motives and for justifiable ends.[11]

In other States the truth is a sufficient defence only in indictments or prosecutions for libel, when the libellous matter was published with good motives and for justifiable ends.[12]

[1] Kan.; Md.; Mass. 1, 16; Minn.; N. H. 1, 22; N. C. 1, 20; Vt. 1, 13; Va.

[2] Del. 1, 5; Ky. 8; Pa.; Tenn.

[3] Vt. 1, 13.

[4] Del.; N. C.; R. I. 1, 20.

[5] The doctrine of the general verdict and evidence of truth in prosecutions for libel grew up under George III but is not expressed in any English constitutional document. The English Stat. 32 Geo. III, C. 60, only dates from 1791. II Taylor, 491. The English law is now similar to the American (note 12) by 6 & 7 Vict. c. 96. See § 132.

[6] Col. 2, 10; Ct. 1, 7; Fla. Decln. Rts. 13; Ga. 1, 2, 1; Ind. 1, 10; Kan. B. Rts. 11; La. 179; Mo. 2, 14; Mon. 3, 10; Nev. 1, 9; N. D. 9; S. C. 1, 21; W. Va. 3, 8.

[7] Ala. 1, 12; Del. 1, 5; Ky. 9; Me. 1, 4; N. M.* 1851, July 12, § 6; Tenn. 1, 19; Tex. 1, 8.

[8] Ark. 2, 6; Cal. 1, 9; Io. 1, 7; Mich. 6, 25; Miss. 13; N. J. 1, 5; N. Y. 1, 8; O. 1, 11; Okla. 3, 22; Utah 1, 15; Wis. 1, 3.

[9] Ind. 1, 10.

[10] R. I. 1, 20.

[11] Fla.; Ill. 2, 4; Kan.; N. D.; Neb. 1, 5; Nev.; S. D. 6, 5; W. Va.; Wy. 1, 20.

[12] Ark. 2, 6; Cal. 1, 10; Io. 1, 7;

In Indiana the provision is simply that the truth may be given in justification in "all prosecutions for libel." [1] And in Pennsylvania, that no conviction shall be had in any prosecution for the publication of papers relating to the official conduct of officers or men in public capacity, or to any other matter proper for public investigation or information, when the jury find that such publication was not maliciously or negligently made.[2]

In many States the jury are to determine the law and the facts, under direction of the court, in all prosecutions for libel; [3] and in some, also in civil suits.[4] And may give a general verdict as in other cases.[5]

The Constitution of California provides that indictments or informations for libels by newspapers are to be tried either in any county where the paper is published or in that of the plaintiff's residence, unless the venue is changed for good cause.[6]

§ 62. *Arms.*[7] — The Constitutions of most States provide that the people shall have the right to bear arms in defence of themselves and the State;[8] and this is perhaps implied in three other States.[9] In others, in defence of themselves only; [10] or, in others, the provision is simply that "they have the right to bear arms." [11] But the Legislature may prescribe the manner in which arms are to be borne; [12] as "with a view to prevent crime," [13] or may forbid the carrying of concealed weapons.[14]

Mich.; Miss.; N. J.; N. Y.; O.; Okla.; S. D. 6, 5; Utah 1, 15; Wis.; Wy. 1, 20.

[1] Ind. 1, 10.

[2] Pa. 1, 7.

[3] Ala., Cal., Col., Ct., Del., Ga., Ky., La., Me., Mich.. Miss.. Mo., Mon., N. D., N. J., N. Y., Pa., S. C., S. D., Tenn., Tex., Utah, Wis., Wy. See White, p. 98.

[4] Col., Ct., Mo., Mon., N. D., S. D., Wy.

[5] N. D.

[6] Cal. 1, 9.

[7] See Art. 29. Compare Eng. Stat. W. & M. S. 2, C. 2. U. S. C. Amt. 2. "The right of feud, or private war, was a right which every Teutonic freeman considered inalienable — a right which entered with him into every political or social organization of which he was a part." (Hannis Taylor, I. 195). The right to arms is probably primordial; but it is definitely recognized in the Bill of Rights, as to subjects "which are Protestants." The basing of this right upon the necessity of militia, as in the Federal Constitution, is not historically correct.

[8] Ala. 1, 26; Ariz.* B. Rts. 5; Ark. 2, 5; Col. 2, 13; Ct. 1, 17; Fla. Decln. Rts. 20; Ind. 1, 32; Ky. 1; Mass. 1, 17; Me. 1, 16; Mich. 18, 7; Miss. 12; Mo. 2, 17; Mon. 3, 13; N. M.* July 12, 1851, § 13; Okla. 3, 26; Ore. 1, 27; Pa. 1, 21; S. C. 1, 26; S. D. 6, 24; Tenn. 1, 26; Tex. 1, 23; Vt. 1, 16; Wash. 1, 24; Wy. 1, 24.

[9] Md. Decln. Rts. 28; N. H. 1, 24; Va. 1, 15. See § 290.

[10] Ida. 1, 11; Kan. B. Rts. 4; O. 1, 4; Utah 1, 6.

[11] Ga. 1, 1, 22; La. 8; N. C. 1, 24; R. I. 1, 22.

[12] Fla., Ga., Ida., Utah.

[13] Tenn., Tex.

[14] Col., Ky., La., Miss., Mo., Mon., N. C., Okla.

§ 63. "*Pinkerton Men,*" *etc.* — No armed person or bodies of men shall be brought into this State for the preservation of the peace or the suppression of domestic violence, except upon the application of the General Assembly, or of the Governor when the General Assembly may not be in session.[1] — No armed police force or representative of a detective agency shall ever be brought into the State for the suppression of domestic violence; nor shall any other body of men be brought in for that purpose except upon application of the Legislature, or the Executive when the Legislature is not in session (as provided for the regular army in the United States Constitution).[2]

No flag other than the United States flag can be carried.[3]

So, the right to bear arms does not authorize individuals or corporations to organize, maintain or employ an armed body of men.[4] No corporation or association shall bring any armed person or bodies of men into this State for the preservation of the peace or the suppression of domestic trouble without authority of law.[5]

§ 64. *Assemblies.*[6] — In all the States except Minnesota and Virginia, the Constitution declares that the people have a right to

[1] Ida. 1, 46; Ky. 225; Mon. 3, 31; N. D. 190; Utah 12, 16; Wash. 1, 24; Wy. 19, 1. As provided for in U. S. C. 4, 4.

[2] Ida. 14, 6; Mon. 3, 31; S. C. 8, 9; Wy. 19, 1.

[3] Wy. 17, 4.

[4] Wash. 1, 24.

[5] Utah 12, 16. The objection to private war is by no means new. The complaint of "retainers" or armed retinue was frequent in feudal times, and was one of the causes of granting the writ *de odio et atia,* when justice was thereby overborne. The Court of Star Chamber was created to suppress such "maintenance" and prevent "assemblies" of private retainers of powerful persons, much as a modern injunction is directed against a mob of strikers. Taswell-Langmead, p. 296.

[6] Founded on U. S. C. Amt. 1; and (as to the right of petition) on Eng. Stat. W. & M. S. 2, C. 2. This right to assemble and the right to petition are somewhat different things. The former right is not expressed in any written constitutional document of England, but it is attributed by Dicey (The Law of the Constitution, p. 258) to the "result of the view taken by the courts as to individual liberty of person and individual liberty of speech." In England both the right to assemble and the right to petition in so far as they are constitutional principles only extend to a peaceable and orderly meeting or petition; in fact the Statute of 13 Charles Second Chap. 5 forbids petitions to the King or Parliament signed by more than twenty or presented by more than ten persons The U. S. Constitutional amendment, however, expresses both rights, "the right of the people peaceably to assemble, and to petition the government for a redress of grievances." This right to assemble is not merely political (McClain, p. 309) but extends to assemblies for religious, social, and business purposes. It would of course include the right to meet and combine for the purpose of nominating or defeating the nomination of any political candidate. Hence an organization of American citizens, rich or poor, for that purpose, cannot properly be termed a conspiracy.

assemble peaceably, consult together and petition the Legislature for the redress of grievances;[1] to instruct their representatives;[2] and "for other proper purposes."[3]

But in one, secret political societies are declared dangerous to liberty, and should not be tolerated.[4]

§ 65. *Emigration.* — In six States the Constitution declares that all persons have a right to emigrate from the State.[5] Or, that they have a right to emigrate from one State to another.[6]

§ 66 *Immigration.* — The Constitution of Alabama declares that immigration shall be encouraged;[7] but by the Constitution of Oregon the Legislature has power to restrain and regulate the immigration into the State of persons not qualified to become citizens of the State.[8]

In a few States there is, by the Constitution, a Commissioner.[9] or a bureau or department of Immigration.[10]

In Delaware the Board of Agriculture is to encourage immigration.[11]

In Texas the Legislature is forbidden to create such a department.[12]

ARTICLE 7. RIGHTS AT LAW

§ 70. *General Rights.*[13] — In nearly all the States the Constitution declares that every person ought to have a certain remedy

[1] Ala. 1, 25; Ariz.* B. Rts. 15; Ark. 2, 4; Cal. 1, 10; Col. 2, 24; Ct. 1, 16; Del. 1, 16; Fla. Decln. Rts. 15; Ga. 1, 1, 24; Ida. 1, 10; Ill. 2, 17; Ind. 1, 31; Io. 1, 20; Kan. B. Rts. 3; Ky. 1; La. 5; Mass. 1, 19; Md. Decln. Rts. 13; Me. 1, 15; Mich. 18, 10; Miss. 11; Mo. 2, 29; Mon. 3, 26; N. C. 1, 25; N. D. 10; Neb. 1, 19; Nev. 1, 10; N. H. 1, 32; N. J. 1, 18; N. M.* 95, 1; 1851, July 12, § 18; N. Y. 1, 9; O. 1, 3; Okla. 3, 3; Ore. 1, 26; Pa. 1, 20; R. I. 1, 21; S. C. 1, 4; S. D. 6, 4; Tenn. 1, 23; Tex. 1, 27; Utah 1, 1; Vt. 1, 20; Wash. 1, 4; W. Va. 3, 16; Wis. 1, 4; Wy. 1, 21.

[2] Ariz., Cal., Fla., Ill., Ida., Ind., Io., Kan., Mass., Me., Mich., N. C., Nev., N. H., N. J., O., Ore., Tenn., Vt., W. Va.

[3] Ala., Ct., Del., Ky., N. D., Pa., R. I., S. D., Tenn., Wy.

[4] N. C.

[5] Ala. 30; Ind. 1, 36; Ky. 24; Ore. 1, 30; Pa. 1, 25 This right is recognized in Magna Carta (c. 42) and is guaranteed by the U. S. Constitution. See Crandall *v.* Nevada, 6 Wall. 35.

[6] Vt. 1, 19.

[7] Ala. 1, 30.

[8] Ore. 1, 32. See § 22. This is doubtless contrary to the Federal Constitution. See also § 22. The right of a State to foster immigration was denied by an executive ruling under Roosevelt's second administration.

[9] Md. 10, 3.

[10] N. C. 3, 17; Va. 143; Wash. 2, 34; Ida. 13, 1.

[11] Del. 11, 7.

[12] Tex. 16, 56.

[13] This provision is founded on Magna Charta, cap. 40: "We will sell to no man, we will not deny to any man either justice or right." Compare also § 130. See Taswell-Langmead, pp. 103, 107. The right to law — as against all, king, officer, or subject — is the cardinal Constitutional right, and has been fully discussed in Part I. See Taylor, I. 516; II. 3, 271.

at law for all injuries to the person, property or character; and to obtain justice freely without being obliged to purchase it, completely and without denial, promptly and without delay.[1] So "without sale, denial or delay,"[2] "or prejudice;"[3] or, by due course of law,[4] "promptly and without delay;"[5] "by due course of law, without sale, denial or delay."[6]

And in many States that all courts shall be open.[7]

So, in four, no person can be deprived of his right to prosecute or defend his own cause in any of the courts of the State.[8]

But all persons except witnesses may be excluded from court room in cases of adultery, rape, etc.[9]

§ 71. *Arrest and Search.*[10] — In all the States but New York the Constitution declares that the people have a right to hold themselves, their houses and possessions without unreasonable search and seizure; consequently, no warrant of search or seizure ought to be issued but upon probable cause supported by oath; and the warrant must describe the thing or person to be seized.[11] Or, that general warrants, whereby an officer may be commanded to search suspected places without evidence of the act committed,

[1] Ark. 2, 13; Col. 2, 6; Ct. 1, 12; Del. 1, 9; Fla. Decln. Rts. 4; Ill. 2, 19; Ind. 1, 12; Ky. 14; Mass. 1, 11; Md. Decln. Rts. 19; Me. 1, 19; Minn. 1, 8; Mo. 2, 10; N. C. 1, 25; N. D. 22; N. H. 1, 14; N. M.* 95, 1; Okla. 2, 6; Ore. 1, 10; Pa. 1, 11; R. I. 1, 5; S. C. 1, 5; Tenn. 1, 17; Vt. 1, 4; W. Va. 3, 17; Wis. 1, 9.

[2] Ida. 1, 18; Miss. 24; Mon. 3, 6; Okla.; Wy. 1, 8.

[3] Ida.

[4] Ala.; Ark.; Ct.; Del.; Fla.; Ill.; Ind.; Kan. B. Rts. 18; Ky.; Mass.; Md.; Me.; Minn.; Miss.; N. C.; N. D.; N. H.; N. M.* 1851, July 12, § 11; Ore.; Pa.; R. I.; S. C. 1, 15; Tenn.; Tex. 1, 13; Vt.; W. Va.; Wis.

[5] Kan.; S. C.; Wash. 1, 10.

[6] Ala. 1, 13; La. 6; Neb. 1, 13; O. 1, 16; S. D. 6, 20; Utah 1, 11.

[7] Ala.; Col.; Ct.; Del.; Fla.; Ida.; Ind.; Ky.; La.; Miss.; Mo.; Mon.; N. C.; N. D.; Neb.; N. M.*; O.; Okla.; Ore.; Pa.; S. C.; S. D.; Tenn.; Tex.; Utah; Vt. 2, 4; Wash.; W. Va.; Wy.

[8] Ala. 1, 10; Ga. 1, 1, 4; Miss. 25; Utah.

[9] Miss.

[10] Compare U. S. C. Amt. 4; Decln. Ind. (22). See II. Hannis Taylor, 382 and Va. B. Rts. 10. This may be said to be the only constitutional principle first established in America (by James Otis, arguing against writs of assistance in Massachusetts) and afterwards adopted in England (by Lord Camden, State Trials, Vol. XIX. p. 1030).

[11] Ala. 1, 5; Ariz.* B. Rts. 7; Ark. 2, 15; Cal. 1, 19; Col. 2, 7; Ct. 1, 8; Del. 1, 6; Fla. Decln. Rts. 22; Ga. 1, 1, 16; Ida. 1, 17; Ill. 2, 6; Ind. 1, 11; Io. 1, 8; Kan. B. Rts. 15; Ky. 10; La. 7; Mass. 1, 14; Me. 1, 5; Mich. 6, 26; Minn. 1, 10; Miss. 23; Mo. 2, 11; Mon. 3, 7; N. D. 18; Neb. 1, 7; Nev. 1, 18; N. H. 1, 19; N. J. 1, 6; N. M.* 95, 1; 1851, July 12, § 7; O. 1, 14; Okla. 2, 30; Ore. 1, 9; Pa. 1, 8; R. I. 1, 6; S. C. 1, 16; S. D. 6, 11; Tex. 1, 9; Utah 1, 14; Vt. 1, 11; W. Va. 3, 6; Wis. 1, 11; Wy. 1, 4. See also U. S. Amt. 4, (and the place to be searched; Okla.).

or to seize a person not named, or whose offence is not particularly described and supported by evidence, are grievous and ought not to be granted.[1] And in Washington "no person shall be disturbed in his private affairs, or his home invaded without authority of law."[2]

§ 72. *Trial by Jury.*[3] — In most States there is a general provision in the Constitution that the right to trial by jury shall remain inviolate.[4]

In a few this provision applies only to civil cases,[5] or only to controversies concerning property and suits between two or more persons [*i. e.*, civil suits].[6] So, the right shall only in civil cases exist when an issue of fact proper for a jury is joined in a court of law.[7] In Texas the Constitution further provides that the Legislature shall pass laws to regulate trial by jury, and maintain its purity and efficiency.

§ 73. *Exceptions.* — (For criminal causes, see § 131.) There is in many States no constitutional right to trial by jury when the amount in controversy does not exceed a certain sum.[8] Or in minor courts; as, in civil cases, before a justice,[9] or in courts not of record. But the right usually exists when the title to real estate is involved.[10] In some States the right is expressly declared to extend to all cases at law, without regard to the amount in controversy.[11]

Some States make an exception to the right to a jury "in cases heretofore used and practised."[12]

[1] Md. Decln. Rts. 26; N. C. 1, 15; N. H.; Tenn. 1, 7; Va. 1, 10; Vt.

[2] Wash. 1, 7. This seems to establish the much discussed "right to privacy."

[3] Compare Decln. Ind. (22) and U. S. C. Amt. 7. For a fuller discussion of the questions of jury trial and due process of law, see §§ 140, 131. Trial by jury is not the judgment of his peers referred to in Magna Carta, c. 39, but grew out of that when it became the usual mode of trial some centuries later. Taswell-Langmead, p. 105. Taylor, I. 281, 310, 331, 332.

[4] Ala. 1, 11; Ariz.* B. Rts. 8; Ark. 2, 7; Cal. 1, 7; Ct. 1, 21; Del. 1, 4; Fla. Decln. Rts. 3; Ga. 6, 18, 1; Ida. 1, 7; Ill. 2, 5; Io. 1, 9; Kan. B. Rts. 5; Ky. 7; Md. Decln. Rts. 5; Mich. 6, 27; Minn. 1, 4; Miss. 31; Mo. 2, 28; Mon. 3, 23; N. D. 7; Neb. 1, 6; Nev. 1, 3; N. J. 1, 7; N. M.* 95, 1; 1851, July 12, § 12; N. Y. 1, 2; O. 1, 5; Okla. 2, 19; Pa. 1, 6; R. I. 1, 15; S. C. 1, 25; S. D. 6, 6; Tenn. 1, 6; Tex. 1, 15; Va. B. Rts. 10; Wash. 1, 21; Wis. 1, 5; Wy. 1, 9.

[5] Ind. 1, 20; Ore. 1, 17; W. Va. 3, 13. See § 131.

[6] Mass. 1, 15; Me. 1, 20; N. C. 1, 19; N. H. 1, 20; Va. 1, 11.

[7] Md. 15, 6; Vt. 1, 12. For criminal causes, see § 131.

[8] In detail, $5. Md. 15, 6; $20, Okla. 2, 19; W. Va. 3, 13; $100, N. H. 1, 20.

[9] W. Va.

[10] N. H.

[11] Ark., Minn., S. D., Wis. This would seem to follow from the silence of the Constitution in other States.

[12] Ill., Mass., Md., Me., Mo., N. H., N. Y., Pa.

The Legislature may alter the law trial by jury as to causes arising on the high seas, or concerning mariners' wages.[1]

In some the Legislature may in civil cases authorize a trial by a jury of less than twelve men.[2] So, in a few States, in inferior courts [as before a Justice of the Peace].[3] So, in New Jersey,[4] in civil suits involving less than fifty dollars, and in Connecticut in cases involving twenty dollars and not more than one hundred dollars, by a jury of six men.[5] And in three States the parties may agree on a jury less than twelve in number.[6] In one no jury is allowed in cases tried before a Justice of the Peace, except on appeal therefrom.[7] A jury in justices' courts, civil or criminal, consists of not more than six.[8] In Kentucky the Legislature may provide for a three-fourths verdict in the Circuit Court.[9]

And by the Constitutions of a few States, in civil actions, three-fourths of a jury may render a verdict.[10] So, two-thirds.[11]

Juries are of eight men, or four in minor courts.[12]

§ 74. *Waiver.*[13] — By the Constitutions of many States the right to a trial by jury may be waived by the parties in all cases in the manner prescribed by law.[14] In some, the right shall be deemed waived, in all civil cases, unless demanded by the parties, or one of them, in the manner prescribed by law.[15]

So, in one State, the Constitution only provides that the right shall be preserved if required by either party.[16]

§ 75. *Suits against the State.*[17] — In many States the Constitu-

[1] Mass., N. H.

[2] Col. 2, 23; Fla. 5, 38; La. 116; Mich. 4, 46; Wy. 1, 9. The constitutional number of a jury was always, and must necessarily be, twelve men. See Taylor, I, 203, 206.

[3] Fla. (six men); Ga. (but not less than five men); Ill.; Io.; Ky. 248 (six men); Mo.; Mon.; N. C. 4, 27 (six men); N. D.; Neb.; Okla. 2, 19 (six men); S. D.; Tex. 5, 17 (six men in the county court); Va.; Wash.; W. Va.

[4] N. J. 1, 7.

[5] Ct.* 679.

[6] Cal., Ida., Mon.

[7] W. Va.

[8] Mon.

[9] Ky. 248.

[10] Cal.; Ida. 1, 7; Mo. 1899, p. 381; Nev.; Okla. 2, 19; S. D.; Tex. 5, 13; Utah; Wash.; 1, 21.

[11] Mon., Mo. (in courts not of record.)

[12] Utah 1, 10.

[13] For criminal cases, see § 132.

[14] Ark. 2, 7; Ariz.* B. Rts. 82; Cal. 1, 7; Del. 4, 23; Fla. Decln. Rts. 2; Ida.; Md. 4, 1, 8; Minn. 1, 4; Mon. 3, 23; N. C. 4, 13; Nev. 1, 3; N. Y. 1, 2; Pa. 5, 27; Vt. 2, 31; Wash. 1, 21; Wis. 1, 5.

[15] Mich. 6, 27; Tex. 5, 10; Utah 1, 10.

[16] W. Va. 3, 13.

[17] For the method of prosecuting claims against the State, in the courts, see also § 653. The Federal courts were forbidden to entertain suits against a State by the eleventh amendment. A State, being sovereign, cannot be sued but with its own consent.

tion provides that the Legislature shall direct a method by which citizens having claims against it may sue the State.[1] No special act authorizing such suit can, however, be passed.[2] In a few, the Supreme Court has, by the Constitution, jurisdiction of claims against the State, but its decisions are merely recommendatory.[3] In others a board is created to audit claims.[4]

In others, the State can never be made defendant in a court of law or equity.[5]

§ 76. *The Common Law.*[6] — By the Constitution of Maryland the people are declared entitled to the common law of England.[7] So, in New York, such parts of the common law as formed the law of the colony, April 19, 1775, are declared in force, if not repugnant.[8]

So, in four States, to such parts of the common law as were in force in the territory, or previously to the adoption of the present Constitution in the State, if not inconsistent with the State Constitution.[9]

So, in Maryland, such English statutes as existed July 4,

[1] Cal. 20, 6; Del. 1, 9; Fla. 3, 22; Ind. 4, 24; Ky. 231; La. 192; N. D. 22; Neb. 6, 22; Nev. 4, 22; Ore. 4, 24; Pa. 1, 11; S. C. 17, 2; S. D. 3, 27; Tenn. 1, 17; Wash. 2, 26; Wis. 4, 27; Wy. 1, 8.

[2] Fla., Ind., Nev., Ore.

[3] Ida. 5, 10; N. C. 4, 9.

[4] The Secretary, Treasurer, and Commissioner of Lands of the State shall constitute a board of State auditors, to examine and adjust all claims against the State not otherwise provided for by general law (Mich. 8, 4). So, the Governor, Secretary of State, and Attorney General (Ida. 4, 18; Mon. 7, 20; Utah 7, 13). They are examined by the auditor, and approved by the Secretary of State, with appeal to the District Court (Neb. 9, 9).

[5] Ala. 14; Ark. 5, 20; Ill. 4, 26; W. Va. 6, 35, and so, where the laws are silent.

[6] Altering the common law, as it has been altered in England, by growth rather than by statute, still prevails in most States. California and the Dakotas, Idaho, Wyoming, Utah, Montana, and Oklahoma have attempted complete codes, however; Georgia, New York, and other States, partial codes. See Blackstone, Book III. p. 126, for the earliest argument against them; Reinsch, Am. Legislatures, for the latest. The effect of a code seems to be to render the law uncertain and increase the number of suits that are carried to the higher courts. The so-called codes of the earlier kings, Edward the Confessor or Henry II., were in no sense codes in this modern sense.

The Constitutional history of England consists mainly in the reassertion of the common English law against Norman ideas, whether in the form of royal prerogative, statute, order-in-council, church authority, chancery, martial or civil law. See Part I. "The laws of the English, the most ancient of modern laws, extend in an unbroken series from the first [written] laws of Ethelbert. . . (600) down to the present time" (Taswell-Langmead, p. 33). They were recognized by William the Conqueror (ibid. 52), formally recognized by every king on his coronation, and for the last time questioned by Charles I. See Taylor, I. 425, 271.

[7] Md. Decln. Rts. 5.

[8] N. Y. 1, 16.

[9] Mich. Sched. 1; N. J. 10, 1; Va. Sched. 1; W. Va. 8, 36; Wis. 14, 13; Wy. 21, 3.

1776, and are, or have been found, applicable. In New York, grants of land made by the King after October 14, 1775, are invalid.[1]

§ 77. *Law Previously in Force.* — By the Constitutions generally, such laws of the colony (in the original thirteen) or territory (in the others) or State, as were in force previous to the Constitution, remain in force afterwards unless repugnant to it, or repealed by the Legislature.[2]

In Kentucky, all laws, not local, which were in force in Virginia, June 1, 1792, are valid in the former State if not repugnant to its Constitution.[3] In Maine all Massachusetts laws in force December 6, 1819.[4] In West Virginia all land titles are valid which existed under the laws of Virginia up to 1863.[5]

§ 78. *Miscellaneous Rights at Law.*[6] — In Nebraska the Constitution provides that the right in all civil cases to be heard in the court of last resort by appeal, etc., shall not be denied.[7]

§ 79. *Venue.*[8] — Every action shall be tried in the county where commenced unless the judges determine that an impartial trial cannot be had.[9]

ARTICLE 8. DEBTORS

§ 80. *Imprisonment for Debt.* — In many States the Constitution provides absolutely that there shall be no imprisonment for debt.[10] In others, no imprisonment for debt in any civil action or mesne or final process,[11] or in any action or judgment founded upon contract.[12] In others, that there shall be no person imprisoned for

[1] N. Y. 1, 17.

[2] Ala. Sched. 1; Ark. Sched. 1; Cal. 22, 1; Col. Sched. 1; Ct. 10, 3; Del. Sched. 18; Fla. 18, 2; Ga. 12, 1, 3; Ida. 21, 2; Ill. Sched. 1; Ind. Sched. 1; Io. 12, 2; Kan. Sched. 4; Ky. Sched. 1; La. 325; Mass. 6, 6; Md. Decln. Rts. 5; Me. 10, 1; Mich. Sched. 1; Minn. Sched. 2; Miss. 274; Mo. Sched. 1; Mon. 20, 1; N. C. 4, 19; N. D. Sched. 2; Neb. 18, 1; Nev. 17, 2; N. H. 2, 89; N. J. 10, 1; N. Y. 1, 16; O. Sched. 1; Okla. Sched. 2; Ore. 18, 7; Pa. Sched. 2; R. I. 14, 1; S. C. 17, 11 & 10; Tenn. 11, 1; Tex. 16, 48; Utah 24, 2; Va. Sched. 1; Wash. 27, 2; W. Va. 8, 36; Wis. 14, 2; Wy. 21, 3.

[3] Ky. 293.

[4] Me. 10, 1.

[5] W. Va. 13, 1.

[6] For the right to counsel, see § 134.

[7] See also §§ 654, 665. Neb. 1, 24.

[8] For criminal cases, see § 133.

[9] Del. 1, 9. See U. S. C. Amt. 6.

[10] Ala. 1, 20; Fla. Decln. Rts. 16; Ga. 1, 1, 21; Ida. 1, 15; Ind. 1, 22; Kan. B. Rts. 16; Md. 3, 38; Minn. 1, 12; Miss. 30; Mo. 2, 16; N. C. 1, 16; Nev. 1, 14; Okla. 2, 13; Ore. 1, 19; S. C. 1, 24; Tex. 1, 18; Utah 1, 16; Wash. 1, 17; Wy. 1, 5.

[11] Ark. 2, 16; Ariz.* B. Rts. 18; Cal. 1, 15; Io. 1, 19; Neb. 1, 20; O. 1, 15; Ore. 1, 15; Tenn. 1, 18.

[12] Mich. 6, 33; N. J. 1, 17; S. D. 6, 15; Wis. 1, 16.

debt in any civil action when he has delivered up his property for the benefit of creditors in the manner prescribed by law.[1]

And a general exception is made in case of fraud.[2] So the Legislature has power to provide for the punishment of fraud, and for reaching property of the debtor concealed from his creditors.[3] Absconding debtors may be imprisoned;[4] or debtors in cases of libel or slander;[5] in civil cases of tort generally;[6] in cases of malicious mischief;[7] or of breach of trust;[8] or of moneys collected by public officers, or in any professional employment;[9] for non-payment of fines, etc.[10]

§ 81. *Debtor Exemption Laws.*[11] — The Constitutions of many States have provisions exempting certain property of resident debtors from attachment, execution or sale by creditors; thus, in detail "that the privilege of the debtor to enjoy the necessary comforts of life shall be reccgnized by wholesome laws exempting a reasonable amount of property;"[12] that the Legislature shall pass liberal exemption laws;[13] that laws shall be passed protecting from forced sale a certain amount of the personal property of adults, male and female;[14] that certain personal property to be designated by law, to the value of five hundred dollars, shall be exempted.[15]

That personal property (of any nature) to the value of $200, in the hands of a husband, a parent, or the infant children of deceased parents, shall be exempted.[16] Personal property (of any nature) to be selected by the debtor, to the value of $500[17] or of $1000;[18] and wearing apparel and tools and implements of trade, to the value of $300, of any person.[19] Personal property of a resident not married or the head of a family, to the value of $200 and his clothing,

[1] Col. 2, 12; Ill. 2, 12; Ky. 18; Mon. 3, 12; N. D. 15; Okla.; Pa. 1, 16; R. I. 1, 11; Vt. 2, 33.

[2] Ariz.*, Ark., Cal., Col., Fla., Ida., Ill., Ind., Io., Kan., Ky., Mich., Minn., N. C., N. D., Neb., Nev., N. J., O., Ore., Pa., R. I., S. C., Tenn., Vt., Wy.

[3] Ga. 1, 2, 6.

[4] Ore., Utah, Wash.

[5] Nev.

[6] Cal., Col., N. D.

[7] Cal.

[8] Ariz.*, Mich.

[9] Ariz.*, Mich.

[10] Mo.

[11] For States where the exemptions of real and personal property are not kept distinct, see §§ 83 *et seq.* The exemption of a farmer's horse and cattle or plow and of an artisan's tools goes back to Magna Carta, c. 20. See Taswell-Langmead, p. 92.

[12] Ind. 1, 22; Minn. 1, 12; Mon. 19, 4; N. D. 208; Nev. 1, 14; S. D. 21, 4; Wis. 1, 17.

[13] Col. 18, 1; Ill. 4, 32.

[14] Cal. 17, 1; Tex. 16, 49; Wash. 19, 1.

[15] Md. 3, 44; Mich. 16, 1.

[16] W. Va. 6, 48.

[17] N. C. 10, 1; S. C. 3, 28.

[18] Ala. 204.

[19] S. C.

and personal property of the head of a family to the value of $500, besides their clothing, are exempt from any process on a debt founded on contract;[1] $1000 worth of personal property owned by the head of a family.[2] And the exemption applies only to heads of families in other States.[3]

Exceptions. — These exemptions do not prevail against artisans' liens on the property claimed as exempt.[4] Nor, against a debt for the purchase money of the exempt property, in the hands of the vendee.[5] Nor, against a levy for taxes.[6] Nor for debts of laborers or servants.[7]

These exemptions may be waived by an instrument in writing.[8]

By the Constitution of North Carolina a husband may insure his life for the sole use and benefit of his wife and children, and at his death the claim shall be paid to the widow and children, or their guardian, for their use, free from all liabilities of the husband or claims of his representatives.[9]

§ 82. *Homestead.* — The same States usually have provisions concerning the homestead exemption; thus, "that the Legislature shall pass liberal homestead laws."[10] That there shall be a homestead exempt, as provided by law.[11] That a homestead in the possession of each head of a family is exempt, with improvements thereon to the value, in all of $1,000,[12] or of $1,500,[13] or even of $5,000.[14]

In other States the laws vary in great detail.[15]

[1] Ark. 9, 1, 2.

[2] Fla. 10, 1.

[3] Cal., S. C.

[4] Ala. 10, 4; Minn. 1889, p. 1. Amt. 1, 12. N. C. 10, 4.

[5] Ark.; W. Va.; Okla. 12, 3.

[6] Fla., S. C., W. Va.

[7] Minn.

[8] Ala. 210.

[9] N. C. 10, 7.

[10] Col. 18, 1; Ill. 4, 32; Mon. 19, 4; N. D. 208; S. D. 21, 4; Wash. 19, 1.

[11] Cal. 17, 1; Nev. 4, 30; Wy. 19, 1.

[12] S. C. 3, 28; Tenn. 11, 11; W. Va. 6, 48.

[13] Utah 22, 1.

[14] Okla. 12, 2.

[15] Thus, in Michigan (16, 2), every homestead, if not exceeding 40 acres of land, and the dwelling house thereon, and the appurtenances to be selected by the owner thereof, and not included in any town; or instead thereof, at the option of the owner, any lot in any city, village, or recorded town plat, or such parts of lots as shall be equal thereto, and the dwelling house thereon and its appurtenances, owned and occupied by any resident of the State, not exceeding in value $1,500, shall be exempt from sale under legal process. In Kansas (15, 9), a homestead to the extent of 160 acres of farming land, or one acre in a town or city, occupied as a residence by the family of the owner, with all improvements, be so exempt. In North Carolina (10, 2), every homestead and buildings thereon, to be selected by the owner, or in lieu thereof a town lot and buildings thereon, owned and occupied by a resident of the State, not exceeding in value $1,000, shall be so exempt In Virginia (190), every householder or

§ 83. *Exceptions.* — The homestead exemption does not avail as against any mortgage or pledge thereon, lawfully obtained;[1] or, as against any lien.[2]

Nor, against any obligation or debt contracted for the purchase of the premises (or property),[3] or contracted for improvements thereon.[4] Nor, against a sale for taxes.[5] Nor against a claim for

head of a family shall be entitled, in addition to the articles now exempt from levy or distress for rent, to hold exempt his real or personal property, or either, to the value of $2,000, to be selected by him.

A married woman is entitled to a homestead, her husband not having sufficient property to constitute one (S. C.). In Arkansas (9, 3–5), the homestead of a resident who is married or the head of a family, not exceeding 160 acres of land outside of a town, with improvements thereon, nor exceeding in value $2,500, but not less than 80 acres, without regard to value; or, if in a town, not exceeding one acre, nor $2,500 in value, but not less than one quarter acre, is exempt. In Texas (16, 50, 51), the homestead of a family, 200 acres in extent, with improvements, or, in a town, lots to the value of $5,000, exclusive of improvements, with the improvements thereon (provided the same be used for the purposes of a home, or as a place of business of the head of the family), is exempt.

In Alabama (205), every homestead not exceeding 80 acres, with improvements thereon, to be selected by the owner, or, in a town, any lot with improvements, not in all exceeding $2,000 in value, owned and occupied by a resident, is exempt. In Georgia (9, 1, 1; 9, 4, 1), there is exempt from levy or sale of the property of every head of a family, or guardian or trustee of a family of minor children, or any aged or infirm person, or person having the care and support of dependent females of any age, who is not the head of a family, realty or personalty, or both, to the aggregate value of $1,600 besides improvements (and besides this, the Constitution recognizes a species of homestead previously existing called *short* homestead. In Florida (10, 1), a homestead to the extent of 160 acres of land, or half an acre in a town, and improvements thereon, owned by the head of a family residing in the State, is exempt. In Louisiana (244), of every head of a family, or person having a mother or father, or person or persons dependent on him for support, there is exempt the homestead *bona fide* owned by the debtor and occupied by him, consisting of lands, buildings, and appurtenances, whether rural or urban; also one work-horse, one wagon, one yoke of oxen, two cows and calves, twenty-five head of hogs, or one thousand pounds of bacon or its equivalent in pork, and on a farm the necessary corn and fodder for a year, and farming implements to the value of $2,000; if the homestead exceed $2,000 in value, the beneficiary is entitled to that amount in case a sale of the homestead under legal process realize more than that sum; but no husband is entitled to a homestead whose wife was and is in the actual enjoyment of property to the value of $2,000. In Oklahoma (12, 1) a homestead of 160 acres in the country or one acre in a city, town, or village, not over $5000 in value, but in no case less than one quarter acre.

[1] Ala. 205; Fla. 10, 4; Mich. 16, 2; Nev. 4, 30; S. C. 2, 28; Va. 190.

[2] Ark. 9, 3; Kan. 15, 9; N. D.; Nev.

[3] Ark.; Fla. 10, 1; Ga. 9, 2, 1; Kan.; La. 245; N. C. 10, 2; Nev.; Okla.; S. C. 2, 28; Tenn. 11, 11; Tex.; Va.; W. Va. 6, 48; Wy. 19.

[4] Fla., Ga., Kan., La., N. D., Nev., Okla., S. C., Tenn., Tex. (such claims for work or materials used in improvements must be evidenced by written contract for with the consent of the wife given as in a deed of the homestead.) W. Va., Wy.

[5] Ark., Fla., Ga., Kan., La., N. C., Nev., Okla., S. C., Tenn., Tex., Va., W. Va., Wy.

services thereon by a laboring person or mechanic,[1] or against laborers' or mechanics' liens thereon,[2] or against a debt incurred by a public officer, fiduciary or attorney-at-law as such,[3] or trustee of an express trust.[4] Nor against a claim for rent, or for the legal fees of an officer,[5] or a debt for the removal of incumbrances thereon.[6]

"The yearly products of the homestead are not exempt as against obligations contracted in the production of the same." [7]

§ 84. *Alienation.* — A homestead cannot be alienated or mortgaged without the joint consent of husband and wife.[8] An instrument of waiver of homestead rights, besides being so signed, must be attested by one witness.[9] In Texas no mortgage, trust-deed, or other lien on the homestead is ever valid, except for the purchase-money therefor or improvements thereon, as in § 83, whether such mortgage, etc., is created by the husband alone or together with his wife; and all pretended sales of the homestead involving any condition of defeasance are void.[10]

All homestead rights may be waived by the debtor in writing except $300 worth of household furniture and provisions, and wearing apparel.[11]

No temporary renting shall change the character of a homestead, no other homestead having been acquired.[12]

§ 85. *Recording.* — The Constitution of Nevada provides that laws shall be enacted requiring homesteads to be recorded.[13]

§ 86. *Duration.* — In some States the homestead estate continues exempt from the owner's debts after his death, during the minority of any of his children.[14] In others, during the life and widowhood of his widow, unless she be the owner of a homestead in her own right.[15] So, it is provided in general terms that it shall inure to the benefit of the widow.[16] So it would seem to be implied in Texas, where the Constitution provides "that on the death of the husband, wife, or both, the homestead descends and vests like other real

[1] Fla., La., Va.

[2] Ala. 207; Ark.; Ga.; N. C. 10, 4.

[3] Ark., La., Va.

[4] Ark.

[5] Va.

[6] Ga.

[7] S. C.

[8] Ala.; Fla. 10, 1; Kan. 15, 9; La. 246; Mich. 16, 2; N. C. 10, 8; Nev. 4, 30; Okla., 12, 2; S. C. 2, 28; Tenn.; Tex.; Wy.

[9] Ala. 210.

[10] Tex. 16, 50. These are surprising innovations.

[11] Ga. 9, 3, 1.

[12] Tex. 16, 51; Okla. 12, 2.

[13] Nev. 4, 30.

[14] Ala. 206; Ark. 9, 6, 10; La. 244; Mich. 16, 3; N. C. 10, 3 Tenn.; W. Va. 6, 48.

[15] Mich. 16, 4; N C. 10, 5.

[16] Ala. 208; Fla. 10, 2; La ; Tenn.

property of the deceased, and shall be governed by the same laws of descent and distribution, but shall not be partitioned among the heirs of the deceased during the lifetime of the husband or widow, or so long as he or she occupy or use the same as a homestead, or the guardian of minor children be permitted so to do by order of court."[1] So, in Arkansas, during her natural life (whether she marry or not), unless she be the owner of a homestead in her own right. In Florida the homestead exemption inures to the widow and heirs of the party enjoying it.[2]

§ 87. *Stay Laws.* — By the Constitution of Virginia no law staying the collection of debts can be passed.[3]

§ 88. *Garnishment.* — By the Constitution of Texas no current wages for personal service shall ever be subject to garnishment.[4]

ARTICLE 9. EMINENT DOMAIN.[5]

§ 90. *General Principles.* — In two States private property is expressly declared by the Constitution to be inviolate.[6] But, in four, subservient to public welfare when necessity demands it.[7]

But it cannot be taken by law[8] without just compensation being made.[9]

§ 91. *Taking for Public Use.* — The Constitutions of many States prescribe specially that no man's property shall be taken,[10] damaged, or destroyed for public use[11] without just compensation being made,[12] or not without the owner's consent or just compensa-

[1] Tex. 16, 52.

[2] Fla. 10, 2.

[3] Va. 194.

[4] Tex. 16, 28.

[5] See also section 15 for the general principle. The principles of this article are covered repeatedly in Magna Carta. Kansas and North Carolina alone have no constitutional provisions covering this article, which has doubtless had its effect in the liberal opinions of Kansas courts upon laws destroying property rights.

[6] Ark. 2, 22; O, 1, 19.

[7] Mass, 1. 10; Me. 1, 21; O.; Vt. 1. 2, See also § 92.

[8] *I. e.* either for public or private use; compare §§ 91-93.

[9] Fla. Decln. Rts. 12; 16, 29; Ind. 1, 21; Mass.; N. M.* 95, 1.

[10] The U. S. Amt. 5 and many States only specify property "taken," not merely damaged, but the distinction should be unimportant. Property damaged is property "taken" in part, though not destroyed. "Taken or applied" (Del.).

[11] *I. e.*, by the State or by a municipal corporation, or, perhaps by a quasi-public corporation. In some States the words "public use" extend, by the context, to takings by a private corporation for a public use (N. J., Ill., Wy., Wash.).

[12] Ala. 23; Ark. 2, 22; Ariz. *B. Rts. 14; Cal. 1, 14; Col. 2, 15; Ct. 1, 11; Fla. 16, 29; Ga. 1, 3, 1; Ida. 1, 14; Ill. 2, 13; Ind. 1, 21; Io. 1, 18; Ky. 242; La. 167; Mass. 1, 10; Me. 1, 21; Mich. 18, 14; Minn. 1, 13; Amt. 1895, 5; Miss. 17; Mo. 2, 21; Mon. 3, 14; N. D. 14; Neb. 1, 21; Nev. 1, 8; N. J.,

tion,[1] or the consent of the owner's representatives (*i. e.*, the legislature) *and* just compensation,[2] or his own consent or that of the representative body of the people.[3]

But reservoirs, storage-basins, irrigation canals, ditches, flumes, and pipes for water drainage, or mining purposes, working mines, as dumps, hoists, shafts, tunnels, etc., are declared a public use in the arid States.[4] So, as to water only,[5] or "any other use necessary for the complete development of the material resources of the State or the preservation of the health of its inhabitants." [6]

§ 92. *Taking by Private Parties.*[7] — Private property cannot constitutionally be taken for private use, or the use of corporations other than municipal, without the consent of the owner, except as below.[8]

But land may be taken by private parties in a manner provided by law for ways of necessity,[9] for drains across another's land,[10] for flumes and aqueducts across another's land.[11] In a few, lands may be taken by private persons or corporations, for a public way.[12] or for works of internal improvement generally.[13]

But the Constitution declares that no man's property can be taken for such private use [14] without just compensation.[15]

No right of way shall be appropriated to the use of a corporation (other than municipal) until full compensation is paid or secured in money.[16]

1, 16; 4, 7, 8; N. Y. 1, 7; O. 1, 19; Okla. 2, 24; Ore. 1, 18; R. I. 1 16; S. C. 1, 17; S. D. 6, 13, 17, 18; Utah 1, 22; Va. 58; Vt. 1, 2; Wash. 1, 16; W. Va. 3, 9; Wis. 1, 13; Wy. 1, 33. See also § 90. Or, in several States, "secured to be made." (Io., Me., Nev., Pa., Minn., Wash.)

[1] Md. 3, 40; N. M.* 1851, July 12, § 14; Tex. 1, 17. These distinctions would appear unnecessary.

[2] Del. 1, 8; Pa. 1, 10; Tenn. 1, 21.

[3] Mass.; N. H. 1, 12; Vt. 1, 9.

[4] Ida.; Wy.

[5] Mon. 3, 15. See § 418.

[6] Ida.

[7] In States having no provisions under this section, the right of eminent domain can probably only be exercised under Sections 90, 91; and land can never be taken for private use. (See Mo. 2, 21.)

[8] Ala. 1, 23; Col. 2, 14; Mo. 2, 20; Okla. 2, 23; S. C. 1, 17; Wash. 1, 16; Wy. 1, 32.

[9] Ala.; Col.; Ga.; Ill. 4, 30; Mich. 18, 14; Miss. 110; Mo.; Mon.; N. J. 1, 16; N. Y. 1, 7; Okla.; Wash.; Wy.

[10] Col. 16, 7; Ida. 1, 14; Ill. 4, 31; Mo.; Mon. 3, 15; N. Y.; Okla.; Wash.; Wy.

[11] Col.; Ida.; Wash.; Wy. See also §§ 91, 418.

[12] Ala.; Ark. 12, 9; Cal. 1, 14; Minn. 10, 4; N. J.

[13] W. Va. 3, 9.

[14] This is probably law in many other States, as included in the provisions of § 91. See § 91, notes.

[15] Ala.; Ark.; Col. 2, 15; 16, 7; Fla. 16, 29; Ga. 1, 3, 1; Ky. 242; Mich.; Minn.; Mo. 2, 21; N. J. 4, 7, 8; N. Y.; O. 1, 19; Okla.; Pa. 16, 8; Wash.; W. Va.; Wy.

[16] Cal.; Fla.; Kan. 12, 4; N. D. 14; Nev. 8, 7; O. 13, 5; S. C. 9, 20; Wash. 1, 16.

In Alabama, that the right of eminent domain shall not be so construed as to allow taxation or forced subscription for the benefit of railroads or any corporations, except municipal.

The fee of land taken for railroad tracks without the consent of the owners remains in them subject to the use for which it is taken.[1]

§ 93. *Compensation.* — The compensation must, in most States, always be paid[2] before[3] the taking.[4] So, when the taking is for public improvements in towns.[5] But not in some States, when the taking is by the State.[6] Nor when the taking is by a municipal corporation.[7] Until the compensation is paid, as above, the rights of the owner are not, in two States, divested.[8]

§ 94. *Jury Trial.* — The amount of compensation for property so taken must be determined by a jury, either in cases of taking by the State,[9] or by public or municipal corporations,[10] or in cases of taking by private parties or corporations, under § 92,[11] or, when any corporation is interested for or against the right of taking.[12]

In Wisconsin, the necessity of the taking must also be ascertained by a jury in cases of taking by municipal corporations against the owner's consent.[13] And so, in Michigan, in all cases where a jury

[1] Ill. 2, 13; Mo.; Okla. 2, 23; S. D. 6, 13. Or highways; S. D. See § 519.

[2] "Except in cases of war, riot, fire, or public peril, or, in Ohio, making or repairing public roads" (O., Nev.). Or, in some States, secured to be paid by a deposit in money or bond; see § 91, note 1. (Io., Mich., O., Pa., Kan., W. Va., Ark., Tex., Ore., Nev., S. C.)

[3] Except, in some States, by the owner's consent. [This would seem to follow in all States, from general principles.]

[4] Ala. 23; 235; Ark. 12, 9; Cal. 1, 14; Fla. 16, 29; Ga.; Ida.; Ind. 1, 21; Io.; Kan. 12, 4; Ky. 242; La.; Md.; Mich. 15, 9; Minn.; Miss. 17; Mon.; N. D. 14; Nev. 1, 8; N. J. 4, 7, 8; O. 1, 19; Okla. 2, 23; Ore. 1, 19; 11, 4; Pa. 16, 8; S. C. 1, 17; S. D. 6, 13; 17, 18; Tex.; Wash.; W. Va.

[5] Mich. 15, 5; Pa.

[6] Cal.; Ind.; Mich.; N. J. 1, 16; Ore. 1, 18; Tex.; W. Va.

[7] Cal.; N. J.; Wash. 1, 16; W. Va.

[8] Col. 2, 15; Mo. 2, 21.

[9] N. D. 14; Io. 1, 18; Col. 3, 4; Md.; O.; Okla. 2, 24; Mo.; Ala.; S. D. Or by commissioners appointed by law: Col., Mo., Okla. On the appeal from preliminary assessment: Ala. Always by a jury when required by the owner; not, as above, by the commissioners: Col. Except when agreed upon by the parties (this would seem to follow in all States). Md., N. D.

[10] Ala.; Col.; Ill. 2, 13, 20; Ky.; Md.; Mich. 15, 15; 18, 2; Mo.; N. Y. 1, 7; O.; Okla.; S. D. On the appeal from preliminary assessment: Ala., Ky. Or by commissioners: Col., Mo., N. Y. Always by a jury when required by the owner; not, as above, by commissioners: Col. Except when agreed upon by the parties: Md., Okla.

[11] Ark., Ala., Cal., Col., Ill., Io., Fla., Ky., Mich., Md., Mo., N. Y., O., Okla., N. D., S. C., W. V., Wash. On the appeal from preliminary assessment Ala., Ky.; Ark. 12, 9. Always by a jury when required by the owner; not, as above, by commissioners: Col. On the appeal from preliminary assessment : Ala., Ky., Okla. Or by commissioners: Col., N. Y., Mo.

[12] Ill. 11, 14; Mo. 12, 4.

[13] Wis. 11, 2.

trial is required by the Constitution. So, in others, in opening private roads.[1]

The question whether the use alleged to be public is really so must be determined by the court, any legislation asserting it to be public notwithstanding.[2]

§ 95. *The Amount of Compensation* must be determined without any reference to any benefit that may be conferred by betterment or otherwise, in some States, in cases of taking of rights of way by a private corporation,[3] or in all cases of taking for public use,[4] or in cases of taking by a municipal corporation.[5]

§ 96. *Appeal* from the preliminary assessment of damage [*i. e.*, by commissioners] can, in some States, never be denied in the case of taking by corporations; and on such appeal the amount must be determined by a jury.[6]

§ 97. *The Exercise of the Right against Franchises.* — The right of eminent domain shall never be so construed as to prevent the legislature from taking the property or franchises of incorporated companies and subjecting them to public use the same as that of individuals.[7]

Article 10. Citizens and Aliens. Language, etc.

§ 100. *Who are Citizens.*[8] — All citizens of the United States resident in the State are, by the Constitution, declared citizens of the State.[9] (For § 101, Forfeiture of citizenship by absence, see Art. 24.)

§ 102. *Alien's Rights.*[10] In two States the Constitution provides

[1] Mon., N. Y.

[2] Col.; Miss. 17; Mo. 2, 20; Okla. 2, 23; Wash. An excellent legislative recognition of its boundaries on the judicial power.

[3] Ark. 12, 9; Cal. 1, 14; Fla. 16, 29; Kan. 12, 4; N. D. 14; O. 13, 5; 1, 19; S. C. 9, 20; S. D. 6, 13; Wash. 1, 16.

[4] Io. 1, 18; O. 1, 19; S. D. 1, 16.

[5] Kan.

[6] Ala. 159; Ky. 242; Okla. 2, 23; Pa. 16, 8; S. D. 17, 18; see § 94.

[7] Ala. 1, 23; Ark. 17, 9; Cal. 12, 8; Col. 15, 8: Ga. 4, 2, 2; Ida. 8; Ill. 11, 14; Ky. 195; Miss. 190; Mo. 12, 4; Mon. 11, 8; 15, 9; N. D. 134; Neb. 11, 6; Pa. 16, 3; S. D. 17, 4; Utah 12, 11; Wash. 12, 10; W. Va. 11, 12; Wy. 10, 9; 10, 10 (4). See § 504.

[8] Founded on U. S. Amts. 14, 1, and consequently true in all States; see also Article 24.

[9] Ala. 2; Ga. 1, 1, 25; Miss. 8; Vt. Amt. 1; W. Va. 2, 3. So, in Alabama, all persons who have duly declared their intention to become citizens of the United States. But in Vermont there is an oath of allegiance required from persons wishing to become freemen (Vt. 2, 21).

[10] For tax laws, see § 334. By the Act of Settlement of William III. no person born out of English dominions

that no distinction whatever can be made between citizens and aliens with respect to the possession, enjoyment, or descent of property, real or personal.[1] Or, in others, between citizens and aliens *bona fide* resident in the State.[2] But in others, this applies only as to mining property.[3]

In Vermont, persons of good character who have come to settle in the State, having first made oath of allegiance to the same, may take, hold, and transfer real estate.[4]

But in others, the legislature shall enact laws limiting the number of acres of land which any alien or corporation controlled by aliens may own within the State.[5]

And in Washington, the ownership of lands by aliens, other than those who in good faith have declared their intention to become citizens of the United States, is prohibited, except where acquired by inheritance, under mortgage, or in good faith in the ordinary course of justice in the collection of debts; and all conveyances of lands hereafter made to any alien directly, or in trust for such alien, shall be void. Every corporation, the majority of the capital stock of which is owned by aliens, shall be considered an alien for the purpose of this prohibition.[6] This does not apply to mining lands or property.

In Oklahoma,[7] no alien or person not a United States citizen may take or own land, and if acquired by devise, descent, etc., he must sell within five years; but this does not apply to Indians nor to aliens who are *bona fide* residents, nor to lands now owned by aliens.

§ 103. *Language.* By the Constitutions of four States, the laws, public records, and written legislative and judicial proceedings shall be conducted, promulgated, and preserved in the English language (only).[8] So, in Oklahoma, schools must be taught in English only.[9]

although naturalized, except such as are born of English parents could be a member of the House of Parliament or enjoy any office, civil or military, or have any granted land from the Crown. This was only repealed by 7 & 8 Vict. c. 66.

[1] Fla. D. Rts. 18; Kan. B. Rts. 17.

[2] Ala. 1, 34; Ark. 2, 20; Cal. 1, 17; Amt. 1893, p. 624; (*Except* that in California a distinction may be made against such aliens as are not eligible to become United States citizens. And see § 22); Col, 2, 27; Io. 1, 22; Mich. 18, 13; Mon. 3, 25; Neb. 1, 25; Nev. 1, 16; Ore. 1, 31; S. D. 6, 14; W. Va. 2, 5; Wis. 1, 15; Wy. 1, 29.

[3] Mon. 3, 25; Wash. 2, 33.

[4] Vt. 2, 39.

[5] Miss. 84; S. C. 3, 35.

[6] Wash. 2, 33.

[7] Okla. 22, 1.

[8] Cal. 4, 24; Ill. Sched. 18; La. 165; Mich. 18, 6.

[9] Okla. 1, 5.

In Colorado, laws are also to be published in Spanish and German.[1] And in Louisiana, the legislature may provide for the publication of laws in the French language, and that judicial advertisements, in certain designated districts, may be made in French. So, in Missouri, certain characters, etc., in the German language.[2] So, in Maryland, proposed amendments to the Constitution, in German.[3]

[1] Col. 18, 8. [2] Mo. 9, 16. [3] Md. 14, 1.

CHAPTER II

BILL OF RIGHTS: CRIMINAL

ARTICLE 12. RIGHTS BEFORE TRIAL

§ 120. *To Hear Accusation.*[1] By the Constitutions of nearly all the States, persons accused of crime have the right to hear the nature and cause of the accusation.[2] And in many they are to have a copy of the accusation furnished them.[3] In Georgia, also, to have a list of the witnesses on whose testimony the charge is founded.[4]

§ 121. *Bailable Offences.* The Constitutions of most of the states provide that all persons shall, before conviction, be admitted to bail, upon giving sufficient sureties, except (where proof of their guilt is evident or the presumption great) for capital offences.[5] Or for murder and treason,[6] or offences punishable with death or im-

[1] The wording of the text is that of the Virginia Bill of Rights, and would apparently give the right to any person arrested and accused *before trial or indictment.* U. S. Amt. 6 confines this right to criminal prosecutions. The former doctrine is preferable, and the principle is an old one, asserted by Coke in 1615, and probably independent of the right to habeas corpus: see § 125.

"No man could be committed to prison but by a legal warrant specifying his offence; and by an usage nearly tantamount to constitutional right, he must be speedily brought to trial by means of regular sessions of gaol delivery." (Taswell-Langmead, p. 294.)

[2] Ala. 1, 6; Ark. 2, 10; Col. 2, 16; Ct. 1, 9; Del. 1, 7; Fla. Decln. Rts. 11; Ill. 2, 9; Ind. 1, 13; Io. 1, 10; Kan. Bill of Rts. 10; Ky. 11; La. 10; Mass. 1, 12; Md. Decln. Rts. 21; Me. 1, 6; Mich. 6, 28; Minn. 1, 6; Miss. 26; Mo. 2, 22; Mon. 3, 16; N. C. 1, 11; Neb. 1, 11; N. H. 1, 15; N. J. 1, 8; N. M. * 50, 7; 95, 1; O. 1, 10; Okla. 1, 20; Ore. 1, 11; Pa. 1, 9; R. I. 1, 10; S. C. 1, 18; S. D. 6, 7; Tenn. 1, 9; Tex. 1, 10; Utah 1, 12; Va. 1, 8; Vt. 1, 10; Wash. 1, 22; W. Va. 3, 14; Wis. 1, 7; Wy. 1, 10.

[3] Ala.; Ark.; Ga. 1, 1, 5; Ill.; Ind.; Io.; Md.; Me.; Mon.; Neb.; O.; Okla.; Ore.; S. D.; Tenn.; Tex.; Utah; Wash.; Wy. Or of the indictment (Fla.).

[4] Compare § 135.

[5] Ala. 1, 16; Ariz.* Bill of Rts. 11; Ark. 2, 8; Cal. 1, 6; Col. 2, 19; Ct. 1, 14; Del. 1, 12; Fla. Decln. of Rts. 9; Ida. 1, 6; Ill. 2, 7; Io. 1, 12; Kan. Bill of Rts. 9; Ky. 16; La. 12; Me. 1, 10; Minn. 1, 7; Miss. 29; Mo. 2, 24; Mon. 3, 19; N. D. 6; Nev. 1, 7; N. J. 1, 10; N. M.* 95, 1; 1851, July 12, § 9; O. 1, 9; Okla. 2 8; Pa. 1, 14; S. C. 1, 20; S. D. 6, 8; Tenn. 1, 15; Tex. 1, 11; Utah 1, 8; Vt. 2, 33; Wash. 1, 20; Wis. 1, 8; Wy. 1, 14.

[6] Ind. 1, 17; Mich. 6, 29; Neb. 1, 9; Ore. 1, 14.

prisonment for life.[1] And so, *after conviction*, except for capital or infamous offences in Louisiana.

§ 122. *Excessive Bail.*[2] The Constitutions of all the States except Illinois provide that excessive bail shall not be required.[3]

§ 123. *Imprisonment of Parties Accused.* In a few States the Constitution provides that no person arrested shall be treated with unnecessary rigor.[4]

§ 124. *Witnesses.* In several States the Constitution provides that witnesses shall not be unreasonably detained;[5] or that they shall not be imprisoned longer than may be necessary for securing their depositions; and thereafter shall be discharged on their own recognizance.[6] Depositions so obtained may be used at the trial if the witness is dead or absent from the State.[7] They shall not be confined in any room where individuals are actually imprisoned.[8] Cf. § 135.

Contempts and their punishment are regulated by the Constitution in Oklahoma and two other States. See § 662.

[1] R. I. 1, 9.

[2] Compare Eng. Stat. 1 W. & M. Sess. 2; U. S. Amt. 8. Excessive bail was one of the abuses complained of in the Bill of Rights, and a usual method under the Stuarts of evading the habeas corpus. The right to bail was granted under the writ *de odio et atia* even before Magna Carta and was the means by which a person imprisoned on a charge of homicide could get released on bail to await the Iter of the King's Justices.

[3] Ala. 1, 16; Ariz.* Bill of Rts. 10; Ark. 2, 9; Cal. 1, 6; Col. 2, 20; Ct. 1, 13; Del. 1, 11; Fla. Decln. of Rts. 8; Ga. 1, 1, 9; Ida. 1, 6; Ind. 1, 16; Io. 1, 17; Kan. Bill of Rts. 9; Ky. 17; La. 12; Mass. 1, 26; Md. Decln. of Rts. 25; Me. 1, 9; Mich. 6, 31; Minn. 1, 5; Miss. 29; Mo. 2, 25; Mon. 3, 20; N. C. 1, 14; N. D. 6; Neb. 1, 9; Nev. 1, 6; N. H. 1, 33; N. J. 1, 15; N. M.* 95, 1; 1851, July 12, § 11; N. Y. 1, 5; O. 1, 9; Okla. 2, 9; Ore. 1, 16; Pa. 1, 13; R. I. 1, 8; S. C. 1, 19; S. D. 6, 23; Tenn. 1, 16; Tex. 1, 13; Utah 1, 9; Va. 1, 9; Vt. 2, 33; Wash. 1, 14; W. Va. 3, 5; Wis. 1, 6; Wy. 1, 14.

[4] Ariz.* 4, 28; Ga. 1, 1, 9; Ind. 1, 15; Ore. 1, 13; Tenn. 1, 13; Utah 1, 9; Wy. 1, 16. Compare § 140. So the Constitution of Rhode Island declares that every man is presumed innocent until proved guilty by the law; and consequently no act of severity not necessary to secure the accused should be permitted. (R. I. 1, 14.) And in Delaware their friends and counsel must be allowed access to the accused. (Del. 1, 12.) "Theoretically torture was never part of the law of England" (Taylor II. 166), but was employed under Elizabeth and Henry VIII. to extort confessions from Roman Catholics by authority of the Privy Council. Coke says the rack was introduced by the Duke of Exeter under Henry VI. and adds: "There is no law to warrant tortures in this land, nor can they be justified by any prescription, being so lately brought in, and it was declined by the judges in the trial of Felton, the murderer of the Duke of Buckingham. (Taswell-Langmead, p. 360.)

[5] Ariz.* Bill of Rts. 10; Ark. 2, 9; Cal. 1, 6; Fla. Decln. of Rts. 8; Mich. 6, 31; N. D. 6; Nev. 1, 6; N. Y. 1, 5; S. C. 1, 19.

[6] Col. 2, 17; Cal.; Mon. 3, 17; Wy. 1, 12.

[7] Mon.

[8] Cal., N. D., Wy.

§ 125. *Habeas Corpus.*[1] Three State Constitutions declare the writ of habeas corpus a writ of right.[2] Two others declare that the writ or remedy ought not to be denied or delayed.[3]

In others, the legislature are to enact laws to render the remedy speedy and effectual.[4] Or the privilege of the writ is to be enjoyed in the most easy, cheap, expeditious and ample manner.[5]

So, North Carolina declares that every person restrained of his liberty is entitled to a remedy to inquire into the lawfulness thereof, and to remove the same if unlawful.[6]

§ 126. *Suspension of Habeas Corpus.*[7] By the Constitutions of most States, the writ can only be suspended where, in cases of

[1] The right to habeas corpus is contained in Magna Carta, C. 39. Its predecessor was known as the writ *de odio et atia,* which, however, was not granted as of right and was often refused except for a money payment. Five centuries of effort to evade this writ, the great guaranty of personal liberty, ended in the Habeas Corpus Act of Charles II. which applies to any person committed and charged with crime and requires any judge at any time to issue the writ, returnable immediately, and within two days to discharge the prisoner if bailable. This statute of Charles II. only covered arrests on a criminal charge. This was only remedied by 56 Geo. III. c. 100. The right to personal liberty — the most precious of all rights — is as old as the Constitution itself. It rests upon the common law which was merely defined and declared by Magna Carta and the stream of statutes which form that enactment (Taswell-Langmead, p. 488). An English subject was always free from lawful detention except upon a criminal charge or conviction or for a civil debt, and the habeas corpus was in theory always a writ of right, but it was doubtful whether it could be issued by a single judge during vacation, and it was only issued by the Court of King's Bench. The Habeas Corpus Act of Charles II. fixed no limit on the amount of bail which might be demanded, which defect was remedied by the Bill of Rights in 1689, and it did not provide against falsehood in the return. (See II. Taylor, pp. 328–383.) The Constitution of the United States, Art. 1, § 9 (2) providing that the privilege of the writ of habeas corpus shall not be suspended, etc., only applies to action by the Federal Government. (See § 126.)

[2] Fla. Decln. of Rts. 7; Tex. 1, 12; Vt. Amt. 12.

[3] Io. 1, 13; N. C. 1, 18.

[4] Tex., Vt.

[5] Fla.; Mass. 2, 6, 7; N. H. 2, 90.

[6] N. C. 1, 18.

[7] Derived from U. S. C. 1, 9 (2). "The privilege of the writ of habeas corpus shall not be suspended, unless when in cases of rebellion or invasion the public safety may require it." This of course only applies to the Federal Government; but is most unfortunately ambiguous as it does not say who is to suspend the writ. The better law is that the President may not suspend the writ, but only Congress; though they may perhaps authorize the President to suspend the writ on finding a special state of facts. It may be questioned, however, whether an act would be constitutional which authorized the President to suspend the writ at his discretion. Habeas corpus will issue from a Federal court to a State court or other authority, but only on the ground that the person detained is deprived of a right secured to him by or under the Constitution of the United States. The President was authorized to suspend the writ by Act of Congress in 1863, 1866, 1867 (McClain, p. 331), but there is no general act to that effect in Revised Statutes.

invasion or rebellion, the public safety requires it.[1] In others, it can never be suspended in any case.[2] "Martial law" of course would suspend it.[3] The writ can only be suspended by the legislature.[4] In other States this is implied by the general provision of § 392; and it is a general constitutional principle.

The manner of its suspension is left to the legislature to determine by law.[5]

§ 127. *Indictment.*[6] In most States, the Constitution provides that no person shall be held to answer for a capital crime [7] or a crime punishable by imprisonment for life [8] or infamous crime or felony [9] or any criminal offence [10] except on indictment or presentment of a grand jury.[11] So, in others, that no person, for any indictable

[1] Ariz.* Bill of Rts. 9; Ark. 2, 11; Cal. 1, 5; Col. 2, 21; Ct. 1, 14; Del. 1, 13; Fla. Decln of Rts. 7; Ida. 1, 5; Ill. 2, 7; Ind. 1, 27; Io. 1, 13; Kan. Bill of Rts. 8; Ky. 16; La. 13; Me. 1, 10; Mich. 4, 44; Minn. 1, 7; Miss. 21; Mon. 3, 21; N. D. 5; Neb. 1, 8; Nev. 1, 5; N. J. 1, 11; N. M.* 95, 1; 1851, July 12, § 10; N. Y. 1, 4; O. 1, 8; Ore. 1, 23; Pa. 1, 14; R. I. 1, 9; S. C. 1, 23; S. D. 6, 8; Tenn. 1, 15; Utah 1, 5; Va. 58; Wash. 1, 13; Wis. 1, 8; Wy. 1, 17.

[2] Ala. 1, 17; Ga. 1, 1, 11; Md. 3, 55; Mo. 2, 26; N. C. 1, 21; Okla. 2, 10; Tex. 1, 12; Vt. Amt. 12; W. Va. 3, 4. Or can only be suspended on the most urgent occasions, and for a limited time (not exceeding in Massachusetts twelve months, and in New Hampshire three months. Mass. 2, 6, 7; N. H. 2, 90).

[3] Compare §§ 293, 392.

[4] Ark, Ct., Ida., Md., Mich., Miss., N. H., R. I., Tenn.

[5] Ida. 1, 5; Neb.

[6] Compare U. S. Amt. 5. A presentment is the notice taken by a grand jury of an offence of their own knowledge without an indictment. Information is a complaint against a person for some criminal or penal offence, filed by the proper officer, on behalf of the people, at his own discretion, on the relation of some private person; not founded on the oath of a jury, although the subsequent proceedings are the same. (Stimson's Law Glossary.) There does not appear to be any constitutional provision requiring an indictment in England, though the effect of a habeas corpus is in most cases to make one necessary. Informations were, however, always unpopular and are rendered very unusual by the effect of recent statutes (4 Blackstone, 311) requiring express directions from the Court of King's Bench. The constitutional provisions of California and other code States would seem to revive the information in all criminal cases.

[7] Ct., Fla., La., Me., Nev., N. M.*, N. Y., O., Okla., R. I. See Note 7 below.

[8] Ct.

[9] All the States previously mentioned except Ct. and La.; and also in Cal., Col., Mo., N. D., and the U. S. Const. Amt. 5 as applying to Federal courts. An indictment is not necessary to due process of law and consequently is not required by the Federal Constitution in the State courts under the Fourteenth Amendment.

[10] Ark., Ill., Io., Ky., Minn., N. C., Neb., N. J., Okla., S. C., S. D., Tenn., Tex., W. Va.

[11] Ariz.* Bill of Rts. 14; Ark. 2, 8; Col. 2, 8; Ct. 1, 9; Fla. Decln. of Rts. 10; Ill. 2, 8; Io. 1, 11; La. 9; Me. 1, 7; Minn. 1, 7; Mo. 2, 12; Amt. 1899, p. 382; N. C. 1, 12; N. D. 8; N. M.* 50, 6; 1851, July 12, § 8; Neb. 1, 10; Nev. 1, 8; N. J. 1, 9; N. Y. 1, 6; O. 1, 10; Okla. 2, 17; R. I. 1, 7; S. C. 1, 17; Tenn. 1, 14; Tex. 1, 10; W. Va. 3, 4; Wy. 1, 13.

offence, shall be proceeded against criminally, by information.[1] In Wisconsin and Minnesota, no person shall be held to answer for a criminal offence without due process of law.[2]

But in the "code" States, offences may usually be prosecuted either by indictment or by information after examination and commitment by a magistrate.[3] Under this statute indictments are practically done away with and all offences are prosecuted by such information,[4] except that a grand jury *may* still be summoned.[5]

Exceptions. But in nearly all these states an exception to the above rule is made in cases arising in the army or navy of the State or the militia, in time of war or public danger,[6] or at any time.[7] An exception is made also in cases of impeachment.[8]

So, of course, in cases of inferior offences not above described,[9] as petit larceny,[10] or in courts not of record,[11] or cases cognizable by a justice of the peace,[12] or by the county court,[13] or police courts,[14] or probate courts,[15] or in cases where the punishment is by fine, or by imprisonment not in the penitentiary.[16]

A person may be proceeded against by information, by leave of court, for oppression or misdemeanor while in office.[17]

Indictments are (of course) unnecessary in cases where the legislature may have dispensed with a grand jury and provided other process by law.[18] But without a constitutional permission, such dispensing would be invalid.

In cases where indictments may be employed, indictment and information are declared concurrent remedies.[19]

[1] Ala. 1, 8; Del. 1, 8; Ky. 12; Miss. 27; Pa. 1, 10.

[2] Minn. Amt. 1903, 269; Wis. 1, 8 and Amt. Presumably the same meaning is intended.

[3] Cal. 1, 8; Ida. 1, 8; La. 9; Mon. 3, 8; Okla.; S. D. 6, 10; Utah 1, 13; Wash. 1, 25.

[4] Ida.; Mon.; Utah; Wash. 1, 26.

[5] But not, by information, after a charge has been ignored by a grand jury. See § 129.

[6] Ala., Ariz.*, Ark., Col., Ct., Del., Fla., Ida., Ill., Io., Ky., La., Me., Minn., Miss., Mo., N. D., Neb., Nev., N. J., N. M.*, N. Y., O., Pa., R. I., S. C., S. D., Tex., U. S., Wy.

[7] Fla., N. Y., N. D., S. D.

[8] Ariz.*, Ark., Fla., Ida., Ill., Me., Minn., N. C., Neb., Nev., N. M.*, N. J., N. Y., O., R. I., S. D., Tenn., Tex.

[9] Ala., La., Miss., N. D., O., and others.

[10] Ala., Nev., N. Y., O.

[11] Ala.; Ark.; Io.; Me.; Minn.; Miss.; Mon. 3, 8; N. J.; N. M.*; R. I. S. D.; W. Va.

[12] Okla.

[13] S. D.; Tex. 5, 17.

[14] D. C.* 1064; Mon.

[15] Ida., Mon.

[16] Ill., Neb., Tex.

[17] Ala., Ky., Miss., Pa.

[18] See § 128.

[19] Col., La., Mo.

§ 128. *Grand Juries.*[1] In some States the Constitution gives the legislature authority to make laws dispensing with a grand jury in any case.[2] In Oklahoma (2, 18) it may make the calling of grand juries compulsory. So "No grand jury shall be summoned unless, in the opinion of the judge of the district, public interest demand it."[3] One hundred resident taxpayers of the county may, in Oklahoma, petition any judge to call one.

A grand jury shall consist of twelve men, any nine of whom may concur to find an indictment or true bill.[4] Of seven men, of whom five may so concur.[5] Of any number from five to fifteen.[6] Eighteen, of whom twelve may so concur.[7] Of eight.[8]

After a charge has been ignored by a grand jury, no information will lie.[9] The Oklahoma Constitution [unnecessarily] specifies that grand juries have power to return indictments for all character and grades of crime, and such other powers as the legislature may prescribe.

ARTICLE 13. RIGHTS AT TRIAL

§ 130. *Rights to Law.*[10] In nearly all the States the Constitution provides that no person can be deprived of his life, liberty, or property

[1] Grand juries are older than petit juries. By the Assize of Clarendon, A. D. 1166, it was ordained that in every county twelve lawful men of each hundred, with four lawful men from each township, should be sworn to present all reputed criminals of their district in each county court, at a time when the persons so presented were tried by the water ordeal (Taswell-Langmead, p. 134). In the course of time the element of popular election in the mode of nominating the grand jury was entirely eliminated. Now, twenty-four freeholders of each county are summoned by the sheriff, of which a certain number, varying from twelve to twenty-three, are sworn. A grand jury in the United States usually consists of twenty-three, but they must all, in the absence of express constitutional provision, concur in order to find a bill of indictment. Taylor traces the Grand Jury to the Hundred Courts of Aethelred, his law providing that the twelve senior thegns go out and swear on the relic that is given them in hand that they will accuse no innocent man nor conceal any guilty one. In other words, they were inquisitors representing the earliest form of a jury of presentment.

[2] Col. 2, 23; Ill. 2, 8; Ind. 7, 17; Io. Amt. 3; N. D. 8; Neb. 1, 10; Ore. 7, 18; S. D. 6, 10; Wy. 1, 9; Wash. In misdemeanors, etc., only: Ala. 1, 8; Miss. 27.

[3] Ida.; Mo. Amt. 1899, p. 38; Mon.; Utah 1, 13; Wash. 1, 26.

[4] Col.; La. 117; Ky. 248; Mo. 2, 28; Okla. 1, 18; Tex. 5, 13; Wy.

[5] Mon.; Ore.; Utah.

[6] Io.

[7] S. C. 5, 22.

[8] Miss.

[9] Ida., Utah.

[10] This provision is founded on Magna Carta, C. 39. Compare also U. S. C. Amts. 5, 14, and §§ 70, 72, 127. The right of a man to law either as against king, officer, or subject, is discussed in Book I., and in matters not criminal under § 70. We are now discussing that protection to a man's person, property, or liberty, which, while it always existed under English

except by due process of law;[1] or by the law of the land or the judgment of his peers.[2] The exact wording may be important as deter-

law, was so clearly expressed in Magna Carta, Chap. 39. "No free man shall be taken, or imprisoned, or disseised, or outlawed, or exiled, or anyways destroyed; nor will we pass upon him (in some translations, "go upon him"), nor will we send upon him, unless by the lawful judgment of his peers, or by the law of the land." In these clauses are contained both habeas corpus and trial by jury, the most effectual securities against oppression which the wisdom of man has hitherto been able to devise. "Henceforth," says Hallam, "it must have been a clear principle of our constitution that no man can be detained in prison without trial. Whether courts framed the writ of Habeas Corpus in conformity with this clause or possessed it already it became from that era the right of every subject to demand it." Coke points out that these clauses, as they stand combined in the second issue of the Charter under Henry III. with the words "No person shall be disseised of his free tenement or liberties, or customs" recite the evils from which the laws of the land are to protect the subject, in the order in which they most affect him. First, the liberty of a man's person. Second, his property, liberties, or free customs, that is, the right to labor or trade as well as other franchises; which inferentially forbids state-created monopolies. Only the third clause, relating to outlawry, may be considered obsolete. The words "Nor will we go upon him," etc., are much disputed. Coke takes the simple meaning that no person is to be condemned at the King's suit, that is, in any criminal or penal suit, but by the judgment of his peers, that is, equals, or according to the law of the land. Others have said that John was in the habit of descending upon his enemies with an armed force, and that this was meant to be forbidden. Whatever was the historical meaning, the former one has grown to be the true one, and the words were used in the times of the Tudors and Stuarts to prevent any condemnation, outlawry, or forfeiture of a subject without the proper forms or law. The words "judgment of his peers or by the law of the land," or as they appear in later confirmations of the charter "due course of law" did not, at the time of the original Charter of John, mean jury trial, although Coke says they meant the lawful judgment, that is, verdict of his equals, or the law of the land, that is, the due course and process of law. It is probable, however, that the words included trial by jury, even in the original charter, as it was used at the time, and there can be no question but that by the interpretation of centuries they have come to mean that both in English and American constitutional history. (See Taswell-Langmead, 107.) The American Supreme Court has decided that the words "due process of law" do not necessarily mean trial by jury, but it is at least probable that they did so mean, in any case where trial by jury was wont to be used; and such is certainly the Constitution in England. In fact, the Supreme Court in rendering this decision do not refer to the fact, nor was it pointed out to them in argument, that the words "judgment of his peers" and "due course of law"

---

[1] Ala. 1, 6; Ariz.* Bill of Rts. 14; Ark. 2, 8; Cal. 1, 13; Col. 2, 25; Ct. 1, 9; Fla. Decln. of Rts. 12; Ga. 1, 1, 3; Ida. 1, 13; Ill. 2, 2; Io. 1, 9; Ky. 14; La. 2; Mich. 6, 32; Minn. 1, 7; Miss. 14; Mo. 2, 30; Mon. 3, 27; N. C. 1, 17; N. D. 13; Neb. 1, 3; Nev. 1, 8; N. M.* 1851, July 12, § 15; N. Y. 1, 6; Okla. 2, 7; S. C. 1, 5; S. D. 6, 2; Tex. 1, 19; Utah 1, 9; Wash. 1, 3; Wy. 1, 6.

[2] Del. 1, 7; Mass. 1, 12; Md. Decln. of Rts. 23; Me. 1, 6; N. H. 1, 15; N. M.* 95, 1; Pa. 1, 9; R. I. 1, 10; Tenn. 1, 8; Va. 1, 8 & 11; Vt. 1, 10; W. Va. 3, 10.

mining rights of trade or labor, freedom of contract, etc. Even in Magna Carta of Henry III. it includes one's "liberties or free cus-

are used interchangeably in the several issues of Magna Carta and in many Acts of Parliament.

In connection with this clause must, of course be read Cap. 40. "To none will we sell, to none will we deny or delay right or justice." (In some translations, "We will sell to no man, we will not deny to any man either justice or right.") See § 70, notes. "These words," says Coke, "are spoken in the person of the King, who, in judgment of law, in all his courts of justice is present, and repeating these words." The words "To none will we sell" were intended to abolish the fines paid in early times for procuring right or judgment. "To none will we deny" referred to the stopping of suits and the denial of writs. "To none will we delay" meant the delays caused either by the counter-fines of defendants, or by the will of the king. Taylor points out (I. 389) that the formula of Magna Carta was almost exactly anticipated in an edict of Conrad II. issued two centuries before in the words "No one shall lose his benefit except according to the custom of our ancestors and by judgment of his peers." And in the so-called laws of Henry I. it is expressed, "Every one is to be judged by his peers of his own county." This would dispose of the trial by jury theory, historically; but it is clearly of not so much importance as it seems. Whatever the clause meant at the time of King John, it has been repeatedly established in seven centuries, either as against king, American Congress or President, that trial by his peers, at least, does mean trial by jury as the word is now understood. The only real doubt is whether "due course of law" does not mean the same thing.

There is considerable doubt whether the law referred to in this section is in England the law of the king or the law of the people. "Pleas of the Crown are criminal prosecutions carried on in the name of the sovereign, who is supposed by the law to be the person injured by every infraction of the public rights of the community." (Blackstone, reported in Taswell-Langmead, p. 93.) On the other hand, as we have discussed in the first part, the English notion of law was the custom or law of the people, written or unwritten, not the command of a king to his subject. Hence, constitutional historians will differ on this point according as they take what we may call the Norman or the Saxon view. The distinction may appear somewhat theoretical, but it was not so in early days when every king upon his accession was compelled to promise to observe the laws or customs of the English or of Edward the Confessor; and for centuries the English people struggled to establish or restore the principle that the people, that is, Parliament, alone could make or unmake a law,— with, of course, the consent of the king, — against the effort of all the kings, at least until the Revolution of 1688 established the principle that the law was theirs and they made it. In England, writs still run "against the peace of the King," but this is probably as much of a formality as the words "The King so wills" at the end of an Act of Parliament. Writs in New York run in the name of "The people of the State of New York by the grace of God free and independent," but in most States they run in the name of the State or Commonwealth as the case may be. (Massachusetts, Pennsylvania, Virginia, and Kentucky are the only "commonwealths;" all the others are States.) As, upon the Declaration of Independence, the right of sovereignty reverted to the people of each colony and not to the States, in the first instance, it may be questioned whether the former is not the better form. It certainly tends less to confusion of thought and socialism.

It is important to note that the right to law in England has always meant the right to the law of one's own country or neighborhood and one's local court. Magna Carta itself has a chapter on this point, C. 34. "The writ called *praecipe* shall not in future be issued so as to cause a freeman to

toms." Thus in New Hampshire and Massachusetts: "arrested, imprisoned, despoiled, or deprived of his property, immunities, or privileges, put out of the protection of the law, exiled, or deprived of life, liberty, or estate."

No person shall be arrested, detained, and punished; or, in Alabama, accused, arrested, or detained, except in cases clearly ascertained by law.[1] And according to the forms by law prescribed.[2]

In several States, no person shall be disfranchised or deprived of *any* rights and privileges as a citizen, unless as provided above respectively.[3]

§ 131. *Jury Trial.*[4] In most States, the Constitution provides

lose his court," and the object of this writ was to prevent a case being removed to the King's Court from the Court Baron or manorial court. In early times the English people had the same dread of centralizing even the judicial power in London, or with the king's person, that the founders of the American Constitution had as against the Federal power. C. 24, however, secured the trial of all serious crimes before the king's justices. "No sheriff, constable, coroner or bailiff of the King shall hold pleas of the Crown."

[1] Ala. 1, 7; Ct. 1, 10; S. C.

[2] Ala.

[3] Ark. 2, 21; Mass.; Md.; Me.; Minn. 1, 2; N. H.; N. C.; N. M.*; N. Y. 1, 1; S. C.; Tenn.; Tex. For lynch law, see § 165.

[4] For civil cases, see Art. 7. The matter of jury trial is partly discussed in the notes to §§ 128 and 130. The original petit jury was a jury of witnesses, not a Saxon institution, but operated from, or suggested by, a procedure of the Norman kings, — the Inquest, of commissioners to verify facts. This Inquest at first belonged to matters not judicial, as, in 1106, Henry I. directed five commissioners to verify certain matters concerning taxation and the customs of the Church by the oath of twelve of the citizens. (Taswell-Langmead, p. 131.) Henry II. applied recognition by jury to every description of business, fiscal and legal. But the use of a jury as now understood is mentioned for the first time in the Constitutions of Clarendon, 1164, where, "when no one could be obtained to accuse a powerful layman amenable to the bishop's jurisdiction, the sheriffs, at the bishop's request, were directed to 'swear twelve lawful men of the neighbourhood to tell the truth, according to their conscience.'" If the jurors chosen were ignorant of the facts, a fresh jury had to be summoned. If some were ignorant or if they could not agree, others were added, which was called "afforcing the jury," until a verdict could be obtained from twelve unanimous witnesses . . . just the opposite of the modern notion. Trial by jury as the word is used in Magna Carta, therefore, must mean a jury of this sort. The English mode of trying facts before the jury arose was that of the ordeal, by water or otherwise; but this was abolished by the fourth Lateran Council in 1215. The Norman method of trial was by battle, but only if the injured prosecutor demanded it. Even before the abolition of the ordeal (says Taswell-Langmead) the practice had grown up of allowing a second or petit jury to affirm the finding of the grand jury; but for a long time the prisoner was not compelled to plead, that is, he might refuse to be tried by jury, in which case he was remanded to prison and submitted to the punishment called *peine forte et dure*, which was abolished in England only so late as George III. and under which Giles Corey was executed in the Salem Witchcraft case. In early times a verdict of a majority might be received, as in some of the new American States, but by the reign of Edward III. the necessity for an unanimous verdict of

that (in criminal prosecutions) all persons accused shall have a speedy and public trial by an impartial jury.[1] And so, in several, of all persons prosecuted by indictment or information.[2] In California, the provision is simply that the accused shall have a speedy and public trial.[3] So, the legislature shall make no law subjecting a person to capital [or infamous, in Mass.] punishment without trial by jury;[4] or, the right to trial by jury shall remain inviolate in criminal cases;[5] no person shall be convicted of any crime but by the verdict of a lawful jury in open court.[6] (Except upon confession, demurrer, etc., in Arizona — an unnecessary exception.)

Exceptions. The legislature may provide other means of trial for offences not infamous,[7] for petty offences,[8] for all offences less than felony, and in which the penalty does not exceed $100 or thirty days' imprisonment; these shall be tried summarily before a justice of the peace.[9] No fine of more than $50 shall be imposed except by a jury.[10]

But in all such cases of trial without a jury there must be a right of appeal.[11]

Laws may be made for the government of the army and navy,

twelve was re-established. As late as Queen Anne the Court of Queen's Bench decided that a jury might give a verdict of their own knowledge, but ought so to inform the Court, that they might be sworn as witnesses; though as early as the year 1450 the mode of procedure by *viva voce* evidence was the same as at present. Taswell-Langmead places the modern principle — that no juror is competent who knows anything as a witness — so late as George I. In old days the jurymen, being witnesses, were guilty of perjury if they gave a wrong verdict; and as late as 1554 the Court, being dissatisfied with a verdict, committed a jury to prison; but in 1670 a London jury, having failed to find William Penn guilty of preaching, was heavily fined, and when one of the jurors brought *habeas corpus*, he was decided by Chief Justice Vaughan to be improperly imprisoned, though return was made that he had been committed for finding a verdict "against full and manifest evidence and against the direction of the Court." (Taswell-Langmead, p. 138.) For the procedure in jury matters, see Art. 65 below.

[1] Ark. 2, 10; Col. 2, 16; Del. 1, 7; Fla. Decln. Rts. 11; Ga. 1, 1, 5; Ida. 1, 13; Ill. 2, 9; Ind. 1, 13; Io. 1, 10; Kan. Bill of Rts. 10; La. 9; Md. Decln. of Rts. 21; Me. 1, 6; Mich. 6, 28; Minn. 1, 6; Mo. 2, 22; Mon. 3, 16; N. D. 13; Neb. 1, 11; N. J. 1, 8; N. M.* 95, 1; 1851, July 12, § 8; O. 1, 10; Okla. 1, 20; Ore. 1, 11; Pa. 1, 9; R. I. 1, 10; S. C. 1, 18; S. D. 6, 7; Tex. 1, 10; Utah 1, 12; Va. 1, 8; Vt. 1, 10; Wash. 1, 22; Wy. 1, 10; and so, as applied to Federal courts, in U. S. Amt. 6.

[2] Ala. 1, 6; Ct. 1, 9; Ky. 11; Miss. 26; N. M.* 50, 7; Tenn. 1, 9; Wis. 1, 7.

[3] Cal. 1, 13.

[4] Mass. 1, 12; N. H. 1, 16; Utah 1, 10.

[5] Col. 2, 23; Fla. Decln. of Rts. 3; Ida. 1, 7; N. Y. 1, 2; Wash. 1, 21; Wy. 1, 9; see also § 72, for other States.

[6] Ariz.* 429; N. C. 1, 13; N. M.* 50, 8; W. Va. 3, 14.

[7] La., Va. (Amt. 1891).

[8] Del. 15, 7; N. C.

[9] Io. 1, 11; S. C. 5, 21.

[10] Tenn. 6, 14.

[11] Io., N. C., S. C.

(and the militia in actual service, in N. H.) without providing for trial by jury.[1]

All cases in which the punishment may not be at hard labor shall, until otherwise provided by law, which shall not be prior to 1904, be tried by the judge without a jury. Cases in which the punishment may be at hard labor shall be tried by a jury of five, all of whom must concur to render a verdict; cases in which the punishment may be capital, by a jury of twelve, all of whom must concur to render a verdict.[2]

Waiver. The Constitution provides that a jury may be waived by consent of both parties in all criminal cases not amounting to felony.[3] So, the accused may in all cases waive jury trial,[4] with the consent of the State's attorney.[5]

§ 132. *Juries.*[6] By the Constitution of Florida the number of the jury may in all cases be fixed by the legislature.[7] So, in other States, in courts not of record,[8] or in cases not punishable by hard labor or death.[9] Juries in the county or other inferior court consist of six men.[10] Not less than five.[11] Eight, in cases not capital, or four, in inferior courts.[12]

The parties may agree on a jury less than twelve in number, in cases of misdemeanor.[13] But otherwise the usual number (twelve) is by the Constitution declared indispensable.[14]

The Verdict of the jury, by the Constitution of several States, must, except as below, be unanimous to convict.[15] But in others, a verdict of five-sixths, in misdemeanors,[16] or two-thirds,[17] suffices. So, in others, nine members of the jury may concur to render a verdict in cases not amounting to felony.[18] By the Constitution of Louisiana, the accused is given the right to challenge peremptorily

[1] Mass., N. H. In other States § 131 does not apply, probably, to cases of military law where allowable. See § 127.

[2] La. 116.

[3] Cal. 1, 7; Ida. 1, 17; Mon. 3, 23.

[4] N. M.* 1851, July 12, § 8; Va. 1, 8.

[5] Va.

[6] See § 73 for juries in civil suits, and § 131, note.

[7] Fla. 5, 38.

[8] Col. 2, 23; Io. 1, 9; Mich. 6, 28; La. 9; Mo. 2, 28; Mon.; Wash. 1, 21; Wy. 1, 9.

[9] Ky. 248; La. 9.; S. C. 5, 22; Mon.; Va. 1, 8.

[10] Mon. 3, 23; Tex. 5, 17; Okla. 1, 19.

[11] Va.

[12] Utah 1, 10.

[13] Cal. 1, 7; Ida.; Mon.

[14] Me. 1, 7; W. Va. 3, 14; Okla.

[15] Md. Decln. of Rts. 21; Me. 1, 7; N. C. 1, 13; Okla., S. C., Utah, Va. 8; Vt. 1, 10.

[16] Ida.

[17] Mon.

[18] Tex. 5, 13; Okla. In such cases the verdict must be in writing and signed by each member concurring.

a number of jurors to be fixed by statute.[1] In Oklahoma, the Constitution (7, 21) provides for a general verdict, though the court may direct a special finding.

The Constitution provides that in all criminal cases whatever [2] the jury shall have the right to determine the law and the facts;[3] but under the direction of the court, as to the law.[4]

§ 133. *Venue.*[5] The Constitutions of many States provide that the jury shall be of the county or district where the alleged offence was committed,[6] and this county, etc., shall have been previously ascertained by law.[7] So, criminal offences must be tried by a jury of the vicinage.[8]

Change of. In several, the power to change the venue is vested in the courts.[9] It is to be exercised in such manner as the legislature provide.[10] And for the same grounds, by State or defendant.[11]

In one, change of venue in criminal cases can only be directed by the legislature, on report of the judges of the Superior Court, in cases of insurrection.[12]

The Constitutions of a few States specially give to the legislature power to provide for change of venue.[13] So, the Constitution specifies that the legislature shall so provide in cases where an impartial trial cannot be had in the county where the crime was committed.[14]

The legislatures are frequently forbidden to enact special or local laws for the change of venue in civil or criminal cases.[15]

In Vermont and Oklahoma no person can be transported out of the State for any offence committed within it.[16]

§ 134. *Counsel.*[17] The Constitutions of all the States except

[1] La. 10.

[2] For libel, see § 61.

[3] Ind. 1, 19; La. 179; Md. 15, 5; Ore. 1, 16.

[4] La., Ore. And, subject to the right of new trial, as in civil cases (Ore.).

[5] By the reign of Henry VII. says Hallam, "the fact of guilt or innocence on a criminal charge was determined in a public court, and in the county where the offence occurred, by a jury of twelve men, from whose unanimous verdict no appeal could be made."

[6] Ala. 1, 6; Ark. 2, 10; Col. 2, 16; Fla. Decln. Rts. 11; Ill. 2, 9; Ind. 1, 13; Kan. Bill of Rts. 10; La. 9; Minn. 1, 6; Miss. 26; Mo. 2, 22; Mon. 3, 16; Neb. 1, 11; N. H. 1, 17; N. M.* 50, 7; O. 1, 10; Okla. 1, 20; Ore. 1, 11; S. D. 6, 7; Tenn. 1, 9; Utah 1, 12; Wash. 1, 22; W. Va. 3, 14; Wis. 1, 7; Wy. 1, 10.

[7] Minn., N. M.*, Wis.

[8] Ky. 11; Mass. 1, 13; Md. 1, 20; Me. 1, 6; Pa. 1, 9; Va. 1, 8.

[9] Ala. 75; Ariz.* 11, 285; Del. 1, 9; Md. 4, 8; Pa. 3, 23; W. Va. In civil or criminal cases. (Ala., Col., Ga., La., Pa., S. C., Tex.)

[10] Ala. 1, 6; Ark.; Col. 5, 37; Ga. 6, 17, 1; Mon.; Okla.; Pa.; Tex. 3, 45.

[11] Mon.

[12] N. H.

[13] Ky.; La. 169.

[14] S. C. 6, 2.

[15] See § 395.

[16] Vt. 1, 21; Okla. 2, 29. See § 141.

[17] This constitutional provision does

Virginia provide either that every person accused may defend by himself and counsel.[1] Or that he may have the assistance of counsel in his defence.[2] Or that he may be allowed counsel,[3] or may be heard by himself or counsel.[4] In several, the above principle, as particularized respectively, extends to any suitor in a court of law, civil or criminal.[5]

§ 135. *Witnesses.*[6] By the Constitutions of most of the States every person accused is entitled to enforce by compulsory process the attendance of witnesses [in his favor],[7] or to call for evidence on his behalf.[8]

not mean that defendant is entitled to have his counsel paid by the State, but it is usually so provided by statute. (McClain Constitutional Law, p. 327.) It does not appear that the right to have counsel is a constitutional right in England. At one time certainly, a defendant was not allowed counsel in cases of treason or felony. Counsel was, however, early allowed by express statutes in trials for treason, and doubtless this and other statutes made a precedent, and now it is required in all cases by 6 & 7 Wil. IV, chap. 114.

[1] Ala. 6; Ariz.* Bill of Rts. 14; Ark. 2, 10; Cal. 1, 13; Col. 2, 16; Ct. 1, 9; Del. 1, 7; Fla. Decln. of Rts. 11; Ga. 1, 1, 4; Ida. 1, 13; Ill. 2, 9; Ind. 1, 13; Ky. 11; Me. 1, 6; Mo. 2, 22; Mon. 3, 16; N. D. 13; Nev. 1, 8; N. H. 1, 15; N. M.* 95, 1; 1851, July 12, § 8; N. Y. 1, 6; O. 1, 10; Ore. 1, 11; Pa. 1, 9; R. I. 1, 10; S. C. 1, 18; S. D. 6, 7; Tenn. 1, 9; Tex. 1, 10; Utah 1, 12; Vt. 1, 10; Wash. 1, 22; Wis. 1, 7; Wy. 1, 10.

[2] Io. 1, 10; La. 9; Mich. 6, 28; Minn. 1, 6; N. C. 1, 11; N. J. 1, 8; W. Va. 3, 14. So in U. S. C. Amt. 6.

[3] Ga. 1, 1, 5; Md. Decln. of Rts. 21; N. C. 1, 11.

[4] Ala. 1, 10; Ariz.* 426; Kan. Bill of Rts. 10; Mass. 1, 12; Mich. 6, 24; Miss. 25, 26; Neb. 1, 11; Nev. 1, 8; N. M.* 50, 7; Okla. 1, 20; Wis. 7, 20.

[5] Fla., Ga., Mich., Miss., Nev., Wis.

[6] The word "witnesses" in the first clause will undoubtedly be extended by judicial construction to include the right to call for evidence, documentary or otherwise. The right to be confronted with witnesses was merely a matter of general common law procedure, hardly in England a constitutional right. Originally witnesses in England testified broadly to the fact, that is, whether the person charged was guilty or not, like a modern jury, or rather to his trustworthiness; this trial by "compurgation" being the alternative to trial by ordeal, which latter was usually employed only when there was strong proof of guilt, or when the accused was unable to procure a sufficient number of compurgators, or had been guilty of perjury on a previous occasion. These compurgators were thus in reality witnesses of character, and the oaths of different men varied in legal value according to their rank or property. Thus, the word of one thegn was as good as that of twelve churls. (Taswell-Langmead, p. 31.) Doubtless these original jury-witnesses gave place to modern witnesses under the jury trial. (Taylor, p. 325.) It does not appear that the right to compel witnesses is a constitutional right in England, but rather a matter of time-honored procedure. White says only since 1688 (p. 103).

[7] Ala. 6; Ark. 2, 10; Cal. 1, 13; Col. 2, 16; Ct. 1, 9; Del. 1, 7; Fla. Decln. Rts. 11; Ga. 1, 1, 5; Ida. 1, 13; Ill. 2, 9; Ind. 1, 13; Io. 1, 10; Kan. Bill of Rts. 10; Ky. 11; La. 9; Md. Decln. of Rts. 21; Me. 1, 6; Mich. 6, 28; Minn. 1, 6; Miss. 26; Mo. 2, 22; Mon. 3, 16; N. D. 13; Neb. 1, 11; N. J. 1, 8; N. M.* 50, 7; 95, 1; 1851, July 12, § 8; O. 1, 10; Okla. 1, 20; Ore. 1, 11; Pa. 1, 9; S. C. 1, 18; S. D. 6, 7; Tenn. 1, 9; Tex. 1, 10; Utah 1, 12; Vt. 1, 10; Wash. 1, 22; W. Va. 3, 14; Wis. 1, 7; Wy. 1, 10.

[8] Ariz.* 426; Mass. 1, 12; N. C. 1, 11; N. H. 1, 15; R. I. 1, 10; Va. 1, 8. So in U. S. C. Amt. 6.

In Maryland it is specially provided that the accused may examine all witnesses under oath. The legislature has power, in several States (except in cases of homicide: Cal.) to provide for the taking of depositions, in the presence of the person accused and his counsel, when there is reason to believe that the witness will not attend the trial.[1] But in most States the old rule prevails and the accused shall be confronted with the witnesses against him.[2] And may give evidence (testify) in his own behalf.[3]

In Oklahoma,[4] in capital cases, defendants must be furnished with a list of the witnesses that will be called in chief by the prosecution two days before the trial, with their post-office addresses.

§ 136. *Criminating Evidence.*[5] The Constitutions of most of the States provide that no person accused shall be compelled to give evidence against himself,[6] or to furnish evidence.[7] So, no person [whether accused or not, it seems] can be compelled to give evidence criminating himself in any court of law,[8] or in any criminal proceeding.[9]

"Any person having knowledge or possession of facts that tend to establish the guilt of any other person or corporation charged with an offense against the laws of the State, shall not be excused

[1] Cal., Col., Mon., Wy. See § 124.

[2] Ala., Ariz.*, Ark., Col., Ct., Del., Fla., Ga., Ill., Ind., Io , Kan., Ky., La., Mass., Md., Me., Mich., Minn., Miss., Mo., Mon., N. C., Neb., N. H., N. J., N. M.* 50, 7; 95, 1; 1851, July 12, § 8; O., Okla., Ore., Pa., R. I., S. C., S. D., 6, 7; Tenn., Tex., Utah, Va., Vt., Wash., W. Va., Wis., Wy. So in U. S. C. Amt. 6.

[3] Ala., Utah, Wash.

[4] Okla. 2, 20. See also § 120.

[5] The word "subject," oddly enough, is retained in some States (Mass., N. H.). The provision is unfortunately ambiguous; does "testify" include furnishing documentary evidence? This came up in the Chicago beef-trust cases and was decided in the affirmative. — This is also not a constitutional right in England, but a rule of common law procedure. (McClain, p. 320.) It applies, however, to all cases, whether civil or criminal, and to all persons, whether "accused" at the time or not; and to the production of books or papers as well as oral testimony. Hence a statute compelling such testimony will be unconstitutional unless it guaranties full immunity from prosecution for any offences so revealed; and testimony actually given under compulsion cannot be used against them.

[6] Ala. 6; Ariz.* Bill of Rts. 14; Ark. 2, 8; Cal. 1, 13; Col. 2, 18; Ct. 1, 9; Del. 1, 7; Fla. Decln. of Rts. 12; Ill. 2, 10; Ind. 1, 14; Kan. Bill of Rts. 10; Ky. 11; La. 11; Mass. 1, 12; Md. Decln. of Rts. 22; Me. 1, 6; Mich. 6, 32; Minn. 1, 7; Miss. 26; Mo. 2, 23; N. C. 1, 11; Neb. 1, 12; Nev. 1, 8; N. H. 1, 15; N. M.* 95, 1; 1851, July 12, § 8; N. Y. 1, 6; O. 1, 10; Ore. 1, 12; Pa. 1, 9; S. C. 1, 17; Tenn. 1, 9; Tex. 1, 10; Va. 1, 8; Vt. 1, 10; W. Va. 3, 5; Wis. 1, 8.

[7] Ga. 1, 1, 6; Mass.; N. H.; R. I. 1, 13; Okla. 1, 21; Va.

[8] Ida. 1, 13; La.; Minn. Amt. 1903, 269; Mon. 3, 18; N. D. 13; S. C. 1, 17; S. D. 6, 9; Utah 1, 12; Va. 1, 8; Wash. 1, 9; Wy. 1, 11. This is the wording in the Federal Constitution; U. S. C. Amt. 5.

from giving testimony or producing evidence, when legally called upon so to do, on the ground that it may tend to incriminate him under the laws of the State; but no person shall be prosecuted or subjected to any penalty or forfeiture for or on account of any transaction, matter, or thing concerning which he may so testify or produce evidence." Okla. 27.

"The records, books, and files of all corporations shall be, at all times, liable and subject to the full visitorial and inquisitorial powers of the State, notwithstanding the immunities and privileges in this Bill of Rights secured to the persons, inhabitants, and citizens thereof." Okla. 28.

In one State, by the Constitution, husband or wife may not in criminal prosecutions be compelled to testify against one another.[1]

§ 137. *Twice in Jeopardy.*[2] In most States the general provision is found that no person, for the same offence can be twice put in jeopardy,[3] in jeopardy of life or limb,[4] in jeopardy of life or liberty,[5] or in jeopardy of punishment.[6]

But it is provided that the accused shall not be deemed to have been in jeopardy if the jury disagree, or the judgment be reversed for error.[7]

But in several the provision is that no person shall, after an

[1] Utah 1, 12. This is the common law.

[2] See also § 668. The phrase "twice in jeopardy" may be defined to be the being confronted with a petit jury when charged with an offence, though the law varies somewhat in different States. In about half the States, the government has the right to appeal in case of mistrial; that is, for error of law, and in all States the accused can be tried again if the jury disagree. It is usually, however, the custom not to try a man more than twice, and thereafter he is released upon bail. President Roosevelt has had introduced a bill giving the government the right of appeal in Federal courts. It might possibly not be constitutional under the 5th Amendment, though the better opinion is to the contrary. The principle probably dates back to the time of the Bill of Rights, though not expressly included therein. The *Habeas Corpus* Act provided that a person once discharged could not be re-arrested for the same offence, which is a somewhat similar principle. The word "limb" in the provision is, of course, obsolete, as all punishments but death and imprisonment have ceased in all States, except, indeed, the whipping-post in Delaware.

[3] Ariz.* Bill of Rts. 14; Cal. 1, 13; Col. 2, 18; Fla. Decln. of Rts. 12; Ida. 1, 13; Ill. 2, 10; Ind. 1, 14; Kan. Bill of Rts. 10; Mon. 3, 18; N. D. 13; Neb. 1, 12; Nev. 1, 8; N. Y. 1, 6; O. 1, 10; Ore. 1, 12; S. D. 6, 9; Utah 1, 12; Va. 1, 8; Wash. 1, 9; Wy. 1, 11.

[4] Ala, 9; Del. 1, 8; Ky. 13; Me. 1, 8; N. M.* 1851, July 12, § 12; Pa. 1, 10; Tenn. 1, 10. So in the U. S. C. Amt. 5. This limits it to capital cases.

[5] Ark. 2, 8; Ga. 1, 1, 8; La. 9; S. C. 1, 17; Tex. 1, 14; Va. 88; W. Va. 3, 5; Okla. 1, 21.

[6] Minn. 1, 7; Miss. 22; Mon.; N. D.; Wis. 1, 8.

[7] Col., Wy.

acquittal, be tried for the same offence,[1] or have his life or liberty again put in jeopardy for the same offence.[2]

But in three, it is specified that such acquittal must be upon the merits.[3] And in Texas, it must be in a court of competent jurisdiction.

Exceptions. But the person may be tried again on his own motion, after conviction.[4] So, in case of mistrial,[5] or if a motion in arrest of judgment is sustained,[6] or, if the jury disagree.[7] Courts may, for reasons fixed by law, discharge the jury and empanel a new one.[8] An appeal is allowed to the State in revenue cases, but not in any case involving the life or liberty of any person.[9]

§ 138. *Attainder.*[10] Most States have a general constitutional provision that the legislature shall pass no bill of attainder,[11] or, that no person can be attainted of treason or felony by the legislature.[12] So, in one, of treason alone.[13]

§ 139. *Miscellaneous.* The Constitutions of two States forbid the issue of commissions of oyer and terminer and gaol delivery.[14] By that of Nebraska the writ of error is declared a writ of right in

[1] Ariz.* 427; Io. 1, 12; Mich. 6, 29; N. H. 1, 16; N. J. 1, 10; N. M.* 50, 9; 95, 1; R. I. 1, 7; Tex.; Okla.

[2] Mo. 2, 23.

[3] Mich., Miss., N. M.*

[4] Ga., La.

[5] Ga., La., Mo.

[6] La.

[7] Ark., Col., Mo., Wy.

[8] Ala.

[9] Va. 88.

[10] Bills of attainder were the usual method by which arbitrary kings or parliaments evaded the right to law described in §§ 70, 131. They could only be passed by Parliament, not by the Crown, but were used by the Stuart kings particularly as a method of getting rid of objectionable subjects. In effect, of course, they were a trial and conviction without hearing, witnesses, jury, or other process of law, — by mere legislative act, and commonly involved both death and forfeiture of property. Impeachment differed from attainder principally in that it was found by the Commons and tried by the laws and applied only to a political personage. Thomas Cromwell in the name of Henry VIII. got a decision from the judges that a bill of attainder would be valid although it condemned a man to death for treason without a hearing, and himself perished by the same act of attainder that he had procured. There is no such thing as an executive attainder; for this reason President Roosevelt's order that the negro soldiers in Texas should be both discharged and forever precluded from holding any civil office was unconstitutional in its latter part.

[11] Ala. 14; Ariz.* Bill of Rts. 19; Ark. 2, 17; Cal. 1, 16; Fla. Decln. of Rts. 17; Ga. 1, 3, 2; Ida. 1, 16; Io. 1, 21; Me. 1, 11; Mich. 4, 43; Minn. 1, 11; N. D. 16; Neb. 1, 16; Nev. 1, 15; N. J. 4, 7, 3; N. M.* 1851, July 12, § 14; Okla. 2, 15; S. C. 1, 8; Tex. 1, 16; Utah 1, 18; Va. 58; Wash. 1, 23; W. Va. 3, 4; Wis. 1, 12. Compare U. S. 1, 9, 10, forbidding such bills both to States and the nation. See also § 142. This might be implied in other States from § 127.

[12] Col. 2, 9; Ct. 1, 15; Ky. 20; Mass. 1, 25; Md. Decln. of Rts. 18; Mo. 2, 13; Mon. 3, 9; Pa. 1, 18; S. D. 6, 22; Vt. 2, 20.

[13] Ala. 1, 19.

[14] Del. 1, 14; Pa. 1, 15.

all cases of felony.[1] So, in Wisconsin, the writ shall never be prohibited by law.[2] In Kentucky, the legislature are authorized to pass laws regulating writs of error in criminal or penal cases.[3] And also, laws regulating the right of challenge of jurors therein.

Article 14. Rights after Trial

§ 140. *Fines and Costs.*[4] The Constitutions of nearly all states provide that excessive fines shall not be imposed nor, except in Connecticut and Vermont, cruel or unusual punishments be inflicted.[5] Nor, in one, excessive costs.[6]

No person shall be compelled to pay costs except after conviction on final trial.[7] In Texas the legislature may by law require fines and costs in prosecutions for misdemeanors to be discharged by manual labor in default of payment.[8]

So, all punishments and penalties should be proportioned to the offence.[9] "Indefinite imprisonment" is forbidden.[10] And in six, reformation, not vindictive justice, is declared to be the principle of the penal code.[11] Further, it is specially declared that sanguinary

[1] Neb. 1, 23.

[2] Wis. 1, 21.

[3] Ky. 2, 39; La. 10.

[4] Copied from U. S. Amt. 8. This principle goes back to Magna Carta, Cap. 20. "A freeman shall only be amerced . . . after the manner of the offence . . . according to the heinousness of it," but the fines referred to in Magna Carta were assessed by the oath of "honest men of the neighbourhood." The constitutional provision refers only to fines imposed in courts of law or by statute. The exact provision is found in the Bill of Rights, paragraph 10, and on this our provision is based, it being a favorite use of the Stuart kings. "Cruel and unusual punishments" were also forbidden by the Bill of Rights; this is a provision aimed at torturing, maiming, and banishment. No punishment remains in any of the States except death and imprisonment with the exception of the whipping post in Delaware; but no mode of putting condemned persons to death under a criminal statute is "cruel or unusual" under the court decisions.

[5] Ala. 15; Ariz.* Bill of Rts. 10; Ark. 2, 9; Cal. 1, 6; Col. 2, 20; Ct. 1, 13; Del. 1, 11; Fla. Decln. of Rts. 8; Ga. 1, 1, 9; Ida. 1, 6; Ind. 1, 16; Io. 1, 17; Kan. Bill of Rts. 9; Ky. 17; La. 12; Mass. 1, 26; Md. Decln. of Rts. 25; Me. 1, 9; Mich. 6, 31; Minn. 1, 5; Miss. 28; Mo. 2, 25; Mon. 3, 20; N. C. 1, 14; N. D. 6; Neb. 1, 9; Nev. 1, 6; N. H. 1, 33; N. J. 1, 15; N. M.* 95, 1; 1851, July 12, § 11; N. Y. 1, 5; O. 1, 9; Okla. 2, 9; Ore. 1, 16; Pa. 1, 13; R. I. 1, 8; S. C. 1, 19; S. D. 6, 23; Tenn. 1, 16; Tex. 1, 13; Utah 1, 9; Va. 1, 9; Vt. 2, 32; Wash. 1, 14; W. Va. 3, 5; Wis. 1, 6; Wy. 1, 14.

The clause about punishment is omitted in a few. (Ct., Vt.)

[6] N. C.

[7] Fla. Decln. Rts. 14; Ga. 1, 1, 10; N. C. 1, 11.

[8] Tex. 16, 3.

[9] Ill. 2, 11; Ind.; Me.; N. H. 1, 18; Neb. 1, 15; Ore.; R. I.; W. Va.

[10] Fla.

[11] Ind. 1, 18; Mon. 3, 24; N. C. 11, 2; N. H.; Ore. 1, 15; Wy. 1, 15.

laws shall not be passed.[1] But the death penalty is in Montana expressly preserved. In all criminal cases when the defendant is insolvent or discharged, the legal costs and expenses, including officers' fees, must be paid by the counties.[2]

That whipping or corporal punishments shall not, in two, be inflicted.[3] No mechanical trade shall be taught to convicts in the State prison, except the manufacture of those articles of which the chief supply for home consumption is imported from other States.[4] But in others, provision is made by the Constitution for punishment by hard labor.[5] In several, the Constitution forbids the letting out of convict labor by contract.[6] In New York, also, the product or profit may not be sold, but may be used by the State or in public institutions.

No citizen shall be outlawed.[7] Banishment from the State or transportation shall not be allowed as a punishment for crime.[8]

The gaols shall be constructed with regard to the health of the prisoners.[9] So, the erection of secure and comfortable prisons, and the humane treatment of prisoners, shall be provided for.[10]

In North Carolina, the Constitution provides that death, imprisonment, fines, removal from office, and disqualification for office, shall be the only punishments known to the laws; convict labor may be employed on public works, or farmed out; but no convict sentenced for murder, manslaughter, rape, or arson shall be farmed out; murder, arson, burglary, and rape may be made punishable by death.[11] In Vermont, punishment for crimes not capital should be by hard labor.[12] Sentence of labor on the highways or public works may be imposed.[13] And convicts may be hired out under State supervision.[14] Michigan makes provision in the Constitution for indeterminate sentences and release of prisoners on parole.[15]

[1] Md. Decln. of Rts. 16; Me.; N. H.

[2] Fla. 16, 9; Amt. 1894.

[3] Ga. 1, 1, 7; S. C. 1, 19.

[4] Mich. 18, 3.

[5] Cal. 10, 6; Ky. 153; N. C. 11, 1; Vt. 2, 37.

[6] Cal.; Ky.; Mon. 18, 2; N. Y. 3, 29; Wash. 2, 29.

[7] Tex. 1, 20.

[8] Ala. 1, 30; Ark. 2, 21; Ga. 1, 1, 7; Ill.; Kan. Bill of Rts. 21; Neb.; O. 1, 12; Tex.; W. Va.; Vt. 1, 21.

"No person shall be transported out of the State for any offence committed within the State, nor shall any person be transported out of the State for any purpose, without his consent, except by due process of law; but nothing in this provision shall prevent the operation of extradition laws, or the transporting of persons sentenced for crime to other States for the purpose of incarceration." Okla. 2, 29.

[9] Del.

[10] Tenn. 1, 32; Wy. 1, 16. See § 124.

[11] N. C. 11, 12.

[12] Vt. 2, 37.

[13] S. C. 5, 33; 12, 6.

[14] S. C. 12, 9.

[15] Mich. 1901, p. 391.

For contempt, see § 668.

§ 141. *Ex Post Facto Laws.*[1] These are, in most of the States, forbidden by the Constitution.[2] So, "no person can be punished but by virtue of a law already established or promulgated prior to the offence."[3] Conversely the repeal or amendment of any criminal statute shall not affect the prosecution or punishment of any crime committed before such repeal or amendment.[4]

§ 142. *Corruption of Blood.*[5] The Constitutions of most States provide that no conviction shall work corruption of blood or forfeiture of estate.[6] But in three, it seems that there may be forfeiture of estate during the life of the offender.[7]

§ 143. *Suicides.* The Constitution declares that the estates of suicides are not forfeit.[8] Such estates descend as in cases of natural death.[9]

§ 144. *Deodands* are in seven States abolished by the Constitution.[10]

[1] The words *ex post facto* are here used as the equivalent of *retroactive* and *retrospective;* and the law is here applied only to *criminal* offences. For civil laws of a similar nature, see §§ 392, 393, Laws impairing the obligations of contracts. The provision against *ex post facto* laws does not expressly appear in the English Bill of Rights, though it was a familiar abuse under the Stuart kings. *Ex post facto* has been decided by the U. S. Supreme Court to refer only to criminal statutes whereby a man is punished for an offence under a law passed after the offence was committed. They are forbidden by the U. S. Constitution, Art. 1, Sec. 9, Clause 3, to the United States, and by Sec. 10, Clause 1, to the States, in the Federal Constitution.

[2] Ala. 22; Ariz.* Bill of Rts. 19; Ark. 2, 17; Cal. 1, 16; Col. 2, 11; Fla. Decln. of Rts. 17; Ga. 1, 3, 2; Ida. 1, 16; Ill. 2, 14; Ind. 1, 24; Io. 1, 21; Ky. 19; La. 166; Mass. 1, 24; Md. Decln. of Rts. 17; Me. 1, 11; Mich. 4, 43; Minn. 1, 11; Miss. 16; Mo. 2, 15; Mon. 3, 11; N. C. 1, 32; N. D. 16; Neb. 1, 16; Nev. 1, 15; N. H. 1, 23; N. J. 4, 7, 3; N. M.* 1851, July 12, § 14; O. 2, 28; Okla. 2, 15; Ore. 1, 21; Pa. 1, 17; R. I. 1, 12; S. C. 1, 8; S. D. 6, 12; Tenn. 1, 11; Tex. 1, 16; Utah 1, 18; Va. 58; Wash. 1, 23; W. Va. 3, 4; Wis. 1, 12; Wy. 1, 35. So, both as to States and nation, in U. S. C. 1, 9 (4); 1, 10 (1).

[3] Ala. 7.

[4] Fla. 3, 32.

[5] Compare U. S. C. 3, 3. The attempt to enact a statute working corruption of blood would probably be held unconstitutional in all the States as part of the unwritten Constitution. This, and the following two sections are probably, therefore, unnecessary.

[6] Ala. 19; Ark. 2, 17; Col. 2, 9; Ct. 9, 4; Del. 1, 15; Fla. Decln. Rts. 23; Ga. 1, 2, 3; Ida. 5, 5 (the clause is clumsily worded, so as to apply only to treason or "attainder"); Ill. 2, 11; Ind. 1, 30; Kan. Bill of Rts. 12; Ky. 20; Md. Decln. of Rts. 27; Me. 1, 11; Minn. 1, 11; Mo. 2, 13; Mon. 3, 9; N. C. 4, 5; Neb. 1, 15; O. 1, 12; Okla. 2, 15; Ore. 1, 25; Pa. 1, 19; S. C. 1, 8; Tenn. 1, 12; Tex. 1, 21; Wash. 1, 15; W. Va. 3, 18; Wis. 1, 12.

[7] Del., Ky., Pa.

[8] N. H. 2, 88; Pa. 1, 19; Vt. 2, 38.

[9] Col. 2, 9; Del. 1, 15; Ky. 21; Mo. 2, 13; Mon. 3, 9; N. H.; Pa.; Tenn. 1, 12; Tex. 1, 21; Vt.

[10] Del. 1, 15; Ky. 21; Mo. 2, 13; N. H. 2, 88; Pa. 1, 19; Tenn. 1, 12; Vt. 2, 38.

§ 145. *Appeals.*[1] By the Constitution of Texas and Virginia the State has no right of appeal in criminal cases,[2] but the defendant has.[3]

§ 146. *Fees and Costs.*[4] No accused person before final judgment shall be compelled to advance money or fees to secure the rights herein guaranteed.[5]

Article 15. Special Provisions Concerning Criminal Offences

§ 150. *Treason*[6] is by the Constitutions of most of the States declared to consist only in levying war against the State, adhering to its enemies, and giving them aid and comfort; there must be two witnesses to the same overt act, in order to convict, or a confession in open court.[7]

§ 151. *Duelling.* By the Constitutions of many States duelling is made a cause of disfranchisement and disqualification to hold office.[8] And in five, it is made, by the Constitution, a criminal offence.[9]

The governor may pardon it after five years.[10]

[1] See Art. 70, and § 137.

[2] Tex. 5, 26; Va. 88. See § 137.

[3] Utah 1, 12; Wash. 1, 22.

[4] This is a new provision although in the Bill of Rights, threats and promises of fines and forfeitures of particular persons before conviction are declared illegal and void.

[5] Utah 1, 12; Wash. 1, 22. See § 140.

[6] Copied from U. S. C. 3, 3. This is also an English constitutional principle, though forfeiture for treason was only abolished under Victoria. The principle requiring two witnesses is as old as Edward VI. and they were required to be confronted with the person charged, although this statute was evaded or disregarded under Queen Elizabeth and the Stuarts. (Taswell-Langmead, p. 308.) In England, of course, treason might and usually did rather consist in words or writings than in acts.

"Imagining the Kings' death" was treason in England, but the better law was that the imagination must be attended with the intent or purpose as manifested by some overt act. Still, the mental act constituted a treason, not the physical one. Thus, the regicides were tried not for beheading King Charles, but for compassing his death, of which the killing was only evidence.

[7] Ala. 18; Ark. 2, 14; Cal. 1, 20; Col. 2, 9; Ct. 9, 4; Del. 6, 3; Fla. Decln. of Rts. 23; Ga. 1, 2, 2; Ida. 5, 5; Ind. 1, 28–29; Io. 1, 16; Kan. Bill of Rts. 13; Ky. 229; La. 162; Me. 1, 12; Mich. 6, 30; Minn. 1, 9; Miss. 10; Mo. 2, 13; Mon. 3, 9; N. C. 4, 5; N. D. 19; Neb. 1, 14; Nev. 1, 19; N. J. 1, 14; Okla. 1, 16; Ore. 1, 24; S. C. 1, 22; S. D. 6, 25; Tex. 1, 22; Utah 1, 19; Wash. 1, 27; W. Va. 2, 6; Wis. 1, 10; Wy. 1, 26.

[8] See §§ 223, 254, 257. It will be noticed that this statute is peculiar to the Southern States.

[9] Ala. 86; Ark. 19, 2; Ga. 2, 4, 2; Ky. 239; Tenn. 9, 3.

[10] Ky. See § 160.

§ 152. *Bribery*[1] of an office-holder, whether accomplished or attempted, is made a felony[2] in the person giving or offering the bribe, by the Constitution of several States.[3] And usually also in the office-holder receiving or offering to receive the bribe.[4] So, of a member of the legislature bribed,[5] or offering or seeking to bribe.[6]

Bribery at elections is, by the Constitution of several States, made a criminal offence in both parties.[7] So, fraud, or other wilful and corrupt violation of election laws.[8] "Any person who shall directly or indirectly offer, give or promise any money or thing of value, testimonial, privilege or personal advantage, to any executive or judicial officer or member of the Legislative Assembly, to influence him in the performance of any of his official or public duties, shall be deemed guilty of bribery, and be punished in such manner as shall be provided by law."[9]

And in many States bribery is cause of disfranchisement or disqualification for office.[10]

§ 153. *Lobbying* is declared a felony by the Constitution in two States.[11] So, no State or county officer shall accept a fee, reward, etc., for lobbying.[12] Lobbying is in California defined to be the seeking to influence the vote of a member of the legislature by bribery, promise of reward, intimidation, or other dishonest means.

§ 154. *Corrupt Legislation.* No State officer or member of the legislature shall directly or indirectly receive a fee or be engaged as

[1] See § 154. The tendency of modern statutes is to make bribery a felony in both the person giving and the person offering the bribe, and more elaborate statutes are being devised to cover all cases of political corruption by influence or otherwise.

[2] A penal offence or a misdemeanor only (La.).

[3] Ark. 5, 35; Col. 5, 41 and 42; Del. 2, 22; La. 183; Md. 3, 50; N. Y. 13, 2 and 3; Pa. 3, 30; Tex. 16, 41; W. Va. 6, 45.

[4] Ark., La., Md., Nev., N. Y., Tex., W. Va.

[5] Cal. 4, 35; Col. 12, 6; La.; Md.; N. Y.; Pa. 3, 29–31; Tex.; W. Va.

[6] Ala.

[7] Ark. 3, 6; Del. 5, 7; Fla. 4, 9; La.; Nev. 4, 10; Tenn. 10, 3.

[8] Ark.

[9] Mon. 5, 42; Pa.; S. D. 3, 23; Wy. 3, 43. So, a member of the legislature who shall solicit, demand, or receive, or consent to receive, directly or indirectly, for himself or for another, from any company, association, or person, any money, office, appointment, employment, or personal advantage for his vote or influence or withholding the same, or with the understanding that his vote, etc., shall be in any way influenced thereby, or who shall solicit or demand such money or other advantage for another, or give or withhold his vote in consideration thereof, is guilty of bribery and shall incur the disabilities and penalties provided in the Constitution for such offence, and such additional punishment as may be provided by law. And so, any person who shall directly or indirectly offer such money (Ala. 79, 80; Pa.).

[10] See §§ 223, 255.

[11] Cal. 4, 35; Ga. 1, 2, 5.

[12] Ala. 101. See also § 154.

counsel, agent, or attorney in the prosecution of any claim against the State,[1] or in advocating any bill or measure.[2] Upon due proof thereof he shall forfeit his seat.[3]

So, the offence of corrupt solicitation of members of the Legislative Assembly, or of public officers of the State, or of any municipal division thereof, and the occupation or practice of solicitation of such members or officers, to influence their official action, shall be defined by law, and shall be punishable by fine and imprisonment.[4]

Any governor of this State who asks, receives, or agrees to receive any bribe upon any understanding that his official opinion, judgment, or action shall be influenced thereby, or who gives or offers, or promises his official influence in consideration that any member of the legislative assembly shall give his official vote or influence on any particular side of any question or matter upon which he may be required to act in his official capacity, or who menaces any member by the threatened use of his veto power, or who offers or promises any member that he, the said governor, will appoint any particular person or persons to any office created or thereafter to be created, in consideration that any member shall give his official vote or influence on any matter pending or thereafter to be introduced into either house of said legislative assembly, or who threatens any member that he, the said governor, will remove any person or persons from office or position, with intent in any manner to influence the action of said member, shall be punished in the manner now, or that may hereafter be, provided by law, and upon conviction thereof shall forfeit all right to hold or exercise any office of trust or honor in this State.[5]

No member of the legislature can be interested directly or indirectly in any contract with the State or a county thereof authorized by a law passed during his term,[6] or within one year thereafter.[7]

The governor is forbidden to receive any compensation or promise thereof for any service rendered or performed while governor, or to be rendered thereafter.[8]

"Any member of the legislature who shall give, offer, or promise

[1] Ore. 15, 7; R. I. 4, 4; Vt. 2, 19.
[2] N. H. 2, 7; Vt.
[3] N. H.
[4] Ala. 81; Mon. 5, 43; S. D. 3, 28; Wash. 2, 30; Wy. 3, 45; Pa. 3, 31.
[5] N. D. 3, 81; S. D. 4, 11; Wy. 4, 10.
[6] Ill. 4, 15; Mich. 4, 18; Miss. 109; Neb. 3, 12; S. D. 3, 12; Tex. 3, 18; W. Va. 6, 15. Compare also § 303.
[7] Ill., Mich., Miss., Neb., S. D.
[8] Tex. 4, 6.

his vote in favor of or against any measure, in consideration that any other member shall give or promise his vote on another measure, shall be guilty of solicitation of bribery, or bribery [if the thing be accomplished]; and such member shall be expelled, and not thereafter be eligible for the legislature, and be liable to such further penalty as may be prescribed by law." [1]

Evidence. By the Constitutions of several, any person may be compelled to testify in any investigation or proceeding to establish bribery or lobbying offences under these three sections; but such testimony cannot be afterwards used against him, except to prove perjury.[2] And the person so testifying is exempted from punishment for his own offence.[3] He may also testify in his own behalf.[4]

§ 155. *Special Crimes.* The Constitution of Texas provides that the legislature shall provide by law for defining and punishing barratry.[5]

Gambling is by the Constitution of Louisiana declared to be a vice, and laws shall be passed to suppress it.[6]

Prize fighting is forbidden.[7]

Polygamy and bigamy are made crimes in the Constitution.[8]

§ 156. *Embezzlement* of public funds or defalcation in public office or trust is, in some, declared a felony by the Constitution.[9] So, misappropriation of the State or school funds.[10] It is a penal offence to borrow, or divert from its purpose, any State fund.[11] Or for a public officer to make a profit out of public money, or to use it for any purpose not authorized by law.[12]

[1] Col. 5, 40; Mon. 5, 41; N. D. 40; Wy. 3, 42.

[2] Cal.; La. 174; Md. 3, 50; N. Y. 13, 3; Pa. 3, 32; S. D. 3, 28; Wash. 2, 30; W. Va. 6, 45; Wy. 3, 44. See also § 239.

[3] Md., W. Va.

[4] N. Y. 13, 4.

[5] Tex. 16, 29. See I. Taylor, 567, for the origin of this offence.

[6] La. 188. See § 426.

[7] S. C. 8, 12.

[8] Ida. 1, 4. See also § 41. The enabling acts admitting the eight new Western States usually provided against polygamy on account of the Mormon influence, and this, with other provisions concerning schools, etc., was made forever irrepealable without the consent of the United States; see Utah 3, 1. This is probably only a moral obligation; a State when once admitted comes in with all the rights of the older States. So far as this section is concerned, Utah could probably amend her Constitution and re-establish Mormonism to-morrow.

[9] Cal. 4, 21; Ida. 18, 2; Amt. Nev. 4, 10; S. C. 10, 12.

[10] Minn. 9, 12.

[11] Tex. 8, 7. The notion that an appropriation could be limited to any definite object was only established in England as late as Charles II. The use of public funds for other purposes than they were originally raised for, although probably contrary to Magna Carta itself, is usual in other countries, so much so that it has been given a special name, *virement*, in France. See Art. 32.

[12] Ark. 16, 3; Cal. 11, 17; Col. 10,

§ 157. *War Exemption.* By the Constitutions of two States, no person shall be prosecuted in any civil or criminal action for any act done by him during the war of secession under orders, or in pursuance of military authority vested in him by the United States, the Confederate States, or the State.[1] The Florida provision is omitted in the new Constitution.

§ 158. *Felony.* The Constitution of Colorado defines felony to mean any criminal offence punishable with death or imprisonment in the penitentiary.[2]

Article 16. Pardons

§ 160. *Pardon Power.*[3] By the Constitution of most States, the governor has power to grant pardons and commutations[4] of sentence after conviction.[5] And so in all the territories, by U.S.R.S. 1841.

In some, the governor may grant pardons as above only by and with the advice of the Council,[6] or Senate,[7] or Board of Pardons.[8]

13; Ga. 5, 2, 5; 7, 9, 1; Ida. 7, 10; Ky. 173; Mo. 10, 17; Mon. 12, 14; Okla. 10, 11; Pa. 9, 14; S. D. 11, 11; Utah 13, 8; Wash. 11, 14; Wy. 11, 14; 15, 8.

[1] Mo. 14, 2; W. Va. 8, 35. The 14th Amendment inferentially terms rebellion a crime. Presumably a Confederate soldier or officer would be liable for acts committed during the Revolution, even if acts of war,—civilly, if not criminally; but there are hardly any instances of such suits being brought, though there are one or two cases where damages have been recovered for acts improperly committed, such as seizures of goods not contraband, or forfeiture of property without due process of law. The statutes and court decisions of the States in rebellion, except in so far as they concern such political matters, have been declared valid by the U. S. Supreme Court.

[2] Col. 18, 4. And the word is always so used in this book. This is a proper definition, at least in the United States; there being no longer any forfeiture or corruption of blood.

[3] Compare U. S. C. 2, 2. The pardon power is not inherent in the executive, like the power to punish for contempts in the judiciary, but it may be questioned whether it would not be exerted even in the absence of a statute. All the States have such statutes, however, and the tendency is more and more to relieve the Executive of the responsibility by creating boards of pardons. The granting of pardons before conviction became an abuse under the Stuarts.

[4] Nothing is said about commutations of sentence (Kan., Mass., Md., Minn., Miss., Neb., N. H., N. J., R. I., Tenn., Vt.) "Under the regulations and restrictions prescribed by law:" (N. Y., O., Ind., Ill., Mich., Wis., Io., Kan., Va., Neb., Del., N. C., Mo., Ark., Cal., Ore., Col., Ga., Ala., N. D., S. D., Wy.)

[5] Ala. 124; Ariz.* 1093; Ark. 6, 18; Cal. 7, 1; Col. 4, 7; Ga. 5, 1, 12; Ill. 5, 13; Ind. 5. 17; Io. 4, 16; Kan. 1, 7; Ky. 77; Md. 2, 20; Mich. 5, 11; Minn. 5, 4; Miss. 124; Mo. 5, 8; N. C. 3, 6; N. D. 76; Neb. 5, 13; N. Y. 77; O. 3, 11; Okla. 6, 10; Ore. 5, 14; S. C. 4, 11; S. D. 4, 5; Tenn. 3, 6; Tex. 4, 11; Va. 73; Vt. 2, 11; Amt. 8; Wash. 3, 9; W. Va. 7, 11; Wis. 5, 6; Wy. 4, 5.

[6] Mass. 2, 2, 1, 8; Me. 5, 1, 11; N. H. 2, 51.

[7] R. I. C. Amt. 2.

[8] Fla. 1895, p. 366, Del. 7, 1; Minn. 1895, 2; S. D. 4, 5; N. J. 5, 10; S. C.

Power to pardon, as above, is, in others, vested in the governor, judges of the Supreme Court, and attorney-general, or a majority of them, of which the governor must be one.[1] Governor, secretary of state, and attorney-general.[2] Governor, secretary of state commissioner of agriculture, controller, attorney-general.[3] Governor, secretary of state, attorney-general and auditor.[4] Presiding judge, secretary of state, and attorney-general.[5] Governor, chief justice, and attorney-general.[6]

In other States, pardons are issued by the governor, upon written recommendation of the lieutenant-governor, secretary of state, secretary of internal affairs, and attorney-general, or any three of them,[7] or a majority of the board,[8] as above,[9] the lieutenant-governor, secretary of state, and presiding judge,[10] or the attorney-general, chief justice, and two electors appointed by the governor.[11]

The Board of Pardons must sit in open session, give published notice of hearings, and record all pardons, etc.; and communicate them to the legislature at each session.[12]

Exceptions. But in California a person twice convicted of felony cannot be so pardoned by the governor without the written recommendation of a majority of the judges of the Supreme Court. And in Kentucky, a person who has participated in a duel may be pardoned only after the expiration of five years from the offence.[13] Restoration to franchise is by a two-thirds vote of the legislature.[14]

§ 161. *What may be pardoned.* In most States all offences may be pardoned, according to § 160, except treason and in cases of impeachment.[15] Or except only in cases of impeachment.[16] Or except only treason.[17] In Vermont, except also murder.

But in some States, no exception is made of either treason or impeachment.[18]

[1] Nev. 5, 14; Utah 7, 12.
[2] Ida. 4, 7.
[3] Fla.
[4] Mon. 7, 9; Ala. 124.
[5] S. D.
[6] Minn.
[7] Pa. 4, 9.
[8] Mon., S. D.
[9] Except minor crimes, S. D.
[10] La. 69.
[11] N. D. Amt. 3.
[12] Ida., Mon., N. D., S. D., Utah, Wy.
[13] Ky. 239.
[14] Miss. 253.
[15] Ark., Cal., Col., Fla., Ga., Ida., Ind., Io., La., Md., Mich., Miss., Mo., N. D., Neb., Nev., N. Y., O., S. D., Tex., Utah, Vt., Wis., Wy. The President of the United States is authorized to pardon even treason (U. S. C. 2, 2, 2), but not impeachment, and this is probably a constitutional principle in England. There can, of course be treason to a State as well as to the United States.
[16] Ala., Del., Ky., Mass., Md., Me., Minn., N. C., N. H., N. J. Okla., Pa., R. I., S. C., Tenn., Va., W. Va.
[17] Ore.
[18] Ct., Ill., Kan.

Treason may, in many States, be pardoned by the legislature; and the governor may suspend the sentence until the end of the session of the legislature next following conviction.[1] So, in two more, except that this power to pardon is vested in the Senate.[2]

§ 162. *The Effect of a Pardon.* In Alabama it does not relieve from civil or political disability unless so specifically expressed in the pardon. But in South Carolina pardon by the governor restores the right of suffrage.[3] In Connecticut, the legislature, by a two-thirds vote of each full house, may restore the privileges of an elector to a person convicted of crime.[4] Or embezzlement.[5]

In two, the governor may remove political disabilities consequent on conviction,[6] or that of holding office (as to duelling only).[7]

§ 163. *Reprieves.* By the Constitutions of most States, the governor is expressly given power to grant reprieves in the same cases (§ 161),[8] but not for more than sixty days.[9] The governor may grant reprieves, after conviction, except in cases of impeachment, until the end of the next session of the legislature.[10] So the Board of Pardons.[11]

§ 164. *Fines and Forfeitures* may, by the Constitutions of most States, be remitted by the governor or other persons in whom the pardoning power is vested (see § 160).[12] So the governor may suspend their collection for a period not exceeding sixty days.[13] So, of fines or forfeitures.[14] But he may not remit other debts due the State.[15]

§ 165. *Lynch Law.* A prisoner lawfully in custody of any officer seized by a mob or other unlawful assemblage and suffering violence or death, the officer is guilty of a misdemeanor and upon conviction shall forfeit his office and be forever disqualified to hold office unless pardoned; and when death ensues to the person lynched

[1] Cal., Fla., Ga., Ida., Ind., Io., Ky., La., Mich., Miss., N. D., Neb., Nev., N. Y., O., Ore., S. D., Utah, Vt., Wis., Wy.

[2] Ark., Tex.

[3] S. C. 2, 6.

[4] Ct. Amt. 17.

[5] S. C. 10, 12.

[6] Ky. 145; Va. 73.

[7] Ky. 240.

[8] Ala., Ark., Cal., Col., Del., Fla., Ga., Ida., Ill., Ind., Io., Ky., La., Md., Me., Mich., Minn., Miss., Mo., Mon., N. C., N. D., Neb., Nev., 5, 13; N. J. 5, 9; N. Y., O., Okla., Ore., Pa. 4, 9; S. C., S. D., Tenn., Tex., Utah, Va., W. Va., Wis., Wy.

[9] Fla., Nev.

[10] Ct. 4, 10; R. I. 7, 4.

[11] Ida.

[12] Ala., Ariz.,* Ark., Del., Fla., Ga., Ida., Ind. 5, 17; Io., Ky., La., Md., Me., Miss., Mon., N. D., Nev., N. J., Ore., Pa. 4, 9; S. C., S. D., Territories, U. S. R. S. 1841; Tex., Utah, Va. 73; Vt. 2, 11; Wash. 3, 11; W. Va., Wy.

[13] Nev.

[14] Fla. 4, 11; N. J. 5, 9.

[15] Md.

the county where it takes place is liable in exemplary damages of not less than $2000 to his representatives. The county may recover back from the parties engaged in said lynching.[1]

The sheriff suffering a lynching to take place is liable to impeachment.[2]

[1] S. C. 6, 6. Statutes of similar import are being adopted in many States.

[2] Ala. 138.

PART II

POLITICAL PROVISIONS

§ 180. *Note.* Compare, generally, with this part the United States Constitution, after which the political systems of the newer States are generally modelled. It has proved, since the first edition (1886) of *American Statute Law,* owing to frequent amendments of this part of the State Constitutions and endless diversity of detail, unwise to attempt herein more than a general statement of the States' frame of government.

ARTICLE 18. RIGHTS OF GOVERNMENT

§ 181. *Authority derived from the People.* The Constitutions of all States except New York and Michigan declare that all political power is inherent in the people,[1] or that Governments derive their just powers from the consent of the governed,[2] or are founded on the authority of those governed.[3] And that the people have at all times the right to make, alter, or reform the government.[4] So, in three, the doctrine of non-resistance is declared to be wrong; and the people ought to reform or abolish the government when other means of redress fail.[5]

[1] Ala. 1, 2; Ark. 2, 1; Cal. 1, 2; Col. 2, 1; Ct. 1, 2; Del. Preamble; Fla. Decln. of Rts. 2; Ga. 1, 1, 1; Ida. 1, 2; Ind. 1, 1; Io. 1, 2; Kan. Bill of Rts. 2; Ky. 4; La. 1; Mass. 1, 5, & 7; Md. Decln. of Rts. 1; Me. 1, 2; Minn. 1, 1; Miss. 5; Mo. 2, 1; Mon. 3, 1; N. C. 1, 2; N. D. 1, 2; Nev. 1, 2; N. H. 1, 1, & 8; N. J. 1, 2; N. M.* 95, 1; July 12, 1851, § 1; O. 1, 2; Okla. 2, 1; Ore. 1, 1; Pa. 1, 2; R. I. 1, 1; S. C. 1, 1; S. D. 6, 26; Tenn. 1, 1; Tex. 1, 2; Utah 1, 2; Va. 1, 2; Vt. 1, 6; Wash. 1, 1; W. Va. 2, 2; 3, 2; Wy. 1, 1. So in the United States Constitution (Preamble; Amts. 9, 10). In England it resides with the Sovereign and Parliament. (Taswell-Langmead, p. 428.) See Decl. Ind., Cl. 3.

[2] Ariz.* Bill of Rts. 1; Ark. 1, 2; Del.; Ga.; Ill. 2, 1; La.; Md.; Mon.; N. C.; Neb. 1, 1; N. H.; S. D. 6, 1; Wash.; Wis. 1, 1. See Decln. Ind. ¶ 3.

[3] Ala., Col., Ct., Ind., Kan., Ky., La., Me., Miss., Mo., Mon., N. M.*, Ore., Pa., S. D., Tenn., Tex., Utah, Wy.

[4] Ala.; Ariz.*; Ark.; Cal.; Col. 2, 2; Ct.; Del.; Fla.; Ga. 1, 5, 1; Ida.; Ind.; Io.; Ky.; Mass. Preamble 1, 7; Md.; Me.; Minn.; Miss. 6; Mo. 2, 2; Mon. 3, 2; N. C. 1, 3; N. D.; Nev.; N. H. 1, 10; N. J.; N. M.*; O.; Okla.; Ore.; Pa.; R. I.; S. C.; S. D. ("In lawful and constituted methods"), Tenn.; Tex.; Utah; Va. 1, 3; Vt. 1, 7; W. Va. 3, 3; Wy. See also Decln. Ind. ¶ 1. See also § 183.

[5] Md. Decln. of Rts. 6; N. H.; Tenn. 1, 2. This seems like an attempt to

§ 182. *Form of Government.* The Constitution of Texas declares that the faith of the people stands pledged to a republican form of government;[1] and that of Kentucky and Wyoming, that absolute, arbitrary power over the lives, liberty, and property of freemen exists nowhere in a republic, not even in the largest majority.[2] Representative government is not necessary, however, in Oklahoma. See § 201.

§ 183. *The object of Government* is declared to be for the security, benefit, and protection of the people,[3] "for the preservation and protection of our liberties,"[4] for their peace, safety, and happiness,[5] for their benefit, or "for the good of the whole,"[6] "for the protection of property,"[7] for their equal protection and benefit,[8] or to protect the citizen in the enjoyment of life, liberty, and property,[9] or, to protect and maintain individual rights.[10] And in New Hampshire, also in the enjoyment of rights of conscience.[11] In Massachusetts, to protect them in the enjoyment of their natural rights generally.[12]

When Government assumes other functions than as above, it is, in Alabama, declared to be usurpation and oppression. So, in Missouri, when it fails of its objects as above, it fails of its chief design.[13] And may be reformed or abolished by a majority of the community.[14]

§ 184. *Officers.* — [As a consequence of § 181] all officers are by the Constitutions of seven States declared to be accountable to the people as their trustees or servants.[15]

establish a constitutional right to revolution! See also §§ 4, 5, 12.

[1] Tex. 1, 2. This is required by U. S. Const. 4, 4. A republican form of government is usually understood to be based upon the suffrages of the people with a representative legislature and an elective non-hereditary executive; while in a pure democracy all the people make the laws and elect the officers directly.

[2] Ky. 2; Wy. 1, 5. This is a good definition of constitutional governments as distinct from a pure democracy.

[3] Ark. 2, 1; Cal. 1, 2; Fla. Decln. of Rts. 2; Ida. 1, 2; Io. 1, 2; Kan. Bill of Rts. 2; Mass. 1, 7; Minn. 1, 1; N. D. 1, 2; Nev. 1, 2; N. H. 1, 10; N. J. 1, 2; O. 1, 2; Okla. 2, 1; R. I. 1, 2; Va. 1, 3; Vt. 1, 7; W. Va. 3, 3.

[4] S. C. Preamble.

[5] Del. Preamble; La. 1; Ind. 1, 1; Ky. 4; Ore. 1, 1; Pa. 1, 2; Tenn. 1, 1; Wy. 1, 1.

[6] Col. 2, 1; Ct. 1, 2; Ga. 1, 1, 1; Ida. 1, 2; La. 1; Md.; Okla.; Decln. of Rts. 1; Me. 1, 2; Miss. 5; Mo. 2, 1; Mon. 3, 1; N. C. 1, 2; N. H. 1, 1; Okla.; R. I.; S. D.; Tex. 2, 2.

[7] Ky.

[8] Ida.; S. D. 6, 26; Utah 1, 2.

[9] Ala. 1, 35; Ariz.* Bill of Rts. 1; Ark. 2, 2; Ga. 1, 1, 2; Ill. 2, 1; Mo. 2, 4; Neb. 1, 1; N. H. 1, 12; S. D. 6, 1; Wis. 1, 1. See also Decln. of Ind. ¶ 4.

[10] Wash. 1, 1. See also § 6.

[11] N. H. 1, 4.

[12] Mass. Preamble.

[13] See also §§ 6, 12.

[14] Va. 1, 3.

[15] Ga. 1, 1, 1; Mass. 1, 5; Md. Decln.

§ 185. *Fundamental Principles* are referred to, and their observance required both of electors and officers.[1]

§ 186. *Representation* is, by the Constitutions of many States, required to be apportioned according to population.[2] And so of representatives to Congress.[3] So, in others, it is to be "founded on principles of equality." [4] To be "equal and uniform." [5] Representation according to population in both houses of the Legislature is in fact provided for in nearly all.[6] In others, as to the lower house only,[7] in Connecticut as to the Senate. In New Hampshire, the representative districts are divided according to population, but the senatorial according to the proportion of direct taxes paid.[8] For Oklahoma, see also § 182.

§ 187. *Gerrymandering.* — See § 218.

§ 188. *Initiative and Referendum.* — See § 309. (See also § 182, note 1.)

Article 19. State Sovereignty

§ 190. *The United States Constitution,*[9] by the Constitutions of a few Southern States, is expressly declared the supreme law of

of Rts. 6; N. H. 1, 8; Va. 1, 2; Vt. 1, 6; W. Va. 3, 2. See § 213.

[1] N. H. 1, 38. See § 5.

[2] Ala. 198, 200, 284; Ariz.* Bill of Rts. 12; Col. 5, 45; Kan. 10, 2; Ky. 33; La. 18, 19; Md. Amt. 1900, 432; Me. Amt. 25; Minn. 4, 2; Mon. 6, 2; N. D. 29 & 35; Neb. 3, 2; Nev. 1, 13; N. Y. 3, 4; S. D. 3, 5; Tex. 3, 25, & 26; Wash. 3, 3; W. Va. 2, 4; Wy. 3, 3.

[3] Mon.; Va. 55; W. Va. 1, 4.

[4] Mass. 2, 1, 3, 1; N. H. 2, 9.

[5] Ky., La.

[6] Ark. 8, 1, 2; Cal. 4, 6; Ct. Amts. 2, 18, 23, 31 (the equality is still imperfect, however); Fla. 7, 3; Ill. 4, 6; Ind. 4, 5; Io. 3, 35; Ky. 33; Mass. Amt. 21–22; Me. 4, 1, 2; Mich. 4, 4; Miss. 4, 34–35; Mo. 4, 2, & 5; Mon. 6, 6; N. C. 2, 4–5; N. D. 29, 35; N. Y. 3, 4–5; O. 11, 2, & 6; Okla. 5, 9 a, & 10 (c); Ore. 4, 6; Pa. 2, 16–17; Tenn. 2, 4–6; Vt. 2, 7; W. Va. 6, 4, & 7; Wis. 4, 3; Wy. 3, 3.

[7] Ga. 3, 3, 2–3; Md. 3, 2–4; N. J. 4, 3, 1; R. I. 5, 1, but each town or city is at least entitled to one member; S. C. 1, 2, and so of the Senate; R. I.

[8] N. H. 2, 9, & 25.

[9] Compare § 391. The Federal Constitution, Art. 6, § 2, reads: "This Constitution, and the Laws of the United States which shall be made in Pursuance thereof; and all Treaties made or which shall be made, under the Authority of the United States shall be the supreme Law of the Land; and the Judges in every State shall be bound thereby, anything in the Constitution or Laws of any State to the contrary notwithstanding." It is therefore quite unnecessary to put similar provisions in the State Constitutions, though it is probably done in memory of the attempted Secession. It will be noted that all treaties made under the authority of the United States shall be the supreme law of the land. But just as a law must be constitutional, it would seem that a treaty should be constitutional, and one made counter to the admitted rights of the States would, according to the better opinion, not be constitutional, at least as between the States and the Federal government.

Treaties stand on no higher footing than acts of Congress and may be imthe land,[1] or that the State is free and independent, subject only to the United States Constitution.[2] So, the United States Constitution is declared part of the State law, anything in the State Constitutions or laws to the contrary notwithstanding.[3] And so of United States laws made under the Constitution,[4] or treaties by the national Government.[5] This is declared irrepealable without the consent of the United States, in the new Western Constitutions, according to their enabling Acts; but this would seem to add no new strength to the clause; cf. § 155, note 8.

§ 191. *Allegiance.* — The Constitutions of North Carolina and the newer States provide that the State shall always remain a member of the American Union.[6] So, that no law shall be passed in derogation of the paramount allegiance of the citizens of the State to the United States Government.[7] And in two, it is declared that the State and United States Constitutions apply as well in war as in peace.[8]

§ 192. *Secession.* — The Constitutions of three States declare that there is no right on the part of the State to secede or dissolve its connection with the Union,[9] and that all attempts at secession ought to be resisted by the State,[10] and by the Federal Government, if necessary, by force of arms.[11]

§ 193. *State Rights.* — But the right of local self-government belonging to the people of each State is in several of the older States

paired by a subsequent law counter to their provisions. Under Art. 2, § 2, the president has power, by and with the advice and consent of the Senate, to make treaties provided two-thirds of the Senate as present concur. They cannot be formally abrogated or modified except by the power that made them, but a law inconsistent with their provisions would, nevertheless, take effect *pro tanto.*

[1] Ariz.* Bill of Rts. 2; Cal. 1, 3; Ga. 12, 1, 1; Ida. 1, 3; Md. Decln. of Rts. 2; Miss. 6; Mo. 2, 2; Mon. 3, 2; N. C. 1, 5; N. D. 3; Nev. Prelim. Act; Okla. 1, 1; S. D. 6, 26; Utah 1, 3; Wash. 1, 2; W. Va. 1, 1; Wy. 1, 35; Ordinance. See also § 193.

[2] Col. 2, 2; Md. Decln. of Rts. 2-3; Tex. 1, 1.

[3] Ga. 1, 4, 2; Ida. Sched. 22; Md.; Territories, U. S. R. S. 1891.

[4] Ariz.* Ga., Md., Territories, W.Va.

[5] Ga., Md., W. Va.

[6] Ariz.* Bills of Rts. 2; Cal. 1, 3; Ida. 1, 3; N. C. 1, 4; N. D. 3; Okla. 1, 1; S. D. 6, 26; Utah 1, 3; Wy. Ordinance; 1, 35. This would seem to be settled, and it is left out in the new Constitution of S. C. and Va.

[7] Fla. Decln. of Rts. 2; Miss. 7; N. C. 1, 7; Nev. 1, 2 ("In the exercise by the United States Government of the constitutional powers as defined by the U. S. Supreme Court").

[8] Md. Decln. of Rts. 44; W. Va. 1, 3.

[9] Fla. Decln. of Rts. 2; N. C. 1, 4; Nev. 1, 2. Similar provisions existed in Alabama and Mississippi, but have been omitted by the new Constitution. In substance this is declared by the 14th Amendment. See § 157, note 1. Compare also § 191.

[10] N. C.

[11] Nev.

declared a constitutional right which the national Government can never infringe.[1] The people of the State have the sole and exclusive right of governing themselves as a free, sovereign, and independent State; and shall exercise and enjoy every power, jurisdiction and right which is not or may not hereafter be, by them, expressly delegated to the United States of America in Congress assembled.[2]

So, in Virginia, that the people have a right to uniform government; and therefore that no government separate from, or independent of, the government of Virginia, ought to be erected or established within the limits thereof.[3]

And that the powers not delegated to the United States by the United States Constitution, nor prohibited by it to the States, are reserved to the State.[4]

ARTICLE 20. CONSTITUTION OF THE STATE GOVERNMENTS

§ 200. *The Three Functions.*[5] — By the Constitutions of nearly all, the powers of Government are divided into three distinct depart-

[1] Col. 2, 2; Ga. 1, 5, 1; Md. Decln. of Rts. 4; Mo. 2, 2; N. C. 1, 3; Tex. 1, 1; Vt. 1, 5; W. Va. 1, 2. See Book I for a full discussion of this principle and its history.

[2] Mass. 1, 4; N. H. 1, 5.

[3] Va. 1, 14.

[4] Md. Decln. of Rts. 3; W. Va. 1, 2. To the State *or* to the people, and so the words run in the U. S. 10th Amendment.

[5] This division of the powers of sovereignty into three departments, legislative, executive, and judicial, and constitutional exclusion of either department from the functions of the other is, with the invention of a delegated legislative authority subject to the judgment of the courts, perhaps the greatest political invention of the founders. (See Book I.) Although doubtless theoretical precedents are to be found in the books of Montesquieu and others, the principle does not exist in the British Constitution, and was really first applied intelligently in our own. The separation of powers is just as clearly expressed in the Federal Constitution as in those of the States, although put more simply and without the negative; that is to say, Article 1, § 1, "All legislative powers herein granted shall be vested in a Congress." Art. 2, § 1, "The executive power shall be vested in a President." Art. 3, § 1, "The Judicial power of the United States shall be vested in one Supreme Court," etc. The Massachusetts provision adds the striking words "To the end it may be a government of laws and not of men," which phrase was praised by Daniel Webster as its "noblest expression." The omission of the provision from the Constitution of New York, with the corresponding omission of the statement (Sec. 183) that the object of government is for the benefit, etc. of the people, is a most striking one. In England the attempt of the kings to resist this principle was in modern times most notable under Charles I. and George III. The effort of James I. in 1616 to interfere with the judiciary, and the resistance of Coke is well described in Taswell-Langmead (pp. 406–407). By the Act of Settlement (12 and 13 William III. c. 2) all judges' commissions are to be during good behavior, and their salaries fixed, and they can only be removed upon address of both houses of Parliament. In 1780

ments, — the legislative, executive, and judicial,[1] "to the end that it be a government of laws, not of men."[2] And in most of these it is declared that no person or collection of persons exercising the functions of one department shall assume or discharge the functions of any other.[3] They (the three departments) ought to be kept as separate from and independent of each other as the nature of a free government will admit.[4]

In the other States the same thing is implied by the distribution of *all* such power in separate articles, as in the United States Constitution.

In others, only that the Legislature can exercise no judicial power not expressly conferred by the Constitution,[5] or that the judges shall have none but judicial duties imposed upon them.[6]

The legislature shall have no power to deprive the Judicial Department of any power or jurisdiction which rightfully pertains to it as co-ordinate department of the Government; but the Legislature shall provide a proper system of appeals, and regulate, by law, when necessary, the methods of proceeding in the exercise of their powers of all the courts below the Supreme Court, so far as the same may be done without conflict with this Constitution.[7]

§ 201. *Political Constitution.* (See 309.) There is in all the States and territories a Legislature.[8] Both the Senate and the House

a resolution was proposed and carried in the House of Commons affirming that the influence of the Crown has increased, is increasing, and ought to be diminished (Taswell-Langmead, p. 550).

[1] Ala. 42; Ark. 4, 1; Cal. 3, 1; Col. 3, 1; Ct. 2; Fla. 2; Ga. 1, 23; Ida. 2, 1; Ill. 3, 1; Ind. 3, 1; Io. 3, 1; Ky. 27; La. 16; Mass. 1, 30; Md. Decln. of Rts. 8; Me. 3, 1; Mich. 3, 1; Minn. 3, 1; Miss. 1, 1; Mo. 3, 1; Mon. 4, 1; N. C. 1, 8; Neb. 2, 1; Nev. 3, 1; N. H. 1, 37; N. J. 3; Okla. 4, 1; Ore. 3, 1; R. I. 3; S. C. 1, 14; S. D. 2, 1; Tenn. 2, 1; Tex. 2, 1; Utah 5, 1; Va. 5 & 39; Vt. 2, 6; W. Va. 5, 1; Wy. 2, 1.

[2] Ala. 43; Mass.

[3] Ala.; Ark. 4, 2; Cal.; Col.; Fla.; Ga.; Ida.; Ill.; Ind.; Io.; Ky. 28; La. 17; Mass.; Md.; Me. 3, 2; Mich. 3, 2; Minn.; Miss. 1, 2; Mo.; Mon.; Neb.; Nev.; N. J.; Okla.; Ore.; S. C.; S. D.; Tenn. 2, 2; Tex.; Utah; Va.; Vt.; W. Va (Except in cases expressly by the Constitution permitted: Ark., Cal., Col., Fla., Ga., Ida., Ill., Ind., Io., Ky., La., Me., Mich., Minn., Mo., Mon., Neb., Nev., Ore., Tenn., Tex., Utah, Wy.)

[4] N. H.

[5] O. 2, 32.

[6] N. D. 96; Wy. 5, 16.

[7] Ida. 5, 13. See also Art. 65, for laws regulating powers of courts in contempt cases.

[8] Ala. 44; Ark. 5, 1; Cal. 4, 1; Col. 5, 1; Ct. 3, 1; Del. 2, 1; Fla. 3, 1; Ga. 3, 1, 1; Ida. 3, 1; Ill. 4, 1; Ind. 4, 1; Io. 3, 1; Kan. 2, 1; Ky. 29; La. 21; Mass. 2, 1, 1, 1; Md. 3, 1; Me. 4, 1, 1; Mich. 4, 1; Minn. 4, 1; Miss. 33; Mo. 4, 1; Mon. 5, 2; N. C. 2, 1; N. D. 52; Neb. 3, 1; Nev. 4, 1; N. H. 2, 2; N. J. 4, 1, 1; N. Y. 3, 1; O. 2, 1; Okla. 5, 1; Ore. 4, 1; Pa. 2, 1; R. I. 4, 2; S. C. 3, 1; S. D. 3, 1; Tenn. 2, 3; Tex. 3, 1; U. S. R. S. 1846; Utah 6, 1; Va. 40; Vt. Amts. 2–3; Wash. 2, 1; W. Va. 6, 1; Wis. 4, 1; Wy. 3, 1. In many,

are in all States elected by the people at the general election day.[1] Vacancies in either House are nearly always filled in the same way by a special election,[2] but in Massachusetts, vacancies in the Senate are filled by special election upon the order of a majority of the senators elected,[3] and in New Hampshire by direct vote of the two Houses. Where there is no majority vote, see § 232.

Each house of the Legislature has a negative on the other.[4] Or the concurrence of both Houses is necessary to the enactment of laws.[5] For other States, see § 304.

The legislative authority of the State shall be vested in a Legislature, consisting of a Senate and a House of Representatives; but the people reserve to themselves the power to propose laws and amendments to the Constitution and to enact or reject the same at the polls independent of the Legislature, and also reserve power at their own option to approve or reject at the polls any act of the Legislature.[6]

There is, in most States, a provision that legislative districts shall be fixed according to population.[7] In some of the older States, however, the districts are fixed by the Constitution, and cannot, apparently, be changed.[8] So, in South Carolina, there must be only one senator from each county.[9] In several States the number of both Senate and House is permanently fixed; thus, for the Senate, forty-four;[10]

the legislature is called the General Assembly (Ark., Col., Ct., Del., Ga., Ill., Ind., Io., Ky., La., Md., Mo., N. C., N. J., O., Pa., R. I., S. C., Tenn., Va., Vt.); in a few, the Legislative Assembly (Mon., N. D., Ore.); in some of the old States, the General Court (Mass., N. H.). In the territories the Senate is called the Council. In some States the House of Representatives is called the Assembly (Cal., Nev., N. Y., Wis.). In others, the House of Delegates (Md., W. Va.).

[1] Ala. 46; Ark. 5, 2–3; Cal. 4, 3–4; Col.; Ct. 3, 3–4; Del. 2, 2, 3; Fla. 3, 3; Ga. 3, 4, 2; Ida. 3, 2; Ill.; Ind. 4, 2; Io. 3, 3 & 5; Kan. 2, 29; Ky. 29, 30, 31; La. 191; Mass. Amts. 3–15; Md. 3, 2 & 6; Me. 4, 2, 1; Mich. 4, 2; Minn. 4, 24; Miss. 34, 35; Mo. 4, 2 & 5; Mon.; N. C. 2; N. D.; Neb. 16, 13; Nev. 4, 3–4; N. H. 2, 11 & 27; N. J. 4, 2, 1; N. Y. 3, 2–5; O. 2, 2; Okla. 5, 9; Ore. 4, 3; Pa. 2, 2; R. I. 8, 1; S. C. 3, 2 & 6; S. D.; Tenn.; Territories, U. S. R. S. 1846; Tex. 3, 3–4; Utah; Va. 41, 42; Vt. Amts. 5–24, 2; Wash.; W. Va. 4, 7; Wis. 4, 4–5; Wy.

[2] Ala. 46; Ark. 5, 6; Cal. 4, 12; Col. 5, 2; Del. 2, 6; Ga. 5, 1, 13; Ill. 4, 2; Ind. 5, 19; Io. 3, 12; Kan. 2, 9; Ky. 152; La. 23; Md. 3, 13; Me. 1897, resolve 259; Mich. 5, 10; Minn. 4, 17; Miss. 77; Mo. 4, 14; Mon. 5, 45; N. C. 2, 13; N. D. 44; Nev. 4, 12; N. H. 2, 15 & 33; N. J. 4, 4, 1; O. 2, 11; Okla. 5, 20; Ore. 5, 17; Pa.; R. I. 8, 9; Amt. 11; S. C. 3, 25; S. D. 3, 10; Tenn. 2, 15; Tex. 3, 13; Utah 6, 13; Va. 47; Wash. 2, 15; W. Va.; Wis. 4, 14; Wy. 3, 4. See also § 232.

[3] Mass. Amt. 24.

[4] Mass.; Me.; N. H. 2, 2; Vt. This is, of course, the case in all the States.

[5] Io. 3, 15; N. Y. 3, 15; R. I. 4, 2.

[6] Okla. 5, 1; Mon. 1905, 61. See also § 309.

[7] S. C. 3, 3. See § 186.

[8] Ct. 1895, p. 712; 1899, p. 1153; Del. 2, 2.

[9] S. C. 3, 6.

[10] Okla. 5, 9.

or fifty.[1] For the House, one hundred;[2] one-hundred and eight;[3] one hundred and fifty.[4]

United States senators must be elected by popular vote whenever the Federal Constitution so permits,[5] and several states have passed resolutions urging Congress to call a convention so to amend;[6] while a few States have statutes authorizing voters to express their preferences for United States senators at ordinary elections.

§ 202. *Executive.* There is in all the States a governor, a secretary of state, and a treasurer.[7] And so in all the territories by U. S. R. S. 1841. In most of the States there is also a lieutenant-governor.[8] In New Hampshire, Massachusetts, and Maine,[9] there still exists an executive council with power to advise the governor; so in North Carolina, the "council" consists of the secretary, auditor, treasurer, and superintendent of public instruction.[10] But in some States the president of the Senate, etc., succeeds to the governor's office when vacant.[11]

There is in most States also an auditor,[12] comptroller,[13] and an attorney-general.[14] In the other States these offices may be provided for by statute. In many States there is a superintendent of public

[1] N. Y. 1902, p. 199; 1898, p. 1550.

[2] Okla. 5, 10.

[3] Io.

[4] N. Y.

[5] Okla. 3, 4.

[6] Io. 1907, p. 185; Neb. 1907, 203; Ore. 1901, p. 476.

[7] Ala. 113; Ark. 6, 1; Ariz.* 1143; Territories, U. S. R. S. 1843; Cal. 5, 1 & 17; Col. 4, 2; Ct. 4, 1 & 18 & 17; Del. 3, 1 & 15; 2, 16; Fla. 4, 1 & 20; Ga. 5, 1, 1; Ida. 4, 1; Ill. 5, 1; Ind. 5, 1; 6, 1; Io. 4, 1 & 22; Kan. 1, 1; Ky. 69, 80, 82; La. 61; Mass. 2, 2, 1, 1; 2, 2, 4, 1; Amt. 17; Md. 2, 1 & 22; 6, 1; Me. 5, 1, 1; 5, 3, 1; Mich. 5, 1; 8, 1; Minn. 5, 1; Miss. 116, 133; Mo. 5, 1; Mon. 7, 1; N. C. 3, 1; N. D. 71, 82; Neb. 5, 1; Nev. 5, 1 & 19; N. H. 2, 40 & 66; N. J. 5, 1; 7, 2, 3, 4; N. Y. 4, 1; 5, 1; O. 3, 1 & 5; Okla. 6, 1; Ore. 5, 1; 6, 1; Pa. 4, 1; R. I. 7, 1 & 12; S. C. 4, 1 & 24; S. D. 4, 1 & 12; Tenn. 3, 1 & 17; 7, 3; Tex. 4, 1; Utah 7, 1; Va. 69, 80, 81; Vt. Amts. 8–10; Wash. 3, 1; W. Va. 7, 1; Wis. 5, 1; 6, 1; Wy. 4, 1 & 11.

[8] Ala. 112; Cal. 5,15; Col. 4, 1; Ct. 4, 3; Del. 3, 19; Ida.; Ill.; Ind. 5, 2; Io. 4, 3; Kan.; Ky. 82; La.; Mass. 2, 2, 2, 1; Mich.; Minn.; Miss. 128; Mo.; Mon.; N. C.; N. D. 72; Neb.; Nev. 5, 17; N. Y.; O.; Okla.; Pa.; R. I.; S. C. 4, 5; S. D. 4, 1; Tex.; Va. 77; Vt.; Wash.; Wis. See § 282.

[9] N. H. 2, 59; Mass. Amt. 16; 2, 2, 3, 1; Me. 5, 2, 1.

[10] N. C. 3, 14.

[11] See § 282.

[12] Ala.; Ark.; Col.; Ida.; Ill.; Ind; Io.; Kan.; Ky.; La. 82; Mass.; Mich.; Minn.; Miss.; Mo.; Mon.; N. C.; N. D.; Neb.; O.; Okla.; Pa.; S. D.; Utah; Va.; Vt. Amt. 1882, p. 108; Wash.; W. Va.; Wy.

[13] Cal.; Ct. 4, 19; Fla.; Ga.; Md.; Nev.; N. J.; N. Y.; S. C.; Tenn.; Tex.

[14] Ala.; Ark.; Cal.; Col.; Del. 7, 1; Fla.; Ga. 6, 10, 1; Ida.; Ill.; Io. 5, 12; Kan.; Ky.; La. 97; Mass. 9, 11; Md. 5, 1; Me. 9, 11; Mich.; Minn.; Miss. 143; Mo.; Mon.; N. C.; N. D.; Neb.; Nev.; N. H. 2, 46; N. J.; N. Y.; O.; Okla.; Pa.; R. I.; S. C.; S. D.; Tenn. 6, 5; Territories, U. S. R. S. 1875; Tex.; Utah; Va. 107; Wash.; W. Va. ; Wis.

instruction,[1] in others, a board of education.[2] And the state Constitutions establish other offices as follows: a secretary of internal affairs;[3] a state engineer or surveyor;[4] a state corporation commission of three members;[5] a state examiner of banks;[6] a commissioner of charities;[7] a state examiner and inspector;[8] a commissioner of insurance;[9] of state prisons;[10] of immigration, labor, and statistics;[11] of charities;[12] of the land office;[13] of agriculture;[14] a canal board;[15] a superintendent of public works;[16] a commissioner of mines;[17] a board of public works;[18] a register of the land office;[19] a state librarian;[20] a superintendent of labor and agriculture;[21] a board of railway commissioners;[22] a board of prison commissioners;[23] a state board of health;[24] a state board of labor may in Virginia be established by law.[25] In the other States, many of these boards or commissions are created by the statutes and are composed of certain specified officers.

There has been a decided movement recently to establish railroad commissions, and in many states they are created by the state Constitution itself; see § 532. For arbitration commissions, see § 456.

Executive officers are, in most States, elected by the people at the general election.[26]

[1] Ala. 13, 7; Ark. 6, 21; Col.; Fla. 12, 2; Ga. 8, 2, 1; Ida.; Ill.; Ind. 8, 8; Kan.; Ky. 91; La. 225; Mich.; Miss. 202; Mo.; Mon.; N. C.; N. D.; Neb.; Nev. 11, 1; Okla.; Ore. 8, 1; Pa.; S. C. 11, 1; S. D.; Utah; Va. 131; Wash.; W. Va.; Wis. 10, 1; Wy.

[2] Cal. 9, 2; Col. 9, 1; Fla. 12, 3; Ida. 9, 2; Io. 9, 1, 1; Mich. 13, 9; Miss. 203; Mo. 11, 4; N. C. 9, 8; Neb. 8, 1; S. C. 11, 2; Tex. 7. 8; Va. 130.

[3] Pa.

[4] Cal.; Nev.; N. Y. 5, 2.

[5] Va. 155.

[6] La. 194.

[7] Okla. 6, 27.

[8] Okla. 6, 19.

[9] N. D. 82; Okla. 6, 22.

[10] N. Y.

[11] Fla.; Ida. 13, 1; Ky.; Md. 10, 3; Va.; Wash.; Okla. 6, 20.

[12] N. Y. 8, 11.

[13] Ark.; Col. 9, 9; Fla. 4, 26; Ky.; Md. 7, 4; Mich.; Neb.; N. Y. 5, 5; Okla. 6, 32; S. D.; Tex.; Wash.

[14] Ala.; Del. 11, 1; Va. 143.

[15] N. Y. 5, 5.

[16] N. Y.

[17] Col. 16, 1.

[18] Md. 12, 1; Va. 4, 17.

[19] Ky.

[20] Md. 7, 3.

[21] Ala.; Del. 11, 1; Ky.; La.; Okla. 6, 31; Md. 10, 1; Mon. 18, 1; N. D.; Va. 143.

[22] Neb., N. D. See in § 532.

[23] Mon. 7, 20; Nev. 5, 21.

[24] Del. 12, 1.

[25] Va. 86.

[26] Ala. 114; Ark. 6, 3; Cal.; Col. 4, 3; Ct. Amts. 4, 5, and 6; Del. 3, 2, & 21; Fla. 4, 20; Ga. 5, 1, 3; Ida. 4, 2; Ill. 5, 3; Ind. 5, 3; 6, 1; Io. 4, 2, & 3; Kan.; Ky. 70; La. 62 & 79; Mass.; Md. 2, 2; Me. 5, 1, 2; Mich. 5, 3; 8, 1; Minn.; Miss.; Mo. 5, 2; Mon. 7, 2; N. C.; N. D. 74; N. H. 2, 41 & 59; Neb.; Nev.; N. Y. 5, 1; O. 3, 1 & 18; Okla.; Ore.; Pa. 4, 2; R. I. 8, 1; S. C.; S. D. 4, 3; Tenn. 3, 2; Tex. 4, 2; Utah 7, 2; Va. 70; Vt. Amt. 1883, p. 107; Wash.; W. Va. 7, 2; Wis. 5, 3; 6, 1; Wy. 4, 3. But in New Jersey the treasurer and comptroller are appointed by the legislature in joint session; and

Vacancies in all executive offices (except the governor or lieutenant-governor, see § 282) are, as a rule, filled either by election or appointment as originally provided.[1] But in some, they are filled by the governor, with the consent of the Senate, if in session [2] (except in Illinois, Montana, North Carolina; and, in Massachusetts, vacancies of the council are filled by the joint vote of the Legislature, or, if not in session, by the governor and council. Mass. Amt. 25.)

In a few States, all state offices for the weighing, gauging, inspecting or measuring any merchandise or produce are forbidden.[3]

§ 203. *Terms of Office.* A senator, by the Constitution of most States, is elected for four years.[4] In many others, for two

the attorney-general and secretary of state are nominated by the governor and confirmed by the senate (N. J. 7, 2, 3, & 4); so, in New York, the superintendents of public works, and of prisons. In Pennsylvania, the secretary of state and attorney-general are appointed by the governor and confirmed by the senate on a two-thirds vote; and so he appoints one superintendent of public instruction and all other officers whom he is given power to appoint (Pa. 4, 8). In Maryland, the comptroller and attorney-general are elected by the people; the secretary of state, librarian, and commissioner of lands appointed by the governor; and the legislature in joint session elects the treasurer. In Delaware, the secretary of state is appointed by the governor and confirmed by the senate (Del. 3, 10); and the treasurer by the legislature (Del. 2, 16). In two States, the secretary of state is appointed by the governor and confirmed by the senate (Tex. 4, 21; W. Va. 7, 3). In Georgia, the school commissioner or superintendent is appointed by the governor. In several, the secretary and treasurer [and commissary] are elected by the legislature in joint ballot (Me.; N. H. 2, 66; Tenn. 3, 17; 7, 3; so, in one, the comptroller (Tenn.); so, in one, the attorney-general (Me. 9, 11). In one, the attorney-general is appointed by the Supreme Court (Tenn.), in one, by the governor and council (N. H. 2, 45). The state boards of charities, lunacy, and prisons are appointed by the governor and confirmed by the senate (N. Y. 8, 12).

In the territories, the governor, secretary, and attorney-general are appointed by the President, and confirmed by the Senate of the United States (U. S. R. S. 1877).

In Maine, the council is elected by the legislature in joint ballot (Me. 5, 2, 2).

In Mississippi, the governor is chosen by votes of the counties or district, each one being entitled to the same number of votes as it is entitled to members in the House, these being designated electoral votes and given to the person receiving in each county or district the highest number; and the person receiving a majority of all the electoral votes and also a majority of the popular vote is declared elected by the House, which may determine the contested vote of counties or districts by a majority vote. If no person have such majorities, the House chooses the governor from the two persons who have received the highest number of popular votes, which election is *viva voce.* (Miss. 140; 141.)

[1] See §§ 202, 211.

[2] Ala. 136; Ark. 6, 23; Col. 4, 6; Del. 2, 9; Ill. 5, 20; Kan. 1, 14; Ky. 76; La. 76; Mich. 8, 3; Minn. 5, 4; Mon. 7, 7; N. C. 3, 13; Neb. 5, 20; W. Va. 7, 17. In R. I., the legislature elects, as in § 232, by *majority vote.* (R. I. Amt. 11.)

[3] Cal. 11, 14; Pa. 3, 27.

[4] Ala. 46; Ark. 5, 3; Cal. 4, 4; Col. 5, 3; Del. 2, 2; Fla. 7, 2; Ind. 4, 3; Io. 3, 5; Kan. 2, 29; Ky. 31; La. 24; Md. 3, 2; Minn. 4, 24; Miss. 34, 35; Mo. 4, 5; Mon. 5, 2; N. D. 27; Nev.

years.[1] In two, for one year.[2] In one, for three years.[3] Half the senators are, in many States, elected at each general election for them, the other half holding over.[4] And so, one-third are elected at each general election, the others holding over.[5] In three States, a representative is elected for four years.[6] But in most States, for two years.[7] In four States, for one year.[8] In about half, the governor holds office for a term of two years.[9] In most others, for four years.[10] In two, for one year.[11] In one, for three years.[12]

The other executive officers, generally, hold office for the same period as the governor in all the States.[13]

§ 204. *Special Qualifications for Senators and Representatives.*[14] The usual qualifications required by the state Constitutions for state senators and representatives fall into three classes: citizenship, age, and residence. Thus, in most States, no person can be state

4, 4; Okla. 5, 9; Ore. 4, 4; Pa. 2, 3; S. C. 3, 6; Tex. 3, 3; Utah 6, 4; Va. 41; Wash. 2, 6; W. Va. 6, 3; Wis. 4, 5 & Amt.; Wy. 3, 2.

[1] Ct. Amt. 16, 2; Amt. 27; Ga. 3, 4, 1; Ida. 3, 3; Ill. 4, 2; Me. Amt. 23; Mich. 4, 2; N. C. 2, 3; Neb. 3, 4; N. H. 2, 24; N. Y. 3, 2; O. 2, 2; S. D. 3, 6; Tenn. 2, 3; Territories, U. S. R. S. 1846; Vt. Amt. 24, 4.

[2] Mass. Amt. 22; R. I. 8, 1.

[3] N. J. 4, 2, 1.

[4] Ark.; Cal. 4, 5; Col. 5, 5; Fla.; Ind.; Io. 3, 6; Ky.; Md. 3, 7–8; Minn.; Mo. 4, 10; Mon.; N. D.; Okla. Ore.; Tex.; Utah; 1, 4; Wash.; W. Va.; Wis.; Wy.

[5] N. J. 4, 2, 2.

[6] Ala.; La.; Miss.

[7] Ark. 5, 2; Cal. 4, 3; Col. 5, 3; Ct. Amt. 27, 1; Del. 2,2; Fla.; Ga.; Ida.; Ill.; Ind.; Io. 3, 3; Kan.; Ky. 31; Md. 3, 6; Me.; Mich. 4, 3; Minn.; Mo. 4, 2; Mon.; N. C. 2, 5; N. D. 33; Neb.; Nev. 4, 3; N. H. 2, 9; O.; Okla.; Ore.; Pa.; S. C. 3, 2; S. D.; Tenn.; Territories*; Tex. 3, 4; Utah 6, 3; Va. 5, 2; Vt.; Wash. 2, 5; W. Va.; Wis. 4, 4.

[8] Mass. 2, 1, 3, 1; N. J. 4, 3, 1; N. Y. 3, 2; R. I.

[9] Ark. 6, 1; Col. 4, 1; Ct.; Ga. 5, 1, 2; Ida.; Io. 4, 2; Kan. 1, 1; Me.; Mich. 5, 1; Minn. 5, 3; N. D. 71; Neb. 5, 1; N. H. 2, 41; N. Y. 4, 1; O. 3, 2; S. C. 4, 2; S. D. 4, 1; Tenn. 3, 4; Tex. 4, 4; Vt. Amt. 24, 3; Wis. 5, 1.

[10] Ala. 116; Cal. 5, 2; Del. 3, 2; Fla. 4, 2; Ill. 5, 1; Ind. 5, 1; Ky. 70; La. 62; Md. 2, 1; Miss. 4, 2; Mo. 5, 2; Mon. 7, 1; N. C. 3, 1; Nev. 5, 2; Okla. 6, 4; Ore. 5, 1; Pa. 4, 3; Territories, U. S. R. S. 1841; Utah 7, 1; Va. 69; Wash. 3, 2; W. Va. 7, 1; Wy. 4, 1.

[11] Mass. 2, 2, 1, 2; R. I.

[12] N. J. 5, 3.

[13] In New Jersey, the treasurer and comptroller hold office for three years, and the attorney-general and secretary of state for five (N. J. 7, 2, 3, & 4). The term of the auditor-general is three years, and of the treasurer two (Pa. 4, 21). In Ohio, the auditor holds office for four years. In Indiana, they all hold office two years, except the lieutenant-governor. In Minnesota, the auditor holds office four years (Minn. 5, 5; Amt. 1883, C. 1). In Maryland, the attorney-general and the superintendent of labor, etc., hold office four years (Md. 5, 1). In several, the treasurer holds office two years (Del. 3, 21; Ill. 5, 2; Ky. 3, 25). And the auditor (Del.).. In Tennessee, the secretary of state holds office four years and the attorney-general, eight. In Nevada, the superintendent of instruction holds office two years (Nev. 11, 1). For citations of other States, see above and § 202. See also § 212.

[14] For religious qualifications, see §§ 46, 47.

senator or representative who is not a citizen of the United States [1] or in some cases a qualified elector of the State, which would seem to mean much the same thing. Maine alone prescribes that he must have been a citizen of the United States for five years.[2]

The residence qualifications vary considerably and are usually greater in the case of a senator than in a representative; thus, no person is eligible for state senator who has not been one year,[3] two years,[4] three years,[5] four years,[6] five years,[7] six years,[8] or seven years [9] resident in the State. In a few States the term used is "citizen" instead of "resident." [10] In others "a qualified elector." [11]

For representatives, the period of residence is one year,[12] two years,[13] three years,[14] four years,[15] and five years; [16] and in several States he must in like manner be a qualified elector,[17] or a citizen.[18]

There is frequently required by the Constitution a term of residence within the senatorial or representative district which is usually also greater in the case of senators than in that of representatives. Thus, in many, a candidate must be resident in the senatorial[19] or representative [20] district at the time of the election; and if he cease to reside in such district he vacates his office.[21] The time of residence required in the district varies in the case of senators, from sixty days,[22] three

[1] Ark. 5, 4; Col. 5, 4; Ga. 3, 5, 1; Ida. 3, 6; Ill. 4, 3; Ind. 4, 7; Io. 3, 5; Mich. 4, 5; Mo. 4, 6; Mon. 5, 3; Ore. 4, 8; S. C. 3, 7; S. D. 3, 3; Tenn. 2, 10; Tex. 3, 6; Utah 5, 1; Wash. 2, 7; Wy. 3, 2.

[2] Me. 4, 2, 6.

[3] Io. 3, 5; Me. 4, 1, 4; 4, 2, 6; Minn. 4, 25; Wis. 4, 6.

[4] Ark.; Ind.; N. C. 2, 7; N. D. 28; S. D.

[5] Ala. 47; Del. 2, 3; Cal. 4, 4; Md. 3, 9; Mo.; Tenn.; Utah.

[6] Ga.; Miss. 42; N. J. 4, 1, 2; Pa. 2, 5.

[7] Ill.; La. 24; Mass. 2, 1, 2, 5; Amt. 22; Tex.; W. Va. 4, 4.

[8] Ky.

[9] N. H. 2, 28.

[10] Cal., Del., Ky., Md., N. C., N. J., Pa., W. Va., Wy.

[11] Ida.; Md.; Minn.; Miss.; Mo.; N. D.; Neb. 3, 5; N. J.; Tex.; Territories, U. S. R. S. 1846; W. Va.

[12] Io.; Me.; Minn. 4, 25; S. C ; Wis. 4, 6.

[13] Ark.; Ga.; Ind.; Ky. 32; Mo.; N. H. 2, 13; N. J. 4, 1, 2; N. D. 34; S. D.; Tex.; Vt. 2, 18.

[14] Ala. 47; Cal. 4, 4; Del. 2, 2; Md. 3, 9; Tenn.; Utah.

[15] Miss. 41; Pa. 2, 5.

[16] Ill.; La. 24.

[17] Ida.; La.; Md.; Minn.; Miss. 41; Mo.; N. C. 2, 8; Neb. 3, 5; N. J.; S. C.; Territories; Tex.

[18] Ky.; Wy.

[19] Ct. 3, 3; Kan. 2, 4; Mass.; Me.; Mich.; Miss.; Neb.; N. H.; Okla. 5, 17; Territories, U. S. R. S. 1846; Va. 5, 5.

[20] Ct. Amt. 3; Kan. 2, 4; Mass.; Mich. 4, 5; Miss.; Neb.; N. H.; Territories; Va. 44; Vt. Amt. 23; Wis.

[21] Ala.; Fla. 3, 8; Ga. 3, 4, 8; La.; Mass.; Me.; Mich.; Miss.; Mo. 4, 13; Neb.; Okla.; Pa.; Tex. 3, 23; Va.; W. Va. 6, 12.

[22] Io. In England at one time members of Parliament had to be resident in the district.

months,[1] six months,[2] one year,[3] to two years.[4] In some States, instead of resident he must be a *qualified elector*,[5] in the district.

In the case of representatives, he must, in like manner, be resident in the district at the time of the election,[6] and upon ceasing to be such resident he loses his office.[7] The time of residence required varies from sixty days,[8] three months,[9] six months,[10] one year,[11] to two years.[12]

Many state Constitutions have also age qualifications for senators or representatives, varying from twenty-one [13] in the case of senators to twenty-five,[14] twenty-six,[15] twenty-seven,[16] or thirty.[17] For representatives, the age varies from twenty-one,[18] to twenty-four,[19] or twenty-five.[20] In Missouri, either senator or representative must have paid a state or county tax within one year before election.

There are certain other miscellaneous special qualifications. (See also Art. 22 and § 304.) Thus, in Massachusetts, the Constitution forbids any property qualification for the Legislature or Council.[21] In Nebraska, no person interested in a contract with, or an unadjusted claim against, the State, can hold a seat in the Legislature.[22] In Delaware, no person concerned in an army or navy contract; and no person who has served as state treasurer is eligible for the Legislature before his accounts as treasurer are settled and discharged.[23] In West Virginia, no salaried officer of a railroad.[24] No person convicted of embezzlement or misuse of the public funds.[25] No person who has

[1] Me., S. C.

[2] Minn.

[3] Ala.; Ark.; Cal.; Col.; Del.; Ga.; Ida.; Ind.; Ky.; Md.; Mo. 4, 6; Mon.; N. C.; Neb.; N. J.; O. 2, 3; Ore.; Pa.; Tenn.; Tex.; Utah; W. Va.; Wy.

[4] Ill., La., Miss.

[5] Fla. 3, 4; Kan.; Mich.; N. D.; Nev. 4, 5; Okla.; S. C. 3, 7; S. D.; Utah; Va.; Wash.; Wis.

[6] Ct. 3, 3; Kan. 2, 4; Mass.; Me.; Mich.; Miss.; Neb.; N. H.; Okla. 5, 17; Territories, U. S. R. S. 1846; Va. 5, 5.

[7] Ala.; Fla. 3, 8; Ga. 3, 4, 8; La.; Mass. Amt. 21; Me.; Mich.; Miss.; Mo. 4, 13; Neb.; N. H.; Okla.; Pa.; Tex. 3, 23; Va.; W. Va.

[8] Io.

[9] Me.

[10] Minn.

[11] Ala.; Ark.; Cal. 4, 4; Col.; Del.; Ga.; Ida.; Ind.; Ky.; Mass. Amt. 21; Md.; Mo.; Mon.; N C.; Neb.; N. J.; O. 2, 3; Ore.; Pa.; Tenn. 2, 9; Tex.; Utah; Vt.; W. Va. 6, 12; Wy.

[12] Ill., La., Miss.

[13] Ore.

[14] Ala.; Ark.; Col.; Ga.; Ill.; Ind.; Io. 3, 5; La.; Md.; Me. 4, 2, 6; Miss.; Mon.; N. C.; N. D.; Okla.; Pa.; S. C.; S. D. (24); Utah; W. Va.; Wy.

[15] Tex.

[16] Del.

[17] Ky., Mo., N. H., N. J., Tenn., Vt.

[18] Ala., Ark., Ga., Ill., Ind., Io., Md., Me., Miss., Mon., N. D., N. J., Okla., Ore., Pa., S. C., Tenn., Tex., Wy.

[19] Del., Ky., Mo.

[20] Col., Ga., S. D., Utah.

[21] Mass. Amt. 13.

[22] Neb. 3, 6. Compare § 154.

[23] Del. 2, 24.

[24] W. Va. 6, 13. See § 204, note 14.

[25] Ga. 3, 4, 7; Kan. 2, 6. See also § 222.

been convicted of bribery, perjury, or other infamous crime,[1] or expelled for corruption.[2] And also, no person who has collected or been intrusted with public money, and has not accounted for the same.[3]

Many qualifications similar to these are, of course, contained in the general provision for disqualification for office.[4]

§ 205. *Special Qualifications for Governor.*[5] Similar qualifications for the governor are prescribed in many state Constitutions; thus, he must be a citizen of the United States.[6] And he must, in some States, have been such citizen for a certain period of time; thus, two years,[7] five years,[8] ten years,[9] twelve years,[10] fifteen years,[11] or twenty years.[12] In Maine, he must be a natural-born citizen of the United States.[13] In others, he must have been resident of the State a certain period of time; thus, one year,[14] two years,[15] three years,[16] four years,[17] five years,[18] six years,[19] seven years,[20] and ten years.[21] And in Maine and the territories, he must continue to reside in the State or territory during his term of office.[22] In a few States, instead of "citizen," the words "qualified elector" are used.[23] The age limitations for the governor vary from twenty-one in States where there is no prescription, to twenty-five in a few,[24] thirty in most,[25] and thirty-five in two.[26]

In a few States the governor is not eligible for re-election for any two successive terms (unless the office devolved upon him);[27] and so in Delaware, he is not eligible for a third time for the office.[28] In

[1] N. D. 38; S. D. 3, 4; Okla. 5, 18.

[2] Okla. 5, 19.

[3] Ky. 45; W. Va. 6, 14.

[4] See § 223.

[5] See also § 221.

[6] Ark. 6, 5; Col. 4, 4; Del. 3, 6; Ida. 4, 3; Minn. 5, 3; Mon. 7, 3; N. D. 73; N. Y. 4, 2; Okla. 6, 3; Ore. 5, 2; Pa. 4, 5; S. D. 4, 2; Tenn. 3, 3; Tex. 4, 4; Va. 71; Wis. 5, 2; Wy. 4, 2.

[7] Io. 4, 6; Neb. 5, 2.

[8] Cal. 5, 3; Ill. 5, 5; Ind. 5, 7; Mich. 5, 2; N. C. 3, 2; S. C. 4, 3.

[9] Ala. 117; Fla. 4, 3; La. 63; Mo. 5, 5; Va. (if of foreign birth).

[10] Del.

[11] Ga. 5, 1, 7.

[12] Miss. 117; N. J. 5, 4.

[13] Me. 5, 1, 4.

[14] Minn.

[15] Col.; Ida.; Io.; Mich.; Miss.; Mon.; N. C.; Neb.; Nev. 5, 3; Okla.; S. C; S. D.

[16] Ore., Va.

[17] Vt. 2, 30.

[18] Cal.; Fla.; Ill.; Ind.; Md. 2, 5; Me.; Miss.; N. Y.; S. C.; Tex.; Utah; Va. 71; W. Va. 4, 4; Wy.

[19] Del.; Ga; Ky. 72.

[20] Ala.; Ark.; Mass. 2, 2, 1, 2; Mo.; N. H. 2, 41; N. J.; Pa. 4, 5; Tenn.

[21] La., Md.

[22] Me., U. S. R. S. 1841.

[23] Ark.; Ct. 4, 1; Fla.; Md.; N. D.; Nev.; S. D.; Utah; 7, 3; Wis.; Wy.

[24] Cal., Minn., Nev.

[25] Ala. Ark., Col., Ct., Del., Ga., Ida., Ill., Ind., Io., La., Md., Me., Mich., Miss., Mon., N. C., N. D., Neb., N. H., N. J., N. Y., Okla., Ore., Pa., S. C., S. D., Tenn., Tex., Utah, Va., W. Va., Wy.

[26] Ky., Mo.

[27] Fla. 4, 2; Ky. 71; La.; Miss. 116; Mo. 5, 2; N. C.; N. J. 5, 3; Okla. 6, 3; Pa. 4, 3; Va. 69; W. Va. 7, 4.

[28] Del. 3, 5.

Tennessee, not more than six years in any term of eight.[1] In Indiana, not more than four years in any term of eight.[2] In Oregon, not more than eight years in any period of twelve.[3] In Georgia he is not eligible for four years after a second term.[4]

Other executive offices must generally have the same qualifications as the governor and this is frequently specified as to the lieutenant-governor.[5]

Several States provide against long periods of service by the treasurer or auditor; thus, the treasurer is not eligible for any two successive terms,[6] or for more than five successive years,[7] or until two years after the end of two successive terms;[8] so the auditor is only eligible for two successive terms;[9] and in Oregon, the treasurer and secretary are not eligible for more than eight years in any period of twelve.[10] There are certain other qualifications for the less important executive offices in several States which it has not seemed worth while to set forth in detail.[11]

§ 206. *Pay of the State Legislature.* Many state Constitutions provide that members of the Legislature shall receive a fixed compensation[12] which generally may not be increased or diminished during the term for which they are elected.[13] In a few States it cannot be altered at all by the Legislature, the salaries being fixed by the Constitution.[14]

Similar principles apply to the pay of all executive officers in several States.[15]

[1] Tenn. 3, 4.

[2] Ind. 5, 1.

[3] Ore. 5, 1.

[4] Ga. 5, 1, 2.

[5] Ala.; Cal. 5, 15; Col. 4, 4; Ct. 4, 3; Del. 3, 19; Ill. 5, 5; Ind. 5, 7; Io. 4, 6; Ky. 82; Mass. 2, 2, 2, 1; Mich. 5, 2; Minn. 5, 3; Miss. 5, 14; Mo. 5, 15; N. C. 3, 2; Neb. 5, 2; Nev. 5, 17; N. Y. 4, 2; Okla. 6, 3 & 15; Pa. 4, 5; S. C. 4, 5; Vt. 2, 30; Wis. 5, 2.

[6] Ky. 93; La. 80; Mon. 7, 1; Mo. 5, 2; Utah; N. D. 82; S. D. 4, 12; Miss.; Wash. 3, 25; Wy. 4, 11.

[7] Col. 4, 21; Mass. 2, 2, 4, 1; Me. 5, 4, 1; Pa. 4, 21.

[8] Ill. 5, 2; Neb. 5, 3.

[9] Col., Pa.

[10] Ore. 6, 1.

[11] Ky. 93; Mon. 7, 3.

[12] Ala. 49; Ariz.* 1139; Ark. 5, 16; Cal. 4, 23; Col. 5, 6; Ct. Amt. 27; Del. 2, 15; Fla. 3, 4; Ga. 3, 9, 1; Ida. 3, 23; Ill. 4, 21; Ind. 4, 29; Io. 3, 25; Kan. 2, 3; Ky. 42; La. 29; Md. 3, 15; Me. 4, 3, 7; Mich. 4, 15; Minn. 4, 7; Miss. 46; Mo. 4, 16; Mon. 5, 5; N. C. 2, 28; N. D. 45; Neb. 3, 4; Nev. 4, 33; N. H. 2, 14; N. J. 4, 4, 7; N. Y. 3, 6; O. 2, 31; Okla. 5, 21; Ore. 4, 29; Pa. 2, 8; R. I. 4, 11; Amt. 11 (1900, p. 146); S. C. 3, 19; S. D. 3, 6; Tenn. 2, 23; Terr. U. S. R. S. 1853; 1878, 329; Tex. 3, 24; Utah 6, 9; Va. 45; Wash. 2, 23; W. Va. 6, 33; Wis. 4, 21; Wy. 3, 6.

[13] Ark.; Cal.; Col.; Ct. 4, 4; Ind.; Io.; Ky. 74; Me.; Minn.; Miss.; Mon. 5, 5 & 8; Nev.; O.; Pa.; S. C.; Utah; Va. 72; Wy. 3, 9.

[14] Mo., Tex.

[15] Ala. 118; Ark. 19, 11; Cal. 5, 19; Col.; Ida. 4, 19; Ill. 5, 23; Kan.; Ky. 235; N. C. 3, 15; N. H. 2, 17; N. D. 84; N. Y.; O. 2, 19; S. D. 21, 2; Utah; Wash. 3, 14; Wy. 4, 13.

When the pay of the Legislature is fixed by the Constitution, or the term for which they are paid limited (see § 277), the provision becomes more important, as in a certain measure determining the length of legislative sessions. Thus, in New Hampshire, in the case of a special session, legislators receive three dollars a day, but for a period not exceeding fifteen days, and the total pay for any regular session is two hundred dollars with mileage. See also § 277. Mileage is given in most States.

This pay would doubtless be understood to be all that a member of a state Legislature could receive in any manner, direct or indirect, for performing the duties of his office without being liable for bribery or malfeasance, and the Constitution of Mississippi expressly provides that no member can take a fee or act as counsel before either House.[1]

Article 21. Of Offices in General

§ 210. *Appointment.* (For the important executive officers and the members of the Legislature, see Art. 20; for the judicial officers, see Art. 65.)

Generally speaking, it may be stated that all State officers except such important executive officers or judges as are elected by the people of the State or the several districts are appointed by the governor,[2] in Massachusetts, Maine, and New Hampshire, with the consent of the Council,[3] and very generally this appointment must be confirmed by the Senate.[4] Other officers are to be appointed or elected as the Legislature may provide.[5] Most State Constitutions provide with considerable detail what officers shall be elected by the people of the several counties, towns, or districts, usually solicitors or district attorneys, sheriffs, registers of deeds and probate, county treasurers, and so on. It has not seemed worth while to go into this matter in more detail.

§ 211. *Vacancies* in any office whatever (except members of the

[1] Miss. 47.

[2] Col. 4, 6; Del. 3, 9; Ida. 4, 6; Ill. 5, 10; La. 71; Md. 2, 10; Minn. 5, 4; Mo. 5, 23; Mon. 7, 7; N. C. 3, 10; Neb. 5, 10; N. J. 7, 2, 9; Pa. 4, 8; Territories, U. S. R. S. 1857; Utah 7, 10; Vt. 2, 11; W. Va. 7, 8.

[3] Mass. 2, 2, 1, 9; 2, 1, 1, 4; Me. 5, 1, 8; N. H. 2, 45.

[4] Col., Del., Ida., Ill., La., Md., Minn., N. C., Neb., N. J., Pa., Territories, Utah, W. Va.

[5] Cal. 20, 4; Fla. 3, 27; Ind. 15, 1; Kan. 2, 19 & 15, 1; Ky. 93; Mo. 14, 9; Neb. 5, 1; Amt. 1883, Nev. 15, 10; N. H. 2, 5; O. 2, 27; Ore. 6, 7; Pa. 12, 1; Tenn. 7, 4; Territories; W. Va. 4, 8; Wis. 13, 9; Wy. 6, 12 (6).

Legislature and the governor or lieutenant-governor or other high executive offices) are usually filled by the governor with the consent of the council, when there is one, or in some States of the Senate, but in other States the whole matter of filling vacancies is left to the Legislature. Where nothing is said, all offices would presumably be filled in the same manner as the original appointment (see § 210). So, vacancies in elective offices are filled at the next regular election.

§ 212. *Tenure.* A few States have the general provision that no office can be granted for a longer term than during good behavior,[1] while in three States no person shall be elected or appointed to office for life or during good behavior, but the terms of all offices shall be for some specified period (except notaries and in the militia).[2] In several States no office can be created by the Legislature for a longer term than four years,[3] or in Texas, two years.[4]

It is usually provided that all officers (except in case of impeachment or suspension) shall continue to discharge their duties until their successors are duly appointed and qualified;[5] and in some States this provision is expressly made of the governor or other executive officers.[6] No law can be passed which shall operate to extend the term of any public officer after his election or appointment.[7]

Rotation in office is still, by the Constitutions of Massachusetts, Maryland, and Virginia, declared to be a necessary principle in a free government.[8]

§ 213. *Pay.* The State Constitutions frequently provide that all officers are to receive a compensation fixed by law, reasonable in amount, and paid at stated periods.[9] In some, a limit of salaries is fixed by the Constitution.[10] In Vermont all offices of profit are for-

[1] Ala. 1, 29; Del. 1, 19; Me. 1, 23; Pa. 1, 24.

[2] Ky. 23; Miss. 20; S. C. 1, 11.

[3] Cal. 20, 16; Fla. 16, 7; Ind. 15, 2; Kan. 15, 2; Miss. 252; Nev. 15, 11; Ore. 15, 2.

[4] Tex. 16, 30.

[5] Ark. 19, 5; Col. 12, 1; Del. 15, 5; Fla. 16, 14; Ind. 15, 3; La. 172; Miss. 136; Mo. 14, 5; O. Sched. 10; Okla. 23, 10; Ore. 15, 1; R. I. 4, 16; Tenn. 7, 5; Tex. 16, 17; Va. 33; W. Va. 4, 6; Wy. 6, 12.

[6] Ark. 6, 1; Ct. 4, 1; Ga. 3, 4, 1; 5, 1, 2; Ill. 5, 1; Io. 3, 3; 4, 2; 5, 12; Kan. 1, 1; Ky. 73; La. 64; Mass. Amt. 17; Md. 2, 1; 5, 1; Minn. 5, 3; 5, 5; Miss. 5, 22; Mo. 5, 2; Mon. 7, 1; N. C. 3, 1; N. D.; Nev. 5, 2; 5, 19; N. J. 7, 2, 3; Pa. 4, 17; R. I. 8, 1; S. C. 4, 2; S. D. 5, 36; Tenn. 3, 4; Tex. 4, 4; 4, 22; 4, 23; Vt. Amt. 21; Wash. 3, 2; Wy. 4, 1.

[7] Col. 5, 30; Del. 15, 4; Ill. 4, 28; Mo. 14, 8; Mon. 5, 31; Okla.; Pa. 3, 13; W. Va. 6, 37; Wy. 3, 32.

[8] Mass. 1, 8; Md. 1, 34; Va. 1, 5.

[9] Ala. 118; Ark. 16, 4; Ky. 96; La. 81; Miss. 103; Mo. 5, 24; Okla. 6, 34; Ore. 13, 1; N. Y. 10, 9; Tex. 3, 44; Va. 83.

[10] Ark. 19, 23; Ky. 246 ($5000); La.; Md. 15, 1; Mich. 9, 1; Amt. 1893, p. 433; S. D. 21, 2.

bidden, but fees or a reasonable compensation may be allowed.[1] In two States all fees and perquisites are forbidden,[2] and the Legislature may not increase the expenses of any office by appointing assistant officers.[3]

§ 214. *Extra Pay.* Very generally this compensation may not be increased or diminished during the term of office; and the Legislature can grant no extra compensation after the service is ended or after the contract is entered into.[4] Nor can it authorize municipal corporations to grant such compensation.[5] In two States, salaries of deceased officers may not be paid beyond the date of death,[6] and it would seem that this must be the law in others.[7]

§ 215. *Farming Offices.* By the Constitutions of three States, no person elected or appointed to any office under the laws of the State or any municipal ordinance shall hold such office without personally devoting his time to the performance of its duties.[8]

§ 216. *Gerrymandering.* The Constitutions of California and Idaho provide that when a congressional district shall be composed of two or more counties, it shall not be separated by any county belonging to another district; nor can a county or city be divided to form congressional districts, except when rendered necessary by excess of population.[9] In four, the congressional districts shall be formed of contiguous counties, &c., and be "compact."[10]

There are in nearly all States provisions of the same nature as to districts electing members of the State Legislature, and in Oklahoma an apportionment made by the Legislature is reviewable by the Supreme Court at suit of any citizen.[11]

§ 217. *Election of United States Officers.* The Constitutions of several States provide that senators shall be elected by the two houses of the Legislature in joint convention, at such time and in such man-

[1] Vt. 2, 25.

[2] La. 180; Okla.

[3] La. 54.

[4] Ala. 68, 98, 118, 281; Ark. 5, 27; Cal. 4, 32; Col. 5, 28 & 30; Ct. Amt. 24; Del. 15, 4; Fla. 16, 11; Ga. 7, 16, 2; Ida. 5, 27; Ill. 4, 19; Io. 3, 31; Ky. 235; La. 47; Md. 3, 35; Mich. 4, 21; Miss. 96; Mo. 4, 48; 5, 24; 14, 8; Mon. 5, 29 & 31; 7, 4; Neb. 3, 16; Nev. 4, 28; 15, 9; N. Y. 6, 12; 3, 28; 10, 9; O. 2, 20 & 29; Okla. 5, 47; 23, 10; Pa. 3, 11 & 13; S. C. 3, 30; S. D. 12, 3; Utah 6, 30; Tex. 3, 44; W. Va. 6, 38; Wash. 2, 25; Wis. 4, 26; Wy. 3, 30; 3, 32; 4, 13.

[5] Ala.; Cal.; Ct.; La.; Mo.; N. Y.; Tex. 3, 53.

[6] Ala.'97; S. C. 3, 32.

[7] Compare also § 395.

[8] Col. 12, 2; Mo. 2, 18; Miss. 267; Okla. 2, 11.

[9] Cal. 4, 27; Ida. 3, 5.

[10] Mon. 6, 3; Va. 55; W. Va. 4, 6; Wy. 3, 46.

[11] Okla. 5, 10 (j).

ner as may be by law provided.[1] In Nebraska the Legislature may provide that at the general election next preceding the expiration of the term of a United States senator, the electors may by ballot express their preference for some person for such office.[2] In Oklahoma [3] the Legislature shall provide for their election by direct vote of the people "at any time the Federal Constitution may permit." By the Constitution of Florida, no person can receive credentials as a member of Congress who has not been five years a citizen of the State and ten years a citizen of the United States and is not a qualified voter.[4]

In Colorado, one representative in Congress is elected for the State at large.[5] Presidential electors must, in Colorado, be elected by the people; and it was so prescribed in the old Constitution of South Carolina, but seems to be omitted from the present one. There is, of course, nothing in the Federal Constitution (Art. 2, 1) to prevent a State from appointing the electors in such manner as the Legislature direct, or by direct choice of the Legislature itself, if the State Constitution were so to provide. Michigan and other States in fact elect them by districts.

Territorial delegates are elected by the people, one from each territory.[6]

§ 218. *Corruption.* State officers may not be interested in contracts awarded by their department.[7]

ARTICLE 22. QUALIFICATIONS FOR OFFICE

§ 220. *Plurality of Offices.* Nearly all the States have provisions that no person can hold at the same time a State office and a national office of trust or profit, or at the same time two State offices of trust or profit, and this applies as well to seats in the Legislature as to other offices. The only exception is commonly that of justices of the peace and officers in the militia. Generally the holding of such other office, State or national, or under any foreign government, would make the person ineligible for a State office; and if already holding a seat in the Legislature or other State office, his acceptance of such

[1] Fla. 3, 31; Minn. 4, 26; Nev. 4, 34; R. I. 4, 18.

[2] Neb. Sep. Prop.

[3] Okla. 3, 4.

[4] Fla. 16, 20.

[5] Col. 5, 44.

[6] U. S. R. S. 1862.

[7] Del. 15, 8. See also § 304.

other office, State or national, would vacate his seat or amount to a resignation. The State Constitutions provide for this subject with endless and, it seems, unnecessary detail.

§ 221. *Age and Citizenship.* There is not usually much provision about age and citizenship qualifications for ordinary offices; but in many States no one who does not possess the qualifications of an elector is eligible for office.[1] A few States make residence in the State for one year a necessary qualification for any office;[2] and in a few others he must continue to reside within the State or forfeit his office.[3] (For judges, see Art. 65.)

A few State Constitutions specially provide that there shall be no property qualification for holding office;[4] and in New Hampshire and South Carolina, every inhabitant of the State having the proper qualification has equal right to be elected into office,[5] but in New Hampshire he must be able to read the State Constitution in English, and to write.

§ 222. *Disqualifications.* The State Constitutions very frequently provide that no person convicted of crime can hold office, and more particularly any person convicted of bribery, election frauds, defalcation of public money, or duelling, the attention of State Legislatures having of late years been especially called to the advisability of such disqualifications. Thus, many States provide generally that no person convicted of felony or infamous crime can hold office,[6] or, in Kentucky, "high misdemeanors." The special crimes thus disqualifying are defalcation or embezzlement of public [7] money,[8] or the case where any person remains liable for public moneys unaccounted for, whether actually convicted of defalcation or not.[9] Bribery is generally a disqualification for holding office, both of the party giving

[1] Ark. 19, 3; Col. 7, 6; Ct. 6, 4; La. 210; Minn. 7, 7; Miss. 250; Mon. 9, 7 & 11; N. H. 1, 14; Nev. 15, 3; N. C. 6, 7; Amt. 1900; O. 15, 4; S. C. 2, 2; 17, 1; Wash. 3, 25; Va. 32; W. Va. 4, 4; Wy. 6, 12 (3).

[2] Ill., Mo., Mon.

[3] Ark. 19, 4; Del. 3, 11; Ky. 234; 235; La.; R. I. 9, 1; Tex. 16, 14.

[4] Cal. 1, 24; Del. 7, 12; Ida. 1, 20; Kan. Bill of Rts. 7; Minn. 1, 17; N. C. 1, 22; Utah 1, 4.

[5] N. H. 1, 11; S. C. 1, 10. See also § 246.

[6] Ala. 60; Ark. 5, 9; Cal. 20, 11; Del. 2, 21; Fla. 6, 5; Ga. 2, 21; Ida. 6, 3; Ill. 4, 4; Ky. 150; La. 202; Minn. 4, 15; Miss. 44; N. C. 6, 5; N. D. 2, 38; Neb. 14, 2; O. 5, 4; Pa. 2, 7; Tex. 16, 2; Wis. 13, 3.

[7] Ky. 45 (for the legislature only).

[8] Ala.; Ark. 5, 9; Cal. 4, 21; Col. 12, 4; Del. 2, 21; Fla.; Ga.; Ida.; La. 182; Nev. 4, 10; Pa.; O. 2, 5; S. C. 10, 12; Wis. 13, 3.

[9] Ark. 5, 8; Col. 12, 3; Ga. 2, 4, 1; Ill. 4, 4; Ind. 2, 10; Io. 3, 23; Ky. 45; La. 182; Md. 3, 12; Mich. 4, 30; Miss. 43; Mo. 2, 19; Neb. 16, 2; O.; Ore. 2, 11; Tenn. 2, 25; Tex. 3, 20.

and the party receiving the bribe.[1] So specially in a few States bribery at elections,[2] but in some only as to the person offering the bribe. The giving or offering a bribe to procure the election or appointment of the guilty party disqualifies him for that term of office in many States,[3] and in a few permanently.[4] So, in some States specially the bribery of members of the Legislature,[5] or "treating." [6]

In Kentucky, corporations bribing or offering bribes forfeit their charters, or foreign corporations their license.[7]

A few States have the general provision that malfeasance in office shall be a disqualification,[8] but it would seem difficult to determine this without process of impeachment, to which the guilty party is nearly always liable. And so, in a few States, corruption in office,[9] malpractice,[10] taking more fees than the law allows,[11] or generally the violation of the oath of office.[12]

Betting on elections was, by the old Constitution of Florida, cause for the disqualification for office, and now in South Carolina, gambling,[13] and in two States, fraud or wilful violation of the laws [14] (whether a candidate for office or not).

Ordinary crimes are not made by the State Constitutions cause for general disqualification for office (see § 206 for disqualification for Legislature), but several State Constitutions so prescribe in case of perjury,[15] and a few in the case of larceny,[16] forgery,[17] and treason.[18] Idaho makes the practice of polygamy or professing Mormonism a cause for disqualification.[19]

Duelling, however, is by the Constitutions of a great many States made cause for disqualification for office, for either fighting a duel

[1] Ala. 60; Ark. 5, 9; Cal. 20, 11; Col. 12, 4; Fla.; Ga. 2, 2, 1; Ill. 4, 4; Ky. 151; La. 183; Md. 3, 50; Minn. 4, 15; Miss. 44; O. 5, 4; Pa.; Tex. 16, 2; Wash. 2, 30; W. Va. 6, 45. The same is implied in other States. See § 152.

[2] Ark. 3, 6 (but there must be a conviction of actual bribery); Ga. 2, 2, 1; Ida. La.; Md. 1, 3; Miss.; Mass, 2, 6, 2; Nev. 4, 10; N. H. 2, 96; Tex. 16, 5.

[3] Ind. 2, 6; Kan. 5, 6; Ky. 150; Mass.; N. H.; Ore. 2, 7; R. I. 9, 2; Tenn. 10, 3; Tex. 16, 5; Vt. 2, 34.

[4] Cal. 20, 10; Pa. 8, 9.

[5] W. Va. In one, only the member of the Legislature is so disqualified (Cal. 4, 35. See § 276.)

[6] Tenn.

[7] Ky. 150.

[8] Cal., Ga.

[9] N. C., Ga.

[10] N. C.

[11] Vt. 2, 25.

[12] Ill. 4, 5; Md. 1, 7; Mo. 4, 15; N. H.; Neb. 14, 1; Okla. 15, 2; S. D. 3, 8; W. Va. 6, 16; Wy. 6, 12 (9). See § 223.

[13] S. C. 17, 8.

[14] Ark. 3, 6; Pa. 8, 9.

[15] Ala.; Cal.; Col. 12, 4; Del.; Fla.; Ill.; Ky.; Minn.; N. C.; O.; Pa.; Tex.

[16] Ga.

[17] Ark., Cal., Tex.

[18] Ga., N. C.

[19] Ida. 6, 3.

as principal,[1] or absence from the State for that purpose,[2] or being a second,[3] or the giving, carrying, or accepting a challenge,[4] or the being engaged in a duel in any State or country as either principal or accessory.[5]

The Constitutions of a few States prescribe that no insane person or idiot can hold office.[6] The provision would seem to be unnecessary.

In two, no minister or preacher of any religious denomination can be a member of the Legislature.[7]

By the United States statutes, no soldier, seaman, or marine in the regular army or navy of the United States can hold a State office.[8]

The Louisiana Constitution disqualifies paupers or inmates of charitable institutions.[9] The same is probably provided by the statutes of most other States.

Idaho has a general provision that the disqualifications for office are the same as for voting.[10] There is an extraordinary provision in Utah. No officer, employee, attorney or agent of any corporation, company, or association doing business under, or by virtue of, any municipal charter or franchise, shall be eligible to or permitted to hold any municipal office in the municipality granting such charter or franchise.[11]

§ 223. *Oath of Office.* Members of the Legislature and other State officers, executive, judicial, or otherwise, are usually required to make oath to support the national and State Constitutions and faithfully discharge the duties of their office. Citations on this point seem unnecessary; but in three New England States they only make oath to bear allegiance to the State, and support the State Constitution.[12] In a few they must make oath that they have not, directly or indirectly, paid, or offered to pay, any consideration, or made any promise, as a reward for the giving or withholding a vote at an election;[13] or for their own election or nomination;[14] that they will not

[1] Ark. 19, 2; Cal. 20, 2; Col. 12, 12; Ga. 2, 4, 2; Ind. 2, 7; Io. 1, 5; Md. 3, 41; Mich. 7, 8; Miss. 19; Mo. 14, 3; N. C. 14, 2; Nev. 15, 3; O. 15, 5; Ore. 2, 9; Pa. 12, 3; S. C. 1, 11; Tenn. 9, 3; Tex. 16, 4; Wis. 13, 2; W. Va. 4, 10.

[2] Col.; Ind.; Kan. 5, 5; Md.; Miss.; Mo.; N. C.; Nev.; Ore.; Tex.

[3] Ark., Cal., Col., Md., Mo., N. C., Nev., O., Pa., Tex., W. Va.

[4] Ark.; Cal.; Col.; Ga.; Ind.; Kan.; Ky. 239; Md.; Mo.; N. C.; Nev.; O.; Ore.; Pa.; S. C.; Tenn.; Tex.; W. Va.

[5] Cal., Ga., Io., Md., Mich., Nev., S. C., Tenn., Tex., W. Va., Wis.

[6] Ga. 2, 2, 1; Ida. 6, 4; La. 202. See § 251.

[7] Md. 3, 11; Tenn. 9, 1.

[8] U. S. R. S. 1860.

[9] La. 202.

[10] Ida. 6, 3.

[11] Utah 12, 17.

[12] Mass. Amt. 6; N. H. 2, 83; Vt. 2, 12; 2, 29.

[13] Del., Ill., Mon., Neb., N. Y., Pa., S. D., Tex., Wy. See also § 154.

[14] Mon., Okla., S. D., Wy.

accept, or directly or indirectly receive, any valuable consideration for the giving or withholding a vote,[1] or for the doing or not doing any duty relating to their office;[2] that they have not been concerned in a duel as above specified;[3] that they have not violated any election law;[4] that they are not disqualified for holding office under the national or State Constitutions;[5] that they will not receive the profits of any other office during their term as governor, member of the Legislature, or judge;[6] that they hold no office of profit or trust under Congress.[7]

Violation of the oath of office is in a few States declared to be perjury.[8] Any officer convicted of having sworn falsely to, or violated, his oath of office forfeits it.[9] And he is always liable to impeachment.

§ 224. *Official Bonds.* The Legislature shall fix the amount of the penalty of all official bonds, and may, as far as practicable, provide that the whole or a part of the security required for the faithful discharge of official duty shall be made by some guarantee company or companies.[10]

§ 225. *Political Tests.* The Constitution of West Virginia declares political tests which require persons, as a prerequisite to the enjoyment of their civil and political rights, to purge themselves by their own oaths of past alleged offences, are repugnant to the principles of a free government, cruel, and oppressive.[11]

ARTICLE 23. ELECTIONS

§ 230. *General Provisions.* The Constitutions of many States declare that all elections should be free.[12] Of five, that they shall

[1] Ill.; Neb.; Pa.; Tenn. 10, 2; W. Va. 6, 16.

[2] Mo., Mon., Okla., Pa., S. D., Wy.

[3] Ky., Nev., S. C., Tex.

[4] Mon., Okla., Pa., Wy.

[5] Fla., S. C.

[6] Md.

[7] Vt. Amt. 1883.

[8] See § 222.

[9] Ill. 4, 5; Md. 1, 7; Neb. 14, 1; Okla.; S. D.; Wy.

[10] Miss. 82.

[11] W. Va. 3, 11. The attempt of the United States Government to disqualify persons from office or employment for having participated in the Rebellion came to naught, partly by voluntary repeal of the proscription, but mainly because decisions of the United States Supreme Court rendered the enforcement of such laws by test oaths impracticable.

[12] Ark. 3, 2; Col. 2, 5; Del. 1, 3; Ill. 2, 18; Ind. 2, 1; Ky. 6; Mass. 1, 9; Md. Decln. of Rts. 7; Mo. 2, 9; Mon. 3, 5; N. C. 1, 10; Neb. 1, 22; N. H. 1, 11; Okla. 3, 7; Ore. 2, 1; Pa. 1, 5; S. C. 1, 10; S. D. 6, 19; Tenn. 1, 5; Utah 1, 17; Va. 1, 6; Vt. 1, 8; 2, 34; Wash. 1, 19; Wy. 1, 27. A principle

be open,[1] or "not secret, nor the ballots counted in secret;"[2] that they shall be equal[3] and frequent.[4] So, in others, that no power, civil or military, shall ever interfere with the free exercise of the right of suffrage.[5]

§ 231. *Votes by Ballot.* The Constitutions of many States provide that all elections shall be by ballot.[6] So, in most, all elections by the people.[7] So, "until the Legislature otherwise direct."[8] And all elections by the Legislature, or by the people in a representative capacity, must be *viva voce*[9] (see also § 306).

The ballot box must be kept in public view.[10] The counting must be public.[11] But the secrecy of the ballot shall be maintained.[12] Voting machines may be used.[13] But ballots may be numbered.[14]

§ 232. *Majority Vote.* By the Constitutions of nearly all, the person having the highest number (*i. e.*, a plurality) of votes is declared elected.[15] And so, a plurality of votes given at any elec-

dating from very early statutes in England, and confirmed in the Bill of Rights.

[1] Col., Mo., Mon., S. C., Wy.

[2] S. C.

[3] Ark., Del., Ill., Ind., Ky., Mass., Ore., Pa., S. D., Tenn., Wash., Wy.

[4] Md.; N. C. 1, 28.

[5] Ark.; Col.; Ida. 1, 19; Mo.; Mon.; Neb.; Okla. 2, 4; Pa.; S. C. 2, 15; S. D.; Utah; Wash.; Wy.

[6] Cal. 1895, p. 407; Del. 5, 1; Ill. 7, 2; Io. 2, 6; Md. 1, 1; Mich. 7, 2; Minn. 7, 6; Neb. 7, 6; N. Y. 2, 5; O. 5, 2; Pa. 1901, p. 882; Utah 4, 8; W. Va. 4, 2; Wis. 3, 3.

[7] Ala. 179; Ariz. * 1358; Ark. 3, 3; Cal. 2, 5; Col. 7, 8; 1905, p. 84; Ct. 6, 7; Amt. 6; Fla. 6, 6; Ga. 2, 1, 1; Ida. 6, 1; Ind. 2, 13; Kan. 4, 1; Ky. 147; La. 203; Mass. 2, 1, 3, 3; Me. 2, 1; Miss. 240; Mo. 8, 3; Mon. 9, 1; N. C. 6, 6; N. D. 129; Nev. 2, 5; N. H. 2, 14 & 42; N. M.* 63, 22; Okla. 3, 6; Pa. 8, 4; R. I. 8, 2; S. C. 2, 1; S. D. 7, 3; Tenn. 4, 4; Tex. 6, 4; Va. 27; Vt. 2, 8; Amt. 19; Wash. 6, 6; Wy. 6, 11.

[8] Ore. 2, 15.

[9] Ala.; Ariz.;* 1112; Ark. 3, 12; Cal. 4, 28; Fla.; Ga. 3, 10, 1; Ind.; Io. 3, 38; Kan.; Ky.; La.; Mich. 4, 11; Minn. 4, 30; Miss. 76; Mo. 8, 6; N. C. 2, 9; N. D. 54; Neb. 3, 8; Nev.; N. Y.; O. 2, 27; Ore.; Pa. 8, 12; S. D. 3, 14; Tenn.; Tex. 3, 41; Va.; Wash. 2, 27; W. Va. 6, 44; Wis. 4, 30.

[10] Va.

[11] La.

[12] Cal., Ida., Ky., N. D., N. Y., Pa., Utah, Va., Wash., Wy.

[13] Col.; Cal.; Ct.; Amt. 23; Utah; Va. 37.

[14] Col., S. D.; Texas 1891, p. 194.

[15] Ala. 115; Ariz.* 1373; Ark. 6, 3; Cal. 5, 4; Col. 4, 3; Ct. Amt. 3; D. C.* 99–100; Del. 3, 3; Ida. 4, 2; Ill. 5, 4; Ind. 5, 5; Io. 4, 4; Kan. 1, 2; Ky. 70; La. 62; Mass. Amt. 14; Md. 2, 3; 15, 4; Me. 4, 1, 5; 4, 2, 5; 5, 1, 3; Amts. Art. 24; Mich. 5, 3; Mo. 5, 3; Mon. 7, 2; N. C. 3, 3; N. D. 74; Neb. 5, 4; Nev. 5, 4; N. J. 5, 2; N. M.* 63, 28; N. Y. 4, 3; 1898, p. 1550; O. 3, 3; Ore. 5, 5; Pa. 4, 2; R. I. Amt. 10; S. C. 4, 4; S. D. 4, 3; Tenn. 3, 2; Territories, U. S. R. S. 1847; Tex. 4, 3; Utah 7, 2; Va. 70; Vt. Amt. 5; Wash. 3, 4; W. Va. 7, 3; Wis. 5, 3; Wy. 4, 3. In some States the above rule applies only to elections of the officers of the executive (see § 202): Ala., Ark., Cal., Ga., Ill.; Kan., Mo., N. C., Neb., Nev., O., Tex., W. Va. In others, only to elections of the governor or lieutenant-governor (Cal., Ct., Del., Ind., Io., Ky., La., Md., Mich., N. J., N. Y., Pa., Tenn., Va., Wis.). In others, only to elections of the Legislature (Ct., Vt.).

tion shall constitute a choice, where not otherwise directed in the Constitution.[1]

When there is no majority for any person for governor, the Legislature in joint session elects him.[2] But only one of the two having the highest votes.[3] So, only, in case of a tie.[4] So, when there is none for lieutenant-governor.[5] Or for the council.[6] And in the case of State senators, when no candidate has received a majority.[7] So, for secretary, treasurer, or attorney-general.[8] Or for treasurer.[9] For secretary of State or comptroller.[10] For vacancies in office, see § 201.

§ 233. *Australian Ballot.* — Ballots must be uniform, with the names of all candidates and the offices to be filled in due order, and have no distinguishing mark or symbol; but any voter may erase any name and insert another.[11] So elections are by "secret official ballot" marked by each voter in private.[12] At all elections by the people, except primaries and municipal elections in small towns which are not held at the same time as a general election, there must be an official ballot which may have a separate device by which the political party or the candidate may be indicated; and the voter may vote for such device at the head of the list thereby voting for the entire ticket, or he may vote for each of the candidates in turn by marking him specially by his name. Ballots must be prepared in secrecy at the polls, and the names of independent candidates may be printed with a device; and names of candidates may be written on the ballot.[13] In other States similar provisions are made by statute.

Cumulative Voting exists by the Constitution of Illinois (each district voting for three representatives) each voter may cast as many votes for each candidate as there are State representatives to be elected, or may distribute his votes, or equal parts thereof, among the candidates as he sees fit.[14]

§ 234. *Election Day*, by the Constitutions of the States (or statutes in some States and the Territories) comes as follows: In nearly all States, on the first Tuesday after the first Monday in

[1] Cal. 20, 13; Fla. 16, 8; Nev. 15, 14; Ore. 2, 16.

[2] Ga. 5, 1, 5; 5, 2, 1; N. H. 2, 41; Vt. 2, 10; Amt. 9. For Mississippi, see § 202, notes.

[3] N. H., R. I.

[4] Ala.; Ct. Amt. 30; Ida.; Ky.; La.; Mon.; N. D.; N. Y.; R. I.; S. C.; S. D.; Utah; Wash.; W. Va. 1891, 153; Wy.

[5] Ct., Vt.

[6] N. H. 2, 60.

[7] Me. 5, 1, 3; N. H. 2, 33.

[8] Ct., R. I.

[9] Ga., Vt.

[10] Ga.

[11] Va. 28.

[12] Ky. 147; Wy. 5, 11.

[13] La. 212.

[14] Ill. 4, 7, and 8.

November, biennially; in the even years;[1] in the odd years.[2] In a few other States it is biennially in the even years but on different days; thus, in Maine on the second Monday in September;[3] in Oregon on the first Monday in June;[4] in Vermont on the first Tuesday in September;[5] in Arkansas on the first Monday in September;[6] in Georgia on the first Wednesday in October; and in Colorado (now changed by statute) on the first Tuesday in October.[7]

In other States, the election is held *annually* on the first Tuesday after the first Monday in November.[8] In a few of the southern States, the elections and terms of office have recently been made quadrennial; thus, in Louisiana, every four years on the Tuesday after the third Monday in April (next in 1908);[9] in Alabama and Mississippi, every four years on the first Tuesday after the first Monday in November (beginning in Mississippi with 1895 and in Alabama with 1902); and see also § 203.[10] But the Legislature, in some States, may fix a different day.[11]

§ 235. *Conduct of Elections.* — The Constitutions of many States provide that the right of suffrage shall be protected by laws regulating elections and prohibiting all undue influences from power, bribery, tumult, or improper conduct.[12] Or, that the Legislature may enact laws concerning the judges, time, place, and manner of elections;[13] that the Legislature shall forbid the sale of intoxicating liquors near the polls.[14] The Legislature shall provide by law against fraudulent voting, etc.[15] In four States, the election officers are sworn not to disclose how any person shall have voted, except in judicial

[1] Ariz.* 1129; Cal. 4, 3; Ct. Amt. 27, 1; Del. 5, 1; Schedule, 7; Fla. 3, 3; 1889, p. 314; 1895, p. 367; Ida. Pol. C.* 770; Ill. 4, 3 and 5, 3; Io. Amt. 1 (1882, No. 12); 1904, p. 207; Kan. 1905, 543; Mich. 4, 34; Minn. 7, 9, Amt. 1883; Mo. 8, 1; Mon.* 1150; N. C. 2, 27; Code, 2668*; N. D. 124; Nev. 4, 3; 15, 5; N. H. 26, 40 ("biennially in November"); N. M.* 1588; O. 1904, p. 640; Okla.* 2906; S. C. 3, 8; S. D. 7, 4; Tenn. 2, 7; Tex.* 1659; Utah 6, 3; 4, 9; Wash. 2, 5; 6, 8; W. Va. Amt. 1884; Wis. 13, 1; Wy. 3, 5; 6, 12 (5).

[2] Ky. 30 & 95; Md. 3, 7; 15, 7; Miss. 102, 252; Va. 41, 42.

[3] Me. 2, 4; Amt. 23.

[4] Ore. 2, 14.

[5] Vt. 2, 8; Amt. 24, 1.

[6] Ark. 3, 8; Jan. 23, 1875, § 1.

[7] Col. 5, 2; 7, 7; Ga. 3, 4, 2.

[8] Col.* 1575; Del. 4, 1; Ind. 2, 14; Kan. 4, 2; Ky. 148; Mass. Amt. 15; Neb. 16, 13; N. J. 4, 1, 3; N. Y. 3, 9; Pa. 8, 2; R. I. Amt. 11 (1890, p. 146); Va.* 109. But note that the terms of office may be biennial; see §§ 201, 202.

[9] La. 206.

[10] Ala. 46; Miss. 102, 140, 252.

[11] Ala., Ga., La.

[12] Ala. 33 and 191; Cal. 20, 11; Ct. 6, 6; Fla. 3, 26; Ky. 150; Nev. 4, 27; Ore. 2, 8; S. C. 1, 9; Tex. 16, 2; Va. 36; W. Va. 4, 11; Wy. 6, 12 (1).

[13] Md. 3, 49.

[14] Ala. 191; Ga. 2, 5, 1; Ky. 154; La. 205.

[15] S. C. 2, 5.

proceedings.[1] So, in one, a voter may vote by sealed ballot if he so choose.[2] All boards, etc., must be bi-partisan.[3] Election managers shall require proof of the payment of taxes, etc.[4] All employers must allow employees four hours in which to vote,[5] between 6 A. M. and 7 P. M. No corporation organized or doing business in this State shall be permitted to influence elections or official duty by contributions of money or anything of value.[6]

§ 236. *Registration.* — The Constitutions of some States have a general provision that there shall be laws to preserve the purity of elections, prevent fraud, and guard against the abuse of the elective franchise.[7] And in many, provision for registration of voters is especially made.[8] Permanent lists are kept, and a certificate given to the voter.[9] A person denied registration may appeal to the courts.[10] But in one, the Constitution expressly forbids registration laws.[11] And in one, no elector shall be deprived of his vote by reason of his name not being registered.[12] And in one, the Legislature shall establish no board or court of registration of voters.[13] Registration must be four months before the election;[14] so, ten days.[15]

§ 237. *Freedom from Arrest.* — In most States, the Constitution provides that electors shall be free from arrest while attending, going to, or returning from the polls, except for treason, felony, or breach of the peace.[16] So, in some, on any civil process.[17] They are not liable to arrest on civil process during election day.[18] Nor are they required to attend court on that day, either as party or witness.[19]

[1] Ark. 3, 3; Col. 7. 8; Mo. 8, 3; Pa. 8. 4.

[2] W. Va. 4, 2. See § 231.

[3] N. Y. 2, 6.

[4] S. C. 2, 4. See § 244.

[5] Ky. 148.

[6] Okla. 9, 40.

[7] Col. 7, 11; Fla. 6, 9; Kan. 5, 4, Ky. 150; Md. 3, 42; Mich. 7, 6; Mon. 9, 9; Nev. 2, 6; N. Y. 2, 4; Okla. 3, 6; Pa. 1901, p. 881; R. I. 2, 6; Tenn. 4, 1; Tex. 6, 4; W. Va. 4, 11.

[8] Ala. 186; Del. 5. 4; Fla. 6, 2; Ga. 2, 2, 1 (such provision may be made by the Legislature); Ind. 2, 2 and 14; Ky. 147; La. 197, 214; Md. 1, 5; Mo. 8, 5; N. C. 6, 3; Amt. 1900, 2; Nev.; N. Y.; Okla. 3, 6; R. I. Amt. 7; Pa. 1901, p. 881; S. C. 2, 4 & 8; Va. 18, 19, 20, 25; Wash. 6, 7; Wis. 3, 1; Amt. (the Legislature must provide for registration in cities and towns); Wy. 6, 12.

[9] S. C.

[10] La. 201; S. C. 2, 5.

[11] Ark. 3, 2.

[12] W. Va. 4, 12.

[13] W. Va. 6, 43.

[14] Miss. 251.

[15] N. Y.

[16] Ala. 191; Ariz.* Bill of Rts. 24; Ark. 3, 4; Cal. 2, 2; Col. 7, 5; Del. 5, 5; Ga. 2, 3, 1; Ill. 7, 3; Ind. 2, 12; Io. 2, 2; Kan. 5, 7; Ky. 149; La. 204; Me. 2, 2; Mich. 7, 3; Miss. 102; Mo. 8, 4; Mon. 9, 4; N. D. 123; Neb. 7, 5; O. 5, 3; Okla. 3, 7; Ore. 2, 13; Pa. 8, 5; S. C. 2, 14; S. D. 7, 5; Tenn. 4, 3; Tex. 6, 5; Utah 4, 3; Wash. 6. 5; Wy. 6, 3.

[17] Ct. 6, 8; Va. 29; W. Va. 4, 3.

[18] Minn. 7, 5; Nev. 2, 4.

[19] Mich., Va., W. Va.

And they are not obliged to perform military duty on election day, except in time of war or public danger.[1]

§ 238. *Contested Elections* are, by the Constitutions of many States, to be tried in a manner to be provided by law.[2] In many others, they are to be tried by the Legislature in joint session.[3] So, in several others, by the Legislature in the manner of law provided.[4] In two States, by a committee of both houses.[5] In one, by the house alone.[6] In others, by the courts of law.[7] But in most of the States, the elections of members of each house of the Legislature are to be determined by such house.[8] In the trial of contested elections, and proceedings for investigating them, no person can refuse to testify on the ground that it will criminate him; but such testimony shall not afterwards be used against him except in proceedings for perjury.[9]

ARTICLE 24. THE RIGHT OF SUFFRAGE

§ 240. *Citizens.*[10] — The right of suffrage (subject to the other conditions in this article) is, by the Constitutions (or statutes) of all

[1] Cal. 2, 3; Ill.; Io. 2, 3; Me. 2, 3; Mich. 7, 4; Mon. 9, 5; N. D.; Neb.; Ore.; S. D.; Utah 4, 4; Va.; Wash.; W. Va.; Wy. 8, 4.

[2] Ark. 19, 24; Col. 7, 12; Ct. 4, 2; Ida. 4, 2; Io. 3, 7; Ky. 38; La. 209; Mon. 7, 2; N. J. 5, 2; O. 2, 21; Tex. 3, 8; W. Va. 4, 11; Wash. 3, 4.

[3] Ark. 6, 4; Col. 4, 3; Mass. 2, 2, 1, 3; Me. 5, 1, 3; Mo. 5, 25; N. C. 3, 3; N. H. 2, 41; R. I. 8, 7; Tex. 4, 3; Va. 4, 2; Vt. Amt. 9; W. Va. 7, 3. See also § 270.

[4] Ala. 115; Ga. 5, 1, 6; Ill. 5, 4; Ind. 5, 6; Io. 4, 5; Ky. 90; Mo.; Neb. 5, 4; Ore. 5, 6; Tenn. 3, 2.

[5] Del. 3, 4; Pa. 4, 2.

[6] Md. 2, 4.

[7] Ariz.* 1384; Mo. 8, 9; N. M.* 1874, 29; Pa. 8, 17; Wy. 6. 2.

[8] N. H. 2, 21 and 34; N. M.* 63, 59. For other States, see § 270. In some States the above provision applies to the contested elections of the governor or other executive officers only (Ala., Ark., Col., Ct., Del., Ill., Mass., Me., N. C., Nev., N. H., N. J., R. I., Tex., Vt.). In others, for members of the Legislature only (Io., Ky., Pa.). In others, for the governor or lieutenant-governor only (Del., Ind., Io., Ky., Md., Miss., Mo., Ore., Tenn., Tex., Va., W. Va.). But in some States these provisions do not apply to contested elections for the governor (Mo., Pa.), or it only applies to elections of executive officers other than governor, &c. (Mo.).

[9] Ark. 3, 9; Col. 7, 9; La. 216; Pa. 8, 10.

[10] In order to give a complete presentation of the subject in this article, the statute provisions of a few States which have no constitutional provisions on the subject are also incorporated. In England all free men voted until 1429. The right to vote even for presidential electors and members of the House is determined by the laws of the States, save only that any one who can vote for the lower House of the State Legislature must be allowed to vote for members of Congress (U. S. C. 1, 2, 1); therefore it will of course vary in the different States of the Union. But by the Fourteenth Amendment any

the States, given to every male (or female, see below) citizen of the United States aged twenty-one.[1] But he must *also* be a citizen of the State.[2] So, of any person naturalized; but he must have been a United States citizen ninety days before the election,[3] or one month before.[4] And in many States, also to every male of foreign birth, aged twenty-one, who has declared his intention to become a citizen according to the United States naturalization laws,[5] at least thirty days before the election;[6] at least one year, and not more than five years, before;[7] at least four months before;[8] or one year, and not more than six, respectively.[9]

In other States, to every male citizen or inhabitant of the State aged twenty-one.[10] He must have been a citizen ninety days.[11] Since the Fourteenth Amendment this provision is of course neutralized; See note 10.

Indians, aged twenty-one, if civilized, and not a member of any tribe, can vote.[12] So, in Michigan, if born in the United States. In

person naturalized in the United States becomes a citizen both of the United States and of the State wherein he resides; therefore the State may not withhold the right to vote except as it may be withheld from other citizens in the State; and never by reason of race, color, or previous condition of servitude (U. S. C. Amts. 14, 1; 15, 1). It would seem, however, that foreigners newly naturalized may be subjected to the same term of residence in the State before being allowed to vote as are required of citizens coming from other States. All limitations of the right of suffrage are indirectly forbidden by the Federal Constitution (Amt. 14, 2). That is to say, the representation of the State in Congress is reduced in proportion to the number of male inhabitants whose right of suffrage is denied or abridged except for participation in rebellion or for other crime. The educational tests, therefore, imposed especially by the newer Constitutions, would seem to be ground of diminishing the representation in Congress of the States adopting them; but this has not yet been done. The right of suffrage is not, however, a natural right, but one of political expediency; hence women, although citizens, do not necessarily vote.

[1] Ala. 177; Ariz.* 1347; Ark. 3, 1; 1891, p. 314; Cal. 2, 1; 1893, p. 543; Col. 7, 1; Ct. Amt. 8; D. C.* 98; Fla. 6, 1; Ga. 2, 1, 2; Ida. 6, 2; Ill. 7, 1; Ind. 2, 2; Io. 2, 1; Kan. 5, 1; Ky. 145; La. 197; Md. 1, 1; Me. 2, 1; Mich. Amt. 1893, p. 438; Minn. 7, 1; Amt. 1895, 3; Miss. 241; Mo. 8, 2; Mon. 9, 2; N. C. 6, 1; N. D. 121; Neb. 7, 1; Nev. 2, 1; N. J. 2, 1; N. M.* 1868, 26, 2; O. 5, 1; Okla. 3, 1; Ore. 2, 2; R. I. 2, 1; Amt. 7; S. C. 2, 3; S. D. 7, 1; Tenn. 4, 1; Territories, U. S. R. S. 1859, 1860; Tex. 6, 2; Utah 4, 2 & 5; Va. 18; Wash. 6, 1; Wis. 3, 1; Amt.; Wy. 6, 2 & 5.

[2] La., S. C.

[3] Cal., Utah.

[4] Pa. 8, 1.

[5] Ariz.* 1412; Ark.; Ind.; Kan.; Mo.; Ore.; S. D.; Terr.; Tex.; Wis.

[6] Neb.

[7] Mo.

[8] Col.

[9] N. D.

[10] Del. 5, 2; Mass. 2, 1, 2, 2; Amt. 3; Mich. 7, 1; N. H. 2, 12 & 27; N. Y. 2, 1; Okla.; Pa. 8, 1; Vt.* 62; W.Va. 4, 1.

[11] N. Y.

[12] Ida., Wis., Minn. In other States, it would follow from §§ 240 or 21, 22, that all Indians not on a reservation

Oklahoma, all Indians vote like whites; in North Dakota, civilized Indians who have two years severed their tribal relation. So, in Wisconsin, persons of Indian blood who have once been declared by Congress citizens of the United States, any subsequent act of Congress to the contrary notwithstanding. So, in Minnesota, persons of mixed white and Indian blood who have adopted the customs and habits of civilization; and Indians also, after an examination by the courts. But in several no Indian not taxed can vote.[1] And in one, no Narragansett can vote.[2]

The Constitutions of a few States still restrict the right of suffrage to white persons (see § 22); but this is void under the Fifteenth Amendment. Mongolians may not vote, if not born in the United States.[3] In four States, women vote in all respects like men.[4] (See also §§ 22, 23.) By the Constitution of others, the Legislature may at any time extend the right of suffrage without regard to sex to persons not here enumerated;[5] but the law must be approved by a majority of the voters at a general election.[6]

"The Legislature shall at its first session after the admission of the State into the Union submit to a vote of the electors of the State the following question to be voted upon at the next general election held thereafter, namely: 'Shall the word "male" be stricken from the article of the Constitution relating to elections and the right of suffrage?' If a majority of the votes cast upon that question are in favor of striking out said word 'male,' it shall be stricken out and there shall thereafter be no distinction between males and females in the exercise of the right of suffrage at any election in this State."[7]

§ 241. *Residence Qualifications.* — By the Constitutions of a few States, a voter must have been resident a certain period of time in the United States.[8] And by the Constitutions of nearly all, to vote at a State election, a person qualified according to § 240 must have

are citizens, there being no provision to the contrary.

[1] Ida.; Me. 2, 1; Miss. 241; Wash. 6, 1.

[2] R. I. 2, 4.

[3] Ida.

[4] Ida. Amt.; Col. 7, 1; Utah 2, 6; 4, 1; Wy. 6, 2.

[5] N. D. 122 (perhaps repealed by Amt. 2); Col. 7, 2 (adopted).

[6] Wis.

[7] S. D. 7, 2. And so, substantially, in Washington (27, 17).

The above question was submitted to the people at the election held in November, 1890, and was rejected in both, in South Dakota by the following vote: for, 22,072; against, 45,682.

[8] Ninety days (Cal.). One year (Ind. 2, 2; Minn. 7, 1; S. D. 7, 1). He must have been a citizen one month (Pa. 8, 1). In one, he must be *born* in the United States, unless he holds a certain amount of real estate in the State (see § 244; R. I. 2, 1 & 2).

been resident for a certain period immediately preceding the election in the State.[1] In England no residence qualification existed until Henry V., and it was repealed under Geo. III.

In one State, residence on State land ceded to the United States is not sufficient (compare § 243).[2] Ministers and teachers are qualified after six months' residence.[3] And by the Constitutions of a few States, a person otherwise qualified must, in order to vote at any election, have been resident in the county or legislative district for a certain period of time before,[4] or in the city or township.[5] So he must be *registered* in the town by June 30 preceding.[6]

§ 242. *Losing a Residence, etc.* — By the Constitutions of many States, no person shall be deemed to have lost a residence for the purpose of voting,[7] by reason of his absence from the State while employed in the service of the United States,[8] or of the State.[9] Or, while engaged in the navigation of the waters of this State or of the United States,[10] or temporarily absent from the State.[11] Or, while

[1] Three months (Me. 2, 1). Four months (Minn.). Six months (Ark. 8, 2; Col. 7, 1; Ida. 6, 1; Ind. 2, 2; Io. 2, 1; Kan. 5, 1; Mich.; Minn.; Neb. 7, 1; Nev. 2, 1; N. H.* 31, 8; N. M.*; Ore. 2, 2; S. D.). One year (Ark. 3, 1; Cal. 2, 1; Col. 1901, 47; Ct. Amt. 8; D. C.* 98 (in the District); Del. 5, 2; Fla. 6, 1; Ga. 2, 1, 2; Ill. 7, 1; Ky. 145; Mass. Amt. 3; Md. 1, 1; Miss. 241; Mo. 8, 2; Mon.; N. D.; N. J. 2, 1; N. Y.; O. 5, 1; Okla. 3, 1; Pa. 8, 1; Tenn. 4, 1; Tex. 6, 2; Utah; Vt.* 61; Wash.; W. Va. 4, 1; Wis. 3, 1; Wy.). For two years (Ala. 178; La.; N. C. 1900, 2; R. I. Amt. 7; S. C. 2, 4; Va. 18). Two and a half years (Mich.).

[2] R. I. 2, 5.

[3] S. C.

[4] Ten days (Ark., Minn.). Thirty days (Del., Ida., Nev., O.* 2945, S. D.). Sixty days (Io., Mo., W. Va., Wy.). Three months (Cal., Del., Ill., N. C., Va., Wash.). Four months (N. Y., Utah). Five months (N. J.). Six months (Ark., Fla., Ga., Ky., Md., N. C., N. D., Okla., Tenn., Tex.). One year (La., Miss., S. C., Va.). "As by law provided" (Col., Mon., Neb., O.).

[5] Sixty days (Ind., Mo., Pa.). Six months (Ct., La., Mass., Md., N. H., R. I.). Thirty days (Cal., Kan., Minn.). One year (Ala., S. D., Va.). In the ward or precinct or election district, ten days (Mich., Minn.). Twenty days (Mich., O.). Thirty days (Ark., Cal., D. C.,* Del., Ill., Ind., Nev., N. Y., Okla., Va., Wash., Wis.). Sixty days (Ky.; Pa. 8, 1; Utah.) Three months (Ala., Md., Me.). Four months (N. C., S. C.). And he does not lose his residence in the old district for a corresponding period (Va.).

[6] R. I. Amt. 11 (1900, p. 149).

[7] Or for the purpose of holding office (Col., Ky., Tex.). Or for any purpose whatever (Ark., Cal., Ind., Wis.).

[8] Ariz.* 1693; Ark. 19, 7; Cal. 2, 4; 20, 12; Col. 7, 4; Ida. 6, 5; Ill. 7, 4; Ind. 2, 4; Kan. 5, 3; Me. 2, 1; Mich. 7, 5; Minn. 7, 3; Mo. 8, 7; Mon. 9, 3; N. D. 125; Nev. 2, 2; N. Y. 2, 3; Ore. 2, 4; Pa. 8, 13; S. C. 2, 7; S. D. 7, 6; Tex. 16, 9; Wash. 6, 4; Wis. 3, 4; Wy. 6, 7. These exceptions do not apply to a person serving out a sentence in the penitentiary for infamous crime.

[9] Ark., Cal., Col., Ida., Ill., Ind., Ky., Me., Mich., Mo., Mon., N. D., Ore., Pa., S. D., Tex., Wash., Wis.

[10] Ariz.,* Cal., Ida., Kan., La., Mich., Minn., Mo., Mon., Nev., N. Y., Ore., Pa., S. C., Wash. Or, in all these last except Idaho and Minnesota, of the waters of the high seas.

[11] Ala. 1, 31; Ariz.*; Ark.; S. C. 1, 12.

confined in prison,[1] or kept at an almshouse or asylum at the public expense.[2] Or while a student in any institution of learning.[3] And in several States no person shall be deemed to have *gained* a residence in the State by reason of his presence, for the various reasons respectively specified.[4]

§ 243. *Army and Navy.* — And in most States it is specially provided that no person shall be deemed to have acquired a residence for the purpose of voting by reason of being stationed in the State while in the military or naval service of the United States.[5] And the same law would seem to be implied (by § 242) in a few other States.

In several, no person in the regular army or navy of the United States can vote (see also below).[6] But those who were soldiers and sailors in the Civil War, if United States citizens, have a special right to vote.[7] *And conversely,* no person in the actual military or naval service of the United States is deemed to have lost his right to vote by reason of his absence (in time of war, except in Nevada); [8] but a manner in which he may vote is to be provided by the Legislature.[9] But in three, only when such person is not in the regular army or navy.[10]

§ 244. *Property Qualification.* — In nine States there is an express constitutional provision that there shall be no property qualification for the right of suffrage.[11] *Except* school elections; [12] elections creating indebtedness.[13] But in one, the Constitution declares that every free man has a right to vote "who has a sufficient

[1] Ariz.,* Cal., Col., Kan., Mich., Minn., Mo., Nev., N. Y., Ore., Pa.

[2] Ariz.,* Cal., Col., Ida., Kan., La., Mich., Minn., Mo., Mon., Nev., N. Y., Ore., Pa., Va., Wash.

[3] Ariz.*; Cal.; Col.; Ida.; Kan.; La.; Mich.; Minn.; Mo.; Mon.; Nev.; N. Y.; Ore.; Pa.; S. C.; Va. 24; Wash.

[4] Ariz.,* Cal., Col., Ida., Kan., La., Mich., Mo., Mon., Nev., N. Y., Ore., Pa., S. C., Wash. So, in Maine, as to paupers or asylum inmates only.

[5] Ark. 3, 7; Del. 5, 2; Ga. 2, 1, 2; Ill. 7, 5; Ind. 2, 3; Io. 2, 4; Ky. 146; La. 175; Me. 2, 1; Mich. 7, 7; Minn. 7, 4; Mon. 9. 6; N. D. 126; Neb. 7, 4; N. J. 2, 1; O. 5, 5; Okla. 3, 2; Ore. 2, 5; R. I. 2, 4; S. D. 7, 7; Territories, U. S. R. S. 1860; Va. 24; Wash. 6, 4; W. Va. 4, 1; Wis. 3, 5; Wy. 6, 8.

[6] Kan. 5, 3; Mo. 8, 11; Ore.; Tex. 6, 1.

[7] R. I. Amt. 6.

[8] Ariz.* 1407; Ct. Amt. 13; Kan. 5, 3; La. 208; Me. 2, 4; Mich. 7, 1; Neb. 7, 3; Nev. 2, 3; N. J. 2, 1; N. Y. 2, 1; Okla.; Pa. 8, 6; R. I. Amt. 4; S. D. 6, 19; Utah 1, 17; Wash.; Wy. 6, 7.

[9] This last clause is not added in a few States (Wash., Wy.).

[10] Ct., Kan., Neb.

[11] Ark. 1, 21; Cal. 1, 24; Ida. 1, 20; Kan. Bill of Rts. 7; Minn. 1, 17; N. C. 1, 22; S. C. 1, 11; Utah 1, 4; 4, 7. In States where there is no express qualification, the same would result from § 240 (except as the Constitution provides).

[12] Ida.

[13] Ida., Utah.

interest in the community."[1] In Virginia, the Legislature may provide a property qualification not exceeding $250 in town or county elections except for members of the Legislature.[2] And in several, there is a provision requiring a voter to have paid certain taxes.[3] See also §§ 245, 246.

And in *municipal elections*, in two States, to determine the expenditure of money or the assumption of debt, no person can vote who does not pay a property tax in such municipality.[4]

And in one, no person can vote in city council or tax or money elections unless he have paid a property tax on property in such town or city to the net value of $134.28.[5]

Exceptions. — No person who served in the army or navy, U. S. A. or C. S. A., is required to have paid such poll tax above required.[6]

§ 245. *Educational Qualifications* of the right of suffrage exist in several States. Thus, no person can vote who cannot read the Constitution and Statutes of the State.[7] No person who cannot read the Constitution of the State in English.[8] No person who cannot write his name;[9] or, in New Hampshire "write"; in Virginia, he must write his application.[10] Who cannot read and speak English.[11] Who cannot read and write any section of the State Constitution.[12] Physical disability is always an excuse.[13]

Except persons who now (1904) have the right to vote, or who were sixty years old January 1, 1904;[14] or who were twenty or became United States citizens before January 1, 1900,[15] or were voters, or over the age of sixty in 1893.[16]

[1] Vt. 1, 8.

[2] Va. 30.

[3] Thus, all taxes except for the year of the election (Ga. 2, 1, 2). He must have paid a State, county, or city tax within two years previous to the election (Pa. 8, 1). He must have paid all poll taxes assessed upon him for the year previous (N. C. 5, 1); for a period of two years preceding (Miss. 241; R. I. 2, 3); three years (Va. 20, 21); to be prescribed by the Legislature (Fla. 6, 8; Tenn. 4, 1; Tex. 1901, p. 322). He must have paid all poll taxes due six months before the election (S. C. 2, 4). No person can vote who is excused from paying taxes at his own request (N.H. 2, 28). He must have paid a tax to the amount of $1, unless he owns real estate in the State (R. I. 2, 1 & 2).

[4] Ida. 1, 20; Tex. 6, 3. (Such a tax may be required also in school elections. See §§363, 372.)

[5] R. I. Amt. 7.

[6] Va. 22.

[7] Ct. Amt. 11; Wy. 6, 9.

[8] Cal. 1893, p. 543; Del. 5, 2; Mass. Amt. 20; Me. 1891, res. 109; Miss. 244; N. H. 1, 11.

[9] Cal., Del., Mass., Me.

[10] Va. 20.

[11] Wash. C. Amt. 1896.

[12] N. C. 1900, 2; S. C. 2, 4; (unless he have paid taxes on $300).

[13] Cal., Mass., Me., Del., N. H., Wy.

[14] N. H.

[15] Del.

[16] Me.

Every inhabitant of the State possessing the qualifications required by the Constitution has an equal right to vote.[1]

In Colorado, the Legislature were authorized to exact an educational qualification after 1890.[2]

§ 246. *Southern State Provisions.* — In Alabama after January 1, 1903, only those persons can register who can either (1) read and write any article of the Constitution of the United States in English, and who are physically unable to work or who have worked or been regularly engaged in some lawful employment, business, occupation, trade, or calling for the greater part of the twelve months next preceding; or else (2) the owner in good faith in his own right, or the husband of such owner, of forty acres of land upon which they reside, or of real estate or personal property assessed to the value of $300, provided the taxes have been paid.[3]

In Louisiana an applicant for registration must be able to read and write and shall make his own written application in English or in his mother tongue, which application contains the essential facts and must be entirely written, dated, and signed by him in the presence of the registration officer without assistance or suggestion from any person, or any memorandum whatever, except the form of application, provided that if unable to write in English he may write the same in his mother tongue from the dictation of an interpreter, or if unable to write by reason of physical disability, the same shall be written at his dictation by the registration officer.

If he be not able to read or write he may nevertheless be entitled to be registered if, at the time he offers to register, he be the bona fide owner of property assessed him in the State at a valuation of not less than $300 on which all taxes shall have been paid, if the property be personal; but he must make oath that he is a citizen of the United States and of the State, over the age of twenty-one, that he possesses the qualifications as to residence prescribed in the general laws, and that he is the owner of property assessed at such valuation.[4]

"*Grandfather Clause.*" — This principle recently adopted in State Constitutions, mainly in Southern States, but also in some Northern States, operates as an exception to the property and educational qualifications. Thus, in New Hampshire, all persons who had the right to vote at the time of the adoption of the new Constitution, 1903, or were sixty years old January 1, 1904. So in Delaware the

[1] S. C. 1, 10.
[2] Col. 7, 3.
[3] Ala. 181, 180.
[4] La. 197 (3) & (4).

educational qualification only applies to persons who become twenty-one years old or are naturalized as United States citizens after January 1, 1900. In Virginia there was a general registration in 1902 and 1903, at which all male citizens of the United States having proper qualifications of age and residence could register if they were either, first, a person who, prior to the adoption of this Constitution, served in time of war in the Army or Navy of the United States or of the Confederate States or of any State of the United States or of the Confederate States; or, second, a son of any such person; or third, a person who owns property upon which, for the year next preceding that in which he offers to register, State taxes aggregating at least one dollar have been paid; or, fourth, a person able to read any section of the State Constitution and give a reasonable explanation of the same, or, if unable to read such section, able to understand and give a reasonable explanation thereof when read to him by the officers. A roll containing the names of all persons thus registered was to be preserved, and persons so enrolled need not register again.[1] In South Carolina, up to January 1, 1898, persons were allowed to register permanently who could read or understand the State Constitution when read to them.[2] In Alabama, up to December 20, 1902, persons who served in the U. S. or C. S. army or navy in the Mexican, Indian, Civil, or Spanish wars; the lawful descendants of such; and "all persons of good character who understand the duties and obligations of citizenship under a republican form of government."[3]

In North Carolina no male person who was, on January 1, 1867, or prior thereto, entitled to vote under the laws of any State in the United States wherein he then resided, and no lineal descendant of any such person shall be denied the right to register and vote by reason of his failure to possess these educational qualifications, provided he have registered prior to December 1, 1908; and the Legislature are to provide for the registration of all persons entitled to vote without such educational qualifications and make a permanent record of such registration on or before November 1, 1908, and all persons so registered shall forever thereafter have the right to vote unless disqualified for other reasons, provided such person have paid his poll tax as required.[4]

On and after the first day of January, A. D., 1892, every elector

[1] Va. 19.
[2] S. C. 2, 4.
[3] Ala. 180.
[4] N. C. Amt. 1900, 2.

shall, in addition to the foregoing qualifications, be able to read any section of the Constitution of the State; or he shall be able to understand the same when read to him, or give a reasonable interpretation thereof.[1]

In Louisiana "no male person who was in 1867, or prior, entitled to vote under the Constitution or statutes of any State of the United States wherein he then resided, and no son or grandson of such person not less than twenty-one years of age at the time of the adoption of this Constitution, and no male person of foreign birth who was naturalized prior to 1898 shall be denied the right to register and vote by reason of his failure to possess the educational or property qualifications prescribed by this Constitution, provided he shall have resided in the State for five years next preceding the date at which he shall apply for registration and shall have registered in accordance with this article prior to 1898; but no person shall be entitled to register under this section after said date."

All registration under this section closed on the 31st of August, 1898, and permanent records of voters so registering were made, and such persons are admitted to register for all elections without possessing the educational or property qualifications otherwise prescribed by this Constitution.[2]

§ 247. *Challenges.* — By the Constitution of Georgia, any voter, on being challenged, must make oath that he has complied with the constitutional requirements.[3]

§ 248. *Primaries.* — Only registered and qualified electors can vote at primaries.[4] The Legislature shall provide by law for the regulation of primaries and punishing fraud at the same.[5]

The Legislature shall enact laws providing for a mandatory primary system, which shall provide for the nomination of all candidates in all elections for State, District, County, and municipal officers, for all political parties, including United States senators. Provided, however, this provision shall not exclude the right of the people to place on the ballot by petition any non-partisan candidate.[6]

§ 249. *Municipal Elections, Special Provision.* — The voter must have been resident four months and paid all taxes due for the preceding fiscal year.[7]

[1] Miss. 244.
[2] La. 197 (5).
[3] Ga. 2, 1, 2.
[4] La. 200; Va. 35.
[5] Cal. 1899, p. 501; La. 215; S. C. 2, 10; Miss. 247.
[6] Okla. 3, 5.
[7] S. C. 2, 12.

No person less than sixty years of age can vote at any election who shall not, in addition to the qualifications herein prescribed, have paid on or before the end of each year, for two years preceding the year in which he offers to vote, a poll tax of one dollar per annum to be used for the public schools; but such taxes are a lien only upon assessed property, and every person liable for such tax before being allowed to vote must exhibit to the registration officers his poll tax for two years.[1]

Article 25. Disfranchisement

§ 250. *General Provisions.* — The Tennessee Constitution declares that no person shall be deprived of the right of suffrage except upon conviction by a jury of some infamous crime previously ascertained and determined by law and judgment thereon by a court of competent jurisdiction.[2] Or, upon lawful conviction of a felony at common law.[3]

§ 251. *Insanity.* — By the Constitutions of most States no insane or idiot person can vote.[4] So, in a few, no person under guardianship.[5] No person in gaol on conviction of a criminal offence.[6] In a few States there are constitutional provisions disfranchising paupers; thus, in some, that no pauper can vote.[7] So, in others, no person kept at a poorhouse or asylum at the public expense.[8] So, in Texas, no pauper supported by any county.

Exception. — But these provisions do not apply to any person who has served in the United States army or navy in time of war and been honorably discharged.[9] Nor to Soldiers' Home inmates.[10]

§ 252. *Crime.* — By the Constitutions of most States, no person convicted of infamous crime can vote.[11] In other States, the Legis-

[1] La. 198.

[2] Tenn. 1, 5. This is propably implied in other States. See § 130.

[3] Ark. 3, 2.

[4] Ala. 182; Ark. 3, 5; Cal. 2, 1; Del. 5, 2; Fla. 6, 4; Ga. 2, 2, 1; Ida. 6, 3; Io. 2, 5; Kan. 5, 2; Ky. 145; La. 202; Minn. 7, 2; Miss. 241; Mon. 9, 8; N. D. 127; Neb. 7, 2; Nev. 2, 1; N. J. 2, 1; O. 5, 6; Okla. 3, 1; Ore. 2, 3; R. I. 2, 4; S. C. 2, 6; S. D. 7, 8; Tex. 6, 1; Utah 4, 6; Va. 23; Wash. 6, 3; W. Va. 4, 1; Wis. 3, 2; Wy. 6, 6.

[5] Fla.; Ida.; Kan.; Mass. Amt. 3; Md. 1, 2; Me. 2, 1; Minn.; N. D.; R. I.; S. D.; Wis.

[6] Ida., Okla.

[7] Del. 5, 2; Mass. Amt. 3; Me. 2, 1; N. H. 2, 28; N. J. 2, 1; R. I. 2, 4; Tex. 6, 1; Va. 23; W. Va. 4, 1.

[8] La. 202; Mo. 8, 8; Okla. 3, 1; S. C. 2, 6; See § 242.

[9] Mass. Amt. 28; Okla. (or the Confederate army).

[10] La.; Mich. Amt. 1893, p. 439.

[11] Ala. 182; Cal. 2, 1; Ct. 6, 3; Ga. 2, 2, 1; Ida. 6, 3; Io. 2, 5; Md. 1, 2; La. 202; N. C. 6, 1; Neb. 7, 2; Nev.

lature may pass laws to such effect,[1] or to disfranchise persons convicted of "other high crimes";[2] or high misdemeanors.[3] So, in several, specially, no person convicted of "felony."[4] And no person confined in public prison.[5] And, specially, no person convicted of larceny can vote;[6] of forgery;[7] treason.[8] No person who has ever borne arms voluntarily against the United States (if, in Nevada, such person was over eighteen at the time).[9] No person guilty of murder;[10] adultery;[11] bigamy;[12] vagrancy;[13] receiving stolen goods;[14] living in adultery;[15] selling or offering votes;[16] other offences connected with the election laws;[17] bartering or selling, or offering to buy votes;[18] burglary;[19] assault and battery on the wife;[20] a bigamist or polygamist;[21] or persons advising polygamy;[22] a person who preaches or advises that the rules of the State are not our supreme law.[23] No person who held civil or military office under the Confederate States;[24] no person who in any manner voluntarily aided or abetted the Rebellion.[25] And no one dishonorably discharged from the United States service.[26] For perjury;[27] malfeasance in office;[28] misdemeanors connected with the right of suffrage;[29] embezzlement of the public funds.[30] For defrauding the United States, or any

2, 1; N. J. 2, 1; Ore. 2, 3; R. I. 2, 4; Tex. 6, 1; Wash. 6, 3; W. Va. 4, 1; Wy. 6, 6. Whether the conviction was in the home State, or any other (Nev.). Compare U. S. Amt. 14, 2.

[1] Ark. 1891, p. 314; Fla. 6, 4; Ill. 7, 7; Ind. 2, 8; Minn. 4, 15; Mo. 8, 10; N. Y. 2, 2; O. 5, 4; Tenn. 4, 2; Wis. 3, 6.

[2] Cal. 20, 11; Tex. 16, 2.

[3] Ky.

[4] Ark. 3, 2; Del. 5, 2; Fla. 6, 4; Ida. 6, 3; Kan. 5, 2; Ky. 145; Minn. 7, 2; Mo.; Mon. 9, 2; N. C.; N. D. 127; Okla. 3, 1; S. D. 7, 8; Va. 23; Wis. 3, 2.

[5] Col. 7, 10; Ky.; La.; Mo. 8, 8; S. C.

[6] Ala. 182; Ct. 6, 3; Fla. 6, 5; Ga. 2, 2, 1; La.; Md. 1, 2; Miss.; S. C. 2, 6; Va. 23; Wis. 3, 6.

[7] Ala.; Cal. 20, 11; Ct. 14, 4; Miss. 241; S. C.; Tex. 16, 2; Va.

[8] Ala.; Ga.; Ida.; Ky.; Minn.; N. D. 127; Neb.; Nev. 2, 1; S. D. 7, 8; Utah; Va.; W. Va., 4, 1; Wis. 3, 2.

[9] Kan. 5, 2; Nev.

[10] Ala.

[11] S. C.

[12] Ala.; S. C.

[13] Ala.

[14] Ala.; S. C.

[15] Ala.

[16] Ala.

[17] Ala.

[18] Ida., Ky.

[19] Ala., Miss., S. C.

[20] Ala., S. C.

[21] Ida.

[22] Ida.

[23] Ida.

[24] Nev.

[25] Kan.

[26] *Except*, in Kansas, persons honorably discharged from the military service of the United States, after April, 1861, and who had served at least one year therein, are not so disfranchised. And in Nevada, the foregoing provisions cease to apply when an amnesty be granted by the United States government.

[27] Ala.; Cal.; Ct.; Minn. 4, 15; Miss.; O.; S. C.; Tex.; Va.

[28] Ala., Cal., Ga.

[29] Mo.; S. C.; Utah 4, 6.

[30] Cal. Amt. 1893, p. 543; Ga.; Miss.; Va.

State government,[1] or fraudulent bankruptcy.[2] Obtaining money under false pretences;[3] robbery;[4] arson;[5] miscegenation, sodomy, or fornication;[6] incest;[7] assault to rape;[8] or to rob;[9] breach of trust.[10] *Unless* legally restored to the rights of citizenship.[11]

§ 254. *Bribery.* — By the Constitutions of many States, no person convicted of bribery can vote;[12] whether giving or receiving the bribe.[13] So, no person guilty of giving or offering to give or receive a bribe.[14] So, no person convicted of bribery at elections, as to both parties.[15] A person giving or offering or receiving a bribe at an election is disqualified to vote *at that election.*[16] No member of the Legislature convicted of bribery can vote.[17] In Pennsylvania, any person convicted of wilful violation of the election laws is deprived of the right of suffrage for four years.[18]

§ 255. *Betting on an Election* disqualifies the persons interested from voting at that election.[19] And in Florida, laws shall be passed to deprive a person convicted of so betting of the right of suffrage absolutely.[20]

§ 256. *Duelling.* — By the Constitutions of several States a person is disfranchised by being concerned in a duel in the same cases in the several States respectively that he would be disqualified to hold office (see § 223).[21] And so, a conviction for duelling is cause of disfranchisement.[22] Or sending or accepting a challenge, or assisting in a duel.[23] But the Legislature on two-thirds vote may remove the disqualification.[24]

[1] Kan.
[2] Ct.
[3] Ala., Miss., S. C., Va.
[4] S. C.
[5] S. C.
[6] Ala., S. C.
[7] S. C.
[8] S. C. 2, 6.
[9] Ala.
[10] S. C.
[11] Fla., Ga., Ida., Kan., Ky., La., Md., Minn., Mon., N. C., N. D., Neb., Nev., N. J., O., Okla., R. I., S. C., S. D., Wash., Wis., Wy.
[12] Ala.; Cal. 20, 11; Ct. 6, 3; Del. 5, 7; Fla. 6, 5; Ga.; Minn.; N. J. 2, 2; N. Y.; O. 5, 4; R. I. 2, 4; S. C.; Tex. 16, 2; Va. 23; Wis. 3, 6. See § 253, notes. For a term not over ten years (Me.).
[13] Del., Miss.
[14] Kan.
[15] Ga.; Ida. 6, 3; Ky.; Md. 1, 3; Me. 9, 13; Va.; W. Va.
[16] Del. 5, 3; N. Y.; Pa., 8, 8; Vt. 2, 34.
[17] Cal. 4, 35.
[18] Pa. 8, 9.
[19] N. Y.; Wis. 3, 6.
[20] Fla. 5, 4.
[21] Cal. 20, 2; Fla. 6, 5; Mich. 7, 8; Miss. 19; Nev. 15, 3; Tex. 16, 4; Wis. 13, 2.
[22] Ct. 6, 3.; Va. 23.
[23] Va.
[24] Va. 57.

ARTICLE 26. REMOVAL OF OFFICERS

§ 260. *By Impeachment.*[1] — By the Constitutions of many States, every civil State Officer may be impeached.[2] So, in Kansas, all officers under the Constitution.[3] All "executive" officers;[4] the governor;[5] lieutenant-governor;[6] secretary of State;[7] treasurer of the State;[8] the council;[9] the auditor;[10] the comptroller;[11] the attorney-general;[12] all attorneys for the State;[13] the superintendent of education;[14] the commissioner of public lands;[15] the railroad commissioners;[16] the surveyor-general;[17] all judicial officers or judges;[18] all judges of the supreme courts;[19] all judges of the superior courts;[20] all judges of the criminal court;[21] all judges of the Court of Appeal;[22] all chancellors.[23] Any such officer may be impeached within two years after his term of office expired.[24] The Constitution forbids impeachment of public officers.[25]

§ 261. *The Causes of Impeachment* are in many States, crime. Thus in detail (for citations, see also in § 260):

Crime (generally).[26] Misdemeanors (generally).[27] Any high

[1] The right of impeachment by the Commons, to be tried by the Lords, existed from early times, in England, but lay dormant from 1449 to 1621 (T.-L. 409).

[2] Ark. 15, 1; Col. 13, 2; Del. 6, 2; Ill. 5, 15; Ind. 6, 7; Io. 3, 20; Ky. 68; Mass. 2, 1, 2, 8; Me. 9, 5; Mich. 12, 1; Miss. 50; Mon. 5, 17; N. D. 196; Neb. 5, 5; Nev. 7, 2; N. H. 2, 37; N. J. 5, 11; O. 2, 24; Okla. 8, 1; Pa. 6, 3; S. D. 16, 3; Utah 6, 19; Va. 54; Vt. 2, 24; Wash. 5, 2; W. Va. 4, 9; Wis. 7, 1; Wy. 3, 18.

[3] Kan. 2, 28.

[4] Ct. 9, 3; Fla.; R. I. 11, 3; S. C.

[5] Ala. 173; Ark.; Cal. 4, 18; Col.; Ct.; Del.; Fla. 3, 29; Ill.; Io.; Kan.; Ky.; La. 217; Minn. 13, 1; Miss.; Mo. 7, 1; Mon.; N. C. 4, 4; N. D.; Nev.; N. H. 2, 39; N. J. ; O. 2, 24; Okla.; Pa.; R. I.; S. C. 15, 5; S. D.; Tenn. 5, 4; Tex. 15, 2; Utah; Va.; Wash.; Wis.; Wy.

[6] Ala., Cal., Fla., La., Mo., Tex., Va.

[7] Ala., Cal., Fla., La., Minn., Mo., Tenn.

[8] Ala., Cal., La., Minn., Mo., Tenn., Tex.

[9] N. H. 2, 62.

[10] Ala., La., Minn., Mo.

[11] Cal., Tenn., Tex.

[12] Ala., Cal., La., Minn., Mo., Tex., Va.

[13] Ark., Tenn.

[14] Ala., La., Mo.

[15] Tex.

[16] La.

[17] Cal.

[18] Col.; Ct.; La.; Md. 4, 4; Mon.; Nev.; N. D.; O.; R. I.; S. C.; S. D.; Tenn.; Utah; Va.; Wash.; Wy.

[19] Ala., Ark., Cal., Fla., Io., Minn., Mo., Okla., Tenn., Tex. See § 551.

[20] Ark., Cal., Fla., Io., Minn., Mo., Tex.

[21] Mo.

[22] Tex.

[23] Ark., Tenn.

[24] N. J.

[25] Ore. 1, 19.

[26] Ark., Col., Ind., La., Mich., Minn., Mo., Mon., N. D., S. D., Utah, Va., Wash., W. Va., Wis., Wy. It may now be regarded as settled that "high crimes and misdemeanors may include misconduct in office which does not in itself constitute a crime." (McClain, p. 61.)

[27] Ark., Col., La., Mich., Minn., Mo.,

crime in office.[1] Any misdemeanor in office.[2] Any offence involving moral turpitude, committed while in office, or connected therewith.[3] Treason.[4] Bribery.[5] Habitual drunkenness.[6] Drunkenness, at any time or place.[7] "Gross immorality."[8] In several, malfeasance[9] or misconduct in office.[10] Corruption in office.[11] Or "favoritism." Extortion in office.[12] Oppression in office.[13] Neglect of official duties.[14] "Maladministration."[15] Incompetency.[16] Incapacity, mental or physical.[17] No causes are specified.[18]

§ 262. *Process of Impeachment.* — By the Constitutions of nearly all, the impeachment is first made by the House of Representatives.[19] In most, a majority of a quorum seems to be sufficient for impeachment in the house as in ordinary votes (see § 304).[20] But in a few, a majority of the members elected.[21] In two, a vote of two thirds of the members present,[22] or elected.[23] And the impeachment is then, in all these States but two, tried by the Senate, sitting as a court, under oath.[24] In many States, with the chief justice of the Supreme Court presiding (in cases of impeachment of the governor).[25]

Two thirds of the senators elected must, in many States, concur

Mon., Utah, Va., Wash., W. Va., Wis., Wy.

[1] Del., Miss., Tenn.

[2] Cal., Fla., Del., Ill., Io., Kan., Ky., Me., Miss., N. D., Neb., Nev., O., Pa., S. D.

[3] Ala., Okla.

[4] Del., Miss.

[5] Del.; Miss.; N. H. 2, 37.

[6] Ala., La., Mo., N. D., Okla.

[7] Neb. 14, 3; S. D.

[8] W. Va.

[9] Ark.; Col.; Io.; La.; Mass. 2, 1, 2, 8; Mo.; Mon.; N. D.; Nev.; N. H.; S. D.; Utah; Va.; Wash.; Wy.

[10] Ala., La., Mich., Minn., N. D., N. H., Okla., S. D., Va., W. Va., Wis.

[11] La.

[12] La.

[13] La., Mo.

[14] Ala., Ind., Okla., Va., W. Va.

[15] Mass.; N. H.; Va.; Vt. 2, 24; W. Va.

[16] Ala., La., Okla., W. Va.

[17] Ind.

[18] S. C.

[19] Ala. 173; Ark. 15, 2; Cal. 4, 17; Col. 13, 1; Ct. 9, 1; Del. 6, 1; Fla. 3, 29; 1897, p. 308; Ga. 3, 6, 3; Ida. 5, 4; Ill. 4, 24; Ind. 6, 7; Io. 3, 19; Kan. 2, 27; Ky. 66; La. 218; Mass. 2, 1, 3, 6; Md. 3, 26; Me. 4, 1, 8; Mich. 12, 1 & 2; Minn. 4, 14; Miss. 49; Mo. 7, 2; Mon. 5, 16; N. C. 4, 4; N. D. 194; Nev. 7, 1; N. H. 2, 16; N. J. 6, 3, 1; N. Y. 6, 13; O. 2, 23; Okla. 8, 3; Pa. 6, 1; R. I. 11, 1; S. C. 15, 1; S. D. 16, 1; Tenn. 5, 1; Tex. 15, 1; Utah 6, 19; Va. 54; Vt. Amt. 25, 3; Wash. 5, 1; W. Va. 4, 9; Wis. 7, 1; Wy. 3, 17.

[20] Ark., Cal., Ct., Ga., Ind., Io., Kan., Ky., Mass., Me., Mo., N. C., N. H., Tenn., Tex., W. Va.

[21] Ala., Col., Ill., Md., Mich., Minn., Mon., N. D., Nev., N. J., N. Y., O., S. D., Utah, Wash., Wis., Wy.

[22] Fla., Miss.

[23] Del., Ind., R. I., S. C., Vt.

[24] Ala.; Ark.; Cal.; Col.; Ct. 9, 2; Del.; Fla.; Ga. 3, 5, 3; Ida. 5, 3; Ill.; Ind.; Io.; Kan.; Ky. 67; La.; Mass. 2, 1, 2, 8; Md.; Me. 4, 2, 7; Mich.; Minn.; Miss.; Mo.; Mon.; N. C. 4, 3; N. D. 195; Nev.; N. H. 2, 37; N. J.; O.; Okla.; Pa. 6, 2; R. I. 11, 2; S. C. 15, 2; S. D. 16, 2; Tenn. 5, 2; Tex. 15, 2; Utah 6, 18; Va.; Vt. Amt. 7; Wash.; W. Va.; Wis.; Wy.

[25] Ala.; Del.; Ida.; Mon.; N. D.; N. H. 2, 39; Okla.; S. D.; Utah; Wash.; Wy.

to convict of the impeachment.[1] In others, two thirds of the senators, &c., present.[2] In four, a vote of a quorum, as in other cases (see § 304).[3] But in Nebraska, the impeachment is first made by the Legislature in joint convention upon resolution in either house; and a majority of elected members must concur; and it is then tried by the judges of the Supreme Court.[4] So, in New York, it is tried by the Senate and the judges of the Court of Appeals.

§ 263. *The Effect of Impeachment* is, by the Constitutions of all but Maryland and Oregon, merely to remove from office; and, in all these States except Rhode Island, Indiana, Michigan, South Carolina, and Oklahoma, to disqualify the person impeached from holding any other State office; and the person impeached, whether convicted or not on the impeachment, is nevertheless liable to indictment, trial, and punishment according to law.[5] But in one State such disqualification only lasts during the term for which he was elected or appointed.[6] In many, when an officer is impeached, he is at once suspended from his office until acquitted.[7] In Tennessee, the Legislature has no power to relieve the person impeached from the above penalties (and see also § 162).[8] He cannot be again impeached for the same offence.[9]

§ 265. *Removal by Address.* — Certain officers may, by the Constitutions of many States, be removed by the Legislature; thus, in many States, judges of the supreme or superior courts,[10] or all judicial officers.[11] So, judges of the supreme court, and all other judicial officers, on recommendation of the governor,

[1] Cal., Col., Del., Ida., Ill., Ind., Kan., La., Md., Mich., Mon., N. D., Nev., N. J., O., R. I., S. C., S. D., Utah, Wash., W. Va., Wy.

[2] Ark.; Ct.; Fla.; Ga. 3, 5, 4; Io.; Ky.; La.; Me.; Minn.; Mo.; N. C.; N. Y.; Okla.; Pa.; Tenn.; Tex. 15, 3; Va.; Vt.; Wis. So in U. S. C. I. 3 (6).

[3] Ala., Mass., Miss., N. H.

[4] Neb. 3, 14.

[5] Ala. 176; Ark. 15, 1; Cal. 4, 18; Col. 13, 2; Ct. 9, 3; Del. 6, 2; Fla. 3, 29; Ga. 3, 5, 5; Ida. 5, 3; Ill. 4, 24; Io. 3, 20; Kan. 2, 28; Ky. 68; La. 218; Mass. 2, 1, 2, 8; Me. 4, 2, 7; Mich. 12, 2; Minn. 13, 1; Miss. 51; Mo. 7, 2; Mon. 5, 17; N. C. 4, 3; N. D.; Neb. 3, 14; Nev. 7. 2; N. H. 2, 38; N. J. 6, 3, 3; N. Y. 6, 3; O. 2, 24; Okla. 8, 5; Pa. 6, 3; R. I. 11, 3; S. C. 15, 3; S. D.; Tenn. 5, 4; Tex. 15, 4; Utah; Va. 54; Vt. Amt. 7; Wash.; W. Va. 4, 9; Wis. 7, 1; Wy.

[6] Ala.

[7] Fla.; La. 219; Mich. 12, 4; Minn. 13, 3; N. D. 198; Neb.; N. J. 6, 3, 2; N. Y.; R. I. 11, 2; S. D. 16, 5; Tex. 15, 5; Utah 6, 20; Wis. 7, 1.

[8] The principle that the power to pardon does not extend to impeachments is embodied in the Act of Settlement, but was claimed in Danby's case, 1679.

[9] N. D. 201; S. D. 16, 8.

[10] Cal. 6, 10; Kan. 3, 15; Miss. 53; N. C. 4, 31; Nev. 7, 3; O. 4, 17; R. I. 10, 4; S. C. 15, 4; Va. 104; Wash, 4. 9; Wis. 7, 13; W. Va. 8, 18; Utah 8, 11.

[11] Ill. 6, 30; Nev.; O.; Wash.

by vote of two thirds of the senate elected.[1] All civil officers,[2] or all executive officers.[3] All officers not liable to impeachment may be removed as provided by law.[4] In a few, a two-thirds vote of both houses elected is necessary,[5] or a three-fourths vote.[6] In others they are removed by a majority vote of elected members in joint committee,[7] or by the governor (or governor and council), upon the address of both houses of the Legislature; thus: all judicial officers or judges;[8] the judges of the supreme and superior courts;[9] all State officers except members of the Legislature;[10] the auditor, treasurer, secretary of state, attorney-general, and chancellors;[11] the attorney-general.[12] In one State, by the governor, on address of two thirds of the full senate, all officers elected by the people except members of the Legislature and judges.[13] Minor judges, by the senate on address by the governor.[14]

The Causes of Removal of officers under this section are by the Constitutions specified to be any reasonable cause,[15] misbehavior in office,[16] any infamous crime,[17] incompetence,[18] neglect of duty,[19] age,[20] mental or bodily infirmity,[21] corruption in office,[22] drunkenness,[23] if habitual.[24]

§ 266. *Removal by the Governor.* — So, in many States, certain officers may be removed by the governor alone, as, namely: any officer whom he has power to appoint,[25] all officers not legislative or judicial,[26] judges,[27] sheriffs,[28] coroners,[29] district attorneys,[30] county

[1] N. Y. 6, 11.

[2] La. 163.

[3] S. C.

[4] Fla. 14, 15; N. D. 197; S. D. 16, 4; Utah 6, 21; Wash. 5, 3; Wy. 3, 19. See also § 268.

[5] Cal., Kan., La., Miss., N. C., N. Y., Nev., O., Utah, Wis., W. Va.

[6] Ill., Wash.

[7] R. I., Va.

[8] Mass. 2, 3, 1; Md. 4, 4; Mich. 12, 6; Mo. 6, 41; N. H. 2, 72; Pa. 5, 15; S. C.; Tex. 15, 8. Two thirds of each house must concur (Ark., Ct., Del., Ky., La., Md., Mich., Miss., Mo., Ore., Pa., S. C., Tex.).

[9] Ark. 15, 3; Ct. 5, 3; Ky. 112, 129; Ore. 7, 20.

[10] Del. 3, 13; La. 220; Me. 9, 5; S. C.

[11] Ark.

[12] Ore.; Va. 107.

[13] Pa. 6, 4.

[14] Cal. 1904, Nov. 8.

[15] Del., Ky., La., Mich., Miss., Nev., Pa., S. C., Wash.

[16] N. D., Ore., Pa., S. D., Wash., Wy., Utah.

[17] N. D., Pa., S. D., Utah, Wy.

[18] N. D., Ore., S. D., Wash., W. Va.

[19] Ore., S. C.

[20] W. Va.

[21] Mo., N. C., W. Va.

[22] Wash., Ore.

[23] S. D.

[24] N. D.

[25] Col. 4, 6; Ill. 5, 12; Md. 2, 15; Neb. 5, 12; Pa. 6, 4 (except judges); W. Va. 7, 10.

[26] Mich. 12, 8.

[27] Md. 4, 4.

[28] N. Y. 10, 1; Wis. 6, 4.

[29] N. Y., Wis.

[30] N. Y., Wis.

clerks,[1] registers of deeds,[2] all public officers.[3] In Florida by the governor, with the concurrence of the senate, all officers not liable to impeachment may be removed; in California by the senate on recommendation of the governor, judges of inferior courts.[4] He may suspend all executive State officers except the lieutenant-governor until the next session of the Legislature.[5] He shall prosecute and suspend officers charged with embezzlement.[6]

The Causes of Removal under this section are specified to be: incompetency;[7] malfeasance in office;[8] misconduct;[9] neglect of duty;[10] conviction in a court of law of incompetency, misbehavior, or neglect in office,or any crime (as to judges only);[11] gross immorality.[12]

§ 267. *Removal by the Courts.* In a few states, certain officers may be removed by the judges of the supreme court.

Thus, judges of the superior court;[13] judicial officers;[14] all officers not liable to impeachment;[15] any judge (except those mentioned in § 260);[16] any prosecuting attorney.[17]

By the judges of the superior courts:—

Minor officers;[18] county or town officers;[19] county judges, attorneys, clerks of court, and justices of the peace.[20] In Oregon, all officers may be tried for incompetence, corruption, malfeasance, or delinquency in office, as for criminal offences; and judgment may be rendered for dismissal from office.[21]

§ 268. *Other Removals from Office.* The Constitutions of other States provide that the Legislature may provide for the removal of inferior officers from office, for malfeasance or nonfeasance of their duties;[22] for official misconduct, incompetence, neglect of duty, or gross immorality,[23] or for any cause.[24]

[1] N. Y.
[2] Wis.
[3] Del. 15, 6.
[4] Cal. 6, 10; Fla. 4, 15.
[5] Va. 73.
[6] S. C. 4, 22.
[7] Col.; Fla.; Ill.; Md.; Neb.; W. Va. 7, 10.
[8] Col., Del., Fla., Ill., Neb., W. Va.
[9] Md., W. Va.
[10] Col., Fla., Ill., Neb., W. Va.
[11] Del., Md.
[12] W. Va.
[13] La. 221; Tex. 15, 6.
[14] Ala. 174.
[15] Tenn. 5, 5.
[16] Ind. 7, 12.
[17] Ind.
[18] La. 222.
[19] Ark. 7, 27; La.; Tex. 5, 24.
[20] Tex. 5, 24; La.
[21] Ore. 7, 19.
[22] Col. 13, 3; Minn. 13, 2; Mo. 14, 7; Mon. 5, 18; N. D. 197; Nev. 7, 4; S. C. 3, 27; S. D. 16, 4; Utah; Wash. 5, 3; Wy. See § 265, 2d paragraph.
[23] W. Va. 4, 6.
[24] Okla. 8, 2; Tex. 15, 7.

Article 27. The Legislature

§ 270. *General Provisions.*[1] — The Constitutions of all the States provide that each house of the Legislature shall judge of the qualifications, elections, and returns of its members, and determine the rules of its own proceedings.[2] "It has all other powers necessary and usual for the Legislature of a free State."[3] In most States, each house shall choose its own officers,[4] except, in many, the president of the senate, which place is filled by the lieutenant-governor,[5] or by the governor or lieutenant-governor;[6] if neither, by the secretary of State.[7]

§ 271. *Quorum.* — By the Constitutions of nearly all, a majority of elected members in either house constitutes a quorum.[8] But in some two thirds is necessary.[9] And in one State, a majority is a

[1] Copied from U. S. C. I, 5. The right to determine contested elections was finally vindicated by the House of Commons against James I. who tried to transfer such cases to his own Court of Chancery, in 1604. (T.-L. pp. 389, 390, 421.) Congress, having delegated powers only, has not succeeded to the unlimited powers of Parliament to punish for contempt. (Reinsch, American Legislatures, 176.)

[2] Ala. 51, 53; Amt. 6; Ariz.* 1110; Ark. 5, 11, 12; Cal. 4, 7 & 9; Col. 5, 10 & 12; Ct. 3, 6 & 8; Del. 2, 8 & 9; Fla. 3, 6; Ga. 3, 7, 1; Ida. 3, 9; Ill. 4, 9; Ind. 4, 10; Io. 3, 7 & 9; Kan. 2, 8; Ky. 38, 39; La. 25; Mass. 2, 1, 2, 4; 2, 1, 3, 10; Md. 3, 19; Me. 4, 1, 5; 4, 2, 5; 4, 3, 3 & 4; Mich. 4, 9; Minn. 4, 3 & 4; Miss. 38 & 55; Mo. 4, 17; Mon. 5, 9 & 11; N. C. 2, 22; N. D. 47 & 48; Neb. 3, 7; Nev. 4, 6; N. H. 2, 24, 34; N. J. 4, 4, 2; N. M.* 63, 35; N. Y. 3, 10; O. 2, 6 & 8; Okla. 5, 30; Ore. 4, 11; Pa. 2, 9 & 11; R. I. 4, 6 & 7; S. C. 3, 11; S. D. 3, 9; Tenn. 2, 11 & 12; Tex. 3, 8 & 11; Utah 6, 10 & 12; Va. 47; Vt. 2, 9; Amt. 6; Wash. 2, 8 & 9; W. Va. 6, 24; Wis. 4, 7 & 8; Wy. 3, 10 & 12. But see § 238.

[3] Mon., N. D., Wy.

[4] Ala.; Ariz.*; Ark.; Cal.; Col.; Ct. 3, 7; Del. 2, 7; Fla.; Ga. 3, 5, 2; 3, 6, 2; Ida.; Ill.; Ind. 2, 10; Io.; Ky. 34; La.; Mass. 2, 1, 2, 7; 2, 1, 3, 10; Md.; Me. 4, 1, 7; 4, 2, 8; Mich. Minn. 4, 5; Miss.; Mo.; Mon. 5, 9; N. C. 2, 18–20; N. D. 31, 36; Neb.; Nev.; N. H. 2, 21 & 36; N. J. 4, 4, 3; N. Y.; O. 2, 8; Okla. 5, 29; Ore.; Pa.; R. I. 5, 2; 6, 4; S. C. 3, 12; S. D.; Tenn.; Tex. 3, 9; Utah 6, 12; Va. 47; Vt.; Wash. 2, 10; W. Va.; Wis. 4, 9; Wy. See U. S. C. I, 2 (5); I, 3 (5).

[5] Ala. 51; Col.; Ct.; 4, 13, Ill.; Ind.; Io. 4, 18; Ky.; La.; Mich.; Minn.; N. C.; Neb.; Nev.; N. Y.; O. 3, 16; Okla. 5, 28; Pa.; Tex.; Va.; Vt.; Wash. 3, 16; Wis. See also § 282.

[6] R. I. 6, 2.

[7] R. I. 6, 3.

[8] Ala. 52; Ark. 5, 11; Cal. 4, 8; Col. 5, 11; Ct. 3, 7; Del. 2, 8; Fla. 3, 11; Ga. 3, 4, 4; Ida. 3, 10; Ill. 4, 9; Io. 3, 8; Kan. 2, 8; Ky. 37; La. 34; Mass. Amt. 33; Md. 3, 20; Me. 4, 3, 3; Mich. 4, 8; Minn. 4, 3; Miss. 54; Mo. 4, 18; Mon. 5, 10; N. C. 2, 2; N. D. 46; Neb. 3, 7; Nev. 4, 13; N. J. 4, 4, 2; N. Y. 3, 10; O. 2, 6; Okla. 5, 30; Pa. 2, 10; R. I. 4, 6; S. C. 3, 11; S. D. 3, 9; Utah 6, 11; Va. 46; Vt. 2, 9; Amt. 6; Wash. 2, 8; W. Va. 6, 24; Wis. 4, 7; Wy. 3, 11. See U. S. C. I, 5, (1). Compare also § 303.

[9] Ariz.* 1116; Ind. 4, 11; Ore. 4, 12; Tenn. 2, 11; Tex. 3, 10.

quorum in the house; but when less than two thirds are present, a two-thirds vote is necessary to any act or proceeding; and in the senate thirteen are necessary to a quorum, and when less than sixteen are present, a vote of ten is necessary.[1]

But a smaller number than a quorum may generally adjourn from day to day and compel the attendance of absent members.[2]

§ 272. *Speech in the Legislature.* — The Constitutions of most States provide that no member of the Legislature for any speech or debate in either house shall be questioned elsewhere.[3] So, in many, that speech in the legislature can be the foundation of no prosecution or action whatever, civil, or criminal, in any other court or place.[4]

§ 273. *Freedom from Arrest.* — By the Constitutions of most States, State senators and representatives are privileged from arrest in all cases except treason, felony, and breach of the peace, during the session of the Legislature, or in going to and returning from the Legislature.[5] For fifteen days before and after the session of the

[1] N. H. 2, 19 & 36.

[2] Ala., Ark., Ariz., Cal., Col., Ct., Del., Fla., Ga., Ida., Ind., Io., Ky., La., Mass., Md., Me., Mich., Minn., Miss., Mo., Mon., N. D., Nev., N. J., O., Okla., Ore., Pa., R. I., S. C., S. D., Tenn., Tex., Utah, Va., Wash., W. Va., Wis., Wy. Notes. 1. So in U. S. 1. 5. 2. But there are often special provisions for finance bills; see Arts. 30, 31.

[3] Ala. 56; Ark. 5, 15; Ariz.* 1118; Col. 5, 16; Ct. 3, 10; Del. 2, 13; Ga. 3, 7, 3; Ida. 3, 7; Ill. 4, 14; Ind. 4, 8; Kan. 2, 22; Ky. 43; La. 28; Md. Decln. of Rts. 10; Me. 4, 3, 8; Mich. 4, 7; Minn. 4, 8; Mo. 14, 12; Mon. 5, 15; N. D. 42; N. J. 4, 4, 8; N. Y. 3, 12; O. 2, 12; Okla. 5, 23; Ore. 4, 9; Pa. 2, 15; R. I. 4, 5; S. D. 3, 11; Tex. 3, 21; Tenn. 2, 13; Utah, 6, 8; Va. 48; Wash. 2, 17; W. Va. 6, 17; Wy. 3, 16. This is an old English constitutional right, finally definitely established in Strode's case and the Stat. 4 Hen. VIII. (Taylor, I. 523). It would probably be deemed part of the "unwritten constitution" where not guaranteed here or in § 60. Freedom of speech was first definitely asserted by Peter Wentworth against Elizabeth in 1576, and is distinctly claimed as the privilege of Parliament in the Protestation of December 18, 1621 (T.-L. 419). A member may, however, be expelled by the House itself, as was the case with Sir Richard Steele in 1714 for writing "a seditious and scandalous libel" (T.-L. 579).

[4] Mass. 1, 21; Md. 3, 18; Neb. 3, 23; N. H. 1, 30; Vt. 1, 14; Wash. 2, 17; Wis. 4, 6.

[5] Ala. 56; Ark. 5, 15; Col. 5, 16; Del. 2, 13; Ga. 3, 7, 3; Ida. 3, 7; Ill. 4, 14; Ind. 4, 8; Io. 3, 11; Kan. 2, 22; Ky. 43; La. 28; Me. 4, 3, 8; Minn. 4, 8; Miss. 48; Mo. 14, 12; Mon. 5, 15; N. D. 42; Neb. 3. 12; N. J. 4, 4, 8; O. 2, 12; Okla. 5, 23; Ore. 4, 9; Pa. 2, 15; S. C. 3, 14; S. D. 3, 11; Tenn. 2, 13; Tex. 3, 14; Utah 6, 8; Va. 48; W. Va. 6, 17; Wy. 3, 16. The Protestation of 1621 puts the right in those words:

"And that every member of the said House hath like freedom from all impeachment, imprisonment, and molestation (other than by the censure of the House itself), for or concerning any speaking, reasoning, or declaring any matter or matters, touching the Parliament, or Parliament business." (T.-L. 419). But it first received distinct legislative recognition under James I. in 1604 (T.-L. 389). Both the right to freedom of speech and freedom from arrest is probably inherent in the Constitution of Parliament and coeval with the first existence of National Councils in England (T.-L. 259). The

Legislature.[1] So ten days before and after.[2] In some they are so privileged from arrest (except as above) at all times while members of the Legislature.[3] This privilege does not, in five States, protect from arrest in cases of violation of the oath of office.[4]

In two they cannot be arrested or held to bail upon mesne process during their attendance upon, going to, or returning from the Legislature.[5] And it is further provided, in a few States, that members of the Legislature are not subject to any civil process during the session of the Legislature and for fifteen days before such session and after its termination.[6] Or for fifteen days before the session.[7] So, in one, their persons are free from arrest and their property from attachment on any civil action during the session and for two days before and after it.[8] And in one other, they are free from arrest in civil process during the session and for four days before and after.[9]

§ 274. *Open Sessions.* — The Constitutions of nearly all the States provide that the doors of each house of the Legislature shall be open, or that the proceedings shall be public[10] *Except* such occasions as may, in the opinion of the House, require secrecy,[11] or except the senate when in executive session.[12] And in a few it is even required that the doors of either house should be open when sitting as

privilege of freedom from arrest is limited to civil causes in England, and it is not available in case of attachment for refusing to obey the writ of habeas corpus. It originally extended to the servants or household of a member, but this was altered by statute in 1770 (T.-L. 263).

[1] Cal., Miss., Mo., Neb., Utah, Va.

[2] S. C., W. Va.

[3] Ariz.* 1118; Cal. 4, 11; Mich. 4, 7; Wash. 2, 16; Wis. 4, 15.

[4] Ala., Col., Mon., Pa., Wy.

[5] N. H. 2, 20 (this is ambiguous, but § 21 seems to confine the word "arrest" to arrests for debt); Mass. 2, 1, 3, 10 (the privilege is here confined to the House of Representatives, by the letter of the Constitution).

[6] Ariz.*; Cal.; Ind.; Kan.; Mich.; Nev. 4, 11; Ore.; Va.; Wash.; Wis.

[7] Ind.; or 10 days before (Ida.).

[8] R. I. 4, 5.

[9] Ct. 4, 10.

[10] Ala. 57; Ark. 5, 13; Ariz.* 1113; Cal. 4, 13; Col. 5, 14; Ct. 3, 11; Del. 2, 11; Fla. 3, 13; Ida. 3, 12; Ill. 4, 10; Ind. 4, 13; Io. 3, 13; Md. 3, 21; Mich. 4, 12; Minn. 4, 19; Miss. 58; Mo. 4, 19; Mon. 5, 13; N. D. 50; Neb. 3, 8; Nev. 4, 15; N. H. 2, 8; N. Y. 3, 11; O. 2, 13; Ore. 4, 14; Pa. 2, 13; S. C. 3, 23; S. D. 3, 15; Tenn. 2, 22; Tex. 3, 16; Utah 6, 15; Vt. 2, 13; Wash. 2, 11; Wis. 4, 10; Wy. 3, 14. One of the original privileges of Parliament was secrecy of its proceedings; and it was only after a prolonged struggle that the right of the public to know what their representatives were doing in Parliament was at length conceded. The Long Parliament in 1641 had permitted the publication of its proceedings, but prohibited the printing of speeches, and it is still in theory a breach of privilege to report debates; but no action for libel will lie for so doing (T.-L. 579–587).

[11] Ala., Ark., Ariz.*, Cal., Col., Ct., Del., Ill., Ind., Io., Md., Mich., Min., Miss., Mo., Mon., N. D., Neb., N. H., N. Y., O., Ore., Pa., S. C., S. D., Tenn., Vt., Wash., Wis., Wy. "In the opinion of two thirds of those present" (O.).

[12] Fla., Nev., Tex., Utah.

committee of the whole.[1] But no person with exception of members of the press and certain officers can be admitted to the floor of either house in session.[2]

§ 275. *Journals.* — The Constitutions of all the States but Massachusetts provide that each house of the Legislature shall keep a journal of its proceedings;[3] and, in all these States except Oregon, publish the same. But, in one, they are only to publish it when required by one fifth of the members.[4] They need not print such parts as may require secrecy.[5] The yeas and nays of the members of either house voting in elections, must in some States be always entered on the journal,[6] and in several States the same is required of other votes[7] (see also § 304). So in others at the request of any one member,[8] or at the request of two members in either house,[9] of two in the senate, or five in the house,[10] of three in either house,[11] of five in either house,[12] of one sixth of the members present in either house,[13] of one fifth of the members present in either,[14] of one fifth of the members elected in either,[15] of one tenth of those present,[16] or, in one, whenever the Constitution requires a two-thirds vote.[17] Any member may dissent from or protest against any act or proceeding he may deem injurious to the public, and have the reasons for his dissent entered on the journal.[18] So, in two, any two or more members may do so.[19]

§ 276. *Expulsion of Members, etc.* — By the Constitutions of

[1] Ark., Col., Del., Ida., Ill., Md., Miss., Mon., Neb., Ore., Pa., S. D., Tenn., Wy.

[2] Ala.

[3] Ala. 55; Ark. 5, 12; Ariz.* 1111; Cal. 4, 10; Col. 5, 13; Ct. 3, 9; Del. 2, 10; Fla. 3, 12; Ga. 3, 7, 4; Ida. 3, 13; Ill. 4, 10; Ind. 4, 12; Io. 3, 9; Kan. 2, 10; Ky. 40; La. 30; Md. 3, 22; Me. 4, 3, 5; Mich. 4, 10; Minn. 4, 5; Miss. 55; Mo. 4, 42; Mon. 5, 12; N. C. 2, 16; N. D. 49; Neb. 3, 8; Nev. 4, 14; N. H. 2, 23; N. J. 4, 4, 4; N. Y. 3, 11; O. 2, 9; Okla. 5, 30; Ore. 4, 13; Pa. 2, 12; R. I. 4, 8; S. C. 3, 22; S. D. 3, 13; Tenn. 2, 21; Tex. 3, 12; Utah 6, 14; Va. 49; Vt. 2, 14; Wash. 2, 11; W. Va. 6, 41; Wis. 4, 10; Wy. 3, 13. See in U. S. Const. 1, 5.

[4] Ct.

[5] Ala., Ark., Ariz.*, Col., Ct., Del., Me., Mich., Miss., Mon., Neb., N. Y., Pa., S. C., S. D., Tenn., Wash., Wis., Wy. Nor proceedings of executive sessions (Utah).

[6] Ark. 4, 14; Cal.; Kan.; Io. 3, 38; Minn.; Miss. 76; Okla. 5, 31; S. C. 2, 24; S. D. 3, 14; Tenn. 4, 4; Wash. 2, 27; W. Va. 6, 44.

[7] Kan., Minn., S. D., Tenn.

[8] Del., N. H., Vt.

[9] Col.; Ind.; Io. 3, 10; Ky.; Mo.; Mon.; Neb.; O.; Ore.; Pa.; Wy.

[10] Ill.

[11] Cal., Ida., Nev., Tex.

[12] Ark., Fla., Md., Tenn., Utah. Of five in the Senate, ten in the house (S. C.).

[13] N. D.; S. D.; Wis. 4, 20.

[14] Ct.; Ga. 3, 7, 6; La. 36; Me.; N. C.; 2, 26; N. J.; R. I.; Va.

[15] Ariz.*, Mich.

[16] Ala., Miss., W. Va.

[17] Ga. 3, 7, 21.

[18] Ala.; Ariz.*; Ind. 4, 26; Io.; Kan. 2, 11; Mich.; N. C. 2, 17; N. H.; O. 2, 10; Ore. 4, 26; S. C.; Tenn. 2, 27; Vt.

[19] Ill.; Minn. 4, 16.

most States, either house of the Legislature may expel any of its members by a vote of two thirds of the elected members.[1] So, in one, by a majority vote of a quorum.[2] But no member can, in many, be expelled a second time for the same cause;[3] except for theft, perjury, etc.[4] Nor, for any cause known to his constituents before his election.[5] The reasons for the expulsion must, in two, be entered on the journal with the names of the members voting.[6] In some, a member expelled for corruption is not thereafter eligible for either house.[7] Each house has, in most States, power to punish its members for disorderly conduct.[8] And in many, either house may punish any person not a member for disorderly or contemptuous conduct, such punishment not to extend beyond final adjournment of the session.[9] It may punish for contempt any person who refuses to attend as a witness or produce papers, etc., before the Legislature, either house, or a committee of either, or to testify as to any matter which may be a proper subject of inquiry by the Legislature.[10] Such punishment is to be by imprisonment.[11] But not over thirty days.[12] Not over ten days.[13] Not over twenty-four hours at a time.[14] No time is specified.[15]

[1] Ala. 53; Ark. 5, 12; Ariz.* 1110; Cal. 4, 9; Col. 5, 12; Ct. 3, 8; Del. 2, 9; Fla. 3, 6; Ga. 3, 7, 1; Ida. 3, 11; Ill. 4, 9; Ind. 2, 8; Io. 3, 9; Ky. 39; La. 25; Md. 3, 19; Me. 4, 3, 4; Mich. 4, 9; Minn. 4, 4; Miss. 55; Mo. 4, 17; Mon. 5, 11; N. D. 48; Neb. 3, 7; Nev. 4, 6; N. J. 4, 4, 3; O. 2, 8; Okla. 5, 30; Ore. 4, 15; Pa. 2, 11; R. I. 4, 7; S. C. 3, 12; Tenn. 2, 12; Tex. 3, 11; Utah 6, 10; Va. 47; Wash. 2, 9; W. Va. 6, 25; Wis. 4, 8; Wy. 3, 12. In many of these States (N. J., Pa., O., Ind., Io., Minn., Va., Ky., Tenn., Ark., Tex., Okla., R. I., Ore., Col., S. C., Ga., Ala., Mon., N. D., Wy.) the provision is ambiguously worded, and so in U. S. C. 1, 5, (2); by custom, however, "two-thirds of the house" should be so interpreted. In a few it is definitely stated to mean members present (Fla., Miss.), and such is general parliamentary law, in vetoes (§ 304) and impeachments; and so by the practice of the U. S. Senate, even on votes of expulsion. It is one of the inherent powers of a Legislature to expel a member, or punish any person for contempt, but in the Wilkes case it was established that a member thus expelled is not thereby disqualified.

[2] Vt. 2, 9.

[3] Ala., Ark., Ariz., Col., Ct., Ill., Ind., Io., Ky., Md., Me., Mich., Minn., Miss., Mo., Neb., O., Ore., Pa., R. I., S. C., Tenn., Tex., Wash., W. Va., Wis.

[4] Miss.

[5] Ariz., Mich., Vt.

[6] Ariz., Mich.

[7] Ala. 54; Ark.; Col.; Mon.; N. D. 2, 38; Okla. 5, 19; Pa.; Wy. See §§ 206, 210.

[8] Ala.; Ark.; Ariz. *1120; Col.; Ct.; Del.; Fla.; Ill.; Ind.; Io.; Ky.; La.; Md.; Me.; Minn.; Miss.; Mo.; Mon.; N. D.; N. H. 2, 21, 32; Nev.; N. J.; O.; Okla.; Ore.; Pa.; R. I.; S. C.; Tenn.; Tex.; Utah; Va.; Wash.; W. Va.; Wis.; Wy.

[9] Ariz.; Fla. 3, 9; Ga. 3, 7, 2; Ky.; Mass. 2, 1, 3, 10–11; Me. 4, 3, 6; Miss. 58; N. D.; Nev. 4, 7; N. H.; S. C. 3, 13; W. Va. 6, 26; and this is the proper rule.

[10] Ky. 39; Okla. 5, 42.

[11] Mass.; Me.; N. D.; N. H.; S. C.; Tenn. 2, 14.

[12] Mass., N. D.

[13] La. 26; Md. 2, 23; Mo.; N. H.

[14] Ill.; Ind. 4, 15; Minn. 4, 18; Neb.; Ore. 4, 16.

[15] Ala., Col., Mon., Wash., Wis., Wy.

Not over forty-eight hours.[1] The house may commit any person to gaol for crime, until duly released by law.[2] And it does not bar a criminal prosecution.[3] Bribery offered or effected of a member of the legislature may be punished bv it directly.[4] For punishment for contempt, see above.

§ 277. *Time of Session.* — There is in three States a general provision of the Constitution that the Legislature should be frequently convened.[5] The regular session of the Legislature is, in six States, once each year.[6] In most States and most territories once every two years; thus in the even year,[7] and in others in the odd year;[8] but often there are adjourned sessions held in the intervening year; in Pennsylvania, such adjourned sessions are, however, prohibited. In a few Southern States only once in four years.[9]

Beginning on the first Monday in January;[10] the first Tuesday;[11] the first Wednesday in January;[12] the first Monday after January 1,[13] the Wednesday after the first Monday in January;[14] the second Wednesday in January;[15] the first Tuesday after the first Monday in January;[16] the first Thursday after the first Monday in January;[17] the second Tuesday in January;[18] the third Monday in January;[19] the first Wednesday of October;[20] the second Monday in January;[21] the second Monday in May;[22] the fourth Wednesday in June;[23] the Tuesday after first Monday in April.[24]

Extra sessions on extraordinary occasions may be convened by the

[1] Tex. 3, 15.

[2] Md. 3, 24.

[3] Mon., N. D., Okla., Wy.

[4] Ky., Mon., N. D., Wy.

[5] Mass. 1, 22; Md. Decln. of Rts. 12; S. C. 1, 3.

[6] Ga. 1891, p. 55; Mass. Amt. 10; N. J. 4, 1, 3; N. Y. 10, 6; R. I. Amt. XI.; S. C. 3, 9.

[7] Ky. 36; La. 23; Md. 3, 14; Miss. 36; Mon. 5, 6; N. D. 53, 55; O. 2, 25; Okla. 5, 27; Va. 46; Vt. Amt. 24, 1.

[8] Ark.* 1875, 39, 1; 3520; Ariz.* 39; Cal. 4, 2; Col. 5, 7; Ct. Amt. 27, 1899, p. 1153; Del. 2, 4; Fla. 3, 2; Ida. 3, 8; Ill. 4, 9; Ind. 4, 9; Io. 3, 2; Amt. 1900; Kan. 2, 25; Me. 4, 3, 1; Amt. 23; Mich. 4, 33; Minn. 3, 4; 4, 1; Mo. 4, 20; N. C. 2, 2; Neb. 3, 3 & 7; Nev. 4, 2; 17, 12; N. H. 2, 32; N. Y. 1898, p. 1550; N. D. 55; N. M., U. S. 1896, 252; Ore.* 2371; Pa. 2, 4; S. D. 3, 2 & 7; Tenn. 2, 8; Tex. 3, 5; Utah 6, 2; W. Va. 6, 18; Wash. 2, 12; 1891, Wis. 20*; 4, 11; 99* Wy. 3, 5.

[9] Ala. 48; Miss. 36. See also § 203. Beginning in 1903 (Ala.) 1892 (Miss.); and there is a "special session" in 1894 and every four years thereafter (Miss.).

[10] Mon., O., Tenn.

[11] Del., Neb., Pa., R. I.

[12] Col., Mass., Me., Mich., N. Y., N. H. So, *after* Jan. 1, Md., Mo.

[13] Ida., Cal.

[14] Ct., Ill., N. C.

[15] Va., W. Va., Wis.

[16] Ky., Minn., N. D., S. D., Miss. Okla.

[17] Ind.

[18] Ala., Kan., N. J., S. C., Wy., Tex.

[19] Nev., N. M.,* Ariz.*

[20] Vt.

[21] Wash., Ark., Io., Ore., Utah.

[22] La.

[23] Ga. 1890, p. 57.

[24] Fla.

governor.[1] But in the newer States the Legislature so called may only legislate on the subject specified in the proclamation.[2] So, in two, the governor may call the Legislature together sooner than the time to which it was adjourned or prorogued, if necessity require.[3]

No session can extend beyond the term of forty,[4] forty-five,[5] fifty,[6] sixty,[7] sixty-one,[8] seventy-five,[9] or ninety days.[10] It must be dissolved by the governor if necessary, seven days before the first Wednesday of January.[11] So, in others, no member will be paid, or paid full rates, for more than a session of seventy-five days,[12] of seventy days,[13] of sixty days,[14] of forty days,[15] or by extra session, thirty days.[16] And the session may be continued for thirty days beyond the time so above limited, upon concurrence of two thirds[17] or three fifths[18] of the members. Unless organization is effected within four days after a quorum is secured, they get no pay.[19]

§ 278. *Adjournment.* — By the Constitutions of all States, neither house can adjourn without the consent of the other for more than three days,[20] or than two days,[21] nor without such consent, to

[1] Ala. 122; Ark. 6, 19; Cal. 5, 9; Col. 4, 9; Ct. 3, 2; Del. 3, 16; Fla. 4, 8; Ga. 5, 1, 13; Ida. 4, 9; Ill. 5, 8; Ind.; Io. 4, 11; Kan. 1, 5; Ky. 80; La. 75; Mass. Amt. 10; Md. 2, 16; Me. 5, 1, 13; Mich. 5, 7; Minn. 5, 4; Miss. 36; Mo. 5, 9; Mon. 7, 11; N. C. 3, 9; N. D. 75; Neb. 5, 8; Nev. 5, 9; N. H. 2, 49; N. J. 5, 6; N. Y. 4, 4; O. 3, 8; Okla. 6, 7; Ore. 5, 12; Pa. 4, 12; R. I. 7, 7; S. C. 4, 16; S. D. 4, 4; Tenn. 3, 9; Tex. 4, 8; Utah 7, 6; Va. 73; Vt. 2, 11; Wash. 3, 7; W. Va. 6, 19; Wis. 5, 4; Wy. 4, 4; U. S. R. S. 1923; 1874, 388 (Territories). But no such extraordinary session can be called in the Territories without the approval of the President of the United States; so, it must be on application of three fifths of the elected members, except on extraordinary occasions (W. Va.) or with advice of the Council (N. C.).

[2] Ida., Mon., Okla., Utah.

[3] Mass. 2, 2, 1, 5; N. H. 2, 49.

[4] Wy. 3, 6.

[5] W. Va. 6, 22.

[6] Ala.; Ga. 1891, p. 55.

[7] Ark. 5, 17; Ariz.;* Col. Amt. 3; Fla. 3, 2; Ky. 42; La. 23; Mon. 5, 5; N. D. 56; Nev. 4, 29; S. D. 3, 6; Utah 6, 16; Va. 46; Wash.; Territories U. S. R. S. 1852; U. S. 1881, 7.

[8] Ind. 4, 29.

[9] Col. 5, 6.

[10] Col. Amt. 3; Md. 3, 15; Minn. Amt. 1889, 1, 2.

[11] N. H. 2, 3.

[12] Tenn. 2, 23.

[13] Mo. 4, 16.

[14] Cal. 4, 2; Del. 2, 15; Ida. 3, 23; Nev. 1891, 11; R. I. Amt. 11 (1900, p. 146); Tex. 3, 24; Va.

[15] Ore. 4, 29; S. C.

[16] La., Miss., Neb., S. C., Utah., Va.; or twenty (Fla.).

[17] Ga.

[18] Va.

[19] Ida. 3, 10. So, only $2 a day after 60 days (Okla. 5, 21).

[20] Ala. 58; Ariz.* 1113; Ark. 5, 28; Cal. 4, 14; Col. 5, 15; Del. 2, 12; Fla. 3, 13; Ga. 3, 7, 24; Ida. 3, 9; Ind. 4, 10; Io. 3, 14; Ky. 41; La. 35; Md. 3, 25; Mich. 4, 12; Minn. 4, 6; Miss. 57; Mon. 5, 14; N. D. 51; Neb. 3, 8; Nev. 4, 15; N. J. 4, 4, 5; Okla. 5, 30; Ore. 4, 11; Pa. 2, 14; S. C. 3, 21; S. D. 3, 16; Tenn. 2, 16; Tex. 3, 17; Utah 6, 15; Va. 46; Vt. Amt. 3; Wash. 2, 11; W. Va. 6, 23; Wis. 4, 10; Wy. 3, 15 (Sundays excepted, O.; Kan.; Minn.).

[21] Ill. 4, 10; Kan. 2, 10; Mass. 2, 1,

any other place than that in which it may be sitting; but in one it may adjourn to such other place by concurrent vote of two thirds present.[1] And in one other, every adjournment or recess taken by the Legislature for more than three days has the effect of an adjournment *sine die*.[2]

Adjournment by the Governor. — In most States, if the two houses disagree with respect to the time of adjournment, the governor may adjourn the Legislature, to such time as he think proper, not beyond the first day of the next regular session,[3] or for more than ninety days,[4] or such time as he think proper,[5] not exceeding four months.[6] So, if either house remain five days without a quorum.[7]

§ 279. *The Place of Session.* — The capital, in all States. But the governor may convene the Legislature elsewhere in case of war or contagious disease, etc., etc.[8]

Article 28. The Executive

§ 280. *Duties of the Governor.* — It is in most States declared to be the duty of the governor to take care that the laws are faithfully executed.[9] He is generally, at the commencement of each session, or from time to time, to give the Legislature information by message of the condition of the State, and recommend such measures as he deems expedient.[10] He must, in some States, present estimates, at the

2, 6; 2, 1, 3, 8; Me. 4, 3, 12; Mo. 4, 23; N. H. 2, 18 & 35; N. Y. 3, 11; O. 2, 14; R. I. 4, 9.

[1] Md.

[2] Mo. 4, 21.

[3] Ark. 6, 20; Cal. 5, 11; Col. 4, 10; Ct. 4, 7; Fla. 4, 10; Ill. 5, 9; Io. 4, 13; Kan. 1, 6; Me. 5, 1, 13; Miss. 121; Neb. 5, 9; Nev. 5, 11; O. 3, 9. But only with assent two thirds elected members each house: Okla. 6, 14; R. I. 7, 6; S. C. 4, 16; Utah 7, 7.

[4] Del. 3, 16; Mass. 2, 2, 1, 6; N. H. 2, 42.

[5] Ga.; Vt.; Amt. 3.

[6] Ky. 81; Pa. 4, 12.

[7] Kan., O., Minn., S. C.

[8] Ala. 4, 8; Ky. 36, 80; La. 75; N. D.; Okla. 6, 14; S. C. 3, 9.

[9] Ala. 120; Ariz.* 1089; Ark. 6, 7; Cal. 5, 7; Col. 4, 2; Ct. 4, 9; Del. 3, 17; Fla. 4, 6; Ga. 5, 1, 12; Ida. 4, 5; Ill. 5, 6; Ind. 5, 16; Io. 4, 9; Kan. 1, 3; Ky. 81; La. 75; Md. 2, 9; Me. 5, 1, 12; Mich. 5, 6; Minn. 5, 4; Miss. 113; Mo. 5, 6; Mon. 7, 5; N. C. 3, 7; N. D. 75; Neb. 5, 6; Nev. 5, 7; N. J. 5, 6; N. Y. 4, 4; O. 3, 6; Okla. 6, 8; Ore. 5, 10; Pa. 4, 2; R. I. 7, 2; S. C. 4, 12; S. D. 4, 4; Tenn. 3, 10; Territories U. S. R. S. 1841; Tex. 4, 10; Utah 7, 5; Va. 73; Vt. 2, 11; Wash. 3, 5; W. Va. 7, 5; Wis. 5, 4; Wy. 4, 4.

[10] Ala. 123; Ark. 6, 8; Ariz.* 1091; Cal. 5, 10; Col. 4, 8; Ct. 4, 8; Del. 3, 15; Fla. 4, 9; Ga. 5, 1, 13; Ida. 4, 8; Ill. 5, 7; Ind. 5, 13; Io. 4, 12; Kan. 1, 5; Ky. 79; La. 74; Md. 2, 19; Me. 5, 1, 9; Mich. 5, 8; Minn. 5, 4; Miss. 122; Mo. 5, 9; Mon. 7, 10; N. C. 3, 5; N. D. 75; Neb. 5, 7; Nev. 5, 10; N. J.; N. Y.; O. 3, 7; Okla. 6, 9; Ore. 5, 11; Pa. 4, 11; S. C. 4, 15; S. D. 4,

commencement of the session, to the Legislature of the amount of money required to be raised by taxation for all State purposes.[1]

§ 281. *Powers of the Governor.* — By the Constitutions of most States, the governor may require information in writing from officers of the executive department upon any subject relating to the duties of their respective officers.[2] So, in a few, from all officers or managers of State institutions.[3] He may, in some, require such information to be given under oath.[4] So, in two, any officer making a false report is guilty of perjury.[5] The governor and council have a negative on each other in nominations and appointments.[6] In Massachusetts the council has only advisory power, except that it succeeds to the duties of governor if the offices of both governor and lieutenant-governor are vacant.[7]

§ 282. *The Lieutenant-Governor*, by the Constitutions of most States, succeeds to the office of governor upon the death, impeachment, or other disability of the latter.[8] But in many (where there is no lieutenant-governor), the president of the senate succeeds the governor.[9] And, after him, the speaker of the house.[10] In others the secretary of state succeeds (so in the territories, U. S. R. S. 1843), and after him the president of the senate.[11] Or, in Delaware, the attorney-general, then the president of the senate *pro tempore*, then the speaker of the house. And in two, the Legislature, in case of vacancy, elects a governor.[12] So, if the vacancy occurs in the first three years of the term, there is an election by the people.[13]

4; Tenn. 3, 11; Tex. 4, 9; Utah; Va.; Wash. 3, 6; W. Va. 7, 6; Wis.; Wy. 4, 4.

[1] Ala.; Col.; Ida.; Ill.; Mo. 5, 10; Mon.; Neb.; Tex.; W. Va. 7, 6.

[2] Ala. 121; Ariz.* 1088; Ark. 6, 7; Cal. 5, 6; Col. 4, 8; Ct. 4, 6; Del. 3, 14; Fla. 4, 5; Ga. 5, 1, 18; Ida. 4, 8; Ill. 5, 21; Ind. 5, 15; Io. 4, 8; Kan. 1, 4; Ky. 78; La. 73; Me. 5, 1, 10; Mich. 5, 5; Minn. 5, 4; Miss. 120; Mo. 5, 22; Mon. 7, 10; N. C. 3, 7; Neb. 5, 22; Nev. 5, 6; O. 3, 6; Okla. 6, 9; Ore. 5, 13; Pa. 4, 10; S. C. 4, 14; Tenn. 3, 8; Tex. 4, 24; Utah 7, 5; Va. 74; Wash. 3, 5; W. Va. 6, 18.

[3] Ala.; Col.; Ida.; Mass. 2, 2, 1, 12; Mo.; Mon.; Neb.; N. H. 2, 56; Utah.

[4] Ala., Col., Ida., Ill., Mon., Tex.

[5] Ala., Mo.

[6] N. H. 2, 46.

[7] Mass. 2, 2, 3, 5 & 6.

[8] Ala. 127; Cal. 5, 16; Col. 4, 13; Ct. 4, 14; Del. 3, 20; Ida. 4, 12; Ill. 5, 17; Ind. 5, 10; Io. 4, 17; Kan. 1, 11; Ky. 84; La. 65; Mass. 2, 2, 2, 3; Mich. 5, 12; Minn. 5, 6; Miss. 131; Mo. 5, 16; Mon. 7, 14; N. C. 3, 12; N. D. 72; Neb. 5, 16; Nev. 5, 18; N. Y. 4, 6; O. 3, 15; Okla. 6, 16; Pa. 4, 13; R. I. 7, 9; 1890, p. 146; S. C. 4, 9; S. D. 4, 6; Tex. 4, 16; Va. 78; Vt. Amt. 8; Wash. 3, 10; Wis. 5, 7. See also § 202.

[9] Ala.; Ark. 5, 18; 6, 12; Del. 3, 14; Fla. 4, 19; Ga. 5, 1, 8; Md. 2, 7; Me. 5, 1, 14; N. H. 2, 48; N. J. 5, 12; Tenn. 3, 12; W. Va. 7, 16.

[10] Ala.; Ark. 6, 13; Fla.; Ga.; Me.; N. J.; Tenn.; W. Va.

[11] Del.; N. D.; Ore. 5, 8; S. D.; Utah 7, 11; Wy. 4, 6.

[12] Md. 2, 6; W. Va.

[13] W. Va.

So, if in the first two years of the term.[1] So, if a year of the term remains unexpired.[2] So, if sixty days before the next election.[3]

The lieutenant-governor is in most States president of the senate, with a casting vote.[4] And in one, he is a member of the council, and president thereof when the governor's chair is vacant.[5] But he cannot grant pardons or reprieves, nor can he command the militia, except as lieutenant-general, but by advice of the senate.[6]

Upon the death, impeachment, or inability of the lieutenant-governor or secretary of State also, the temporary president of the senate is, in most States, governor *pro tempore*.[7] But in one, the council, or a majority of it, has the power of the governor.[8] And in others, the secretary of state succeeds.[9] And so, by succession, in several, the speaker of the house succeeds the president of the senate.[10] And the secretary of state the speaker.[11] In Rhode Island the Legislature elects from the persons having the highest votes, as in § 232.[12]

ARTICLE 29. THE MILITIA

§ 290. *General Provisions.* — In four State Constitutions it is declared that every member of society is bound to yield his personal service, or an equivalent thereto, to the State for the defence of life, liberty, and property.[13] But in many States it is declared that a person conscientiously opposed to bearing arms will not be compelled thereto if he will pay an equivalent.[14] But in a few it seems

[1] Ky. 85.

[2] Ark. 6, 14.

[3] Ala.

[4] Ala. 117; Cal. 5, 15; 1897, p. 646; Col. 4, 14; Ct. 4, 13; Del. 3, 19; Ida. 4, 13; Ill. 5, 18; Ind. 5, 21; Io. 4, 18; Kan. 1, 12; Ky. 83; La. 67; Mich. 5, 14; Minn. 5, 6; Miss. 129; Mo. 5, 15; Mon. 7, 15; N. C. 3, 11; N. D. 77; Neb. 5, 17; Nev. 5, 17; N. Y. 4, 7; O. 3, 16; Okla. 6, 15; Pa. 4, 4; S. C. 4, 5 & 6; S. D. 4, 7; Tex. 4, 16; Va. 79; Vt. Amt. 6; Wash. 3, 16; Wis. 5, 8.

[5] Mass. 2, 2, 2, 2.

[6] Vt.

[7] Cal.; Ct. 4, 15; Col. 4, 15; Ida. 4, 14; Ill. 5, 19; Io. 4, 19; Kan. 1, 13; Ky. 85; La. 68; Mich. 5, 13; Minn.; Miss.; Mo. 5, 17; Mon. 7, 16; N. C.; N. D. 31; Neb. 5, 18; Nev.; N. Y.; O. 3, 17; Okla. 6, 15; Pa. 4, 14; R. I. 7, 10; S. C.; Tex. 4, 17; Utah.

[8] Mass. 2, 2, 2, 6.

[9] Ky. 87; La.; N. D.; S. D.; Wash.; Wis.

[10] Cal., Col., Ida., Ill., Io., Kan., Miss., Mo., Mon., Neb., N. H., N. Y., O., Okla.

[11] Del.

[12] R. I. Amt. 11.

[13] Mass. 1, 10; N. H. 1, 12; Ore. 1, 27; Vt. 1, 9.

[14] Col. 17, 5; Ida. 14, 1; Ill. 12, 6; Ind. 12, 6; Io. 6, 2; Ky. 220; La. 300; Me. 7, 5; Mo. 13, 1; N. D. 188; N. H. 1, 13; Ore. 10, 2; S. C. 13, 1; Tenn. 1, 28; 8, 3; Tex. 16, 47; Vt.; Wash. 10, 6.

that he may be compelled to bear arms in time of war, as the exemption applies only to militia duty in time of peace.[1] "Upon such terms as may be prescribed by law," he will be relieved from such service.[2] And in Maine, Quakers and Shakers and clergymen are excused. In several, the militia is declared the proper and natural defence of a free State.[3]

§ 291. *The Militia* consists in most States of all able-bodied male persons (citizens, Io., Mich., or inhabitants, Fla., N. Y., and Ore.) between the ages of eighteen and forty-five,[4] twenty-one and forty-five,[5] or twenty-one and forty.[6] In a few, they must in addition be white.[7] In others, the whole matter (otherwise) is left to the Legislature to be determined by law.[8] But there must always be 10,000 men fully equipped, disciplined and ready for action.[9] The Legislature shall provide for maintaining an organized militia conforming as nearly as practicable to the regulation for the government of the United States army.[10] "Not incompatible with the Constitution or laws of the United States." [11]

§ 292. *Civil Power.* — The military is, in all States except New York, declared forever subordinate to the civil power.[12]

[1] Col.; Ida. 15, 7; Ill.; Io.; N. D.; Ore.; S. D.; Wash. 10, 6.

[2] Fla. 14, 1; Kan. 8, 1; Mich. 17, 1; Mo.; N. C. 12, 1; N. Y. 11, 1; Wy. 17, 1.

[3] Ga. 10, 1, 1; La. 6; Md. Decln. of Rts. 28; N. C. 1, 24; N. H. 1, 24; S. C. 1, 26; Tenn. 1, 24; Va. 13.

[4] Ala.; Ark. 11, 1; Col. 17, 1; Fla. 14, 1; Ida. 14, 1; Ill. 12, 1; Ind. 12, 1; Io. 6, 1; Ky. 219; Mich. 17, 1; Miss. 214; Mo. 13, 1; Mon. 14, 1; N. D. 188; O. 9, 1; Ore. 10, 1; S. C. 13, 1; S. D. 15, 1; Utah 15, 1; Wash. 10, 1; Wy. 17, 1.

[5] Kan. 8, 1.

[6] N. C. 12, 1.

[7] Ind., Kan., O.

[8] Ala. 271; Cal. 8, 1; Ga. 10, 1, 1; Ida. 14, 2; Ky. 220; La.; Md. 9, 1; Minn. 12, 1; Mon. 14, 1; Miss. 215; Neb. 13, 1; Nev. 12, 1; N. D. 190; N. J. 7, 1, 1; N. Y. 11, 2; Okla. 5, 40; Pa. 11, 1; S. D. 15, 2; Tex. 16, 46; Wis. 4, 29.

[9] N. Y. 11, 3.

[10] Ida. 14, 2; Ky. 221; Mon. 14, 2; S. D. 15, 2-3; Utah 15, 2; Wy. 17, 2.

[11] N. D. 189; Wash. 10, 2.

[12] Ala. 27; Ark. 2, 27; Ariz.* Bill of Rights 3; Cal. 1, 12; Col. 2, 22; Ct. 1, 18; Del. 1, 17; Fla. Decln. Rts. 21; Ga. 1, 1, 19; Ida. 1, 12; Ill. 2, 15; Ind. 1, 33; Io. 1, 14; Kan. Bill of Rts. 4; Ky. 222; La. 14, 173; Mass. 1, 17; Md. Decln. of Rts. 30; Me. 1, 17; Mich. 18, 8; Minn. 1, 14; Miss. 9; Mo. 2, 27; Mon. 3, 22; N. C. 1, 24; N. D. 12; Neb. 1, 17; Nev. 1, 11; N. H. 1, 26; N. J. 1, 12; N. M.* 1851, July 12, § 16; O. 1, 4; Okla. 2, 14; Ore. 1, 27; Pa. 1, 22; R. I. 1, 18; S. C. 1, 26; S. D. 6, 16; Tenn. 1, 24; Tex. 1, 24; Utah 1, 20; Va. 13; Vt. 1, 16; Wash. 1, 18; W. Va. 3, 12; Wis. 1, 20; Wy. 1, 25. Compare Eng. Stat. 1 W. & M. Sess. 2; also Declaration of Independence. See § 240, note. Martial law and courts martial are no part of the common law of England. It was complained of in the Petition of Right, but is not expressly forbidden in the Bill of Rights. In this country the Federal Constitution makes no specific mention of it, but it is doubtless forbidden by the ordinary constitutional provisions requiring due process of law

§ 293. *Martial Law* is in one State declared inconsistent with a free government and is not "confided" to any department of the State government.[1] And in several, no person can be subjected to martial law except the army, navy, or militia in actual service.[2] In one, martial law is to be employed only when occasion necessarily requires it.[3] But in three, it seems any person may be subjected to martial law by authority of the Legislature.[4]

§ 294. *Standing Armies.*[5] — The Constitutions of most of the States provide that standing armies are dangerous to liberty and ought not to be kept up in time of peace.[6] And in time of war the appropriation for such army cannot be for a longer term than two years,[7] or even one year.[8] But in several, it seems standing armies may be kept up at any time with the authority of the Legislature.[9]

§ 295. *Billeting Soldiers.*[10] — By the Constitutions of all but Vermont, New York, Wisconsin, Virginia, and Mississippi, no soldier can be quartered in any house without the consent of the owner, except in time of war; and then only (in all these States except Louisiana) in the manner by law prescribed.[11]

(Amts. 5 and 14). When so-called martial law is enforced at the will of the commanding officer it will not, in ordinary cases, prevent the person tried from being tried again at the common law; nor will it exempt the officers or soldiers carrying out orders under martial law from being responsible for their acts in the ordinary manner. At most it is lawful in the enemy's country in time of actual warfare. There is, however, a New York decision to the effect that in that state a statute providing for courts martial is constitutional. It will be noted that the New York Constitution alone has no provision that the military is forever subordinate to the civil power (see § 292). People *v.* Daniel, 50 N. Y. 274.

[1] Tenn. 1, 25.

[2] Mass. 1, 28; Md. Decln. of Rts. 32; Me. 1, 14; N. H. 1, 34; S. C. 1, 26; Tenn. 1, 25; Vt. 1, 17; W. Va. 3, 12.

[3] R. I. 1, 18.

[4] Mass.; N. H.; S. C.

[5] "The existence of a standing army in time of peace is contrary to law. It is legalized each year for a year by the Army Act; as are the punishments and procedure for the maintenance of discipline, which are also contrary to the common law. Hence the Parliament has to be summoned once a year." Anson, Law and Customs of the Const. I, 248. Henry II. promised never to employ mercenary soldiers in England, though he kept a force of 10,000 Brabançons and many Welsh and Galwegians. He faithfully kept his promise, but John's mercenary army, though raised to repel the French invasion of 1213, was one of the greatest occasions of his downfall. (1 Stubbs, 588.)

[6] Ark. 2, 27; Cal. 1, 12; Io. 1, 14; Kan. Bill of Rts. 4; Ky. 22; Mass. 1, 17; Me. 1, 17; Minn. 1, 14; N. C. 1, 24; N. D. 12; Nev. 1, 11; N. H. 1, 25; O. 1, 4; Pa. 1, 22; S. C. 1, 26; Tenn. 1, 24; Va. 13; Vt. 1, 16; Wash. 1, 31; W. Va. 3, 12.

[7] Io., Nev.

[8] Ala. 27.

[9] Ala.; Del.; Ky.; Mass.; Md. Decln. of Rts. 29; Me.; N. H.; Pa.; S. C.

[10] U. S. C. Amt. 3.

[11] Ala. 28; Ark. 2, 27; Ariz. B. Rts. 4; Cal. 1, 12; Col. 2, 22; Ct. 1, 19; Del. 1, 18; Fla. 16, 23; Ga. 1, 1, 19; Ida. 1, 12; Ill. 2, 16; Ind. 1, 34; Io. 1, 15; Kan. Bill of Rts. 14; Ky. 22; La.

§ 296. *Privileges of Militia.* — Members of the militia are, by the Constitutions of several States privileged from arrest during their attendance at musters and elections and in going to and returning from them, *except* in cases of treason, felony, and breach of the peace.[1] And in several, no person can be imprisoned for a militia fine in time of peace.[2]

§ 297. *The Governor is Commander-in-Chief* of the militia (and army and navy of the State), by the Constitutions of all States.[3] And so, in the territories, by U. S. R. S., 1841. *Except,* in many, when they are called into the United States service.[4] But he is not, in a few, to command in person in the field unless he is advised to do so by resolution of the Legislature.[5] And he is not, without legislative authority or their consent, to lead or order the militia out of the State.[6] Officers are to be appointed as by law.[7] Captains and subalterns are to be nominated by the field officers and appointed by the governor and council.[8] No officer can be removed except by court martial or upon address of both houses to the governor.[9] The officers appoint their respective aids and the captains and subalterns their non-coms.[10]

§ 298. *Purposes of the Militia.* — The governor may, by the Constitutions of most States, call out the militia to execute the laws, to suppress insurrection, and to repel invasion.[11] So, in Louisiana,

173; Mass. 1, 27; Md. Decln. of Rts. 31; Me. 1, 18; Mich. 18, 9; Mo. 2, 27; Mon. 3, 22; N. C. 1, 36; N. D. 12; Neb. 1, 18; Nev. 1, 12; N. H. 1, 27; N. J. 1, 13; O. 1, 13; Okla. 2, 14; Ore. 1, 28; Pa. 1, 23; R. I. 1, 19; S. C. 1, 26; S. D. 6, 16; Tenn. 1, 27; Tex. 1, 25; Utah 1, 20; Wash. 1, 31; W. Va. 3, 12; Wy. 1, 25.

[1] Ala. 275; Ark. 11, 3; Ill. 12, 4; Miss. 220; Mo. 13, 5; N. D. 193; S. C. 13, 2; S. D. 15, 5; Wash. 10, 5.

[2] Cal. 1, 15; Io. 1, 19; Mich. 6, 33; Nev. 1, 14; N. J. 1, 17.

[3] Ala. 131; Ark. 6, 6; Cal. 5, 5; Col. 4, 5; Ct. 4, 5; Del. 3, 8; Fla. 4, 4; Ga. 5, 1, 11; Ida. 4, 4; Ill. 5, 14; Ind. 5, 12; Io. 4, 7; Kan. 8, 4; Ky. 75; La. 183, 73; Mass. 2, 2, 1, 7; Md. 2, 8; Me. 5, 1, 7; Mich. 5, 4; Minn. 5, 4; Miss. 119, 219; Mo. 5, 7; Mon. 7, 6; N. C. 3, 8; N. D. 75; Neb. 5, 14; Nev. 5, 5; N. H. 2, 50; N. J. 5, 6; N. Y. 11, 6; O. 3, 10; Okla. 6, 6; Ore. 5, 9; Pa. 4, 7; R. I. 7, 3; S. C. 4, 10; S. D. 4, 4; Tenn. 3, 5; Tex. 4, 7; Utah 7, 4; Va. 73; Vt. 2, 11; Wash. 3, 8; W. Va. 7, 12; Wis. 5, 4; Wy. 4, 4; 17, 5.

[4] Ala., Ark., Col., Ct., Del., Fla., Ida., Ill., Ky., La., Me., Miss., Mo., Mon., N. C., N. D., Neb., Nev., O., Okla., Pa., R. I., S. C., S. D., Tenn., Tex., Utah, Wash., W. Va., Wy.

[5] Ala., Ky., Md., Mo.

[6] Mass., Me., Mon., N. H.

[7] Ida.; N. D. 191; Wash. 10, 2; Wy. 17, 3. Or elected (Ala. 271).

[8] N. H. 2, 47.

[9] N. H. 2, 52.

[10] N. H. 2, 53.

[11] Ala. 131; Ark. 11, 4; Cal. 8, 1; Col. 4, 5; Fla. 14, 4; Ida. 4, 4; Ill. 5, 14; Ind. 5, 12; Kan. 8, 4; La. 301; Md. 2, 8; Mich. 5, 4; Minn. 5, 4; Miss. 217; Mo. 5, 7; Mon. 7, 6; N. C. 12, 3; N. D.; Neb. 5, 14; Nev. 12, 2; Okla. 6, 6; Ore. 5, 9; S. C. 13, 3; S. D.; Tex. 4, 7; Utah; Va. 73; Wash. 10, 2; W. Va. 7, 12; Wy. 17, 5.

"when the public service requires it." But so, in three, only when the Legislature declare by law that the public safety requires it.[1] So, in Tennessee, only with special enactment of the Legislature; or in Texas, to protect the frontier, or the public health.[2] And, in five, to preserve the public peace.[3]

§ 299. *Miscellaneous Provisions.* — (See also § 63.) The California Constitution provides that all military organizations receiving State support should carry under arms no device or flag of any nation other than the United States or State flag.[4] The legislative assembly shall provide by law for the establishment of volunteer organizations of the several arms of the service, which shall be classed as active militia, and no other organized body of men shall be permitted to perform military duty in this State, except the army of the United States, without the proclamation of the governor of the State.[5]

[1] Mass. 2, 2, 1, 7; N. H. 2, 50; Tenn. 3, 5.
[2] Okla.
[3] Ark., Fla., La., S. C., Wy.
[4] Cal. 8, 2; Ida. 14, 5; Wy. 17, 4.
[5] N. D. 190.

PART III

LEGISLATION

ARTICLE 30. PROCESS OF LEGISLATION

§ 300. *Bills.* — (See also §§ 201, 310.) By the Constitutions of many States, no law can be passed except by bill;[1] and bills may generally originate in either house of the Legislature,[2] but they may be amended, altered, or rejected in the other house.[3] (The same is probably implied in all other States; see § 303.) But not, in some States, so as to change the original purpose of the bill,[4] nor upon or after the last reading.[5]

§ 301. *Form of Bills.* — The Constitutions of most States prescribe that no law shall relate to more than one subject, and that this shall be expressed in the title,[6] indicating clearly the subject matter.[7] *Except*, in a few, general appropriation bills,[8] and in two,

[1] Ala. 61; Ark. 5, 21; Cal. 4, 15; Col. 5, 17; Ida. 3, 15; Ind. 4, 1; Kan. 2, 20; Md. 3, 29; Miss. 60; Mo. 4, 25; Mon. 5, 19; N. D. 58; Neb. 3, 10; Nev. 4, 23; N. Y. 3, 14; Pa. 3, 1; Tex. 3, 30; Va. 50; Wash. 2, 18; Wis. 4, 17; Wy. 3, 20. After the Conquest English legislation was based on petitions addressed to the king by the House of Commons; this resulted in their not always getting the legislation they desired, so that it soon became the practice to accompany the petition with the precise law asked for. Later, laws were made by Ordinances or Orders in Council without the consent of Parliament. (T.-L. p. 249.)

[2] Ariz.* 1114; Cal.; Fla. 3, 14; Ida. 3, 14; Ill. 4, 12; Ind. 4, 17; Io. 3, 15; Kan. 2, 12; Md. 3, 27; Me. 4, 3, 9; Mich. 4, 13; Miss. 59; Mo. 4, 26; N. D. 57; Neb. 3, 9; Nev. 4, 16; N. Y. 3, 13; O. 2, 15; Ore. 4, 18; S. C. 3, 15; S. D. 3, 20; Tenn. 2, 17; Tex. 3, 31; Va.; W. Va. 6, 28; Vt. Amt. 3; Wash. 2, 20; Wis. 4, 19. See, however, § 309.

[3] Ala., Ark., Cal., Col., Fla., Ida., Ill., Ind., Io., Kan., Md., Me., Miss., Mo., N. D., Neb., Nev., N. Y., O., Ore., Pa., S. C., S. D., Tenn., Tex., Va., Wash., W. Va., Wis.

[4] Ala.; Ark.; Col.; Mo.; N. D. 58; Pa.; Tex.; Wash. 2, 38; Wy. 3, 20.

[5] N. Y.

[6] Ala. 45; Cal. 4, 24; Col. 5, 21; Del. 2, 16; Fla. 3, 16; Ga. 3, 7, 8; Ida. 3, 16; Ill. 4, 13; Ind. 4, 19; Io. 3, 29; Kan. 2, 16; Ky. 51; La. 31; Md. 3, 29; Mich. 4, 20; Minn. 4, 27; Mo. 4. 28; Mon. 5, 23; N. D. 61; Neb. 3, 11; Nev. 4, 17; N. J. 4, 7, 4; O. 3, 16; Okla. 5, 57; Ore. 4, 20; Pa. 3, 3; S. C. 3, 17; S. D. 3, 21; Tenn. 2, 17; Tex. 3, 35; Utah 6, 23; Va. 52; Wash. 2, 19; W. Va. 6, 30; Wy. 3, 24.

[7] Miss. 71.

[8] Ala., Col., Del., Mo., Mon., Okla., Pa., Tex., Utah, Wy. See § 311.

the principal provision only applies to private or local bills.[1] But, in several States, if there are other subjects in the bill not embraced in the title, the bill is nevertheless good *pro tanto* as to those that are.[2] By the Constitutions of three States, every act is to be plainly worded, avoiding, so far as possible, the use of technical terms.[3] And by that of Louisiana, the Legislature shall never adopt any system or code of laws by general reference to such code, but shall in all cases recite at length the provisions enacted (compare § 307).[4] Every statute is a public law unless otherwise declared.[5]

§ 302. *Passage of Bills.*[6] — By the Constitutions of some States, no bill shall be considered for passage unless it has first been referred to a committeee and reported therefrom.[7] And in Texas, no bill shall be passed unless so referred and reported at least three days before the final adjournment of the Legislature. *Except* if the committee refuses or fails to report a bill "within a reasonable time" any member may call it up.[8]

Reading of Bills. — Every bill must ordinarily, by the Constitutions of most States, be read by sections on three different days in each house of the Legislature.[9] But in case of urgency, either house

[1] N. Y. 3, 16; Wis. 4, 18.

[2] Cal., Col., Ida., Ill., Ind., Io., Mon., N. D., Ore., Tex., W. Va., Wy.

[3] Ida. 3, 17; Ind. 4, 20; Ore. 4, 21.

[4] La. 33.

[5] Del. 2, 23.

[6] While these directions as to the method of passing laws are mandatory in form, they are binding only on the conscience of the legislative body. The courts, in the very nature of things, are obliged to accept the enactment of the law as conclusive proof of the compliance of the Legislature with the necessary formalities, and cannot consider questions of fact relative to the regularity of procedure. It has been expressly decided that such matters will not be inquired into by the courts. In Kilgore *v.* Magee, 85 Pa. 401 (1877), it was contended that an act of Assembly had been so altered during its passage as to change its original purpose, and also that the required forms had been disregarded. As to this the court said: "In regard to the legislation required by the constitution, we think the subject is not within the pale of judicial inquiry. So far as the duty and the consciences of the members of the Legislature are involved, the law is mandatory. They are bound by their oaths to obey the constitutional mode of proceeding, and any intentional disregard is a breach of duty and a violation of their oaths. But when a law has been passed and approved and certified in due form, it is no part of the duty of the judiciary to go behind the law as duly certified to inquire into the observance of form in its passage. The presumption applies to the act of passing the law, that applies generally to the proceedings of any body whose sole duty is to deal with the subject. The presumption in favor of regularity is essential to the peace and order of the State." T. R. White, The Constitution of Pennsylvania, p. 212.

[7] Ala. 62; Col. 5, 20; Ky. 46; La. 39; Miss. 74; Mo. 4, 27; Mon. 5, 22; Pa. 3, 2; Tex. 3, 37; Va. 50; Wy. 3, 23.

[8] Ky.

[9] Ala. 63; Ark. 5, 22; Ariz.* 1117; Cal. 4, 15; Col. 5, 22; Fla. 3, 17; Ga. 3, 7, 7; Ida. 3, 15; Ill. 4, 13; Ind. 4, 18; Kan. 2, 15; Ky. 46; La. 39; Md.

may dispense with such rule, on a vote of four fifths of the members present,[1] three fourths,[2] two thirds,[3] or of a majority of those elected.[4] But in Minnesota and Florida, every bill must have been read at least twice at length, in order to pass either house. Provision may be made by law for reading by title only.[5] And every bill, in order to become a law, must, in many States, have been read at length on its final passage,[6] on its second reading,[7] its first,[8] or on its first and third.[9] It must be printed for the use of members,[10] and no amendment is allowed on the last reading.[11]

Of Private or Local Bills,[12] there must, by the Constitutions of several States, be notice given; as by thirty days' publication of the bill in the locality affected before its introduction into the legislature,[13] or in others four weeks' notice by such publication.[14] In one State, the manner of notice is expressly left to the Legislature to determine.[15] All private or local bills must, in Georgia, originate in the lower house, and be referred to a committee.[16] There is a permanent joint committee on special private or local legislation.[17]

§ 303. *Voting*.[18] — By the Constitutions of most States no bill [19] can become a law unless on its final passage it receive in each House a vote of a majority of "each house," [20] or of the members elected.[21]

3, 27; Mich. 4, 19; Minn. 4, 20; Miss. 59; Mo. 4, 26; N. C. 2, 23; N. D. 63; Neb. 3, 11; Nev. 4, 18; N. J. 4, 4, 6; O. 3, 16; Okla. 5, 34; Ore. 4, 19; Pa. 3, 4; S. C. 3, 18; S. D. 3, 17; Tenn. 2, 18; Tex. 3, 32; Utah; Va. 50; W. Va. 6, 29. It seems the readings need not be on different days (Mich.); and the first two may be on the same day (N. D., S. D.).

[1] Tex., Va., W. Va.

[2] O.

[3] Ark., Cal., Fla., Ida., Ind., Kan., Md. (of the members elected), Minn., Miss., Nev., Okla., Ore. But only so far as to allow all three readings on the same day (Ark.).

[4] Ky.

[5] S. C. So on the first reading (Fla.).

[6] Ala.; Cal.; Fla.; Ida.; Ind.; Io. 3, 17; Kan.; Mich.; Miss.; Nev.; N. Y. (implied) 3, 15; Ore.; W. Va.

[7] Fla., S. C.

[8] Ky.

[9] N. D., S. D.

[10] Ky.; Ida. 3, 15; Mon.; N. Y.; Wy. It must have been "upon their desks in its final form three calendar legislative days" (N. Y.).

[11] N. Y.

[12] See also §§ 395, 501.

[13] Ark. 5, 26; Ga. 3, 7, 16; La. 50; Mo. 4, 54; N. C. 2, 12; Okla. (four weeks); Pa. 3, 8; Tex. 3, 57 (60 days); Fla. 3, 21.

[14] Ala. 106; Okla. 5, 32.

[15] N. J. 4, 7, 9.

[16] Ga. 3, 7, 15.

[17] Miss. 89; Va. 51.

[18] Notes. Whether by ballot or not, see § 231. See also § 314.

[19] So, also, of joint resolutions (Kan., Md.).

[20] Ala. 63; Ark. 5, 22.

[21] Cal. 4, 15; Col. 5, 22; Del 2, 10; Ga. 3, 7, 14; Ill. 4, 12; Ind. 4, 25; Io. 3, 17; Kan. 2, 13; La. 39, 40; Md. 3, 28; Mich. 4, 19; Minn. 4, 13; Mo. 4, 31; N. D. 65; Neb. 3, 10; Nev. 4, 18; N. J. 4, 4, 6; N. Y. 3, 15; O. 2, 9; Okla. 5, 34; Ore. 4, 25; Pa. 3, 4; S. D. 3, 18; Tenn. 2, 18; Utah 6, 22; Wash. 2, 22; Wy. 3, 25.

In others, of a majority of the members present,[1] and this would be implied in States where the Constitution is silent, as in the United States Congress. In two, a majority vote including two fifths of the members elected.[2]

The names of the members so voting for or against a bill on its final passage must usually be entered in the journals.[3]

In many States, a member who has a personal or private interest in any measure or bill, proposed or pending, must disclose the fact to the house of which he is a member, and cannot vote thereon.[4]

All votes on the final passage of any measure shall be subject to reconsideration for at least one whole legislative day, and no motion to reconsider such vote shall be disposed of adversely on the day on which the original vote was taken, except on the last day of the session.[5]

§ 304. *Veto Power.* — In all States but Rhode Island and North Carolina, and in the territories[6] the Constitution provides that every bill or every joint or concurrent resolution, except for adjournment,[7] passed by the legislature shall be presented to the governor before it becomes a law; and if he approves he is to sign it.[8] Except in Missouri, resolutions for amending the Constitution. The governor may generally veto a bill, by returning it with his objections to the house in which it originated,[9] or in Kansas, to the house of representatives. It will then become a law, by an ordinary ma-

[1] Ariz.* 1117; Fla. 3, 17; Ida. 3, 15; Mon. 5, 24.

[2] Ky. 47; Va. 50.

[3] Ala.; Ark.; Ariz.*; Cal.; Col.; Del.; Fla.; Ga.; Ida.; Ill.; Io.; Kan.; Ky. 46; La.; Md.; Mich.; Minn.; Mo.; Mon.; N. D.; Neb.; Nev.; N. J.; N. Y.; O.; Okla.; Pa.; S. D.; Tenn. 2, 21; "By yeas and nays": Utah 6, 22; Va.; Wy. The same would follow in other States from § 275.

[4] Ala. 82; Col. 5, 43; Del. 2, 20; La. 52; Ky. 57; Mon. 5, 44; N. D. 43; Okla. 5, 24; Pa. 3, 33; Tex. 3, 22; Wash. 2, 30; Wy. 3, 46. See also § 154.

[5] Miss. 65.

[6] U. S. R. S. 1842.

[7] Ala.; Ark. 6, 16; Ariz.*; Col. 5, 39; Del.; Ga.; Kan.; Ky. 89; La. 78; Mass.; Me.; Mich.; Minn. 4, 12; Mo. 5, 14; Mon. 5, 40; Neb.; N. H. 2, 44; Okla.; Pa. 3, 26; S. C.; Tenn.; Tex. 4, 15; Va.; Wy. 3, 41.

[8] Ala. 125; Ark. 6, 15; Cal. 4, 16; Col. 4, 11; Ct. 4, 12; Del. 3, 18; Fla. 3, 28; Ga. 5, 1, 17; Ida. 4, 10; Ill. 5, 16; Ind. 5, 14; Io. 3, 16; Kan. 2, 14; Ky. 88; La. 41, 76; Mass. 2, 1, 1, 2; Md. 2, 17; Amt. 1890, 394; Me. 4, 3, 2; Mich. 4, 14; Minn. 4, 11; Miss. 72; Mo. 4, 39; Mon. 7, 12; N. D. 79; Neb. 5, 15; Nev. 4, 35; N. H. 2, 43; N. J. 5, 7; N. Y. 4, 9; O. 1902, p. 962; Okla. 6, 11; Ore. 5, 15; Pa. 4, 15; S. C. 4, 23; S. D. 4, 9; Tenn. 3, 18; Tex. 4, 14; Utah 7, 8; Va. 76; Vt. Amt. 11; Wash. 3, 12; W. Va. 7, 14; Wis. 5, 10; Wy. 4, 8. And so in U. S. C. I. 7.

[9] Ala.; Ark.; Ariz.*; Cal.; Col.; Ct.; Del.; Fla.; Ida.; Ill.; Ind.; Io.; Ky.; La.; Mass.; Md.; Me.; Mich.; Minn.; Miss.; Mo. 4, 39; Mon.; N. D.; Neb.; Nev.; N. H.; N. J.; N. Y.; O.; Okla.; Ore.; Pa.; S. C.; S. D.; Tenn.; Tex.; Utah; Va.; Vt.; Wash.; W. Va.; Wis.; Wy.; Territories, U. S. R. S., 1842.

jority vote in each house,[1] or a majority of the elected members of each house,[2] of three fifths of the elected members of each house,[3] two thirds of the members present in each house [4] (the provision is ambiguous, however, on these points in some States, though, by custom, it means the members *present* [5]), two thirds of the elected members of each house,[6] two thirds of the elected members of the house which originated the bill, and of a majority in the other house,[7] or two thirds of the members present, and a majority of those elected, in each house.[8] The votes must in this case be entered on the journal [9] by yeas and nays. Any bill may be vetoed in part.[10]

§ 305. *Pocketed Bills.* — In most States, if a bill be kept a certain length of time by the governor, without returning it, it will become a law except in case of adjournment by the Legislature; as, three days, Sundays excepted,[11] five days,[12] six days,[13] or ten days.[14] But Sundays apparently are not excepted in some States.[15] But in most States, if the Legislature adjourn before the time respectively limited above, the bill does not (except as below) become a law.[16] In several States, however, the bill does become a law if not returned by the governor within five days after the adjournment,[17] ten days after,[18] fifteen,[19] twenty,[20] thirty days after; [21] or, within two [22] or three

[1] Ct.

[2] Ala., Ark., Ind., Ky., N. J., Tenn., Vt., W. Va.

[3] Del., Md., Neb.

[4] Fla.; Ga. 5, 1; Ida.; Mass.; Me.; Minn.; Miss.; Mon.; N. H.; Ore.; S. C.; S. D.; Tex.; Wash.; Wis.; Territories. So in U. S. C. I. 7.

[5] Ga., Miss., S. C.

[6] Cal., Col., Ill., Kan., La., Mich., N. D., Nev., N. Y., O. (and it must not be less than on the original passage); Okla., Pa., Utah, Wy.

[7] Mo.

[8] Va.

[9] See also § 303.

[10] (See § 310.) O., Va., Wash.

[11] Ct., Ind., Io., Kan., Minn., N. D., Nev., N. M., Okla., S. C., S. D., Wy., Wis.

[12] Ark., Fla., Ga., Ida., La., Mass., Me., Miss., Mon., Neb., Nev., N. H., N. J., Ore., Tenn., Utah, Va., Vt., Wash., W. Va., Wy.

[13] Ala., Md.

[14] Ariz.; Cal.; Col.; Del.; Ill.; Ky.; Mich.; Mo. 4, 40; N. Y.; O.; Pa.; Tex.

[15] Col., La., Mass., Mo., Pa.

[16] Ala.; Ark.; Cal.; Col.; Ct.; Del.; Fla.; Ga.; Ill.; Ind.; Io.; Kan.; Ky.; La.; Mass. Amt. 1; Md.; Me.; Mich.; Minn.; Miss.; Mo. 5, 12; Mon.; N. D.; Neb.; N. H.; N. J.; N. Y.; O.; Okla.; Ore.; Pa.; S. C.; S. D.; Tenn.; Tex.; Va.; Vt.; W. Va.; Wis.; Wy.; and the territories. In Vermont it does not become a law if the Legislature adjourn within three days after its presentment to the governor.

[17] Ind., Ky., Neb., Ore., S. D., W. Va.

Sundays are excepted, except in Ark., Fla., Ill., Ind., Neb., N. Y., S. D., W. Va., Tex.

[18] Fla., Ill., Ida., Ky., Nev., S. D., Utah, Wash.

[19] Mon., N. D., Wy.

[20] Ark., Tex.

[21] Col.; Mo.; N. J.* 1880; 173; Pa.

[22] Ala., S. C.

days after the next meeting of the Legislature,[1] or ten days after.[2] And in California,[3] the bill becomes a law *if* returned and signed within ten days after the adjournment, in Oklahoma fifteen days, in New York thirty days after. So, in Michigan, if returned signed within five days of the adjournment, the bill having been passed in the last five days of the session; or, in Minnesota, if passed in the last three days of the session, if signed within three days of the adjournment; and in Iowa, if returned within thirty days after.

§ 306. *General Restrictions.* — By the Constitutions of several States, no new bill can be introduced into either House after the first thirty [4] or fifty [5] days of the session; or, not during the last three days of the session.[6] In others, not within the last ten days, except by a two-thirds vote of a full house.[7] And in one, no bill can be passed by either house on the day prescribed for adjournment,[8] nor be presented to the governor within two days of the final adjournment,[9] nor within the last twenty days except on special message of the governor.[10]

By the Constitutions of three States, after a bill or resolution has been considered and defeated in either house, no bill the same in substance shall be passed during that session,[11] or be again proposed without the consent of a majority of the house which rejected it.[12] In New Mexico and Arizona, all laws passed by the territorial Legislature and governor must be submitted to Congress, and, if disapproved, shall be void.[13]

There can be no legislation at special sessions on subjects *other* than those designated in the Governor's proclamation except on two-thirds vote of each House.[14]

In other States these matters are usually provided for by the Legislature itself.

§ 307. *Amendments, Repeals, and Revisions.* — The Constitutions of many States provide that no law shall be revived, altered, or amended by reference to its title only; but the act revived, and

[1] Me., Miss.
[2] Ill.
[3] Sundays excepted.
[4] Col. 5, 19, Amt. 1887.
[5] Cal. 4, 2 (unless by the consent of two-thirds of the members).
[6] Ark. 5, 34; Miss. 67.
[7] Md. 3, 27; Wash. 2, 36.
[8] Minn. 4, 22.
[9] Ind. 5, 14.
[10] Minn. Amt. 1889, p. 2.
[11] Ga. 3, 7, 13 (without the consent of two thirds of the house which rejected it); Tenn. 2, 19; Tex. 3, 34.
[12] La. 38.
[13] U. S. R. S. 1850.
[14] Ala. 76; Ida.; Mon.; Okla.; Utah. (See § 277.)

sections altered or amended, shall be enacted and published at length.[1] And the sections so amended shall, in three, be repealed.[2] So, in two States, no act shall be passed which shall provide that any existing law or any part thereof shall be made or deemed a part of said act, or shall be applicable, except by inserting it in such act.[3] But in two others, all acts which repeal, revive, or amend former laws, shall recite in their caption or otherwise the substance of the act repealed or revived.[4] Amendments may not turn a general law into a special, private, or local one.[5]

§ 308. *When Acts take Effect.* — In some States the Constitution provides that laws go into effect immediately upon publication,[6] or on the fortieth day after final passage,[7] the sixtieth day,[8] or the ninetieth day,[9] or ninety days after the end of the session;[10] or sixty days after;[11] on the July 1st after the passage of the law,[12] the July 4th following,[13] or the June 1st following.[14] In Louisiana, on the day of publication in the place where the State journal is published; elsewhere, twenty days thereafter.[15] In other States the Legislature is to prescribe the time when its acts take effect.[16] In several, the Legislature are to provide for the speedy publication of laws.[17] The above rules are subject to exception in several States "if the Act so provide."[18]

No law can be in force until published.[19] In three States, no law shall be passed the taking effect of which shall be made to depend upon any authority, except as provided in the Constitution.[20]

But in some States the Legislature may, "in case of emergency" provide that any law shall go into effect sooner than the time re-

[1] Ala. 45; Ark. 5, 23; Cal. 4, 24; Col. 5, 24; Fla. 3, 16; Ida. 3, 18; Ill. 4, 13; Ind. 4, 21; Kan. 2, 16; Ky. 51; La. 32; Md. 3, 29; Mich. 4, 25; Miss. 61; Mo. 4, 33 & 34; Mon. 5, 25; N. D. 64; Neb. 3, 11; Nev. 4, 17; N. J. 4, 7, 4; O. 2, 16; Okla. 5, 57; Ore. 4, 22; Pa. 3, 6; Tex. 3, 36; Utah 6, 22; Va. 52; Wash. 2, 37; W. Va. 6, 30; Wy. 3, 26.

[2] Kan., Neb., O. This seems unnecessary.

[3] N. J.; N. Y. 3, 17.

[4] Ga. 3, 7, 17; Tenn. 2, 17.

[5] Va. 64. See § 394.

[6] Ind. 4, 28; Wis. 7, 21.

[7] Tenn. 2, 20.

[8] Miss. 75.

[9] Col. 5, 19.

[10] Ky. 55; Mich, 4, 20; Mo. 4, 36; Neb. 3, 24; Okla. 5, 58; Ore. 4, 28; S. D. 3, 22; Tex. 3, 39; Va. 53; Wash. 2, 31; W. Va. 6, 30.

[11] Fla. 3, 18; Ida. 3, 22; Utah 6, 25.

[12] Ill. 4, 13; N. D. 67.

[13] Io. 3, 26.

[14] Md. 3, 31.

[15] La. 42.

[16] Kan. 1, 19.

[17] Col. 18, 8; Io.; Kan.; La.; Mich. 4, 36; Neb.; Nev. 15, 8; N. Y. 6, 23; Utah 6, 25; Wis.

[18] Md., Miss., Ore., Tenn.

[19] Kan., Wis.

[20] Ind. 1, 25; O. 2, 26; Ore. 1, 21. But see § 309.

spectively above limited,[1] as by a two-thirds vote of all members elected to each house,[2] a four-fifths vote,[3] or a majority of those elected.[4]

No amendment to bills by one house shall be concurred in by the other, except by a vote of a majority thereof, taken by yeas and nays; and the names of those voting for and against recorded upon the journals; and reports of committees of conference shall in like manner be adopted in each house.[5]

"Emergency" is strictly defined in Oklahoma.[6]

§ 309. *Referendum and Initiative.* — Some States impliedly forbid the referendum in their Constitutions (see §§ 201, 300).[7] Six have adopted it: Montana, Nevada, Oklahoma, Oregon, South Dakota, and Utah[8] — all new or far western States; and in

[1] Col., Fla., Ida., Ind., Io., Ky., Mich., Mo., Neb., Ore., S. D., Tex., Utah, Va., Wash., W. Va.

[2] Col., Ill., Mich., Mo., N. D. (present), Neb., Okla., S. D., Tex., Utah, Wash., W. Va.

[3] Va.

[4] Ky.

[5] Miss. 62.

[6] "No act shall take effect until ninety days after the adjournment of the session at which it was passed, except enactments for carrying into effect provisions relating to the initiative and referendum, or a general appropriation bill, unless, in case of emergency, to be expressed in the act, the Legislature, by a vote of two-thirds of all members elected to each House, so directs. An emergency measure shall include only such measures as are immediately necessary for the preservation of the public peace, health, or safety, and shall not include the granting of franchises or license to a corporation or individual, to extend longer than one year, nor provision for the purchase or sale of real estate, nor the renting or encumbrance of real property for a longer term than one year. Emergency measures may be vetoed by the Governor, but such measures so vetoed may be passed by a three-fourths vote of each House, to be duly entered on the journal" (Okla. 3, 58).

[7] "No law, except such as relates to the sale, loan, or gift of vinous, spirituous, or malt liquors, bridges, turnpikes, or other public roads, public buildings or improvements, fencing, running at large of stock, matters pertaining to common schools, paupers, and the regulation by counties, cities, towns, or other municipalities of their local affairs, shall be enacted to take effect upon the approval of any other authority than the General Assembly, unless otherwise expressly provided in this Constitution" (Ky. 60).

[8] "The legislative power shall be vested in a Legislature — except that the people expressly reserve to themselves the right to propose measures, which measures the Legislature shall enact and submit to a vote of the electors of the State, and also the right to require that any laws which the Legislature may have enacted shall be submitted to a vote of the electors of the State before going into effect (except such laws as may be necessary for the immediate preservation of the public peace, health or safety, support of the State government and its existing public institutions).

"*Provided*, that not more than five per centum of the qualified electors of the State shall be required to invoke either the initiative or the referendum.

"This section shall not be construed so as to deprive the Legislature or any member thereof of the right to propose any measure. The veto power of the executive shall not be exercised as to measures referred to a vote of the

Oregon the secretary of state complains that the laws adopted by

people. This section shall apply to municipalities" (S. D. 3, 1).

"The legal voters, or such fractional part thereof, of the State of Utah as may be provided by law, under such conditions and in such manner and within such time as may be provided by law, may initiate any desired legislation and cause the same to be submitted to a vote of the people for approval or rejection, or may require any law passed by the Legislature (except those laws passed by a two-thirds vote of the members elected to each house of the Legislature) to be submitted to the voters of the State before such law shall take effect.

"The legal voters or such fractional part thereof as may be provided by law, of any legal subdivision of the State, under such conditions and in such manner and within such time as may be provided by law, may initiate any desired legislation and cause the same to be submitted to a vote of the people of said legal subdivision for approval or rejection, or may require any law or ordinance passed by the law-making body of said legal subdivision to be submitted to the voters thereof before such law or ordinance shall take effect" (Utah 6, 1, Amt.).

"The legislative authority of the State shall be vested in a Legislature, consisting of a Senate and a House of Representatives; but the people reserve to themselves the power to propose laws [and amendments to the Constitution in Oklahoma and Oregon] and to enact or reject the same at the polls independent of the Legislature, and also reserve power at their own option to approve or reject at the polls any act of the Legislature" (Mon. 1905, 61; Okla. 5, 1; Ore. 4, 1, Amt. 1899, p. 1129).

"*Except*, that the people may not propose laws relating to appropriations, constitutional amendments, or local or special laws [as enumerated in § 395] and they have no right to approve or reject acts of the Legislature which are necessary for the immediate preservation of the public peace, health or safety, or laws relating to appropriations of money, or laws for the submission of constitutional amendments or local or special laws as above." (Mon.).

"The first power reserved by the people is the Initiative, and eight per cent of the legal voters of the State shall be required to propose any measure by petition; provided, that two-fifths of the whole number of the counties of the State must each furnish as signers of said petition eight per cent of the legal voters in such county, and every such petition shall include the full text of the measure so proposed. Initiative petitions shall be filed with the Secretary of State, not less than four months before the election at which they are to be voted upon" (Mon.).

"The second power is the Referendum, and it may be ordered either by petition signed by five per cent of the legal voters of the State; provided, that two-fifths of the whole number of the counties of the State must each furnish as signers of said petition five per cent of the legal voters in such county, or, by the Legislative Assembly as other Bills are enacted" (Mon.).

"Referendum petitions shall be filed with the Secretary of State, not later than six months after the final adjournment of the Session of the Legislative Assembly which passed the Bill on which the Referendum is demanded. The veto power of the governor shall not extend to measures referred to the people by the Legislative Assembly or by Initiative Referendum petitions" (Mon.).

"All elections on measures referred to the people of the State shall be had at the biennial regular general election, except when the Legislative Assembly, by a majority vote, shall order a special election. Any measure referred to the people shall still be in full force and effect unless such petition be signed by fifteen per cent of the legal voters of a majority of the whole number of the counties of the State, in which case the law shall be inoperative until such time as it shall be passed upon at an election, and the result has

initiative are "full of bad spelling, punctuation, omissions, and

been determined and declared as provided by law. The whole number of votes cast for governor at the regular election last preceding the filing of any petition for the Initiative or Referendum, shall be the basis on which the number of the legal petitions and orders for the Initiative and for the Referendum shall be filed with the Secretary of State; and in submitting the same to the people, he, and all other officers, shall be guided by the General laws and the Act submitting this amendment, until Legislation shall be especially provided therefor. The enacting clause of every law originated by the Initiative shall be as follows:

"'Be it enacted by the people of Montana':

"This section shall not be construed to deprive any member of the Legislative Assembly of the right to introduce any measure" (Mon.).

" By the Oklahoma Constitution, the initiative consists in the proposal by eight per cent of the legal voters of any legislative measure, and in the same manner fifteen per cent may propose amendments to the State Constitution by petition. Every such petition must include the full text of the measure proposed. The referendum may be ordered except as to laws necessary for the immediate preservation of the public peace, health or safety, either by petition signed by five per cent of the voters, or by the Legislature as other bills are enacted. The ratio and per cent to be based on the total number of votes cast at the last general election for the State office receiving the highest number of votes. Referendum petitions must be filed with the Secretary of State not more than ninety days after the final adjournment of the session of the Legislature which passed the bill on which the referendum is demanded. The governor has no veto power on measures voted on by the people. The elections upon such measures are held at the next election held throughout the State except when the Legislature or governor order a special election, and must be passed by a majority of votes cast, whereupon, apparently, it takes effect immediately. The referendum may be demanded by the people against one or more items, sections, or parts of any act of the Legislature as well as on a complete act, and the filing of a petition against a part does not delay the remainder of the act from becoming law. Otherwise the referendum, apparently, suspends its operation. These powers of initiative and referendum are further reserved to the local voters of every county and district in the State as to all local legislation or action in the administration of county and district government in and for their respective counties and districts. The manner of such powers to be prescribed by general laws. The requisite number of petitioners for the initiative and referendum in counties and districts to be twice the ratio to the whole number of legal voters in such county or district as herein provided for the State at large. Any measure rejected by the people through initiative or referendum cannot be again proposed by the initiative within three years by less than twenty-five per cent of the legal voters. This reservation of the powers of initiative and referendum does not, however, deprive the Legislature of the right to repeal any law, propose or pass any measure which may be consistent with the Constitution of the State and of the United States. Laws shall be provided to prevent corruption in making, procuring and submitting initiative and referendum petitions" (Okla. 5, 2–8).

"The powers of the initiative and referendum, reserved by this Constitution to the people of the State and the respective counties and districts therein, are hereby preserved to the people of every municipal corporation now existing or which shall hereafter be created within this State, with reference to all legislative authority which it may exercise, and amendments to charters for its own government in accordance with the provisions of this Constitution.

"Every petition for either the initiaative or referendum in the government

repeated words;" and an important amendment to the Constitu-

of a municipal corporation shall be signed by a number of qualified electors residing within the territorial limits of such municipal corporation, equal to twenty-five per centum of the total number of votes cast at the next preceding election, and every such petition shall be filed with the chief executive officer of such municipal corporation.

"When such petition demands the enactment of an ordinance or other legal act other than the grant, extension or renewal of a franchise, the chief executive office shall present the same to the legislative body of such corporation at its next meeting, and unless the said petition shall be granted more than thirty days before the next election at which any city officers are to be elected, the chief executive officer shall submit the said ordinance or act so petitioned for, to the qualified electors at said election; and if a majority of said electors voting thereon shall vote for the same, it shall thereupon become in full force and effect.

"When such petition demands a referendum vote upon any ordinance or any other legal act other than the grant, extension, or renewal of a franchise, the chief executive officer shall submit said ordinance or act to the qualified electors of said corporation at the next succeeding general municipal election, and if, at said election, a majority of the electors voting thereon shall not vote for the same, it shall thereupon stand repealed.

"When such petition demands an amendment to a charter, the chief executive officer shall submit such amendment to the qualified electors of said municipal corporation at the next election of any officers of said corporation, and if, at said election, a majority of said electors voting thereon shall vote for such amendment, the same shall thereupon become an amendment to and a part of said charter, when approved by the Governor and filed in the same manner and form as an original charter is required by the provisions of this article to be approved and filed" (Okla. 18, 4).

"The legislative authority of the State shall be vested in a legislative assembly, consisting of a Senate and House of Representatives, but the people reserve to themselves power to propose laws and amendments to the Constitution, and to enact or reject the same at the polls, independent of the legislative assembly, and also reserve power at their own option to approve or reject at the polls any act of the legislative assembly. The first power reserved by the people is the initiative, and not more than eight per cent of the legal voters shall be required to propose any measure by such petition, and every such petition shall include the full text of the measure so proposed. Initiative petitions shall be filed with the Secretary of State not less than four months before the election at which they are to be voted upon. The second power is the referendum, and it may be ordered (except as to laws necessary for the immediate preservation of the public peace, health or safety) either by petition, signed by five per cent of the legal voters, or by the legislative assembly, as other bills are enacted. Referendum petitions shall be filed with the Secretary of State not more than ninety days after the final adjournment of the session of the legislative assembly which passed the bill on which the referendum is demanded. The veto power of the governor shall not extend to measures referred to the people. All elections on measures referred to the people of the State shall be had at the biennial regular general elections, except when the legislative assembly shall order a special election. Any measure referred to the people shall take effect and become the law when it is approved by a majority of the votes cast thereon, and not otherwise. The style of all bills shall be: 'Be it enacted by the people of the State of Oregon.' This section shall not be construed to deprive any member of the legislative assembly of the right to introduce any measure. The whole number of votes cast for justice of the Supreme Court at the regular election last preceding the filing

tion requiring constitutional amendments proposed by initiative to be submitted to the people at the next election, and calling for a constitutional convention, is not included in the Oregon law of 1907, though adopted by the people June 4, 1906. It is yet too early to judge of the effect in the other States. In Delaware the Legislature "are to provide a system of advisory initiative and referendum." [1]

Article 31. Form of Revenue Bills

§ 310. *Origin.* — All bills for raising revenue must, by the Constitutions of most of the States, originate in the lower house; but the senate may generally propose amendments as in other bills.[2] But no new matter not relating to the revenue can be so introduced.[3] The governor may, in most States, veto certain items in an appropriation bill and allow the others to become a law.[4] In several States,

of any petition for the initiative or for the referendum shall be the basis on which the number of legal voters necessary to sign such petition shall be counted. Petitions and orders for the initiative and for the referendum shall be filed with the secretary of state, and in submitting the same to the people he and all other officers shall be guided by the general laws and the act submitting this amendment until legislation shall be especially provided therefor" (Ore. 1899, p. 1129, Amt. to IV. 1).

"Whenever ten per centum or more of the voters of this State, as shown by the number of votes cast at the last preceding general election, shall express their wish that any law or resolution made by the Legislature be submitted to a vote of the people, the officers charged with the duties of announcing and proclaiming elections and of certifying nominations or questions to be voted on, shall submit the question of the approval or disapproval of said law or resolution to be voted on at the next ensuing election wherein a State or Congressional officer is to be voted for, or wherein any question may be voted on, by the electors of the entire State.

"When a majority of the electors voting at a State election shall by their votes signify approval of a law or resolution such law or resolution shall stand as the law of the State and shall not be overruled, annulled, set aside, suspended, or in any way made inoperative except by the direct vote of the people. When such majority shall so signify disapproval, the law or resolution so disapproved shall be void and of no effect" (Nev. 1901, p. 139).

[1] Del. 1905, 53.

[2] Ala. 70; Ark. 6, 17; Col. 5, 31; Del. 8, 2; Ga. 3, 7, 10; Ida. 3, 14; Ind. 4, 17; Ky. 47; La. 37; Mass. 2, 1, 3, 7; Me. 4, 3, 9; Minn. 4, 10; Mon. 5, 32; Neb. 3, 9; N. H. 2, 17; N. J. 4, 6, 1; Okla. 5, 33; Ore. 4, 18; Pa. 3, 14; S. C. 3, 15; Tex. 3, 33; Vt. Amt. 3; Wy. 3, 33. This principle was fully established in England as early as 1407 (T.-L. p. 248). It is also contained in the United States Constitution (I. 7 (1)). See also § 300.

[3] Del.; Ky.; Me.; Vt.; Miss. 69.

[4] Ala. 126; Ark.; Cal. 4, 16; Col. 4, 12; Del. 3, 18; Fla. 4, 18; Ga. 5, 1, 16; Ida. 4, 11; Kan. 1903, 545; Ky. 88; La. 77; Md. Amt. 1890, 194; Minn. 4, 11; Miss. 73; Mo. 5, 13; Mon. 7, 13; N. D. 80; Neb. 5, 15; N. J. 5, 7; N. Y. 4, 9; Okla. 6, 12; Pa. 4, 16; S. C. 4, 23; S. D. 4, 10; Tex. 4, 14; Utah 7, 8; Va. 76; Wash. 14, 12; W. Va. 7, 15; Wy. 4, 9.

no appropriation bill can be passed in the last five[1] or ten[2] days of the Legislative session, or not after the first forty days but by unanimous consent.[3]

§ 311. *The General Appropriation Bill* may contain only, in some States, appropriations for the ordinary expenses of the State in its legislative, executive, and judicial departments.[4] So, in several, for the general expenses of government.[5] And in a few, for the interest on the public debt,[6] for the sinking fund,[7] for public schools,[8] or public charities.[9] In more detail, it may contain appropriations for salaries of State officers generally,[10] of the Legislature, or for the "civil list";[11] for the cost of collecting the revenue;[12] for institutions under the exclusive control and management of the State;[13] for the support of the eleemosynary institutions of the State.[14] It may not contain any other enactment or provision unless it relate specifically to some particular appropriation.[15]

§ 312. *Other Appropriation Bills* must, by the Constitution of a few States contain no provisions on any other subject;[16] and so, in one, of all bills for raising revenue;[17] so, they must, in other States, contain only one item or subject.[18]

They must, in several, be for a certain specified purpose;[19] and it is not sufficient to refer to any other law to fix such purpose.[20] So, no appropriation can be made under the title of "contingent";[21] all must specify the sum appropriated,[22] and none may last six months beyond the next meeting of the Legislature.[23] No moneys shall be issued out of the treasury but for the necessary defence and support of the State government and the protection of the inhabitants.[24]

[1] Ala.; La. 57; Miss. 68; Okla.; Wy. 3, 22. See also § 306.

[2] Mon. 5, 21.

[3] N. D. 60.

[4] Ala. 71; Ark. 5, 30; Col. 5, 32; Ga. 3, 7, 9; Miss. 69; Mon. 5, 33; N. D. 62; Pa. 3, 15; S. D. 12, 2; Wy. 3, 34.

[5] Cal. 4, 29; La. 55; Neb. 3, 19; Ore. 9, 7.

[6] Ala.; Col.; Ga.; La.; Miss.; Mo. 4, 43; Mon.; N. D.; Pa.; S. D.; Wy.

[7] Mo.

[8] Ala., Col., Ga., La., Miss., Mo., Mon., N. D., Pa., S. D., Wy.

[9] La.

[10] Cal.; Ill. 4, 16; Neb.; Ore.; W. Va. 6, 42.

[11] Mo.

[12] Mo.

[13] Cal., Ga.

[14] Mo.

[15] N. Y. 3, 22.

[16] Ala. 71; Fla. 3, 30; Ga. 3, 7, 9; La. 55; Miss. 69; Okla. 1, 16; Pa. 3, 15; S. D. 12, 3.

[17] Del. 8, 2.

[18] Ala.; Ark. 5, 30; Cal. 4, 34; Col. 5, 32; Ga.; La.; Miss.; Mon.; Pa.; N. D. 62; S. D.; Wy. 3, 33.

[19] Ark. 5, 29; Cal.; La. 56; Mo. 10, 19; N. Y. 3, 21; Okla. 5, 55; S. C. 4, 23.

[20] Mo., N. Y.

[21] La.

[22] N. Y.

[23] Miss. 64. See also § 300.

[24] Mass. 2, 2, 1, 11; N. H. 2, 56.

In one the *general* appropriations (§ 311) must be made first, and take precedence of any others.[1]

§ 313. *Voting.* — The Constitutions of several provide that a bill appropriating money or property for private or local purposes must receive a vote of two thirds of the elected members of each house.[2] So, in two, an appropriation for charitable or educational institutions not under the absolute control of the State.[3] In two, a bill appropriating money for extraordinary purposes (not included in §§ 311, 335) requires a two-thirds vote in each house.[4] The yeas and nays must always be entered on the journal, on the passage of a bill appropriating money;[5] and three-fifths of each house are necessary to a quorum.[6] So, in two, such act must be voted for by a majority[7] or two thirds of the members[8] elected to each house, or of three fifths of those present.[9] So, any act releasing, discharging, or commuting any claim or demand of the State[10] must have a majority vote of members elected, or of a quorum of three fifths, as above.[11]

§ 314. *Tax Bills.* — The Constitutions of several States require that every law imposing a tax shall state distinctly the object of the same, to which only it shall be applied.[12] So, in a few, of a bill creating a debt.[13] And it is not sufficient to refer to any other law, to fix such object.[14]

In several, all taxes must be levied and collected by general laws.[15]

In two, a bill imposing a tax must receive the necessary vote in a quorum of three fifths of each house, to be entered in the journal (as in § 313);[16] and in one of a majority of a quorum of two thirds of the elected members, in the house.[17] In one other, it must be read three several times in each house, and pass the three readings on different days, the yeas and nays of the second and third readings entered in the journal.[18] In others, a bill imposing a tax for

[1] Mo. 4, 43.
[2] Io. 3, 31; Mich. 4, 45; Miss. 60; N. Y. 3, 20; R. I. 4, 14.
[3] Ala. 73; Pa. 3, 17.
[4] Ark. 5, 31; S. D. 12, 2. See also § 314.
[5] Ga. 3, 7, 12; N. Y. 3, 25; Wis. 8, 8.
[6] N. Y., Wis.
[7] Ky. 46; Miss. 64; Va. 50.
[8] S. D. 12, 2.
[9] Miss. 70.
[10] Va. 50. See also § 304.
[11] N. Y.
[12] Ark. 16, 11; Io. 7, 7; Kan. 11, 4; Ky. 180; Mich. 14, 14; N. C. 5, 7; N. D. 175; N. Y. 3, 24; O. 12, 5; Okla. 10, 19; Ore. 9, 3; S. C. 10, 3; S. D. 11, 8; Va. 50; Wash. 7, 5; Wy. 15, 13. See also § 330.
[13] Col. 11, 4; Ga. 7, 4, 1; Ky. 178; N. Y. 7, 4; Nev. 9, 3; Pa. 9, 5.
[14] Io., Mich., N. Y., Va.
[15] Col. 10, 3; Ga. 7, 2, 1; Ky. 171; Mo. 10, 3; Pa. 9, 1; Tex. 8, 3. See § 395.
[16] N. Y. 3, 25; Wis. 8, 8.
[17] Vt. 2, 9.
[18] N. C. 2, 14.

extraordinary objects (not included in § 335) requires a two-thirds vote in each house,[1] or a majority of the members elected.[2]

§ 315. *State Debt Bills.*[3] — Bills providing for a loan to the State or creating a State debt require the assent of two thirds of the elected members of each house,[4] or of three fourths,[5] or of a majority of members elected,[6] or of a majority of members present; but three fifths are, in such case, necessary to a quorum (as in § 313).[7] They must be read three times, like tax bills (see § 314).[8] The law must state the purpose for which the money is borrowed.[9]

§ 316. *State Aid Bills.* — In four States the Legislature [10] has no power to give or lend the credit of the State in aid of any person or corporation, unless the law be approved by direct vote of the people.[11] So, law creating a State debt must be approved by the people at a general election; [12] and in South Carolina it must receive a two thirds vote.

Article 32. Appropriations [13]

§ 320. *Warrants, etc.* — By the Constitutions of most States, no money shall be paid out of the treasury except upon appropriations duly made by law specifying the purpose, etc. (see Art. 31).[14] And there must be warrants drawn by the proper officer.[15] And in

[1] Ark. 5, 31.

[2] Va.

[3] See also § 314. For temporary loans, see § 360.

[4] Minn. 9, 5.

[5] Del. 8, 3.

[6] Kan. 11, 5; Wis. 8, 6.

[7] N. Y. 3, 25; Wis. 8, 8.

[8] N. C. 2, 14.

[9] Del.; Mon.; N.Y. 7, 5; Okla. 10, 16.

[10] Compare § 326. Also Art. 36.

[11] Ark. 10, 6; Ky. 50; N. C. 5, 4; S. C., 10, 11.

[12] Ky.; Mon. 13, 2; S. C. See also §§ 309, 361.

[13] See U. S. C. 1, 9. The appropriation of supplies to objects specified in the law dates from 1353, but was only put in practice occasionally, and at long intervals. An account of the expenditure of the last subsidy was required from Richard II; and the principle that an appropriation should be diverted to no other purpose was expressly asserted by the Commons under Henry VI, and finally vindicated in 1665 under Charles II. Since then it has been "an undisputed principle, recognized by frequent, and at length constant practice," that "supplies granted by parliament are only to be expended for particular objects specified by itself." (Hallam, Const. Hist., vol. ii. p. 356.)

[14] Ala. 72; Ark. 5, 29; 16, 12; Ariz.* Bill of Rts. 25; Cal. 4, 22; Col. 5, 33; Del. 8, 6; Fla. 9, 4; Ga. 3, 7, 11; Ida. 7, 13; Ill. 4, 17; Ind. 10, 3; Io. 3, 24; Kan. 2, 24; Ky. 58, 230; La. 45; Md. 3, 32; Me. 5, 4, 4; Mich. 14, 5; Minn. 4, 12; 9, 9; Miss. 60; Mo. 4, 43; Mon. 5, 34; 13, 2; N. C. 14, 3; N. D. 186; Neb. 3, 22; Nev. 4, 19; N. J. 4, 6, 2; N. Y. 7, 8; O. 2, 22; Okla. 5, 55; Ore. 9, 4; Pa. 3, 16; S. C. 10, 9; S. D. 11, 9; Tenn. 2, 24; Tex. 8, 6; Va. 186; Vt. 2, 17; Wash. 8, 4; W. Va. 10, 3; Wis. 8, 2; Wy. 3, 35; 16, 7. So in U. S. C. 1 9, (7).

[15] Ala.; Cal.; Col.; Ill.; Mass. 2, 2, 1, 11; Mo. 10, 19; Mon.; Neb.; N. D.; N. H. 2, 55; Pa.; S. D.; W. Va.; Wy.

a few States, no appropriation can be made for a longer term than two years;[1] so in others, the warrant must be issued within two years[2] or two and a half years of the act of appropriation.[3] Money raised by taxation, loan, or assessment for any purpose shall not be diverted to any other purpose except by authority of law.[4]

No appropriation shall be made, nor any expenditure authorized, by the Legislature, whereby the expenditure of the State during any fiscal year shall exceed the total tax then provided by law, and applicable to such appropriation or expenditure, unless the Legislature making such appropriation shall provide for levying a sufficient tax, not exceeding the rates allowed in [§ 336], to pay such appropriation or expenditure within such fiscal year. This provision shall not apply to appropriations or expenditures to suppress insurrection, defend the State, or assist in defending the United States in time of war.[5]

§ 321. *State Accounts.* — By the Constitutions of most States, a regular statement and account of receipts and expenditures of public moneys must be published annually,[6] semi-annually,[7] or after every session of the Legislature, with the laws,[8] or in such manner as by law directed.[9]

§ 322. *Private Appropriations, Claims, and Debts.* — The Constitution of Illinois provides that the Legislature shall make no appropriation of money out of the treasury in any private law.[10] So, in Texas, that no appropriation for private or individual purposes shall be made.[11] In Mississippi, no law granting a donation, etc. without a two-thirds vote of members elected in each house.[12] So, in several States, no appropriation of money or grant of property can be made by the State to any individual or corporation, municipal or otherwise.[13] And by the Illinois Constitution, the Illinois and

[1] Ark., Kan., La., Mo., Mon., O., Tex., Va.

[2] Kan., Mo., N. Y., Wash.

[3] Okla.

[4] Ky. 18; O.; N. D. 130; S. D. 10, 2.

[5] Ida. 7, 11; Mon. 12, 12.

[6] Ala. 72; Del. 8, 6; Ky. 230; N. C. 14, 3; S. C. 19, 8; S. D. 11, 12; Tex. 12, 4; Tex. 16, 6; Utah 13, 6; Wash. 7, 7; W. Va. 10, 3. Quarterly: Ga.; La.; Mon. 12, 13.

[7] Ky. 53; Miss. 137.

[8] Cal. 4, 22; Fla. 3, 19; Ga. 3, 7, 11; Ill. 4, 17; Ind. 10, 4; Io. 3, 18; Md. 3, 32; Me. 5, 4, 4; Mich. 18, 5; Minn. 9, 11; Miss. 113; Mon. 7, 19; Neb. 3, 22; Nev. 4, 19; Ore. 9, 5; S. C.; Tenn. 2, 24; Va. 10, 18; Vt. 2, 28.

[9] Ark. 19, 12; Ct. 4, 21; Kan. 15, 5; Mo. 10, 19; O. 15, 3; S. D.; Tex.

[10] Ill. 4, 16. See also § 395.

[11] Tex. 16, 6. Compare Art. 39.

[12] Amt. 1906, 238.

[13] Ga. 7, 16, 1; Ky. 177; Mo. 4, 46;

Michigan Canal can never be sold or leased but by vote of the people.[1] *Except* that in two States a grant of aid may be made in case of a public calamity.[2] And a right of way through public land may, in one, be granted to a railroad or canal.[3]

The Constitutions of two States provide that the Legislature shall not audit nor allow any private claim or account;[4] nor, in several, authorize the payment of any claim against the State under an agreement or contract made without the authority of law.[5] Or of any such claim against a municipality;[6] and all such private or special contracts are void.[7] Nor, in a few, can money be paid on any claim the subject matter of which is not provided for by preexisting laws.[8] Such claim may, however, be allowed on a two-thirds vote of the full Legislature.[9] So, in two, no special act making compensation to a person claiming damages against the State can be passed.[10]

In Maryland, the Legislature can appropriate no money in payment of a private claim over $300 unless proved before the comptroller and reported on by him.[11] And in Indiana (10, 7), the State is freed from all liability on account of Wabash & Erie Canal stock.

Exceptions. But, in a few States, the Legislature may appropriate for expenses incurred by private persons in suppressing insurrection or repelling invasion.[12]

The Constitutions of several States provide that the Legislature shall have no power to release or extinguish, or to authorize the releasing or extinguishing, in whole or in part, any indebtedness or liability, of any corporation or individual to the State,[13] or to any municipal corporation therein.[14] This follows, practically, in other States, from the provisions of § 395.[15]

So, in several, the Legislature have no power to release, alienate,

N. D. 185; Neb. (of land only) 3, 18; N. J. 1, 20; Tex. 3, 51. See also § 326.

1 Ill. Sep. § 3.

2 Mo., Tex.

3 La. 58.

4 Ariz.* B. Rts. 27; Mich. 4, 31; N. Y. 3, 19.

5 Cal. 4, 32; Ill. 4, 19; Ky. 58; La. 47; Miss. 96; Mo. 4, 48; Mon. 5, 29; S. D. 12, 3; Tex. 3, 53; Utah 6, 30; W. Va. 6, 38.

6 Cal.; Ky. 162; La.; Tex.

7 Cal., Ill., Ky., La., Mo., S. D., W. Va.

8 Ark. 5, 27; Col. 5, 27 & 28; Fla. 16, 11; Io. 3, 31; Nev. 4, 28; O. 2, 29; Pa. 3, 11; Tex. 3, 44.

9 Ark., Fla., O.

10 Ind. 4, 24; Ore. 4, 24.

11 Md. 3, 52.

12 Ill., Miss., S. D., W. Va.

13 Ala. 100; Ark. 5, 33, 12, 12; Col. 5, 38; Ill. 4, 23; Ky. 52; La. 59; Miss. 100; Mo. 4, 51; Mon. 5, 39; Okla. 5, 53; S. D. 3, 24; Tex. 3, 55; Utah 6, 27; Wy. 3, 40.

14 Ala., Col., Ill., Ky., La., Miss., Mon., Okla., Wy.

15 Cal., Md.

or alter the lien held by the State upon any railroad,[1] or as against any corporation.[2] And in Illinois, specially of the Illinois Central Railroad, no lien, contract, obligation, or liability in the original charter, shall ever be released or impaired.[3]

In one State, no claim shall be allowed (by the Legislature or other body or officers acting for the State) against the State which would be barred by lapse of time if made against a private person; *except* that a claim may be so prosecuted within two years of the removal of a legal disability of the claimant.[4]

The Legislature shall not authorize payment to any person of the salary of a deceased officer beyond the date of his death;[5] nor retire any officer on pay, or part pay, or make any grant to such retiring officer.[6]

§ 323. *Charitable and Sectarian Appropriations.* — The Constitutions of a few States provide that no appropriation shall be made for private, charitable, educational, or benevolent purposes to any person or community or any corporation not wholly under the State authority;[7] nor to any denominational or sectarian institution;[8] except by a vote of two-thirds the members elected;[9] and see § 313.

Exceptions. But in California, grants of aid may be made to orphan or indigent asylums in accordance with a uniform rule. And in Pennsylvania, to asylums for soldiers' widows or orphans.[10]

§ 324. *Internal Improvement.* — By the Constitutions of a few States the State cannot be interested in works of internal improvement, or "engage in them"[11] except on two-thirds vote of the people;[12] nor, in Alabama, loan its credit in support of such works;[13] nor, in several States, create or contract debts for them;[14] nor be a party to carrying on such works.[15]

But the Tennessee Constitution declares that a well-regulated system of internal improvement should be encouraged by the Legislature.[16]

[1] Ark. 5, 33; Mo. 4, 50; Pa. 3, 24; Tex. 3, 54.
[2] Pa.
[3] Ill. Sep. § 1.
[4] N. Y. 7, 6.
[5] Miss. 92.
[6] Miss. 93.
[7] Ala. 73; Cal. 4, 22; Col. 5, 34; La. 53; Mon. 5, 35; Pa. 3, 17; S. C. 11, 9; Va. 67; Wy. 3, 36. See also §§ 44, 54.
[8] Wy.
[9] Ala.
[10] Pa. 3, 19.
[11] Mich.; N. D. 185; S. D. 13, 1; Wy. 16, 6.
[12] N. D., Wy.
[13] Ala. 93.
[14] Ala.; Md. 3, 34; Minn. 9, 5; O. 12, 6; Wis. 8, 10. See, however, § 361.
[15] Ala.; Kan. 11, 8; Md.; Mich. 14, 9; Minn.; Wis.
[16] Tenn. 11, 10.

§ 325. *Miscellaneous Restrictions.* — The Constitution of Texas provides that the State shall make no appropriation for a bureau of, or to encourage or assist, immigration.[1] Not for war debts of the State or any county, city, or town.[2]

§ 326. *Loans of Credit, etc.*[3] — The State, by the Constitutions of most of the States, cannot lend money or its credit to any individual, association, or corporation, municipal or otherwise, whatever.[4] *Except* corporations for religious or charitable purposes; or for the support of the poor.[5] So, specially, it cannot loan, etc., to railroads or canals.[6]

Nor, in many, can the State become a stockholder or bondholder in any corporation,[7] in any bank,[8] railroad,[9] or highway.[10]

The Constitution provides, in general terms, that the State may not be interested in any private or corporate enterprise,[11] or internal improvement.[12]

Nor, in many, can it assume the debts of any (individual or) municipal corporation;[13] except, in several, when incurred in time of war for the benefit of the State.[14]

Nor, in Tennessee, can any bonds of the State be issued to any railroad which is in default in paying interest on bonds previously loaned to it, or has sold them for less than par.[15]

Limitations. But in North Carolina, the credit of the State may be so loaned, contrary to the above rules, upon vote of the people.

§ 327. *Money.* — The Constitution of Texas provides that the

[1] Tex. 16, 56. See § 202.

[2] Va. 186. See U. S. C. Amt. 14.

[3] Compare § 316. See also Art. 36.

[4] Ala. 93; Ark. 16, 1; Cal. 4, 31; Col. 11, 1–2; Del. 8, 4; Fla. 9, 10; Ga. 7, 5, 1; Ida. 8, 2; Ill. 4, 20; Ind. 11, 12; Io. 7, 1; Ky. 177; La. 58; Md. 3, 34; Me. 9, 14; Mich. 14, 6; Minn. 9, 10; Miss. 258; Mo. 4, 45; Mon. 13, 1; N. C. 5, 4; N. D. 185; Neb. 14, 3; Nev. 8, 9; N. J. 4, 6, 3; N. Y. 7, 1; 8, 9; O. 8, 4; Okla. 10, 11; Pa. 9, 6; S. C. 10, 6; S. D. 13, 1; Tenn. 2, 31; Terr. U. S. 1886, 818; Tex. 3, 50; Utah 6, 31; Va. 185; Wash. 12, 9; 8, 5; W. Va. 10, 6; Wis. 8, 3; Wy. 16, 6.

[5] N. D., S. D.

[6] Ill. Sep. § 3; Wy. 3, 39; 10, 10 (5).

[7] Ariz.* Bill of Rts. 27; Ark. 12, 7; Cal. 12, 13; Col.; Fla.; Ga.; Ida.; Ind.; Io. 8, 3; Ky.; La.; Mich. 14, 8; Miss.; Mo. 4, 49; Mon.; N. D.; Nev.; O.; Okla.; Ore. 11, 6; Pa.; S. C.; S. D.; Tenn.; Utah; Va.; Wash.; W. Va.; Wy.

[8] Ill., Ind., Kan., Mo., Tenn. See § 530.

[9] Ky.

[10] Ky.

[11] Ala., La., Va. See § 324.

[12] Va.

[13] Ark. 12, 12; Cal.; Col.; Ga. 7, 8, 1; Ida. 12, 3; Ill.; Ind. 10, 6; Io.; Ky. 176; La.; Mon. 13, 5; Nev. 9, 4; O. 8, 5; Okla. 10, 14; Ore. 11, 8; Pa. 9, 9; S. D.; Tex.; Utah 14, 6; W. Va.; Va.

[14] Ark., Ga., Ida., Io., Ky., Nev., O., Okla., Ore., Pa., S. D.

[15] Tenn. 2, 23.

State shall have no power to issue treasury notes or warrants intended to circulate as money.[1]

§ 328. *Embezzlement, etc.* (See § 156.) — The Legislature shall provide by law for the establishment and maintenance of an efficient system of checks and balances between the officers of the Executive Department, and all commissioners and superintendents, and boards of control of State institutions, and all other officers entrusted with the collection, receipt, custody, or disbursement of the revenue or moneys of the State whatsoever.[2]

Article 33. Taxation

§ 330. *General Principles.*[3] — In the Constitutions of several States it is declared that every member of society is bound to contribute his proportion to the expenses of the government; but no part of his property can be taken without his own consent or legislative authority.[4]

So, in many, no tax, impost, duty, or charge can be levied except in pursuance of a law;[5] or by consent of the people,[6] or their representatives in the Legislature.[7] Taxation can be for public purposes only;[8] and must be levied under general laws.[9]

[1] Tex. 16, 7. See U. S. C. 1, 10.

[2] Okla. 5, 60.

[3] Compare Art. 9. The history of English taxation, as distinct from feudal aids, begins with the imposition of the Dane-geld, A. D. 1008. The first tax on personal property was the Saladin tithe, A. D. 1188 (see Historical Digest). The English constitutional principles affecting taxation are fully discussed in Book I.; in substance, that no tax, direct or indirect, shall be imposed upon the people or upon their property, real or personal, which has not been voted or assented to by the House of Commons; second, that all taxes must be for the common benefit or the general advantage of the Realm. To these, American Constitutional Law may be said to have added a third principle, that taxes shall be proportionate and uniform. The Federal Government has practically no power of direct taxation; this remains with the people of the States. Otherwise the powers of taxation belong both to the Federal and the State governments; though the Federal power is subject to the broad limitation that it may be exercised only by Congress and to pay the debts and provide for the common defence and general welfare of the United States; and that all indirect taxes shall be uniform throughout the United States, and direct taxes, if any, imposed upon the States according to their respective numbers, now excluding only Indians not taxed.

[4] Del. 8, 1; Mass. 1, 10; Md. Decln. of Rts. 14 & 15; N. H. 1, 12; Okla. 10, 14; Va. 1, 6; Vt. 1, 9; Wy. 15, 13; 13, 3.

[5] Ark. 16, 11; Fla. 9, 3; Kan. 11, 4; Ky. 171; Mo. 10, 1; Mon. 12, 16; N. D. 175; O. 12, 5; Ore. 9, 3; S. C. 8, 3; 10, 3; Wash. 7, 5.

[6] Mass. 1, 23; Me. 1, 22; N. C. 1, 23; N. H. 1, 28; Ore. 1, 32; S. C. 1, 7; S. D. 6, 17; Wy. 1, 28.

[7] La. 224; Mass.; Md.; Me.; N. C.; N. H.; Ore.; S. C.; S. D.; Wy.

[8] Ky. 171; Minn. Amt. 1907, p. 18; 9, 1; S. C.; S. D. 10, 2. See note 1.

[9] Ida. 7, 5; Ky.; Mon.; Okla.; Va. 168.

And in Vermont, previous to any law for a tax, the purpose for which the tax is levied ought not to appear of more importance to the community than the money would be if not collected.

By the Constitution of Arkansas, "the State's ancient right of eminent domain, and of taxation, is expressly and fully conceded." [1] In Georgia, taxation is declared to be a sovereign right of the State, absolutely inalienable.[2]

In several, the Legislature has no power to release (in Louisiana, postpone) the inhabitants of, or property in, any town or county from payment of State or county taxes;[3] except in case of great public calamity,[4] and by a two-thirds vote of each house.[5] So, in others, the power to tax shall not be surrendered or suspended by any act, contract, or grant to which the State is a party;[6] so, specially, of the power to tax corporations and their property.[7]

And in several, no power to levy taxes can be delegated to individuals or private corporations.[8] See § 340.

In Illinois, the Constitution provides that the specification therein of the objects and subjects of taxation shall not deprive the General Assembly of the power to require other subjects or objects to be taxed in such manner as may be consistent with the principles of taxation fixed in the Constitution.[9]

§ 331. *Taxable Property.* — In many States, the Constitution declares that all property, real and personal and mixed, is taxable.[10]

In others, taxes "shall be levied upon such property as is described by law." [11] "Polls, estates, and other classes of property, including franchises and property when passing by will and inheritance." [12]

[1] Ark. 2, 23.

[2] Ga. 4, 1, 1.

[3] Cal. 11, 10; Col. 10, 8; Ill. 9, 6; La. 212; Mo. 10, 9; Neb. 9, 4; Tex. 8, 10.

[4] La., Tex.

[5] Tex.

[6] Cal. 13, 6; Ga.; Ida. 7, 7; Ky. 175; Me. 9, 9; Minn.; Mon. 12, 6; N. D. 178; Okla. 10, 5; Wash. 11, 9; Wy. 15, 14. And this applies also to municipal taxation (N. D.).

[7] Ark. 16, 7; Col. 10, 9; Ga. 7, 2, 5; Ida. 7, 8; La. 228; Miss. 182; Mo. 10, 2; Mon. 12, 7; Pa. 9, 3; S. D. 113; Tex. 8, 4; Va. 64; Wash. 7, 4. These two provisions show the desire to escape the impairment of contract clause of the Federal Constitution, and prevent the granting or bargaining away of the sovereign right of taxation, in conformity with the views of a persistent minority in the United States Supreme Court.

[8] Ala. 212; Cal. 11, 13; Col. 5, 35; Ga. 4, 1, 1; Pa. 3, 20. Compare § 340.

[9] Ill. 9, 2.

[10] Cal. 13, 1; Col. 10, 3; Fla. 9, 1; Ind. 10, 1; Ky. 174; Minn. 9, 3; Mon. 12, 16; N. C. 5, 3; N. D. 176; Nev. 10, 1; O. 12, 2; S. C. 10, 13; Tenn. 2, 28; Utah 13, 2; Va. 168; Wash. 7, 1; W. Va. 10, 1.

[11] Ida. 7, 3; Mich. 14, 11; Wis. 8, 1.

[12] N. H. 2, 6.

In one, the personal property of residents of the State is taxable in the county or city where the resident *bona fide* resides for the greater part of the year; and not elsewhere, except goods and chattels "permanently located."[1] But in two, all property is to be assessed where situated (except rolling stock, etc., of railroads).[2]

Land and the improvements thereon are to be separately assessed.[3] Mortgages, except mortgages by railroads, etc., are taxed to the owner, and the property less the value of the mortgage to the mortgagor.[4] Mortgages may be taxed where the land is.[5]

In Texas, all property of railroads in towns shall bear its share of municipal taxation;[6] and all property of railroads shall be taxed.[7]

The property of all corporations shall, by several State Constitutions, be subject to taxation the same as that of individuals;[8] so of corporations for pecuniary profit only.[9] But this shall not be construed so as to authorize the taxation of the stocks of any company or corporation when the property of such company or corporation represented by such stocks is within the State and has been taxed.[10]

"The Legislature shall provide for taxing all moneys, credits, investments in bonds, stocks, joint stock companies, or otherwise; and also for taxing the notes and bills discounted or purchased, moneys loaned and all other property, effects or dues of every description, of all banks and of all bankers, so that all property employed in banking shall always be subject to a taxation equal to that imposed on the property of individuals."[11]

In Maryland, the Legislature are to provide for the taxation of the revenue of foreign corporations doing business in the State.[12]

[1] Md. 3, 51.

[2] Cal. 13, 10; Tex. 8, 11.

[3] Cal. 13, 2; Wy. 15, 1; Del. 8, 7.

[4] Cal. 13, 4.

[5] Md. Amt. 1898.

[6] Tex. 8, 5.

[7] Mon.; Tex. 8, 8. See § 540.

[8] Ala. 217; Col. 10, 10; Fla. 16, 16; Ida. 7, 8; Io. 8, 2; Ky.; Miss. 181; Mon. 12, 7; Nev. 8, 2; O. 13, 4; S. D. 11, 2; Utah 13, 10; Wash. 7, 3. See § 330. This provision would not, however, be held to preclude franchise taxes, or taxes on the capital stock, and the imposition of such in addition to a property tax is not double taxation. Already, by the year 1903, such taxation existed by law in: Ala., Col., Del., Mass., Me, N. J., N. Y., N. C., Tex., Vt., Wash., W. Va. See Report Committee on Corporation Laws, Massachusetts, 1903, pp. 273–279.

[9] Ala., Io.

[10] Mon. 12, 17.

[11] S. D. 11, 4.

[12] Md. 3, 58. See in § 509. There is no Constitutional limit to the power of imposing a franchise tax on foreign corporations, even to the point of driving them from the State; property taxes, however, must be identical with those imposed on home corporations. In 1903 such taxes existed in ten States: Ala., Col., Mass., N. C., N. Y., O., Tex., Vt., Wash., W. Va. These principles do not, however, hold of

In three States, mines and mining claims may not be directly taxed, but only their proceeds.[1] Coal lands not being mined are to be taxed according to value.[2] All mines are to be taxed according to gross product, and the land (except improvements) is exempt.[3] So, the *net* proceeds; but the land is taxed at the price paid the United States.[4] There is a special and separate assessment of coal or mineral land.[5]

The Legislature may provide for a special mode of valuation and assessment for railroads, and railroad (and other corporate) property.[6]

§ 332. *Exemptions.* — The following are the constitutional exemptions from taxation (there are these and many others existing by statutes; indeed the older States have not deemed it advisable to put such matters in the Constitution):

(A) Burying-grounds.[7]

(B) Public schoolhouses;[8] school buildings and apparatus;[9] libraries and grounds used for school purposes.[10]

(C) Churches;[11] church property used for religious purposes;[12] public hospitals;[13] parsonages.[14]

(D) Academies;[15] colleges, universities, and seminaries of learning;[16] public libraries;[17] books, paintings, and statuary, kept in a free public hall;[18] institutions of purely public charity;[19] of education;[20] or free museums.[21]

interstate commerce corporations. See Mass. Corporation Committee Report, Digest by F. J. Macleod, p. 295, *ut supra*.

[1] Col. 10, 3; Nev. 10, 1; Wy. 15, 3. See § 519.

[2] Wy. 15, 2.

[3] Wy. 15, 3.

[4] Mon. 12, 3; Utah 14, 4.

[5] Va. 172.

[6] Ky. 182; Miss. 112. See § 519.

[7] Ala. 91; Ark. 16, 5; Col. [c] 10, 5; Ga. [b] [c] 7, 2, 2; Ill. [b] 9, 3; Ky. [c] 170; La. [c] 230; Minn. 9, 3; Mo. 10, 6; Mon. [c] 12, 2; N. C. [b] 5, 5; N. D. 176; Neb. [b] 9, 2; O. [b] 12, 2; Okla. 10, 6; Pa. [b] 9, 1; S. C. 10, 4; S. D. 11, 6; Tex. [b] [c] 8, 2; 1905, p. 410. Utah 13, 3; Va. [c] 183; W. Va. [b] 10, 1; Wy. [c] 15, 12 [a].

[8] Cal. 13, 1; Col.; La. [c]; Minn.; O. [b]; Okla.; S. C.; Tex

[9] Ala.; Ark.; Ga. [b] [c]; La.; S. C.; Tex.

[10] Ark.; Col.; Ga. [b] [c]; La. [c]; Minn. 1907, ix; N. D.; S. C.; Va.

[11] Ark.; Ga. [b] [c]; Ky.; La. [c]; Minn.; Mon.; O. [b]; Pa. [b]; S. C.; Tex.; Utah; Va.; Wy.

[12] Cal. 1899, p. 447; Col.; Ky.; Minn.; Utah; Wy.

[13] Minn., Mon., S. C.

[14] Ky.; La. 1902, 129; Va.; Wy.

[15] Ga. [b] [c]; Minn.; S. C.; Va.

[16] Ga. [b] [c]; La. [c]; Minn.; S. C.; Va.

[17] Cal. 1893, p. 658; Col. 10, 4; Ga. [b]; Ida. 7, 4; Ky.; La.; Mon.; Okla.; S. C.; Utah; Va.; Wy.

[18] Ga. [b] [c]; Ky.; La. [c].

[19] Ga. [b] [c]; La.; Minn.; O. [b]; Pa. [c]; S. C.; Tex. [b].

[20] Ky. [c].

[21] Cal., Okla.

(E) Public property used exclusively for any public purpose;[1] or for any municipal purpose;[2] all public property.[3]

(F) So, any property (real or personal), held for educational or scientific[4] or literary purposes;[5] or charitable purposes;[6] or religious purposes;[7] by agricultural or horticultural societies.[8] So, lots in towns, within one mile of the limits, to one acre in extent; and lots one mile or more distant from towns to five acres in extent, with buildings thereon, used exclusively for religious, school, or purely charitable purposes;[9] for lodge purposes;[10] for public monuments or historical collections.[11]

(G) In several, lands the property of the United States are exempt;[12] all property exempt by United States laws;[13] all property belonging to the State;[14] all property belonging to the United States;[15] all property belonging to municipal corporations;[16] the property of religious or charitable corporations, or of educational "corporations."[17]

(H) In a few Western States, the Legislature may exempt for a time the increase in value of private lands caused by the planting of hedges, orchards, and forests;[18] so, "a limited amount of improvements on land";[19] so, fruit or vines planted 4 or 5 years respectively.[20]

(I) The personal property of every individual is exempt, to the

[1] Ark.; Kan. 11, 1; Ky. 170; Minn.; Nev. [b] 10, 1; O. [b]; Ore. [b] 9, 1; Pa. [b]; Tenn. [b] 2, 28; Tex. 11, 9; Va.; W. Va. [b].

[2] Ind. [b] 10, 1; Kan.; Va. 10, 1; S. C.

[3] Ala.; Ga. [b] [c]; La. [c]; Mon.

[4] Ala. 91; Cal.; Fla. [b] 9, 1; Ill. [b]; Ind. [b]; Kan.; La.; Mon.; N. C. [b]; N. D.; Neb. [b]; Nev. [b]; Okla. 91; Ore. [b]; S. C. [b]; S. D.; Tenn. [b]; Tex.; Va.; W. Va. [b].

[5] Fla. [b]; Ind. [b]; Kan.; N. C. [b]; Nev. [b]; Ore.; S. C. [b] 10, 1; Tenn. [b]; W. Va. [b].

[6] Ala.; Ark.; Col.; Fla. [b]; Ill.; Ind. [b]; Kan.; Ky.; Mon.; N. C. [b]; N. D.; Neb. [b]; Nev. [b]; Ore. [b]; S. C. [b]; S. D.; Tenn. [b]; Tex.; Va. [b]; W. Va. [b].

[7] Ala. [b]; Fla. [b]; Ill. [b]; Ind. [b]; Kan.; Ky.; N. D.; Neb. [b]; Nev. [b]; N. C. [b]; Okla.; Ore. [b]; S. C. [b]; S. D.; Tenn. [b]; Va.; W. Va. [b].

[8] Ala.; Ill. [b]; Mo. [b] 10, 6; Mon.; Neb. [b]; S. D.

[9] Ala.; Mo. [b].

[10] Va.

[11] La.

[12] Ida.; Kan. Ordinance; Minn. 2, 3; Mo. 14, 1; Mon.; Nev. Ordinance; N. D. 176; Okla.; S. D. 115; Utah; Wash. 7, 2; Wis. 2, 2; Wy.

[13] Cal. 13, 1; Utah; Wash.

[14] Ala.; Cal.; Col. 10, 4; Ida.; Ill.; Mo.; Mon.; N. C.; Neb.; N. D.; Okla.; S. D.; Tenn.; Utah; Va.; Wy.; Wash.

[15] Cal.; Ida.; Mon.; N. D.; S. D.; Terr. U. S. R. S. 1851; Utah; Wash.; Wy.

[16] Ala.; Cal.; Col.; Fla. [b]; Ida.; Ill. [b]; Ind. [b]; La. [c]; Mo.; Mon.; N. C.; N. D.; Neb.; Nev. [b] 8, 2; Okla.; S. C.; S. D.; Tex. 8, 1; Utah; Va.; Wash.; Wy.

[17] Fla. [b]; Nev. [b].

[18] Col. 18, 7.

[19] Ida. 7, 2.

[20] Cal. 1893, p. 623.

value of $200;[1] $100;[2] $250, if with a family;[3] of $1,000;[4] household property to the value of $500;[5] of $250;[6] $200 of heads of families;[7] $300;[8] of every widow or disabled person, $200.[9]

(J) Growing crops are exempt.[10] So, the direct products of the soil in the hands of the producer;[11] and of his immediate vendee.[12] And no articles manufactured of the produce of the State shall be taxed otherwise than to pay inspection fees.[13] Supplies for home or farm use are exempt.[14]

(K) All wearing apparel is exempt; arms for muster; all household furniture; mechanical instruments of mechanics, and agricultural implements of farmers; libraries; scientific instruments; but the total value of exemptions under this paragraph cannot exceed $300.[15]

(L) Such property as the Legislature may except for the public welfare.[16]

(M) For a period of 10 years from 1900, mining and manufacturing property in factories where five hands are employed and (up to 1904) certain railroads.[17] So, railroads constructed between 1905 and 1909.[18] See also § 331.

(N) Provision shall be made by general laws whereby cities and towns may be authorized to aid and encourage the establishment of manufactories, gas works, water works, and other enterprises of public utility other than railroads, within the limits of said cities or towns, by exempting all property used for such purposes, from municipal taxation for a period not longer than ten years.[19]

(O) The General Assembly may authorize any incorporated city or town to exempt manufacturing establishments from municipal taxation for a period not exceeding five years, as an inducement to their location.[20] So the Legislature may grant a general exemption from taxation to manufacturing corporations or enterprises of public utility for one year.[21]

[1] Kan. (of every *family*); Minn.; N. D.; O. b; S. D.
[2] Cal. 1904, Nov. 8; Okla.
[3] Ky.
[4] Tenn.
[5] La.
[6] Ky. 170; Okla.; Tex. 8, 1.
[7] Col. 1899, p. 89.
[8] Wash. b Amt. 1900.
[9] Fla. 9, 9.
[10] Cal., Ky., Okla.
[11] Ky.; Tenn. 2, 30; Tex. 8 19 (1879, p. 192).
[12] Tenn.
[13] Tenn. 2, 30.
[14] Tex.
[15] N. C. b.
[16] Del. 8, 1; Wash.
[17] La. 206.
[18] La. 1904, 16.
[19] Miss. 192.
[20] Ky. 170; Okla. 10, 6.
[21] Miss. 82.

(P) Cities and towns may exempt by ordinance, except for school purposes, manufactories, for five years from their establishment, upon majority vote of all the qualified electors at a special election.[1] State or municipal bonds are made exempt from taxation.[2]

(Q) Except as above, all laws exempting property from taxation are, in several States, void.[3]

§ 333. *Taxes Equal.*[4] — The Constitutions of many States provide that taxation shall be "equal and uniform" throughout the State or throughout each municipality levying a tax;[5] or "proportional and reasonable."[6]

Lands belonging to persons resident out of the State cannot, in several, be taxed higher than lands belonging to residents.[7]

The Legislature shall not enact any law which will permit any person, firm, corporation, or association to pay a privilege, license, or other tax to the State of Alabama, and relieve him or it from the payment of all other privilege and license taxes in the State.[8]

§ 334. *Valuation and Assessment.* — In most States the Constitution provides that all taxes levied shall be assessed in exact proportion to the value[9] of the property.[10]

[1] S. C. 8, 8.

[2] O. 1904, p. 652.

[3] Ark. 16, 6; Col. 10, 6; Ga. 4, 2, 4; Ky. 3; Mo. 10, 7; Mon. 12, 1; Okla. 5, 50; Pa. 9, 2; S. D. 11, 7; Tex.

Notes. (a) See also §§ 394, 395; these same States being apt to restrict their legislatures' powers to enact special laws. (b) In these States the Constitution only provides that this property may be exempted by law. (c) In these States, only burying-grounds, etc., which are not held for personal or corporate profit, or are "actually occupied." (S. C.)

[4] *I. e.*, in the same class of subjects (Col., Minn., Pa., Mo., Va., Ga., Del.); but "no one species of property can be taxed higher than another species, of the same value" (Ark., Tenn., W. Va.); except license or corporation taxes (Mich. 1900, p. 15). (See, however, § 339). This principle generally applies only to property taxation; not inheritance or license taxes, or other excises.

[5] Ala. 217; Ark. 16, 5; Col. 10, 3; Del. 8, 1; Fla. 9, 1; Ga. 7, 2, 1; Ida. 7, 5; Ind. 10, 1; Kan. 11, 1; Ky. 171; La. 225; Mich. 14, 11; Minn. 9, 1; Miss. 112; Mo. 10, 3; Mon. 12, 2 & 11; N. C. 5, 3; N. D. 176; Nev. 10, 1; N. J. 4, 7, 12; Okla. 10, 5; Ore. 1, 32; 9, 1; Pa. 9, 1; S. C. 10, 1; S. D. 6, 17; Tenn. 2, 28; Tex. 8, 1; Va. 16, 8; Wash. 7, 2; W. Va. 10, 1; Wis. 8, 1; Wy. 1, 28.

[6] N. H. 2, 5.

[7] Ida. 21, 19; Kan. Ordinance; Minn. 2, 3; Mo. 14, 1; N. D. 203 (2); Nev. Ordinance; Okla. 1, 3; S. D. 22 (2); Terr. U. S. R. S. 1851; Wash. 26, 1 (2); Wis. 2, 2; Wy. Ordinance.

[8] Ala. 221.

[9] *I. e.*, the *cash* value (Ky., La., Mich., Minn., N. C., N. D., Okla., S. D.).

[10] Ala. 211; Ark.; Cal. 13, 1; Ga.; Ida. 7, 2; Ill. 9, 1; Ind.; Ky. 172; La.; Mass. 2, 1, 1, 4; Me. 9, 8; Mich. 14, 12; Minn.; Miss. 112; Mo. 10, 4; N. C.; N. D. 179; Neb. 9, 1; N. H.; N. J. 4, 7, 12; Okla. 10, 8; Ore. 9, 1; S. C. 3, 29; S. D. 11, 2; Tenn.; Tex.; Utah 13, 3; Va. 169; Wash.; W. Va.; Wy. 15, 11.

The Legislature is to provide for a just valuation, no time being specified.[1] Every five years;[2] every ten years.[3]

In Louisiana, the assessment of all property shall never exceed the actual cash value thereof. Taxpayers have a constitutional right of testing the correctness of their assessments in the courts. The valuation put on property for purposes of State taxation must be taken as the proper valuation for local taxation.[4]

In California, cultivated and uncultivated land of the same quality and similarly situated are to be assessed at the same value;[5] so, plowing is not an improvement to be taxed.[6] The value or rental value of the buildings as well as the land must be included in all assessments.[7] Grain held in elevators, grown in the State, may be specially taxed.[8]

§ 335. *Purposes of Taxation.* — (See § 330, note [1]). The Constitutions of many States prescribe certain limits to the taxing power. Thus taxes can be levied, only for the ordinary expenses of the State Government and Public State Institutions;[9] for the costs of collecting the revenue;[10] to pay any deficiency in the finances of the previous year;[11] to pay the interest on the State debt;[12] to pay the principal of the State debt.[13] So, in Texas, for the benefit of a sinking fund, which (tax?) shall not be more than two per cent of the State debt. Special taxes (§ 337) only are levied for these purposes,[14] or for educational purposes generally.[15] For the support of free schools;[16] to suppress insurrection, repel invasion, and defend the State in time of war;[17] to protect the frontier,[18] for the necessary defence of the government;[19] for the erection and repairs of public buildings;[20] for maintaining and erecting levees;[21]

[1] Col. 10, 3; Fla.; Ida. 7, 5; Mon. 12, 1; Nev. 10, 1; R. I. 4, 15; S. C. 10, 1; Utah; Wash.; Wy.

[2] Mich. 14, 13; N. H. 2, 6; Va. 171.

[3] Mass. 2, 1, 1, 4; Me. 9, 7.

[4] La. 225.

[5] Cal. 13, 2.

[6] N. D. 177.

[7] Del. 8, 7. This seems like an attack on the "single-tax" theory.

[8] N. D. Amt. 5.

[9] Ark. 3, 31; Col. 10, 2; Fla. 9, 2; Ga. 7, 1, 1; Kan. 11, 3; Ky. 171; La. 227; Mass. 2, 1, 1, 4; Mich. 14, 1; Minn. 9, 2; N. D. 174; Nev. 9, 2; N. H. 2, 5; Okla. 10, 2; Ore. 9, 2; S. C. 102; S. D. 11, 1; Tex. 3, 48; Utah 13, 2; Va. 188; Wash. 7, 1; W. Va. 10, 5; Wis. 8, 5.

[10] Tex.

[11] Minn.; Nev.; Okla. 10, 3; Ore. 9, 6; S. C.; S. D.; Wash. 7, 8; W. Va; Wis.

[12] Ark., Fla., Ga., La., Mich., Okla., Ore., S. D., Tex., Va., Wash., W. Va.

[13] Ark., Fla., Ga., La., Mich., Okla., S. D., Utah, Va., Wash., W. Va. See § 362.

[14] Mich.

[15] Ga., La., Mich.

[16] Ark., Tex., W. Va.

[17] Ark., Ga., La.

[18] Tex.

[19] Mass., N. H.

[20] Tex.

[21] La. 238.

to supply Confederate soldiers with wooden legs and arms;[1] with pensions.[2] For the enforcement of quarantine regulations;[3] to preserve the public health;[4] to provide "such revenue as may be needful."[5]

Taxes can be levied for public purposes only.[6] No tax can be levied for paying the interest on the bonds of any chartered company.[7] But taxes for other purposes may be enacted according to the provisions of § 314.[8] And (see § 13) the State of Oklahoma is expressly authorized to impose taxes to pay for its socialistic experiments (see § 6); and levy such taxes separately.[9]

§ 336. *Amount of State Tax.* — (See also § 341.) The Constitutions of a few States limit the amount of State taxation for any one year,[10] to a proportion varying from one and a half mills to one cent on the dollar.[11]

This rate may, however, be increased for a definite rate and time, by majority vote at a general election,[12] or an election of the property-tax-payers.[13]

§ 337. *Special State Taxes.* — The Constitutions of a few States give the Legislature authority to levy a special tax in aid of the common schools; thus, in Florida, not less than one tenth per cent;[14] not greater than one-fifth per cent.[15]

§ 338. *Poll-Tax.* — By the Constitutions of two States, poll-taxes are declared oppressive and prohibited.[16]

[1] Ga.

[2] La.

[3] Tex.

[4] La.

[5] Neb. 9, 1.

[6] Ky.; Minn.; Mo. 10, 3; Mon. 12, 11; Okla. 10, 14; S. C. 8, 3; Tex. 8, 3; Wy. 13, 3. See § 330, note 1.

[7] Fla. 9, 7.

[8] Ark.

[9] Okla. 10, 13 & 14.

[10] Exclusive of the tax to pay interest on the State debt (Mo., Tex., N. D., Wy.), or the tax to support State educational or charitable institutions (Wy.).

[11] Thus one and a half mills when the State valuation is $300,000,000 (Ida.), or $900,000,000 (Mo.), and never over two mills (Mo.); three mills where it is $100,000,000; five mills when $50,000,000; and never over ten mills (Ida. 7, 9). So, four mills when $300,000,000, five mills when $200,000,000, and never over eight mills (Utah 13, 7). So, one and a half mills when $300,000,000, two and a half mills when $1,000,000,000, and never over three mills (Mon. 12, 9). Two mills, always (S. D. 11, 1; Va. 189) until 1907, with one other mill for schools, and a half mill for persons thereafter as by law to be provided (Va.). Three and one half mills (Tex. 8, 19, Amt. 1883; Okla. 10, 9). Four mills when the State valuation reaches $100,000,000; until then, six mills (Col. 10, 11). Four mills, always (N. D. 174; Wy. 15, 4). Five mills except for defence in case of invasion, etc. (Ga. 1903, p. 21). Six mills (La. 232). Ten mills, or one per cent (Ark. 16, 8).

[12] Ida. 1905, p. 441; Mon.

[13] Utah.

[14] Fla. 12, 6.

[15] Ark. 14, 3; Nev. Amt. 1887, p. 169.

[16] Md. Decln. of Rts. 15; O. 12, 1.

But in many States, the Constitution provides that a poll-tax may or shall be imposed, not to exceed $1 per head,[1] $1.50 per head,[2] $2 per head,[3] or $4 per head.[4] Nor less than fifty cents per head,[5] $2 per head,[6] or $1 per head.[7] Nothing is said about the amount.[8]

Poll-taxes may be imposed on all male inhabitants between the ages of twenty-one and sixty,[9] twenty-one and fifty,[10] over twenty one,[11] or on all voters.[12]

Except paupers,[13] idiots,[14] insane persons,[15] the aged or infirm,[16] and Indians not taxed, or uncivilized.[17]

Poll-taxes are, in several States, to be applied exclusively to the common-school fund,[18] or, in North Carolina, to purposes of education; and part of it, not more than one fourth, to the poor.[19] They must be used in the county where collected.[20] One dollar may be authorized, additional to the State tax, for the public schools in any county, city, or town.[21]

§ 339. *Income and License Taxes.* — The Constitutions of a few States specify (unnecessarily) that income taxes may be imposed;[22] and they may be graduated.[23]

But, by one, the tax is limited to such incomes as exceed $600 a year;[24] and, in two, it cannot be imposed on incomes derived from taxed property.[25]

License Taxes, Special, Specific, or Occupation taxes, may, by the Constitutions of some States be imposed. As, in detail, upon pedlers,[26] hawkers,[27] auctioneers,[28] brokers,[29] pawnbrokers,[30] merchants,[31] com-

[1] Ark. 14, 3; Fla. 9, 5; Ga. 7, 2, 3; La. 231; R. I. Amt. 7; S. C. 11, 6; Tenn. 2, 28; W. Va. 10, 2.
[2] Ala. 194; Ky. 180; N. D. 180; Va. 173.
[3] Miss. 243; N. C. 5, 1; Okla. 10, 18; Wy. 15, 5.
[4] Nev.
[5] Tenn.
[6] Cal. 13, 12; Nev. 2, 7.
[7] Tex. 7, 3.
[8] Del. 8, 5; Ida. 7, 2.
[9] Cal., La., Nev., S. C. Tex.
[10] N. C., N. D.
[11] Ark., Va., W. Va.
[12] R. I.
[13] Cal., N. C., N. D.
[14] Cal., N. D.
[15] Cal., N. D.
[16] N. C., Tenn., W. Va.
[17] Cal., N. D., Nev.
[18] Ark., Cal., Fla., Ga., La., Miss., R. I., S. C., Tex., W. Va. So $ 1; balance to the county (Va.).
[19] N. C. 5, 2.
[20] Del.
[21] Va.
[22] Cal. 13, 11; Ky. 174; N. C. 5, 3; Okla. 10, 12; S. C. 10, 1; Tenn. 2, 28; Tex. 8, 1; Utah 13, 12; Va. 170.
[23] Okla., S. C.
[24] Va.
[25] N. C., Tenn.
[26] Ark. 16, 5; Ill. 9, 1; Neb. 9, 1; Tenn. 2, 28.
[27] Ark., Neb.
[28] Ill., Neb.
[29] Ill., Neb.
[30] Va.
[31] Ill., Tenn.

mission merchants,[1] showmen,[2] jugglers,[3] innkeepers,[4] liquor dealers,[5] grocery keepers,[6] toll bridges,[7] ferries,[8] insurance business,[9] telegraph business,[10] express business,[11] venders of patents.[12] Generally, upon all persons or corporations using franchises or privileges.[13] Upon corporations generally,[14] banks, and banking companies,[15] railroads,[16] upon destructive domestic animals.[17] Generally, upon all business which cannot be reached by the *ad valorem* system.[18] So, upon trades, or professions.[19] So, generally, upon persons or corporations doing business.[20] "Gross revenue, franchise, stamp, registration, production, or other specific taxes." [21]

Such taxes must be uniform upon each class upon which they operate,[22] but in South Carolina they may be graduated. They cannot be imposed on mechanical or agricultural pursuits; [23] or upon persons selling their own farm products.[24] In Louisiana, they may be imposed on all persons *except* clerks, laborers, clergymen, school teachers, those engaged in mechanical, agricultural, horticultural, and mining pursuits, and manufacturers of anything except liquor, tobacco, etc., and cotton-seed oil.[25] License taxes imposed by cities and towns shall be graded.[26]

Collateral inheritance taxes are permitted in the Constitution, not to exceed 2½ per cent; [27] 3 per cent for direct inheritances over $10,000, 10 per cent on collateral.[28] Unlimited, direct or collateral, and may be graded.[29] 5 per cent, and graded.[30]

[1] Ill., Neb.
[2] Ark., Ill., Neb.
[3] Ill., Neb.
[4] Ill., Neb.
[5] Ill., Neb.
[6] Ill.
[7] Ill., Neb.
[8] Ark., Ill., Neb.
[9] Ill., Neb.
[10] Ill., Neb.,
[11] Ill., Neb.
[12] Ill., Neb.
[13] Ark.; Ill.; Ky.; N. C. 5, 3; Tenn.; Va.; W. Va. 10, 1.
[14] Mich. 14, 10; Mo. 10, 21. See Art. 65.
[15] Kan. 11, 2; Minn. 9, 4.
[16] Mo. 10, 5.
[17] Ga. 7, 2, 1; S. C.
[18] Va. 170.
[19] N. C.
[20] Fla. 9, 5; Ida. 7, 2; Ky. 181; Mon. 12, 2; Okla.; S. C. (Graduated); Tex. 8, 1; Utah 13, 12.
[21] Okla.
[22] Neb.
[23] Tex. *Quaere* whether this is "equal protection of the law."
[24] Minn. 1907, p. xi.
[25] La. 229.
[26] S. C. 8, 6.
[27] Ala. 219.
[28] La. 235.
[29] Okla.
[30] Minn. 1893, 1 Amt.

ARTICLE 34. MUNICIPAL FINANCE AND TAXATION

§ 340. *General Principles.* — By the Constitutions of many States, the Legislature may not impose taxes upon counties, cities, or other municipalities, or upon the inhabitants or property thereof; but may by law [1] vest in the corporate authorities thereof the power to tax.[2] So, counties and townships shall have such powers of local taxation as may be prescribed by law.[3]

The principles of taxation are generally the same in municipal as in State taxation.[4] Taxes must be levied in pursuance of a law and for public purposes specified therein.[5]

So, in several, such taxes must be uniform as to persons and property (except as in § 342)[6], and must be levied according to the value of the property.[7]

So, taxes for municipal purposes may be levied on all property subject to State taxation;[8] and the valuation of property for municipal purposes must be the same as for State purposes,[9] or not greater than the valuation for State purposes.[10]

The Legislature shall provide by law such a system of county finance as shall cause the business of the several counties to be conducted on a cash basis. It shall also provide that whenever any county shall have any warrants outstanding and unpaid, for the payment of which there are no funds in the county treasury, the County Commissioners, in addition to other taxes provided by law, shall levy a special tax, not to exceed ten (10) mills on the dollar of taxable property, as shown by the last preceding assessment, for the creation of a special fund for the redemption of said warrants.[11]

§ 341. *Amount of Municipal Tax.* — (See also § 343.) The Constitutions of a few States limit the amount of municipal taxation for any one year. Thus the rates of county taxation, from five mills to two and one half per cent.[12] But municipal corporations generally

[1] Usually, by *general* laws only; see also §§ 313, 330, 395, 600.

[2] Cal. 11, 12; Col. 10, 7; Fla. 9, 5; Ida. 7, 6; Ill. 9, 9–10; Ky. 181; La. 224; Mo. 10, 10; Mon. 12, 4; Neb. 9, 6–7; Okla. 10, 20; S. C. 10, 5; S. D. 11, 10; Tenn. 2, 29; Utah 13, 5; Wash. 7, 9; W. Va. 10, 9; Wy. 11, 12.

[3] Ark. 2, 23; Minn. 11, 5; S. C. 8, 6.

[4] Fla.; La. 243; S. D. 10, 2; Tenn.; Wy. 13, 3.

[5] S. D.

[6] Ill. 6, 9; N. C. 7, 9; Neb.; S. C.; S. D.; Wash.; W. Va.

[7] N. C.; Tenn.

[8] Mo. 10, 11; Mon. 12, 5.

[9] La. 225; Mon.

[10] Mo.; Mon.

[11] Ida. 7, 15.

[12] Not over one half per cent on the

may levy a greater rate than as above limited, with a vote of the *property* tax-payers at an election;[1] or of the electors of the county generally;[2] or of three-fifths vote of such electors.[3]

So, in some, the tax rate of towns or cities is limited to from not more than one half per cent to two per cent or even more.[4]

Except, taxes to pay valid indebtedness now existing or hereafter renewed.[5]

The Legislature shall restrict the powers of cities and towns to

valuation, real and personal (Ala. 215; Ark. 16, 91); eight mills (Okla. 10, 9); three fourths per cent (Ill. 9, 8); ninety-five cents per $100 (W. Va. 10, 7); one per cent (La. 233); twelve mills (Wy. 15, 5); one and one half per cent (Neb. 9, 5); two per cent in any city over 100,000 or county containing such city (N. Y. 1901, p. 1804). Not more than one-half the State tax, *i. e.*, one fourth per cent (Tex. 8, 9, Amt. 1883). Not more than twice the State tax, except for special purpose, and with the special approval of the Legislature (N. C. 5, 6). The rate in counties not exceeding $6,000,000 in valuation shall not in the aggregate exceed one half per cent; in counties between $6,000,000 and $10,000,000, it must not exceed four tenths per cent; in counties between $10,000,000 and $30,000,000, not greater than one half per cent; in counties over $30,000,000, not more than thirty-five hundredths per cent (Mo. 10, 11). No county, city, or town may incur debt or loan credit to an extent of more than ten per cent of the value of the real estate (N. Y. 8, 10). There is a complicated sliding scale according to population of cities, etc., varying from $1.50 per $100, to 50 cents (outside the school tax: Ky. 157).

Except that, in some States, certain taxes are not to be included in the amounts respectively above limited; as, "special taxes authorized by law" (Ala.); taxes for free schools (Ark. 14, 3; N. Y.; Va.); for debts already incurred (Ala., Ark., Ill., Neb., Tex., W. Va., Wy.); for the erection of public buildings; but such taxes must not exceed one half per cent in any one year; and not over fifteen hundredths per cent, for roads and bridges (Tex.).

There is a three mills county road tax; a seven mills school tax; and a poll-tax of $1 (Ark. 1897, p. 93; 1905, p. 833). So, a three mills school tax (Fla. 1903, p. 637).

[1] La.

[2] Ill., Neb.

[3] W. Va.

[4] Thus, not more than one half per cent in any one year (Ala. 215; Ark. 12, 4). Eight mills (Wy. 15, 6). No town not having a special charter can so levy a tax of more than one-fourth per cent (Ill. 11, 4), and cities having more than 10,000 population, not more than two and a half per cent (Tex. 11, 5). Counties, cities, and towns, twenty-five cents per $100 for county, city, or town purposes, fifteen cents for roads and bridges, twenty-five cents for public buildings, streets, sewers, water, etc. (Tex, 1899, p. 171). The rate in cities and towns having over 30,000 inhabitants may not exceed in the aggregate one per cent; between 10,000 and 30,000 inhabitants, not over six-tenths per cent; between 1,000 and 10,000, not over one-half per cent; under 1,000 not over one-quarter per cent; and in school districts, for school purposes, not over four-tenths per cent; but for school purposes these rates may be increased by a majority vote of tax-paying voters at a special election, and for the erection of public buildings, by a two-thirds vote of all voters at such an election (Mo.). Similar provisions are found in Oklahoma, and the rates are: townships not over one half per cent; cities and towns, one per cent; school districts, one half per cent; total thirty-one and one half mills (Okla. 10, 9, & 10). For New York, see above, note 12.

[5] Ala., Ark., Mo., Wy.

levy taxes and assessments to borrow money and contract debts.[1] And this is done, in fact, in many other States.

§ 342. *Prescribed Purposes.* — In Wisconsin, the Constitution provides that each town and city shall raise, by tax, annually, for the support of the common schools, a sum not less than half the sum received for such purposes from the State school fund.[2] In North Carolina, no county, town, etc., shall levy a tax, except for its necessary expenses, without a special vote of the electors.[3] In Arkansas the Legislature may, by general law, authorize school districts to levy, by a vote of the qualified electors, a tax for school purposes, not to exceed one half per cent.[4] In Georgia, counties may levy taxes for schools under special authority of the Legislature and a two-thirds vote of the county.[5] In Texas, counties may raise a special tax for common schools not exceeding one fifth per cent.[6] In Florida it must be from three to five mills.[7]

Counties, towns, etc., may levy taxes for their current annual expenses,[8] for educational purposes,[9] for the interest and sinking fund of debts already created,[10] for the building and repair of courthouses, gaols, bridges, and other necessary conveniences for the people of the county.[11] The Constitution of South Carolina provides that there shall be an annual tax of three mills per dollar in each county for the support of public schools.[12]

In other States these matters are left to statutes.

§ 343. *Special Taxes* for local improvements may be made either by general assessment,[13] or by betterment tax on contiguous property.[14] But only for sidewalks and sewers, and not in excess of the benefit.[15]

But such betterment taxes must be consented to by a majority of property holders in the locality affected, and they must be *ad valorem* and uniform.[16] So, in Louisiana, a special tax not exceeding one half per cent, nor for more than ten years, may be levied in aid of railroads or public improvements by vote of a majority of the tax-payers.[17]

[1] S. C. 8, 3.
[2] Wis. 10, 4.
[3] N. C. 7, 7.
[4] Ark. 14, 3.
[5] Ga. 8, 4, 1.
[6] Tex. Amt. 1883.
[7] Fla. 12, 8.
[8] Tex. 11, 6.
[9] Ga. 7, 6, 2.
[10] Tex.
[11] Ga.
[12] S. C. 11, 6.
[13] Ill. 9, 9; Neb. 9, 6.
[14] Ala. 222, 223; Ark. Amt. 1907, p. ix; 19, 27; Cal. 11, 19: Col. 1891, p. 89; 1903, p. 74; Ill.; Minn. 9, 1; Neb.; Okla. 10, 7; S. D. 11, 10; Va. 170; Wash. 7, 9.
[15] Ala., Va.
[16] Ark.
[17] La. 242.

The betterment tax must be collected before the work is commenced.[1] License taxes may be imposed by towns, etc., under legislative authority.[2]

§ 344. *Power to Contract Loans, etc.* — The Constitutions of several States provide that the power of municipal corporations to tax, borrow money, contract debts, or loan credit, shall be restricted so as to prevent the abuse of such power.[3] So, it may only be for schools, roads, bridges, indebtedness, current expenses, etc.[4]

But in Nevada, that there can be no restriction on the power of municipalities to tax, borrow, loan, etc , for the purpose of getting a water supply.

§ 345. *Loans of Credit, etc.* — By the Constitutions of most States, no town, county, or municipality can give money or property to any corporation having for its object a dividend of profits;[5] or to any individual or corporation whatever;[6] or to any railroad corporation specially.[7] Nor can it loan its money or credit to such corporations respectively.[8] (So, no county can loan its credit to any association or corporation but by special act with notice, etc., see § 346.)[9]

No county, city, or town, etc., may incur any debt above its annual revenue without a two-thirds vote at a special election; and a tax with sinking fund of twenty years must be provided.[10] It may not become a party to, or interested in, any work of internal improvement except roads.[11]

Nor, in several, can such town, etc., become security for such corporation;[12] nor become a stockholder or bondholder in such private corporation.[13]

[1] Cal.

[2] Ky. 181, Amt. 1902, 50.

[3] Ala. 222, 226; Ark. 12, 3; Kan. 12, 5; Mich. 15, 13; Miss. 80; N. C. 8, 4; N. D. 130; Nev. 8, 8; N. Y. 12, 1; O. 13, 6; Ore. 11, 5; S. C. 8, 3; S. D. 10, 2; Wis. 11, 3; Wy. 13, 3.

[4] S. C.

[5] Ida. 12, 4; N. H. 2, 5; Okla. 10, 17.

[6] Ala. 94; Ark. 12, 5; Cal. 4, 31; Col. 11, 2; Del. 8, 8; Fla. 9, 10; Ga. 7, 6, 1; Ida. 8, 4; Ill. separate section; Ind. 10, 6; Ky. 179; La. 58; Miss. 183; Mo. 4, 47; 9, 6; Mon. 13, 1; N. D. 185; N. J. 1, Amt. 19 & 20; N. Y. 8, 10; O. 8, 6; Ore. 11, 9; Pa. 9, 7; S. D. 13, 1; Tex. 3, 52 & 11, 3; Utah 6, 31; Wash. 8, 7; Wis. 11, 3; Wy. 16, 6.

[7] Ct. Amt. 25; Neb. 14, 2; Utah; Wy. 3, 39; 10, 10 (5).

[8] Ala.; Ark. 16, 1; 1903, p. 484; Cal.; Col. 11, 1; Ct.; Del.; Fla.; Ga.; Ida.; Ill.; Ind.; Ky.; La.; Miss.; Mo.; Mon.; N. D.; Nev. 8, 10; N. H.; N. J.; N. Y.; O.; Okla.; Ore.; Pa.; S. D.; Tenn. 2, 29; Terr. U. S. 1886, 818, 2; Tex.; Utah; Va.; Wash.; Wy.

[9] Md. 3, 54.

[10] Ida. 8, 3.

[11] Va.

[12] Cal., Col., La., N. H., N. J., Terr.

[13] Ala.; Ark.; Cal.; Col. 11, 2; Ct.; Del.; Fla.; Ga.; Ida.; Ill.; Ind.; Ky.; La.; Miss.; Mo.; Mon.; N. D.; Neb. 12, 1; Nev.; N. H.; N. J.; N. Y.; O.; Okla.; Ore.; Pa.; S. D.; Tenn.; Terr.; Tex.; Va.; Wash.; Wy.

Except, it may own stock or bonds of railroad companies;[1] or of any corporation, if the stock be paid for at the time of subscription;[2] or for gas, lighting, sanitary, water, or school purposes, provided it "own its just proportion of the property so erected and receive its proportionate income."[3]

Nor can the Legislature authorize such town, etc., so to do.[4] The same would follow from the constitutional provisions in other States.

So, no municipality can become a stockholder, directly or indirectly, in any bank.[5]

In other States no municipality can become indebted or issue bonds to aid a railroad for more than ten per cent of its valuation;[6] and five per cent additional, on a two-thirds vote.[7] (See § 346.)

Except for the necessary support of the poor.[8]

§ 346. *Limitations on Section* 345. — But in some States a county, town, etc., may give or lend its property or credit, or own stock, notwithstanding § 345, on vote of the electors under authority of law;[9] or on a three-fourths vote of the electors;[10] or by act of the Legislature approved also by the next Legislature after publication in the locality interested;[11] or for constructing roads and bridges;[12] or by a vote of property owners, for ten years, if the appropriation be not more than five mills on the valuation.[13]

See also § 332.

ARTICLE 35. COLLECTION OF TAXES

§ 350. *Sworn List.* — By the Constitution of California every tax-payer is required to make an annual statement of his taxable property under oath.[14]

§ 351. *Sale for Taxes.* — The Constitution of Louisiana provides that there shall be no forfeiture for the non-payment of taxes.[15]

But there must be a sale of so much as is necessary.[16] Such sale of real estate must be after order or judgment of some court of record.[17]

There must, in two, be reasonable notice to the owner.[18] And, in

[1] Nev.
[2] Ind.
[3] Ida. 12, 4.
[4] Ala., Cal., Fla., Ga., Ky., Mo., N. H., O., Tex. But see Tex. Amt. 1903, p. 247.
[5] Io. 8, 4.
[6] Minn. 9, 14; Neb. (see § 346).
[7] Neb.
[8] N. D.; N. Y.
[9] Neb. 14, 2.
[10] Tenn. 2, 29.
[11] Md. 3, 54.
[12] Ky.
[13] La. 270.
[14] Cal. 13, 8.
[15] La. 233.
[16] La.; Tex. 8, 13.
[17] Ill. 9, 4.
[18] Ill. 9, 5; La.

two others, the occupant must always have personal notice by service before the time of redemption expires.[1]

§ 352. *Redemption.* — By the Constitutions of a few States, the owner, tenant, etc., of real estate sold for taxes may redeem at any time within two years from the sale;[2] at any time within one year therefrom.[3] Upon payment of twice the purchase-money;[4] of the price plus twenty per cent and costs.[5]

The right of redemption from all sales of real estate, for the non-payment of taxes, or special assessments, of any and every character whatsoever, shall exist, on conditions to be prescribed by law, in favor of owners and persons interested in such real estate, for a period of not less than two years.[6]

§ 353. *Tax-titles.* — By the Constitution of Louisiana, all tax deeds are *prima facie* evidence of the sale; and no sale can be annulled for informality except on payment or tender of the price plus ten per cent interest.[7] In Texas, the deed vests a good title in the purchaser, subject to be impeached only for actual fraud.[8] The courts are "to apply liberal principles in favor of tax titles." [9]

§ 354. *State Boards of Equalization* are provided for, consisting of the Governor, Secretary of State, Attorney-General, State Auditor, and State Treasurer, whose duties shall be prescribed by law. The Board of County Commissioners for the several counties of the State shall constitute Boards of Equalization for their respective counties, whose duty it shall be to equalize the valuation of the taxable property in the county under such rules and regulations as shall be prescribed by law.[10]

The State Board for Equalization, etc., is composed of the State Treasurer, Auditor, and Secretary.[11]

Such boards exist in many States by statute.

Article 36. State Debts

§ 360. *Temporary Loans.* — By the Constitutions of most States, the Legislature may authorize a temporary loan, to meet casual deficits, etc., not exceeding with all other such debts, $50,000;[12]

1 Ill.; Neb. 9, 3.
2 Ill. 9, 5; Neb. 9, 3; Tex. 8, 13.
3 La. 233.
4 Tex.
5 La.
6 Miss. 79.
7 La. 233.
8 Tex. 8, 13.
9 Miss. 79.
10 Ida. 7, 12; Mon. 12, 15.
11 Wy. 15, 10.
12 Ariz. * Bill of Rts. 25; Md. 3, 34; Mich. 14, 3; Ore. 11, 7; R. I. 4, 13.

$100,000;[1] $200,000;[2] $250,000;[3] $300,000;[4] $400,000;[5] $500,000;[6] $750,000;[7] $1,000,000;[8] or the amount of such loans is not limited.[9]

But in Alabama, until such loan is paid, no new one can be negotiated. (The same follows in all States, unless the whole debt be less than the sum allowed.)

And in several, every such law shall provide annual taxes sufficient to pay the debt, principal and interest, in two years;[10] in five years;[11] in ten years;[12] thirty years;[13] when due;[14] annual taxes sufficient to pay the interest.[15]

Such provision for taxes and appropriation to meet the debt are irrepealable until the debt is paid.[16] See § 362. For the method of enacting such laws, see § 315.

§ 361. *Other Debts* may, by the Constitutions of most of the States, be created for the following purposes only:[17] to repel invasion or suppress insurrection,[18] to pay the State debt,[19] principal and interest,[20] or interest only.[21] The amount of such debts is not limited.[22] Also, for the erection of public buildings[23] (but not to an amount over $50,000); for public improvements (not over the limit prescribed in § 360);[24] for canals;[25] for the improvement of highways.[26]

And debts for purposes not above mentioned, but distinctly speci-

[1] Col. 11, 3; Mon. 13, 2; Neb. 14, 1; N. J. 4, 6, 4; S. D. 13, 2; Wis. 8, 6.

[2] Ga. 7, 3, 1; N. D. 182; Tex. 3, 49; Utah, 14, 1.

[3] Ill. 4, 18; Io. 7, 2; Minn. 9, 5; Mo. 4, 44.

[4] Ala. 213; Cal. 16, 1; Me. 9, 14; Nev. 9, 3.

[5] Wash. 8, 1; Okla. 10, 23.

[6] Ky. 49.

[7] O. 8, 1.

[8] Kan. 11, 5; N. Y. 7, 2; Pa. 9, 4.

[9] Del. 8, 3; Ind. 10, 5; N. C. 5, 4; S. C. 10, 11; Va. 184; W. Va. 10, 4. So in the other States, the power to borrow money being inherent in their sovereignty.

[10] Mo.

[11] Wis.

[12] Minn.

[13] N. D.

[14] Kan.

[15] Neb.

[16] Kan., Minn., Neb., Wis.

[17] *I. e.*, exclusive of temporary loans.

[18] Ala. 213; Cal.; Col.; Del. 8, 3; Fla. 9, 6; Ga. 7, 12, 1; Ida. 8, 1; Ill.; Ind.; Io. 7, 4; Kan. 11, 7; Ky.; La. 46; Md.; Me.; Mich. 14, 4; Minn. 9, 7; Mon.; N. C.; N. D.; Neb. 14, 1; Nev.; N. J.; N. Y. 7, 3; O. 8, 2; Okla. 10, 24; Ore.; Pa.; R. I.; S. D.; Terr., U. S. 1886, 818; Tex.; Utah, 14, 2; Va.; Wash. 8, 2; W. Va.; Wis. 8, 7; Wy. 16, 1. See § 315.

[19] Ala.; Ark. 16, 1; Del.; Fla.; Ga.; Ky.; Mo.; N. Y.; O.; Pa; Terr.; Tex.; Va.; W. Va.

[20] Va., W. Va.

[21] Ind.

[22] N. Y. 7, 4.

[23] Col. See § 324.

[24] Kan. 11, 5.

[25] N. Y. 7, 10.

[26] N. Y. 7, 12; Amt. 1905. Such debt may not exceed fifty million dollars, and counties may be required to pay thirty-five per cent and towns fifteen per cent of the cost, towards a sinking fund of two per cent.

fied in the bill, may be incurred, in many States, if the law is passed and ratified according to §§ 315, 363, and provision for payment made according to § 362;[1] so, of debts exceeding the amount limited in § 360.[2] But otherwise no debts can be incurred except as in §§ 360, 361.[3] The amount of such debts is limited to one per cent of valuation;[4] one and one-half per cent.[5]

In Maine, the Constitution authorized a special war debt of $3,500,000.[6] Three States are forbidden to issue any interest-bearing treasury warrants or scrip;[7] *except* for the redemption of bonds previously issued, or for such debts as are expressly authorized by the Constitution.[8] A recent Arkansas amendment forbids all interest bearing "evidences of indebtedness" both to the State, counties, cities, and towns, except on vote of the people, in cities of the first and second class.[9]

§ 362. *Payment of Debts.* — In several States, no debt[10] can be contracted by the Legislature unless authorized by a law which shall at the same time make provision by taxation, etc., for its payment; thus: —

For its payment, principal and interest, when due;[11] or within ten years;[12] thirteen years;[13] fifteen years;[14] within twenty years;[15] twenty-five years;[16] thirty years;[17] thirty-five years;[18] or fifty years;[19] for the payment of the interest (only), when due.[20]

And this part of the law, is, by the Constitutions of these States declared irrepealable until the debt is paid.[21] In some States there are also constitutional provisions for a sinking fund.[22]

§ 363. *Ratification by the People.* — An act authorizing a State

[1] Cal.; Ida.; Ill.; Io. 7, 5; Kan. 11, 6; Ky. 50; Md.; Mon.; N. C.; N. J.; N. Y.; R. I.; S. C.; Wash.; Wy.

[2] Cal., Mo., Mon., Nev., N. D., Okla., S. D.

[3] Ark.; Col.; Minn. 9, 7; Mo.; Neb.; O. 8, 3; Wis. 8, 4.

[4] Wy. 16, 1; Terr., U. S. 1886, 818, 3.

[5] Ida.

[6] Me. 9, 15.

[7] Ark. 16, 1; S. C. 10, 7; Va. 10, 13.

[8] S. C.; Va.

[9] Ark. 1903, p. 484.

[10] Except debts incurred to meet a casual deficit (§ 360), or except debts incurred to repel invasion or suppress insurrection (§ 361).

[11] Io. 7, 6; Kan. 11, 5–6; Minn. 9, 5; Mon. 13, 2; Neb.; S. D. 13, 2; Va. 187.

[12] S. D. 11, 1.

[13] Me.; Minn.; Mo. 4, 44.

[14] Col. 11, 4; Md. 3, 34; Mo. 4, 44.

[15] Cal. 16, 1; Ida. 8, 1; Io. 7, 5; Nev. 9, 3; Utah, 13, 2; Wash. 7, 1; 8, 3.

[16] Okla. 10, 4.

[17] Ky. 50; N. D. 182.

[18] N. J. 4, 6, 4.

[19] N. Y. 7, 4.

[20] Ill. 4, 18; N. C. 5, 4; S. C. 10, 11.

[21] Cal.; Col.; Ida.; Ill.; Io. 7, 6; Kan.; Md., Minn.; Mon.; N. D.; Nev.; N. J.; N. Y.; S. D. The provision seems hardly necessary.

[22] Ga. 7, 14, 1; Ky. 48; Mich. 14, 2; Pa. 9, 11; Va. 10, 8.

debt, under §§ 361, 362, must in several States be ratified by the people at a general election;[1] and it requires a two-thirds vote of the people.[2]

§ 364. *Limitations on the State's Power to contract Debts. — Rebellion Debts.* — By the Constitutions of two Southern States, the State shall never assume, pay, or authorize the collection of any debt or obligation, express or implied, incurred in aid of rebellion against the United States.[3] See § 31, and compare U. S. C. Amt. XIV, 4. So, no county, city, or municipal corporation shall levy or collect any tax for the payment of any debt created for the purpose of aiding rebellion against the State or the United States.[4]

All debts must be by State bonds of an amount not under $50 each, on interest, payable in not more than forty years.[5]

§ 365. *Repudiation.* — The Constitution of North Carolina provides that all debts authorized or bonds issued by the Legislature of 1868–1870, or under the Convention of 1868 (except such as were issued to fund the old debt), shall never be paid, unless the law proposing payment be ratified by the people at a special election.[6] And the Constitution of Missouri provides that the claims audited by virtue of the Act of 1874 to adjust the war debt of the State or any similar act shall never be paid by the State until they are paid to the State by the United States.[7]

But in Arkansas, the Constitution prescribes that the Legislature shall, from time to time, provide for the payment of all just and legal debts of the State.[8] Compare also § 362. By an amendment, however, the "Holford" bonds of 1869 are repudiated.[9]

ARTICLE 37. MUNICIPAL DEBTS

§ 370. *Purposes.* — (See also § 362.) Some Constitutions provide that no county, city, or village shall contract debts except for county, city, and village purposes;[10] for making and repairing public roads and bridges;[11] for erecting necessary public buildings;[12] for school,

[1] Cal.; Ida.; Ill.; Io.; Kan. 11, 6; Ky.; Mon.; N. J.; N. Y.; Okla.; R. I.; Wash.; Wy. 16, 1.

[2] Mo.; S. C. 10, 11.

[3] Ga. 7, 11, 1; N. C. 1, 6.

[4] N. C. 7, 13.

[5] S. C. 10, 11.

[6] N. C. 1, 6.

[7] Mo. 4, 52.

[8] Ark. 16, 2.

[9] Ark. 1879, p. 149.

[10] N. Y. 8, 10; Utah 14, 4; Wash. 8, 6.

[11] Col. 11, 6; Mo. 1905, p. 39.

[12] Col., Mo.

water, sanitary, and lighting.[1] No county can borrow money for the purpose of taking stock (§ 345);[2] so no county can contract debts in the construction of railways, canals, or works of internal improvement, except as in § 346.[3] No county, city, or other municipality can ever issue interest-bearing evidences of indebtedness, except in payment of debts previously (to 1874) existing.[4] In Texas, counties and cities bordering on the Gulf may levy taxes and issue loans for the erection of sea-walls, breakwaters, and for sanitary purposes.[5] In Colorado, school-districts may contract a loan upon a majority vote of the tax-payers therein.[6] In Louisiana, various purposes are particularly specified, and in Michigan, county roads.[7]

The Legislative Assembly shall have no power to pass any law authorizing the State, or any county in the State, to contract any debt or obligation in the construction of any railroad, nor give or loan its credit to or in aid of the construction of the same.[8]

§ 371. *Amount.* — There is an increasing tendency to limit by Constitution the amount of municipal debts; thus, in Virginia no county or city can in the aggregate be indebted or contract debts to an amount exceeding 18 per cent on its assessed valuation;[9] in New York, 10 per cent on the realty;[10] in others, 8 per cent;[11] 7 per cent;[12] 5 per cent;[13] 4 per cent;[14] 3 per cent;[15] 2 per cent;[16] $1\frac{1}{2}$ per cent;[17] $\frac{3}{10}$ per cent or $\frac{6}{10}$ per cent in counties having a valuation under $5,000,000.[18] In Kentucky there is a sliding scale according to six classes of cities ranging from 10 per cent to 2 per cent of valuation;[19] in California no county, city, or town is permitted to contract any debt in excess of the annual expenditure except by vote of the people.[20] No county in Oregon may create debts to exceed $5,000.[21] In South Carolina there is also a provision that there may be no debt upon any "territory" (of overlapping municipalities)

[1] Ida. 12, 4.
[2] Ind. 10, 6.
[3] Md. 3, 54.
[4] Ark. 16, 1.
[5] Tex. 11, 7.
[6] Col. 11, 7.
[7] La. 281; 1906, 122; Mich. 1899, p. 478.
[8] Mon. 5, 38.
[9] Va. 127.
[10] N. Y. 8, 10.
[11] S. C. 8, 7.
[12] Ga. 7, 7, 1; Pa. 9, 8; Wash. 8, 6.
[13] Ill. 9, 12; Io. 11, 3; Me. Amt. 22; Mo. 10, 12; Mon. 13, 6 (of counties); N. D. 183; Okla. 10, 26; W. Va. 10, 8; Wis. 11, 3.
[14] Utah 14, 4 (of cities and towns only).
[15] Col. 11, 8; Mon. 13, 5; S. D. 13, 4 (of cities and towns only in Colorado).
[16] Ind. 13, 1; Mon. 13, 6; Wy. 16, 3. Utah 14, 4 (of counties only).
[17] Wash. 8, 6.
[18] Col. 11, 6.
[19] Ky. 158.
[20] See § 372.
[21] Ore. 11, 10.

over 15 per cent.[1] All bonds in excess of this limit are usually declared void.[2]

Except, in Oregon, to repel invasion or suppress insurrection; or, in Indiana, to provide for the protection of the people in time of war or great public calamity, on a petition of a majority of the property-owners in number and value; or, in Missouri, to erect a court-house or gaol; or, in New York, North Dakota, Wyoming, and Colorado, to supply water to the city or town; or in North Dakota, sewerage works; or, in Montana, of cities and towns for sewerage or water supply owned by the municipality, by act of Legislature, and on popular vote.[3] Such water bonds may only run 20 years, with sinking-fund, etc.[4]

But in Colorado, counties, in Oklahoma and North Dakota cities and towns, may incur debt to a greater amount than as above limited by a majority vote of the tax-payers in such county.[5] In Oklahoma such debts may be created for "purchasing or constructing public utilities to be owned by the city," etc. So any county, town, etc., may incur an additional indebtedness not exceeding 10 per cent[6] upon the valuation of the year preceding (1) for the purpose of providing water and sewerage for irrigation, domestic uses, and other purposes; provided that a city where the population is 8,000 or more may incur an additional debt not exceeding 8 per cent for the purpose of constructing electric railways, electric lights, or other lighting plants, provided further that no county, town, etc., shall be included within such district without the majority vote of the electors, and no such debt shall be incurred for any of the purposes in this section provided unless by a majority vote of the electors of such county, town, etc.;[7] (2) for water, light, and sewerage works owned by the municipality;[8] (3) for county roads.[9]

§ 372. *Voting.* — No municipality can, in a few States, contract any debt (except a temporary debt, incurred in anticipation of income) without the assent of two thirds of its voters at a special election;[10] or a majority;[11] of three fifths, at any elec-

[1] S. C. 10, 5.

[2] Mon.; N. D.; N. Y.; Okla. 10, 29.

[3] But not over 4 per cent on the valuation (N. D., Wy.).

[4] N. Y.

[5] But only to double such amount (Col.) or 8 per cent instead of 5 per cent and by a two-thirds vote (N. D.).

[6] Eight per cent (Utah).

[7] S. D. 13, 4, as amended.

[8] Utah 14, 4; Wash. 8, 6.

[9] Three per cent (Mich. 1899, p. 478).

[10] Ga. 7, 7, 1; Ida. 8, 3; Ky. 157; Mo. 10, 12; 9, 19.

[11] Cal. 1891, p. 523; Mon. 14, 5; Wy. 16, 4.

tion;[1] of a majority of the *tax-payers;*[2] both in number and amount;[3] of the electors, and under a law;[4] on a petition by a majority of the freeholders; and they must have paid all taxes, State and local, for the preceding year.[5]

§ 373. *Payment.* — A municipality creating a debt must, by the Constitutions of several States, at the same time provide for its payment, principal or interest, and make provision for a tax or a sinking-fund therefor, to be fully paid, when due, or at maturity;[6] within fifteen years;[7] twenty years;[8] twenty-five years;[9] thirty years;[10] thirty-four years;[11] forty years.[12] The sinking-fund must be of two per cent annually.[13]

§ 374. *Collection of Municipal Debts.* — By the Constitutions of several Western States, private property shall not be liable to be taken and sold for the payment of corporate debts of municipal corporations.[14] The New England law is otherwise.

§ 375. *No bond* or evidence of debt of any county, or bond of any township or other political subdivision shall be valid unless the same have indorsed thereon a certificate signed by the county auditor, or other officer authorized by law to sign such certificate, stating that said bond, or evidence of debt, is issued pursuant to law and is within the debt limit.[15]

Article 39. Matter of Legislative Power

§ 390. *The State Legislatures* during the Revolution had unlimited legislative power. They are now restrained, principally, by Articles I. 10, II. 1, and IV., and Amendments XIII., XIV., and XV. of the Federal Constitution (but see Appendix, Z, AZ), and by the State Constitutions, and in the latter we find an ever-increasing tendency to limit legislative power. See Book I; Book III. § 1.

§ 391. *In General.* — Some of the older States have provisions in the Constitution attempting to define generally the duties of the

[1] Okla. 10, 26; Wash. (does not apply to debts under the lower limit in § 371); W. Va. 10, 8.

[2] Col. 11, 8; La. 281; S. C. 2, 13; Utah 14, 3.

[3] La.

[4] Ala. 104.

[5] S. C.

[6] N. D. 184; S. C. 8, 7; S. D. 13, 5.

[7] Col. 11, 8 (of a city or town only).

[8] Ida.; Ill. 9, 12; Mo. 10, 12; Wis. 11, 3.

[9] Okla.

[10] Ga. 7, 7, 2; Pa. 9, 10.

[11] W. Va. 10, 8.

[12] Cal.; Ky. 159; La.

[13] Tex. 11, 5.

[14] Cal. 11, 15; Col. 10, 14; Ill. 9, 10; Mo. 10, 13; Mon. 12, 8; Neb. 9, 7; Wy. 11, 13.

[15] N. D. 187; Wy. 16, 8.

Legislature and the purposes and objects of legislation;[1] as, "for the redress of public grievances, and for making such laws as the public good may require;"[2] or, "all manner of wholesome and reasonable order, laws, statutes, ordinances and directions as they may judge for the benefit and welfare of this State."[3] "To encourage private and public institutions, rewards, and immunities, for the promotion of agriculture, arts, sciences, commerce, trades, manufactures, and natural history of the country; to countenance and inculcate the principles of humanity and general benevolence, public and private charity, industry and economy, honesty and punctuality, sincerity, sobriety and all social affections and generous sentiments, among the people."[4] So, in several States, the Legislature are to pass such laws as may be necessary to carry into effect the provisions of the Constitution.[5] The Legislature are to pass such laws as will foster and aid the agricultural, mining, and manufacturing interests of the State.[6] They shall provide, as far as practicable, by general laws, for all matters usually appertaining to private or local legislation.[7] So, for all matters specified in § 395.[8]

But no law or tax may, in Michigan, be enacted by the State or any municipal corporation for any internal improvement except by the city of Grand Rapids to improve its river navigation.[9]

The legislative power of the Territories extends to all rightful subjects of legislation not inconsistent with the Constitution and laws of the United States.[10]

The allowable province of legislation other than its general constitutional limitations will, however, be best defined by the limitations and restrictions on legislation contained in this chapter.

§ 392. *Suspending Laws.*[11] — By the Constitutions of most States, laws can only be suspended by the Legislature[12] or by authority

[1] Ga. 3, 7, 22; Me. 4, 3, 1; Vt. 2, 9.

[2] N. H. 1, 31.

[3] N. H. 2, 5; Mass. 2, 1, 1, 4.

[4] N. H. 2, 82.

[5] Col. Sched. 4; Ill. Sched. 19; Io. 12, 1; Md. 3, 56; Mo. Sched. 15; N. D. 68; N. J. 10, 12; Okla. 5, 45; Tex. 3, 42; W. Va. Sched. 22; Wy. 21, 14. The question whether a State Constitution is self-executing is elsewhere discussed; see § 2, note.

[6] Ark. 10, 1.

[7] Me. 4, 3, 13.

[8] Ala. 104; Io. 3, 30; Md. 3, 33; Miss. 88; N. J. 4, 7, 11; N. Y. 3, 18; S. C. 3, 34; W. Va. 6, 39; Wis. 4, 32.

[9] Mich. 1893, p. 431. See also § 324.

[10] U. S. R. S. 1851.

[11] This matter has been fully discussed in Book I. The dispensing power of the king was claimed by James II.; denied in a memorable speech by Chief Justice Jones, who was thereupon dismissed; and finally prohibited in the Bill of Rights a few years later. See § 127 for *habeas corpus;* § 88 for stay laws.

[12] Ala. 21; Ark. 2, 12; Del. 1, 10; Ind. 1, 26; Ky. 15; La. 188; Mass. 1,

derived from the Legislature;[1] and not for the benefit of any private association, corporation or individual.[2]

§ 393. *Laws Impairing Contracts.*[3] — By the Constitutions of nearly all, the Legislature are forbidden to pass laws impairing the obligation of contracts,[4] or destroying the remedy for their enforcement, and cannot revive any rights or remedy barred by lapse of time, etc.[5]

By that of Louisiana, vested rights may not be divested, unless for purposes of public utility, adequate compensation being first made (compare Article 9). So, in one other, no laws taxing retrospectively sales, purchases, or other acts previously done, can be passed.[6] But the Legislature may, in Ohio, by general laws, authorize courts to carry into effect, upon such terms as are just and equitable, the manifest intention of parties and officers, by curing omissions, defects, and errors in instruments and proceedings arising out of their want of conformity with the laws of the State.[7] In New Hampshire retrospective laws for the decision of civil causes are forbidden;[8] so of retrospective laws taking away a cause of action, or destroying a defence.[9]

§ 394. *Laws to be General.*[10] — In many States, the Constitution provides that there shall be no special, local, or private law in any case for which provision has been (or can be[11]) made by general law.[12] Or, in several, in any case where the relief sought can be given by any State court.[13] And whether a general law can be made applicable or not is declared, in Missouri, Minnesota, Kansas, and Alabama, to be a judicial question, despite any legislative assertion to the con-

20; Md. Decln. of Rts. 9; Me. 1, 13; N. C. 1, 9; N. H. 1, 29; N. M.* 1851, July 12, § 19; O. 1, 18; Ore. 1, 22; Pa. 1, 12; S. C. 1, 13; S. D. 6, 21; Tex. 1, 28; Va. 7; Vt. 1, 15.

[1] Del., Ky., La., Mass., Md., Me., N. H., N. M.,* Ore., Pa., S. C., S. D., Vt.

[2] Ala. 108; Va. 64.

[3] U. S. C. 1, 10. See § 141, note 1.

[4] Ala. 22; Ark. 2, 17; Ariz.* Bill of Rts. 19; Cal. 1, 16; Col. 2, 11; Fla. Decln. of Rts. 17; Ga. 1, 3, 2; Ida. 1, 16.; Ill. 2, 14; Ind. 1, 24; Io. 1, 21; Ky. 19; La. 166; Me. 1, 11; Mich. 4, 43; Minn. 1, 11; Miss. 16; Mo. 2, 15; Mon. 3, 11; N. D. 16, 5; Neb. 1, 16; Nev. 1, 15; N. J. 4, 7, 3; N. M.* 1851, July 12, § 14; O. 2, 28; Okla. 2, 15; Ore. 1, 21; Pa. 1, 17; R. I. 1, 12; S. C. 1, 8; S. D. 6, 12; Tenn. 1, 20; Tex. 1, 16; Utah 1, 18; Va. 58; Wash. 1, 23; W. Va. 3, 4; Wis. 1, 12; Wy. 1, 35.

[5] Ala. 95; Okla. 5, 52. See § 630.

[6] N. C. 1, 32.

[7] O. 2, 28.

[8] N. H. 1, 2, 3.

[9] Ala.; Fla. 3, 33; Okla. 5, 52.

[10] Compare also §§ 17, 391.

[11] Cal.; Ill.; Ky.; Minn. 1891, p. 19; Mo.; Tex.; Wy.; Okla.

[12] Ala. 105, 109; Ark. 5, 25; Cal. 4, 25; Col. 5, 25; Ga. 1, 4, 1; Ill. 4, 22; Ind. 4, 23; Kan. 2, 17; 1905, 543; Ky. 59; Md. 3, 33; Miss. 87; Mo. 4, 53; Mon. 5, 26; N. D. 70; Neb. 3, 15; Nev. 4, 21; Pa. 3, 7; S. C. 3, 34; S. D. 3, 23; Okla. 5, 59; Terr. U. S. 1886, 818; Tex. 3, 56; Utah 6, 26; Va. 51; W. Va. 6, 39; Wy. 3, 27.

[13] Ala.; Ark.; Ky. 60; Miss.; Pa.; Va. 5, 20; W. Va.

trary. In some, every statute is a public law unless otherwise declared in the statute itself.[1]

Nor can the Legislature indirectly enact a special or local law by the partial repeal of a general law.[2] But laws repealing local or special laws may be passed.[3] A general law is one which applies to the whole State.[4]

So, in Georgia, no general law affecting private rights can be varied in any particular case, by special legislation, except with the free consent, in writing, of all persons to be affected thereby.[5] And in Texas, no man, or set of men, shall ever, by special law, be exempted or relieved from any public duty imposed by general laws.[6] In New Jersey, no general law shall embrace any provision of a private, special, or local character.[7] No special law may exempt any person etc., from the operation of any general law.[8]

§ 395. *Local or Special Laws*[9] in most States and in many cases are forbidden by the State Constitutions.

Land: Thus, in detail, are forbidden, in the several States, all such laws laying out or opening roads or highways;[10] vacating streets, roads, plats, and public squares;[11] authorizing or pro-

[1] Ind. 4, 27; Ore. 4, 27; S. C. 6, 4.

[2] Ala.; Ky. 60; La. 49; Miss.; Mo.; Minn.; N. D.; Pa. 3, 7.

[3] Ky.; La.; Mo.; Minn.; N. D.; Pa.; S. D. 14; Utah.

[4] Ala. 110.

[5] Ga. 1, 4, 1.

[6] Tex. 16, 43.

[7] N. J. 4, 7, 4.

[8] Ala. 104.

[9] The distrust of the people of their representatives is in nothing more shown than in the increasing number of matters they are forbidden to meddle with; these restrictions will be found generally noted under their several subjects. The growing adoption of the initiative and referendum (see § 309) is a more noteworthy instance still. Finally, the Southern and Western States have found it necessary to expressly forbid their Legislatures from passing local or special laws in an immense variety of matters. Connecticut, Massachusetts, New Hampshire, and Vermont have no such restrictions, but otherwise they are now common to every State in the Union, and in some instances extend to forty or fifty different restrictions in one State alone. The most concise classification the author has been able to make mounts up to one hundred and twenty matters upon which special legislation is forbidden, throughout the States and Territories. The statement in the text is believed to be substantially accurate, though it would be well in any case where a State is referred to, to consult the exact wording of the constitutional provision to which reference is made.

[10] Cal. 4, 25; Col. 5, 25; Del. 2, 19; Ida. 3, 19; Ill. 4, 22; Ind. 4, 22; Io. 3, 30; Ky. 59; La. 48; Minn. 4, 33; Amt. 1881, p. 22; 1891, p. 19; Miss. 90; Mo. 4, 53; Mon. 5, 26; N. D. 69; Neb. 3, 15; N. J. 4, 7, 11; N. Y. 3, 18; Okla. 5, 46; Ore. 4, 23; Pa. 3, 7; Terr. U. S. 1886, 818; Tex. 3, 56; Utah 6, 26; Wash. 2, 28; W. Va. 6, 39; Wis. 4, 31; Wy. 3, 27.

[11] Ark. 5, 24; Cal.; Col.; Del.; Fla. 3, 20; Ida.; Ill.; Ind.; Io.; Ky.; La.; Mich. 4, 23; Minn.; Mo.; Mon.; N. D.; Neb.; Nev. 4, 20; N. J.; N. Y.; Okla.; Ore.; Pa.; S. D. 3, 23; Terr.; Tex.; Utah; W. Va.; Wy.

viding for the sale or conveyance of real estate;[1] or of any property;[2] and so, in others, "providing for the sale or conveyance of the real estate of persons under disability;"[3] so of their personal estate;[4] and in a few others, "providing for the sale of real estate of persons under disability by executors, administrators, guardians, or trustees;"[5] or "affecting the estates of minors or persons under disability;"[6] or providing for the sale of church property, or property held for charitable use.[7]

Draining swamps:[8] or for ditches;[9] relating to fences;[10] or the straying of livestock;[11] declaring streams navigable;[12] or relating to water-courses.[13]

Changing the law of descent:[14] giving effect to informal or invalid deeds or wills;[15] authorizing deeds to be made for lands sold for taxes.[16]

Liens: authorizing the creation, extension, or impairing of liens.[17]

Relating to cemeteries, graveyards, or public grounds not of the State.[18]

Money: in relation to interest on money.[19]

Persons: legitimating any children (in Tennessee, any person) not born in lawful wedlock;[20] changing the name of any person;[21] or of any place;[22] or corporation;[23] adopting any *child;*[24] constitut-

[1] Ala. 104; Ark.; Mich.

[2] Ala.

[3] Cal.; Col.; Fla.; Ida.; Ill.; Ky. 63; Minn.; Miss.; Mon.; Neb.; Nev.; N. J. 4, 7, 7; Utah; Va.; Wash. W. Va.; Wis.; Wy.

[4] Minn., Miss., Wash., Wis.

[5] Ind.; Md. 3, 33; Ore.

[6] Cal., Ida., La., Minn., Mo., Mon., N. D., Okla., Pa., Terr., Tex., Wash., Wy.

[7] W. Va.; S. C. Amt. 1905, 482.

[8] N. Y.

[9] Del.

[10] Del., Ky., Va.

[11] Del., Ky., Va.

[12] Ky., Va.

[13] Ala.

[14] Ala., Cal., Col., Ida., Ill., Ky., La., Minn., Miss., Mo., Mon., N. D., Neb., N. J., Okla., Pa., Terr., Tex., Utah, W. Va., Wy.

[15] Ala., Cal., Col., Fla., Ida., Ky., La., Md., Minn., Mo., Mon., N. D., Okla., Tex., Wash., Wy.

[16] W. Va.

[17] Cal., Ida., Ky., Mo., Mon., N. D., Okla., Pa., Tex., Wy.

[18] Mo., Okla., Pa., Tex.

[19] Ala., Cal., Col., Ida., Ill., Ind., Ky., La. Minn., Miss., Mo., Mon., N. D. Neb., N. Y., Ore., Pa., Tex., Utah, Va., Wash., W. Va., Wy.

[20] Ala.; Ark.; Cal.; Fla.; Ida.; Ky.; La.; Minn.; Miss.; Mo.; Mon.; N. C. 2, 11; N. D.; Okla.; Pa.; S. C. 3, 34; Tenn. 11, 6; Terr.; Tex.; Wy.

[21] Ala., Ark., Cal., Fla., Ida., Ill., Ind., Io., Ky., La., Md., Minn., Miss., Mo., Mon., N. C., N. D., Neb., Nev., N. Y., Okla., Ore., Pa., S. C., S. D., Tenn., Tex., Terr., Utah, Va., Wash., Wis., Wy.

[22] Cal., Ida., Ill., Ky., Minn., Miss., Mo., Mon., Neb., Okla., Pa., S. C., Tex., Utah, Wy., or lake or river: Minn.

[23] Ala., Mon., N. D., S. D., Va.

[24] Ala., Cal., Fla., Ida., Ky., La., Md., Minn., Mo., Okla., Pa., S. C., Tenn., Tex.

ing one person the heir of another;[1] declaring any person of age;[2] "emancipating minors;"[3] relieving femes coverts.[4]

Divorce: granting divorces;[5] concerning alimony.[6]

Franchises: granting to any person or corporation any exclusive privilege, immunity, or franchise;[7] or any special exemption from a general law.[8]

Granting to any person or corporation the right to lay down railroad tracks;[9] to railroads, bridges, etc., conferring power of eminent domain;[10] for granting State lands.[11] Providing for building bridges, or chartering bridge companies;[12] *except* bridges across streams forming the boundary of the State.[13]

Chartering or licensing ferries:[14] booms, dams, or fisheries.[15]

Chartering, or licensing roads or turnpike companies:[16] incorporating railroads;[17] or other works of internal improvement.[18]

Creating corporations, generally (Ida., Minn., S. C., Wash.), or amending, renewing, extending, or explaining the charters thereof;[19] remitting forfeiture of the charter of a private corporation except, etc.[20] See §§ 501, 504. Authorizing the construction of street railways.[21]

Regulating labor, trade or manufacturing,[22] mining,[23] or agriculture.[24] Creating banks[25] (see § 550); insurance companies;[26] or loan and trust companies.[27]

Debts: providing or changing methods for the collection of debts,

[1] Fla., Minn., Miss., S. D., Utah, Wash., Wis.

[2] Ala., Cal., Col., Ida., Ky., Minn., Mo., Mon., N. D., Okla., Tex., Wash., Wy.

[3] La.

[4] Ky.

[5] Ala.; Ark.; Cal.; Col.; Fla.; Ida.; Ill.; Ind.; Ky.; La.; Md.; Miss.; Mo.; Mon.; N. C. 2, 10; N. D.; Neb.; Nev.; O.; Okla.; Ore.; Pa.; S. D.; Tenn. 11, 4; Tex.; Utah; Va.; W. Va.; Wy.

[6] N. C. See also § 430.

[7] Cal., Col., Ill., La., Minn., Mo., Mon., N. D., Neb., N. J., N. Y., Pa., S. D., Terr., Utah, Va., Wy. See § 16.

[8] Va.

[9] Col., Ill., Ky., Miss., Mo., Mon., N. D., Neb., N. J., N. Y., Pa., Terr., Wy.

[10] Miss.

[11] Ala., Miss.

[12] Ala., Cal., Col., Ida., Ill., Ky., La., Miss., Mo., Mon., N. D., Neb., N. Y., Okla., Pa., Tex., W. Va., Wy.

[13] La., Mo., N. Y., Pa., Tex., or the Hudson or East River (N. Y.).

[14] Ala., Cal., Col., Ida., Ill., Ky., La., Minn., Miss., Mo., Mon., N. D., Neb., Okla., Pa., S. D., Tex., Utah, Wash., W. Va., Wis., Wy.

[15] Ky., Miss., Va.

[16] Ala., Cal., Ida., Ky., Miss., Mon., N. D., Wy.

[17] Okla., Tex.

[18] Okla., Tex.

[19] Ala., Ky., La., Minn., Miss., Mo., Pa., S. C., Terr. U. S. R. S. 1889, Va., Wis.

[20] Va.

[21] La.

[22] Ky., La., Mo., Pa., Tex., Va.

[23] Ky., Mo., Pa., Tex., Va.

[24] La.

[25] Ala. 247; Mon.; N. Y. 8, 4; S. C.; Wy.

[26] Mon., Wy.

[27] Mon., Wy.

enforcing judgments, or prescribing the effect of judicial sales of real estate.[1] Exempting property from execution.[2]

Officers: legalizing the unauthorized or invalid acts of any officer or agent of the State or a municipality,[3] *except* as *against* the State.[4]

Criminal: regulating the jurisdiction, fees, powers, or duties of aldermen, justices of the peace, constables, magistrates, etc.[5]

Juries: selecting or impanelling grand or petit jurors;[6] or exempting from jury duty.[7]

Any laws for the punishment of crimes and misdemeanors;[8] pardoning or commuting the sentence of any criminal;[9] concerning liquor or allowing local option;[10] remitting fines, penalties, or forfeitures;[11] restoring to citizenship any person convicted of infamous crime.[12]

For the protection of game or fish.[13] *But* in others, such laws may be enacted to apply only to localities specially designated.[14]

Municipal: laws locating or changing county seats;[15] or erecting new townships or counties;[16] or changing county or township lines;[17] or school districts.[18]

"Providing for the bonding of cities, towns, or other municipalities."[19]

Incorporating villages and towns;[20] towns only;[21] or cities.[22] Or, in several, amending the charters thereof.[23] "For the organization

[1] La., Mo., Pa., Tex., Va.

[2] Ala.

[3] Cal., Ida., Ky., La., Mo., N. D., Wash.

[4] Cal., Ky., N. D., Wash.

[5] Ala., Cal., Col., Fla., Ida., Ill., Ind., Minn., Miss., Mo., Mon., N. D., Neb., Nev., Ore., Pa., Terr., Tex., Utah, Wy.

[6] Cal., Col., Fla., Ida., Ind., Ky., Miss., Mon., N. D., Neb., Nev., N. J., N. Y., Okla., Ore., S. C., Tex., W. Va., Wy.

[7] Ala., Terr.

[8] Ala., Cal., Fla., Ida., Ind., Ky., Mon., N. D., Nev., Ore., Terr., Utah, Va., Wy.

[9] Ariz.,* Bill of Rts. 28.

[10] Ky.

[11] Ala., Cal., Col., Ida., Ill., Ky., La., Minn., Mo., Mon., N. D., Neb., Okla., Pa., S. D., Terr., Tex., Utah, Wash., W. Va., Wy.

[12] Ala., Cal., Ida., Ky., Mon., N. C., N. D., Terr., Wy.

[13] Col., Ill., Ky., Neb., S. C.

[14] Cal. Amt.; Tenn. 11, 13; Tex. 3, 56.

[15] Ala., Cal., Col., Ida., Ill., Io., Ky., Minn., Mo., Mon., N. D., Neb., N. Y., Okla., S. D., Terr., Tex., Utah, Va., Wash., W. Va., Wis., Wy.

[16] Ga., Mo., N. Y., Pa.

[17] Ga. 11, 1, 3; Mo.; Pa.; Va. 128; Wash.; Minn.

[18] Ala., Del., S. C.

[19] Ala., Neb.

[20] Ala.; Ill.; Minn.; Mo.; N. D; Neb.; N. Y.; Okla.; Pa.; S. C.; S. D. Terr.; Tex.; Utah; Va. 117; Wash.; W. Va.; Wy.

[21] Ill., Io., Mo., Neb., Pa., S. D., Tex., W. Va., Wis., Wy.

[22] Ala., Ill., Io., Mo., N. D., Neb., Okla., Pa., S. C., S. D., Terr., Tex., Utah, W. Va., Wy.

[23] Ala., Ill., Mo., N. D., Neb., Okla., Pa., S. C., S. D., Terr., Tex., Utah, W. Va., Wy., Wis.

and classification of municipal corporations."[1] Authorizing municipal corporations to pass laws inconsistent with general laws.[2]

Regulating county and township business;[3] or the affairs of municipalities generally;[4] or the election of county or township officers;[5] or their compensation;[6] in relation to the fees and salaries of any officer;[7] *except*, that compensation may be suitably graded in proportion to population and necessary services required.[8]

Creating or altering fees or salaries during the term for which the officer is appointed;[9] regulating costs, charges, or fees;[10] authorizing extra compensation to any public officer, agent, or contractor after his service has been rendered or the contract entered into.[11] Creating offices, or prescribing the powers and duties of municipal officers.[12]

Taxes, schools: for the assessment or collection of taxes for either State or municipal purposes;[13] or for a private purpose;[14] exempting property from taxation;[15] or from levy or sale;[16] exempting any person from jury, road, or civil duty.[17]

Providing for the management of the common schools;[18] or for their support;[19] or for the apportionment of the school fund.[20]

For extending the time for the collection of taxes;[21] for otherwise relieving any assessor or collector of taxes from due performance of his duties, or his sureties from liability.[22]

Refunding money paid into the State treasury.[23]

[1] S. C. 8, 1.

[2] Ala. 89.

[3] Cal., Col., Ida., Ill., Ind., Mo., Mon., N. D., Neb., Nev., N. J., Pa., S. D., Tex., Utah, W. Va., Wy.

[4] Mo., Okla., Tex.

[5] Cal., Fla., Ill., Ind., Ky., Minn., N. D., Neb., Nev., N. J., N. Y., Ore., Wy.

[6] Ill. 10, 12; Ind.; S. C. (county only); Minn.

[7] Cal., Col., Fla., Ind., Ky., Minn., Mon., N. D., Okla., Wy.

[8] Ind.

[9] Ida.; Ill. 4, 22; Neb.; N. J.; N. Y.; S. D.; Terr.; Utah; Va. See § 214.

[10] Ala. 96.

[11] Mich. 4, 21; Va. See also § 214.

[12] Cal., Fla. (except municipal), Ida., Minn., Mo., Mon., N. D., Okla., Pa., Tex., Wy.

[13] Ala.; Cal.; Fla.; Ida.; Ind.; Io.; Ky.; Minn.; Mo.; Mon.; N. D.; Nev.; N. J. 4, 7, 12; Ore.; Terr.; Tex. 8, 3; Utah; Va.; Wash.; Wis.; Wy.

[14] Minn.

[15] Ala.; Cal.; Ida.; La.; Minn.; Miss.; Mo.; Mon.; N. Y.; N. D.; Neb. 9, 2; Okla.; Pa.; Tex.; Va.; Wy.

[16] Miss.

[17] Miss.; S. C. Amt. 1905, 482.

[18] Cal., Col., Ida., Ill., Ky., La., Minn., Mo., Mon., N. D., Neb., N. J., Okla., Pa., S. D., Terr., Utah, Wash., Wy.

[19] Ind., La., Minn., Mo., N. J., Okla., Ore., Pa., Tex.

[20] Minn., Wash., Wis.

[21] Cal., Ida., La., Md., Minn., Mo., Mon., N. D., Okla., Tex., Va., Wash., Wis., Wy.

[22] Ky., La., Mo., Okla., Tex.

[23] Cal., Ida., Ky., La., Md., Miss., Mo., Mon., Nev., Okla., Pa., Tex., Va.

Releasing persons from debts due to the State, or to any municipality therein;[1] or to any person or corporation therein;[2] *unless* such special law is recommended by the governor or treasury department.[3] See § 323.

Releasing taxes or title to forfeited lands.[4]

Regarding elections.[5]

Procedure: regulating the practice in the courts;[6] or their jurisdiction;[7] except as to municipal courts.[8] Concerning any civil or criminal actions.[9]

Providing for the change of venue in civil,[10] or in criminal proceedings.[11]

Changing the rules of evidence in judicial proceedings.[12]

Prescribing the limitations of civil[13] or criminal actions.[14]

Granting pensions.[15]

§ 396. *Laws to be Uniform.* — All general laws, or laws of a public nature, must by the Constitutions of many States be uniform in their operation throughout the State.[16]

Article 40. Land Laws

§ 400. *Tenure.* — By the Constitutions of a few States all land is declared allodial.[17] And so, in four, the ultimate property in land is declared to vest in the people, by right of sovereignty.[18]

And all land to which the title fails by defect of heirs reverts[19] or

[1] Ida.; Ky. 52; Md.; Mon.; N. D.; S. D. 3, 23; Nev.; Utah 6, 27; Va.; Wash.; Wy.

[2] Cal.

[3] Md.

[4] W. Va.

[5] Ala.; Cal.; Col.; Fla.; Ida.; Ill.; Ind.; Ky.; La.; Minn.; Mo.; Mon.; N. D.; Neb.; Nev.; N. Y.; Okla.; Ore.; Pa. 3, 7; 8, 7; Terr.; Tex.; Va.; W. Va.

[6] Cal., Col., Fla., Ill., Ida., Ind., Ky., La., Miss., Mo., Mon., N. D., Neb., Nev., Okla., Ore., Pa., Terr., Tex., Utah, Va., W. Va., Wy.

[7] Ky., Mo., Okla.

[8] Fla.

[9] La.

[10] (As below, except in Arkansas).

[11] Ala., Ark., Cal., Fla., Ida., Ill., Ind., Ky., La., Miss., Mo., Mon., N. D., Neb., Nev., N. J., N. Y., Okla., Ore., Pa., Terr., Tex., Utah, Va., Wy.

[12] Col., La., Mo., Mon., N. D., Okla., Pa., Tex., Va. Wy.

[13] Ala., Cal., Col., Ida., Ky., Mo., Mon., N. D., Okla., Tex., Wash., Wy.

[14] Ala., Ida., Ky., Okla., Tex., Wash.

[15] Va.

[16] Ariz.* Bill of Rts. 17; Cal. 1, 11; Fla. 3, 21; Ga. 1, 4, 1; Ind. 4, 23; Io. 1, 6; 3, 30; Kan. 2, 17; N. D. 11; Nev. 4, 21; O. 2, 26; Okla. 5, 59; S. C. 3, 34; Utah 1, 24; Wis. Amt. 4, 32; Wy. 1, 34.

[17] Ark. 2, 28; Minn. 1, 15; N. Y. 1, 12; Wis. 1, 14.

[18] N. Y. 1, 10; S. C. 14, 3; Wis. 9, 3.

[19] This word is improperly used, and misleading. See § 401, note 7.

escheats to the people.[1] The proceeds of escheated lands (or other property) are, by many State Constitutions, to be applied to the public schools.[2]

So the property of the State liquor dispensary.[3]

§ 401. *Feudal Tenures.* — With all their incidents, are abolished by the Constitutions of a few States.[4]

So, in two, all fines, quarter-sales, and like restraints upon alienations are especially declared void.[5]

Except in one, rents and certain services heretofore lawfully created;[6] and except the liability to "escheat"[7] for lack of heirs.[8]

§ 402. *Entails, Primogeniture, and Perpetuities.* — Entails are, by declaration in two of the Territories, entirely abolished;[9] so, in two States, the Legislature is to regulate entails so as to prevent perpetuities.[10]

By the Constitutions of several States perpetuities[11] are forbidden;[12] *except* for eleemosynary purposes.[13]

And the law of primogeniture may never be in force.[14]

§ 403. *Mortmain.*[15]— The Constitution of Maryland declares all

[1] Mich. 13, 3; N. Y.; S. C.; Wis.

[2] Cal. 9, 4; Col. 9, 5; Fla. 12, 4; Io. 9, 2, 3; Kan. 6, 3; Mich.; Mo. 11, 6; Neb. 8, 3; Nev. 11, 3; Ore. 8, 2; S. C. 11, 11; W. Va. 12, 4.

[3] S. C. 11, 12.

[4] Ark. 2, 28; Minn. 1, 15; N. Y. 1, 11; Wis. 1, 14.

[5] N. Y. 1, 14; Wis.

[6] N. Y.

[7] Land being allodial (§ 400), it follows that there can be, properly speaking, no escheat. The word is, however, commonly used in America, and will hereafter be used in this book, to mean both escheat proper and the vesting of the State's title by right of sovereignty.

[8] N. Y. 1, 13.

[9] Ariz.* Bill of Rts. 23 (except as in § 1313); N. M.* 1851, July 12, § 17.

[10] N. C. 2, 15; Vt. 2, 36.

[11] Compare also § 580.

[12] Ark. 2, 19; Cal. 20, 9; Mon. 19, 5; N. C. 1, 31; Nev. 15, 4; N. M.*; Okla. 2, 32; Tenn. 1, 22; Tex. 1, 26; Wy. 1, 30.

[13] Cal., Mon., Nev.

[14] N. M.*; Okla. 2, 32; Tex.

[15] No corporation shall be created or licensed in this State for the purpose of buying, acquiring, trading, or dealing in real estate other than real estate located in incorporated cities and towns and as additions thereto; nor shall any corporation doing business in this State buy, acquire, trade, or deal in real estate for any purpose except such as may be located in such towns and cities and as additions to such towns and cities, and further except such as shall be necessary and proper for carrying on the business for which it was chartered or licensed, nor shall any corporation be created or licensed to do business in this State for the purpose of acting as agent in buying and selling land: Provided, However, That corporations shall not be precluded from taking mortgages on real estate to secure loans or debts or from acquiring title thereto upon foreclosure of such mortgages or in the collection of debts, conditioned that such corporation or corporations shall not hold such real estate for a longer period than seven years after acquiring such title: And Provided, Further, That this section shall not apply to trust companies taking only the naked title to real estate in this State as a trustee, to be held solely as security for indebtedness pursuant to such trust: And Provided,

gifts, sales, and devises of land or personal property to religious sects or for religious uses, without the prior or subsequent sanction of the Legislature, void;[1] so of devises and legacies only.[2]

Except, in two States, a sale, etc., of land for a church, parsonage, or cemetery, and actually so used;[3] but such land must not, in Maryland, exceed five acres in extent.

The United States laws provide that in the Territories no religious or charitable association or corporation shall hold real estate of a greater value than $50,000.[4]

§ 404. *Monopolies* are by the Constitutions of several States declared odious and forbidden; see § 580. But municipalities etc., may regulate slaughtering in Louisiana.

§ 405. *Long Leases.* — In a few States there are constitutional provisions forbidding leases or grants of agricultural land reserving rent, for a longer period than twelve years;[5] fifteen years;[6] or twenty-one years.[7]

§ 406. *Record of Conveyances.* — In Vermont the Constitution provides that all conveyances of land shall be recorded;[8] so, in Louisiana, all mortgages;[9] all deeds and mortgages recorded are *prima facie* evidence of their proper execution.[10]

So, in Louisiana, all "privileges" on real estate; but privileges for expenses of last illness or taxes need not be recorded, and they lapse in three years.

§ 407. *Lands of the United States.* — The new States have constitutional provisions to forbid the Legislature from interfering with the title of the United States to its lands in the State;[11] or from interfering with any laws Congress may find necessary for securing the title of such land to *bona fide* purchasers.[12]

In the Territories, no law can be passed "interfering with the primary disposal of the soil."[13] The Indian reservations are secured to National Government control.[14]

Further, That no public service corporation shall hold any land, or the title thereof, in any way whatever in this State, except as the same shall be necessary for the transaction and operation of its business as such public service corporation. Okla. 22, 2.

[1] Md. Decln. of Rts. 38.

[2] Miss. 270.

[3] Md.; Mo. 2, 8.

[4] U. S. R. S. 1890.

[5] Mich. 18, 12; N. Y. 1, 13.

[6] Wis. 1, 14.

[7] Minn. 1, 15.

[8] Vt. 2, 35.

[9] La. 186.

[10] Fla. 16, 21.

[11] Ida. 21, 19; Kan. Ordinance; Minn. 2, 3; Mo. 14, 1; N. D. 203 (2); Nev. Ordinance; Okla. 1, 3; S. D. 22, 1; Utah 3, 2; Wash. 26, 25; Wis. 2, 2.

[12] Kan., Minn., Mo., Wis.

[13] U. S. R. S. 1851.

[14] Ida., N. D., Okla., S. D., Wash.

§ 408. *Public Lands.* — In four States the Constitution provides that no public land of the State shall be sold or granted except to actual settlers; [1] and not donated to private corporations or individuals or railroads.[2] Lands and public tracts are only sold at market value.[3] The price may not be less than $10 an acre.[4]

The settler must occupy the land for three years in order to perfect his title.[5]

The amount granted is eighty acres to a single man, one hundred and sixty to the head of a family; [6] one hundred and sixty acres to any individual; [7] eighty acres to any settler; [8] three hundred and twenty acres.[9]

The right of the State to mines and minerals is, in Texas, released by the Constitution; [10] but in Arizona "the precious metals are the jewels of sovereignty, and inhere in the sovereign power; no person can acquire absolute title to any public domain in which such metals may be found without the express consent of such power." [11]

In Texas the State may grant lands to railway companies, under special restrictions.[12]

No entry by warrant can now be made, and possession for ten years or payment of taxes for five years since 1865 gives good title as against the State.[13] There are similar numerous provisions in the newer States as to School land; [14] but practically all the State land is now taken up. In New York, there are constitutional provisions rendering invalid purchases or contracts for the sale of lands with Indians.[15] There are frequently Commissioners of Public Lands provided for.[16]

No claim to any public lands by any trespasser thereon by reason of occupancy, cultivation, or improvement thereof, shall ever be recognized; nor shall compensation ever be made on account of any improvement made by such trespasser.[17]

[1] Cal. 17, 3; Fla. 16, 5; Mon. 19, 7; Tex. 14, 4.

[2] Ala. 99; Miss. 95; S. C. 3, 31. Nor sold at a less price than to individuals. This, however, shall not prevent the Legislature from granting a right of way, not exceeding one hundred feet in width, as a mere easement, to railroads, across State land, and the Legislature shall never dispose of the land covered by said right so long as such easement exists: Ala.; Miss. 95; S. C. 3, 31.

[3] Mon. 19, 3; S. D. 8, 7; Utah 20, 1; Wash. 16, 1.

[4] Ida., Mon.

[5] Tex. 14, 6.

[6] Tex.

[7] Ida.

[8] Fla.

[9] Cal.

[10] Tex. 14, 7.

[11] Ariz. Bill of Rts. 21.

[12] Tex. 14, 3–5.

[13] W. Va. 13, 2 & 3.

[14] S. D. Art. 8.

[15] N. Y. 1, 15.

[16] Wash. 3, 24. See § 201.

[17] N. D. 163; S. D. 8, 10.

§ 409. *A Forest Preserve* "as now fixed by law" is to be kept wild and never leased, sold, or timber cut, or be taken by any corporation public or private.[1]

The Legislature shall enact laws to prevent the destruction of and to preserve the forests on the lands of the State, and upon any part of the public domain, the control of which may be conferred by Congress upon the State.[2]

State Highways may be provided for by law;[3] so, in Michigan the Constitution provides for county or town roads and for State wagon roads;[4] and in many States for a State highway Commission.[5]

Article 41. Navigable Waters and Easements

§ 410. *Navigable Waters,* by the Constitutions of a few States, shall forever remain public highways, free to the citizens of the States and the United States, without impost or toll.[6]

So, the Constitution declares that no person or corporation can obstruct the navigation of the navigable waters of the State;[7] and no navigable stream can be dammed or bridged without authority of law; and no law shall prejudice the right of individuals to the free navigation of such stream, or preclude the State from further improvement of it.[8]

§ 411. *Special Streams.* — The Constitutions of some States specially declare certain streams navigable, and forever free, as in four States the Mississippi;[9] and in three of them, navigable waters leading into the Mississippi;[10] and in one, navigable waters leading into the St. Lawrence;[11] and so, navigable waters bordering the State, with the rivers leading into the same.[12]

§ 412. *Jurisdiction.* — In several States the Constitution provides that the State shall have concurrent jurisdiction on all rivers bordering on the State so far as they form the boundary of the State and any other State.[13] The State owns the tide and shores of natural

[1] N. Y. 7, 7.

[2] Col. 18, 6; Mon. 19, 3; Utah, 18, 1.

[3] Cal. 1901, p. 960; Minn. 1897, 333; N. Y. 1903, p. 1454.

[4] Mich. 1893, p. 434, 1899, p. 478; Mich. 1905, p. 531.

[5] See § 202.

[6] Ala. 24; Minn. 2, 2; S. C. 1, 28; 14, 1; Wis. 9, 1. See Book I., Chap. II.

[7] Cal. 15, 2; Miss. 81.

[8] Mich. 18, 4.

[9] Minn. 2, 2; Mo. 1, 1; Tenn. 1, 29; Wis. 9, 1.

[10] Minn., Mo., Wis.

[11] Wis.

[12] Miss., N. C.

[13] Ind. 14, 2; Minn. 2, 2; Mo. 1, 1; S. C. 14, 1; Wis. 9, 1.

waters to high-tide line, and on natural rivers and lakes to ordinary high water.[1]

§ 413. *Water Front.* — By the Constitution of California, the right of eminent domain exists in the State to all frontages on navigable waters; and no person or corporation can exclude the right of way to such water, when required for a public purpose; and all tide lands within two miles[2] of any incorporated city or town, fronting on the waters of any harbor used for navigation, shall be withheld from grant or sale to any person or corporation;[3] so of water front, and rights beyond the harbor lines; and wharf leases may not be for more than 30 years.[4]

§ 414. *Wharves.* — In two States, the Constitutions provide that no tax, toll, impost, or wharfage shall be imposed, demanded, or received from the owner of any merchandise or commodity, for the use of the shores, or any wharf erected on the shores, or in or over the waters of any navigable stream, unless the same be authorized by the Legislature.[5]

§ 415. *Drains.* — In two States the Legislature are authorized to pass laws permitting the owners or occupants of lands to construct drains and ditches for agricultural and sanitary purposes across the lands of others.[6]

§ 416. *Franchises.* —(See §§ 502, 536.) The right to collect rates for water furnished to a municipality is declared to be a franchise, not to be exercised except by authority of law and in the manner by law prescribed.[7] The county commissioners may empower reasonable maximum rates for the use of water, whether furnished by persons or corporations;[8] so, in Idaho, the Legislature;[9] and in Texas, the right to regulate tolls or freights, for the use of roads, bridges, ferries, landings, or wharves, shall always remain in the Legislature.[10]

No railway, gas, water, telephone, light, etc., company shall construct its works in, over, or under the streets without consent of the municipal authorities is first obtained;[11] so, in California, the Legislature shall pass laws to regulate the charges of telegraph or gas companies, wharfingers, and warehousemen, where there is a public use.[12]

[1] Wash. 17, 1.
[2] So, substantially, within one mile (Wash. 15, 1–2).
[3] Cal. 15, 3.
[4] Wash. 15, 2.
[5] Ala. 24; S. C. 1, 28.
[6] Ill. 4, 3, 1; N. Y. 1, 7. See also § 92. Drainage is declared a public use (S. D., 1903, 70).
[7] Cal. 14, 2; Ida. 15, 2.
[8] Col. 16, 8.
[9] Ida. 15, 5.
[10] Tex. 12, 3.
[11] Ky. 163.
[12] Cal. 4, 33.

"No municipal corporation shall ever grant, extend, or renew a franchise, without the approval of a majority of the qualified electors residing within its corporate limits, who shall vote thereon at a general or special election; and the legislative body of any such corporation may submit any such matter for approval or disapproval to such electors at any general municipal election, or call a special election for such purpose at any time upon thirty days' notice; and no franchise shall be granted, extended, or renewed for a longer term than twenty-five years.

"Whenever a petition signed by a number of qualified electors of any municipal corporation equal to twenty-five per centum of the total number of votes cast at the next preceding general municipal election, demanding that a franchise be granted, extended, or renewed, shall be filed with the chief executive officer of said corporation, the chief executive officer shall, within ten days thereafter, call a special election, at which he shall submit the question of whether or not such franchise shall be granted, extended, or renewed, and if, at said election, a majority of the said electors voting thereon shall vote for the grant, extension, or renewal of such franchise, the same shall be granted by the proper authorities at the next succeeding regular meeting of the legislative body of the city.

"Every municipal corporation within this State shall have the right to engage in any business or enterprise which may be engaged in by a person, firm, or corporation by virtue of a franchise from said corporation." [1]

§ 417. *Hunting and Fishing.* — The Constitution of Vermont provides that the inhabitants shall have liberty at seasonable times to hunt, fish, and fowl on lands not enclosed.[2]

The Legislature may establish fish and game districts and laws to regulate the same.[3]

§ 418. *Use of Water.* — Several Western Constitutions declare that the water of every natural stream (not heretofore lawfully appropriated) within the State is the property of the public.[4] But the right to divert the unappropriated waters of any such stream to beneficial uses shall never be denied; priority of appropriation shall give the better right as between those using the water for the same pur-

[1] Okla. 18, 5.

[2] Vt. 2, 40. William Rufus three times promised his people the right of free hunting, which was claimed as an English liberty.

[3] Cal. 1901, p. 948.

[4] Ariz.* Bill of Rts. 22; Col. 16, 5; Ida. 15, 1; Wy. 8, 1.

pose; and if the water is insufficient, those using it for domestic purposes have the preference; and those using it for agricultural purposes have the preference over manufacturers.[1] No individual or corporation shall have the right to appropriate streams or ponds exclusively to their own private use except as may be provided by law.[2]

The use of the waters of the State for irrigation, mining, and manufacturing purposes shall be deemed a public use.[3]

The use of all waters now appropriated, or that may hereafter be appropriated for sale, rental, or distribution; also of all water originally appropriated for private use, but which after such appropriation has heretofore been, or may hereafter be sold, rented, or distributed, is hereby declared to be a public use, and subject to the regulation and control of the State in the manner prescribed by law.[4] For Idaho, see also note.[5]

All flowing streams and natural water-courses shall forever re-

[1] Col. 16, 6.

[2] Ariz.*

[3] Wash. 21, 1.

[4] Ida. 15, 1; Mon. 3, 15.

[5] "And in any organized mining district, those using the water, for mining purposes or milling purposes connected with mining, shall have preference over those using the same for manufacturing or agricultural purposes. But the usage by such subsequent appropriators shall be subject to such provisions of law regulating the taking of private property for public and private use, as referred to in section fourteen of Article I., of this constitution." (Ida. 15, 3.)

"Whenever any waters have been, or shall be, appropriated or used for agricultural purposes, under a sale, rental, or distribution thereof, such sale, rental or distribution shall be deemed an exclusive dedication to such use; and whenever such waters so dedicated shall have once been sold, rented or distributed to any person who has settled upon or improved land for agricultural purposes with the view of receiving the benefit of such water under such dedication, such person, his heirs, executors, administrators, successors, or assigns, shall not thereafter, without his consent, be deprived of the annual use of the same, when needed for domestic purposes, or to irrigate the land so settled upon or improved, upon payment therefor, and compliance with such equitable terms and conditions as to the quantity used and times of use, as may be prescribed by law." (Ida. 15, 4.)

"Whenever more than one person has settled upon, or improved land with the view of receiving water for agricultural purposes, under a sale, rental, or distribution thereof, as in the last preceding section of this article, provided, as among such persons priority in time shall give superiority of right to the use of such water in the numerical order of such settlements or improvements; but whenever the supply of such water shall not be sufficient to meet the demands of all those desiring to use the same, such priority of right shall be subject to such reasonable limitations as to the quantity of water used and times of use as the Legislature, having due regard, both to such priority of right and the necessities of those subsequent in time of settlement or improvement, may by law prescribe." (Ida. 15, 5.)

main the property of the State for mining, irrigating, and manufacturing purposes.[1]

Water being essential to industrial prosperity, of limited amount, and easy of diversion from its natural channels, its control must be in the State, which, in providing for its use, shall equally guard all the various interests involved.[2]

All existing rights to the use of any of the waters in this State for any useful or beneficial purpose, are hereby recognized and confirmed.[3]

Municipal corporations shall have the same right as individuals to acquire rights, by prior appropriation and otherwise, to the use of water for domestic and municipal purposes, and the Legislature shall provide by law for the exercise upon the part of incorporated cities, towns, and villages of the right of eminent domain for the purpose of acquiring from prior appropriators, upon the payment of just compensation, such water as may be necessary for the well-being thereof and for domestic uses.[4]

The Legislature shall have power and shall provide for a system of levees, drains, and ditches and of irrigation in this State when deemed expedient, and provide for a system of taxation on the lands affected or benefited by such levees, drains, and ditches and irrigation, or on crops produced on such land, to discharge such bonded indebtedness or expenses necessarily incurred in the establishment of such improvements; and to provide for compulsory issuance of bonds by the owners or lessees of the lands benefited or affected by such levees, drains, and ditches or irrigation.[5]

§ 419. *Riparian Rights.* — There are special provisions for levees, etc., in Louisiana.[6]

Article 42. Personal Property

§ 420. *Record.* — By the Constitution of Louisiana, "privileges" may exist without record, except in cases where the Legislature prescribe otherwise.[7]

§ 421. *Seal.* — By the Constitution of Arkansas private (*i. e.* not corporate) seals are abolished, and no distinction shall exist between

[1] N. D. 210.
[2] Wy. 1, 31.
[3] Utah 17, 1.
[4] Wy. 13, 5.
[5] Okla. 16, 3.
[6] La. 290.
[7] La. 187.

sealed and unsealed instruments, in contracts between individuals, until otherwise provided by law.[1]

§ 422 *Interest.*[2] — The Constitution of Tennessee provides that the Legislature may fix the rate of interest, and such rate shall be uniform throughout the State, and may also provide for a conventional (*i. e.*, to be specially contracted for) rate of interest not to exceed ten per cent.[3] So, in Arkansas, the Constitution fixes the legal rate, in contracts where no rate is specified, at six per cent; but shall pass a law limiting the rate for which individuals may contract to ten per cent.[4] In Texas the legal rate is, by the Constitution, made six per cent; the special contract rate is limited at ten per cent; and all over ten per cent is declared usurious, and the Legislature are to pass usury laws.[5] In Maryland the legal rate is six per cent until otherwise provided by the Legislature.[6]

§ 423. *Money.* — The Constitutions of New Hampshire and Massachusetts provide that the money mentioned in the Constitution shall be computed at 6*s.* 8*d.* to the ounce of silver.[7]

§ 424. *Trust Funds.* — By several State Constitutions, the Legislature is forbidden to pass laws to authorize the investment of trust funds in the bonds or stock of private corporations.[8]

§ 425. *Stock-jobbing.* — The California Constitution provides that the Legislature shall pass laws to regulate or prohibit the buying or selling of the shares of the stock of corporations in any stock board;[9] and that all contracts for the sale of stock on a margin or for future delivery are void, and the money paid therefor may be recovered.

§ 426. *Lotteries.* — Are prohibited by the Constitutions of nearly all; and in all these States (except R. I., Wis., Neb., Md., Fla., Ida., S. D., and Wash.) the sale of lottery tickets is forbidden;[10] so, in several of "gift enterprises;[11] pool selling;[12] or all other forms of gambling.[13]

[1] Ark. Sched. 1.

[2] See also § 395.

[3] Tenn. 11, 7.

[4] Ark. 19, 13.

[5] Tex. 16, 11; Amt. 1891, p. 196.

[6] Md. 3, 57.

[7] Mass. 2, 6, 3; N. H. 2, 96.

[8] Ala. 74; Col. 5, 36; Mon. 5, 37; Pa. 3, 22; Wy. 3, 38. See also § 519.

[9] Cal. 4, 26.

[10] Ala. 65; Ark. 19, 14; Ariz.* Bill of Rts. 27; Cal. 4, 26; Col. 18, 2; Del. 2, 17; Fla. 3, 23; Ga. 1, 2, 4; Ida. 3, 20; Ill. 4, 27; Ind. 15, 8; Io. 3, 28; Kan. 15, 3; Ky. 226; La. 178; Md. 3, 36; Mich. 4, 27; Minn. 4, 31; Miss. 98; Mo. 14, 10; Mon. 19, 2; N. D. Amt. 1; Neb. 3, 21; Nev. 4, 24; N. J. 4, 7, 2; N. Y. 1, 9; O. 15, 6; Ore. 15, 4; R. I. 4, 12; S. C. 17, 7; S. D. 3, 25; Tenn. 11, 5; Tex. 3, 47; Uta. 6, 28; Va. 60; Wash. 2, 24; W. Va. 6, 36; Wis. 4, 24.

[11] Ala., Cal., Col., Ill., Mo., Mon., Neb., S. D., Tex., W. Va.

[12] Del., N. Y.

[13] Del., Neb., N. J., N. Y.

ARTICLE 43. LAW OF PERSONS

§ 430. *Marriage.* — By the Constitutions of many States, the Legislature can grant no divorce,[1] nor allowance of alimony;[2] and in one all absolute divorces are forbidden.[3]

But in two, the Legislature may enact general laws regulating divorce and alimony;[4] so, of course, in all other States. In one, no contract of marriage otherwise duly made shall be invalid for want of conformity to the requirements of any religious sect.[5] In one, no absolute divorce can be granted except on the concurrent verdicts of two juries at different terms of the court; and the last jury shall determine the disabilities and rights of the parties.[6]

§ 431. *Age of Consent.* — "No unmarried woman shall legally (*sic*) consent to sexual intercourse who shall not have attained the age of 14." [7]

§ 432. *Names.* — In Tennessee the Legislature has no power to change the names of persons, or to pass acts adopting or legitimating persons, but shall confer this power on the courts.[8]

§ 433. *Warehouses.* By the Constitutions of two States all elevators or storehouses where grain or other property is stored for a compensation, whether the property stored be kept separate or not, are declared *public warehouses.*[9]

The owners or managers of public warehouses are required to make public statements of grain or goods stored, and the warehouse receipts issued; and are not to mix grain with grain of inferior grade; and the owner is to be always at liberty to examine such property stored, and the books of the warehouse relating thereto.[10]

§ 434. *Warehouse Receipts.* — The Constitution of Illinois declares that the Legislature shall pass laws to prevent the issue of false and fraudulent warehouse receipts;[11] and (in Kentucky also) laws for the inspection of grain,[12] and "for the protection of producers," etc.[13]

[1] Del. 2, 18; Io. 3, 27; Kan. 2, 18; Mich. 4, 26; Minn. 4, 28; N. H. 2, 75; N. J. 4, 7, 1; N. Y. 1, 9; O. 2 32; S. C. 17, 3; Tenn. 11, 4; Wash. 2, 24; Wis. 4, 24. See also § 395.

[2] Del.

[3] S. C.

[4] N. C. 2, 10; Tenn.

[5] Cal. 20, 7.

[6] Ga. 6, 15, 1–2.

[7] S. C. 3, 33.

[8] Tenn. 11, 6. See § 395.

[9] Ill. 13, 1; Ky. 206.

[10] Ill. 13, 2 & 3.

[11] Ill. 13, 6.

[12] Ill. 13, 7; Ky. 206.

[13] Ky.

§ 435. *Drawbacks and Rebates.* — (See also § 416.) By the Constitution of Texas, all drawbacks and rebatement of insurance, freight transportation, carriage, wharfage, storage, compressing, baling, repairing, or for any other kind of labor or service, of or to any cotton, grain, or other produce, to any carrier, shipper, merchant, or factor not the owner thereof, are prohibited.[1]

§ 436. *Carriers.* — The Constitution of Illinois provides that all railroads and other common carriers shall weigh or measure grain at points where it is shipped, and receipt for the full amount, and shall be responsible for the delivery of such amount to the owner or consignee thereof at the place of destination.[2]

§ 437. *Cattle and Stock.* — The Legislature may pass laws for the regulation of live-stock and the protection of stock-raisers, having a local application; and also pass general and special laws for the inspection of cattle, stock, and hides, and the regulation of brands; *provided* that any local law thus passed shall be submitted to the freeholders of the section to be affected thereby and approved by them.[3]

§ 438. *Physicians.* — The Constitutions of three States provide that laws may be passed prescribing the qualifications of medical practitioners, and to punish for malpractice (but, in Texas, that no preference shall be given to any one school of medicine).[4]

Article 44. Health and Morality

§ 440. *Live Stock.* — The Legislature shall pass all necessary laws to provide for the protection of live stock against the introduction or spread of pleuro-pneumonia, glanders, splenetic or Texas fever, and other infectious or contagious diseases. The Legislature may also establish a system of quarantine or inspection, and such other regulations as may be necessary for the protection of stock owners and most conducive to the stock interests within the State.[5]

§ 441. *Board of Health* (see also § 202). — There shall be established by law a State board of health and a bureau of vital statistics in connection therewith, with such powers as the Legislature may direct.[6] Boards of Health shall be created by the Legislature wherever they may be necessary, with power to make such regu-

[1] Tex. 16, 25. See also § 524.
[2] Ill. 13, 4.
[3] Tex. 16, 23.
[4] La. 178; Tex. 16, 31; Wash. 20, 2.
[5] Ida. 16, 1; Wy. 19, 1.
[6] Wash. 20, 1.

lations as shall protect the health of the community and abate nuisances.[1]

§ 442. — *Inspection Laws.* — No State office shall be continued or created for the inspection or measuring of any merchandise, manufacture or commodity; but any county or municipality may appoint such officers when authorized by law.[2]

§ 443. *Dealing in Futures.* — The pernicious practice of dealing or gambling in futures on agricultural products or articles of necessity, where the intention of the parties is not to make an honest and *bona fide* delivery, is declared to be against public policy; and the Legislature shall pass laws to suppress it.[3]

§ 444. *Fire Protection.* — The Legislature shall enact laws to secure the safety of persons from fires in hotels, theatres, and other public places of resort.[4]

§ 445. *Liquor Traffic, General Regulation of,* is declared to belong to the police jurisdiction; and the State may enact laws regulating their sale and use [5] or regulating and prohibiting their sale.[6]

§ 446. *Prohibition* of the manufacture and sale (or giving away) of intoxicating liquors is found in several State Constitutions.[7]

Except for medical, mechanical, and scientific purposes; [8] and except cider.[9]

In Colorado only the sale of spurious or drugged liquors is forbidden.[10]

§ 447. *Local Option.* — Some Constitutions provide that the Legislature shall enact a law whereby the qualified electors of any city, county, town, or precinct may, by a majority vote, prohibit the sale of liquors within the prescribed limits.[11]

In other States they may do so [12] or the dispensary system may be established.[13]

The County Commissioners, not oftener than once in two years upon petition of one fourth the registered voters, must call an election (special) to determine whether or no intoxicating liquors or beer shall be sold in the county.[14]

[1] S. C. 8, 10.
[2] Ala. 77.
[3] La. 189.
[4] Miss. 83.
[5] La. 181.
[6] S. C. 8, 11; W. Va. 6, 46; Va. 62.
[7] Io. Amt. 1882, p. 178; Kan. Amt. 1881, p. 323; Me. Amt. 1885, p. 339; Okla. 1, 7 (as to Indian reservations); p. 95 (separate article applying to the whole State); N. D. 217; O. 15, 9.
[8] Kan., Me., N. D., Okla.
[9] Me.
[10] Col. 18, 5.
[11] Ky. 61; Fla. 19, 1; Tex. 1891, p. 196.
[12] Va. 62; Del. 13, 1.
[13] Va.
[14] Fla. 19, 1.

§ 448. *Dispensary System.* — This is expressly authorized under the Constitution of a few States, and has been carried into execution in South Carolina, as to sales exceeding one half-pint, between sunrise and sunset, not to be drunk on the premises.[1]

§ 449. *Vagrant Laws* are required to be enacted by the Constitution of Texas.[2]

Poor Laws. — There are in a few States constitutional provisions for the support of the poor by counties, and for State asylums for orphans, deaf, blind, insane, or inebriates.[3]

ARTICLE 45. LABOR

§ 450. *General Principles.* — The Legislature shall pass necessary laws for the protection of persons working in mines, factories, and other employments dangerous to life and deleterious to health; and fix pains and penalties for the enforcement of same.[4]

The rights of labor shall have just protection through laws calculated to promote the industrial welfare of the State.[5]

The Legislature shall prohibit the political and commercial control of employees.[6]

The Legislature shall provide for the protection of the employees of all corporations doing business in this State from interference with their social, civil, or political rights by said corporations, their agents or employees.[7]

"The Legislature, by appropriate legislation, shall provide for the enforcement of the provisions of this article." [8]

§ 451. *Day's Work.* — A few Western Constitutions prescribe an eight-hour day in all public work.[9]

[1] S. C. 8, 11.

[2] Tex. 3, 46.

[3] Ala. 88; Ark. 19, 9 & 19; Col. 8, 1; Fla. 13, 1 & 3; Ida. 10, 1; Kan. 7, 4; La. 174; Miss. 86; Mon. 10, 1; Okla. 17, 3; Amt. 1887; Nev. 13, 1 & 3; N. C. 11, 8–10; S. C. 12, 1 & 3; Tex. 11, 2; 16, 8 & 42 & 54; S. D. 14, 1; Wash. 13, 1.

[4] Ida. Amt. 13; Okla. 23, 5; Wash. 2, 35. See also § 14.

[5] Utah 16, 1.

[6] Utah 16, 3.

[7] Miss. 191.

[8] Utah 16, 7.

[9] Cal. 20, 17; Amt. 1901, 959; Col. 1903, ch. 49; Ida. 13, 2; Mon. 1903, 49; Okla. 23, 2; Utah 16, 6; Wy. 19, 1. Statutes to this effect exist in several other States. For the general subject of labor legislation see the author's "Handbook to the Labor Laws of the United States." No American legislature has yet ventured to prescribe the hours of labor of adult males in general occupations, and it would be clearly unconstitutional. The last English law of the sort was under Elizabeth (see Book II). The same is true of the regulation of wages by law. The labor of minors may be regulated or prohibited in any or all occupations; and so

§ 452. *Wages.* — The Louisiana Constitution prescribes that no law shall be passed fixing the price of manual labor.[1]

§ 453. *Public Work.* — But in New York, by a recent amendment, "the Legislature may regulate and fix the wages or salaries, the hours of work or labor, and make provision for the protection, safety, and welfare of persons employed by the State or by any county, city, town, village, or other civil subdivision of the State, or by any contractor or subcontractor performing work, labor, or services for the State or for any city, county, town, village, or other civil division thereof." [2]

§ 454. *Special Employments.* — A few Western States provide in their Constitutions for an eight-hour day in mines,[3] smelters,[4] or underground employment generally;[5] or even in mills or factories,[6] or in dangerous employments.[7]

§ 455. *Women and Children.* — Children under sixteen,[8] twelve,[9] or fourteen,[10] may not work in mines,[11] workshops, or factories;[12] nor, if under fifteen, in places dangerous to life or health or injurious to morals.[13] The Kentucky Constitution specifies (unnecessarily) that the Legislature may fix such age.[14]

No women or girls of any age may work in mines.[15]

§ 456. *Wage-payments.* — All wage-earners in this State employed in factories, mines, workshops, or by corporations, shall be paid for their labor in lawful money. The general assembly shall prescribe adequate penalties for violations of this section.[16]

§ 457. *Liens.* — The Constitutions of three States provide that mechanics, artisans, and material men of every class shall have a lien upon the building and articles repaired by them for the value of their labor or material.[17] And in two, also, upon personal property,

of women; at least as to unhealthy or immoral trades, except perhaps in the women-suffrage States or those whose Constitutions require identical laws for the two sexes (see §§ 20, 23–25).

[1] La. 51.

[2] N. Y. 12, 1; Amt. 1905.

[3] Col. 1901, 48; Mon. 1903, 49; Wy. 19, 1. Similar laws are constitutional when their object is to protect the health of the public; if only that of the men employed, *quaere.*

[4] Col., Mon.

[5] Col., Mon.

[6] Mon.

[7] Col., Mon.

[8] Mon.; Okla. 24, 4.

[9] N. D. 209; Col. 16, 3.

[10] Utah 16, 1; Wy. 9, 3.

[11] Mon., N. D., Col.

[12] N. D.

[13] Okla. 23, 3.

[14] Ky. 243.

[15] Utah, Wy.

[16] Ky. 244. In the absence of a constitutional provision, statutes to this effect have usually been held unconstitutional; but not so in Massachusetts; and there is old English precedent for the principle. See Historical Digest.

[17] Cal. 20, 15; N. C. 14, 4; Tex. 16,

for labor done upon it;[1] or, in others, upon the subject-matter of their labor.[2]

So, in two others, that the Legislature shall pass laws to protect laborers on public works, railroads, and canals against failure of the contractors to pay their current wages when due, and to make the corporation or individual for whose benefit the work is done responsible for their ultimate payment.[3]

§ 458. *Blacklists.* — The exchange of blacklists by railroad companies or other corporations, associations, or persons, is prohibited.[4]

§ 459. *Strikes and Boycotts.* — There is as yet no Constitutional provision relating to these matters. For injunctions, contempts, etc., see § 662.

§ 460. *Factories, Mines, etc.* — The Legislature are required to pass laws for the protection of miners[5] (as by escapement shafts, ventilation, etc.), or workmen in factories,[6] or employments dangerous to life and deleterious to health,[7] or on railroads.[8]

§ 461. *State Inspectors* of mines,[9] factories, etc., are in some States provided for in the Constitution.

§ 462. *Employers' Liability.* — (See also § 535.) The right of action to recover damages for injuries resulting in death, shall never be abrogated, and the amount recoverable shall not be subject to any statutory limitation.[10]

The defence of contributory negligence or of assumption of risk shall, in all cases whatsoever, be a question of fact, and shall, at all times, be left to the jury.[11]

37. Statutes to this effect are universal.

[1] Cal., N. C.

[2] Ida. 13, 6.

[3] La. 185; Tex. 16, 35.

[4] Utah 16, 4; N. D. 212; Wy. 1, 22.

[5] Ark. 19, 18; Col. 16, 2; Ida. 13, 2; Ill. 4, 29; Utah 16, 6; Wash. 2, 35; Wy. 9, 2; Okla. 23, 5. So, for their drainage (Col. 16, 3).

[6] Wash., Ida., Okla.

[7] Wash., Ida.

[8] Okla.

[9] Wy. 9, 1. See § 202.

[10] N. Y. 1, 18; Okla. 23, 7; Utah 16, 5; Wy. 10, 4. So, "for any injury to person or property caused by wilful failure to comply with the provisions of this article, or laws passed in pursuance hereof, a right of action shall accrue to the party injured, for the damage sustained thereby, and in all cases in this state, whenever the death of a person shall be caused by wrongful act, neglect or default, such as would, if death had not ensued, have entitled the party injured to maintain an action to recover damages in respect thereof, the person who, or the corporation which would have been liable, if death had not ensued, shall be liable to an action for damages notwithstanding the death of the person injured, and the legislature shall provide by law at its first session for the manner in which the right of action in respect thereto shall be enforced." In mines only (Wy. 9, 4).

[11] Okla. 23, 6.

Any provision of a contract, express or implied, made by any person, by which any of the benefits of this Constitution is sought to be waived, shall be null and void; and so of any such provision stipulating for notice or demand other than such as may be provided by law, as a condition precedent to establish any claim, demand, or liability.[1]

It shall be unlawful for any person, company, or corporation to require of its servants or employees, as a condition of their employment or otherwise, any contract or agreement whereby such persons, company, or corporation, shall be released or discharged from liability or responsibility on account of personal injuries received by such servants or employees while in the service of such person, company, or corporation, by reason of the negligence of such person, company, or corporation, or the agents or employees thereof; and such contracts shall be absolutely null and void.[2]

§ 463. *Prison Labor.* — All labor of convicts confined in the State's prison, shall be done within the prison grounds, except where the work is done on public works under the direct control of the State.[3] So the contracting out of prison labor is prohibited.[4]

§ 464. *Alien Labor.* — No person, not a citizen of the United States, or who has not declared his intention to become such, shall be employed upon, or in connection with, any State or municipal works.[5]

§ 465. *Arbitration.* — The Legislature may establish boards of arbitration, whose duty it shall be to hear and determine all differences and controversies between laborers and their employers which may be submitted to them in writing by all the parties.[6] Such boards of arbitration shall possess all the powers and authority in respect to administering oaths, subpœnaing witnesses, and compelling their attendance, preserving order during the sittings of the board, punishing for contempt, and requiring the production of papers and writings, and all other powers and privileges, in their nature applicable, conferred by law on justices of the peace.[7]

[1] Okla. 23, 8–9.

[2] Mon. 15, 16; Wy. 10, 4; 19, 1.

[3] Ida. 13, 3; Ky. 253; Utah 16, 3. The Legislature shall provide by general law for the working of public roads by contract or by county prisoners, or both. Such law may be put in operation only by a vote of the board of supervisors in those counties where it may be desirable (Miss. 85).

[4] Miss. 223; Okla. 23, 2; Utah 16, 3.

[5] Ida. 13, 5; Wy. 19, 1. Such provisions may, if a treaty exists, contravene the Federal Constitution.

[6] Ida. 13, 7; Wy. 19, 1.

[7] Ida. So, the Legislature shall provide by law for a Board of Labor, Conciliation and Arbitration, which shall fairly represent the interests of both

ARTICLE 50. PRIVATE CORPORATIONS

§ 500. *Definition.* — The word *corporation*, as here used, is declared by the Constitutions of many States to mean all associations or joint stock companies having any of the powers or privileges of corporations not possessed by individuals or partnerships.[1]

§ 501. *General Principles.* — All powers and franchises of corporations are derived from the people and are granted by their agent, the government, for the public good and general welfare, and the right and duty of the State to control and regulate them for these purposes is hereby declared. The power, rights, and privileges of any and all corporations may be forfeited by wilful neglect or abuse thereof. The police power of the State is supreme over all corporations as well as individuals.[2] (See § 506, also.) "Being creatures of the State endowed for the public good with a portion of its sovereign powers, they must be subject to its control."[3] The size and functions of all corporations should be so limited and regulated as to prevent fictitious capitalization, and provision should be made for the supervision and government thereof.[4] No exclusive privileges can be granted to a corporation.[5]

§ 502. *Creation.* — By the Constitutions of most States, the Legislature is forbidden, generally, to create corporations[6] or to

capital and labor. The Board shall perform duties, and receive compensation as prescribed by law (Utah 16, 2). By statute, such boards exist in many States.

[1] Ala. 241; Cal. 12, 4; Ida. 11, 16; Kan. 12, 6; Ky. 208; La. 268; Mich. 15, 11; Minn. 10, 1; Miss. 199; Mo. 12 11; Mon. 15, 18; N. Y. 8, 3; N. C. 8, 3; N. D. 144; Okla. 9, 1; Pa. 16, 13; S. C. 9, 1; S. D. 17, 19; Utah 12, 4; Va. 153; Wash. 12, 5. In Delaware (9, 4) nothing in the Constitution applies to religious corporations, whose rights remain unaltered except where therein otherwise provided. Oklahoma and Virginia except municipal corporations from this article and define the term *charter* and *license* — the latter term, in Virginia, referring to foreign corporations (§ 505).

[2] Wy. 10, 2.

[3] Wy. 1, 30.

[4] N. H. 2, 82.

[5] Io. 8, 12; Territories. See also § 16.

[6] Ala. 229; Ark. 12, 2; Cal. 12, 1 & 7; Col. 15, 2; Del. 9, 1; Fla. 1899, p. 1357; Ida. 11, 2; 3, 19; Ind. 11, 13; Ill. 11, 1; Io. 8, 1; Kan. 12, 1; La. 275; Me. 4, 3; Md. 3, 48; 1890, 195; Mich. 15, 1 & 8; Minn. 10, 2; Miss. 178, 179; Mo. 12, 2; Mon. 15, 2; Neb. 13, 1; Nev. 8, 1; N. J. 4, 7, 11; N. Y. 8, 1; N. C. 8, 1; N. D. 131; O. 13, 1; Okla. 9, 38; Ore. 11, 2; R. I. Amt. 9; S. C. 9, 2; S. D. 17, 1; Tex. 12, 1; Tenn. 11, 8; Utah 12, 1; Va. 154, 167; W. Va. 11, 1; Wash. 12, 1; 2, 28; Wis. 11, 1; Wy. 10, 1; Territories U. S. R. S. 1889; 1886, 818. In Rhode Island an exception is made of corporations created with the power to exercise the right of eminent domain or acquire franchises in the streets and highways, which *must* be created by special Act upon petition and notice according to law (§ 302).

license foreign corporations [1] by special act. (See also § 395.) Banking corporations may, however, in three States still be created by special act.[2]

So, the Legislature "shall provide by general laws" for the creation of municipal,[3] educational,[4] charitable, religious, and literary [5] corporations, or for manufacturing,[6] mechanical,[7] industrial,[8] mining,[9] agricultural,[10] draining,[11] "other useful companies," [12] or for the creation of corporations generally [13] (this last would follow from the principal provision above), or for conducting the business of insurance, banks of discount and deposits (but not of issue), loan, trust, and guaranty associations, railroads, wagon roads, irrigating ditches, the colonization and improvement of lands in connection therewith.[14] Nor can the Legislature by special act change or amend any franchise or charter (save as to corporations above excepted),[15] or remit the forfeiture of a charter now existing.[16]

The Legislature shall pass no law for the benefit of a railroad or other corporation (or any individual or association of individuals) retrospective in its operation, or which imposes on the people of any municipality a new liability in respect to transactions or considerations already past.[17]

In Delaware a general or special incorporation act must have a two-thirds vote of all the members elected in each house; in Rhode Island it must be continued to the next Legislature, and public

And in other States an exception is made of municipal corporations (Col., Del., Ida., La., Md., Me., Mich., Mon., Minn., N. C., N. D., Nev., N. Y., Ore., S. C., Tex., Wis., Territories U. S. 1878, 168) "which are under the control of the State" (Col., Ida., Mon., N. D.); of cases where there is no general act (Me., Md., N. C., N. Y., Wis.); of educational, charitable, penal, or reformatory corporations (Ark., Col., Del., Ida., Ill., Mo., Mon., Neb., N. D., S. C., S. D.); but such corporations if specially chartered must, except in Montana, be under State control. It will be noted that in the northern and eastern States the whole matter of corporations is left to the Legislature to determine by law; while the following States endeavor to cover the subject substantially in their Constitutions: Del., La., Ky., Ida., Mon., Okla., N. D., S. C., S. D., Utah, Wash., Va., Wy.

[1] Okla.

[2] Del., Ind., Md.

[3] Cal. 11, 6.

[4] Fla. 3, 25; Territories.

[5] Territories.

[6] Territories.

[7] Fla.

[8] Territories.

[9] Fla., Territories.

[10] Fla.

[11] Territories.

[12] Fla.

[13] Ala., Miss., N. D., S. C., S. D., Va.

[14] Territories.

[15] Ala., Cal., Col., Del., Ida., Ill., La., Mich., Miss., Mo., Mon., Neb., Nev., S. C., S. D., Utah, Va., Wash. And see §§ 503, 395.

[16] Ala.; Cal.; La. 262; Miss.; Mo. 12, 3; Mon.; N. D. 13, 3; S. C. 9, 17; S. D. 17, 3; Utah; Wash. See, however, § 503.

[17] Col. 15, 12; Ida. 11, 12; Mo. 12, 19; Mon. 15, 13.

notice given of its pendency.[1] No law can create, renew, or expend the charter of more than one corporation.[2] In Georgia the Legislature has *no* power to create private corporations, but shall prescribe the manner in which such powers shall be exercised by the Secretary of State.[3] So in Virginia, charters are granted by the Corporation Commission (see § 532, note 6).[4]

§ 503. *Repeal.* — And all general [5] or even special [6] laws for the creation of corporations may be altered or repealed. So (see also § 16), no law shall be passed granting irrevocably any franchise, privilege, or immunity.[7] But in Arizona no corporation can be dissolved or its rights impaired except by judicial proceedings.[8] In others, the Legislature shall by general law provide for the revocation or forfeiture of the charters of all corporations for the abuse, misuse, or nonuser of their corporate powers, privileges, or franchises, any procedure for such forfeiture, etc., to be taken by the attorney-general.[9] All privileges or franchises, and rights to collect freights, fares, tolls, or wharfage are subject to control.[10] But they are not to be repealed, etc., so as to impair or destroy vested corporate rights,[11] or work injustice to the corporators or the corporation's creditors.[12] In Iowa and Michigan such repeal, etc., must have a vote of two-thirds present [13] or elected[14] in each house of the Legislature. All corporations must organize and commence business within two years of the charter, etc., or it becomes void.[15]

§ 504. *Existing Corporations.* — Some newer State Constitutions specifically provide that no general or special law,[16] or no exemption

[1] Del. 9, 1; R. I. 4, 17.

[2] S. D. 17, 9.

[3] Ga. 3, 7, 18; Amt. 1891, p. 59.

[4] Va. 156.

[5] Ala. 229, 238; Ark. 12, 6; Cal. 11, 6; 12, 1; Col. 15, 3; Ga. 1, 3, 3; 12, 1, 5; Ida. 11, 2 & 3; 12, 1; Io. 8, 12; Kan. 12, 1; Me. 4, 3, 14; Md. 3, 48 (except banks); Miss. 88, 178; Mon. 15, 3; Mich. 15, 1; N. J. 4, 7, 11; N. Y. 8, 1; Nev. 8, 1; Neb. 13, 1; N. C. 8, 1; N. D. 131; O. 13, 2; Okla. 9, 47; Ore. 112; Pa. 16, 10; S. C. 9, 2; S. D. 17, 9; Tenn. 11, 8; Utah 12, 1; Va. 154; Wash. 12, 1; Wy. 10, 1; Wis. 11, 1. See also § 394. But only by general law: Del., Me., N. D., S. C. Compare § 502.

[6] Ark., Del., Md., Me., Miss., Mon., Nev., N. Y., N. C., Okla., Ore., Pa., S. D., Utah, Wash., Wis., Wy. And so doubtless in the others.

[7] Ala. 22; Ky. 3; S. D. 6, 12; Utah 1, 23; Wash. 1, 8. For other States see § 16, notes 1 & 2.

[8] Ariz.* B. Rts. 29.

[9] Del. 9, 1; Ky. 205; Va. 154.

[10] Tex. 1, 17; 12, 5. See also §§ 416, 501, 506.

[11] Ga., Ore., Tenn.

[12] Ala., Ark., Col., Ga., Ida., Miss., Okla., Pa., S. D. (as to corporations existing when the Constitution was adopted). These provisions would seem meaningless.

[13] Io. 8, 12.

[14] Mich. 15, 8.

[15] Miss. 180.

[16] Ala. 231; Ark. 17, 8; Ga. 4, 2, 3; Ida. 11, 7; Ky. 190; La. 262; Md. 1890,

or remission of forfeiture,[1] or renewal or extension,[2] or alteration or amendment [3] of a charter shall be enacted except on condition that any corporation availing itself of it shall thereafter hold its charter subject to the provisions of the Constitution. So, no corporation can do business until it accepts the Constitution.[4] The acceptance of any amendment usually brings the corporation under the general law.[5] These restrictions do not of course apply to municipal corporations.[6]

Existing charters or grants of special or exclusive privileges under which a *bona fide* organization had not taken place at the time of the adoption of the Constitution, or twelve months thereafter,[7] are declared void.[8] The property and franchises of corporations are subject to eminent domain like that of individuals.[9]

§ 505. *Foreign Corporations.* — Several States provide that no corporation organized out of the State shall be allowed to transact business within the State which is forbidden to domestic corporations,[10] or, on more favorable conditions than are prescribed by law to similar corporations organized in the State.[11] But such companies may be licensed, or taxed, on a different principle from home corporations,[12] so it be uniform, or other conditions may be imposed.[13] No foreign corporation can condemn land,[14] or conduct the business of a public service corporation within the State.[15] They must usually

p. 195; Miss. 179; N. D. 133; Okla. 9, 11; Pa. 16, 2; S. C. 9, 17; S. D. 17, 3; Utah 12, 2. This is applied specifically also to railroads: Ala. 246; Col. 15, 7; Mo. 12, 21; Mon. 15, 8; Tex. 10, 8; Wy. 10, 6; or express or transportation companies: Mon., Wy. Or telegraph: Wy.

[1] Ala., La., Md., Miss., N. D., S. C., S. D.

[2] Del. 9, 2; La.; Mich. 15, 8; Va. 158.

[3] Ala., Del., La., Miss., N. D., S. C., S. D., Va.

[4] Wy. 10, 5; 10, 10 (6).

[5] Md., Miss., Okla., S. C.

[6] Ida., Mich.

[7] Ala. 230; Miss. 180.

[8] Ark. 12, 1; Col. 15, 1; Ida. 11, 1; Ill. 11, 2; Ky. 191; Mo. 12, 1; Mon. 15, 1; N. D. 132; Neb. 13, 6; Okla. 9, 46; Pa. 16, 1; S. D. 17, 2; S. C. 9, 16; Utah 12, 2; Wash. 12, 2; Wy. 10, 3; W. Va. 11, 3.

[9] Va. 159. For other States see § 97.

[10] Okla. 9, 44; Va. 163.

[11] Ark. 12, 11; Cal. 12, 15; Ida. 11, 10; Ky. 202; Mon. 15, 11; Okla.; Va.; Utah 12, 6; Wash. 12, 7. No point of constitutional law is more vexed than this. Does a foreign corporation come into a State with all its charter powers, or only such as the State law permits its own corporations? It is clear that a State may by express statute exclude such corporation entirely. Otherwise, the better opinion is that a definite prohibition of such powers, or a clear line of policy forbidding such corporations of its own creation, will also suffice so to limit or exclude foreign companies.

[12] Ark. 12, 11; La. 242.

[13] Okla. 9, 44; Va.

[14] Ark.

[15] Va.

file a copy of their charter, etc., with the Secretary of State,[1] or other official. In Virginia no foreign corporation can do business in the State until it has obtained a license from the corporation commission.[2] In Texas no such corporation except a national bank can do banking or discounting business in the State.[3]

§ 506. *Business, Ultra Vires, etc.* — All corporations doing business in a State may as to such business be regulated, limited, or restrained by law[4] (see also § 503); so, the police power of the State shall never be so abridged or construed as to permit corporations to conduct their business in such manner as to infringe the equal rights of individuals or the general well-being of the State.[5] No corporation can engage in any business other than that expressly authorized by its charter or the law under which it was formed:[6] and not in more than one line of business.[7]

"The Legislature shall provide for the protection of the employees of all corporations doing business in the State from interference with their social, civil or political rights by said corporations or their agents or employees."[8]

§ 507. *Office in the State, Reports, etc.* — A few State Constitutions provide that railroads,[9] or all business corporations[10] doing business in the State must have an office in the State for the transaction of business, where transfers of stock may be made and the stock books shall be kept open. They must file a list of officers and stockholders with the Corporation Commission showing addresses and amount of stock held by each.[11]

And foreign corporations in particular must have an authorized office and agent in the State upon whom process may be served.[12]

Failure to pay franchise taxes or make reports for two successive

[1] Ala. 232; Utah 12, 9. See § 507.

[2] Va. 157.

[3] Tex. 1903, p. 249.

[4] Utah, 12, 1; Wash. 12, 1; Wy. 10, 1.

[5] Cal. 12, 8; Col. 15, 8; Ga. 4, 2, 2; Ida. 11, 8; Ky. 195; La. 263; Miss. 190; Mo. 12, 5; Mon. 15, 9; N. D. 134; Pa. 16, 3; S. D. 17, 4; Va. 159.

[6] Ala. 233; Cal. 12, 9; Ky. 192; La. 265; Mo. 12, 7; N. D. 137; Pa. 16, 6; S. C. 9, 12; S. D. 17, 7; Utah, 12, 10; Wy. 10, 6. This is but the common law.

[7] Wy.

[8] Miss. 191.

[9] Ark. 17, 2; Ill. 11, 9; La. 273; Mo. 12, 15; Neb. 11, 1; N. D. 140; Pa. 17, 2; S. D. 17, 12; Tex. 10, 3.

[10] Cal. 12, 14; Ky. 194; La. 264; Mon. 15, 11; S. C. 9, 4; Utah 12, 9. (*Except* mercantile corporations: S. C.) And so of canals (Ark. Pa.); turnpikes (Ark.); banks (Kan. 13, 6.)

[11] Okla. 9, 43.

[12] Ark. 12, 11; Ala. 232; Col. 15, 10; Del. 9, 5; Ida. 11, 10; Ill.; Ky.; La.; Mon.; N. D. 136; Okla.; S. C.; S. D. 17, 6; Utah.

years operates a revocation or annulment of its charter, or, if a foreign corporation, its license (§ 505).[1]

§ 508. *Suits.* — All corporations may sue and be sued in the courts like natural persons.[2] Suits may be brought against a foreign corporation in any county where it does business,[3] and service be made on an agent anywhere within the State.[4] Every license or charter granted to a mining or public service corporation, foreign or domestic, shall stipulate that it will submit any difference with its employees to arbitration as shall be provided by law.[5]

§ 509. *Liabilities of Stockholders.* — (For banks, see § 555.) The Constitutions of several States provide that stockholders shall in no case be liable otherwise than for unpaid stock owned by them;[6] so, each stockholder is liable for the amount of stock held or owned by him.[7] In Nevada no stockholder is individually liable for the debts of the corporation.[8]

But in a few he is liable over and above his stock to a further sum equal in amount to such stock;[9] in California, for his aliquot share for all the debts and liabilities of the corporation;[10] and in Michigan he is individually liable for all labor performed for the corporation or association.[11]

In others, dues from corporations or their stockholders are to be secured in a manner provided by law.[12]

Trust Funds. — No act of the Legislative Assembly shall authorize the investment of trust funds by executors, administrators, guardians, or trustees in the bonds or stock of any private corporation.[13]

§ 510. *Voting.* — Stockholders have one vote for each share, for each person to be elected, by person or by proxy,[14] and may cumulate their votes on one candidate or distribute them as they see

[1] Va. 157.

[2] Ala. 240; Cal. 12, 4; Kan. 12, 6, Mich. 15, 11; Minn. 10, 1; Mon. 15, 18; Neb. 13, 3; Nev. 8, 5; N. Y. 8, 3; N. C. 8, 3; Utah 12, 4; Wash. 12, 5.

[3] Ala. 232; Cal. 12, 16.

[4] Ala., Okla. Or in the county of the plaintiff's residence or where the cause of action arose (Okla.).

[5] Okla. 9, 42. A striking clause.

[6] Ala. 236; Ida. 11, 17; O. Amt. 1902, p. 961; S. C. 9, 18; Wash. 12, 4. *Except* banking, or insurance companies (Wash.).

[7] Minn. 10, 3 (except in mechanical or manufacturing companies).

[8] Nev. 8, 3.

[9] Kan. Amt. 1905, 542; Utah 12, 18; Wash. 12, 11 (of banks, insurance, and joint stock companies); S. C. 9, 18 (of banks). *Except* in railway corporations (Kan.).

[10] Cal. 12, 3.

[11] Mich. 15, 7.

[12] Ala.; Cal. 12, 2; Ida. 11, 17; Ind. 11, 14; Kan.; Mon. 15, 19; Mo.; Nev.; N. C. 8, 2; Tex. 12, 2.

[13] Ala. 74; Mon. 5, 37; Wy. 3, 38.

[14] Cal.; Ida. 11, 4; Ill. 11, 3; Ky. 207; Miss. 194; Mon. 15, 4; Mo. 12, 6; N. D. 135; Neb. 13, 5; S. C. 9, 11; S. D. 17, 5; W. Va. 11, 4.

fit.[1] But no person engaged or interested in a competing business, either as director, stockholder, or individually, may so be elected without a majority stock vote.[2]

§ 511. *Directors are liable* jointly and severally to creditors and stockholders for moneys embezzled or misappropriated by officers of the corporation during their term of office.[3]

§ 512. *Issue of Stock.* — The usual constitutional provision is that no corporation may issue stock or bonds except for money, labor done, or money or property actually received; [4] and all fictitious increase of stock or indebtedness shall be void.[5] In a few States stock can only be issued to actual subscribers therefor.[6] Whenever any issue of stock or bonds is made the corporation must file a detailed statement of the plans, payments, etc., of such issue with the Corporation Commission.[7]

§ 513. *Increases of Stock* may only be made under general laws with the consent of a majority of the stock,[8] given at a special meeting after due notice [9] (usually thirty [10] or sixty [11] days).

And the same law applies in a few State Constitutions to an increase of bonded indebtedness.[12]

[1] Cal.; Ida.; Ill.; Ky.; Miss.; Mon.; Mo.; N.D.; Neb.; Pa. 16, 4; S. C.; S. D.; W. Va.

[2] Miss.

[3] Cal. 12, 3.

[4] Ala. 234; Ark. 12, 8; Cal. 12, 11; Col. 15, 9; Del. 9, 3; 1901, 1; Ida. 11, 9; Ky. 193; La. 266; Mo. 12, 8; Mon. 15, 10; N. D. 138; Okla. 9, 39; Pa. 16, 7; S. D. 17, 8; Tex. 12, 6; Utah 12, 5. So in others, of railroads only: Ill. 11, 13; Neb. 11, 5; S. C. 9, 10; Miss. 196; Wash. 12, 6; or "transportation companies" (Miss.). Such money or property must further be applied to the purposes for which the corporation was created, and not be received at greater value than the market price (Ky.).

[5] Ark., Ala., Cal., Col., Ida., Ill., Ky., La., Miss., Mo., Mon., Neb., N. D., Okla., Pa., S. C., S. D., Tex., Utah, Wash. And the corporation issuing it forfeits its charter (La.).

[6] Utah, Wash.

[7] "The Legislature shall enact general laws regulating and controlling all issues of stock and bonds by corporations. Whenever stock or bonds are to be issued by a corporation, it must file with the State Corporation Commission a sworn statement setting forth fully and accurately the basis, or financial plan upon which such stock or bonds are to be issued; and where such plan includes services or property (other than money), received or to be received, it must accurately specify and describe, in the manner prescribed by the Commission, the services and property, together with the valuation at which the same are to be received" (Va. 167).

[8] Ala. 234; Ark. 12, 8; Cal. 12, 11; Col. 15, 9; Ida. 11, 10; La. 267; Mon.; Mo. 12, 8; Okla. 9, 38; Pa. 16, 7; S. D. 17, 8; Utah; Wash.; Va. 167. In others the restriction only applies to railroads (Ill. 11, 13; Neb. 11, 5).

[9] Okla., Utah, Wash.

[10] Ala., Col., La.

[11] Ark., Cal., Ida., Ill., Mo., Mon., Neb., N. D., Pa., S. D.

[12] Ala., N. D., Okla., S. D.

§ 514. *Preferred stock* cannot be issued without the consent of two thirds,[1] or even all,[2] of the stockholders.

§ 515. *Time.* — A few State Constitutions limit the duration of corporations to thirty,[3] or ninety-nine [4] years.

§ 516. *Real Estate* may be held by any corporation, usually such as it actually occupies in the exercise of its franchises,[5] or as is necessary and proper for the carrying on of its legitimate business.[6] Otherwise no corporation may hold land for more than a limited period of time.[7] The Mississippi Constitution simply provides that the Legislature may limit or restrict the acquiring or holding of land by corporations.[8]

§ 517. *Assignment of Franchise.* — Western States provide that the Legislature shall pass no law permitting the leasing or alienation of any franchise so as to relieve it or the property held thereunder from the liabilities of the lessor or grantor, lessee or grantee, contracted or incurred in the operation and use of such franchise or any of its privileges.[9]

§ 518. *Consolidation, Combination, etc.* (see also Article 58). — In Georgia the strict principle is laid down that the Legislature may not authorize any corporation to buy shares or stock in any other corporation in the States or elsewhere, or to make any contract or agreement with such corporation with the effect or purpose of lessening competition or encouraging monopoly, and all such contracts etc., are void.[10] In Oklahoma, it may not own stock in any corporation engaged in the same line of business, or competitive, unless pledged, etc., and then it may not be voted and must be sold within a year.[11]

So, no incorporated company, or any association of persons or stock company in the State shall directly or indirectly combine or make any contract with any other incorporated company, foreign or domestic, through their stockholders or the trustees or assignees of such stockholders, or in any manner whatsoever for the purpose of fixing the price or regulating the production of any article of commerce or of produce of the soil, or of consumption by the people,

[1] Ala. 237.

[2] Mo. 12, 10.

[3] Mich. 15, 10 (except railroads, plankroads, and canals).

[4] Miss. 178.

[5] Mich. 15, 12.

[6] Cal. 12, 9; Ky. 192; La. 265; Mo. 12, 7; S. D. 17, 7.

[7] Thus, five years (Cal., Ky.), six years (Mo.), or ten years (La., Mich.).

[8] Miss. 84.

[9] Cal. 12, 10; Ida. 11, 15; Ky. 203; Mon. 15, 17; Utah 12, 7; Wash. 12, 8.

[10] Ga. 4, 2, 4.

[11] Okla. 9, 41.

and the Legislature are required to pass laws for the enforcement thereof, by adequate penalties, to the extent, if necessary for that purpose, of the forfeiture of their property and franchise,[1] and, if foreign corporations, prohibiting them from carrying on business in the State.[2] (See § 581.)

"No corporation, company, person, or association of persons in the State shall directly combine or form what is known as a trust."[3]

"Monopolies and trusts shall never be allowed in this State."[4] So, "the Legislature shall enact laws preventing" such combinations, etc.[5] (See § 581.)

"There shall be no consolidation or combination of corporations of any kinds whatever to prevent competition, to control or influence productions or prices thereof, or in any manner to interfere with the public good and general welfare."[6]

"No person, corporation, etc., engaged in the production, manufacture, distribution, or sale of any commodity in general use shall for the purpose of creating a monopoly or destroying competition discriminate between different persons or corporations, or different sections, communities, or cities, by selling at a lower rate in one than in another, allowance made for the difference if any in the grade, quantity, or quality, and in the actual cost of transportation from the point of production or manufacture."[7]

§ 519. *Taxation of Corporations.* — (See § 330.) By the Virginia Constitution,[8] provision shall be made by general laws for the payment of a fee by every domestic corporation, upon the granting, amendment, or extension of its charter, and by every foreign corporation upon obtaining a license to do business; and also for an annual registration fee of from $5 to $25, irrespective of other taxes, upon every corporation for the privilege of carrying on its business in the State (and this seems to apply to foreign corporations as well), and upon failure to pay the tax for two years the license to do business is revoked or the charter annulled.

"The Legislature shall, by general law, provide for the payment to the State of a franchise tax by corporations organized under the

[1] Ida. 11, 18; Mon. 15, 20; S. D. 17, 20; Wash. 12, 22. Or "regulating the transportation thereof" (Mon., S. D., Wash.).

[2] Mon.

[3] Mon.

[4] S. D., Wash.

[5] Ala. 103; Ky. 198; La. 190; Miss. 198; N. H. 2, 82; Okla. 5, 44; S. C. 9, 13; Va. 165. See Art. 58.

[6] Wy. 10, 8.

[7] Okla. 9, 45.

[8] Va. 157.

laws of this State, which shall be in proportion to the amount of capital stock; and for the payment of a franchise tax by foreign corporations, but such franchise tax shall be based on the actual amount of capital employed by this State. Strictly benevolent, educational or religious corporations shall not be required to pay such a tax.[1] In other States corporations are taxed on their property in like manner as individuals.[2]

"The word property as used in this article is hereby declared to include moneys, credits, bonds, stocks, franchises, and all matters and things (real, personal, and mixed), capable of private ownership, but this shall not be construed so as to authorize the taxation of the stocks of any company or corporation when the property of such company or corporation represented by such stocks is within the State and has been taxed."[3] (See § 331.)

Shares of stock of Delaware corporations "owned by persons or corporations without the State shall not be subject to taxation by any law now existing or hereafter to be made."[4]

Article 52. Railroads

(See, for General Provisions, Article 50.)

§ 520. *Highways.* — The Constitutions of many States declare all railroads to be public highways;[5] and so, in a few, canals[6] or turnpikes;[7] and "free to all persons for the transportation of their persons or property thereon under the regulations prescribed by law."[8]

§ 521. *Carriers.* — And these State Constitutions usually, with others, declare railroads to be common carriers,[9] and so also of canal,[10] pipe line,[11] express,[12] telegraph and telephone,[13] or other transportation companies,[14] or sleeping cars.[15]

[1] Ala. 232.

[2] Miss. 181; Fla. 16, 16. See also § 330.

[3] Mon. 12, 17; Utah 13, 2.

[4] Del. 9, 6.

[5] Ala. 242; Ark. 17, 1; Col. 15, 4; Ill. 11, 12; Ida. 11, 15; La. 272; Miss. 184; Mo. 12, 14; Mon. 15, 5; Neb. 11, 4; N. D. 142; Okla. 9, 6; Pa. 17, 1; S. D. 17, 15; Tex. 10, 2; W. Va. 11, 9; Wy. 10, 10 (2).

[6] Ala., Ark., Pa.

[7] Ark.

[8] Ark. 17, 3; Col. 15, 6; Ill.; Neb.; W. Va.

[9] Ala.; Ark. 17, 1; Cal. 12, 17; Col. 15, 4; Ida. 11, 5; La.; Miss. 184, 195; Mo.; Mon.; N. D. 142; Pa.; S. C. 9, 3; S. D.; Tex.; Utah 12, 12; Wash. 12, 13, and 19; Wy. 10, 7.

[10] Ala., Ark., Cal., Ida., Mon., Pa., S. C., Wash.

[11] Okla., Wy.

[12] Ala., Ida., Mon., Miss., N. D., S. C., Wy.

[13] Ala.; Ky. 199; Miss.; Mon.; S. C.; Wash.; Wy.

[14] Ala., Cal., Ida., Miss., Mon., N. D., S. C., S. D., Utah, Wash., Wy.

[15] Ida., Miss.

And as such they are subject to legislative control,[1] taxation,[2] and liability,[3] which last can never be limited by law, nor shall a carrier be permitted to contract himself out of it.[4]

In Oklahoma and Virginia this applies to all public service corporations; and the terms "transmission" and "transportation" company are defined.

§ 522. *Legislative Control.* — The newer State Constitutions give the legislature express power to make laws establishing reasonable maximum rates of fare and freight,[5] or generally to control or regulate the rates within the State.[6] In other States, to correct abuses and prevent unjust discrimination or extortion.[7] This power may never be surrendered nor abridged.[8] In a few, this power is or may be given to the railroad [9] or corporation commission.[10] And it extends also to transportation,[11] steamboat,[12] express,[13] or "transmission" (telegraph and telephone) companies,[14] canals,[15] or pipe lines.[16] But always with appeal to the courts; [17] and the rate fixed stands, pending appeal.[18] In Oklahoma the Constitution requires a two-cent rate for passengers, unless the corporation commission exempt a railroad because unable at that rate to earn a "just compensation." [19]

In California, a railroad, having once lowered its rates to compete with another carrier, cannot put them up again without the consent of the railroad commissioners.[20]

§ 523. *Short-Haul Clause.* — By a few State Constitutions no railroad may charge, for freight or passengers, a greater amount for a less distance than a greater, in the same direction,[21] of which

[1] Cal.; Ida.; Ky.; Miss. 186; Mon.; N. D.; S. D.; Utah; Va. 164; Wash.

[2] S. C.

[3] S. C.

[4] Ky. 196; Neb.; S. C.

[5] Ala. 243; Ill. 11, 12; Ida. 11, 5; Mich. 19 A, 1; Mo. 12, 14; Neb. 11, 4; Tex. 10, 2; Wash. 12, 18; Utah 12, 15; W. Va. 11, 9; Va. 158.

[6] Mon. 15, 5; N. D. 142; S. D. 17, 15; Va. 164; S. C. 9, 13.

[7] Ark. 17, 10, 1897, p. 92; Ala. 243; Fla. 16, 30; Ill. 11, 15; Ky. 196; Ga. 4, 2, 1; Miss. 186; Mo. 12, 14; Neb. 11, 7; N. D.; Tex. 10, 2; Utah; Wash.; W. Va. 11, 9; S. C. 9, 13; S. D. 17, 17.

[8] Va. It may be enforced if necessary by forfeiture of the franchise (S. C.).

[9] Cal. 12, 22; Ky. 209; Tex. 1889, p. 171. See § 532.

[10] Neb. 1905, 233; Okla. 9, 4; S. C., 9, 13; Va. (subject to the paramount authority of the Legislature).

[11] Ida., Miss.

[12] Ky.

[13] Ida., Miss.

[14] Okla., Va.

[15] Ala., Ark.

[16] Okla. So, all public service companies: Fla., Okla., Va.

[17] N. D., Okla., Va.

[18] N. D., Okla., Va. See § 532.

[19] Okla. 9, 37.

[20] Cal. 12, 20.

[21] Ark. 17, 3; Cal. 12, 21; Ida. 11, 6; Ky. 218; Mo. 12, 12; Mon. 15, 7; Okla. 9, 30; Pa. 17, 3; S. C. 9, 5; Wash. 12, 15; Va. 160.

the lesser is part; and as to freight, etc., of the same class.[1] But the railroad commission may make order exempting from this condition,[2] as at competitive points,[3] etc. In Oklahoma and Virginia this principle applies to both transportation or "transmission" companies.

§ 524. *Discrimination.* — Besides the general prohibition of § 522, we find a usual constitutional provision that no (undue or unreasonable [4]) discrimination in charges or facilities for transportation shall be made by any railroad [5] between places or persons, or in the facilities for the transportation of the same classes of freight or passengers,[6] or by abatement, drawback, rebate,[7] etc.

All individuals, associations, and corporations similarly situated, shall have equal rights to have persons or property transported on and over any railroad, transportation, or express route in this State [8] (except that preference may be given to perishable property [9]), and to employees and ministers.[10]

No railroad, express, or transportation company, nor any lessee, manager, or other employee thereof, shall give any preference to any individual, association, or corporation, in furnishing cars or motive power,[11] or for the transportation of money or other express matter.[12]

All railway lines shall receive, load, unload, transport, haul, deliver, and handle freight of the same class for all persons, associations, or corporations from and to the same points and upon the same conditions, in the same manner and for the same charges, and for the same method of payment.[13]

No railway, transfer, belt line, or railway bridge company

[1] Expressed in a few, but doubtless implied in all. "This section shall not prevent the Railroad Commission from making such competitive rates as shall, in their judgment, be just and equitable between the railroads and the public, at all junctional and competitive points or at points where water competition controls the traffic, or at points where the competition of points located in other States may make necessary the prescribing of different rates for the protection of the commerce of this State." (S. C.) So, substantially, in Oklahoma.

[2] Okla., Ky., S. C., Va.

[3] Okla., Va.

[4] Ark.; Cal.; Col.; Ida. 11, 6.

[5] Or transportation (Ida.; La. 286; Mon. 15, 7; S. C. 9, 5; Wash. 12, 15; canal (Pa.); express (Ida., Mon.); turnpike (Ark.); or transmission (telegraph, etc.) company (S. C.; Va.).

[6] Ark.; Cal. 12, 21; Col.; Ida.; La.; Mon.; Pa. 17, 3; S. C.; Wash.

[7] Ala. 245; Cal.; Ida.; Mon.; Pa.; S. C.; Wash.

[8] Ida. 11, 6; Mon. 15, 7.

[9] Ida.

[10] Wy. 10, 2.

[11] Ark. 17, 6; Col. 15, 6; Ida.; Mo. 12, 23; Mon.; Pa. 17, 7.

[12] Ida., Mon.

[13] Ky. 215.

shall make any exclusive or preferential contract or arrangement with any individual, association, or corporation for the receipt, transfer, delivery, transportation, handling, care, or custody of any freight, or for the conduct of any business as a common carrier.[1]

The Legislature shall pass laws against abuses, discrimination, and excessive charges by railroads, canals, and turnpike companies for freight or passengers.[2]

"No rebate or bonus shall be paid, directly or indirectly, or any act done which shall mislead the public as to the real rates charged or received for freight or passage."[3] (See also § 435.)

Common carrier corporations, enjoying a right of way, shall carry the productions of the country on equal terms.[4]

§ 525. *Passes, Commutations, etc.* — But excursion or commutation tickets may be issued at reduced rates[5] and charitable service rendered free of cost.[6]

Free passes, or reduced rates, to State officials or members of the Legislature are in a few States forbidden by the Constitution;[7] and so to anybody, except officers or employees,[8] or ministers.[9] Acceptance of such a pass causes forfeiture of the office.[10]

§ 526. *Connections.* — In many States railroad companies are given a constitutional right to connect with or cross any other;[11] to construct and operate its railroad between any designated points

[1] Ky. 214. So in Washington (12, 21): "Railroad companies now or hereafter organized or doing business in this State, shall allow all express companies organized or doing business in this State, transportation over all lines of railroad owned or operated by such railroad companies upon equal terms with any other express company, and no railroad corporation organized or doing business in this State shall allow any express corporation or company any facilities, privileges, or rates for transportation of men or materials or property carried by them, or for doing the business of such express companies, not allowed to all express companies."

[2] Ark. 1897, p. 92; Ky. 196; Utah 12, 15; Wash. 12, 18. Compare § 522.

[3] Ga. 4, 2, 5.

[4] Minn. 10, 4.

[5] Ark.; Cal.; Ida.; La. 287; Mo.; Mon.; Okla. 9, 30; Pa.; S. C.; Wash.

[6] La., Okla.

[7] Ala. 244; Ark. 17, 7; Cal. 12, 19; Mo. 12, 24; Ky. 197; La. 191; Fla. 16, 31; Miss. 188; Okla. 9, 2; Wash. 2, 39; 12, 20; N. Y. 13, 5; Va. 161. And so as to steamboats (La., Ky.); telegraph or telephone (La., N. Y., Va.); or any public service corporation or common carrier (Ky., La.).

[8] Okla. 9, 13; Pa. 17, 8; La. 287.

[9] La., Okla.

[10] Ala., Cal., Ky., La., Mo., N. Y., Va.; Wis. 1901, 437. It is made a crime (Okla.).

[11] Ala. 242; Ark. 17, 1; Cal. 12, 17; Col. 15, 4; Ida. 11, 5; Ky. 216; La. 271; Miss. 184; Mo. 12, 13; Mon. 15, 5; N. D. 143; Okla. 9, 2; Pa. 16, 12; S. C. 9, 6; S. D. 17, 16; Tex. 10, 1; Va. 166; Wash. 12, 13; Wy. 10, 10 (1). "In such a manner as to transfer cars" (Ky., Wash.).

within the State [1] and to connect with railroads of other States at the State line.[2]

And in several States this principle is extended to telegraph or telephone [3] companies and canals.[4] Any such company must receive and transport the passengers and freight [5] (or even the cars, loaded or empty [6]), of such other company without delay or discrimination.

A railway must deliver grain at any elevator or warehouse which can be reached by its tracks and allow other warehouses or coal-banks to make connection.[7]

§ 527. *Consolidations and Combinations.* — Most State Constitutions provide that no railroad may consolidate with a competing or parallel line,[8] or acquire it by purchase, lease, or otherwise,[9] or own or control its stock,[10] or pool its earnings with it,[11] or operate it; [12] nor may the officers of one act as the officers of the other.[13]

In two States no railroad may consolidate with another organized in another State.[14] In other States it may do so, but will still be liable to the home jurisdiction.[15]

Nor shall any railroad company or other common carrier combine or make any contract with the owners of any vessel that leaves or makes port in this State, or with any common carrier, by which combination or contract the earnings of one doing the carrying are to be shared by the other not doing the carrying.[16]

Notice of a proposed consolidation must be given to all the stockholders of both roads,[17] usually sixty days.[18] An attempt to evade

[1] Ida., Miss., Mon., N. D., Okla., S. D., Wash., Wy.

[2] Ida., Miss., Mon., N. D., Okla., S. D., S. C., Wash., Wy.

[3] Ala., Col., Pa., Okla., S. C.

[4] Ala.

[5] Ark.; Ala.; Cal.; Ky. 213; La.; Mich. 19 A, 1; Miss.; Mo.; N. D.; Okla.; Pa.; S. C.; S. D.; Tex.; Utah 12, 12; Va.; Wash.; Wy.

[6] Okla., S. C., Va.

[7] Ill. 13, 5.

[8] Ark. 17, 4; Col. 15, 5 and 13; Ill. 11, 11; Ky. 201; Mich. 19 A, 2; Mo. 12, 17; Mon. 15, 6 & 7 & 14; Neb. 11, 3; N. D. 141; Okla. 9, 8; Pa. 16, 12; S. C. 9, 7; S. D. 17, 14; Tex. 10, 5; Utah 12, 13; Wash. 12, 16; W. Va. 11, 11. And so of telegraph companies (Ala. 239; Col.; Ky.; Neb.; Pa.; S. C.; S. D. 17, 11); telephone (Ala., Ky., Mon.); canals (Ark., Pa.); bridges (Ky.); express (Mon.); common carrier (Ky.); or transportation (Mon., S. C.); or "any other corporation" (Mon.). Any public service company (Okla.). And it applies also to corporations of other States, or of the United States, having lines in the State (Okla.).

[9] Ark., Mo., Okla., Pa., S. C., Tex., W. Va.

[10] Okla., S. C. 9, 19.

[11] Ky., Mon.

[12] Ky., Mon.

[13] Ark., Mo., Mon., Okla., Pa., Tex.

[14] Okla. 9, 9; Tex. 10, 6; S. C. 9, 8.

[15] Col. 15, 14; Ida. 11, 14; Ky. 200; La. 274; Mo. 12, 18; Mon. 15, 11. And so of telegraph (Col., Ky., Ida., Mon.); telephone (La.); express (Ky., Ida., Mon.); transportation (Mon.); or any other corporation (Ky., Ida.).

[16] Cal. 12, 20; Ky. 201; Wash. 12, 14.

[17] Ill., Mich., Neb., N. D., Mo., S. D.

[18] La., N. D., S. D.

the provisions of this section, by lease or otherwise, forfeits the charter.[1] The question whether the roads are parallel or competing is one of fact, to be determined by a jury.[2] The provisions of this article may not be evaded by holding companies, control of stock, etc.[3]

§ 528. *The Rolling Stock* and movable property of railroads are declared to be personal property; and the Legislature may pass no law exempting it from execution,[4] or ordinary direct taxation.[5] And so its earnings are subject to ordinary attachment or trustee process.[6]

§ 529. *Location.* — No railroad, etc., organized in another State can exercise the right of eminent domain or acquire land or right of way until duly incorporated in the State.[7] (See also §§ 505, 538.)

No railroad company shall construct or operate a railroad within four miles of any existing town or city without providing a suitable depot or stopping place at the nearest practical point for the convenience of said town or city, and stopping all trains doing local business at said stopping place. No railroad company shall deviate from the most direct practical line in constructing a railroad for the purpose of avoiding the provisions of this section.[8] Proper depots must be maintained for freight and passengers; and protecting devices at grade crossings.[9]

The exclusive right to build or operate railroads parallel to its own or any other line of railroad shall not be granted to any company.[10]

§ 530. *Office and Officers, Reports, etc.* — "Every railroad corporation organized or doing business in this State under the laws or authority thereof shall have and maintain a public office or place

[1] N. D., S. D.

[2] Ark., Mo., Pa., S. C.

[3] Nothing prohibited in this Article shall be permitted to be done by any corporation or company, persons or person, either for its or their own benefit or otherwise, by its or their holding or controlling in its or their own name or otherwise, or in the name of any other person or persons, or other corporation or company whatsoever, a majority of the capital stock, or of bonds having voting power, of any railroad or transportation company, or corporation created by or existing under the laws of this State, or doing business within this State (S. C. 9, 19).

[4] Ark. 17, 11; Ill. 11, 10; Ky. 212; Miss. 185; Mo. 2, 16; Neb. 11, 2; Okla. 9, 7; S. D. 17, 13; Tex. 10, 4; W. Va. 11, 8; Utah 12, 14; Wash. 12, 17.

[5] Utah, Wash.

[6] Ky.

[7] Ky. 211; Neb. 11, 8; Okla. 9, 31.

[8] Wy. 10, 10 (9). So, not within half a mile of a town of three hundred people (W. Va. 11, 10); and "it may not pass within three miles of a county seat, without passing through the same" if the town will give right of way, etc., unless prevented by natural obstacles (Miss. 187; Okla. 9, 14; Tex. 10, 9).

[9] Okla. 9, 26 & 27.

[10] Va. 166.

in this State for the transaction of its business, where transfers of its stock shall be made, and in which shall be kept for public inspection books in which shall be recorded the amount of capital stock subscribed, and by whom; the names of the owners of its stock, and the amount owned by them respectively; the amount of stock paid in, and by whom; the transfers of said stock; the amount of its assets and liabilities; and the names and place of residence of its officers. The directors of every such railroad corporation shall annually make a report, under oath, to the auditor of public accounts or some officer or officers to be designated by law, of all their acts and doings, which report shall include such matters relating to railroads as may be prescribed by law, and the Legislature shall pass laws enforcing by suitable penalties the provisions of this section."[1]

"Every railroad corporation or association operating a line of railroad within this State shall annually make a report to the auditor of State of its business within this State, in such form as the Legislature may prescribe."[2]

A majority of the directors must be resident in the State.[3]

No president, officer, director, agent, or employee of a railroad or canal shall be interested, directly or indirectly, in furnishing it material or supplies, or in the business of transportation of freight or passengers as a common carrier over the company's works.[4]

§ 531. *Ultra Vires.* — No company doing the business of a common carrier can engage in mining or manufacturing articles for transportation over its works; nor directly or indirectly engage in any other business; nor hold land except such as is necessary to its business.[5]

§ 532. *Railroad Commissioners* are established by the Constitutions of several States[6] (see also § 202). In Oklahoma, Virginia, and South Carolina the "Corporation Commission" have charge of all "transporting and transmitting companies."[7] But in Oklahoma,

[1] N. D. 140; Okla. 9, 6 (report to be made to the Corporation Commission); S. D. 17, 12. And so of all public service corporations (Okla.).

[2] Ark. 17, 13; W. Va. 11, 7; Wy. 10, 10 (3).

[3] Ill. 11, 11.

[4] Ark. 17, 5; Cal. 12, 18; Mo. 12, 22; Pa. 17, 6.

[5] Ky. 210; Okla. 9, 12; Pa. 17, 5. But mining or manufacturing companies may carry their product over their own railways or canals not exceeding fifty miles in length (Pa.).

[6] Cal. 12, 22; Ky. 209; La. 283; Neb. 1905, 233; S. C. 9, 14. So, "they may be established by the Legislature," N. D. 142; Tex., 1889, p. 171, 1893, p. 213; Wash. 12, 18.

[7] The Virginia and Oklahoma Constitutional provisions concerning the Corporation Commission are so prolix that it is impossible to give more than an abstract in the note. Briefly stated

the legislature may repeal Art. 9 §§ 18–34, being practically all constitutional provisions relating to railroads, after January, 1909 (9, 35).

they are as follows: The State Corporation Commission consists of three members appointed by the Governor (Va.), elected by the people (Okla.), for six years respectively, one going out each two years. No person can hold office as a member of such Commission while employed by or holding any office in any transportation or transmission company or financially interested therein (Okla., Va.), or engaged in practising law (Va.), or in any other business (Okla.), although at least one of the Commission must have the qualifications prescribed for a judge of the Circuit Court of Appeals (Va.). Then there are provisions much like the Massachusetts statutes concerning the Railroad Commission as to their rules, sittings, officers, etc.: Okla. 9, 16–19; Va. 155. After 1908 the Legislature may provide for the election, instead of the appointment, of the members of such Commission (Va.).

The Corporation Commission issues all charters and amendments or extensions thereof for domestic corporations and all licenses to do business for foreign corporations (Va.) and has general supervision and control, with power to require evidence and reports, etc. (Okla., Va.). They may prescribe rates, charges, classifications of traffic, and rules and regulations, and may require railroads, etc., to establish such public services as may be reasonable, and all other rates or charges shall be void, and may inspect books and papers, require evidence under oath, etc. (Okla. 9, 28; Va.). Before fixing any rate or making any order directed against one or more companies by name, such company shall be given ten days' notice with an opportunity to be heard; and of general orders directed not against any specific company, there must be four weeks' publication in a capital newspaper with notice of hearing (Okla., Va.). Nothing in this section is to interfere with the paramount authority of the Legislature (Va.). But the authority of the Commission to make rates, subject to appeal to the courts, is paramount (Okla.). Nor to impair any right heretofore or hereafter conferred by law upon the authorities of any city, town, or county to fix rates or prescribe regulations, etc., as to rates of public service corporations therein (Okla., Va.). The Commission has the general powers of a court of record, may administer oaths, compel the attendance of witnesses and the production of papers, and punish for contempt, etc. (Okla. 9, 19; Va.). From any action of the Commission prescribing rates, charges, or other orders an appeal may be taken by the corporation or by the Commonwealth to the Supreme Court but prior to the reversal of such order by the Court no action of the Commission is delayed or suspended until a suspending bond shall first have been executed and filed with and approved by the Commission, payable to the Commonwealth to secure all charges which such company may collect or receive pending the appeal in excess of those fixed by the final decision. All such appeals have precedence in the Court of Appeals. No new evidence may be introduced upon the appeal. If the Court reverse the order of the Commission affecting rates, etc., it shall substitute therefor such order as it deem reasonable, which substituted order has the same force and effect as if entered by the Commission originally. The right of any person to institute in the ordinary courts any action or suit against any transportation or transmission company for any claim or cause of action is not extinguished or impaired by reason of any fine or other penalty which the Commission may impose upon such company, but in no such proceeding shall the reasonableness or justness of any rate or order, etc., made by the Commission within the scope of its authority and then in force, be questioned. The Commission makes annual reports to the Governor, etc. (Va. 156–157; Okla. 9, 20–25). And in Oklahoma they must report the cost of road, rebuilding cost or "re-

The Constitution of Louisiana provides for a Railroad, Express, Telephone, Telegraph, Steamboat, and Sleeping Car Commission to be composed of three members to be elected from the State Districts, which Commission has power to adopt or change reasonable and just rates, charges, and regulations, to govern the tariffs and service of such several companies, to prevent them from charging any greater compensation in the aggregate for the like kind of property or passengers for a shorter than a longer distance over the same line unless specially authorized by the Commission; to require suitable depots, switches, and appurtenances, to inspect railroads and require them to keep their tracks, etc., in a safe condition, and to fix and adjust rates between branch or short lines and the great trunk lines with which they connect. The Commission may further adopt reasonable rules, regulations, etc., may hear and determine complaints, and regulate investigations, and compel the attendance of witnesses and compel the production of testimony, etc., and punish for contempt as fully as is provided by law for the district courts. Railroads and other companies dissatisfied with the decision or rate may appeal to the Supreme Court of the State. The powers of the Commission go only to matters within the State lines.[1]

The Legislature is empowered to add to or enlarge the powers of such Commission; and no person in the service of any such railway or other company can be a Commissioner.[2]

§ 534. *Liabilities.* — The fellow-servant doctrine as to employees of railroads is done away with by some new State Constitutions;[3] and railroads are responsible for all damages to persons or property to their employees as to others.[4]

The Constitution of Arkansas provides that all railroads shall be responsible for all damages to person or property, under such regulations as are prescribed by the Legislature; and that the Legislature shall require, by suitable laws, the necessary means and appliances to secure the safety of passengers on railroads and other public conveyances.[5]

valuation," debt, stock, bonds, prices received therefor, salaries and wages paid, etc., at once to the Attorney General, and in their annual reports (Okla. 9, 29). And they must investigate and report, when necessary, to the Interstate Commerce Commission (Okla. 9, 32).

[1] La. 283–285.

[2] La. 287, 288.

[3] Okla. 9, 36; S. C. 9, 15; Va. 162; Miss. 193. And also of mines (Okla.).

[4] S. C., Miss.

[5] Ark. 17, 12; 19, 18.

And it is unlawful for any person or corporation to require of its employees, as a condition of their employment or otherwise, any contract or agreement whereby the company is released from liability on account of personal injuries received by such employees while in its service, by reason of the negligence of the company or its servants; and such contracts are void.[1]

§ 535. *Damages for Death.* — (See also § 462.) Four new Constitutions provide for damages for death whether instantaneous or not, in cases where damages would be liable had death not occurred; and contracts to waive the benefit of this section are made void.[2]

The Constitutions of other States provide that every person or corporation that may commit a homicide, through wilful act or omission or gross neglect, shall be responsible in exemplary damages to the surviving husband, widow, or heirs, notwithstanding any criminal proceedings that may or may not be had.[3]

And in others, that no act of the Legislature shall limit the amount to be recovered for injuries resulting in death, or for injuries to person or property; and in case of death resulting therefrom, the right of action shall survive for the benefit of such persons as the Legislature may prescribe (see § 462).[4] And also, that no act shall prescribe

[1] Col. 15, 15; Wy. 10, 4.

[2] Okla.; S. C. 9, 15; Va. 161; Miss. 193. Thus: "Every employee of any railroad corporation shall have the same rights and remedies for any injury suffered by him from the acts or omissions of said corporations or its employees as are allowed by law to other persons not employees, when the injury results from the negligence of a superior agent or officer, or of a person having a right to control or direct the services of a party injured, and also when the injury results from the negligence of a fellow servant engaged in another department of labor from that of the party injured, or of a fellow servant on another train of cars, or one engaged about a different piece of work. Knowledge by any employee injured of the defective or unsafe character or condition of any machinery, ways, or appliances shall be no defence to an action for injury caused thereby, except as to conductors or engineers in charge of dangerous or unsafe cars or engines voluntarily operated by them. When death ensues from any injury to employees, the legal or personal representatives of the person injured shall have the same right and remedies as are allowed by law to such representatives of other persons. Any contract or agreement, expressed or implied, made by any employee to waive the benefit of this section, shall be null and void; and this section shall not be construed to deprive any employee of a corporation, or his legal or personal representative, of any remedy or right that he now has by the law of the land. The General Assembly may extend the remedies herein provided for to any other class of employees." (Miss. 193; S. C. 9, 19.) Other provisions are substantially similar (Okla. 9, 36; Va. 162).

[3] Ky. 241; Tex. 16, 26; Wy. 10, 4.

[4] Ark. 5, 32; Ky. 54; Pa. 3, 21. The Legislature are to prescribe to whom the damages belong (Ky.).

any limitation of time within which such suits shall be brought against corporations, different from those fixed by general laws for actions against natural persons.[1]

Whenever the death of a person shall result from an injury inflicted by negligence or wrongful act, then, in every such case, damages may be recovered for such death, from the corporations and persons so causing the same. Until otherwise provided by law, the action to recover such damages shall in all cases be prosecuted by the personal representative. The same shall form part of the personal estate of the deceased person.[2]

§ 536. *Street Railways.* — The Constitutions of several States provide that no law shall be passed authorizing the construction of a street railroad [3] in a town or city without the consent of one-half in value of the abutting property owners,[4] or the consent of the local authorities [5] or of the electors,[6] and this consent is also required for gas, water, telephone, light companies, etc.,[7] or any public service. *Except,* however, a petition may be brought, in New York, in the Supreme Court, in case the consent of property owners cannot be obtained.

§ 537. *Telegraph Companies.* — Any association or corporation organized for the purpose, or any individual, shall have the right to construct and maintain lines of telegraph and telephone within this State, and connect the same with other lines; and the Legislature shall, by general law of uniform operation, provide reasonable regulations to give full effect to this section.[8] No telegraph or telephone company shall consolidate with any other, etc. (See § 527.)

Cities and towns may, however, control the location of such companies.[9]

Said companies shall receive and transmit each other's messages without delay or discrimination.[10]

Railroad corporations organized or doing business in this State shall allow telegraph and telephone corporations and companies to

[1] Pa.

[2] Ky. 241.

[3] And so of telegraph or telephone (N. D., S. C., Utah, Wy.), electric (S. C., Wy.), gas (S. C.), or water companies (S. C.).

[4] N.Y. 3, 18; Tex. 10, 7; W. Va. 11, 5.

[5] Ala. 220; Col. 15, 11; Ga. 3, 7, 20; Ill. 11, 4; Ky. 163; Mo. 12, 20; Okla. 9, 10; Pa. 17, 9; S. C. 8, 4.

[6] Neb. 13, 2.

[7] Ala., Ky. See note 5.

[8] Ala. 239; Ida. 11, 13; Ky. 199; Mon. 15, 14; S. D. 17, 11; Wash. 12, 19; Wy. 10, 10 (7).

[9] Ky.

[10] Ky.; N. D. 142; Okla. 9, 5; S. D.; Wash. 12, 19. See also § 526.

construct and maintain telegraph lines on and along the rights-of-way of such railroads and railroad companies, and no railroad corporation organized or doing business in this State shall allow any telegraph corporation or company any facilities, privileges, or rates for transportation of men or material, or for repairing their lines, not allowed to all telegraph companies. The right of eminent domain is hereby extended to all telegraph and telephone companies. The Legislature shall, by general law of uniform operation, provide reasonable regulations to give effect to this section.[1]

§ 538. *Foreign railroads* (see also §§ 505, 529) or telegraph lines shall do no business within this State without having an agent or agents within each county through which such railroad or telegraph line shall be constructed upon whom process may be served.[2]

In South Carolina and Mississippi no foreign road can operate in the State. (See also § 529.)[3]

§ 539. *Local Aid.* — Neither the State, nor any county, township, school district, or municipality shall loan or give its credit or make donations to or in aid of any railroad[4] or telegraph line.[5] Provided, that this section shall not apply to obligations of any county, city, township, or school district, contracted prior to the adoption of this Constitution.[6] (See also §§ 326, 335, 345, 370.)

§ 540. *Taxation.* — (See § 528.) State franchise taxes may be imposed, and the Legislature in its discretion may make the same in

[1] Wash. 12, 19.

[2] Wy. 10, 10 (8).

[3] "The General Assembly shall not grant to any foreign corporation or association a license to build, operate, or lease any railroad in this State; but in all cases where a railroad is to be built or operated, or is now being operated, in this State, and the same shall be partly in this State and partly in another State, or in other States, the owners or projectors thereof shall first become incorporated under the laws of this State; nor shall any foreign corporation or association lease or operate any railroad in this State, or purchase the same or any interest therein. Consolidation of any railroad lines and corporations in this State with others shall be allowed only where the consolidated company shall become a domestic corporation of this State. No general or special law shall ever be passed for the benefit of any foreign corporation operating a railroad under any existing license of this State or under any existing lease, and no grant of any right or privilege and no exemption from any burden shall be made to any such foreign corporation, except upon the condition that the owners or stockholders thereof shall first organize a corporation in this State under the laws thereof, and shall thereafter operate and manage the same and the business thereof under said domestic charter." (Miss. 197; S. C. 9, 8.)

[4] Mon. 5, 37; Wy. 3, 39; 10, 5.

[5] Wy.

[6] Wy.

lieu of taxes upon other property of a transportation, industrial, or commercial corporation; but when such franchise tax is imposed upon a corporation doing business in the State, or whenever all the capital, however invested, of a State corporation is taxed, the shares of stock shall not be further taxed.[1]

"The franchise, roadway, roadbed, rails, and rolling stock of all railroads operated in this State shall be assessed by the State Board of Equalization at their actual value, and such assessed valuation shall be apportioned to the counties, cities, towns, townships, and districts in which said roads are located, as a basis for taxation of such property, in proportion to the number of miles of railway laid in such counties, cities, towns, townships, and districts." [2]

"The Legislative Assembly may, by law, provide for the payment of a per centum of gross earnings of railroad companies to be paid in lieu of all State, county, township, and school taxes on property exclusively used in and about the prosecution of the business of such companies as common carriers, but no real estate of said corporations shall be exempted from taxation in the same manner and on the same basis as other real estate is taxed, except roadbed, right of way, shops, and buildings used exclusively in their business as common carriers; and whenever and so long as such law providing for the payment of a per centum on earnings shall be in force, that part of § 179 of this article relating to assessments of railroad property shall cease to be in force." [3]

In Virginia the State Corporation Commission are to assess the real estate, rolling stock, and personal property of railroads, the canal bed, real estate, and boats of canals, and such property shall be taxed for State, county, city, town, and district purposes as authorized by law at such rates of taxation as may be imposed by them respectively on the real estate and personal property of natural citizens, provided that no tax shall be laid upon the net income; but such railway or canal shall also pay an annual State franchise tax equal to one per centum upon its gross receipts, which tax shall be in lieu of all other taxes or charges upon the franchises or shares of stock or property except the annual fee, etc. When the road or canal does not lie wholly within the State, the tax shall be equal to one per cent of the gross transportation receipts earned within the State, ascertained by determining the average gross per mile over its

[1] Va. 170. See O. 1904, p. 652.
[2] Mon. 12, 16; N. D. 179.
[3] N. D. 176.

whole extent and multiplying the result by the number of miles operated in the State, with a reasonable deduction for excess of value for terminal facilities, etc., in other States.[1]

§ 541. *Switches etc.* — The Oklahoma Constitution provides that any person or corporation may construct spur tracks to its mine, mill, etc., and compel the railway to maintain the switch.[2]

ARTICLE 55. BANKS

§ 550. *State Banks Forbidden.* — The Constitutions of a few States forbid the creation or renewal of corporations with banking or discounting privileges.[3] And in several, any act establishing banks must first be approved by a majority of the people, at a general election.[4] State banks are forbidden in Illinois; and, in other States, the State may not hold stock in any bank.[5] See also § 326. Any banking law may be amended or repealed.[6] But in others, such corporations may be formed under general laws,[7] though such banking law must receive a two-thirds vote of the Legislature.[8]

So, in a few, no special charter can be granted for banking purposes.[9] (See also § 395 and § 502.)

§ 551. *Money and Banknotes.* — In several, no corporation or individual can circulate as money anything but the lawful money of the United States.[10] So, all banknotes must be redeemable in the lawful money of the United States,[11] or in gold and silver.[12] No note can be issued of less than one dollar.[13] Banknotes are allowed, secured by State or United States bonds.[14]

§ 552. *Specie Payments.* — In several, the Legislature can pass no law sanctioning the suspension of specie payments by banks.[15]

[1] Va. 176–179.

[2] Okla. 9, 33.

[3] Ore. 11, 1; Wis. 11, 4.

[4] Io. 8, 5; Ill. 11, 5; Kan. 13, 8; Mich. 15, 2; Mo. 12, 26; O. 13, 7; Wis. 11. 5.

[5] Ala. 253; Ind. 11; Ill.; Kan. 13, 5; Mo. 12, 25.

[6] Kan. 13, 9.

[7] Ala. 248; Cal. 12, 5; Minn. 9, 13; Miss. 181; Okla. 14, 1; S. C. 9, 9; Tex. 1904, p. 249; W. Va. 11, 6; Wy. 3, 27.

[8] Minn.

[9] Ind. 11, 2; Kan. 13, 1; N. Y. 3, 4; S. C.

[10] Ark. 12, 10; Cal.; Nev. 8, 6; Ore.; Wash. 12, 11.

[11] Kan. 13, 4.

[12] Ala. 249.

[13] Kan. 13, 7.

[14] Ala. 248; S. D. 18, 1.

[15] Ala. 249; Ind. 11, 7; Ill. 11, 7; Io. 8, 11; Mich. 15, 6; Minn. 9, 13; N. Y. 8, 5.

§ 553. *Security of Notes.* — (See also § 551.) In many, the Legislature are to provide by law for the registry of all bills or notes issued as money, and shall require ample security for their redemption in specie.[1]

§ 554. *Insolvency of Banks.* — The Constitution makes it a crime for any officer or owner of a private or public bank to assent to the reception of deposits or the creation of debts by such bank after he has knowledge that it is in insolvent or failing circumstances, and he is individually responsible for such debts or deposits.[2] The bill-holders have preference over all other creditors of an insolvent bank.[3]

§ 555. *Stockholders* of a bank are, in a few States, individually liable for its debts, over and above their stock, to the amount of the stock held by them.[4] But in others, they are liable only to the amount of their unpaid stock.[5] In one, to double such amount of stock.[6] And in one, they are liable for all debts of the bank contracted while they are officers or such stockholders, each for his proportion, according to the amount of stock owned by him.[7]

§ 556. *Interest.* — The Constitution of Indiana provides that no bank shall receive, directly or indirectly, a greater rate of interest than is allowed to individuals loaning money.[8] In Oklahoma, the article on banking provides that it shall be six per cent, or by contract, ten per cent.[9]

§ 557. *Limitation of Charter.* — By the Constitutions of two, every bank shall be required to cease all banking operations within twenty years from the time of its organization and promptly close its business.[10]

§ 558. *Trust Companies* and individuals are included in the provisions of the banking law.[11] No trust company or bank may own or hold stock in another such company except by *bona fide* pledge, and then must dispose of the same within one year as in § 518.[12]

[1] Ind. 11, 3; Ill. 11, 8; Io. 8, 8; Kan. 13, 2; Mich. 15, 4; Minn. 9, 13; N. Y. 8, 6; N. D. 145; Pa. 16, 9; S. D. 18, 20.

[2] Ky. 204; La. 269; Mo. 12, 27; Wash. 12, 12.

[3] Ala. 250; Io. 8, 10; Ind. 11, 8; Mich. 15, 5; Minn. 9, 13; Kan. 13, 4; N. Y. 8, 8.

[4] (See also § 509.) Ind. 11, 6; Ill. 11, 6; Io. 8, 9; Neb. 13, 7; N. Y. 8, 7; S. C. 9, 18; S. D. 18, 3; Tex. 1904, p. 249; Utah 12, 18; Wash. 12, 11. For a year after they sell their stock. (S. D., Tex.) Stock must be paid up in cash (Tex.). (See also § 512.)

[5] Kan.; Md. 3, 39.

[6] Minn. 9, 13.

[7] Mich. 15, 3.

[8] Ind. 11, 9.

[9] Okla. 14. 2.

[10] Ind. 11, 10; S. D. 18, 2.

[11] Ala. 255.

[12] Okla. 9, 41.

§ 559. *Reports* (semi-annual) must be made to the State banking officer.[1]

ARTICLE 56. INSURANCE COMPANIES

§ 560. *Deposit.* — The Georgia Constitution provides that all foreign or domestic life-insurance companies doing business in the State shall deposit $100,000 in good securities with the comptroller of the insurance commissioners of this State or the State where they are chartered; and all companies must make semi-annual reports.[2]

ARTICLE 57. MISCELLANEOUS CORPORATIONS

§ 570. *Religious.* — In one State, no religious corporation can be established in the State except such as may be formed under a general law for the purpose of holding title to such real estate as may be allowed them by law.[3] In one other, the title to all property of religious corporations vests in trustees, elected by their members.[4] The Legislature shall not grant a charter of incorporation to any church or religious denomination, but may secure the title to church property to an extent to be limited by law.[5]

§ 571. *Co-operative.* — The Legislature shall provide by suitable legislation for the organization of mutual co-operative associations or corporations.[6]

ARTICLE 58. TRUSTS, MONOPOLY, ETC.

§ 580. *General Principles.* — (See also §§ 518, 526.) "It shall be the duty of the General Assembly from time to time, as necessity may require, to enact such laws as may be necessary to prevent all trusts, pools, combinations, or other organizations, from combining to depreciate below its real value any article, or to enhance the cost of any article above its real value."[7]

"The General Assembly shall enact laws to prevent all trusts, combinations, contracts, and agreements against the public welfare."[8]

[1] Ala. 254.
[2] Ga. 3, 12, 1 & 3 & 5.
[3] Mo. 2, 8.
[4] Kan. 12, 3.
[5] Va. 6, 47.
[6] Wy. 10, 10.
[7] Ky. 198.
[8] S. C. 9, 8; Miss. 198; Va. 165.

"Full and fair competition in the trades and industries is an inherent and essential right of the people, and should be protected against all monopolies and conspiracies which tend to hinder or destroy." [1]

The Legislature shall define what is an unlawful combination, monopoly, trust, act, or agreement, in restraint of trade, and enact laws to punish persons engaged in any unlawful combination, monopoly, trust, act, or agreement, in restraint of trade, or composing any such monopoly, trust, or combination.[2]

§ 581. *Monopolies and Perpetuities* are "contrary to the genius of a free State and should not be allowed." [3] And so, in others, of "monopolies and trusts," [4] or monopolies simply.[5]

In California, the Constitution declares that the holding of large tracts of land, uncultivated and unimproved, by individuals or corporations, is against the public interest, and should be discouraged by all means not inconsistent with the rights of private property.[6]

Any combination between individuals, corporations, associations, or either, having for its object or effect the controlling of the price of any product of the soil or any article of manufacture or commerce, or the cost of exchange or transportation, is prohibited and hereby declared unlawful and against public policy,[7] and any and all franchises heretofore granted or extended, or that may hereafter be granted or extended in this State, whenever the owner or owners thereof violate this article, shall be deemed annulled and become void.[8]

All just power possessed by the State is hereby granted to the General Court to enact laws to prevent the operations within the State of all persons and associations, and all trusts and corporations, foreign or domestic, and the officers thereof, who endeavor to raise the price of any article of commerce or to destroy free and fair competition in the trades and industries through combination, conspiracy, monopoly, or any other unfair means; to control and regulate the acts of all such persons, associations, corporations, trusts, and officials doing business within the State; to prevent

[1] N. H. 2, 82.

[2] Okla. 5, 44.

[3] Wy. 1, 30. (See also § 518.)

[4] S. D. 17, 20; Wash. 12, 32.

[5] Ark. 2, 19; Ida. 2, 32; N. M. *1851, July 12, § 17; La. 276 (except slaughtering businesses which may be regulated by cities); N. C. 1, 31; Md. Decl. Rts. 41; Okla. 2, 32; Tenn. 1, 22; Tex. 1, 26; Wy. 1, 30.

[6] Cal. 17, 2.

[7] N. D. 146; Utah 12, 20. So in Minnesota, but as to food products only (Minn. 1889, 1).

[8] N. D. So the legislature shall pass laws to forfeit, etc. (Utah.)

fictitious capitalization; and to authorize civil and criminal proceedings in respect to all the wrongs herein declared against.[1]

The Legislature shall provide by law for the regulation, prohibition, or reasonable restraint of common carriers, partnerships, associations, trusts, monopolies, and combinations of capital, so as to prevent them or any of them from making scarce articles of necessity, trade, or commerce, or from increasing unreasonably the cost thereof to the consumer, or preventing reasonable competition in the calling, trade, or business.[2]

It shall be unlawful for persons or corporations, or their legal representatives, to combine or conspire together, or to unite or pool their interests for the purpose of forcing up or down the price of any agricultural product or article of necessity, for speculative purposes; and the Legislature shall pass laws to suppress it.[3]

ARTICLE 60. MUNICIPAL CORPORATIONS [4]

§ 600. *Local Government.* — It is in many States provided that the Legislature shall provide by general law for the organization of cities, towns, and municipalities, their powers and duties.[5] The same would follow in other States from § 395 and § 502.

And so, in several, that the Legislature shall create a uniform system of county, town, and municipal government;[6] not dividing cities into more than four classes,[7] or three classes,[8] or six.[9]

So, in others, the Legislature may confer upon organized townships, incorporated cities and villages,[10] and upon the board of supervisors of the several counties,[11] such powers of a local, legislative, and administrative character as they deem proper.

"The Legislature shall not delegate to any special commission, private corporation or association any power to make, supervise, or interfere with any municipal improvement, money, property, or

[1] N. H. 2, 82.

[2] Ala. 103.

[3] La. 190.

[4] For financial provisions, see Arts. 34, 37.

[5] Ark. 12, 3; Cal. 11, 6; 1895, p. 450; Ida. 12, 1; 18, 5; 1895, p. 257; Ill. 10, 5; Kan. 12, 5; Ky. 156; Mich. 15, 13; Miss. 88; Mo. 9, 7; Neb. 10, 4 and 5; N. D. 167, 170; N. C. 8, 4; Nev. 8, 8; O. 13, 6; Okla. 10, 4; S. D. 18, 1, 9; Utah 11, 4; Va. 117; Wash. 11, 10; Wis. 1891, p. 731; Wy. 11, 2 & 4.

[6] Cal. 11, 4; Fla. 3, 24; Ga. 11, 3, 1; Ida.; Ky. 156; Mo. 9, 7; Nev. 4, 25; Okla. 18, 1; S. D.; Utah 11, 5; Wis. 4, 23; Wy.

[7] S. D. 10, 1.

[8] N. Y. 12, 1.

[9] Ky.

[10] Kan. 2, 21; Mich. 4, 38; Wis. 4, 22.

[11] Kan.; Mich.; N. Y. 3, 27; Wis.

effects, whether held in trust or otherwise, to levy taxes, to select a capitol site, or to perform any municipal functions."[1]

In a few States the Constitution provides that any county may by vote adopt the township form of government.[2]

Counties are usually to be governed by a board of county commissioners;[3] called, in Michigan, the "board of supervisors."

Townships are, in one, governed by a board of trustees, consisting of a clerk and two justices of the peace, elected by the voters thereof.[4]

In a few, the Constitution provides that the Legislature may charter cities in towns having more than 10,000,[5] 12,000,[6] or 20,000[7] inhabitants.

In two, any city having a population of more than 20,000[8] or 100,000[9] may frame a charter for itself (by a special process, subject to certain restrictions). And the States are rapidly adopting constitutional provisions permitting all cities and towns to frame their own charters.[10]

§ 601. *Municipalities.* — The Constitutions of a few States provide that each organized county shall be a body corporate, with such powers and immunities as shall be established by law;[11] and so each organized township.[12]

All suits and proceedings by or against a county or township shall be in the name thereof.[13]

[1] Utah 6, 29; Wy. 3, 37; Mon. 5, 36; S. D. 3, 26.

[2] Cal.; Ill.; Mo. 9, 8; Neb. 10, 5; N. D. 170; Wash. 11, 4.

[3] Ida. 18, 10; Ind. 6, 10; Ill. 10, 6; Miss. 170; Mon. 16, 4; Nev. 4, 26; N. Y. 3, 26; N. D. 172; Mich. 10, 6; Pa. 14, 7; Wash. 11, 5.

[4] N. C. 11, 5.

[5] Mass. C. Amt. 2.

[6] Pa. 15, 1; Tex. 11, 4.

[7] Minn. 11, 2.

[8] Wash. 12, 10.

[9] Cal. 11, 8; Mo. 9, 16.

[10] Thus, California has a novel provision, followed in Oklahoma, whereby any city or town may, through a board of fifteen chosen freeholders, frame its own charter, which, if approved by the Governor as constitutional, is then submitted to the electors and adopted by a majority vote. (Cal. 1889, p. 231; 1891, p. 533; 1901, p. 950; Okla.)

In Colorado the charters of the city of Denver and all cities of the first class are contained in a Constitutional Amendment which provides further that it may at any time be amended [or abolished?] by the voters of the respective cities. It also provides for the ownership and operation of public utilities. (Col. 1901, p. 46.)

In Minnesota (1895, p. 4), a charter may be adopted by a board of fifteen freeholders and a four-sevenths vote.

In Missouri (1901, p. 263), by thirteen, with a three-fifths vote.

In Oregon, on initiative petition, June 4, 1906, Art. 11, § 2 of the Constitution was amended so that any municipality is given the exclusive right to enact and amend its charter, subject only to the Constitution and the criminal laws.

Town Organization (Mo. 1901, p. 267) is elaborately provided for.

[11] Ga. 11, 1, 1; Mich. 10, 1; Okla. 17, 1; S. C. 7, 9.

[12] Mich. 11, 2; N. C. 7, 4.

[13] Ga., Mich.

Any county, city, town, or township may make and enforce within its limits all local, police, sanitary, and other regulations not in conflict with general laws.[1]

No municipal corporation can be authorized by the Legislature to pass laws inconsistent with the general laws of the State.[2]

§ 602. *Officers.* — The following persons are, by the Constitution, declared ineligible to hold municipal offices: persons in default as collectors or custodians of money or property of such municipality.[3] In cities or counties having more than 200,000 inhabitants, no person can at the same time have a State office and a municipal office, or two municipal offices together in any municipality.[4] The fees or salaries of municipal officers cannot, in two States, be increased or diminished during their terms.[5] They must reside in their respective counties or towns.[6] In one, they must have so resided one year.[7] They must be qualified electors.[8]

§ 603. *Citizens' Rights.* — By the Constitution of Arkansas, any citizen of any county, city, or town may institute suits in behalf of himself and all others interested to resist an illegal exaction.[9]

§ 604. *Specified Systems of City, County, or Town Government* exist in the Constitutions of a few States.[10]

§ 605. *Franchises.*[11] — The right to collect rates for water furnished to a municipality is, in California, declared to be a franchise, not to be exercised except by authority of law and in the manner by

[1] Cal. 11, 11; Ida. 12, 2; Wash. 11, 11.

[2] Ala. 89.

[3] Ill. 9, 11.

[4] Mo. 9, 18.

[5] Cal. 11, 19; Ill.

[6] Ore. 6, 8.

[7] Col. 14, 10.

[8] Col.

[9] Ark. 16, 13.

[10] Thus, the New York Constitution divides cities into three classes: the first class above 250,000, the second class above 50,000, and the third class below 50,000. All laws relating to cities are divided into general and special city laws; general city laws being those which relate to all the cities of one or more classes, and special city laws those which relate to a single city or to less than all the cities of a class. No special city law can be passed except a certified copy be sent to the Mayor, and fifteen days thereafter the Mayor returns such bill to the House, passing it on to the Governor with his certificate stating whether the city has or has not accepted the same. The Legislature may provide for the concurrence of the legislative body in cities of the first class. In both the other classes the Mayor and legislative body must act concurrently. If a bill relate to more than one city, it must be sent to all. If it be not accepted or returned without acceptance, it may, nevertheless, again be passed by both branches of the Legislature, and shall then be subject only to the action of the Governor. (N. Y. 12, 2.)

Municipal elections must be held on the Tuesday succeeding the first Monday in November in the odd year, but this does not apply to cities of the third class nor to elections of judicial officers. (N. Y. 12, 3.)

[11] See also §§ 435, 536.

law prescribed.[1] So, in Colorado the county commissioners, and in Idaho the Legislature, may empower reasonable maximum rates for the use of water, whether furnished by persons or corporations.[2] And in Texas the right to regulate tolls or freights, for the use of roads, bridges, ferries, landings, or wharves, shall always remain in the Legislature.[3] So, in California the Legislature shall pass laws to regulate the charges of telegraph or gas companies, wharfingers, and warehousemen, where there is a public use.[4]

"The rights of no city or town in and to its water front, wharf property, public landings, wharves, docks, streets, avenues, parks, bridges, and other public places, and its gas, water, and electric works shall be sold except by an ordinance or resolution passed by a recorded affirmative vote of three-fourths of all the members elected to the council, or to each branch thereof where there are two, and under such other restrictions as may be imposed by law; and in case of the veto by the mayor of such an ordinance or resolution, it shall require a recorded affirmative vote of three-fourths of all the members elected to the council, or to each branch thereof where there are two, had in the manner heretofore provided for in this article, to pass the same over the veto. No franchise, lease, or right of any kind to use any such public property or any other public property or easement of any description, in a manner not permitted to the general public, shall be granted for a longer period than thirty years. Before granting any such franchise or privilege for a term of years, except for a trunk railway, the municipality shall first, after due advertisement, receive bids therefor publicly, in such manner as may be provided by law, and shall then act as may be required by law. Such grant, and any contract in pursuance thereof, may provide that upon the termination of the grant the plant as well as the property, if any, of the grantee in the streets, avenues, and other

[1] Cal. 14, 2; Ida. 15, 2. So, "No municipal corporation shall, directly or indirectly, lease, sell, alien, or dispose of any water-works, water-rights, or sources of water supply now or hereafter to be owned or controlled by it; but all such water-works, water-rights, and sources of water supply now owned or hereafter to be acquired by any municipal corporation, shall be preserved, maintained, and operated by it for supplying its inhabitants with water at reasonable charges: Provided, That nothing herein contained shall be construed to prevent any such municipal corporation from exchanging water-rights, or sources of water supply, for other water-rights or sources of water supply of equal value, and to be devoted in like manner to the public supply of its inhabitants." (Utah 11, 6.)

[2] Col. 16, 8; Ida. 15, 6.

[3] Tex. 12, 3. The common law; see Book I.

[4] Cal. 4, 33.

public places shall thereupon, without compensation to the grantee, or upon the payment of a fair valuation therefor, be and become the property of the said city or town; but the grantee shall be entitled to no payment by reason of the value of the franchise; and any such plant or property acquired by a city or town may be sold or leased, or, if authorized by law, maintained, controlled, and operated by such city or town. Every such grant shall specify the mode of determining any valuation therein provided for, and shall make adequate provision by way of forfeiture of the grant, or otherwise, to secure efficiency of public service at reasonable rates, and the maintenance of the property in good order throughout the term of the grant. Nothing herein contained shall be construed as preventing the General Assembly from prescribing additional restriction on the powers of cities and towns in granting franchises or in selling or leasing any of their property, or as repealing any additional restriction now required in relation thereto in any existing municipal charter."[1]

No franchises may be granted for more than a fixed period of time, twenty[2] or thirty[3] years, and there must always be due advertisement and a public bidding.[4]

§ 606. *Police Power.* — Any county or incorporated city or town may make and enforce, within its limits, all such local, police, sanitary, and other regulations as are not in conflict with its charter or with the general laws.[5]

[1] Va. 125.

[2] Ky. 164.

[3] Ala. 228; Va. Of cities, etc., over 6000 population, and *except* railroads other than street (Ala.).

[4] Ky.

[5] Cal. 11, 11; Ida. 12, 2.

PART IV

JUDICIAL SYSTEM

ARTICLE 65

§ 650. *General Principles.* — Nearly all States provide in their Constitutions for the separation into three departments, and all in fact apply the common law, though Louisiana preserves its French Code [1] and New Mexico some Spanish law.

§ 651. *Courts.* — The system of all the States is substantially the same, except that the older States are more apt to leave the establishment of courts to the Legislature than to prescribe it in the Constitution. Only seven States apparently still have a separate Court of Chancery.[2] In many States, however, like Massachusetts, equity jurisdiction, though administered in the Supreme Court or Superior Courts, is kept separate from the common law; and different sittings are held. In other States [3] common law and chancery are declared to be fused. Nearly all the States have a Supreme Court and Superior, Circuit, or District Courts. Some States [4] interpose a Court of Appeals between the Superior Courts and the Supreme Court, while in New York there is a Court of Appeals above the Supreme Court. The words "Circuit" or "District" are in some States used for the courts corresponding to the County Courts in other States, which are below the Superior Court. Most States have a separate Probate, Orphans' or Surrogate's Court, but in the West probate jurisdiction is commonly given to the superior courts or the county courts. There are furthermore many city, municipal, police, or corporation courts, frequently, in the large cities, created by special law; while in the country there are justices of the peace or magistrates with, in the West, minor jurisdiction in civil cases not involving the title to real

[1] See §§ 76, 200.

[2] Ala. 139; Del. 4, 1; Mich. 6, 1; Miss. 152; N. J. 6, 1; Tenn. 6, 1; Vt. 2, 4. See, however, § 671.

[3] Cal., Ct., Ga., Ida., Mich., N. C., N. Y., O., S. C. See § 671.

[4] Cal., Ga., Ill., La.

estate, or in criminal cases not amounting to felony, but always with appeal to a higher court.

It might be wished that the States could adopt a more uniform system or at least adopt the same names; in this book the terms "Supreme Court," "Superior Court," "County Court," "Probate Court," "Chancery Court," or "Justices of the Peace" have been used as typical names for the system above described; when there is a Court of Appeals above the Supreme Court that term is used. In New Hampshire alone there are no constitutional provisions affecting the establishment of courts, the whole matter being left to the Legislature;[1] while in Kentucky, and presumably others, the Legislature may establish no courts except those provided in the Constitution.[2] A few State Constitutions provide that land registration courts may be established by the Legislature.[3] In the absence of such a provision it may be questioned whether such courts, which purport to deprive a land owner of his title without notice and hearing, are constitutional in States, or in any case consistent with the Fourteenth Amendment.[4]

§ 652. *Jurisdiction.* — The general division of jurisdiction has been indicated above. When there is a Court of Appeals above the Supreme Court, it has only appellate jurisdiction, and in most States the Supreme Court has no original jurisdiction except to issue habeas corpus, mandamus, prohibition, certiorari, procedendo, quo warranto, injunction, supersedeas, and other prerogative or remedial writs; and in some States it has jurisdiction of suits against the State.[5]

In a few States the opinion of the Supreme Court may be required upon important questions of law and upon solemn occasions by either branch of the Legislature or by the governor and council.[6] This practice of requiring opinions from the Supreme Court was copied from the English Parliament; but it may be questioned whether it is advisable or, when required by statute, even constitutional. At all events such opinions are not regarded as a binding precedent, and being given without the argument of counsel and

[1] N. H. 2, 4.

[2] Ky. 135.

[3] Fla. 5, 17; S. D. 5, 21; Va. 100.

[4] Tyler *v.* Judges, 175 Mass. 71; s. c. 179 U. S. 405.

[5] Ida. 5, 10; Neb. 6, 2; N. C. 4, 9. So, often, by statute; and see § 75.

[6] Col. (Amt.) 6, 3; N. H. 2, 73; Mass. 2, 3, 2; Me. 6, 3; R. I. Amt. 12. By the Governor, upon questions concerning the State Constitution: Fla. 4, 13; or concerning important questions of law: S. D. 5, 13.

the light that comes from a real issue between the litigant parties are entitled to little more respect than if given by the judges in their private capacities; indeed they have given rise to a singular amount of doubtful law, notably that in Massachusetts upon a compulsory weekly payment law, and that in Colorado against the eight-hour law in mines.[1]

§ 653. *Opinions on Appeal.* — When a judgment or decree is reversed or confirmed by the Supreme Court, every point fairly arising upon the record of the case shall be considered and decided, and the reasons therefor shall be concisely stated in writing, signed by the judges concurring, filed in the office of the clerk of the Supreme Court, and preserved with a record of the case. Any judge dissenting therefrom may give the reasons of his dissent in writing over his signature.[2]

It shall be the duty of the court to prepare a syllabus of the points adjudicated in each case, which shall be concurred in by a majority of the judges thereof, and it shall be prefixed to the published reports of the case.[3]

§ 654. *Judges.* — Generally speaking, the States have not followed the example of Massachusetts and of both the English and the United States Constitution, in making all judges independent of popular election and irremovable during good behavior. Four States only still provide that all judges shall be appointed by the governor[4] or by the governor and council;[5] but a few other States require this specially of the judges of the Supreme Court,[6] though they must be confirmed by the Senate or, in Connecticut, the Legislature. In three other States Supreme Court judges are elected by the two Houses of the Legislature in joint convention,[7] and in the Territories and District of Columbia appointed by the President and confirmed by the Senate. In all the other States the judges of the Supreme Court are elected by the people of the entire State. Yet, in 1798, none of the States chose their judges by popular election, and in most States their tenure was for life (Smith, View of Constitutions, p. 33).

[1] *Re* Eight-Hour Law, 39 Pac. 328; Op. Justices, 163 Mass. 589. See James B. Thayer's Legal Essays, Chapter 2.

[2] N. D. 101; S. C. 5, 8; Utah 8, 25; W. Va. Amt. 1, 5. See § 666.

[3] N. D. 102. These provisions, if statutes, would hardly be constitutional.

[4] Del. 4, 3.

[5] Mass. 2, 2, 1, 9; Me. 5, 1, 8; N. H. 2, 45.

[6] Ct. Amt. 26; Miss. 145; N. J. 7, 2, 1.

[7] R. I. 10, 4; S. C. 5, 2; Va. 91; Vt. 2, 9; Amt. 10.

Judges of the Superior Courts are in all the States except the four above mentioned elected by the people, though in several they are elected by the Legislature in joint convention,[1] and in others appointed by the Governor and confirmed by the Senate.[2] And so generally of the minor judges.

The terms of office of judges vary from a life tenure as in Massachusetts, New Hampshire, and Rhode Island, through definite periods ranging from twenty-one years in Pennsylvania to two years in Vermont; but the usual term seems to be six years in the case of judges of the Supreme Court, and four years for judges of the Superior Court, and two years for justices of the peace.

The Constitutions usually provide that a judge of the Supreme Court shall be of a certain age, varying from twenty-five to thirty-six, and that he must be a citizen of the United States or the State. A few State Constitutions provide that he shall be learned in the law;[3] others that he shall have practised a certain number of years. By the Constitutions of nearly all the States, judges must receive a regular fixed compensation, but no other fees or perquisites; and this may not be increased nor diminished during their term of office. Four States provide for the retirement of judges after they have attained the age of seventy years.[4] Some State Constitutions prescribe that no judge can sit in a case where he is interested or related to the parties.[5] In like manner a few State Constitutions provide that no judge shall practise law or act as attorney;[6] and that he shall not sit in appeal upon any decision made by him or by any Court of which he was at the time a member,[7] or in which he acted as counsel.[8] If a judge absent himself from the State for sixty days, he forfeits his office.[9] For appeals, see § 78.

[1] Ga. 6, 3, 2; N. J. 7, 2, 2; S. C. 5, 13; Va. 96.

[2] Fla. 5, 8, 1901, p. 360; Miss. 153; N. J. 7, 2, 1.

[3] This principle was early established in England. See Historical Digest, Book II.

[4] Ct. Amt. 12; Md. 4, 3; N. H. 2, 77; N. Y. 6, 12.

[5] Ark. 7, 20; Del. 4, 16; Md. 4, 7; Miss. 165; N. D. 100; Tenn. 6, 11; S. C. 5, 6; Tex. 5, 11; Utah 8, 15. This constitutional provision seems hardly necessary, it being the judicial duty of a judge in any such case to recuse himself; if he were not to do so, it is probable his judgment would be reversed upon appeal.

[6] Ark. 7, 25; Cal. 6, 22; Col. 6, 18; Ala. 162; Kan. 3, 13; Neb. 6, 14; N. Y. 6, 20; N. D. 117; S. D. 5, 31; Va. 105; Wash. 5, 19; W. Va. 8, 16; Wy. 5, 25.

[7] Ark.; Ill. 6, 11; Md. 4, 15; N. J. 6, 2, 5; N. Y. 6, 3; Ore. 7, 6; S. C. 5, 6; W. Va. 8, 29; Utah 8, 13.

[8] Ark.; Md. 4, 7; S. C.; Tenn. 6, 11; Tex. 5, 11; Utah 8, 13.

[9] Cal. 6, 9; Mon. 8, 37. So ninety days, but the governor may give him leave of absence "in case of extreme necessity" (Utah 8, 27; Wash. 4, 8).

ARTICLE 66. REMEDIAL LAWS

§ 660. *Laws General.* — All laws relating to courts must, by a few of the Constitutions, be general and of uniform operation.[1] So, in several, the jurisdiction of all courts of the same grade or class, so far as regulated by law.[2] So, also, the practice of such courts.[3] And the effect of their judgments, decrees, or process, shall be uniform.[4]

§ 661. *Arbitration.* — The Constitutions of several States provide that the Legislature shall pass laws allowing parties to determine suits by arbitration.[5] So, in others, that the Legislature may establish "courts of conciliation."[6] So, in one, that they may refer suits to a practising lawyer as referee.[7] But such arbitrators, referees, or courts may not render final judgment obligatory on the parties, except upon submission by the parties and their agreement to abide such judgment.[8] So there must always be an appeal to the Supreme Court from boards of compulsory arbitration.[9]

§ 662. *Contempts.*[10] — The Legislature may regulate the exercise by the courts of the right to punish for contempt;[11] in Oklahoma, it shall do so.[12] In one it is provided that the Legislature shall have power to regulate by law the punishment of contempts not committed in the presence or hearing of the courts, or in disobedience of process.[13] Punishment may not extend to imprisonment in penitentiary.[14]

"The Legislature shall pass laws defining contempts and regulating the proceedings and punishment in matters of contempt: Provided, That any person accused of violating or disobeying, when not in the presence or hearing of the court, or judge sitting as such, any order of injunction, or estaint (*sic*), made or entered by any court

[1] Col. 6, 28; Ga. 6, 9, 1; Ida. 5, 26; Ill. 6, 29; Mon. 8, 26; Neb. 6, 19; Pa. 5, 26; S. D. 5, 34. See § 395.

[2] Col., Ga., Ill., Neb., Pa.

[3] Col., Ga., Ill., Neb., S. D.

[4] Col., Ga., Ill., Neb., Pa., S. D.

[5] Ala. 84; Col. 18, 3; Ky. 250; La. 176; S. C. 6, 1; Tex. 16, 13.

[6] Ida. 13, 72; Ind. 7, 19; Mich. 6, 23; N. D. 120; O. 4, 19; Utah 16, 2; Wis. 7, 16; Wy. 5, 1; 19, 1.

[7] Fla. 5, 20.

[8] Ind., N. D., O., Wis., Wy.

[9] Mon. 8, 36; Wy. 5, 28.

[10] The origin of the Chancellor's power to enforce the writ of injunction has been fully discussed in Book I. A bill similar to the Oklahoma statute has for many years been before Congress.

[11] Va. 63.

[12] Ga. 1, 1, 20; La. 177; Okla. 2, 25.

[13] Ark. 7, 26.

[14] S. C. 1, 19.

or judge of the State shall, before penalty or punishment is imposed, be entitled to a trial by jury as to the guilt or innocence of the accused. In no case shall a penalty or punishment be imposed for contempt until an opportunity to be heard is given."[1]

§ 663. *Attorneys.* — By the Constitution of Indiana, every person of good moral character, being a voter, shall be entitled to admission to practise in the courts.[2] But in most States they must have some education in the law, or pass an examination.

§ 664. *Codes.* — (See also § 308.) The Constitutions of a few States provide for codes of civil and criminal practice.[3] So, in three, for codes of the general laws.[4] The Constitution of one State provides that no general revision of the laws shall hereafter (1850) be made, and that, when a reprint is necessary, the Legislature shall appoint a suitable person to collect such acts as are in force and arrange them without alteration.[5] But in several, the Constitution provides that there shall be a revision and digest every ten years;[6] every twelve years, beginning with 1902.[7]

§ 665. *Speedy Decisions.* — The Constitution of California provides that no judge of the Supreme or Superior Courts shall receive his salary until he make affidavit that no cause in his court remains undecided that has been submitted for decision for the period of ninety days.[8] So he must decide all cases within ninety days "after submission."[9] So, in one other, such judges must file their decisions within sixty days after the end of the term at which the causes were heard,[10] so, thirty days,[11] or six months.[12] And in Georgia, the Supreme Court must dispose of every case at the first or second term after the writ of error is brought.[13] Every point in the record must be decided, and the reason concisely stated in writing.[14]

§ 666. *Opinions.* — All judges must state the law and reasons of their decisions.[15] Concurring and dissenting opinions must not be published;[16] in other States, they *may* be.[17] Reports are provided

[1] Okla. 2, 25.
[2] Ind. 7, 21.
[3] Ind. 7, 20; O. 14, 2; S. C. 6, 5; Wis. 7, 22.
[4] Ala. 85; Ind.; S. C.
[5] Mich. 18, 15.
[6] Mo. 4, 41 (1875); S. C.; Tex. 3, 43 (1879).
[7] Ala. 85.
[8] Cal. 6, 24.
[9] Wash. 4, 20.
[10] S. C. 4, 17.
[11] Ida. 5, 17.
[12] Okla. 7, 5.
[13] Ga. 6, 2, 6.
[14] Okla. 7, 5; Wash. 4, 2. See also § 653. Such provisions have been held unconstitutional when made by statute.
[15] Cal. Nov. 8, 1904; La. 91; N. D.
[16] La. 92. See also § 653.
[17] N. D., Utah.

for by the Constitution.[1] Judges must prepare a "syllabus."[2] A majority or quorum is necessary to any decision.[3] Upon a constitutional question or one involving State or Federal rights, the Supreme Court may call for the advice of the judges of the Circuit Court.[4]

ARTICLE 67. PROCEDURE[5]

§ 670. *Forms of Action.* — In several States, the Constitution provides that there shall be but one form of civil action.[6]

§ 671. *Equity.* — (See also § 651.) In several States, the Constitution provides that the Legislature shall abolish the distinction between law and equity proceedings.[7] So, in two others, law and equity may be administered in the same action.[8] And in Georgia, the Legislature may confer (and has conferred) upon the common-law courts all the powers of courts of equity.[9] But in Iowa, the Constitution provides that the law and equity jurisdiction (though often vested in the same courts) shall be kept distinct.[10] In two States, the testimony in equity is to be taken in the same manner as at law.[11]

§ 672. *Feigned Issues* are abolished by two State Constitutions.[12]

§ 673. *Juries: Qualifications.* — (For religious qualifications, see § 45.) The Constitution of Tennessee provides that no political test can be required for jurors;[13] in New Hampshire, that great care should be taken that none but qualified persons should serve on juries, and that they should be fully compensated;[14] so, in Vermont, that great care should be taken to prevent corruption or partiality in the choice of juries.[15]

§ 674. *Disqualifications.* — By the Constitution of one State, no person can serve on a jury who is not a qualified elector of the State, or cannot read and write.[16] And so, in others, the Legislature are

[1] La.; Mon. 8, 32; N. Y. 6, 21; S. D. 5, 12; Utah 8, 23; Wash. 4, 21.

[2] N. D. 102; Utah 8, 26. See p. 233, n. 14.

[3] Cal. 6, 2; Ida. 5, 3; Mon. 8, 5. N. D.; R. I. Amt. 12; Okla. 7, 3; S. D. 7, 5; Utah; Wy. 5, 5; Wash. 4, 2.

[4] S. C. 5, 12.

[5] See also §§ 137, 535, and Arts. 12, 13, 14, 15, generally.

[6] Ida. 5, 1; Mon. 8, 28; N. C. 4, 1; Nev. 6, 14; O. 14, 2; Utah 8, 19.

[7] Ida. 5, 1; Mich. 6, 5; N. C. 4, 1; O. 14, 2; S. C. 6, 3.

[8] Mon. 8, 28; Nev. 6, 14.

[9] Ga. 6, 4, 2.

[10] Io. 5, 6.

[11] N. Y. 6, 3; Wis. 7, 19.

[12] Ida. 5, 1; N. C. 4, 1.

[13] Tenn. 1, 6.

[14] N. H. 1, 21.

[15] Vt. 2, 31.

[16] Miss. 264.

to pass laws excluding persons from serving on juries in the same cases in which they are excluded from voting.[1]

In detail, all persons convicted of bribery are excluded from serving on juries.[2] All persons convicted of treason;[3] of perjury;[4] of forgery;[5] of larceny;[6] generally, all persons convicted of infamous crimes;[7] of "other high crimes";[8] all persons "under interdiction."[9] *Unless* they are restored to civil rights.[10]

§ 675. *Charging the Jury.* — Several State Constitutions provide that the judge shall not charge juries as to matter of fact,[11] nor comment thereon,[12] but they may state the testimony and declare the law.[13] So, they shall declare the law.[14] So, the judges of the Supreme Courts shall instruct the jury in the law.[15]

§ 676. *Amendments* are, by the Constitution of Delaware, to be allowed by the courts on such terms as they deem reasonable, in civil cases.[16]

§ 677. *Witnesses: Parties.* — The Constitutions of two States provide that parties may be witnesses.[17] And in one, that parties may be compelled to testify by the opposing party.[18]

Criminating evidence may be required in bribery cases, the witness being immune.[19]

§ 678. *Parties Deceased.* — But in one State, in actions by executors, administrators, and guardians in which judgment may be rendered either for or against them, neither party shall be allowed to testify against the other as to any transactions with, or statements to, the intestate, testator, or ward, unless called to testify thereto by the opposite party or required by the Court.[20]

§ 679. *Depositions.* — The Constitution of Delaware provides that evidence of witnesses aged or infirm, or about to leave the State, may be taken on interrogatories; and, that the courts shall have power to obtain evidence from without the State.[21]

[1] Cal. 20, 11; Nev. 4, 27; Tex. 16, 2.
[2] La. 159; Nev.; Tex.
[3] La.
[4] La., Nev., Tex.
[5] La., Nev., Tex.
[6] Nev.
[7] La.
[8] Nev., Tex.
[9] La.
[10] Nev.
[11] Ark. 7, 23; Cal. 6, 19; Del. 4, 22; La. 179; Nev. 6, 12; S. C. 5, 26; Tenn. 6, 9; Wash. 4, 16. See also § 132.
[12] Wash.
[13] Cal., Nev., S. C., Tenn.
[14] Ark. Wash.
[15] R. I. 10, 3.
[16] Del. 4, 24. A provision of this sort appears first in the Mass. Body of Liberties, 1641.
[17] Ark. Sched. 2; Io. 1, 4.
[18] Io.
[19] La. 184.
[20] Ark. Sched. 2.
[21] Del. 4, 24. See also § 124.

§ 680. *Limitations.* — The Legislature has no power to revive any right or remedy which may have become barred by lapse of time or any statute.[1] In Wisconsin, no appropriation can be made for any claim against the State, except judgments, unless filed within six years after the claim accrued.[2] In Tennessee, the time between May 6, 1861, and Jan. 1, 1867, shall not be computed in any case affected by the Statutes of Limitation, nor shall any writ of error be affected by such lapse of time.[3] So, in Florida, as to civil suits, the time between Jan. 10, 1861, and Oct. 25, 1865.[4] There is no prescription against the State, in civil matters.[5]

§ 681. *Payment into Court* may, by the Constitution of Delaware, be made by the defendant at any time pending an action for debt or damages; and the plaintiff not accepting it shall recover no costs, if he recover no greater sum on the final decision.[6]

§ 682. *Abatement.* — The Constitution of Delaware provides that no action of which the cause survives shall abate by the death of a party.[7]

[1] Miss. 97. See also § 395.
[2] Wis. Amt. 8, 2.
[3] Tenn. Sched. 4.
[4] Fla. 15, 3.
[5] La. 193; Miss. 104.
[6] Del. 4, 25.
[7] Del. 4, 26.

Part V

CONSTITUTIONAL AMENDMENTS

Article 99. Process of Amendment

§ 990. *How Proposed in the Legislature.* — Amendments to the Constitution may, in most States, be proposed in either house.[1] But in one, they can only be proposed in the senate, and only on every tenth year, beginning with 1880.[2] In one other, they can only be proposed in the house.[3] They must be ratified by a majority of the members present in each house,[4] or elected;[5] by three fifths of the elected members of each house;[6] by two thirds of a quorum of each house;[7] by two thirds of the elected members of each house;[8] by a majority of the elected members of each house of two successive Legislatures;[9] by a majority of the senators and two thirds of the representatives, present and voting thereon, of two successive Legislatures;[10] by a majority of the elected members of each house and two thirds of the members of each house of the next succeeding Legislature;[11] by three fifths of the first Legislature and two thirds of the next, as in Tennessee;[12] by two thirds of the elected members of the first Legislature, and also of the next;[13] by two thirds of the elected senators and a majority of the elected members of the house, in the Legislature proposing them, and by a majority of the elected

[1] Ala. 284; Ark. 19, 22; Cal. 18, 1; Col. 19, 2; Del. 16, 1; Fla. 17, 1; Ga. 13, 1, 1; Ida. 20, 2; Ill. 14, 2; Ind. 16, 1; Io. 10, 1; Kan. 14, 1; Ky. 256; La. 321; Mass. Amt. 9; Md. 14, 1; Mich. 20, 1; Minn. 1897, 185; Mon. 19, 9; N. D. 202; Nev. 16, 1; N. J. Art. 9; N. Y. 14, 1; O. 16, 1; Okla. 24, 1; Ore. 17, 1; Pa. 18, 1; S. C. 16, 1; S. D. 23, 1; Tenn. 11, 3; Utah 23, 1; Va. 196; Wash. 23, 1; W. Va. 14, 2; Wis. 12, 1; Wy. 20, 1.

[2] Vt. Amt. 25, 1.

[3] Ct. Art. 11.

[4] Minn. 14, 1.

[5] Ark.; Mo. 15, 1–2; Okla.

[6] Ala.; Fla.; Ky.; Md. 14, 1; Neb. 15, 1; O.; S. D.

[7] Me. 10, 2; Miss. 273.

[8] Cal. 18, 1; Col.; Ga.; Ida.; Ill.; Kan.; La.; Mich.; Mon.; Nev.; Amt. 1887, p. 170; S. C.; Tex. 17, 1; Utah; W. Va.; Wash.; Wy.

[9] Ind.; Io.; N. D.; Ore. 17, 1; N. J.; N. Y.; R. I. 13, 1; Va.; Wis.

[10] Mass. Amt. 9.

[11] Tenn. 11, 3.

[12] N. C. 13, 2.

[13] Del., Pa.

members of each house of the next Legislature.[1] After being proposed as above, they are to be published and must be ratified by two thirds of each house at the next Legislature.[2] In New Hampshire there is no provision for proposing single amendments.

§ 991. *Ratification by the People.* — In all the States except Delaware the proposed amendment, having passed the Legislature according to § 690, must then be ratified by a majority vote of the people at the next election,[3] or by a three-fifths vote at such election,[4] or a two-thirds vote.[5]

§ 992. *Ratification by the Legislature.* — And in one State, the proposed amendment, having passed both the Legislature and the people according to §§ 990, 991, must again be ratified by a majority of the elected members of each house of the next Legislature after the election by the people ratifying it.[6] But *quaere* whether this is valid.

§ 993. *Restrictions.* — In two, the Legislature cannot propose amendments to more than one article in any one session;[7] nor to the same article oftener than once in four years.[8] Not more than two[9] or three[10] can be voted upon at the same time. The same amendment cannot be submitted to the people oftener than once in five years;[11] once in six years.[12] Not more than three can be so submitted at the same election.[13] If two or more are submitted at the same time, the electors must be permitted to vote on each separately.[14] While an amendment approved by one Legislature is awaiting the action of the next, no other can be proposed.[15] No amendment shall relate to more than one subject.[16]

§ 994. *General Revision.* — There is, in most States, provision for a general revision of the Constitution by a convention called for that purpose. Thus, whenever two thirds (or in Alabama, Iowa, Kentucky, Michigan, Missouri, New Hampshire, New York, Tennessee, Virginia, Wisconsin, West Virginia, a majority; and in Nebraska, three fifths) of the elected members of each house of the

[1] Vt.

[2] Ct.

[3] For citations, see § 990.

[4] R. I. Art. 13.

[5] N. H. 2, 98.

[6] S. C. 16, 2.

[7] Col., Ill., not more than three, Mon.

[8] Ill.

[9] Ky.

[10] Mon.

[11] N. J.; Pa.

[12] Tenn.

[13] Ark., Kan., Mon.

[14] Fla. 17, 1; Ga. 13, 1, 1; Ida, 20, 2; Ind. 16, 2; Io. 10, 2; Kan.; Ky.; La.; Md.; Minn.; Mon.; Neb.; N. J.; N. D.; O.; Okla.; Pa.; S. C. 16, 2; S. D.; Utah; Wash.; W. Va.; Wis.; Wy.

[15] Ind.

[16] Ky.

Legislature vote that such convention is necessary, the question is referred to the people; if they vote at the next election [1] for the convention, the Legislature is to provide for holding the same.[2] In Oklahoma the Constitution may be revised at any time if the Act calling the convention be approved by the people, on a referendum or upon an initiative petition therefor.[3] And in some, the question of holding such a convention is regularly submitted to the people at stated times, at a general election; as, every ten years, beginning with 1870;[4] every twenty years, beginning with 1916;[5] with 1871;[6] with 1887;[7] every sixteen years, beginning with 1866;[8] every seven years.[9] The delegates to such constitutional convention are, in all these States, to be elected by the people. They must be double the number of the Legislature,[10] or the same as the House,[11] or thrice the Senate, and fifteen at large.[12] Such provisions are interesting, but frequently not effective. One generation can hardly bind the next, even to vote upon a new Constitution; if the Legislature fail to set the machinery in motion, nothing can be done.

§ 995. *Ratification.* — The Constitution, as so amended by the convention, must then be ratified by the people at a general election;[13] at a special election called for the purpose.[14] In others, apparently, it goes into effect at once.

§ 996. *Amendments to the United States Constitution* may not, by the Constitutions of Florida and Tennessee, be ratified by any convention or assembly (Legislature) of the State which was not elected after such amendment was submitted.[15]

[1] The popular vote for the convention must equal one-fourth of that thrown at the last election (Ky.).

[2] Ala. 286; Cal. 18, 2; Col. 19, 1; Del. 16, 2; Fla. 17, 2; Ga. 13, 1, 2; Ida. 20, 3; Ill. 14, 1; Io. 10, 3; Kan. 14, 2; Ky. 258 (by a majority of *two successive* houses); Me. 4, 3, 15; Mich. 20, 2; Minn. 14, 2; Mo. 15, 3; Mon. 19, 8; N. C. 13, 1; Neb. 15, 2; Nev. 16, 2; N. H. 2, 98; N. Y. 15, 2; O. 16, 2; S. C. 16, 3; S. D. 23, 2; Tenn.; Utah 23, 2; Va. 197; Wash. 23, 2; W. Va. 14, 1; Wis. 12, 2; Wy. 20, 3.

[3] Okla. 23, 2 & 3.

[4] Io.

[5] N. Y.

[6] O. 16, 3.

[7] Md. 14, 2.

[8] Mich.

[9] N. H. 2, 98, 99 (beginning 1903).

[10] Ida., Wy.

[11] Mon., Utah., Wash.

[12] N. Y.

[13] Md.; Neb.; O.; W. Va. 14, 1.

[14] Cal.; Col.; Ida. 20, 4; Ill.; Mo.; Mon.; N. Y.; Utah 23, 3; Wash. 23, 3; Wy. 20, 4.

[15] Fla. 16, 19; Tenn. 2, 32.

INDEX

A

B

C

D

E

F

G

H

I

J

K

L

M

N

Q

R

S

T

U

V

W

Y

The University Press, Cambridge, U. S. A.

www.ingramcontent.com/pod-product-compliance
Lightning Source LLC
LaVergne TN
LVHW091523200926
848483LV00002B/287
* 9 7 8 1 5 8 4 7 7 3 6 9 6 *